Nietzsche as Political Philosopher

Nietzsche Today

Volume 3

Nietzsche as Political Philosopher

Edited by
Manuel Knoll and Barry Stocker

DE GRUYTER

ISBN 978-3-11-055471-7
e-ISBN 978-3-11-035945-9
ISSN 2191-5741

Library of Congress Cataloging-in-Publication Data
A CIP catalog record for this book has been applied for at the Library of Congress

Bibliographic information published by the Deutsche Nationalbibliothek
The Deutsche Nationalbibliothek lists this publication in the Deutsche Nationalbibliografie; detailed bibliographic data are available in the Internet at http://dnb.dnb.de.

© 2017 Walter de Gruyter GmbH, Berlin/Boston
This volume is text- and page-identical with the hardback published in 2014.
Typesetting: Meta Systems Publishing & Printservices GmbH, Wustermark
Printing and binding: Hubert & Co. GmbH & Co. KG, Göttingen
♾ Printed on acid-free paper
Printed in Germany

www.degruyter.com

Contents

Abbreviations —— ix

Manuel Knoll and Barry Stocker
Introduction: Nietzsche as political philosopher —— 1

I. The Variety of Approaches to Nietzsche's Political Thought

Rolf Zimmermann
The "Will to Power": Towards a Nietzschean Systematics of Moral-Political Divergence in History in Light of the 20th Century —— 39

Rebecca Bamford
The Liberatory Limits of Nietzsche's Colonial Imagination in *Dawn* 206 —— 59

Nandita Biswas Mellamphy
Nietzsche's Political Materialism: Diagram for a Nietzschean Politics —— 77

II. Democratic, or Liberal, or Egalitarian Politics in Nietzsche

Paul Patton
Nietzsche on Power and Democracy circa 1876–1881 —— 93

Lawrence J. Hatab
Nietzsche's Will to Power and Politics —— 113

Barry Stocker
A Comparison of Friedrich Nietzsche and Wilhelm von Humboldt as Products of Classical Liberalism —— 135

Donovan Miyasaki
A Nietzschean Case for Illiberal Egalitarianism —— 155

III. Aristocratic, or Anti-Liberal, or Non-Egalitarian Politics in Nietzsche

Renato Cristi
Nietzsche, Theognis and Aristocratic Radicalism —— 173

Don Dombowsky
Aristocratic Radicalism as a Species of Bonapartism: Preliminary Elements —— 195

Phillip H. Roth
Political and Psychological Prerequisites for Legislation in the Early Nietzsche —— 211

Manuel Knoll
The "Übermensch" as a Social and Political Task: A Study in the Continuity of Nietzsche's Political Thought —— 239

IV. Ethics, Morality, and Politics in Nietzsche

Keith Ansell-Pearson
Care of Self in *Dawn*: On Nietzsche's Resistance to Bio-political Modernity —— 269

Daniel Conway
"We who are different, we immoralists…" —— 287

Christian J. Emden
Political Realism Naturalized: Nietzsche on the State, Morality, and Human Nature —— 313

Tamsin Shaw
The "Last Man" Problem: Nietzsche and Weber on Political Attitudes to Suffering —— 345

V. Physiology, Genealogy, and Politics in Nietzsche

Razvan Ioan
The Politics of Physiology —— 383

Tom Angier
On the Genealogy of Nietzsche's Values —— 405

Evangelia Sembou
Foucault's use of Nietzsche —— 431

Notes on Contributors —— 449

Name Index —— 455

Subject Index —— 465

Abbreviations

Primary sources from Nietzsche are cited in the main text by abbreviation according to the standard conventions listed here. Nietzsche's works are typically cited by section number and, in the cases of EH, GM, and TI, an additional reference to the chapter title or essay number (see below). References to Z include the part number and chapter title (often abbreviated), e.g., Z I Reading. Prefaces of works are referenced by a "Preface" after the abbreviated title, e.g., TI Preface. All passages from Nietzsche's *Nachlass* are cited from KSA or KGW, starting with the abbreviation NL, followed by KSA/KGW, the volume number, the manuscript number, and then fragment number in brackets, e.g., NL, KSA 7, 5[103]. In some cases the page number of KSA was added. Nietzsche's letters are cited according to volume and letter number as they appear in KGB, e.g., KGB III/1, Bf. 213.

The English translations of Nietzsche's works used in the articles are listed in the respective bibliographies.

A	The Antichrist
AOM	Assorted Opinions and Maxims
BAW	Historisch-kritische Gesamtausgabe: Werke (5 vols., edited by Joachim Mette)
BGE	Beyond Good and Evil
BT	The Birth of Tragedy out of the Spirit of Music [BT Attempt]
CW	The Case of Wagner
D	Daybreak
DS	David Strauss, the Writer and the Confessor
DW	The Dionysian Worldview
EH	Ecce Homo [EH Wise, EH Clever, EH Books, EH Destiny]
FEI	On the Future of Our Educational Institutions
GM	On the Genealogy of Morals (Cited by essay number followed by section number)
GS	The Gay Science
GSt	The Greek State
HC	Homer's Contest
HH I	Human All Too Human I
HL	On the Uses and Disadvantages of History for Life
KGB	Nietzsches Briefwechsel:. Kritische Gesamtausgabe
KGW	Nietzsche Werke: Kritische Gesamtausgabe
KSA	Sämtliche Werke: Kritische Studienausgabe
NCW	Nietzsche contra Wagner
NL	Drafts, Fragments, and Sketches from the *Nachlass*
PPP	The Pre-Platonic Philosophers
PT	On the Pathos of Truth
PTAG	Philosophy in the Tragic Age of the Greeks

SE	Schopenhauer as Educator
TI	Twilight of the Idols [TI Arrows, TI Socrates, TI Reason, TI Fable, TI Morality, TI Errors, TI Improving, TI Germans, TI Skirmishes, TI Ancients, TI Hammer]
TL	On Truth and Lie in an Extra-Moral Sense
TM	De Teognide Megarensi (= BAW 3, pp. 21–64)
WB	Richard Wagner in Bayreuth
WP	The Will to Power
WPH	We Philologists
WS	The Wanderer and His Shadow
Z	Thus Spoke Zarathustra

[Z I Adder, Z I Flies, Z I Goals, Z I Hinterworldly, Z I Idol, Z I Metamorphoses, Z I Prologue, Z I Teachers, Z I Virtue, Z I War, Z I Women, Z II Human Prudence, Z II Isles, Z II Priests, Z II On Self-Overcoming, Z II Redemption, Z II Scholars, Z II Tarantulas, Z III Convalescent, Z III Riddle, Z III Tablets, Z III Gravity, Z IV Beggar, Z IV Cry of Distress, Z IV Men]

Manuel Knoll and Barry Stocker
Introduction: Nietzsche as political philosopher

1 The scholarly debate about Nietzsche's political preferences and affinities

In the last decades the interest in Nietzsche's philosophy has become a truly global phenomenon. This has led to a huge amount of literature and different interpretations. In 2003, a German scholar even published a book on the different receptions and discussions of Nietzsche's thought in France, Italy, and the Anglo-Saxon world between 1960 and 2000 (Reckermann 2003). Until now, the interest in Nietzsche's philosophy has not decreased. On the contrary, scholars keep discovering new areas of his work worth examining. In 2012, an edited volume was published on Nietzsche's philosophy of science with contributions from numerous international Nietzsche-scholars (Heit/Abel/Brusotti 2012).

In the Anglo-Saxon world, it was in particular the achievement of Walter Kaufmann's and Arthur Danto's books that Nietzsche received the attention and recognition as a philosopher he is still enjoying today (Kaufmann 1950, Danto 1965). Kaufmann rehabilitated Nietzsche from his usurpation by the Nazis and the Fascists, and from the distorted interpretation he had undergone with the aid of the Nietzsche-archive and his sister Elisabeth Förster-Nietzsche. However, Kaufmann's interpretation depoliticized Nietzsche's thought, which led to the assumption "that Nietzsche was not a political thinker at all, but someone who was mainly concerned with the fate of the solitary, isolated individual far removed from the cares and concerns of the social world" (Ansell-Pearson 1994, p. 1).

This view prevailed in Anglo-Saxon studies for several decades. It was mainly Tracy Strong's book *Friedrich Nietzsche and the Politics of Transfiguration*, published in 1975, which opened the way for several monographs on Nietzsche's political philosophy (Strong 2000).[1] However, again in 1994 Keith Ansell-Pearson remarked in his *Introduction to Nietzsche as Political Thinker*: "Inquiry into the political dimension of Nietzsche's thought still remains the most contentious and controversial aspect of Nietzsche-studies" (Ansell-Pear-

---

[1] For an overview and summary of the content of the publications between 1960 and 2000 see Reckermann 2003.

son 1994, p. 2; cf. Ansell-Pearson 1991). In the meantime in Germany, one of the main centers of research on Nietzsche, Henning Ottmann's voluminous "Habilitationsschrift" on *Philosophie und Politik bei Nietzsche* had appeared in 1987. Like Ansell-Pearson's book, Ottmann's study concludes that Nietzsche is clearly a political thinker (Ottmann 1999; Ansell-Pearson 1994, p. 1).[2] This is also the argument of Daniel Conway's book *Nietzsche & the Political* from 1997, in which he took Nietzsche seriously as a political thinker (Conway 1997). According to Conway, Nietzsche's "commitment to the position known as *perfectionism*" is at the center of his political thinking: Nietzsche "locates the sole justification of human existence in the continued perfectibility of the species as a whole, as evidenced by the pioneering accomplishments of its highest exemplars" (Conway 1997, pp. 6f.; cf. Siemens 2008, p. 235).

One might think that after the publication of these three important monographs, among others, the issue of Nietzsche's relation to politics was settled. On the contrary, not only has this issue remained a topic for heated debates, but new disputes concerning Nietzsche and political thought arose. In 1998, Thomas Brobjer argued for *The Absence of Political Ideals in Nietzsche's Writings* (Brobjer 1998). Along the same lines, Brobjer claimed in 2008 that Nietzsche was "not interested in or concerned with politics", or that he was an "a-, supra- and anti-political thinker" (Brobjer 2008, p. 205). Brobjer's text from 1998 received a critical reply from Don Dombowsky, in which he put forward several arguments against Brobjer's interpretation (Dombowsky 2001, cf. Brobjer's response 2001).

In 2002, Brian Leiter maintained that Nietzsche "has no political philosophy, in the conventional sense of a theory of the state and its legitimacy. He occasionally expresses views about political matters, but, read in context, they do not add up to a theoretical account of any of the questions of political philosophy" (Leiter 2002, p. 296). In line with Leiter, Tamsin Shaw claimed in her book on *Nietzsche's Political Scepticism* that Nietzsche "fails to articulate any positive, normative political theory" (Shaw 2007, p. 2).[3] For Shaw, Nietzsche

---

[2] Ottmann 1999, p. vii: "Vielleicht darf man auch in Zukunft zweifeln, ob Nietzsche zu den 'Klassikern' der Politik gerechnet werden wird. Nicht zweifeln darf man an der politischen Wirkung seiner Gedanken, und nicht zweifeln sollte man am politischen Gehalt des Werkes selbst. Es gibt bei Nietzsche eine politische Philosophie. Man darf sie nur nicht suchen wollen auf der Heerstraße der politischen Strömungen der Zeit".

[3] According to Shaw, it is a "fact" that Nietzsche abstains from developing his insights into morality, culture, and religion "into a coherent theory of politics" (Shaw 2007, p. 1). Similarly, already Bernard Williams had claimed that Nietzsche "did not move to any view that offered a coherent politics" (Williams 1993, p. 10). The politics Williams has in mind and asks for is a politics "in the sense of a coherent set of opinions about the way in which power should

"articulates a deep political skepticism that can be best described as a skepticism about legitimacy" (Shaw 2007, p. 2). As a consequence of the process of secularization, modern pluralist societies cannot reach a consensus on values and normative beliefs, which makes "a form of politics that is genuinely grounded in normative authority" impossible (Shaw 2007, p. 3). Therefore, the political authority we need cannot be based on a consensus and a normative authority. However, for their stability modern states require some shared values and normative beliefs. Hence, they have to produce the consensus through coercive means and ideological control. This dilemma is the basis for Nietzsche's skepticism about legitimacy.

In 2008 the voluminous edition *Nietzsche, Power and Politics: Rethinking Nietzsche's Legacy for Political Thought* was published (Siemens/Roodt 2008). In this volume several authors claim that Nietzsche is a "suprapolitical" (*überpolitisch*) thinker. These interpretations gave rise to questions regarding the content and extent of the traditional concept of politics. According to the editors of this volume,

> it is no exaggeration to say that Nietzsche's significance for political thought has become the single, most hotly contested area of Anglophone Nietzsche research: Is Nietzsche a political thinker at all – or an anti-political philosopher of values and culture? Is he an aristocratic political thinker who damns democracy as an expression of the herd mentality – or can his thought, especially his thought on the Greek *agon*, be fruitfully appropriated for contemporary democratic theory? (Siemens/Roodt 2008, p. 1)

In the Anglo-Saxon world, the controversial issue of Nietzsche's political preferences and affinities has been debated since the late 1980s. Already Tracy Strong had attempted a "left-wing" reading of Nietzsche in his book, and reflected on a political stance that could be based on Nietzsche, though avoiding the aristocratic elements of his thought (Strong 1975). Contrary to such an understanding, a continued reading among scholars of various countries interprets Nietzsche as an aristocratic political thinker, and characterize his politics with the term "aristocratic radicalism", which Georg Brandes created for Nietzsche's position in 1887 and which Nietzsche himself approved of in a letter to Brandes as "the shrewdest remark that I have read about myself till now" (Middleton 1996, p. 279). In his book *Nietzsche and the Politics of Aristocratic Radicalism*, Bruce Detwiler announced:

> While aristocratic conservatives and egalitarian radicals have been plentiful in recent times, it is difficult to think of another modern of Nietzsche's stature whose political ori-

---

be exercised in modern societies, with what limitations and to what ends" (Williams 1993, pp. 10f.).

entation is both as aristocratic and as radical as his. Among modern philosophers Nietzsche stands virtually alone in his insistence that the goal of society should be the promotion and enhancement of the highest type even at the expense of what has traditionally been thought to be the good of all or of the great number. (Detwiler 1990, p. 189)

In his monograph of 1999, *Nietzsche contra Democracy*, Fredrick Appel argued that Nietzsche displays a "radically aristocratic commitment to human excellence", and tried to show "how Nietzsche's politics emerge out of his concern for the flourishing of the 'higher', 'stronger' type of human being" (Appel 1999, pp. 2, 13). Don Dombowsky associates Nietzsche's political theory "with conservative or aristocratic liberalism (Alexis de Tocqueville, Jacob Burckhardt and Hippolyte Taine)", and understands him as "a disciple of Machiavelli" (Dombowsky 2004, pp. 3, 5). Other aristocratic elements of Nietzsche's political thought are his judgment that people are fundamentally unequal and have unequal value, and his aristocratic conception of distributive justice, which is based on this anthropological fundament, and which is embodied in Nietzsche's early and late conceptions of a good social order (Knoll 2009a and Knoll 2010; cf. Appel 1999, p. 2).

Other scholars spotted in Nietzsche affinities to democratic, or liberal political views. In his book *Nietzsche and Political Thought*, Mark Warren understands Nietzsche as the "first thoroughgoing postmodern" in the sense that Nietzsche does not simply break "with modernist categories and ideas", but that he "reconceives central ideals of modern rationalism", and thus should be viewed as "critically postmodern" (Warren 1988, p. X). According to Warren's argument, "Nietzsche did not give his own philosophy a plausible political identity. He failed to elaborate the broad range of political possibilities that are suggested by his philosophy in large part owing to unexamined assumptions about the nature of modern politics" (Warren 1988, p. 246). This judgment leads Warren at the end of his book to speculate about a way how "to supplement Nietzsche's insights with a positive political vision" (Warren 1988, p. 246). William E. Connolly holds his perspective on Nietzsche to be "pertinent" to Warren's study (Connolly 1988, p. 189). At the close of his book on *Political Theory and Modernity*, Connolly reflects on the need for a radical or "radicalized liberalism", which he defines by enumerating several features: "Such a perspective would stand to Nietzsche as Marx stood to Hegel: in a relation of antagonistic indebtedness. It would appreciate the reach of Nietzschean thought as well as its sensitivity to the complex relations between resentment and the production of otherness, but it would turn the genealogist of resentment on his head by exploring democratic politics as a medium through which to expose resentment and to encourage the struggle against it" (Connolly 1988, p. 175).

Contrary to Warren and Connolly, David Owen and Lawrence J. Hatab argue that Nietzsche doesn't belong in the liberal tradition. According to "the central thesis" of Owens's book *Nietzsche, Politics and Modernity*, "it is at the very least plausible to argue that Nietzsche's political thinking offers a significant critique of liberalism and articulates an alternative vision of politics which has much to give" (Hatab 1995, p. 169; cf. Owen 1994). Hatab stresses in his monograph *A Nietzschean Defense of Democracy* that "we cannot hide or ignore Nietzsche's antidemocratic argument and its potent challenge to traditional political principles" (Hatab 1995, p. 2). However, he tries to show "that democracy *is* compatible with Nietzsche's thought, that democracy can be redescribed in a Nietzschean manner" as "an ungrounded, continual contest" (Hatab 1995, pp. 2, 4; italics by Hatab). For Hatab, we can find features of an "agonistic democracy"[4] in Nietzsche's works. While these are essential for Hatab's understanding of democracy, for him democracy doesn't depend on "such problematic notions as the universal 'human nature', a 'common good' and especially 'human equality'" (Hatab 1995, p. 4). Hatab's study is more than simply an interpretation of Nietzsche, but a Nietzschean and postmodern approach to democracy, which he defends as the best political system.

Surprisingly, Frederick Appel doesn't include Hatab's book among the interpretations he mentions in *Nietzsche contra Democracy*. However, he puts forward several arguments against all "progressive" and "left-wing" readings of Nietzsche. One of his "central claims" is that Nietzsche's "radically aristocratic commitments pervade every aspect of his project, making any egalitarian appropriation of his work exceedingly problematic" (Appel 1999, p. 5). Why bother with adapting Nietzsche's political thought for democratic purposes "when there are so many other thinkers past and present with less dubious credentials who could provide ready inspiration?" (Appel 1999, p. 5). Like Appel, Don Dombowsky opposes and criticizes "efforts in contemporary Anglo-American political philosophy to read Nietzsche as consonant with liberal democratic pluralism" (Dombowsky 2004, p. 2). To be sure, the controversy filled debate about Nietzsche's political preferences and affinities will continue. Many of the papers included in this volume are instructive contributions to this debate (cf. part 5 of this introduction).

---

4 The term "agonistic democracy" was first introduced by William Connolly (1991, p. X; cf. Hatab 1995, p. 263, fn. 1). Hatab acknowledges that much of Connolly's work "is a precedent for my efforts" (Hatab 1995, p. 263, fn. 1).

2 A brief overview of Nietzsche's political philosophy

Though not all scholars acknowledge this fact, Nietzsche's multi-facetted works undoubtedly contain a political philosophy. According to his aphoristic and anti-systematic style of thought and presentation, Nietzsche nowhere gives a comprehensive account of his political philosophy. The only exception is his early essay *The Greek State*, which was published posthumously as a part of a collection of five short essays entitled *Five Prefaces to Five Unwritten Books* which Nietzsche offered to Cosima Wagner for Christmas 1872. This essay is an almost exact copy of a part of a long fragment Nietzsche had written for an early version of *The Birth of Tragedy*, which came out at the beginning of 1872 (NL, KSA 7, 10[1], pp. 333–349). *The Greek State* can be understood as a complementary work to *The Birth of Tragedy*, because in it Nietzsche reflects on the social and political bases of his theory of art and culture. The essay is a well elaborated text and most of its basic ideas are repeated in *Beyond Good and Evil* and *The Antichrist*.

Nietzsche understands his essay as an interpretation of Plato's perfect state, in whose general conception he recognizes the "marvelously grand hieroglyph of a profound secret teaching of the connection between state and genius, which is to be interpreted eternally" (GSt, KSA 1, p. 777). For Nietzsche, as opposed to some modern contractarians or contractualists, the origin of the state is not a contract, but a violent conquest and a sudden subjugation. Accordingly, he calls the "original founder of the state" the "military genius" and the "conqueror with the iron hand" (GSt, KSA 1, pp. 775, 770). The foundation of the state leads to the enslavement of the conquered people and to the abolition of "the natural bellum omnium contra omnes" (GSt, KSA 1, p. 772). In line with his early account of the origin of the state, he pronounces in *On the Genealogy of Morality*:

> I used the word 'state': it is obvious who is meant by this – some pack of blond beasts of prey, a conqueror and master race, which, organized on a war footing, and with the power to organize, unscrupulously lays its dreadful paws on a populace which, though it might be vastly greater in number, is still shapeless and shifting. In this way, the 'state' began on earth: I think I have dispensed with the fantasy which has it begin with a 'contract'. (GM II 17)

In the *The Greek State*, Nietzsche conceives of the state as a means of coercion in order to initiate the social process and to uphold it. In his view, this is the true meaning of the state. Through the "iron clamp of the state" the masses of people are squeezed together and are also well separated, which constitutes a social structure that has the shape of a pyramid (GSt, KSA 1, p. 769). Analogously, war produces a separation of the estate of soldiers in military castes, which constitute a pyramidal order of rank. In the estate of soldiers, which for Nietzsche is "the image [*Abbild*], even perhaps the archetype of the state", as well as in society, the lowest stratum is the broadest, while the top of the pyramid is constituted by one or a few men only. The fundamental goal of the "military proto-state" is the generation of the military genius (GSt, KSA 1, p. 775). The general purpose of every state is for Nietzsche the "Olympian existence and the constantly renewed generation and preparation of the genius" (GSt, KSA 1, p. 776). Nietzsche criticizes Plato for putting only "the genius of wisdom and knowledge" on top of his perfect state and for excluding the ingenious artist under the influence of Socrates. In opposition to Plato, Nietzsche proclaims that the purpose and meaning of the state is to generate the genius "in its most general sense" (GSt, KSA 1, pp. 775f.). For Nietzsche, the existence of a "small number of Olympian men", who produce the high culture, presupposes slavery. According to his provocative and generalizing thesis, slavery belongs "to the essence of a culture" (GSt, KSA 1, p. 767). The estate of the slaves, the lowest stratum of the social pyramid, has to do the additional work, which is necessary in order to exempt the few ingenious producers of culture from the struggle of existence. With the term "slavery" Nietzsche not only means the slaves of the ancient world but the contemporary "anonymous and impersonal" "factory-slavery" (WS 288, cf. D 206).

The ultimate basis of Nietzsche's early theory of the state is the "artists' metaphysics" that he developed in *The Birth of Tragedy*, which was inspired by Schopenhauer's *The World as Will and Representation* (BT Attempt 5, cf. BT Attempt 7). According to this "artists' metaphysics", the last causes of the state are the Apollinian and Dionysian art impulses of nature, in which exists "an ardent longing for illusion, for redemption through illusion" (BT 4, KSA 1, p. 38). In order to achieve redemption through art, nature forges the "conqueror with the iron hand" as a tool for the establishment of the state. While the state is the means of nature to "bring society about", society is its means to bring the genius and art about. The final goal of nature and its "omnipotent art impulses" is its "redemption through illusion". Nietzsche talks about "how enormously necessary the state is, without which nature would not succeed in achieving, through society, her salvation in illusion [*Erlösung im Scheine*]" (BT 4, KSA 1, p. 38; cf. GSt, KSA 1, p. 767).

Though in his later works Nietzsche moves away from his early "artists' metaphysics", he takes up central thoughts of *The Greek State* in a slightly modified form. State and society must not be an end in itself, but have to be means for the goal of the "elevation of the type 'man'" (BGE 257). In his later works, Nietzsche speaks hardly any more of the generation of the genius, but rather of the production or breeding of a higher type of man or overman, which his Zarathustra is teaching together with the "eternal recurrence of the same". The generation of a higher type of man is only possible in an aristocratic society, "which believes in a long ladder of order of rank and difference in worth between man and man and that needs slavery in some sense" (BGE 257). According to Nietzsche, a "good and healthy aristocracy" is not a "function" of the commonwealth, but its "meaning and supreme justification" (BGE 258). Its "fundamental faith" has to be that the whole society and thus the masses of common people serve as an "instrument" and "substructure and scaffolding", which allows "a selected kind of being to raise itself to its higher task and generally to a higher existence" (BGE 258).

For Nietzsche, a true aristocracy is not concerned with descent or ancestry. The honor of the "new nobility" that he is aspiring to doesn't originate from where its members are coming from, but from where they are going (Z III Tablets 11 and 12). As an elite of higher men the "new nobility" should distinguish itself from the masses by affirmation of life, strength, health, self-mastery, spirit and free spirit, creative power, magnanimity, and courage. One of the main tasks of the "new nobility" is to counteract "nihilism", which is for Nietzsche a necessary development and consequence of occidental values. In its essence "nihilism" means the process that "the highest values devalue themselves" (NL 1887, KSA 12, p. 350). The "new nobility" should counteract nihilism through the creation and positing of new values and a new morality that should be created by the philosophers of the future are an expression of their "will to power" (BGE 210–211, BGE 202–203). Nietzsche desires the "new nobility" to be a European and Europe ruling nobility which should pursue a "grand politics" of global creation, education and breeding of man in the tradition of Plato. This "grand politics" should replace the "petty politics" of the nation states and "the divided will of its dynasties and democracies" (BGE 208, 209–212).

In *The Anti-Christ* Nietzsche presents once more his vision of a good social and political order. He finds the model for this vision in the old Indian legal code of Manu.[5] The good order of Manu is a hierarchical and pyramidal order of castes, which distinguishes between three castes in analogy to the natural inequality of men. This is why Nietzsche understands the "order of castes" as the "sanctioning of a natural order, a natural law of the first rank": "Nature, not Manu, separates from one another the predominantly spiritual type, the predominantly muscular type and temperamental type, and a third type distin-

---

[5] For Nietzsche's source and reception of the legal code of Manu, and for the debate about whether it constitutes Nietzsche's political ideal, see fn. 32 in Knoll's essay in this volume.

guished neither in the one nor the other, the mediocre type – the last as the great majority, the first as the elite" (A 57). One of the tasks of the highest caste, which Nietzsche glorifies, is to rule the political community. Nietzsche conceives of the second caste in rank as the "noble warriors", and as "the executive of the most spiritual order" (A 57). The members of the lowest caste, the caste of the "mediocre", have to specialize and to do the work which is necessary for the sustenance of the whole society (A 57). According to Nietzsche's interpretation, Manu's good social order is very similar to the good and just city that Plato outlines in the *Politeia*, which is also based on the fundamental inequality of men. In the end, as in his early works, Nietzsche identifies the goal of society and state as the creation of grand individuals and a high culture:

> The order of castes, order of rank, only formulates the supreme law of life itself; the separation of the three types is necessary for the preservation of society, for making possible higher and highest types, – inequality of rights is the condition for the existence of rights at all. – A right is a privilege [*Vorrecht*]. The privilege of each is determined by his sort of being (*Art Sein*). [...] Injustice never lies in unequal rights, it lies in the claim to 'equal' rights. (A 57)

The last statement demonstrates that Nietzsche rejects the liberal and socialist thought on equality of his epoch as well as democracy as a political system. He derives the political "poison of the doctrine 'equal rights for all'" from Christian value judgments, and in particular from the "lie of equality of souls", by which the "aristocratic basic convictions [*Aristokratismus der Gesinnung*] have been undermined most deeply" (A 43). The "democratic movement", which "inherits the Christian", is, for Nietzsche, "not merely a form assumed by political organizations in decay but also a form assumed by man in decay, that is to say in diminishment, in process of becoming mediocre and losing his value" (BGE 202–203). Nietzsche holds the "democratization of Europe to be "unstoppable [*unaufhaltsam*]" (WS 275).

Already in *Human, All Too Human*, Nietzsche states his prognostic conviction, that "modern democracy is the historical form of the decay of the state" (HH I 472). Contrary to "absolute tutelary government", democratic government cannot counteract the decay of religion, which is caused by Enlightenment. If the "belief in a divine order of political matters" fades away, and if the state thus loses its religious foundations, in the long run the "attitude of veneration and piety towards it" will be shattered. Another "consequence of the democratic conception of the state" is "the liberation of the private person", who regards the secular state only under considerations of utility, which, connected with a too rapid changing of competing men and parties, with the "distrust towards everything that rules", and with the empowerment of private societies and private enterprises, leads to the decay and death of the state. However, Nietzsche is not troubled by this outlook. The fact that "prudence and self-interest of men" are highly developed, prevents chaos from ensuing, rather, "an invention more suited to their purpose than the state was, will gain victory over the state" (HH I 472).

Human, All Too Human is the first book of Nietzsche's middle period, in which his thought is oriented more towards the positive sciences and Enlightenment, and in which he is less radical and more willing to compromise. In this period, which ends with *The Gay Science*, Nietzsche not only criticizes democracy, but reflects on it in a subtle and nuanced way (WS). He even publishes thoughts that are close to liberalism, which he usually rejects to a great extent. For example, Nietzsche states that "the" individual is the "original purpose of the state", which he defines as "a prudent institution for the protection of the individuals against each other" (HH I 235). Against socialism, which, similarly to despotism, "desires an abundance of state power", he phrases the motto: "As little state as possible" (HH I 473). Nietzsche's thoughts on liberalism and democracy from his middle period are hardly compatible with the non-egalitarian and aristocratic political views of his early and late writings. Maybe the most likely explanation for this incompatibility is that Nietzsche's views shifted over the course of his life. In regard of the close similarities of Nietzsche's early and late political views, however, such an interpretation implies that Nietzsche moved away from his early political preferences in the late 1870s and then back to them in the later 1880s.

In *Zarathustra*, Nietzsche criticizes the state as the "new idol". The various aspects of this critique are difficult to interpret. After "the death of God", after "the belief in the Christian God has become unbelievable", the State occupies the empty place which was held before by God (GS 343). The consequence is an esteem and veneration of the State which Nietzsche holds to be unjustifiable. He designates the State as a cold and compulsively lying monster, which tries to lure men to render him services. However, the state does not deserve people serving him and make him the purpose of their lives. According to Nietzsche, also wealth, power, and the satisfaction of manifold desires, the aims of life in a state, are not worth striving for. As an alternative, he advises leading a free life far from the state. While he usually conceives of the state as a means for a higher type of human being, he states in *Zarathustra* that "where the state ceases" the "rainbow and bridges to the Overman" are to be seen (Z I Idol).

For the liberal and democratic political thought that prevails today, Nietzsche's "aristocratic radicalism" might appear at best as an anti-modern provocation or as a reactionary utopia. To be sure, Nietzsche's radical non-egalitarianism is in central aspects incompatible with contemporary, mostly egalitarian, political philosophy. However, his view that the state has to serve culture and should be regarded as a means for the generation of outstanding individuals is not without interest for today's politics. Nietzsche's views prompt the questions of whether modern democracies are spending enough money to promote culture and whether the promotion of culture shouldn't be stipulated as one important purpose of a state. Likewise, one could ask, going back to Nietzsche, whether modern states shouldn't contribute more to promote elites, and through which qualities these elites should be singled out. Of remaining actuality is Nietzsche's critique of Europe's "petty politics" of nation states and of nationalism, which he holds to be "the most <u>anti-cultural</u> sickness and unreason there is" (EH CW 2).

3 Nietzsche's Relation to some of the Political Ideas of his Time

Nietzsche did not write a treatise of political philosophy and he dismissed the political ideologies of his time, particularly liberalism (HH I 304), socialism (HH I 473), and nationalism (HH I 475). He condemned the modern drive to egalitarianism, but did not support any concrete program of political reaction, that is for the restoration of the aristocratic-monarchical world as it existed before modern egalitarianism. His thought was largely directed against the religious beliefs which political reaction placed at the centre. His criticisms of slaves (GM I), or any kind of lower class, were also criticisms of the religious beliefs that the priests, a category of masters, encouraged the slaves to follow (GM I 6). One problem Nietzsche faced, in any desire he might have had for a reactionary political process, was that – as will be argued in this section – it would be likely to lead him into the world of modern egalitarianism, at least in the sense of equality of individual rights.

This section does not attempt a comprehensive survey of the political doctrines and thinkers of Nietzsche's time who had some influence on him, as that would be an entire monograph in itself. Such work would need to cover the historical-sociological and political thought of Hyppolite Taine, the liberal social Darwinian Herbert Spencer (whose Darwinism expressed itself with regard to selection of social structures not racial selection), the more racist social Darwinians such as Ernst Haeckel, the political thought (including anti-Semitism) of Richard Wagner, the political aspects of Arthur Schopenhauer's philosophy and so on.

Nietzsche admired Napoleon (HH I 164, TI Skirmishes 44), and may have sympathised with French Bonapartists of his time (Dombowsky 2008, Dombowsky's essay in this volume), but Napoleon started off as a Jacobin, and always claimed to carry on the values of the French revolution, which he achieved by spreading the Civil Code throughout the nations he conquered. Dombowsky's essay in this volume acknowledges the connection between Napoleon and the Civil Code, but claims its egalitarian liberal aspects were undermined by Napoleon's demand for the final role in interpreting its laws. However, the supremacy of the sovereign over judges in interpreting law is a constant of the civil law tradition going back to its origins in Roman law, and carrying on through the democratic era. In the democratic era, sovereignty belongs to the national assembly rather than the monarch, but structurally this is the same and makes no difference to the citizen facing the state law courts. Though Napoleon was taken as an enemy by the leading French liberals, he was also the enemy of the conservative aristocracies and monarchies of Europe; and in the Hundred Days following his escape from Elba, he worked with Benjamin Constant on a more liberal version of Bonapartism. His nephew Napoleon III undermined republicanism and liberal democracy, but kept many of the forms, and favoured social welfare reforms. His career ended in ignominy when Bismarck tricked him into starting the Franco-Prussian War.

Nietzsche's other obvious hero, and representative of an old aristocratic Europe was Goethe (TI Skirmishes 49–51), but again we find that the nearest thing Nietzsche could find to an anti-liberal hero was entangled in liberalism in his own time, and through his later influence on liberal thinking. Goethe stood for an old Germany of a mosaic of small and large states with all different kinds of traditional governments and laws, under the loose sovereignty of the Habsburg Emperors in Vienna. These emperors exercised direct sovereignty mostly in their personal lands partly without and partly within the Holy Roman Empire of the German Nation, the strange and archaic sounding name for this peculiar system of multiplied traditional laws and political forms. Goethe himself was the chief minister of the Duchy of Saxe-Weimar. So we can see Goethe as the great representative of a pre-democratic, pre-liberal and pre-egalitarian Europe, because of his political role in an absolutist princely state and the links he makes between freedom and heroes of the medieval world in his literary output. Is that the sum of his influence? A glance at Ludwig von Mises' brief book of 1927, *Liberalism*, intended to revive the liberalism of the classical liberals, shows that Goethe appears with Schiller in the aesthetic aspects of liberalism, in an appreciation of the great individual, and so of the greatness of the inner individual, and of all individuals in general. Mises notes Goethe's positive attitude towards commercial life including a rather un-Nietzschean enthusiasm for double-entry book keeping (Mises 1985, p. 97). In Mises' view: "Liberal thinking permeates German classical poetry, above all the works of Goethe and Schiller" (Mises 1985, p. 196). We might take Goethe backwards into the pre-egalitarian world, but he was taken up in the egalitarian world, and he was part of its emergence.

The very idealisation of the medieval world in Goethe, Schiller and other German writers of the Enlightenment and Romantic eras as one of heroic individuality and the pluralism of states, itself undermined the customary nature of that world, and the sense of belonging to a hereditary order rather than possessing a self-founding individual excellence. Nietzsche's own thought is formed by awareness of that transition, which he projects back into Ancient Athens in *The Birth of Tragedy*. In Nietzsche's account, the bourgeois world is already emerging in Euripides and is very apparent in Meneander (BT 11). The Platonic dialogue is the route to the novel (BT 14), where the insights of tragedy have disappeared under tendencies to naturalism and logical schematism.

Looking at other anti-egalitarian heroes in Nietzsche, we find Julius Caesar (TI Skirmishes 38), whose power was based on a kind of democratic dictatorship, which sounds peculiar writing now when democracy is so associated with liberalism and separation of powers. However, it used to be widely thought that there was a complicity between the power of the democratic mob and the absolute ruler who ignores the restraining power of the aristocracy, laws and ancient offices, as when Caesar subordinated the Senate and other republican institutions to his will. There was an element of democratic revolution in Caesar's rise to power, and the institutionalisation of his power by Augustus, at least in the sense that the will of the Roman poor was given more weight than in the republican system compared with the senatorial class. Some of Nietzsche's remarks about aristocracy and the virtues of Rome might lead us to think that he admired the aristocratic power of the republican period, but even if we do accept this then we have a model for Nietzsche in the Roman Republic, which was the model for both the French and American Revolutions.

Nietzsche quotes Charles the Bold of Burgundy, referring to his enemy Louis XI of France as the universal spider, in the context of the hubris of self-examination (GM III 9). The universal spider with which Nietzsche contended in politics was not a king, but was democracy, in the sense of equality and of political participation, which he could not resist and which he contributed to in resisting. If this sounds like a strange claim, let us look at some of the words of the great prophet of democracy, of its virtues and its vices, Alexis de Tocqueville, in the Introduction to the first volume of *Democracy in America*.

> Once the work of the mind had become a source of power and wealth, every addition to knowledge, every fresh discovery, and every new idea became a germ of power within reach of the people. Poetry, eloquence, memory, the graces of the mind, the fires of the imagination and profundity of thought, all things scattered broadcast by heaven, were a profit to democracy, and even when it was adversaries of democracy who possessed these things, they still served its cause by throwing into relief the natural greatness of man. Thus its conquests spread along with those of civilisation and enlightenment, and literature was an arsenal from which all, including the weak and poor, daily chose their weapons. Running through the pages of our history, there is hardly an important event in the last seven hundred years which has not turned out to be advantageous for equality. The Crusades and the English wars decimated the nobles and divided up their lands. Municipal institutions introduced democratic liberty into the heart of the feudal monarchy; the invention of firearms made villein and noble proud on the field of battle; printing offered equal resources to their minds; the post brought enlightenment to hovel and palace alike; Protestantism maintained that all men are equally able to find the path to heaven. America, once discovered, opened a thousand new roads to fortune and gave any obscure adventurer the chance of wealth and power. If, beginning at the eleventh century, one takes stock of what was happening in France at fifty-year intervals, one finds that each time a double revolution has taken place in the state of society. The noble has gone down in the social scale, and the commoner gone up; as the one falls, the other rises. Each half century brings them closer, and soon they will touch. And that is not something peculiar to France. Wherever one looks one finds the same revolution taking place throughout the Christian world. Everywhere the diverse happenings in the lives of peoples have turned to democracy's profit; all men's efforts have aided it, both those who intended this and those who had no such intention, those who fought for democracy and those who were the declared enemies thereof; all have been driven pell-mell along the same road, and all have worked together, some against their will and some unconsciously, blind instruments in the hands of God. (Tocqueville 1988, pp. 11f.)

Nietzsche himself fits well into much of what Tocqueville discusses. Nietzsche's own claims to represent an aristocratic point of view, this son of a provincial pastor, is an effect of the coming together of noble and commoner status to which Tocqueville refers. The works of written imagination referred to by Tocqueville celebrate aristocracy in the first place, but then as he says are taken to cover the natural greatness of man, a greatness that can be inside anyone. Nietzsche's father was a Lutheran pastor, and as Tocqueville says it is Protestantism that spread the idea that all humans are equal in finding a way to salvation.

Nietzsche felt special because of a legend that his family was of aristocratic Polish origins (Frenzel 1966, p. 10), but there is no independent confirmation, and the whole idea is really a fantasy belonging to an age in which the commoner-noble status distinction is questioned. Thomas Hardy's novel of 1891, *Tess of the d'Urbervilles*, refers in its title to a rural lower class family which decides that it should replace its plebeian name of Durbeyfield with d'Urberville like a local aristocratic family, because of a rumoured Norman aristocratic ancestry deep in the Middle Ages. The comical self-elevation to the aristocracy is followed up by the trauma of Tess' rape by the son of a family which had purchased the d'Urberville name, as part of its own self-elevation from merchant class to aristocracy. Hardy was both a very philosophical novelist, and a great social observer amongst writers, and does capture with some wit and some pathos the reality of the lower and middle class wish to approach aristocratic status in the nineteenth century. Hardy himself was a reader of Nietzsche. Though there seem to be positive echoes of Nietzsche's philosophy in Hardy's literature, his direct remarks on Nietzsche's thoughts were mostly critical, and he was one of those who thought Nietzsche to blame for Prussian-German militarism and nationalism (Williamson 1978). There is no reason to believe he was aware of Nietzsche's own tendency to assume aristocratic antecedents, but he would probably have been amused to find he had accidentally satirised them in *Tess of the d'Urbervilles*.

Following Tocqueville's classic account, Nietzsche's own criticisms of democracy add to the growth of democracy, as his own poetic exploration of inner individuality is itself serving the democratic ideal of the individual. As Tocqueville argues in *Democracy in America*, democracy both brings about a respect for the rights of the individual and a self-centred individualism which threatens the moral coherence of the democratic society. In some respects, Nietzsche's exploration of immoralism and self-determining individuality is an example of that dangerous individualism, though it has a concern with the cultivation of the self and self-mastery, distinct from the vulgarity that Tocqueville associates with democratic individualism.

The aristocratic feudal world of the Middle Ages itself creates the conditions for democracy through the growth of cities with political institutions of self-government, wars which undermine the nobility, a church which promotes spiritual equality and provides a career path for poor but clever children. The culture of that world, including the spread of imaginative literature, spills over into all parts of society, so that those who are below the aristocracy become part of the world of literary culture, which itself tends to cultivate empathy and egalitarian individualism, even if it does begin with the adventures of knights. It is in this context that we should think of Nietzsche's enthusiasm for Goethe, the poet and thinker who stood between feudalism and liberalism, that is between admiration for the heroism of some medieval knightly figures, and the more bourgeois liberties of the modern world. Nietzsche himself notes the growth of empathy, of concern for the welfare and sensitivities of others, for example with what he suggests is a changing attitude to the sufferings of Don Quixote in Cervantes' novel (GM II 6). The main topic of *On the Genealogy of Morality II* is of how morality and legal codes are descended from customs and codes requiring punishments of extreme physical cruelty, and it is surely hard not to see Nietzsche as repelled as well as fascinated by that cruelty itself, and in any case preferring the individual who rises above urges for cruelty which are the source of *ressentiment*.

Who does Nietzsche look to as his heroes in the era of growing democracy and equality? Is it a list of ultra-reactionary conservatives, or at least conservatives suspicious of democratic enthusiasm? In such a case we would expect an appreciation of Edmund Burke and Joseph de Maistre on the literary side, and an appreciation of Klemens von Metternich and Otto von Bismarck on the political leadership side. Burke and de Maistre are completely absent from Nietzsche's writings, as is Metternich. Only Bismarck gets any attention (D 167, GS 104), and that is of a negative kind, since Nietzsche does not support the German nationalist aspects of Bismarck's politics, or Bismarck's style of government. For Nietzsche, Bismarck was a symbol of vulgarity and opportunism. One monarch of Nietzsche's time gets some appreciation, and that is the briefly reigning Kaiser Friedrich III (EH Z 1), the one Hohenzollern Emperor who favoured the liberals at home and Anglophile policies abroad. The first edition of *Human, All Too Human* was dedicated to Voltaire, who Nietzsche finds to be an Olympian alternative to Rousseau (HH I 463), but who nevertheless was a popular hero of his time due to his defiance of monarchical absolutism. Mirabeau the Younger, a prominent figure on the moderate liberal side of politics in the early stages of the French Revolution, is mentioned with admiration (GM I 10). Another French revolutionary, the rather more resolutely republican Lazare Carnot, gets an admiring mention (D 167). Carnot survived into the Empire period as a senior figure in the state, but kept his distance from the Emperor system.

Looking beyond European writers, Nietzsche took a great interest in Ralph Waldo Emerson, the Transcendentalist who promotes a kind of individualism based on historical progress towards perfection, which had a strong influence on American literature (including Herman Melville and Nathaniel Hawthorne), educational ideas, and political thought, as well as philosophy (SE 8, TI Skirmishes 13; cf. Zavetta 2008, Conant 2001, Cavell 1990). Emerson was an inspiration to the Abolitionist movement in America, and strongly associated with a democratic form of veneration of the individual and the individual search for perfection, though he was not an enthusiast for democracy. The universalism of Emerson's thought made it influential on the shape of democratic thinking. His influence can be seen even now in "democratic perfectionism", a strain of liberal political philosophy in which liberalism is seen as connected with moral ideas of virtue and self-perfection, rather than value neutrality in morals. Melville's *Moby-Dick* takes a great deal of inspiration from Emerson with regard to

Transcendentalism and the idealisation of the common man seen as part of the process of self-perfection, alongside the darker visions Melville explores.

The literary and political ways of taking Emerson in a democratic direction parallel what happens when Nietzsche is taken up politically, in a way that goes beyond a focus, however scholarly, on his gestures towards a version of Platonic elitism. Those who have done the most work on Nietzsche's connections with twentieth century totalitarianism do not find that his thought was well understood by totalitarian leaders; and that while parts of Nietzsche's thought anticipate parts of totalitarian thought, much of it undercuts totalitarian ways of thinking (Golomb/Wistrich 2002).

4 Selected Influences of Nietzsche on Political Thought

Given the vast quantity of material on Nietzsche from the point of view of political thought, along with the huge amount of material by political and social thinkers to some degree influenced by Nietzsche, including controversies about how far and in what way these thinkers have been influenced by Nietzsche, this part tries to illuminate the general issues, by concentrating on a contrast. That is the contrast between the fragmented and tentative ways in which Nietzsche influenced later authoritarian conservative elitism in the form of "Traditionalism", and the more complete and systematic ways Nietzsche has influenced those who wish to be engaged with liberal and democratic thought, in order to deepen and extend it. For the former group, some traditionalist thinkers will be discussed briefly, while for the latter group three major Nietzschean French philosophers will be discussed in comparative detail.

The influence of Nietzsche on political theory has not been towards Platonic elitism or political autocracy on the whole, largely the influence has been the opposite direction. The most obvious way that we can link Nietzsche with elitist and autocratic politics is the way that Nietzsche's name was used by Fascist and Nazi totalitarians, but there is no reason to believe that Nietzsche would have approved of mass political movements based on extreme nationalism, belief in racially pure populations and militarism, all things condemned by Nietzsche. In addition, Fascism and Nazism were mass movements whose leaders manipulated the masses, and so never completely left mass democratic politics behind as they always refer to national or people's will of some kind. The best known Nazi leaning commentator on Nietzsche, Adolf Baeumler, has not become a central reference in Nietzsche studies after his work of the twenties and thirties.

Thomas Mann was very attached to Nietzsche during his ultra-conservative years, but the influence is still clear in his later more liberal years. Some similar comments apply to W.B. Yeats, who had rather "traditionalist" esoteric-authoritarian-elitist interests in combination with his appreciation for Nietzsche. Further links can be made between Nietzsche and "traditionalist" ultra-conservative thought in Julius Evola, Stefan George, and others, but this has not resulted in any great academic study of Nietzsche's work, and the esotericist aspects of Traditionalism are at odds with the materialism and empiricism of Nietzsche's thought. Leo Strauss, who was broadly speaking traditionalist in orientation throughout his career, and was sympathetic to Fascism for a while, had some encounter with Nietzsche's thought, but of a very critical kind. Mircea Eliade makes some references to Nietzsche in his philosophy of religion and history, and was a pro-Fascist Traditionalist for a while, but the connection with the extreme right in Romania was finished by the time of his major intellectual achievements. Traditionalism, as with all other possible bridges between Nietzsche and totalitarian and extreme elitist political thought, provides some possible lineages, but nothing that can be taken as a systematic connection.

Since Traditionalism is the closest posture in the modern world to a movement for the Platonist dominance of an intellectual-aristocratic elite, its lack of fit with Nietzsche studies must have a qualifying effect on how we regard the Platonist form of elitism in Nietzsche. Another qualification is that the Platonist politics is at odds with Caesarism and Bonapartism, as the later phenomena refer to rule by someone of political and military strength, not rulers blessed with access to higher truths. In metaphysics Nietzsche argues for a dissolve of Platonism, and this must be in some tension with the metaphysical assumptions which underlie any belief in a guiding intellectual aristocracy with access to pure truths. This complete distance from Platonism is expressed most succinctly by Nietzsche in "How the Real World Became a Myth" in *Twilight of the Idols* (TI Fable), and passages of those kind must be taken into account in any discussion of Platonist politics in Nietzsche. On this basis, as we shall see, Foucault, Deleuze and Derrida arrive at a less "Platonist" reading of Nietzsche's politics. It is not so much that we should deny any leanings in that direction from Nietzsche, but that we must be very conscious of how it does not fit well with other parts of his thought, and this might be why he never published the text where the Platonist politics is most clear, *The Greek State*. Themes from *The Greek State* appear in later writings, but not as a fully developed account of the state.

One way of thinking about Nietzsche's politics is how it influenced the political thought of the most important of those thinkers, who have been deeply concerned with Nietzsche. Max Weber is an intriguing example, but the nature and extent of Nietzsche's influence is controversial. Weber's biographer Joachim Radkau minimizes this influence (Radkau 2009, pp. 167f.), but several authors have argued in detail that Weber's work is inspired by Nietzsche's thought (Eden 1983, Gerner 1994, Peukert 1989, Schwaabe 2010). For Wilhelm Hennis, the problem of the fate of humankind under the conditions of modernity is a leading question of Weber's thought. Hennis argues, that Weber takes up this question from Nietzsche, and that this problem is also at the centre of Nietzsche's thought (Hennis 1987, cf. Knoll's essay in this volume). Weber himself writes of politics that it is a "self-evident fact" that "the will to power is a driving motive of the leaders in parliament" (Weber 1988, p. 350), as well as: "Politics is: struggle [*Kampf*]" (Weber 1988, p. 329; cf. Weber 1988, p. 335, 337). Tamsin Shaw's contribution to the current volume deals with Nietzsche's influence on Weber, so readers can find more information and supporting argument on this topic there.

Other aspects of democratic and liberal ways of thinking about Nietzsche can be found in contributions to the present volume by Lawrence Hatab, Donovan Miyaski, Paul Patton, Nandita Biswas Mellamphy, Barry Stocker, and Rolf Zimmerman. As suggested above, any attempt to summarize the whole of the reception and reworking of Nietzsche's political thought is an impossible task within the space available, so the more democratic and liberal ways of thinking about Nietzsche will be examined in this section through a limited group of linked thinkers who themselves offer important challenges to democratic and liberal politics.

The class of those who have much to say about Nietzsche, and about political thought in ways that have much influence, notably includes three French thinkers who knew each other and had mutual influence: Foucault, Deleuze, Derrida. While it is not a straight forward matter to classify the political thought of these three, they are all in some way democratic and egalitarian in questions of political rights, and are far from Platonic aristocratic-elitism. They all take from Nietzsche a concern with difference, pluralism, conflict and change in the sphere of politics, so that in their thinking Nietzsche becomes the source of critique of fixed forms, rigid hierarchies, and submission to political sovereignty of any kind. Nietzsche becomes in these philosophers the source of the most persistent critique of authoritarianism and despotism, in a mode of a joyful celebration of multiplying differences and dissolving identities. Foucault's more politically significant texts include *Discipline and Punish* (Foucault 1977), which has many overtones of *On the Genealogy of Morality*, which – as explained above – is very compatible with "liberal" horror at legalised cruelty, particularly in the second essay. Thoughts about how Foucault carries on from

Nietzsche's theory of Will to Power and transforms his idea of genealogy can be found in Evangelia Sembou's contribution to the current volume. Foucault's Nietzsche inspired thoughts in this context include the following passage:

> [...] the notions of institutions of repression, rejection, exclusion, marginalization, are not adequate to describe, at the very centre of the carceral city, the formation of the insidious leniencies, unavowable petty cruelties, small acts of cunning, calculated methods, techniques, 'sciences' that permit the fabrication of the disciplinary individual. In this central and centralized humanity, the effect and instruments of complex power relations, bodies and forces subjected by multiple mechanisms of 'incarceration', objects for discourses that are themselves elements for this strategy, we must hear the distant roar of battle. (Foucault 1991, p. 308)

As with Nietzsche, there is a mixture of fascination and horror with regard to past cruelties, combined with the suggestion that human Enlightenment values may have produced as much cruelty in more dispersed and less dramatic ways. Foucault's whole critique of the understanding of theories of legal sovereignty clearly includes a taking up of Nietzsche, and while it is directed against a large current of "liberal" theory, it is articulated in the service of a critique of unrestrained state and social power which can itself be taken as a contribution to "liberal" thought of another kind. Liberalism since the Enlightenment is portrayed, by Foucault, as deeply complicit with a power of control through visibility and rationalisation, but in the service of a resistance to the cruelty of power which extends liberal sensibilities. The book that made Foucault famous, *History of Madness* (also known as *Madness and Civilisation*), has a Nietzsche influenced respect for the insights of madness, as something connected with tragedy, in opposition to the confinement, constraints, and rational controls placed on it later.

> The world of the early seventeenth century is strangely hospitable to madness. Madness is there, in the hearts of men and at the heart of things, an ironic sign blurring the distinction between the real and the chimerical, but with barely a memory of great tragic threat. (Foucault 2006, pp. 42f.)

As with the critical attitude to modern punishment, there is both a challenge to liberalism, taken up in the more left wing interpretations of Foucault, and a suggestion of how liberalism can be deepened, expanded, and pluralized through liberal encounters with Foucault. Foucault's own political engagements included a period of participation in the Maoist left, but he denies that he was a Marxist in any of his writings. Other periods of his life include engagement with a wide range of protests against power, and towards the end of his writing career a growing engagement with liberal, or liberal related, concepts (Foucault 2001, Foucault 2003, Foucault 2010).

Gilles Deleuze wrote one of his earlier books about Nietzsche (Deleuze 1983) and had an enduring interest in Nietzsche's thought. In his Nietzsche study, he does not present a Nietzschean political philosophy, or deny that Nietzsche might favour some Caesarist or Platonist form of government, but his way of writing about power and force in Nietzsche takes the reader's attention from such approaches to Nietzsche to an idea of Nietzsche as philosopher of pluralism, difference and becoming.

Deleuze's later work suggests that such metaphysical, or naturalist, pluralism is a model for social and political action and ways of thinking.

> Thus reactive force is: 1) utilitarian force of adaptation and partial limitation; 2) force which separates active force from what it can do, which denies or turns against itself (reign of the weak or of slaves). And, analogously, active force is: 1) plastic, dominant and subjugating force; 2) force which goes to the limit of what it can; 3) force which affirms its difference, which makes its difference an object of enjoyment and affirmation. Forces are only concretely and completely determined if these three pairs of characteristics are taken into account simultaneously. (Deleuze 1983, p. 61)

> It is no surprise, therefore, to find that every Nietzschean concept lies at the crossing of two unequal genetic lines. Not only the eternal return and the Overman, but laughter, play and dance. In relation to Zarathustra laughter, play and dance are affirmative powers of transmutation: dance transmutes heavy into light, laughter transmutes suffering into joy and the play of throwing (the dice) transmutes low into high. But in relation to Dionysus dance, laughter and play are affirmative powers of reflection and development. Dance affirms becoming and the being of becoming; laughter, roars of laughter, affirms multiplicity and the unity of multiplicity; play affirms chance and the necessity of chance. (Deleuze 1983, pp. 193f.)

From the political point of view, Deleuze's emphasis on limits, difference, affirmation, laughter, play, dance, becoming, multiplicity, chance, enjoyment, and transmutation, can be taken against authority, hierarchy, sovereignty, rationalism, and elitism in the state and in political life. Society can be seen as something conditioned by the multiplicity of constantly transforming forces, in which hierarchies and sovereignty relations can only be temporary, and are always under challenge. So whatever Nietzsche advocated in the way of Platonist politics or Caesarism can be seen as itself challenged by the Nietzschean emphasis on difference, becoming, and multiplicity. Forces flow through social organisations in ways which constantly disorder them, and suggest a politics of anti-authoritarian self-transformation, along with existential challenges to authority. This understanding of social and political thought can be seen in Deleuze in a series of later texts beginning with *Anti-Oedipus* (Deleuze 1984), which he co-authored with Félix Guattari. These texts use references to Nietzsche, along with Freud, Marx, and many others. The overall effect is that of a form of libertarianism strongly influenced by Marxist theory and revolutionary politics, confirmed by Deleuze's own political interests.

Derrida, unlike Foucault and Deleuze, did write directly on the political aspects of Nietzsche's thought, most significantly in *Politics of Friendship* (Derrida 1997)

> Shall we say that this responsibility which inspires (in Nietzsche) a discourse of hostility towards 'democratic taste' and 'modern ideas' is exercised against democracy in general, modernity in general; or that, *on the contrary*, it responds in the name of a hyperbole of democracy or modernity to come, before it, prior to its coming – a hyperbole for which the 'taste' and 'ideas' would be, in this Europe and this America then named by Nietzsche, but the mediocre caricatures, the talkative conscience, the perversion and the prejudice – the 'misuse of the term' *democracy*? Do not these lookalike caricatures – and precisely because they resemble it – constitute the worst enemy of what they resemble, whose name they have usurped? The worst repression, the very repression which one must, as close as possible to the analogy, open and literally *unlock*? (Derrida 1997, p. 38; italics by Derrida)

So Derrida presents two ways of taking Nietzsche's criticisms of democracy and modernity: we can take them straight and literally; we can take them as a strategy for attacking the bad imitations of democracy and modernity. When Derrida states two apparently opposing options, a common gesture of his (Stocker 2006, ch. 8), he prefers the second option, but always argues that the two options can never be completely separated from each other, and there can never be a complete triumph of the one over the other. So Derrida offers us a model for interpreting Nietzsche on democracy, which is that he is both the harshest critic of bad democracy and the greatest admirer of the real thing. Other passages from *Politics of Friendship* look at how, for Nietzsche, this is an alternative between the relation that neighbours and the relationship that friends have, to be found in *Thus Spoke Zarathustra*. The relation between neighbours is a relationship of mutual dependency between the mediocre, which is non-conflictual to the point of banality. The relation between friends is one of tension between two isolated individuals seeking their own elevation in character through struggle. This is such an ideal and difficult relationship to find that Derrida puts it in the context of the idea, going back to antiquity, that there is no such thing as a friend (Derrida 1997). He traces it back through the republican thinkers Montaigne and Cicero to Aristotle, so that the ideal of the friend is embedded in the ideal of the republic, which is appropriate to antique republicanism, the precedent for modern ideas of republicanism, democracy and liberty.

The implication of what Derrida says is that we take Nietzsche as someone contrasting the heroic republicanism of antiquity with the modern imitations, which even fail to be modern in their weak forms of repetition as poor imitation. There is a lot Derrida leaves unsaid here, even throughout the book as a whole, as he concentrates on the typically deep engagement with, and interlacing of, particular texts by Nietzsche, Aristotle, Montaigne, Blanchot and so on. What is left unsaid includes the whole field of the relation between what Constant referred to as the liberty of the ancients and the liberty of the moderns (Constant 1988). Constant thought of ancient liberty as more concerned with citizenship of a republic with shared institutions and customs, independent of external powers; and considered modern liberty to be defined by individualism, freedom from the state, and commercial life. Stocker's essay in this volume on Humboldt and Nietzsche explores some of the issues around the way that modern liberalism emerges from this sense of a less heroic, more self-centred version of the heroic forms of liberty in the past based on constant existential struggles with tyrants, enemy states, nature itself, and divine forces. Alternatives to "egalitarian liberalism" within current political theory such as "communitarianism" and "republicanism", itself are still formed within that contrast, and the same applies even for "Marxism" in modern theory, which has often become an attempt to reconcile egalitarianism and collectivism with capitalist political economy and individualism, particularly under the label of "Analytic Marxism", but also of "post-Marxism".

We can find some direct indications in Nietzsche that he is concerned with a contrast between heroic antique republican liberties and modern liberties of comfort. He gives a big indication that this is the way he is thinking in *On the Genealogy of Morality* I, when he quotes from the Funeral Speech of Pericles to the ancient Athenians (GM I 11), as recorded and possibly to some degree invented by Thucydides. Nietzsche quotes favourably from Pericles on his pride in how the wickedness of the Athenians is known to the world as well as their goodness. That is in the middle of a speech which is in praise of democracy as it appears in Athens. This is an instance of the heroic republicanism of the ancients, heroism in the sense that is disturbing to the moderns of pride, which is the power of a people, its toughness and unity of will, may be known to other peoples in painful ways, though maybe that pride is still there in more submerged forms.

Pericles represents the opposite pole to Platonic philosophical rule on the face of it. He was elected constantly by the Athenian people to provide military and governmental leadership. That is in a democracy where all free men who were descended from Athenians on both sides had the votes, so it was an electorate where day labourers and the owners of tiny farms had more votes than aristocrats and philosophers combined. Plato, however, appears to have respected Pericles as a leader and an individual, and since Pericles was a man of great culture, connected with the most famous families in Athens, he had some of the qualities of Plato's ideal ruler. That raises the question of how far democracy is the opposite of Platonic philosopher rule. Of course, Plato, like other aristocrats and oligarchs of the time, identified democracy with irrational passions, economic greed and corruption of the law, but even so the *Laws* at least show some appreciation of participatory government, as does Aristotle in the *Politics* (cf. Knoll 2009b). Even these critics of democracy found that it often had to be tolerated in at least limited form, in order to establish an enduring state. That idea was fully developed by the later Roman republicans, Polybius and Cicero. Polybian and Ciceronian republicanism aims to combine democracy with aristocracy and monarchy in a mixed government, extending the ideas of Plato and Aristotle. In the early modern age, Machiavelli's republican ideal of the mixed constitution is composed of exactly these three elements (Knoll/Saracino 2010). That understanding of a republic as a mixed form of government indicates that separation and opposition of democracy in relation to aristocracy and monarchy is not a straightforward operation.

Moving into Nietzsche's own time, enthusiasm for democracy could be combined with aristocratic suspicion of the uneducated majority, and of uncontrolled majorities in general. Those anxieties were expressed in the idea of the tyranny of the majority in Tocqueville (1988) and then in John Stuart Mill (*On Liberty* in Mill 1998). For Mill, democracy had to be combined with education of the poorer classes and barriers against abuse of power by temporary majorities, driven by plebeian ignorance and indifference to liberty (*Considerations on Representative Government* in Mill 1998). Despite the scorn heaped on Mill by Nietzsche, we can see there was much in common between them. Dana Villa discusses the relation between Mill, Nietzsche, Max Weber, Leo Strauss, and Hannah Arendt, with regard to antique citizenship and focused on Socrates in *Socratic Citizenship* (Villa 2001), showing an important way to deal with Nietzsche's place in political philosophy. That is unless we wish to consign him to some place irrelevant to most contemporary political thought, that of a very reactive nineteenth century ultraconservative railing against democracy and equality, with no contribution to make to the design of modern political institutions, modern political thought, and modern political culture.

Even if we are to take Nietzsche's most elitist and pro-slavery comments as definitive of his political thinking, he was concerned with liberty, in a manner focused on the maximum flourishing of the highest kind of self, and concern with liberty for a few tends to spill over into ideas of liberty for all. The spill over process, of course, refers to the effects of the thought of Nietzsche and others, rather than the intentions of the authors concerned. That is all part of the process Tocqueville describes of the inevitable step by step triumph of democracy. John Locke wrote from the point of view of the Whig aristocracy, but his political theory was taken as an inspiration for democratic revolution. The English barons forced King John to sign *Magna Carta* for their own selfish reason in 1215, but demanded rights for all free men within England, rights which eventually applied to the lowest in status as velleinage, a form of serfdom, declined and disappeared. This spill over from an elite to the whole population in mass democracy has been repeated many times over, and when Nietzsche writes about the Overman, at least in some respects his presentation provides a model, willingly or not, for citizenship in a mass democracy, in the forms of political engagement suggested by Foucault, Deleuze and Derrida. We can think of Nietzsche's famous comment about liberal institutions betraying liberty in *Twilight of the Idols* (TI Skirmishes 38), and reflect on how that applies to the liberty of all members of a political community.

In this context it is particularly important to consider Nietzsche's friendship with Jacob Burckhardt, and the kind of aristocratic liberty Burckhardt discusses in *The Greeks and Greek Civilization* (Burckhardt 1998) and *The Civilization of the Renaissance in Italy* (Burckhardt 1944). Though his thought is aristocratic in orientation, it includes an awareness of the cost for the lowest classes in the formation of aristocratic dominated political communities, and that has been compared with the liberalism of Mill and Tocqueville (Kahan 1992). Particularly in that context, we can see that Hannah Arendt is a prime source of thought about how antique and aristocratic concepts of liberty can become part of a participatory mass democracy (Arendt 1990, Arendt 1998), and therefore an important source of thought about how to take up Nietzsche's political theory, as Villa suggests (Villa 2001, Villa 2008). In the field of Nietzsche commentary, the key references here, apart from Villa, are Lester Hunt in libertarian thought (Hunt 1993) and William E. Connolly in egalitarian liberal thought (Connolly 2002, Connolly 2008), along with authors in this volume such as Hatab, Patton, and Miyasaki. However, the democratic and liberal ways of thinking about Nietzsche constitute only one side of the controversy filled debate about Nietzsche's political preferences and affinities. In the present volume contributions by Bamford, Cristi, Dombowsky, Roth, and Knoll present arguments for the more radical aristocratic and anti-liberal interpretations of Nietzsche's politics.

5 Organisation and Contents of the Book

The book begins with a section on the variety of possible approaches to Nietzsche's political thought, starting with Rolf Zimmermann's *The "Will to Power":*

Towards a Nietzschean Systematics of Moral-Political Divergence in History in Light of the 20th Century. Zimmermann offers a broad survey of the ways of thinking about Nietzsche politically and using his ideas to analyse politics. Zimmermann looks at the different possible political readings of Nietzsche's own texts, the ways he is taken up politically, and how we can use Nietzsche's thought to understand political movements in the twentieth century. There is an authoritarian elitist element in Nietzsche's thought that can be taken in an anti liberal-democratic direction, but does not have to be, since respect for elites can be part of liberal democratic thought. The First World War had a major effect on the way that Nietzsche was understood politically, since it suited both sides to present Nietzsche as the inspiration for a German anti-liberal attitude as opposed to the liberal democracies on the Allied side. After that it was then possible to go further and see Nietzsche as the inspiration for Nazism. However, we can see in Max Weber's turn to liberal republicanism after the war a way of incorporating Nietzsche's belief in a political elite within democratic thought. Nietzsche's relation to totalitarianism of all forms is more that he diagnosed their possibility than that he advocated such systems.

In *The Liberatory Limits of Nietzsche's Colonial Imagination in "Dawn" 206*, Rebecca Bamford looks at *Dawn* as example of a therapeutic approach by Nietzsche to philosophy, which reaches a limit to its applicability in its attitude to colonialism, leading us to the anti-egalitarian Nietzsche. Nietzsche suggests that European workers should either become "Chinese" in obedience and willingness to work, or should migrate out of Europe. Nietzsche treats the land to be colonized as empty, so suitable for the European working class. There is an indifference both to working class Europeans and to the people living in the lands to be colonized. The acts of colonization are therapeutic for the colonisers and the European elites, and they are indifferent to the concerns of the native populations negatively effected by colonization. Nietzsche's notebooks are full of the merits of colonialism for a while, so this is not a small scale thing for him. The colonization makes the grand unity and future of Europe possible.

In *Nietzsche's Political Materialism: Diagram for a Nietzschean Politics*, Nandita Biswas Mellamphy looks at the political implications of Nietzsche's thought through François Laruelle's encounter with Nietzsche, an encounter which is functional rather than engaged in close reading. That is Laruelle seeks to clarify the conflicting consequences of Nietzsche's thoughts, rather than aim at an interpretation governed by coherence. This follows the ways that Foucault, Deleuze and others had read Nietzsche through bending and reusing his ideas, and goes beyond them in examining Nietzsche's thought as the intersection of two poles, which can be called Dionysian and Apollinian, and which produces a space structured by four points. In that way of reading Nietzsche, we can see that he produces both fascist and anti-fascist readings. The apparently fascist ideas in Nietzsche come from following a way of thinking until it is undermined, so that the strongest result of Nietzsche's thought for politics is a positing followed by undermining of fascism. This refers to the Dionysian non-identity pole of Nietzsche as opposed to the Appollinian pole.

The book then moves on to those contributions which emphasize a more democratic, or liberal, or more egalitarian politics in Nietzsche. In *Nietzsche's Will to Power and Politics*, Lawrence Hatab argues that the Nietzschean understanding of politics is based in the struggles of the Will to Power, and that the agonistic nature of politics on this basis has implications for democratic politics. Hatab's argument is that while Nietzsche was not a democrat, he could not avoid the reality that political ideas of struggle and hierarchy enter into democratic politics. There are two ends to this. At one end is the argument that Nietzsche's political thought is not as antithetical to democracy as he liked to claim; the other end of the argument is that democratic politics is not as egalitarian and free of violent oppositions as it is often taken to be. On this point, Hatab takes Locke as an example of an early democratic thinker whose attitude to land in North America is that it is wasted by the native population and is therefore open to development by more advanced peoples. Hatab also refers to Foucault as part of the argument for understanding the dark side of democracy and Enlightenment, where Nietzsche's ideas can be seen to be relevant.

In *Nietzsche on Power and Democracy circa 1876–1881*, Paul Patton examines three texts from the late 1870s and early 1880s, where Nietzsche is most sympathetic to democracy: *Daybreak, The Wanderer and His Shadow, Human, All Too Human*. There is an idea of "democracy to come" in these texts, where Nietzsche suggests a hope for forms of democracy in which the worst aspects of political life have been overcome. Negative aspects of democracy include the existence of political parties for Nietzsche. For Nietzsche, parties aim to force individuals to accept an idea of the common good which cannot be real, since all parties have different views of it. Nietzsche believes that what is good is not what forces individuals into a restrictive form of common good, but is rather what will enable citizens to realise differences from others and maintain distance. Nietzsche takes a critical view of the state as oppressive and restrictive of human growth, but it is wrong to assume that Nietzsche takes that thought in an anti-political or anarchistic direction. Nietzsche aims for better forms of organisation and power in the future.

In *A Comparison of Friedrich Nietzsche and Wilhelm von Humboldt as Products of Classical Liberalism*, Barry Stocker argues that the anti-liberal interpretations of Nietzsche both give too much importance to a literal interpretation of Nietzsche's most provocatively anti-egalitarian statements; and attribute too much of an egalitarian and anti-heroic way of thinking to liberal thought. That is such interpretations assume that classical liberals from Locke to J.S. Mill are more egalitarian and anti-heroic than they are in reality. Stocker takes up a comparison between Nietzsche and Wilhelm von Humboldt to demonstrate compatibility between at least some part of Nietzsche's political thinking and a large part of classical liberal thought. The comparison refers to Humboldt's rejection of anything more than the most minimal state and his admiration for ancient heroic virtues, both of which attitudes Humboldt shared with Nietzsche. Like Nietzsche, Humboldt regarded the modern focus on minimizing suffering and avoiding war with suspicion, since such an attitude detracts from the kind of strength that ancient peoples had. Both share a vision of the greatness of the human individual when set free of conformity and an interventionist state.

In *A Nietzschean Case for Illiberal Egalitarianism*, Donovan Miyasaki argues that we can accept Nietzsche's illiberalism while rejecting his anti-egalitarianism. Though it is illiberal egalitarianism, Miyasaki has a starting point in the liberal egalitarianism of John Rawls, in order to show how Rawlsian ways of thinking can be adapted to ends which are not entirely those of Rawls himself. So while Rawls argues that the principle of social and economic organization should benefit the worst off in that society, Miyasaki proposes that we adopt the principle that the best off will not be harmed. The argument is that the highest kind of people will benefit from egalitarianism. Their exceptional qualities will not be threatened by the possibility of the lower kind of people unifying against them, if the lower people have nothing to gain in terms of redistribution of economic goods. This is egalitarianism which is normative rather than descriptive, because while it prescribes equal social and economic outcomes, it does not assume equality of value between different humans.

The book then moves on to a section which contains a sequence of contributions that emphasize the aristocratic, or anti-liberal, or non-egalitarian view of Nietzsche, beginning with Renato Cristi's *Nietzsche, Theognis and Aristocratic Radicalism*. Cristi suggests that a decisive moment in the history of Nietzsche's political thought can be found in his reading of the poetry of Theognis, which laments the triumph of plebeians who have acquired commercial power, and political power through democracy, over the Megarian aristocracy. So everything across Nietzsche's development can be contextualized through Theognis along with Homer as a poet of early aristocratic values. Cristi also refers to the label of "aristocratic radical", which Georg Brandes suggested to Nietzsche and that Nietzsche accepted. So all of Nietzsche's comments on social and political matters can be seen as the expression of belief in the rule by an aristocracy or oligarchy, which would be the rule of the best over the valueless lower orders. Any attempt to think of Nietzsche as an apolitical cultural thinker, as Walter Kaufmann suggested, or as someone whose ideas can be used for democracy, as Lawrence Hatab argues, ignores the radical commitment of Nietzsche to aristocratic values.

In *Aristocratic Radicalism as a Species of Bonapartism: Preliminary Elements*, Don Dombowsky makes the case for a Caesarist-Bonapartist reading of Nietzsche's politics, which he regards as one form of Nietzsche's "aristocratic radicalism". This is justified through the use of Napoleon's own preferred symbols in connection with the figure of Zarathustra, along with the suggestion that Zarathustra's multiplicity of selves makes him structurally similar to Bonaparte. Dombowsky argues that the Civil Code was given a very conservative interpretation by Bonaparte, and he only allowed his own views to serve as interpretations. The plebiscitary-democratic aspect of Bonapartism was only allowed to intrude very occasionally. Bonapartism can be regarded as a return of the old regime for these reasons, and as aristocratic, because of the role of the nobility in it. Bonapartism emphasizes patriarchy and the militarization of the whole of society, views we should then attribute to Nietzsche.

In *Political and Psychological Prerequisites for Legislation in the Early Nietzsche*, Phillip H. Roth looks at the early Nietzsche as an aesthetic thinker attempting an inversion of Plato. The inversion of Plato comes in the replacement of metaphysical ideals with aesthetic ideals. This still leaves Nietzsche as a political Platonist who believes in the rule of an elite over the rest of society. However, in Nietzsche the elite is aesthetic according to values expounded in *Birth of Tragedy*. For Nietzsche, Socrates is anti-Greek, so the proper polity will not be based on the Socratic values which lead Plato to expel poets from the ideal state. The aestheticism fits with an ideal of deception, in which the purpose of laws is concealed behind the wish to benefit the psychological preservation of artistic geniuses and to allow them to rule. Nietzsche simplifies the three fold structure of the hierarchy of Plato's republic, so there is just a twofold distinction between rulers and the lower classes who serve them. The rulers make up laws which suit themselves and impose them on the lower classes in the spirit of deception which an aesthetic perspectival view promotes.

In *The "Übermensch" as a Social and Political Task: A Study in the Continuity of Nietzsche's Political Thought*, Manuel Knoll takes issue with the scholarly tradition of an individualistic understanding of the "Übermensch". Knoll argues that the idea of the "Übermensch", which Nietzsche introduces in *Thus Spoke Zarathustra,* is continuous with Nietzsche's thought from beginning to end, and is consistently focused on the idea of a higher kind of human. This continuity starts with an early interest in Plato's politics, which are the inspiration for Nietzsche's own political thought, even as he rejects Plato's metaphysics. Nietzsche believed that for Plato the guardians of the ideal state are a higher kind of human, and Nietzsche stayed true to this vision while taking Platonic metaphysics as a major object of attack. This continuity ends with *The Anti-Christ*, in which Nietzsche conceives of the social order, as in *Beyond Good and Evil*, primarily as a means for making possible higher and highest men. The idea of the "Übermensch" strictly speaking in Nietzsche begins with the idea of the death of God, so that something else has to be found to give meaning to the world. That something emerges as the *Übermensch* who is the "meaning of the earth", existing as *Übermenschen*, who are the different kinds of higher humans in all fields of human life.

The book then moves on to contributions concerning Nietzsche's moral and ethical thought in relation to politics. In *Care of Self in "Dawn": On Nietzsche's Resistance to Bio-political Modernity*, Keith Ansell-Pearson looks at Nietzsche's thoughts about ethics and the self in *Dawn* in relation to Foucault's views about care of the self and biopolitics. For Foucault, care of the self refers to an art of living which precedes law and absolute moral requirements, and in which the self creates itself. Biopolitics refers to Foucault's concerns that the state had become a means of imposing the prolongation of life on individuals, which becomes an instrument of interference and control. Nietzsche, like Foucault, goes back to the ancient ethical thinkers, not in order to follow any of them, but to look at examples in Epictetus, and others, of care of self. Epictetus provides an example for Nietzsche of a kind of ethics in which we do not subordinate ourselves to concern with others, but are focused on perfecting *our* self. Nietzsche's aim is to draw our attention to the pleasure of existence, so a kind of liberty outside state and law.

In *"We who are different, we immoralists..."*, Daniel Conway concentrates on "immoralism" at the end of Nietzsche's writing career, particularly with regard to *Twilight of the Idols* and *Ecce Homo*. He argues that Nietzsche's thought on morality after *Thus Spoke Zarathustra* is committed to an "immoralist" position, not so much as a rejection of morality, but rather as a challenge to the way that moral concepts are deep inside our sense of historical identity. Immoralism becomes more a means of contesting morality as moralism. But immoralism does not completely reject morality. Morality as moralism is caught up in a narrow intolerant assumption of what morality is, which excludes different possibilities. The more immoralist position favours plurality of what morality means, combined with a grand conception of the salvationist role of immoralism for humanity. Nietzsche's criticisms of "morality" have a particular target which is the Christian church, and Nietzsche wishes to show that the church cannot live up to its own morality, so undermining its claims to have a compelling morality.

In *Political Realism Naturalized: Nietzsche on the State, Morality, and Human Nature*, Christian J. Emden considers the relation of Nietzsche's naturalism to his morality and his realism in politics. Emden extends the discussion of political realism from the role of states in international relations to a general claim regarding politics as a struggle for power distinct from morality. He puts that forward as part of Nietzsche's view of politics and combines it with Nietzsche's view of moral community as dependent on political power relations. Emden argues that this analysis is dependent on Nietzsche's philosophical naturalism, because it is in naturalizing moral concepts that Nietzsche is led to understand humans as power seeking. Though Nietzsche is a realist with regard to politics, it is a mistake to see him as a moral anti-realist. Nietzsche refers to the different moral standards of masters and slaves. That argument in Nietzsche rests on a capacity of masters to recognize their own advantage. The morality of masters rests on epistemic privilege with regard to understanding how to follow self-interest through moral codes. The epistemic superiority as a basis for morality introduces a realist aspect into Nietzsche's moral theory.

In *The "Last Man" Problem: Nietzsche and Weber on Political Attitudes to Suffering*, Tamsin Shaw discusses the fear of the "last man" in Nietzsche and brings his wish to overcome it into comparison with the hope for a charismatic leader in Weber. Both Nietzsche and Weber are concerned with a loss of the acceptance of sacrifice and suffering, for ourselves and for others, as modern societies move towards eudaimonic ideas of minimizing suffering. In earlier stages of history, humans could accept suffering as necessary to some overall good. Nietzsche's and Weber's concern with this problem has its roots in the religious discussion of theodicy, that is the justification of the existence of God in relation to the suffering in the world. The problem Nietzsche and Weber discuss appears because there is no God to justify suffering, and a non-heroic rejection of all suffering is spreading. The growth of utilitarian and hedonistic thought confronts Nietzsche with the possibility of human decay when suffering can no longer be accepted, the mentality of the "last man". Weber's idea of the charismatic political leader is an attempt to provide a positive alternative to Nietzsche's "last man", but should be seen as unnecessary within Weber's own thought because of his acceptance of materialist causation in history.

The collection concludes with some contributions on the methodological side of Nietzsche, with regard to how the uses of genealogy and of physiology appear in Nietzsche's use of political concepts, and how such methods can be applied to the understanding of Nietzsche's thought. In *The Politics of Physiology*, Razvan Ioan follows the interaction between Nietzsche's study of physiology and his political ideas, and the way this interaction changed over time. He argues that we cannot reduce all of Nietzsche's thought to physiology, and that some part of his references to physiology are metaphorical. However, not all such references are metaphorical, some are symptomatic and some are causal. The place of physiological explanation is causal in relation to politics, in the sense that Nietzsche thinks physiology should be used in politics to select better humans. Nietzsche studied the major books of that time in the discipline. At the time of *On the Genealogy of Morality*, this led Nietzsche to an interest in the hierarchy of the organism, of the rank of different cells in the body, which connected with his views of the social hierarchy of master and slave. Nietzsche's later research into physiology led him to a more radical view of hierarchy, which requires the destruction of the lower forms of life in war.

In *On the Genealogy of Nietzsche's Values*, Tom Angier raises questions about Nietzsche's use of genealogical method, concluding that it is fatally flawed by a failure to distinguish between the value of moral concepts and the origin of those concepts, so that there is a genetic fallacy. However, there is a proper way of using genealogy, and we see how this works by using the work of Norbert Elias on German culture in the time of Nietzsche. German culture of that time is troubled by a split between values of power and aesthetic values. Power is concerned with war and the might of the state, while the aesthetic is concerned with the beauty of art objects, and non-power related values. Elias showed how the nineteenth century German Middle Class was divided between those values and was concerned with the relationship between them. We can see that tension in Nietzsche, as he gives value both to power and to art, leaving Nietzsche commentators in an awkward situation as they try to decide whether Nietzsche's values are more oriented to creativity through power or through art.

In *Foucault's use of Nietzsche*, Evangelia Sembou draws attention to the differences between Foucault and Nietzsche, and the need to understand that though Foucault learned from Nietzsche, his thought is often more distinct from Nietzsche than early acquaintance might suggest. Overall, Foucault was a modernist who continued the project of Kantian Enlightenment, even though coming after Nietzsche. It is Nietzsche, the earlier thinker, who was more the post-modernist who opposed Enlightenment. We cannot understand the modernist/postmodernist distinction as defined by succession in time, but by different reactions to Enlightenment, so that a critical early attitude to Enlightenment can be said to be postmodernist, while a later positive attitude to Enlightenment can be said to be modernist. That is why Nietzsche can be postmodernist and Foucault can be modernist. In Foucault there is an endlessness of interpretation in his understanding of "genealogy", while in Nietzsche genealogy goes back to will to power as the final point of reference, and therefore has a natural basis. Foucault creatively misreads Nietzsche when he fails to distinguish between the place of origin and the place of purposes in genealogy. There is a real origin for Nietzsche, in a way there is not for Foucault, and what Nietzsche focuses on is the changes in purpose of the meaning of existing practices. Foucault sees the changes in meaning and purpose as showing that the practice has no origin, so that for Foucault it is the change which is everything.

Bibliography

Ansell-Pearson, Keith (1991): *Nietzsche contra Rousseau*. Cambridge: Cambridge University Press.
Ansell-Pearson, Keith (1994): *An Introduction to Nietzsche as Political Thinker. The Perfect Nihilist*. Cambridge: Cambridge University Press.
Appel, Fredrick (1999): *Nietzsche contra Democracy*. Ithaca, London: Cornell University Press.
Arendt, Hannah (1990): *On Revolution*. London: Penguin.
Arendt, Hannah (1998): *The Human Condition*. Chicago: University of Chicago Press.
Brobjer, Thomas H. (1998): "The Absence of Political Ideals in Nietzsche's Writings. The Case of the Laws of Manu and the Associated Caste-Society". In: *Nietzsche-Studien* 27, pp. 300–318.
Brobjer, Thomas H. (2001): "Nietzsche as Political Thinker. A Response to Don Dombowsky". In: *Nietzsche-Studien* 30, pp. 394–396.
Brobjer, Thomas H. (2008): "Critical Aspects of Nietzsche's Relation to Politics and Democracy". In: Herman W. Siemens/Vasti Roodt (eds.): *Nietzsche, Power and Politics: Rethinking Nietzsche's Legacy for Political Thought*. Berlin, New York: de Gruyter, pp. 205–227.
Burckhardt, Jacob (1944): *The Civilization of the Renaissance in Italy*. S.G.C. Middlemore (trans.). Oxford: Phaidon Press.
Burckhardt, Jacob (1998): *The Greeks and Greek Civilization*. Oswyn Murray (ed.), Sheila Stern (trans.). New York: St Martin's Griffin.
Cavell, Stanley (1990): *Conditions Handsome and Unhandsome: The Constitution of Emersonian Perfectionism*. Chicago: University of Chicago Press.
Conant, James (2001): "Nietzsche's Perfectionism: A Reading of Schopenhauer as Educator". In: Richard Schacht (ed.): *Nietzsche's Postmoralism: Essays on Preludes to Nietzsche's Philosophy of the Future*. Cambridge: Cambridge University Press, pp. 181–257.
Connolly, William E. (1988): *Political Theory and Modernity*. Oxford, New York: Basil Blackwell.
Connolly, William E. (2002): *Identity/Difference: Democratic Negotiations of Political Paradox*. Minneapolis: University of Minnesota Press.
Connolly, William E. (2008): "Nietzsche, Democracy, Time". In: Herman W. Siemens/ Vasti Roodt (eds.): *Nietzsche, Power and Politics: Rethinking Nietzsche's Legacy for Political Thought*. Berlin, New York: de Gruyter, pp. 109–141.
Constant, Benjamin (1998): "The Liberty of the Ancients Compared with that of the Moderns". In: Benjamin Constant: *Constant: Political Writings*. Biancamaria Fontana (ed.). Cambridge: Cambridge University Press.

Conway, Daniel (1997): *Nietzsche & the Political*. London, New York: Routledge.
Danto, Arthur Coleman (1965): *Nietzsche as Philosopher*. New York, London: Macmillan, Collier-Macmillan.
Deleuze, Gilles (1983): *Nietzsche and Philosophy*. Hugh Tomlinson (trans.). London: Athlone Press.
Deleuze, Gilles/Guattari, Félix (1984): *Anti-Oedipus: Capitalism and Schizophrenia*. Robert Hurley, Mark Steen, and Helen R. Lane (trans.). London: Athlone Press.
Derrida, Jacques (1997): *Politics of Friendship*. George Collins (trans.). London: Verso.
Detwiler, Bruce (1990): *Nietzsche and the Politics of Aristocratic Radicalism*. Chicago, London: University of Chicago Press.
Dombowsky, Don (2001): "A Response to Thomas H. Brobjer's 'The Absence of Political Ideals in Nietzsche's Writings'". In: *Nietzsche-Studien* 30, pp. 387–393.
Dombowsky, Don (2004): *Nietzsche's Machiavellian Politics*. Basingstoke et. al.: Palgrave Macmillan.
Dombowsky, Don (2008): "Nietzsche as Bonapartist". In: Herman W. Siemens/Vasti Roodt (eds.): *Nietzsche, Power and Politics: Rethinking Nietzsche's Legacy for Political Thought*. Berlin, New York: de Gruyter, pp. 347–369.
Eden, Robert (1983): *Political Leadership and Nihilism: A Study of Weber and Nietzsche*. Tampa: University Press of Florida.
Foucault, Michel (1991): *Discipline and Punish: The Birth of the Prison*. Alan Sheridan (trans.). London: Penguin.
Foucault, Michel (2001): *Fearless Speech*. Joseph Pearson (ed.). Los Angeles: Semiotext(e).
Foucault, Michel (2003): *"Society Must Be Defended". Lectures at the Collège de France. Mauro Bertani and Alessandro Fontana (eds.), David Macey (trans.). 1975–1976*. New NY: Picador.
Foucault, Michel (2008): *History of Madness*. Jean Khlafa (ed.), Jonathan Murphy and Jean Khalfa (trans.). London: Routledge.
Foucault, Michel (2010): *The Birth of Biopolitics: Lectures at the Collège de France, 1978–1979*. Michel Senellart (ed.), Graham Burchell (trans.). New York: Palgrave Macmillan.
Frenzel, Ivo (1966): *Friedrich Nietzsche in Selbstzeugnissen und Bilddokumenten*. Reinbek: Rowohlt.
Gerner, Andrea (1994): *Wissenschaft und Leben. Max Webers Antwort auf eine Frage Friedrich Nietzsches*. Göttingen: Vandenhoeck & Ruprecht.
Golomb, Jacob/Wistrich, Robert S. (2002): *Nietzsche, Godfather of Fascism? On the Uses and Abuses of Philosophy*. Princeton: Princeton University Press.
Hatab, Lawrence (1995): *A Nietzschean Defense of Democracy. An Experiment in Postmodern Politics*. Chicago, La Salle (Illinois): Open Court.
Heit, Helmut/Abel, Günther/Brusotti, Marco (eds.) (2012): *Nietzsches Wissenschaftsphilosophie. Hintergründe, Wirkungen und Aktualität*. Berlin, Boston: de Gruyter.
Hennis, Wilhelm (1987): *Max Webers Fragestellung. Studien zur Biographie des Werkes*. Tübingen: Mohr Siebeck.
Hunt, Lester (1993): *Nietzsche and the Origin of Virtue*. London: Routledge.
Kahan, Alan S. (1992): *Aristocratic Liberalism: The Social and Political Thought of Jacob Burckhardt, John Stuart Mill and Alexis de Tocqueville*. New York: Oxford University Press.
Kaufmann, Walter (1950): *Nietzsche: Philosopher, Psychologist, Antichrist*. Princeton: Princeton University Press.

Knoll, Manuel (2009a): "Nietzsches Begriff der sozialen Gerechtigkeit". In: *Nietzsche-Studien* 38, pp. 156–181.
Knoll, Manuel (2009b): *Aristokratische oder demokratische Gerechtigkeit? Die politische Philosophie des Aristoteles und Martha Nussbaums egalitaristische Rezeption*. Munich: Fink.
Knoll, Manuel (2010): "Nietzsches 'aristokratischer Radikalismus'. Seine Konzeption des Menschen, der Verteilungsgerechtigkeit und des Staates". In: Hans-Martin Schönherr-Mann (ed.): *Der Wille zur Macht und die 'große Politik' – Friedrich Nietzsches Staatsverständnis*. Baden-Baden: Nomos, pp. 35–67.
Knoll, Manuel/Saracino, Stefano (2010) (eds.): *Niccolò Machiavelli – Die Geburt des Staates*. Stuttgart: Franz Steiner.
Leiter, Brian (2002): *Routledge Philosophy Guidebook to Nietzsche on Morality*. London: Routledge.
Middleton, Christopher (ed./transl.) (1996): *Selected Letters of Friedrich Nietzsche*. Indianapolis: Hackett.
Mill, John Stuart (1998): *On Liberty and Other Essays*. John Gray (ed.). Oxford: Oxford University Press.
Mises, Ludwig von (1985): *Liberalism*. Ralph Raico (trans.). Irvington: The Foundation for Economic Education.
Ottmann, Henning (1999): *Philosophie und Politik bei Nietzsche*. 2nd improved and enlarged edition. Berlin, New York: de Gruyter.
Owen, David (1994): *Maturity and Modernity. Nietzsche, Weber, Foucault and the Ambivalence of Reason*. London, New York: Routledge.
Owen, David (1995): *Nietzsche, Politics and Modernity. A Critique of Liberal Reason*. London, Thousand Oaks, New Delhi: Sage Publications.
Peukert, Detlev (1989): *Max Webers Diagnose der Moderne*. Göttingen: Vandenhoeck & Ruprecht.
Radkau, Joachim (2009): *Max Weber: A Biography*. Patrick Camiller (trans.). Cambridge: Polity Press.
Reckermann, Alfons (2003): *Lesarten der Philosophie Nietzsches. Ihre Rezeption und Diskussion in Frankreich, Italien und der angelsächsischen Welt 1960–2000*. Berlin, New York: de Gruyter.
Schwaabe, Christian (2010): "Das Schicksal des Menschen im Schatten des toten Gottes. Zur Bedeutung Friedrich Nietzsches für Max Webers Diagnose der Moderne". In: Hans-Martin Schönherr-Mann (ed.): *Der Wille zur Macht und die 'große Politik' – Friedrich Nietzsches Staatsverständnis*. Baden-Baden: Nomos, pp. 235–252.
Shaw, Tamsin (2007): *Nietzsche's Political Skepticism*. Princeton, Oxford: Princeton University Press.
Siemens, Herman W. (2008): "Yes, No, Maybe So ... Nietzsche's Equivocations on the Relation between Democracy and 'Grosse Politik'". In: Herman W. Siemens/Vasti Roodt (eds.): *Nietzsche, Power and Politics: Rethinking Nietzsche's Legacy for Political Thought*. Berlin, New York: de Gruyter, pp. 231–268.
Siemens, Herman W./Roodt, Vasti (eds.) (2008): *Nietzsche, Power and Politics: Rethinking Nietzsche's Legacy for Political Thought*. Berlin, New York: de Gruyter.
Stocker, Barry (2006): *Derrida on Deconstruction*. London: Routledge.
Strong, Tracy B. (2000): *Friedrich Nietzsche and the Politics of Transfiguration*. 3rd enlarged edition. Urbana, Chicago: University of Illinois Press.

Tocqueville, Alexis de (1988): *Democracy in America*. J.P. Mayer (ed.), George Lawrence (trans.). New York: Harper Perennial.
Villa, Dana (2001): *Socratic Citizenship*. Princeton: Princeton University Press.
Villa, Dana (2008): "How Nietzschean was Arendt?". In: Herman W. Siemens/Vasti Roodt (eds.): *Nietzsche, Power and Politics: Rethinking Nietzsche's Legacy for Political Thought*. Berlin, New York: de Gruyter, pp. 395–409.
Warren, Mark (1988): *Nietzsche and Political Thought*. Cambridge, London: MIT Press.
Weber, Max (1988): "Parlament und Regierung im neugeordneten Deutschland (Mai 1918)". In: Max Weber: *Gesammelte Politische Schriften*. Gesammelte Aufsätze Vol. 7. Tübingen: UTB/Mohr Siebeck, pp. 306–443.
Williams, Bernard (1993): *Shame and Necessity*. Berkeley: University of California Press.
Williamson, Eugene (1978) "Thomas Hardy and Friedrich Nietzsche: The Reasons". In: *Comparative Literature Studies* XIV(4), pp. 403–413.
Zavatta, Benedetta (2008): "Nietzsche and Emerson on Friendship and Its Ethical-Political Implications". In: Herman W. Siemens/Vasti Roodt (eds.): *Nietzsche, Power and Politics: Rethinking Nietzsche's Legacy for Political Thought*. Berlin, New York: de Gruyter, pp. 511–540.

I. The Variety of Approaches to Nietzsche's Political Thought

Rolf Zimmermann
The "Will to Power": Towards a Nietzschean Systematics of Moral-Political Divergence in History in Light of the 20th Century*

Clarifications of the central concepts of Nietzsche's work represent a never-ending task. The "will to power" in particular is ambiguous in various respects. Without an explication of its meaning or its different meanings, there can be little success in developing the moral and political relevance of Nietzsche's thought. In the following, I attempt to integrate two main lines of interpretation. In the first section, I take up Nietzsche's plea for a historical view on morality as a frame for all further considerations. Within this general approach, I give clarifications of Nietzsche's view of man as a value-driven animal and I analyze "will to power" by distinguishing individual and collective meanings. Political implications, on the collective level, can be discussed with regard to two conceptions that may be explicated in the sense of a liberal and an authoritarian ideal type. At the same time, we must face the problem as to whether Nietzsche's anti-egalitarianism could be consistently integrated into a constitutional democracy of whatever kind. This problem has to be considered anew when we direct our attention to the 20th century.

The second section deals more specifically with moral-political developments in the 20th century, by analyzing in outline form the new moralities of Bolshevism and Nazism as foundations for socio-political orders. On the one hand, such a reading of moral development can demonstrate in terms of historical experience the importance of Nietzsche's insight into divergent moral-defining "wills to power", thereby denying any hope for objectivist foundations of morality. On the other hand, however, there is, within a Nietzschean paradigm, the crucial question as to how to cope with experiences of the 20th century not available to Nietzsche himself. This question, I think, points to distinctions in respect of antithetic conceptions of equality, one group under a totalitarianism heading, the other under the heading of a individualistic meaning of equality compatible with constitutional democracy. Against this background the shortcomings of Nietzsche's critique of liberal egalitarianism can be recognized not only conceptually, but also historically. A Nietzschean systematics of moral-political divergence in history, however, remains fruitful.

---

* I am very grateful to Sandra Walker for correcting my English.

1 On Interpreting "Will to Power" and Nietzschean Politics

1.1 Meanings of "Will to Power"

Now, firstly, let me remind you of Nietzsche's emphasis on a historical approach to philosophy as already stated in *Human, All Too Human* through denying the view of man as an "aeterna veritas" (HH I 2). This line of thought reappears prominently in *Beyond Good and Evil* in which Nietzsche attacks the tendency of moral philosophers to rationalize only the belief in the dominant morality of their time and to neglect a comparative study of a plurality of moralities in history. Thereby, he maintains, the true problem of morality is missed (BGE 186). I agree with this line of thought that can be vindicated, as we shall see, quite independently of a critical view of several details of Nietzsche's conception of morality.

To focus on this conception, it is illuminating to have a look at Nietzsche's critique of Schopenhauer's moral philosophy that states the moral principle of "Neminem laede" as a truth of thousands of years: "Injure no one; on the contrary help everyone as much as you can!" For Nietzsche this principle is not only invalid in view of its presumed a-historical character, but, more specifically, because of its failure with respect to the phenomenon of "will to power". In Nietzsche's words it is "absurdly false and sentimental" to proclaim such a principle "in a world whose essence is will to power." (BGE 186) Here we have in a nutshell what can be called the Nietzsche-paradigm of moral philosophy: to understand problems of morality in terms of history and simultaneously in terms of "will to power".

If we try to discuss this paradigm and its relation to politics in more detail, we have to put aside, as a first step, the broader meaning of "will to power" in its metaphysical sense. As is well known, Nietzsche used the term "will to power" in the context of his studies in natural science in order to construe a somehow inner principle of the world, particularly with regard to the totality of organic life, in addition to or in combination with the concept of power in physics, or other scientific descriptions (BGE 36, GS 349). It seems evident that those speculations can no longer claim systematic interest. Therefore, as Nietzsche occasionally says himself, it is the human realm that defines the leading perspective on "will to power" (NL, KSA 11, p. 563).[1] We should follow this path too.

---

[1] Cf. the differenciating explications in: Gerhardt 1996, ch. VII.

If we do so, we have to cope with the difficulty that Nietzsche nowhere gives explicit definitions of "will to power". I propose, therefore, for the sake of further argument and interpretation, four meanings of "will to power" as an analytical tool. The meanings are
1. "will to power" as self-actualization of one's own abilities and potentialities
2. "will to power" as normative self-assurance in contrast to others
3. "will to power" as exercising power over others
4. "will to power" as exercising power over others through violence

Note in advance that except for the first, all meanings are relational in meaning ("in contrast to", "over"). Note also that all the meanings can be applied to individuals as well as to collectives. With regard to the first meaning, it is the individual dimension that should be considered primarily. The individual self-actualization of human potentialities evidently corresponds to the latin "potentia" or the greek "dýnamis" and can be read in German as "Kraft" or "Macht". Self-actualisation in the individual perspective does not lead inevitably to power in contrast to others or to power over them. This can be exemplified best by looking at the fine arts and their outstanding representatives.[2] The "genius" can be taken as a model for the unfolding of human potentialities to perfection. At the same time, however, this unfolding has to be seen as a process of forming oneself, of domesticating the strength or power one is able to mobilize through the discipline of reason. In a telling reflection in *Daybreak* (D 548) Nietzsche praises the "victory over power" (*Sieg über die Kraft*) that the genius has to win by reason, and he declares the degree of reason in the power for the decisive criterion by which the degree of venerability for the genius is stated.[3]

The model of the genius has general significance for the reading of "will to power" qua self-actualization, because it exposes in an ideal-typical way that "will to power" always transcends physical power or mere self-preservation. "Will to power" is life in a process of self-overcoming, the inner relation of life and will is not "will to life" but essentially "will to power" (Z II Of Self-Overcoming, KSA 4, p. 147f.; cf. BGE 188). The broader spectrum of human talents is equally open to self-development, but – as Nietzsche comments – "only a few have inherited and cultivated such a degree of toughness, endurance, and energy that they really become a talent, *become* what they are – that is, release it in works and actions". (HH I 263). Therefore, to follow the maxim

---

[2] It is, however, not sufficient as in Reginster 2007 to concentrate on the individual perspective and the emphasis on "creativity" alone.
[3] Rightly stressed by Kaufmann 1968, p. 197.

"become what you are" is not at all a easy thing to realize, and it points to a distinction of rank depending on individual success in self-actualization qua forming oneself.

The rather general description of "will to power" in the individual perspective thus far is emphasized by Zarathustra with regard to distinction of rank (cf. BGE 30, 62, 221) and striving for high values. This marks the interface between "will to power" qua self-actualization and – the above second meaning – normative self-assurance in contrast to others. The standards by which Zarathustra proclaims his distinction of rank are value-standards that he tries to impose because the "world revolves about the inventors of new values" (Z I Flies, KSA 4, p. 65). In addition, he explains that neither individuals nor collectives can abstain from adhering to certain values. For, according to Zarathustra, there is "no greater power on earth than good and evil" (Z I Goals, KSA 4, p. 74), and it is necessary that every people identifies with a "table of goods" as expression of its "will to power". Self-actualization of a collective in terms of values is normative self-presentation and self-assurance in contrast to other collectives that attend to different values. Thus the *Genealogy of Morals* is, in the first instance, a genealogy that explicates divergent valuations of "good" and "evil" or "bad" as spread over a plurality of collectives. The collective, the "herd", is older than the "I"; the collective represents the good conscience that can be contrasted by the "I" only as bad conscience. The individual, therefore, is the latest creation and has to live not only in relation to the collective by defending and developing its individuality, but by recognizing the change of values and the chance of influencing or creating value-change (Z I Goals, KSA 4, p. 75).

The creation of values, however, is not only a subject that is articulated in various ways by Zarathustra, but defines the kernel of Nietzsche's view of man. As he puts it in the *Genealogy*: "[...] man designated himself as the being who estimates values, who evaluates and measures, as the 'measuring animal'" (GM II 8, KSA 5, p. 306: "das abschätzende Tier an sich"). Similarly man is for Zarathustra the "evaluator" ("der Schätzende", Z I Goals, KSA 4, p. 75; cf. NL, KSA 11, p.124: "Grundprobleme der Ethik"). The capacity of man to set values in various respects of individual and collective life distinguishes him from the animal. The human world, therefore, is essentially a world of value-guided activities that lead to results of power-relations qua value-comparison and value-domination.[4] Human existence is always guided by adhering to certain

---

[4] Especially in discussions of Nietzsche's "naturalism" it is important to keep the dimension of human value commitments apart from empiricist-scientific reductions. Cf. Clark/Dudrick 2006.

values and by making sense of human life in identifying with values. In general, therefore, "will to power" determines the existential dimension of human self-interpretation in terms of values.⁵ To sum up, I would propose as a definition for "will to power" in the relational sense that it is equivalent to the self-identification with certain valuations and the striving for dominance of these valuations over others. This can be called normative self-assurance in relation to others as I put it above. By the same token, it seems possible to add to this reading the other noted meanings in the sense of different degrees of value-guided power over others, or even violent domination.⁶

Now we can use the foregoing conceptual frame of "will to power" to deal with the following problems: Firstly, Nietzsche's morality in its nearer contents; second, types of Nietzschean politics, third, Nietzsche and the 20th century. This last point I shall deal with separately in the second section.

1.2 Morality and Communicative Power

To begin with some key concepts of Nietzsche's moral values, it seems illuminating to introduce Nietzsche's already stated "distinction of rank" in contrast to the morality he often attacks sharply. This is egalitarian universalism, especially as represented by utilitarianism. Nietzsche insists

> that the 'general welfare' is no ideal, no goal, no notion that can be at all grasped, but is only a nostrum ... that the requirement of one morality for all is really a detriment to higher men ... that there is a distinction of rank between man and man, and consequently between morality and morality. They are unassuming and fundamentally mediocre species of men, these utilitarian Englishmen. (BGE 228)

In the same vein, however, Nietzsche's critique of egalitarianism pertains to a Kantian type of universalism as well as to a morality of compassion in the sense of Schopenhauer. All these moralities are dependent on a concept of human equality that is conceived for all men, and, therefore, all of them are considered by Nietzsche as variants of Christian morality (NL, KSA 12, pp. 340, 355, 558).

The ensuing question is whether Nietzsche's critique of mediocrity in favour of a qualitative hierarchy between men is sufficient to denounce a concept

---

5 I see self-interpretation in terms of values as the leading perspective for analyzing "will to power" as "interpretation". It may, however, be possible to combine this view with a more comprehensive reading of "will to power" as "interpretation": Müller-Lauter 1999, pp. 68–88.
6 Cf. BGE, 211: The philosopher as value creator, dominator, law-giver.

of human equality in principle. I do not think so, and it is important to state why. The reason is that Nietzsche merges his critique of levelling tendencies of his time with a conceptual equation of mediocrity and equality. He seems unaware of the possibility of an individualistic concept of equality that can be opposed to a collectivistic-levelling reading.[7] Ironically enough, we can read in the texts of the utilitarian John Stuart Mill a Nietzsche-like critique of levelling tendencies, in order to beware of the "tyranny of the majority" without the consequence of denying human equality in principle.[8]

Additionally, one can argue that it may even be a condition of Nietzsche's distinction of rank itself that the higher self-realization of men in works and actions should be judged freely against the background of opportunities equally open to all. An individualistic concept of equality does not exclude at all the recognition of outstanding works or social elites. The ranking of persons according to standards of "greatness" would remain possible too, but even Zarathustra would have to endure controversies in setting standards of valuation, and he would not automatically be in a position to decide on human values in the last instance.

If we try to integrate Nietzsche's value-standards into a frame of moral equality between men, they become the status of normative ideals in a spectrum of other value concepts. Consequently, the "will to power" qua self-assurance of ideals of high personalities in the light of outstanding examples of the "genius" has to be located in a process of communicative competition intended not only to strengthen the self-assurance of elitist values, but to reduce possible value-alternatives step by step.

There are passages in Nietzsche that could be cited in favour of such a process. Thus he makes in *Daybreak* the appeal to the people of Europe to give signs to each other with regard to their disbelief in God in order to combine in a power situated across nations and social classes (D 96). Such a unification of enlightened people in Nietzsche's sense could work for a new power of values in contrast to Christianity, and could be able to inaugurate their own moral order by convincing others. It may be helpful to compare the dynamics of conflicting value-powers with Hannah Arendt's concept of communicative power reading as follows:

---

[7] Cf. Nietzsche's polemics aginst "suffrage universel" which criticizes the subordination of the "higher" to the "lower". Evidently, he misses the point that democratic equality may function as a condition for the recognition of the "higher" by the "lower" (NL, KSA 11, p. 69).
[8] For this context and the liberal ideal type below see the paper of Barry Stocker in this volume.

> Power is what keeps the public realm, the potential space of appearance between acting and speaking men, in existence. The word itself, its Greek equivalent *dynamis*, like the Latin *potentia* ... or the German *Macht* ... indicates its 'potential' character. Power is always ... a potential and not an unchangeable, measureable, and reliable entity like force or strength. (Arendt 1998, p. 200).

Communicative power in this sense stands for the unfolding of collective *potentia* that overcomes other value-orientations, and is capable of dominating them, but, in principle, such a confrontation can be conceived of in the dimension of a fight with arguments or polemics.[9] It is not least, Nietzsche's distinction and polemical use of master morality and slave morality that delivers key words for such a confrontation. Analogously his praise of higher mankind, or the utopia of the *Übermensch*, taken as moral ideals are part of such normative conflicts.

1.3 Types of Nietzschean Politics

But how to think of moral controversies and alternatives in the more specific terms of politics? To answer this second question, I propose to build ideal types in the sense of Max Weber. I hold that it is useful to discuss Nietzschean politics by distinguishing between a quasi liberal and an authoritarian ideal type; the liberal type is compatible with constitutional democracy in a broad sense, the authoritarian, or rather dictatorial, is not. To speak of a liberal ideal type may sound strange in view of Nietzsche's attacks on liberalism and human rights, but there are systematic grounds on which it can be explicated. The crucial point is as to how to consider the essentials of Nietzsche's morality in relation to constitutional democracy.

The liberal ideal type[10] results if we take Nietzsche's critique of equality primarily as a critique of uniformity and levelling tendencies, and if we confine his plea for high values of human development to a radical voice of public opinion. Such a voice may create communicative power over mediocrity, with-

---

[9] Cf. NL, KSA 11, pp. 86f: Here Nietzsche speaks of "Die neue Aufklärung. Gegen die Kirchen und Priester gegen die Staatsmänner gegen die Gutmüthigen Mitleidigen gegen die Gebildeten und den Luxus in summa gegen die Tartüfferie. gleich Macchiavell". Cf. also the illuminating characterization of "agonistic" democratic practice in Hatab 2008, p. 63.

[10] To give a short reminder of Weber's concept one can say that an ideal type (*Idealtypus*) is a unified analytical construct which can claim validity not in terms of correspondence with reality but only in terms of adequacy. It is designed to open perspectives for organizing empirical or conceptual research. It has nothing to do with "normative ideals". You can also conceive of an ideal type of "Mafia".

out denying democratic institutions as such. This is equivalent to the acceptance of a democratic basis for dealing with conflicts and social problems, at least in principle. It is not at all necessary to idealize such a basis, but even the German *Kaiserreich* under Bismarck was a state under the rule of constitutional law that respected the equality of men, albeit with restrictions in relation to suffrage and democratic participation, not to speak of the relation to the egalitarian norms in the present German constitution. Consequently, to integrate Nietzsche's morality into constitutional democracy is only possible by repudiating his critique of human equality in *sensu stricto* and by dismissing his critique of representative constitutions (BGE 199).

The other ideal type of Nietzschean politics is much more radical in its anti-egalitarian tendency and combines with his critique of Christianity and French Revolution in terms of moral decay. From this perspective, the revolution in France stands not only for a break with royal or aristocratic rule and tradition, but for the rebellion of the mob and the slaves that continues the Jewish inauguration of slave-morality and the Christian heritage of this morality (BGE 46, Z IV Beggar). It suffices for my purposes to cite Nietzsche's thesis that the Jews succeeded in establishing a transvaluation of values that undertook

> the reversal of the aristocratic value equation (good=noble=powerful=happy=blessed) ... It is they who have declared: 'the miserable alone are the good; the poor, the powerless, the low alone are the good. The suffering, the deprived, the sick, the ugly are the only pious ones, the only blessed, for them alone is there salvation ...' (GM I 7)

This morality of resentment was integrated into the Christian creed that continued the Jewish slave-revolt in morals (BGE 195) and combined with forces in the French Revolution. The Jewish "<u>great</u> policy of revenge" (GM I 8) is responsible for the ever lasting moral struggle of "Rome against Judaea, Judaea against Rome" (GM I 16), and the disastrous outcome for Nietzsche is that Judaea won the epochal historical trophy in the event of the Revolution in France.

For Nietzsche, however, the epochal moral game is not over altogether. There is new hope for a transvaluation of values in his sense because "God is dead" (GS 125). The fading away of religious belief in the 19th century, to be sure, is not at all a phenomenon unknown to other thinkers of the age. Therefore, it is crucial to understand why Nietzsche is interpreting the death of God as passionately as he does. The reason is that for Nietzsche the death of God indicates an existential move in the moral self-interpretation of man. God stands for the absolute instance of the old morality in Jewish-Christian terms, and therefore his death opens new horizons to found human morality anew.

The death of God is the promise of a new dawn of day (GS 343) that can lead to the transvaluation of values as represented by Zarathustra.

In Nietzsche's view moral authority has the structure of giving commands binding humans in form of a belief in absolute authority (TI Skirmishes 5). The disappearance of absolute authority, the death of God, therefore, is the loss of old morality and the beginning of other forms of moral self-interpretation and self-assurance. In this perspective, the death of God is the birth of a new image of man and a new morality that is spelled out by Zarathustra. The establishing of a new table of values points to an open future of moral revolution that strictly negates human equality (Z II Tarantulas) and denounces equal rights as well as the weakness of democratic institutions (TI Skirmishes 37–39). This line of political conception may be combined with the role of the philosopher as a law-giver for the future and as an adviser for authoritarian rule (BGE 211, 207) – reminiscent of historical examples such as Caesar or Napoleon. Therefore, evidently, we can speak of an authoritarian ideal type of Nietzschean politics[11] in contrast to the liberal ideal type I described first. Both types, I think, will suffice as a framework for my further analysis of Nietzsche and the 20th century.[12]

2 Towards a Nietzschean Systematics of Moral-Political Divergence in History

2.1 Against mainstream receptions of Nietzsche

As a starting point, we can follow Nietzsche's own vision of the basic problems of the near future. Quite consistently with his thesis of the death of God, he presumes that the future will be influenced by conflicts relating to the moral self-image of man and he even equates the struggle for possibly divergent self-images of man with "great politics". To cite a well-known passage from *Ecce Homo*:

> For when the truth squares up to the lie of millenia, we will have upheavals, a spasm of earthquakes, a removal of mountain and valley such as have never been dreamed of. The notion of politics will then completely dissolve into a spiritual war, and all configurations of power from the old society will be exploded – they are all based on a lie: there will be

---

[11] This ideal type corresponds to the complex of Bonapartism discussed in the paper of Don Dombowsky in this volume.
[12] My construction of ideal types could be differentiated further with regard to the material discussed in: Siemens 2008.

wars such as there have never yet been on earth. Only since I came on the scene has there been great politics on earth. (EH Destiny 1; cf. BGE 208)

"Great politics" thus conceived becomes the fight for basic moral values of a certain kind.[13] The spiritual war Nietzsche is imagining for the future plays on the level of his own conception of morality in opposition to the "great policy" of Jewish revenge or Christian morality as militantly criticized in Nietzsche's *Antichrist*.[14] But, evidently, there may be other basic moral values participating in such an existential war for new human self-definition in terms of values, because, as we know, it is the destiny of man to evaluate and to develop moral self-interpretation.

In addition, the spiritual war Nietzsche speaks about is not at all a matter without hard power or violence, not the least if "all configurations of power from the old society will be exploded".[15] But even if such phrases may be taken more symbolically in light of the priority of spiritual power set over physical power or violence, it is indubitable that, by the same token, Nietzsche thinks of war in terms of sacrificing men for higher goals (GM II 12), and that the belligerent instincts he favours are designed also for bloody results (TI Skirmishes 38; NL, KSA 9, p. 556; NL, KSA 11, pp. 75, 88, 98; NL, KSA 13, p. 638).

Now, as is often done, one can discuss Nietzsche's outlook on the 20th century in terms of prophetic anticipation of *Weltanschauungskriege* (world view wars) or in terms of his influence on Italian Fascism or German National Socialism (cf. Golomb/Wistrich 2002, Aschheim 1992). These, to be sure, are possible perspectives with regard to a story of the reception of Nietzsche's philosophy in political terms, a story that could be broadened equally to studies of a "Jewish Nietzscheanism" (Stegmaier/Krochmalnik 1997) or to Nietzsche-receptions in Bolshevism (Rosenthal 2002).

My own perspective, however, is quite different. I propose, first of all, to read the radical movements of the 20th century, especially Bolshevism and National Socialism (NS), in terms of their own new moralities that gained force

---

[13] This moral meaning of "great politics" should be distinguished from more conventional uses of the term that can be found in Nietzsche's texts too. Thus he comments on a people to engage in "great politics" in the context of war (H I 481) or on developments towards a sublimation of enmity in "great politics" relating to the new "German Reich" (TI Morality 3). Other sources could be added.

[14] See the dramatic scenario of Nietzsche's moral critique of Christian morality developed by Daniel Conway in this volume.

[15] Already in 1883 we can read that "moral war" will occur in a bloody way (NL, KSA 10, p. 263f.): "Neben den Religionskriegen her geht fortwährend der Moral-Krieg: d.h. Ein Trieb will die Menschheit sich unterwerfen; und je mehr die Religionen aussterben, um so blutiger und sichtbarer wird dies Ringen werden. Wir sind im Anfange!"

in actual history in order to build socio-political formations. In doing so, these movements verified in a systematically relevant way Nietzsche's paradigm of moral philosophy that is defined by insight into the appearance of divergent moralities in history conflicting with each other – divergent "wills to power". This very insight of Nietzsche can be vindicated quite independently of critical objections to his moral-political philosophy in detail. In systematic terms, therefore, it is much more relevant to interpret developments of actual history within a conceptual frame set forth by Nietzsche in an arguable general sense, instead of searching for "influences" of Nietzsche on actual history dozens of years after his lifetime.

In order to underline my priorities, let me give a short characterization of the intellectual scenario that developed around World War I. Intellectuals were forced to take a stance on the war. One of the supporters in Germany was Thomas Mann, who claimed to follow Nietzsche's critique of Western culture and declared that the essence of the German soul is deeply directed against politics in the Western democratic sense (Mann 1956). German culture in contrast to French or Western civilization was a widespread ideological figure which dominated the so called "Ideen von 1914" (Ideas of 1914), a nationalist proclamation of intellectuals to support war by denying the universalist spirit of the French Revolution.

An extreme voice in this context was Werner Sombart who designated the war of 1914 as the war of Nietzsche. He developed a basic opposition between heroes and merchants, the latter standing for the English character and the universalist spirit of the revolutions of the 18th century, the former for the Germans. To be a German means to be a hero and the spirit of the hero was traced back to the philosophy of Nietzsche (Sombart 1915). Conversely, Nietzsche was blamed for German militarism in Great Britain and the US (Martin 2006).

Such an appropriation of Nietzsche seems typical for a historical situation in which intellectuals try to cope with realities of their time by searching for intellectual sources, or authorities serving their own interests, or ideologies. To be sure, Nietzsche was a critique of the English thought in form of utilitarianism, but his anti-universalism conflicts with Kant or Schopenhauer as well. Additionally, Nietzsche's elitism can be stressed in favour of belligerent virtues he proclaimed, primarily in a spiritual, but also in a physical sense. This line of thought, however, contrasts with his critique of German nationalism and the *Kaiserreich*.

It is surely a cogent diagnosis to consider World War I as the "great seminal catastrophe of the 20th century" (G. F. Kennan), as it is adequate to consider this war a catastrophe of the reception of Nietzsche's philosophy by making him a "Fascist" *avant la lettre*. There may be little doubt that World War I induced a mainstream reception of Nietzsche on behalf of right-wing tendencies and anti-Western attitudes, which continued in the Weimar Republic and under Nazi-rule. But quite contrary to an alleged inner coherence of such a line of reception, there exists no clear inner logic in a Nietzschean conception of politics facing the problems of actual history in and after World War I. If we return to the above ideal types of politics, this can be demonstrated with regard to Max Weber, a thinker of comparable quality to Nietzsche and influenced by him in various respects.

Leaving his former militant nationalism behind, Max Weber reflected the German defeat by formulating a new peaceful ideal of the German nation and by arguing for the acceptance of a republican constitution in the tradition of Western democracies (Weber 1988, pp. 453–456). Additionally, however, he advanced in his political theory the conception of a elitist leadership called "plebiszitäre Führerdemokratie" (plebiscitary leadership democracy), because he felt an urgent need to combine the egalitarian elements of constitutional democracy with high standards of personal leadership and charismatic qualities (Weber 1976, p. 156). This Weberian construction we can take as a model as to how to combine the above liberal ideal type with the authoritarian ideal type, by reflecting seriously on historical experience. This is not to say that Nietzsche would have approved of such a model, but he could have done so by revising strict anti-egalitarianism and some dictatorial fantasies. It would be a caricature of Nietzsche's intellectual capacities to formulate in his name a position concerning the outcomes, and consequences, of the hard historical experience induced by World War I.

This reflection shows the difficulty, if not impossibility, of assigning to Nietzsche political identifications of actual history after his time in any direct way. The attempts to do so grew out of attitudes of intellectuals, or politicians, who defined themselves primarily in relation to social and political parties and formations of their own time. We should, therefore, look at the dominant moral-political forces of the 20th century in their own terms.

2.2 The Reading of National Socialism and Bolshevism in Nietzschean Terms

Before going into details, let me pause for a methodological remark. As it is consistent in view of Nietzsche's moral philosophy to speak of a plurality of moralities, it may sound strange to include Bolshevism or Nazism in the discourse of moralities, not least with regard to the atrocities committed in their name. But this points only to distinctions we should bear in mind when speaking of moralities. There are three levels of research. To begin with, we can ask in a rather formal way what is to be understood by a general concept of morals or morality without deciding in advance what is to be judged as the "true" or only "acceptable" sort of morals. On this level, we can speak of a set of norms or imperatives shared by a community to regulate its social life and a corresponding set of sanctions, which are mutually accepted in cases of deviations seen as relevant. A nearer clarification of this level of research is not my aim here. Instead I follow the perspective of Nietzsche in order to analyze the different ways for filling a possible formal concept of morality with moral content.[16] It is important to stress the question of a formal concept of morality, because this helps avoid an unreflected limitation in an already accepted morality and it opens the view towards a study of different moral self-interpretations of humans.

This defines the second level of research which concerns the following considerations. Here it is relevant to discern different conceptions of morality as manifested in NS (National Socialism), Bolshevism, and the universalist paradigm of Western communities and to assess them comparatively. To my mind, however, we can only arrive at results in this field if we combine historical research focusing on NS and Bolshevism with a philosophical sensitivity to moral questions (Zimmermann 2005, Zimmermann 2008). Finally, the third level of research relates to the question of justification for the morality we ourselves identify with: egalitarian universalism. This question cannot be discussed here systematically.

To begin with National Socialism, we have to recognize that the core of this movement is defined by a radical anti-universalism in terms of denying any moral rights to certain collectives or groups. The pivotal characteristic of Nazism is its denunciation of Judaism or the Jews and its permanent struggle against the "Jewish enemy". Nazism denies the Jews the right to exist and leaves the path of moral unity of the human species, with its exterminating strategies and practices. Mankind refers no longer to all human beings, but is separated into those who are real humans and those who are not. Nazism constructs an enmity toward the Jews as a homogeneous collective that incorporates certain essential qualities as a people or race, in strict contrast to the Aryan-German collective designated the "Volksgemeinschaft" (people's community). The Jews obstruct the mission of the Aryan-German race, to advance its creative and idealistic potential, and dispute the principle of history that consists of a never-ending struggle between races.

---

[16] A general social concept of morality which formally points out the reciprocity of claims is already developed by Strawson 1974. A recent version of a formal concept of morality can be found in Tugendhat 2010.

The construct of adversarial qualities in collectivistic terms of race leads to a view of the Jews, as a "spiritual race", that is responsible for a universalistic picture of man brought to power in the French Revolution under the idea of equality. This is the reason that the Nazis' fight against the Jews is a struggle against a universalistic self-image of man. Not least, the radicalism of this type of anti-Semitism provides the leading motive for the Holocaust.

I propose the term "rupture of species" ("Gattungsbruch": Zimmermann 2005, ch. 1) to characterize the radicalism of Nazism in moral terms. This term is meant to signify the overthrowing of traditional moral limits, in order to transform mankind into a new world of moral otherness. With regard to the everyday support, or silent toleration of the persecution of Jewish people in Germany, and elsewhere one can refer to a process of moral dissolution as a failure of species-commitment. In the long run, however, it was not only the "Jewish" ideas of human equality that were supposed to be abolished, but also the Christian-humanistic tradition. The historian Saul Friedländer has classified the radical anti-Semitism of Nazism as "redemptive anti-Semitism," which attempts to "liberate" the Aryan-German community and the whole of mankind from the Jews (Friedländer 1997, ch. 3). The moral transformation I have characterized enables us to speak similarly of a morality of redemption. The religious meaning of "redemption" is converted to a mundane project of this world. There is no longer otherworldly redemption and the Last Judgment is exercised in real history.

In a similar way, we can study the development of a morality of redemption in Bolshevism. It is no accident that a Tsheka bulletin declared the old systems of "ethics and humanity" obsolete as early as 1919 and proclaimed a new ethics of "absolute humanity", the ideal of which is said to legitimize bloody violence. Notwithstanding its own characteristics, the Stalinist era was part of the Bolshevist project as a whole. Stalin spoke of engineers of the soul to build a new type of man, a phrase rather similar to Lenin's dictum that man could be made in a way the Bolsheviks desired him to be. Trotsky's utopian construction of a higher social-biological type shows the same spirit (Trotsky 1924). On the level of Bolshevist principles the family resemblance of Lenin, Stalin, and Trotsky is much more far-reaching than on the level of concrete political struggle between Trotsky and Stalin (Zimmermann 2008, chs. 1, 2).

It is, therefore, possible to learn many aspects of Bolshevik morality by studying Trotsky's texts on moral questions. He emphatically proclaimed the "Transformation of morals" (Trotsky 1923) and continued his Bolshevik conception in the essay "Their morals and ours" (Trotsky 1938). Some main points of Trotsky's argument are: Civil war "explodes into mid-air all moral ties between the hostile classes", the revolutionary party can only succeed in "complete independence from the bourgeoisie and their morality", the class struggle is a life-or-death struggle by violent means, the Bolsheviks are the "inveterate warriors of the socialist idea" who see "no contradiction between personal morality and the interests of the party", the party is "everything" to a Bolshevik in view of the highest "aims of mankind" etc.

The uncompromising spirit of Trotsky's moral views, and his credo of the party's role in advancing historical progress, are not so far away from Stalinist voices in the same field. It is true that Trotsky cannot be blamed for Stalin's liquidation-policy, as it is true that his moral writings can serve as an ideal type for Bolshevik morality. It is important to realize how this conception denounces the universalist reading of Marxism in favour of the construction of a homogenous community. Whatever "true" Marxism may be, there is a universalist type of Marxism, which contradicts the utopian project of Bolshevism and Stalinism that aims at the transformation of the social revolution into a particularistic movement of social and moral discrimination, with ongoing practices of physical extermination. The universalist diction of Marxism is then given the function of an ideological make-believe of emancipation. The Bolshevist particularism has lost any criteria of social mediation or moral tolerance. The true New Man and the true mankind are only achievable by radicalizing extermination to the last class enemy. As in the case of NS, mankind is normatively restricted by Bolshevism. The extermination policy of Bolshevism differs from Nazism because the latter was focussed on one main *active* enemy, the Jews. On the contrary, Bolshevism was directed towards a plurality of enemies (nobility, bourgeoisie, kulaks, counterrevolutionaries), who had to be fought against and annihilated. Thus the extermination strategy in Bolshevism is more appropriately characterized as a development of successive "sociocides" to purify society. This matches the term "cultural racism" which is proposed by historians for Stalinism (Baberowski/Doering-Manteuffel 2006, p. 89).

Hannah Arendt was one of the first to come to see Nazism as being strictly incompatible with Western moral traditions and to give a reading of it as an order of its own (Arendt 1950). In the same spirit she developed her comparative studies of the era of Stalinism (Arendt 1951, part III). I further propose to consider these oppositions in a systematic fashion by taking into account the fact that Nazism as well as Bolshevism/Stalinism had succeeded with constituting a type of revolutionary moral order which, in contrast to other forms, one might call a form of moral sozialization or communitarization. To simplify matters, I will speak of divergent moral orders and characterize them in the sense of Weberian ideal types. To begin with, I give a comparison of the Western type of morality with Nazism:

First, there has to be a basic moral self-understanding as a moral centre, defining obligations for the respective I-orientations or We-orientations. For the Western universalistic type, this means that every woman and man ascribes the same moral status to herself, or himself, as to every other woman and man and is led by the self-understanding as a member of a We-community, in which every member follows just this self-understanding. The relevant self-understanding becomes manifest in the reciprocal recognition of equal rights, for every member of whatever community. Nazism sets a centre of its own against this universalistic centre. The Germans or the Aryans claim a higher moral status than Non-Germans, or Non-Aryans, and follow the self-understanding of a We-community which gives dominance to an order of normative inequality under racial standards. The particularistic self-understanding is strictly opposed to any universalistic conviction, which is seen as "Jewish" in principle.

Secondly, there is a network of social norms and institutions tied to the moral centre. For the universalistic type, some of the elements of this network are a civil life free of violence, social and public protection against discrimination of whatever kind, and a system of law founded on human rights, which also defines constraints in respect of the political sphere of constitutional democracy both in domestic and foreign affairs. Contrary to this setting, Nazism aims for the strengthening of the German-Aryan community under the guidance of the "Führer" ("Führerprinzip": leadership principle). Neither domestic nor foreign affairs are limited by law, the interests of the people's community ("Volksgemeinschaft") are given priority over all other considerations. Carl Schmitt, one of the leading jurists and intellectuals of the Nazi period, created the doctrine of "Der Führer schützt das Recht" (The leader defends the law), thus giving the leader authority on a higher sphere of lawmaking, where he is in a position to create the "true" law of the community (Schmitt 1934).

Thirdly, there is its relation to violence which characterizes a certain type of moral order. The universalistic type requires – note that I am speaking of ideal types – reconciling conflicts within a community by means of non-violent processes and by respecting the state monopoly of legitimate violence. For the Nazi morality type, violence is a legitimate means of enforcing the homogeneity of the community against its enemies, defined in racial terms or other "unhealthy" elements. This corresponds with Hitler's opinion that the violent fight for race domination in the context of a global struggle is the true human right of a community. Even the constitutional law is overridden in order to secure the place of the Germans in history (Hitler 1937, p. 105). By the same token, wars of aggression are declared actions of self-defense. Compared with this, the universalistic type limits military power and violence to situations of self-defense, and demands respect for the law of nations.

Analogously we can summarize the Bolshevik morality as follows: First, there is a basic moral self-understanding of every man as being part of an exclusive community of proletarian equals, which is held to be morally superior to all other forms of socialization hitherto known. Secondly, there is the revolutionary party as the leading level of authority for all social norms and institutions, defining the priorities of communist development and setting rules of law (including criminal law) on all levels. Thirdly, there is the party's monopoly on organizing violence in the name of the state and in the interest of revolutionary progress to secure the homogeneity of proletarian socialization against all class enemies however defined on national or international levels.

Now, given the comparative descriptions of egalitarian universalism, Nazi-morality and Bolshevist-morality, we come to see the moral history of the 20th century clearly in Nietzschean terms, namely as a history of divergent moralities in conflict with each other, a history of divergent "wills to power" realizing themselves in socio-political forms without precedence, and thereby showing the value-forming capacity of man in disastrous results. The normative self-assurance of egalitarian universalism, became a question of actual war in confrontation with Nazism and was followed by the Cold War in confrontation with Stalinism. My overview strengthens a Nietzschean systematics of moralities in history, and, at the same time, implies a critique of Kantian or whatever objectivistic or monistic moral theories. In contrast to these theories the Nietzschean paradigm can be convincingly tied together with research on the actual moral history of man, a history that points to a revision of the belief in the a-historical status of egalitarian universalism, as well as the assumption that liberalism is the basic default position of the West. Conversely, "liberalism is a highly contingent position, under furious attack for much of the twentieth century" (Fritzsche/Hellbeck 2009). Consequently, we would have to speak of egalitarian universalism equally as a historical phenomenon, in short as "historical universalism", specifically related to the history of human rights since the 18th century (Zimmermann 2009).

To sum up, we can, I think, arrive at the following rather dialectical assessment:

On the one hand, there remains Nietzsche's seminal paradigm of discussing morality in terms of a history of value-concepts qua "wills to power". On the other hand, there are the shortcomings of Nietzsche's own "higher morality". Notwithstanding the conceptual problems I presented above in relation to Nietzsche's critique of egalitarianism, there are quite different forms of egalitarian norms in the 20th century to be criticized in Nietzschean terms: proletarian egalitarianism of the Bolsheviki, racial-collectivist egalitarianism of the Nazis. Beyond the scope of Nietzsche's historical imagination, actual history in the 20th century developed fatal forms of egalitarianism in combination with radical anti-universalism. Not only conceptually, therefore, but also historically, Nietzsche's critique of liberalism misses the crucial point of individualistic equality as basis for constitutional democracy in a universalist spirit. If we concede further that meanwhile constitutional democracy may have been pragmatically accepted as "the worst form of government except all the others that have been tried" (Churchill), it goes without saying that Nietzschean ideas of authoritarian claims in politics are idle.

To honor the spirit of Nietzsche means to be open to crucial historical experience. Therefore, we should take seriously the intimate connection between moral philosophy and history which Nietzsche so emphatically stresses:

> Have you experienced history in yourselves, convulsions, earthquakes, sadness wide and protracted, happiness that strikes like lightening? Have you been foolish with fools great and small? Have you really borne the delusions and the burden of the good men? And the burden and the singular happiness of the most evil as well? If so, speak of morality, but not otherwise! (D 545)

Bibliography

Arendt, Hannah (1950): "The Aftermath of Nazi Rule: Report from Germany". In: *Commentary* 10, pp. 342–353.
Arendt, Hannah (1951): *The Origins of Totalitarianism*. New York: Harcourt Brace Jovanovich.
Arendt, Hannah (1998): *The Human Condition*. 2nd edition. Chicago: University of Chicago Press.
Aschheim, St. E. (1992): *The Nietzsche Legacy in Germany 1890–1990*. Berkeley, Los Angeles, Oxford: University of California Press.
Baberowski, Jörg/Doering-Manteuffel, Anselm (2006): *Ordnung durch Terror*. Bonn: Dietz.
Clark, Maudemarie/Dudrick, David (2006): "The Naturalisms of Beyond Good and Evil". In: Keith Ansell-Pearson (ed.): *A Companion to Nietzsche*. Oxford: Blackwell, pp. 148–167.
Friedländer, Saul (1997): *Nazi Germany and the Jews*. Vol. 1: *The Years of Persecution 1933– 1939*. New York: Harper Collins Publishers.
Fritzsche, Peter/Hellbeck, Jochen (2009): "The New Man in Stalinist Russia and Nazi Germany". In: Manfred Geyer/Sheila Fitzpatrick (eds.): *Beyond Totalitarianism. Stalinism and Nazism Compared*. New York: Cambridge University Press, pp. 302–341.
Gerhardt, Volker (1996): *Vom Willen zur Macht*. Berlin, New York: de Gruyter.
Golomb, Jacob/Wistrich, Robert S. (eds.) (2002): *Nietzsche, Godfather of Fascism? On the Uses and Abuses of a Philosophy*. Princeton, Oxford: Princeton University Press.
Hatab, Lawrence J. (1995): *A Nietzschean Defense of Democracy*. Chicago, La Salle: Open Court.
Hitler, Adolf (1937): *Mein Kampf*. Munich: Zentralverlag der NSDAP.
Kaufmann, Walter (1968): *Nietzsche: Philosopher, Psychologist, Antichrist*. 3rd edition. Princeton: Princeton University Press.
Mann, Thomas (1956): *Betrachtungen eines Unpolitischen*. Frankfurt: Fischer.

Martin, Nicolas (2006): "Nietzsche as Hate-Figure in Britain's Great War: 'The Execrable Neech'". In: Fred Bridgham (ed.): *The First World War as a Clash of Cultures*. Rochester: Camden House, pp. 147–166.
Müller-Lauter, Wolfgang (1999): "Nietzsches Lehre vom Willen zur Macht". In: Wolfgang Müller-Lauter: *Nietzsche-Interpretationen I*. Berlin, New York: de Gruyter, pp. 25–95.
Nietzsche, Friedrich (2003): *Daybreak*. Reginald J. Hollingdale (trans.). Cambridge: Cambridge Texts.
Nietzsche, Friedrich (2003): *Thus spoke Zarathustra*. Reginald J. Hollingdale (trans.). London: Penguin Classics.
Nietzsche, Friedrich (2007): *Ecce Homo*. Duncan Large (trans.). Oxford: Oxford World's Classics.
Nietzsche, Friedrich (2008): *Beyond Good and Evil*. Helen Zimmern and Paul V. Cohn (trans.). London: Wordsworth Classics.
Nietzsche, Friedrich (2008): *Genealogy of Morals*. Douglas Smith (trans.). Oxford: Oxford World's Classics.
Nietzsche, Friedrich (2008): *Human, All Too Human*. Helen Zimmern and Paul V. Cohn (trans.). London: Wordsworth Classics.
Reginster, Bernard (2007): "The will to Power and the Ethics of Creativity". In: Brian Leiter/ Neil Sinhababu (eds.): *Nietzsche and Morality*. Oxford: Clarendon Press.
Rosenthal, Bernice G. (2002): *New Myth, New World. From Nietzsche to Stalinism*. Pennsylvania: Pennsylvania State University Press.
Schmitt, Carl (1934): "Der Führer schützt das Recht". In: *Deutsche Juristen-Zeitung* 39(15), pp. 945–950.
Siemens, Herman W. (2008): "Yes, No, Maybe So … Nietzsche's Equivocations on the Relation between Democracy and 'Große Politik'". In: Herman W. Siemens/Vasti Roodt (eds.): *Nietzsche, Power and Politics*. Berlin, New York: de Gruyter, pp. 231–268.
Sombart, Werner (1915): *Händler und Helden*. Munich, Leipzig: Duncker & Humblot.
Stegmaier, Werner/Krochmalnik, Daniel (eds.) (1997): *Jüdischer Nietzscheanismus*. Berlin, New York: De Gruyter.
Strawson, Peter F. (1974): "Social Morality and Individual Ideal". In: Peter F. Strawson: *Freedom and Resentment and Other Essays*. London: Methuen, pp. 26–44.
Trotsky, Leon (1923): "The Transformation of Morals". http://www.marxists.org/archive/trotsky/1923/10/morals.htm
Trotsky, Leon (1924): "Literature and Revolution". http://marxists.org/archive/trotsky/1924/lit_revo/index.htm
Trotsky, Leon (1938): "Their Morals and Ours".http://marxists.org/archive/trotsky/1938/morals/morals.htm
Tugendhat, Ernst (2010): *Anthropologie statt Metaphysik*. 2nd edition. Munich: Beck.
Weber, Max (1976): *Wirtschaft und Gesellschaft. Studienausgabe*. Tübingen: J. B. Mohr (Paul Siebeck).
Weber, Max (1988): "Deutschlands künftige Staatsform". In: Max Weber: *Gesammelte Politische Schriften*. Tübingen: J. B. Mohr (Paul Siebeck), pp. 448–483.
Zimmermann, Rolf (2005): *Philosophie nach Auschwitz. Eine Neubestimmung von Moral in Politik und Gesellschaft*. Reinbek: Rowohlt.
Zimmermann, Rolf (2008): *Moral als Macht. Eine Philosophie der historischen Erfahrung*. Reinbek: Rowohlt.
Zimmermann, Rolf (2009): "Moralischer Universalismus als geschichtliches Projekt". In: *Erwägen Wissen Ethik* 20, pp. 415–485.

Rebecca Bamford
The Liberatory Limits of Nietzsche's Colonial Imagination in *Dawn* 206

In addition to ongoing debate within the scholarly literature, there is some evidence in Nietzsche's own works that he engages in forms of thinking that are not compatible with a politics of liberation. There is an especially perplexing aphorism in *Dawn* where Nietzsche seems to actively recommend engaging in colonization for therapeutic purposes (D 206). While this is only one aphorism amongst hundreds, the sentiments that Nietzsche expresses therein present us with a challenging interpretative puzzle. If Nietzsche advocates colonial occupation, then we need to address whether or not this poses a hard limit on his philosophy's capacity to contribute to liberatory political projects. Moreover, if Nietzsche does endorse colonial occupation, then as Ure (2013) has recently proposed, though for different reasons, we may need to reassess the utility of Nietzsche's political therapy. Given that Nietzsche's apparent endorsement of colonialism occurs in *Dawn*, which both Ure and Holub (1998) distinguish from Nietzsche's later works and which they use to ground their appreciation of Nietzsche's therapeutic focus on health promotion, this issue is pressing. In this chapter, I present a close critical assessment of the aphorism in question, *Dawn* 206, and place this aphorism into the context of Nietzsche's philosophical concerns in *Dawn* and in his wider philosophy. In so doing, I aim to provide a clearer account of the liberatory limits of the therapeutic dimension of Nietzsche's philosophy.

The importance of therapy in Nietzsche's philosophy has been receiving increasing critical attention, including in some recent critical literature focusing on the importance of Nietzsche's so-called middle period works, *Human, All Too Human, Dawn,* and *The Gay Science*. As Michael Ure has pointed out, Nietzsche makes significant use of the Hellenistic analogy between "the arts of medicine and philosophical therapy" to ground an ethics of "self-analysis and self-cultivation" in these works (Ure 2008, p. 59). Ure concurs with previous analysis suggesting that Nietzsche's so-called middle period involves experimentation with the philosophy of Greek and Roman antiquity for therapeutic purposes (Ure 2008, p. 6). Specifically, Ure claims that the care of the self, which is recognized in Nietzsche's earlier writings, is combined with a new focus on modern depth psychology in texts such as *Dawn* (Ure 2008, p. 7).[1]

---

[1] On the view that Nietzsche anticipates some of the key ideas of depth psychology, see e.g. Robert C. Holub (1999).

This combination generates Nietzsche's pursuit of what Ure calls "mature individualism," in which psychological self-observation functions as therapy for a naïve and limiting narcissism about the origins and constitution of the ego (Ure 2008, pp. 3, 6). Ure shows that, for Nietzsche, if we do not engage in therapy, then we will remain in a state of unhealthy narcissism characterized by three symptoms: (i) melancholic longing for death; (ii) the desire for and fantasy of revenge that restores the illusion of the ego's omnipotence; (iii) *Mitleid* as defended by Rousseau or Schopenhauer, which is tied to the desire for revenge because of its function in restoring the ego's feeling of self-affection at the expense of others (Ure 2008, p. 12; cf. Ure 2006, p. 68).

The political aspect of the therapeutic dimension of Nietzsche's philosophy has on balance received less attention than its ethical aspect.[2] This is especially the case with regard to the question of the relevance of the therapeutic dimension of Nietzsche's thought to the politics of liberation. Nietzsche's thinking on colonialism has been addressed by Ofelia Schutte, whose work focuses on Nietzsche's relevance to projects of liberation, including liberation from colonialism and its continuing legacy worldwide, and liberation from androcentrism; her work has been described as involving a project of intellectual translation of Latin American philosophy into the Northern philosophical context (Alcoff 2004, p. 145).[3] Schutte's critical analysis of liberation politics in Latin America has brought Nietzsche's philosophy into dialogue with important Latin American political philosophers such as José Carlos Mariátegui (Schutte 1993). Schutte has consistently defended the view that Nietzsche's philosophy may contribute to a politics of liberation, in the context of anti-colonial and feminist liberatory projects. Of the trajectory of her arguments across many years on this front, she writes,

> [...] Nietzsche can be very helpful, but Nietzsche alone is clearly insufficient to take us where we want to go politically. I do want to say that, after my experiences with Latin American and feminist liberation movements, I would not want to take the journey with-

---

[2] Ure (2013) seeks to redress this. He claims that Nietzsche's philosophy is fundamentally therapeutic in orientation. Ure's account first examines how Nietzsche develops a neo-Stoic political therapy that opens up the possibility of individual freedom from emotional turmoil to all in his so-called middle period works. Subsequently, Ure's account shows how this therapy changes to a "bio-political" one that seeks only to heal higher types, as Nietzsche incorporates evolutionary theory into his wider philosophy.

[3] In addition to Schutte's substantial body of work on this topic, Joseph Pugliese (1996) has drawn attention to the utility of Nietzsche's philosophy for identifying and articulating the logic of colonial practices. Pugliese contends that Nietzsche's comment on the way in which reason effaces its unreasonable origins in *Dawn* 1 can be used to reveal that what the colonizer calls bringing 'reason' to the colonized counts as violence (Pugliese 1996, p. 283).

out Nietzsche. Historically we see that sectors of liberation movements may turn into self-righteous moral and political forces, at which point a strong dose of Nietzschean undermining of absolutes may be just the remedy needed (Schutte 2004, p. 183).

Here and elsewhere Schutte is critical of Nietzsche's political commitments. Yet she is consistent in promoting the liberatory value of Nietzsche's "taboo-breaking" – his philosophical resistance to diverse forms of "conceptual orthodoxies" (Schutte 2004, p. 183). Schutte's particular reverence for Nietzschean thinking in the liberatory context stems from Nietzsche's ontological challenge to dualistic thinking (Schutte 2004, p. 184). She distinguishes between the psychological and existential components of liberatory political movements, and holds that with regard to the psychological component of such movements, thinking in terms of dualisms and binaries are not conducive to health and well being (Schutte 2004, p. 184; see also Schutte 1984). Schutte's reasoning, drawn from her reading of Nietzsche's philosophy, is that "binaries and dualisms put our thinking on 'automatic pilot'," thereby obstructing our reasoning in the liberatory context (Schutte 2004, p. 184). This approach to reading Nietzsche is of course directly compatible with Ure's treatment of Nietzsche as engaging in ethical and political therapy (Ure 2008 and Ure 2013).

The specific political consequences of Schutte's reading of Nietzschean psychology include the point that even when a person or a specific group is threatened by others, there is no obligation to think in binary oppositional hierarchical terms (where one part of the binary is treated as superior and the other part treated as inferior, as happens for example in the case of 'Christians vs. infidels') (Schutte 2004, p. 185). Schutte thinks that, following Nietzsche in rejecting binary oppositional thinking in the political context, we can respond to danger pragmatically, without involving an ideology of danger as inextricably linked to evil, and of liberation from danger as linked to good (Schutte 2004, p. 185). In her view, the pragmatic advantages of not conceptualizing political struggles in terms of binary oppositions includes some support for resistance to manipulation of the masses through rhetoric (as religious and political leaders often use binary oppositions such as good vs. evil to consolidate power and manipulate the masses), and also, more generally, support for continuing refusal to allow our thinking in political matters to become a matter of automatic pilot, which runs a substantial risk of fostering anti-liberatory thinking. Lawrence J. Hatab has also acknowledged the pragmatism of Nietzsche's politics, emphasizing appearances rather than foundations, and connects this feature of Nietzsche's philosophy with Arendt's conception of action (Hatab 1995, p. 240).

However, some of the available scholarship has suggested that Nietzsche's thinking is not commensurate with democratic theory, or with projects commensurate with a politics of liberation.⁴ Robert C. Holub has acknowledged his skepticism about Nietzsche's capacity to contribute to struggle for freedom from the legacy of colonialism. Holub draws attention to Nietzsche's surprisingly consistent affirmation for his brother-in-law Bernhard Förster's colonial ambitions in the available correspondence (Holub 1998, p. 38). With regard to Nietzsche's philosophy, Holub shows (i) that Nietzsche's remarks on colonialism cannot be separated from his epoch, particularly the Second Empire and the intense pressure that it created for Germany to participate in the race for colonial power in the nineteenth century, and (ii) that Nietzsche's remarks also cannot be separated from his reliance on antidemocratic thought and other concepts developed in his writings, such as biologism, will to power, and the transvaluation of all values (1998, p. 49). For Holub, it is clear that Nietzsche's philosophy incorporates a colonialist imagination that speaks against the liberatory value of Nietzsche's philosophy in this context. Holub sums up his identification of the later Nietzsche as essentially comfortable with colonialism by claiming that it is difficult to find aspects of "Nietzsche's 'untimely' colonial imagination" that can mitigate the oppressive legacy of colonialism, either in the nineteenth century or today (Holub 1998, p. 49).

More recently, Linda Martín Alcoff has raised concerns about Schutte's efforts to incorporate Nietzsche's philosophy into anti-colonial and feminist liberation projects. One of Alcoff's particular concerns is whether liberation can be achieved through the use of decontextualized, metaphilosophical tools, which is how she classifies Schutte's presentation of Nietzsche's resistance to unhealthy binary thinking. Alcoff's concern is grounded in the question of whether Nietzsche's taboo breaking is always liberatory, even when particular taboos, or conceptual orthodoxies, are justifiable (Alcoff 2004, p. 151). She suggests (though does not provide textual evidence to support her claim) that Nietzsche often seems to give an affirmative response to this concern on the basis that resisting orthodoxy consistently reveals the contingency of beliefs and customs; yet Nietzsche's way of doing this work is often itself highly contextual. For Alcoff, this movement from the general to the contextual undercuts the logic of Schutte's position that Nietzsche's liberatory value is located in his resistance to binary thinking; consistent affirmation of resistance to binary thinking seems to leave a door open for us to affirm too much, potentially

---

4 Lawrence J. Hatab (1995) and Alan Schrift (2000) hold that Nietzsche's work may still serve as a resource for democratic theory. Dombowsky (2002) challenges their views, proposing that "[t]he closest we may get Nietzsche to democracy is through Bonapartism: autocratic will in the guise of popular rule" (Dombowsky 2002, p. 290).

including political positions that oppose liberatory projects (Alcoff 2004, pp. 152f.).

As already mentioned, Schutte herself is honest about her dissatisfaction with certain facets of Nietzsche's political philosophy. With this dissatisfaction in mind, she refers us to a distinction between monumental and critical history that Nietzsche draws in *On the Uses and Disadvantages of History for Life* (Schutte 2000, p. 12). Schutte lays out Nietzsche's distinction as follows: the monumental historian identifies high moments or deeds in history that it is worth emulating in order to provide energy for future-oriented action, while the critical historian "annihilates" aspects of the past by examining them and condemning them, in order to overturn the past and make continuing life possible (Schutte 2000, p. 12). She argues that colonialism is an excellent example of a case where monumental history cannot guide our political reasoning, because even though extension of a superpower's dominion over other cultures and peoples may count as monumental, it is not ethically justified (Schutte 2000, pp. 12f.). Nietzsche's concept of critical history, on the other hand, helps Schutte to defend Nietzsche's liberatory value from calls that his politics is ethically suspect: the critical historian has the necessary theoretical framework to enable adoption of a stance authorizing the dissolution of the legacy of colonial oppression, and hence, critical history may provide the ethical justification missing from the monumental account (Schutte 2000, p. 13). The dissonance between monumental and critical history may be resolved, Schutte thinks, by appeal to Nietzsche's perspectival epistemology (Schutte 2000, p. 13). This appeal ties in effectively with Schutte's acknowledgement of Nietzsche's pragmatism, though Schutte herself does not spell out this dimension of her reading of Nietzsche (Schutte 2004).

In light of this, the problem at hand changes from the question of whether Nietzsche affirms colonialism to the question of why he does in a given context. Even given that Nietzsche affirms colonialism in D 206, then if we follow Schutte's reasoning that binary thinking runs counter to Nietzsche's philosophical-therapeutic aims, our response would not involve immediate application of a value hierarchy and denial of Nietzsche's position on a binary basis (e.g. 'colonialism is bad; anti-colonialism is good'). Instead, our approach would be based on pragmatism: we would pay close critical attention to the reasons why he does so in a specific situation. The ethical concerns with an affirmation of colonialism raised by Holub and Alcoff – and indeed by Schutte herself – would not be simply be set aside, but would no longer be a matter of a single determination based on an either/or choice (Nietzsche for or against colonialism). If Schutte's reclamation of Nietzsche's concept of critical history is clearly understood as tied to the adoption of perspectival epistemological warrant, then in this particular case, we might be able to resolve the ethical concern (Schutte 2000, p. 13).

In order to accomplish this, we need to turn to the textual evidence. Nietzsche's concerns in *Dawn* involve a strong focus upon health, and the trajectory of his philosophical work in the text is certainly therapeutic. His proposals concerning health-promoting interventions are made in two (interrelated) contexts at the level of the individual: physical and psychological. For example, he claims that physical interventions such as changing the diet, or engaging in hard physical labor, can count as effective treatment for afflictions of the soul (D 269). He also claims that our task in *Dawn* is a psychological one, as it involves us in calming "the invalid's fantasy to the extent that he at least does not suffer <u>more</u>, as heretofore, from thinking about his disease than from the disease itself" (D 54).

Nietzsche ties his concern for health directly to his critique of conventional morality. Nietzsche's campaign against "the morality of unselfing" in *Dawn* targets selflessness and degeneration, which conflict with things that Nietzsche thinks are natural and essential to human flourishing, such as overflowing energy (EH D 2). Nietzsche works to encourage us to engage in moral actions – and to avoid immoral actions – for new and different reasons, in order for us to learn to think and feel differently about matters ethical (D 103). This therapeutic process aims to help us imagine new possible virtues for the future (D 551). We need to engage in therapy because, Nietzsche contends, we live within a period in which sciences such as physiology, medicine, and sociology, and also the science of solitude, are not yet able to reconstitute the existing laws of life and action (D 453). Nietzsche is clear that each individual is expected to take responsibility for their own health; as he suggests, acting as our own physicians is likely to lead to improved health outcomes, as we are less likely to disregard our own prescriptions than those of some other individual (D 322).[5]

Approximately half way through D 206, Nietzsche makes a curious proposal. He declares that the workers of Europe "ought in future to declare themselves as <u>a class</u> a human impossibility" and that they should leave Europe and travel to other lands. Nietzsche specifies that the problem faced by the workers is one that is based on the increasing mechanization and corporatization of production. He makes ironic use of the classical phrase "good news" to bring the problem to life:

---

[5] Some remarks in these two paragraphs are based on remarks made in my previous work (Bamford, 2012).

> — Poor, cheerful, and independent! — These things can exist side by side; poor, cheerful, and a slave! — these things can also exist — and I can think of no better news for the workers in today's factory servitude: provided they don't feel that it's altogether a <u>disgrace</u> to be <u>used</u> and <u>used up</u>, in the way this happens, as a wheel in the machine and, as it were, a stopgap to plug the hole in human inventiveness! Phooey! (D 206)

The workers are to leave, Nietzsche contends, in order to free themselves and Europe from increasing decadence, and from their "impersonal enslavement" of this "factory servitude". Thus far, the aphorism seems commensurate with goals of liberation.

Let me briefly marshal the parts of the aphorism that contain Nietzsche's specific recommendations concerning travel to other lands, for the sake of clarity. First, Nietzsche writes of the European factory workers that,

> [...] everyone ought to think to oneself: 'Better to emigrate, to seek in wild and fresh parts of the world to become <u>master</u>, and above all master of myself; to keep moving from place to place as long as any sign of slavery whatsoever still beckons to me; not to avoid adventure and war and, if worst should come to worst, to be ready for death [...]' (D 206)

This certainly advocates emigration in pursuit of liberation, but it does not amount to a direct claim that the workers should engage in colonial oppression as a means to their own liberation. However, Nietzsche next makes a series of claims that do seem to suggest a colonizing solution for these workers. As he writes,

> [...] within the European beehive, they ought to precipitate an age of grand swarming-out such as has never been seen before and, through this freedom of domicile in the grand style, to protest against the machine, against capital, and against the choice currently threatening them of <u>having</u> to become either slave of the state or slave of a party of insurrection. May Europe be relieved of a quarter of its inhabitants! This will bring relief to it and to them! Only in faraway lands, through the ventures of swarming migrations of colonists, will one come to recognize just how much common sense and fairness, how much healthy distrust mother Europe has incorporated into her sons — these sons who were no longer able to endure being near her, the stupefied old crone, and were in danger of becoming as grumpy, irritable, and addicted to pleasure as she herself is. Outside Europe, Europe's virtues will be journeying along with these workers; and what inside the homeland began to degenerate into dangerous ill humor and criminal tendencies, will outside, take on a wild beautiful naturalness and will be called heroism. (D 206)

Nietzsche uses the imagery of worker bees to illustrate the mindlessness of factory work, and its pernicious effect upon the workers of Europe. He contrasts this with a Romantic image of the free, healthy, colonist who is able to explore wild and beautiful new lands. If we combine these contrasting images with Nietzsche's earlier claim on mastery in this aphorism, then it does seem to be the case that he is encouraging the workers to become colonial masters in these "wild and fresh" parts of the world. The workers are being exhorted to become masters "above all" of themselves – but this exhortation does not set aside, or diminish, that they are also being exhorted to engage in *colonial* mastery.

Moreover, we should not overlook that Nietzsche's "wild and fresh" lands are presented to us in the aphorism as *empty*, not as occupied – or even potentially occupied – by indigenous peoples. One mention that Nietzsche does make – in passing – about indigenous peoples occurs during a broader discussion of belief in intoxication in *Dawn* 50, and concerns the "firewater myth": the stereotype of the Native American who is constitutionally far more prone than Europeans to developing a problematic dependence on alcohol, or 'firewater.'[6] Nietzsche writes that "[j]ust as the natives these days are quickly corrupted and destroyed by 'firewater,' so too has humanity as a whole been corrupted by the spiritual firewaters of intoxicating feelings and by those who keep alive the craving for such feelings" (D 50). The purpose of this aphorism is to draw our critical attention to the psychological problem of lack of control of nervous energy and hatred of the environment, the age, and the entire world, by those people who live for "sublime and enraptured" moments in the belief that these moments are their "true self."

We can, I think, analogize the unreflective attitude that characterizes these unhealthy people in D 50 to the unhealthy workers in D 206, who are prevented from thinking independently by their industrial de-individualization. In both cases, Nietzsche's stated concern is with finding a way to promote the health of these individuals. Developing our awareness of the intoxication phenomenon in D 50 presents us with an opportunity to reflect on the notion that intoxication is not a helpful solution for such individuals; this intoxication is not health promoting, as it encourages the intoxicated to remain bound to a narrow and misguided view of the world and their place within it, ruling them out of pursuit of meaningful development. It seems as though D 50 remains true to the broader therapeutic concerns that Nietzsche expressed in *Dawn*. However, this remark on "natives" in D 50 is made in passing, and involves an unchallenged opposition between the European and the native, suggesting that colonizing logic is at work here. Nietzsche's claim in D 50 also gives us reason to think that Nietzsche is comfortable with adopting the stereotype of the drunken Native American – itself a product of colonizing logic – unreflect-

---

[6] The basis of this stereotype in the history of racial and colonial oppression is recognized in contemporary bioethics (See Dingel/Koenig 2008).

ively, in order to further his therapeutic agenda. This lack of reflection undercuts the therapeutic work that D 50 sets out to perform.

The same issue is evident in D 206. Following this claim on the heroism of the colonizing worker, Nietzsche makes another highly problematic claim regarding the possible introduction of what he characterizes as distinctively 'Chinese' values:

> Perhaps we will also bring in the Chinese at this point: and they would bring along the ways of thinking and living that are suitable for diligent ants. Indeed they could in general assist in transfusing into the blood of a restless and worn out Europe a little Asian calm and contemplation — and what is surely needed most — Asian perseverance. (D 206)

This claim also stereotypes, in that it fallaciously uses a particular trait or set of traits to characterize a particular nationality or a racial/ethnic identity. Moreover, the claim betrays another instance of Nietzsche's colonialism at work: the Chinese as a people, and "Asian characteristics," are presented as a resource to be used for the benefit of Europe. This claim strikes an especially odd note given Nietzsche's earlier complaint concerning the de-individualizing effect of the process of mechanization on the workers of Europe, who are being turned into just so much human resources by this process: each worker is being treated as a "wheel in the machine" and a "stopgap," not a person. As Holub argues, if we substitute the word 'Germany' for the word 'Europe' in this part of the aphorism, the sentiments that Nietzsche is expressing mirror almost perfectly some of the sentiments expressed by his brother-in-law, Bernhard Förster, in his writings on his proposed colony – Nueva Germania – in Paraguay, and on nineteenth century German colonial ambitions more generally (Holub 1998, p. 42).

Despite these remarks and their context, there has been some resistance to characterizing Nietzsche as a colonialist in *Dawn*. Discussing *Dawn* 206 in the broader context of Nietzsche's interest in promoting health, Adrian Del Caro observes that Nietzsche is committed to the view that we should attempt to free ourselves of our immediate environment if this environment is not conducive to our health (Del Caro 2004, p. 112). As pointed out above, Holub explicitly acknowledges the colonizing logic present in *Dawn* 206 (Holub 1998, p. 42). However, and in tension with his other remarks on the aphorism, Holub also claims that Nietzsche's "focus in this passage is ultimately the health of Europe" (Holub 1998, p. 42). Holub bases his assessment of *Dawn* 206 as fundamentally health promoting, rather than as fundamentally dedicated to promoting European colonialism, on the timing of *Dawn's* composition. As he discusses, *Dawn* was (except for the Preface of 1886) composed in Genoa between November 1880 and May 1881, prior to 1884 – which year, he argues, marks the beginning of the German colonial empire (Holub 1998, p. 42).[7] Holub also claims that Nietzsche's writings after 1884 suggest that his thoughts were focused less on health promotion and more on "European subjugation of the world" (Holub 1998, p. 42). In addition to appealing to a range of Nietzsche's letters from this period to support his reasoning, Holub draws on evidence from GS 362 to further substantiate a distinction between Nietzsche's affinity to colonialism pre- and post-1884. In GS 362, Nietzsche lauds Napoleon's reclamation of Renaissance ideas, and specifically the fact that in the wake of Napoleon,

> [...] the man has again become master over the businessman and the philistine — and perhaps even over 'woman' who has been pampered by Christianity and the enthusiastic spirit of the eighteenth century, and even more by 'modern ideas.' (GS 362)

As Holub contends in light of this, Nietzsche's hope is that Napoleon's Renaissance "granite" may become master over the national movement in Germany, and in so doing, render the possibility of a unified Europe accessible (Holub 1998, p. 44). Building on this claim, Holub ties only Nietzsche's post-1884 writings, and in particular Nietzsche's concept of the 'Good European,' to the logic of colonization and European domination.

These discussions of *Dawn* 206 presented by Del Caro and Holub are helpful, but in the end, they are unsatisfying with regard to clarifying the liberatory value of the aphorism. Both Del Caro and Holub seem to agree that the focus of the aphorism is on therapy, and specifically on the role of therapy in promoting health. Both of them seem to agree that Nietzsche is not interested in development of a colonialist agenda for its own sake in the aphorism. However, in light of my discussion thus far, it is not clear what specific evidence is available to justify these conclusions; neither Del Caro nor Holub supply further support for their conclusions that the aphorism is not fundamentally colonialist.

It seems clear to me that in *Dawn* 206 (and indeed elsewhere in the text), Nietzsche has incorporated a version of Holub's colonialist imagination into his philosophy. However, I think it is possible to acknowledge this about the aphorism without branding Nietzsche a colonialist *tout court*. I propose to place Nietzsche's remarks into the broader context of the philosophical work to which these remarks contribute. In so doing, I will show how the rationale informing Nietzsche's thinking in this aphorism is commensurate with the anti-binary and pragmatist defense that Schutte provides of his wider therapeutic philosophy and its liberatory value.

---

[7] For information on the order of *Dawn*'s composition, see also Schaberg (1995, p. 77).

One of the difficulties with understanding *Dawn* 206 concerns how to read Nietzsche's final remark on the Chinese. It is not clear to whom the 'we' in this remark refers: the workers? To the decadent denizens of old Europe? To the progenitors of a revitalized version of Europe? Given that the discussion in *Dawn* 206 has been directed at solving a problem of increasing ill health of European factory workers, and of Europe considered holistically, and given that earlier in the passage, Nietzsche explicitly criticized the "socialist pied pipers who want to inflame" the workers with "mad hopes" to be "prepared and nothing more," the most plausible explanation is that the 'we' refers to the progenitors of a new and healthy Europe. Such progenitors, Nietzsche contends elsewhere, will be characterized by independent exercise of the power of the lawgiver (D 187). Yet Nietzsche also admits that many people will struggle to achieve genuine self-rule; some people – even and especially including philosophers – may ultimately falter in their efforts to achieve self-rule, and may seek instead to become institutions (D 542).[8] As Nietzsche writes,

> [...] it is always necessary [...] to draw out the physiological phenomenon behind moral judgments and moral presumptions, so as not to become the fools of piety and the damagers of knowledge. For it occurs not infrequently that an old man enters into the illusion of undergoing a great moral regeneration and rebirth and from out of this feeling pronounces judgments on his work and the course of his life as if he had only now grown clairvoyant: and yet standing behind the trumpeters of this feeling of well-being and these confident judgments is not wisdom but fatigue. Belief in one's own genius may well be described as its most dangerous indication, which tends to overtake these great and semi-great men only on this life's borderline: belief in an exceptional position and exceptional rights. The thinker, stricken with such a belief, considers it permitted from now on to make it easier on himself and, as genius, to decree more than to prove ... (D 542)

Nietzsche's concern in this aphorism with making things easier on thinkers, and with turning critical engagement into an institution that may not itself be critiqued, also reflects Schutte's concerns with dualistic, binary, frameworks for critical assessment resulting in our thinking being placed on automatic pilot (Schutte 2004, p. 184). Self-rule is not a matter of determining a rule and then abandoning the effort of thinking through problems in favor of following this rule, but is rather the act of continuously questioning and reflecting. Once this process ceases, as Nietzsche points out, the thinker erects in his own teaching a boundary marker (D 542). If they did engage in the great "swarming-out" that Nietzsche advocates in D 206, then no matter the extent to which

---

8 Keith Ansell-Pearson has drawn attention to this feature of the text in order to defend Nietzsche's intellectual integrity (Ansell-Pearson 2009, p. 24).

Nietzsche might romanticize the image of the heroic colonist, the workers of Europe would certainly not be making things easier on themselves.

Another important thing to note about Nietzsche's claim concerning "Asian perseverance" in the aphorism is that it treats perseverance as a virtue. Given the focus at hand is on an ethics of self-analysis and self-cultivation, this raises the question as to what kind of virtue is really intended here. Nietzsche develops a specific way of thinking about virtue that is based on a distinction between the ethical – which for Nietzsche is tied to health – and the merely moral. Of this distinction, he writes in *Antichrist* that,

> What is good? – All that heightens the feeling of power, power itself in man.
> What is bad? – All that proceeds from weakness.
> What is happiness? — The feeling that power increases — that a resistance is overcome.
> Not contentment, but more power; not peace at all, but war; not virtue, but proficiency (virtue in the Renaissance style, virtù, virtue free of moralic acid).
> The weak and ill-constituted shall perish: first principle of our philanthropy. And one shall help them to do so.
> What is more harmful than any vice? Active sympathy for the ill-constituted and weak — Christianity ... (A 2).

Virtue, in this passage from *Antichrist*, is described in terms of proficiency that is free from "moralic acid," and is directly tied to the promotion of health. It is this same type of virtue – *virtù* – that Nietzsche is pointing us towards in his remark on the potential value of Asian perseverance to Europe in *Dawn* 206.[9] As he claims, behaviors that detract from the increasing collectivization and determination of the workers through capitalizing forces in old Europe emerge, in the colonized lands, as virtues – and these virtues are free from what he calls "moralic acid" in *Antichrist* 2. Calm, contemplation, and perseverance are virtues likely to be involved in therapeutic self-analysis and self-cultivation – even given the discriminatory tone that this appeal to "Asian" virtue strikes in contemporary ears.[10]

---

[9] Schoeman (2007, p. 19) draws attention to Nietzsche's frequent use of the concept of *virtù*, which is referred to as 'moraline-free' as it is to be distinguished from the type of virtue promoted by herd mentality.

[10] Kaufmann (1974, p. 293) reads this claim concerning the addition of Chinese blood into Europe as proposing an advantage. While not commenting on the association with the Chinese that Nietzsche makes in this section, Mervyn Sprung points out that Nietzsche's advocacy of a philosophy of self-liberation in Dawn is in keeping with the Indian Buddhist tradition, commenting specifically on Dawn 96 as an example of Nietzsche's praise of Buddhist philosophy of self-redemption (Sprung 1991, 80). André van der Braak (2011, p. 4) concurs with this assessment, adding that Nietzsche considered the Buddha to be a great physician for this reason, even while he treated Buddhist views on health as being opposed to his project of life-affirmation.

This focus on virtue recalls Nietzsche's claim that his proposal to the workers has the capacity to invigorate Europe by returning a "pure air" to it. It is tempting to read this part of the aphorism as a suggestion that those remaining in Europe will enter into some form of solidarity with the workers. However, accepting this reading would involve a significant misunderstanding of the text. Nietzsche's main reason for rejecting the socialist movement in Europe at this time is based on his identification of the loss of inner value – or indeed of the possibility of such value being nurtured in and for the future – at the expense of outwardly valuable things such as money and prestige. As Nietzsche writes to the workers,

> [...] you always have ringing in your ear instead the fife of the socialist pied pipers who want to inflame you with mad hopes, who enjoin you to be prepared and nothing more, prepared at any moment such that you are waiting and waiting for something external, but otherwise you continue to live in every way the same as you had otherwise lived before — until this waiting turns to hunger and thirst and fever and madness, and finally the day of the bestia triumphans rises in all its glory? (D 206)

Socialism cannot provide the therapy that the sickening workers require, Nietzsche contends here, because socialism is simply another way in which the deindividualization of humanity, the turning of humanity into a resource, is being expressed in contemporary culture. Socialism is not an exception to the ongoing prioritization of outer capital at the expense of inner, personal, value.

Emphasizing the centrality of health and therapy in Nietzsche's thinking in *Dawn* suggests another reason as to why the workers of Europe, if conceived of as a class – and remembering the alternative translations for the German term *Stand* – would be ethically justified in declaring their situation, or condition, to be impossible (Smith 2012, p. 330).[11] Notice that in Nietzsche's construction of this example, the workers are tacitly encouraged, through the process of industrialization and through associated language use, to think of themselves as cogs in a corporate machine. As Nietzsche writes to the workers of this disgrace, seeking to draw attention to their problem,

> To let oneself be talked into believing that through a heightening of this impersonality within the mechanical workings of a new society the disgrace of slavery could be turned into a virtue! Phooey! To set a price for oneself whereby one becomes no longer a person but merely a cog! Are you co-conspirators in the current folly sweeping over nations, which, above all else, want to produce as much as possible and to be as rich as possible?

---

11 The epigraph to Dawn 206 is given as, "The impossible class" (Der unmögliche Stand). As Smith notes, the German word "Stand" may be translated as "class" or sometimes as "condition" or "situation."

> Your concern ought to hold out to them a counter-reckoning: what vast sums of genuine <u>inner</u> value are being squandered on such a superficial external goal! (D 206)

The process of industrial mechanization involves the systematic de-individualization of all of the factory workers, encouraging them not to think independently at all. This process of de-individualization runs directly counter to Nietzsche's promotion of an ethics of self-analysis and self-cultivation in pursuit of health.

Given this, it seems more reasonable to accept that the purity in question in D 206 concerns the capacity for what, hearkening back to *Antichrist* 2, we may call virtuous and healthy – moralic-acid-free – self-rule (Schoeman 2007). Nietzsche makes it explicit that for Europeans, in the absence of the workers who heed his call to emigrate, his proposal will necessarily engage them in unlearning some of the needs that they have developed as an effect of the process of industrialization. This involves self-rule on the part of the Europeans left behind: once our worker-dependent needs are no longer so easy to satisfy we will be prompted to pursue critical self-reflection and self-cultivation. In the following aphorism, Nietzsche makes some remarks that further substantiate this reading, when he claims that if a German,

> … is forced to stand on his own and throw off his torpor, if it is no longer possible for him to disappear like a numeral within a sum … then he will discover his powers: then he will turn dangerous, evil, profound, daring, and he brings to the light of day the hoard of sleeping energy he carries inside himself in which no one else (not even he himself) believed (D 207).

Later in the same aphorism, Nietzsche reinforces this point by claiming that if a German is placed in a position that facilitates him to achieve great things, he can and will achieve them – but for the moment, Germans remain in "the embryonic state of something <u>higher</u>."

If we prioritize the therapeutic context of Nietzsche's remarks in our reading of D 206, then we can also note that his proposal that the workers of Europe should declare themselves to be "an impossibility <u>as a class</u>" does not require Nietzsche's consistent commitment to any political ideology, including a colonialist one. To be consistent with his therapeutic aims, Nietzsche need only commit himself to the logical consequences of advocacy of an ethics of self-analysis and self-cultivation that he thinks may result in improved health. Nietzsche's ethical commitments may of course result in a range of political consequences, but he does not need to advocate any specific political action or ideology in order to make available a therapy based on individual self-analysis. Moreover, resulting political consequences remain subject to the same pragmatic-therapeutic evaluation as prior decisions (in the case of our example, the claim that the workers should become colonists). In other words, Nietzsche need not be ideologically committed *tout court* to colonialism or indeed to a specific anti-colonial political agenda, in order to do beneficial therapeutic work that deploys a colonialist strategy in D 206.

This claim is not the same as, but recalls the structure of, Schutte's acknowledgement of the pragmatism of Nietzschean politics of liberation (Schutte 2004). In this specific case, Nietzsche does not need to be worried about the issue of workers' rights as stakeholders in a given industry, because pursuit of this issue would take it for granted that workers do indeed exist as a de-individuated class comprising numerous individuals engaged to complete work tasks of a specific type. Pursuit of workers' rights does nothing in particular to address the health of each individual, or to promote each individual's therapeutic engagement in self-analysis and self-cultivation. Accordingly, instead of defending socialism, or encouraging some other form of collective action within the industrial context, Nietzsche encourages the workers to declare themselves to be a "human impossibility" as a class, or as a condition or situation, and emigrate from Europe, colonizing other lands, in order to make themselves and their condition humanly possible.

In laying out the therapeutic ethical context of *Dawn* in greater detail, I have been showing why Nietzsche's colonialist remarks in D 206 are commensurate with his broader therapeutic concerns. Nietzsche seems certain that the workers would be better off – healthier – as colonists, though as mentioned above, he does not discuss what the indigenous inhabitants of the wild and fresh new lands to be colonized might have to say about their new masters. This is the point at which we might be tempted to conclude by affirming that despite its commensurability with his wider therapeutic aims, there remains a substantial and insuperable ethical objection to Nietzsche's colonial imagination. I do not think there is sufficient evidence in the aphorism to charge Nietzsche with the promotion of colonial *domination*; instead, the ethical failure lies in Nietzsche's *lack of attention* to the rights and needs of indigenous peoples. However, leaving matters here would involve our failure to learn the therapeutic-philosophical lesson concerning the importance of self-rule and critical thought to the promotion of health.

It might still be possible to set the 'lack of attention' objection to one side in the specific context of aphorism 206 of *Dawn*, as Del Caro and Holub ultimately appear to do. To provide some justification for this, we could argue that in the aphorism, Nietzsche's specific concern is with the health of the workers of Europe and with Europe itself; he does not specify colonization of any specific land occupied by any specific peoples or mastery over any specific peoples, merely colonization of some wild and fresh land for the sake of achieving the specific beneficial psychological effects of becoming colonists upon the workers and upon Europe. So, although this is highly improbable, it is logically possible that a deserted island not claimed by any country would qualify as an appropriate colonial target, given the conditions Nietzsche specifies for colonization in the aphorism. Yet this response is not the most satisfying one available; it is certainly not likely to satisfy anyone raising a principled ethical objection to Nietzsche's colonial imagination on the basis of its lack of care for indigenous peoples. Introducing a series of articles that grapple with this problem in contemporary contexts, Ivison, Patton and Sanders point out the need to acknowledge that it is unclear whether or not political theory in the liberal Western tradition can provide appropriate space in which indigenous peoples can articulate their aspirations (Ivison/Patton/Sanders 2000, p. 2). While it is certainly legitimate to question whether a theorist such as Nietzsche can offer a substantial response to the question of the rights of indigenous peoples in the case of his call for colonization, doing no more than making this acknowledgement merely signals the end of the conversation, and does not yield a sufficiently fine-grained sense of the limits of the liberatory value of Nietzsche's thinking, especially with regard to D 206.

A more satisfying way of responding is to treat the ethical concern about Nietzsche's neglect of the needs of indigenous peoples in the self-critical and self-cultivating spirit of his philosophical therapy, so that at the least, we can identify more precise limits to Nietzsche's liberatory value. To sketch out a way forward, we need to briefly examine the concept of resistance. Alcoff distinguishes between the 'Caliban' view of resistance in postcolonial theory, where resistance to the colonizer occurs "within the interstices of the dominant culture" – Caliban is forced to speak his captor's tongue, and as a result is able to curse his master – and the 'indigenous' view of resistance, where resistance to the colonizer involves using rationalities, languages, and ways of being that existed prior to the advent of colonization (Alcoff 2004, pp. 154f.). Alcoff sees a tension between these two poles in Schutte's Nietzschean approach to resistance.

Responding to Alcoff's concerns regarding her reliance on Nietzsche, Schutte emphasizes the importance of overcoming binaries in analyzing the concept of resistance. She denies that the Caliban view of resistance merely involves Caliban using his master's tools, arguing instead that (i) Caliban is not a deficient Prospero but an agent who has already transformed these tools, and (ii) that Caliban's voice does not ideologize itself as a victim, but as an agent using language to communicate (Schutte 2004, p. 186). She also points out that the Caliban position is not the only characterization of alterity available to postcolonial discourse, reclaiming a female alterity by pointing to José Martí's conception of Latin America as a single mother (rather than as a dependent wife) whose children (encompassing all races) will stand equally with the United States and with Europe (Schutte 2004, p. 187).

Nietzsche proposes that European workers engage in an act of colonization in order to accrue psychological health benefits for themselves. Their colonizing act would also benefit the rest of Europe. There is a tension between the needs of (possible) indigenous peoples and the workers-as-colonizers in the aphorism. If we accept this tension then another one arises, this time between the ethical and political aspects of the aphorism, and within the wider context of the therapeutic dimension of Nietzsche's philosophy. On this reading, Nietzsche's work in D 206 has liberatory value – but only to Europeans. Their liberation is at the expense of an act of colonial imagination, and at the expense of (possible) indigenous peoples dwelling in the lands that he proposes that European workers should colonize.

However, if we were to move beyond the specific context of this aphorism and to consider another specific case, then it remains possible that the therapeutic dimension of Nietzsche's philosophy might have further liberatory value beyond the European context. Further work in support of this claim would explore the degree to which the concept of resistance may draw upon – and inform – Nietzsche's concept of pessimistic strength, and whether Nietzsche's discussions of pessimistic strength can go beyond monumental history to critical history. An example of the liberatory relevance of pessimistic strength that supports this proposal occurs in *Twilight of the Idols*. Resonating with Nietzsche's concern in D 542 that we may fail in the effort of self-rule and may instead seek to establish ourselves and our moral laws as institutions, Nietzsche expresses the concern that "liberal institutions stop being liberal as soon as they are set up" – and so, unfortunately, cannot be relied upon to guarantee freedom (TI Skirmishes 38). Instead, he suggests, we should look for freedom in places where the greatest resistance is constantly overcome (TI Skirmishes 38).

Bibliography

Alcoff, Linda Martín (2004): "Schutte's Nietzschean Postcolonial Politics". In: *Hypatia* 19(3), pp. 144–156.

Ansell-Pearson, Keith (2009): "On the Sublime in Dawn". In: *The Agonist* 2/1 (March), pp. 5–30.

Ansell-Pearson, Keith (2011): "Afterword". In: Friedrich Nietzsche: *Dawn*. Brittain Smith (trans.). Stanford, CA: Stanford University Press, pp. 363–408.

Bamford, Rebecca (2012): "Daybreak". In: Paul C. Bishop (ed.): *A Companion to the Works of Friedrich Nietzsche*. Rochester, NY: Boydell & Brewer [Camden House], pp. 139–157.

Del Caro, Adrian (2004): *Grounding the Nietzsche Rhetoric on Earth*. Berlin, New York: de Gruyter.

Dingel, Molly J./Koenig, Barbara A. (2008): "Tracking Race in Addiction Research". In: Barbara A. Koenig/Sandra Soo Jin Lee/S. Richardson (eds.): *Revisiting Race in a Genomic Age*. New Brunswick, NJ: Rutgers University Press, pp. 172–197.

Dombowsky, Don (2002): "A response to Alan D. Schrift's 'Nietzsche For Democracy?'". In: *Nietzsche-Studien* 31, pp. 278–290.

Hatab, Lawrence J. (1995): *A Nietzschean Defense of Democracy: An Experiment in Postmodern Politics*. Chicago and La Salle, IL: Open Court.

Holub, Robert C. (1995): "Nietzsche and the Women's Question". In: *The German Quarterly* 68(1), pp. 67–71.

Holub, Robert C. (1998): "Nietzsche's Colonialist Imagination: Nueva Germania, Good Europeanism, and Great Politics". In: Sara Lennox/Susanne Zantop (eds.): *The imperialist imagination: German colonialism and its legacy*. Sara Friedrichsmeyer, Ann Arbor, MI: The University of Michigan Press.

Holub, Robert C. (1999): "The Birth of Psychoanalysis from the Spirit of Enmity: Nietzsche, Rée, and Psychology in the Nineteenth Century". In: Jacob Golomb/Weaver Santaniello/Ronald Lehrer (eds.): *Nietzsche and Depth Psychology*. Albany, NY: State University of New York Press, pp. 149–170.

Ivison, Duncan/Patton, Paul/Sanders, Will (2000): "Introduction". In: Duncan Ivison/Paul Patton/Will Sanders (eds.): *Political Theory and the Rights of Indigenous Peoples*. Cambridge: Cambridge University Press, pp. 1–22.

Kaufmann, Walter (1974): *Nietzsche: Philosopher, Psychologist, Antichrist*. 4th edition. Princeton, NJ: Princeton University Press.

Nietzsche, Friedrich (1974): *The Gay Science*. Walter Kaufmann (trans.). New York: Vintage.

Nietzsche, Friedrich (1990): *Antichrist*, in *The Twilight of the Idols and The Antichrist*. R. J. Hollingdale (trans.). London: Penguin.

Nietzsche, Friedrich (1998): *Twilight of the Idols*. Duncan Large (trans.). Oxford: Oxford University Press.

Nietzsche, Friedrich (2012): *Dawn*. Brittain Smith (trans.). Stanford, CA: Stanford University Press.

Pugliese, Joseph. (1996): "Rationalized Violence and Legal Colonialism: Nietzsche 'contra' Nietzsche". In: *Cardozo Studies in Law and Literature* 8(2), pp. 277–293.

Schaberg, William H. (1995): *The Nietzsche Canon: A Publication History and Bibliography*. Chicago and London: University of Chicago Press.

Schoeman, Marinus. (2007): "Generosity as a central virtue in Nietzsche's ethics.". In: *South African Journal of Philosophy* 26(1), pp. 17–30.

Schrift, Alan D. (2000): "Nietzsche For Democracy?". In: *Nietzsche-Studien* 29, pp. 220–233.

Schutte, Ofelia (1984): *Beyond Nihilism: Nietzsche Without Masks*. Chicago, IL: The University of Chicago Press.

Schutte, Ofelia (1993): *Cultural Identity and Social Liberation in Latin American Thought*. Albany, NY: State University of New York Press.

Schutte, Ofelia (2000): "Continental philosophy and postcolonial subjects". In: *Philosophy Today* 44 (SPEP Supplement), pp. 8–17.

Schutte, Ofelia (2004). "Response to Alcoff, Ferguson, and Bergoffen," *Hypatia* 19(3), 182–202.

Ure, Michael (2008): *Nietzsche's Therapy: Self-Cultivation in the Middle Works*. Lanham, MD: Lexington Books.

Ure, Michael (2013): "Nietzsche's Political Therapy". In: Keith Ansell-Pearson (ed.): *Nietzsche and Political Thought*. London: Bloomsbury, pp. 161–178.

Nandita Biswas Mellamphy
Nietzsche's Political Materialism: Diagram for a Nietzschean Politics

> Nietzsche invents, in a latent manner, a new discipline that we will call 'Political Materialism', destined to occupy and displace the positions of 'Historical Materialism'. He provides his object by posing all reality (equivalent to Relations-of-Production and Superstructures) as power and Relations-of-Power [...]. Contrary to Marxism, which perceives politics by mediation and delegation [...], with the Eternal-Return/Will-to-Power ER/WP machine [dispositif] Nietzsche provides the possibility of a plastic politics, of an internal political determination [which is] neither too broad or transcendent, nor too narrow and restrictive, of the Relations-of-Power upon which practical empirical fields are deduced, specified and qualified. (Laruelle 1977, pp. 31, 25)[1]

In his very complex but novel and enlightening 1977 treatise on Nietzschean politics, the French philosopher François Laruelle articulates a theory of political materialism in Nietzsche's thinking, which I will try to elucidate in this brief essay. Unlike other French interpretations of Nietzsche by those such as Foucault and Deleuze – and even Bataille and Klossowski – Laruelle's early text on Nietzsche has not yet been translated into English and is relatively unknown in Anglophone philosophical circles. My overall aim is to offer an introductory sketch of Laruelle's specifically political vision of Nietzsche and to tease out some of its more novel aspects, especially in relation to Foucault's and Deleuze's respective interpretations of Nietzsche. So, while the present attempt is only cursory and general (though I am currently developing a detailed and extended comparison between Laruelle's interpretation of Nietzsche and those of other French thinkers in a work provisionally entitled Nietzsche's Avatars), it does tend to emphasize Laruelle's version and vision of Nietzsche over others. The reason is quite simple: what seems to be most valuable about this reading is its specifically diagrammatic approach to Nietzschean thinking. Rather than as linguistically- or discursively-derived mediations that have political effects, Laruelle identifies the technical substructure that would permit Nietzschean concepts such as will to power and eternal recurrence to act as primary, internal and unmediated elements of political power. In fact, for Laruelle, it this transvaluation of the very notion of 'political' (from external to internal, mediated to unmediated) which is the technical hallmark of 'Nietzsche-thinking'. In this sense, Laruelle's perspective is rather unique and hereti-

---

[1] All translations from the French original are mine.

cal insofar as he takes Nietzsche to be a theoretical object with material effects, rather than as a historical subject or interpreter expressing his thoughts.

From the outset, Laruelle makes it clear that what he means by Nietzsche's 'thinking' does not refer primarily to what Nietzsche said or wrote – or neglected to say or write – but rather to the way in which Nietzsche's thinking functions, i.e. operates. Needless to say, with this type of agenda, Laruelle's interpretation does not focus on the hermeneutic, exegetical or doctrinal dimensions of Nietzsche's many explicit political statements; indeed one of Laruelle's main contentions is that although these signifying elements in no way need be repressed or suppressed, they are nevertheless secondary features of the fundamental design or layout (agencement) of Nietzsche's thinking. The basic and most important characteristic – the one that makes Nietzsche's political thinking unique from Laruelle's point of view – is the operation of an elementary and fundamentally non-signifying force-mechanics that activates the virulence of Nietzsche's thought. To 'philosophize with a hammer' and to 'smash idols' become the basic (that is to say, inherent and internal) political work of Nietzsche's elaboration of the will-to-power:

> Where does Nietzsche's revolutionary virulence come from, his power to destroy ontological codes? From what he produces solely from fluent syntax [...]: fluid schemas for morphing statements [...]. Our task: [...] [to] take up a mechanism, at once theoretical and practical, which fulfills the function of a Nietzschean mode of thinking that produces materials or even 'Nietzschean' articulations. (Laruelle 1977, pp. 74f.)

At the heart of Laruelle's notion of Nietzschean political materialism is the contradiction qua opposing tendencies produced by the basic mechanics of power-quanta, or will-to-power. Rather than diagramming Nietzsche's thinking within a dialectical structure of two interacting terms motivated by the engine of negation or negativity toward synthesis (as in dialectical and/or historical materialisms), Laruelle conceives of a four-fold or chiasmus – 'X' – structure: one pole diagrams the movement of 'mastery' (of the will to 'say no', to domination leading to the will-to-knowledge, to truth, to order, to form, to individualization and to unification), and thus expresses a 'fascistic' tendency; the other overlapped but coexisting (yet unrelated and unmediated) pole diagrams the movement of 'rebellion' (of the will to say 'yes' to everything, to squander, to exceed without recuperation, to forget, to affirm). While in traditions of dialectical materialism the engine of historical movement is the synthesis that results from the contradictory relations between two terms, (e.g. thesis/antithesis; master/slave, negation/affirmation), Laruelle posits that in Nietzschean political materialism, contradiction between opposing tendencies finds no mediation at all (the only 'relation' is one of duplicity rather than of duality says

Laruelle), and is instead unsynthesizable, hence basically non-signifiable (that is, not essentially characterized by signification and not essentially given to meaning). Using Nietzsche's own terminology, it could be said – although Laruelle himself does not say this – that the one Apollonian pole, driven by the "principle of individuation" (BT 1, 2) tending towards selection, individualization and formalization, plots the human, anthropocentric and biological movement involved in such processes as cognition and signification; while the other Dionysian pole is driven by the movement of overcoming the principle of individuation: that is, of affirming and activating pre-individual (and thus overhuman) potentialities that break up the human, anthropocentric and biological (e.g. cognition and signification), tending instead towards multiplicity, de-individualization and heterogeneity. "Knowledge is a tool of power [...]. The meaning of 'knowledge': [...] the concept is to be regarded in a strict and narrow anthropocentric and biological sense" (NL, KGW VIII/3, 14[122]).

It is most important in Laruelle's reading that both poles are operative in Nietzsche's thought; the one does not annul or sublate the other, but instead crosses over or perhaps – even better – double-crosses the other. This betrayal (or "duplicity" as Laruelle calls it) accounts for the presence of both fascistic and subversive tendencies in a Nietzschean mode of thinking. It is in this duplicity that Laruelle develops a theory regarding the inherently political function of the Nietzsche's thinking on life and will-to-power.

> Nietzsche is, in a double sense, the thinker of fascism:[2] he is, in a certain way, a fascistic thinker, but he first and foremost the thinker of the subversion of fascism. The Nietzsche-thought is a complex political process with two 'contradictory' poles (without mediation): the subordinate relation of a secondary fascistic pole (Mastery) to a principal revolutionary pole (Rebellion). Nietzsche became fascist to better defeat fascism, he assumed the worst forms of Mastery to become the Rebel. [...] We are all fascist readers of Nietzsche, we are all revolutionary readers of Nietzsche. Our unity is a contradictory relation a hierarchy without mediation), just as Nietzsche's unity is a contradictory and 'auto-critical' unity. Nietzsche puts the Master and the Rebel in a relation of duplicity rather than of duality. He liquidates the opposition of monism (the philosophy of the Master or the Rebel) and dualism (the mediated contradiction of Master and Rebel). (Laruelle 1977, p. 9)

---

2 It is worth noting that Laruelle never defines the term 'fascism' directly, although "Thesis 1" of his 1977 work on Nietzsche historically qualifies the term 'Fascism' as an "epoch" (Laruelle 1977, p. 9). Generally speaking, references to 'fascism' and 'fascistic' by Laruelle are meant to evoke "tendencies" of power in Nietzsche's thinking, for example, the tendency toward 'domination' or 'mastery' (what Laruelle calls "a process of fascisization"), or conversely the tendency toward 'resistance to' and 'rebellion against' domination (i.e. Nietzschean 'affirmation').

Gilles Deleuze appears to make a similar point in his treatment of Nietzsche's 'nomadic thought', but his characterization differs quite significantly from that of Laruelle: although Deleuze also ascribes twin characterizations – the nomad and the despot – he calls the nomadic 'extrinsic' and the despot 'intrinsic', whereas for Laruelle both poles are intrinsic and inherent to Nietzsche's thinking. "The nomad and his war-machine stand opposite the despot and his administrative machine, and the extrinsic nomadic unity opposite the intrinsic unity. And yet they are so interrelated or interdependent that the despot will set himself the problem of integrating, internalizing the nomadic war-machine, while the nomad attempts to invent an administration for his conquered empire. Their ceaseless opposition is such that they are inextricable from one another" (Deleuze 2004, p. 259). For Deleuze both the nomadic and the despotic mediate one another, such that for Deleuze, Nietzsche's most profound contribution is "to have made thought a nomadic power" (Deleuze 2004, p. 260). But for Laruelle, it is the ambiguity or fundamental irreducibility/irresolvability of Nietzsche's notion of will-to-power which is described as the internal duplicity between conflicting tendencies resulting in both fascistic and subversive expressions, that defines the inherently political aspect of Nietzsche's thinking.

> [There is] [n]o question of taking refuge in a historical and neutral reading, nor in the labour of a Nietzschean reading, without having to enter as contradictorily and without mediation in an intense scene of forces, pulsions, relations of power that are no longer textual or signifying "in the last instance" (Laruelle 1977, p. 11) [...] If this complex relation is regularly amputated and mutilated by interpreters, it is precisely because it accounts for the formula by which Nietzsche has posed, a priori, the internal possibility of the falsification of his thought, [a] constitutive falsification (Laruelle 1977, p. 14) [...] Why is our complex political conjecture where a fascistic line crosses with an otherwise continued subversive line interested in a Nietzsche-thinking ...? Because the specificity of Nietzsche is to tie [...] this process of fascisization [...] and the political and materials conditions of its subversion [...] Few have understood the meaning of the greatest of misunderstandings, to know that Nietzsche prefers flowing with the adversary as long as the adversary drowns: the messenger dies in his message, this is the message of Zarathustra" (Laruelle 1977, p. 17) [...] [For] the possibility of producing, in the same stroke, contradictory effects according to readers, the possibility of inoculating some with fascist poison which creates for others the revolutionary remedy of resistance ... for example for the same utterances to receive a fascistic sanction (in the past) and a revolutionary one (now), you have to go looking for it in the quadripartite operation of his thought. This internal duplicity of the two poles in relation to immediate contradiction and its plasticity makes Nietzsche superior to Marx for reflecting on the political problems of our times. (Laruelle 1977, pp. 28f.)

Laruelle departs from 'post-structuralist' accounts of Nietzsche that focus on discourse and the discursive/constructivist aspects of Nietzsche's thinking. For instance in 'Nietzsche, Genealogy, History', Michel Foucault conceives of power almost entirely within the schema of relation, the body being "the inscribed surface of events (traced by language and dissolved by ideas)" and the task of genealogy being the exposing of "a body totally imprinted by history and the process of history's destruction of the body" (Foucault 1977, p. 148). For Foucault, the process of bodily inscription is the "single drama" that stages the "repeated play of dominations" in the genealogy of the human (Foucault 1977, p. 150), and so Foucault's interpretation of Nietzschean genealogy focuses on this 'signifying' tendency.[3] In Nietzsche and Philosophy, Deleuze touches on the non-signifying dimensions of Nietzsche's thinking (much more so than does his essay on nomad thought): "Dionysus and Apollo are therefore not opposed as the terms of a contradiction but rather as two antithetical ways of resolving it; Apollo mediately, in the contemplation of the plastic image, Dionysus immediately in the reproduction, in the musical symbol of the will" (Deleuze 1983, p. 12). But even though Deleuze recognizes the non-mediating, non-discursive pole in Nietzsche's thinking, his conception of 'force' still seems to privilege the individuating, formalizing, hence discursive dimension, such that his articulation of the political nature of Nietzsche's thought is directly tied to its individuating and mediated tendency: "Every force is related to others and it either obeys or commands. What defines a body is this relation between dominant and dominated forces. Every relationship of forces constitutes a body – whether it is chemical, biological, social or political" (Deleuze 1983, p. 40). Although Deleuze does aver that every body "is always the fruit of chance" (Deleuze 1983, p. 40), his conception of the mechanics of active and

---

[3] One can, however, detect the 'presence' of a non-signifying or 'agrammatical' tendency in Foucault's thought, as I have argued (Biswas Mellamphy/Mellamphy 2005) and as Judith Butler (1989, 1997) has suggested. While Butler's point is that this is an unintended consequence of Foucault's reading, I would follow Laruelle is seeing this as a strength and the sign of a strong Nietzscheanism in Foucault's thinking: "The risk of renormalization is persistently there" writes Butler in her discussion of Nietzsche and Foucault, but so is "the possibility of a reversal of signification" (Butler 1997, pp. 93f.). "[P]olitically mobilizing what Nietzsche, in the Genealogy of Morals, called the 'sign chain', Foucault 'opens the way for an inauguration of signifying possibilities that exceed those to which the term has been previously bound', explains Butler (1997, p. 94). But just as we noted at the beginning of our study that the agrammatical or affective body is neither 'stable and self identical' nor 'a body prior to [...] inscription' (but rather, an 'inherently untidy' body inextricably bound to – double-bound, indeed double-crossed by – the 'body proper'), so in this case, in this conclusion, must we note that the possibilities inherent in and afforded by this 'abjected', 'abnormal', 'agrammatical' body exceed signification itself: they are, as such, an inauguration not of 'signifying possibilities' but of insignificant ones, of possibilities beyond signification, possibilities not yet significant" (Biswas Mellamphy/Mellamphy 2005, p. 47).

reactive forces is fundamentally relational such that 'chance' becomes ever-mediated in the process of bodily individuation. For Laruelle, however, the non-signifying, subversive pole of Nietzsche's thought is not mediated by the other individuating pole; in fact, for Laruelle, this is precisely why it can be dominant in its activity of subverting signification. Deleuze's conception cannot give autonomy to the non-discursive.

A revealing expression of the consequences of Deleuze's schema can be found in 'Nomad Thought', where he writes that "if Nietzsche does not belong in philosophy, perhaps it is because he is the first to conceive of another kind of discourse, a counter-philosophy, in other words, a discourse that is first and foremost nomadic, whose utterances would be produced not by a rational administrative machine – philosophers would be the bureaucrats of pure reason – but by a mobile war-machine" (Deleuze 2004, p. 259). By contrast, in Laruelle's diagram, what is truly unique about Nietzsche's thinking is the autonomy and non-mediated power of the non-signifying pole that nonetheless disrupts and infects the expression of every signifying and informational event. "From the outset, it is necessary to think the possibility of mastery outside of (or apart from) discourse, not only as force, but as power of resistance or power of the Other, so as to not fall back under the law of the signifier with a exoteric concept of power and libido (natural energy)" (Laruelle 1977, p. 58).

Let us turn to the question of which 'materials' would constitute a Nietzschean 'materialism', and ask how this materialism could be conceived as inherently 'political'. According to Nietzsche, "all organic functions can be traced back to this will-to-power" (BGE 36); will-to-power can neither be conceptualized monadically nor reductively, as in materialistic atomism in which the source of causation lies is some kind of indivisible substance or monad ("as an atomon": see BGE 12), nor can it be conceptualized in terms of a deductive nomological model (e.g. a universal law): rather, for Nietzsche will-to-power is nothing other than the play of unequal and colliding force quanta, the transient but ongoing "establishment of power relationships" (NL, KGW VII/3, 36[18]), i.e. the struggle "between two or more forces" (NL, KGW VIII/1, 2[139]) of "unequal power" (NL, KGW VIII/3, 14[95]). Forces are not knowable "in themselves" but only in their effects ("Has a force ever been demonstrated?: no, only effects translated into a completely foreign language"; NL, KGW VIII/1, 2[159]). Forces can only be *known* – 'unified', 'signified' – because they have "form-shaping" tendencies and capacities (NL, KGW VII/2, 26[231]); they are not 'things' but the movement of pre-individual affective 'potentialities'; they are the condition for the formation of what we call 'things'. By 'pre-individual', I borrow a term from Gilbert Simondon to describe the differential but latent fund qua information that continuously modifies biological and psychical processes of individuation.[4] Christoph Cox has used the term 'pre-individual' to characterize Nietzsche's musical ontology in which the "genesis of Individuals" arises from Dionysian "pre-individual forces and materials" (Cox 2006, p. 500) that are not inherently subjective or objective but out of which the struggle for individuation arises:

> [O]ut of the simplest forms striving toward the most complex, out of the stillest, most rigid, coldest forms toward the hottest, most turbulent, most self-contradictory, and then returning home to the simple out of this abundance, out of the play of contradictions back to the joy of concord, still affirming itself in this uniformity of its courses and its years, blessing itself as that which must return eternally, as a becoming that knows no satiety, no disgust, no weariness: this, my Dionysian world of the eternally self-creating, the eternally self-destroying (NL, KGW VII/3, 38[12]).

The pre-individual is not an undifferentiated state but precisely a differential collision between a dominating or mastering tendency and a subordinating tendency. This pre-individual force-mechanics – which constitutes the will-to-power – is the basic, immanent, matter of phenomenal reality and that which gives statements and discursive formations their signifying charge and political effects. Of the published works, it is in the Gay Science that we find the clearest articulation of these points:

> Origin of knowledge. — Over immense periods of time the intellect produced nothing but errors. A few of these proved to be useful and helped to preserve the species: those who hit upon or inherited these had better luck in their struggle for themselves and their progeny. Such erroneous articles of faith, which were continually inherited, until they became almost part of the basic endowment of the species, include the following: that there are enduring things; that there are equal things; that there are things, substances; bodies; that a thing is what it appears to be (GS 110) [...] Those, for example, who did not know how to find often enough what is 'equal' as regards both nourishment and hostile animals — those, in other words, who subsumed things too slowly and cautiously — were favoured with a lesser probability of survival than those who guessed immediately upon encountering similar instances that they must be equal [...]. In order that the concept of

---

[4] "[T]he individual is to be understood as having a relative reality, occupying only a certain phase of the whole being in question – a phase that therefore carries the implication of a preceding preindividual state, and that, even after individuation, does not exist in isolation, since individuation does not exhaust in the single act of its appearance all the potentials embedded in the preindividual state. Individuation, moreover, not only brings the individual to light but also the individual-milieu dyad. In this way, the individual possesses only a relative existence in two senses: because it does not represent the totality of the being, and because it is merely the result of a phase in the being's development during which it existed neither in the form of an individual nor as the principle of individuation" (Simondon 1992 p. 300; see also Simondon, 2005).

> substance could originate — which is indispensable for logic though in the strictest sense nothing real corresponds to it — it was likewise necessary that for a long time one did not see nor perceive the changes in things. The beings that did not see precisely had an advantage over those that saw everything 'in flux' (GS 111) [...] We have arranged for ourselves a world in which we can live– by positing bodies, lines, planes, causes and effects, motion and rest, form and content; without these articles of faith nobody now could endure life. But that does not prove them. Life is no argument. The conditions of life might include error (GS 121).

The instinct for self-preservation motivates the will-to-knowledge and accounts for why, in Nietzsche's thinking of force, reactive forces gain expression and can dominate over active forces. "All thought, judgment, perception, considered as comparison, has as its precondition a '<u>positing</u> of equality', and earlier still a '<u>making</u> equal'. The process of making equal is the same as the process of incorporation of appropriated material in the amoeba" (NL, KGW VIII/1, 5[65]). Making things 'equal' and 'substantive' allows endurance beyond the particular life-cycle of an organism, and although this permits the development of the 'organs of knowledge' (NL, KGW VIII/3, 14[122]), it is generally a condition of distress which curtails the instinct for the expansion of power. A basic premise of Nietzsche's 'naturalism' would be that "in nature it is not conditions of distress that are dominant but overflow and squandering, even to the point of absurdity. The struggle for existence is only an exception, a temporary restriction of the will to life"; "growth and expansion [...] – in accordance with the will-to-power" "is the will of life" (GS 349). Hence 'culture' can become "transfigured <u>physis</u>" (SE 3) to the extent that, following Laruelle's chiasmus diagram, the force-mechanics of the Dionysian pre-individual, a-signifying tendencies of will-to-power continuously subvert the mastering, signifying, individuating Apollonian tendencies of the will-to-knowledge. "In order for a particular species to maintain itself and increase its power, [...] a species grasps a certain amount of reality in order to become master of it, in order to press it into service" (NL, KGW VIII/3, 14[122]).

Knowledge is a product of experience, but unlike Kant – who claimed that knowledge was the product of transcendental faculties like understanding, reason, imagination – for Nietzsche, knowledge is product of will-to-power, which is not just sense-data qua lived experience, because sense-data is already a 'translation' or 'transcription' of pre-individual force-mechanics. While interpretations of Nietzsche often characterize his thinking within a philosophy of subjectivity, the subject is a fiction of the will-to-knowledge's mastering tendency towards signification. It is will-to-power that interprets, not a subject: "The will-to-power <u>interprets</u> (– it is a question of interpretation when an organ is constructed –): it defines limits, determines degrees, variations of power" (NL, KGW VIII/1, 2[148]); "[t]he mistake lies in the fictitious insertion of a subject" (NL, KGW VIII/1, 2[142]). "Linguistic means of expression are useless for expressing 'becoming'; it accords with our inevitable need to posit a crude world of stability, of 'things', etc. [...] There is no 'will': there are treaty drafts of will that are constantly increasing or losing power" (NL, KGW VIII/2, 11[73]). Humans are animals that communicate linguistically and symbolically, but from the physiological view of will-to-power, language and knowledge are already 'translations' (from the verb *übertragen*) or modifications of a process in which collisions of force-quanta are represented and signified as nerve-stimuli, then as image and then as concept. "First images ... Then words, applied to images. Finally concepts, possible only when there are words – the collecting together of many images in something nonvisible but audible (word)" (NL, KGW VII/2, 25[168]). "I am afraid we are not rid of God because we still have faith in grammar" (TI Reason 5).

The chiasmus structure (the duplicitous but non-mediated poles of mastery and subversion) also apply to cognitive processes which are, according to Nietzsche, largely being 'directed' by non-cognitive events. Even the 'inner world' of subjective perception, as such, should be treated as a phenomenality (NL, KGW VIII/2, 11[113]), effects of the two complicitous tendencies. In such a schema, 'becoming-conscious' would imply the tendency toward mastery (e.g. of unifying 'consciousness' as 'thinking' and 'knowing'), which is a 'fascistic' reactive tendency in Laruellian terms, whereas the opposing tendency is oriented toward actively subverting, complexifying, and breaking up the dominating tendencies of consciousness: "everything that enters consciousness as "unity" is already tremendously complex" (NL, KGW VIII/1, 5[56]); "[e]verything of which we become conscious is arranged, simplified, schematized, interpreted through and through – the actual process of inner 'perception', the causal connection between thoughts, feelings, desires, between subject and object, are absolutely hidden from us – and are perhaps purely imaginary" (NL, KGW VIII/2, 11[113]). Moreover, the granularity of the active, non-cognitive subversive tendency is finer than its cognitive counterpart; the coarser cognitive tendency accomplishes its 'mastering' function by 'making equal' (that is, schematizing, organizing, simplifying, making familiar) dynamic differences of fine detail so that the organs of sense-awareness can accomplish their representational functions. "The entire apparatus of knowledge is an apparatus for abstraction and simplification" (NL, KGW VII/2, 26[61]); only those perceptions that are useful to the organic development of the species are selected to become-conscious; "this means: we have senses for only a selection of perceptions – those with which we have to concern ourselves in order to preserve ourselves." (NL, KGW VIII/1, 2[95])..."We have projected the conditions of our preservation as predicates of being in general." (NL, KGW VIII/2, 9[38]); "The coarser organ sees much apparent equality"; "the spirit wants equality, i.e., to subsume a sense impression into an existing series [...] the will to equality is the will-to-power – the belief that something is thus and thus (the essence of judgment) is the consequence of a will that as much as possible shall be equal" (NL, KGW VIII/1, 2[90]).

Will-to-power is not transcendental (e.g. it does not have its source in innate ideas that exist in the mind prior to experience), nor is it merely sensual/empirical (e.g. it is not derived from the senses and the senses alone). Rather, will-to-power is immanent, im-mediate, proto-material (conceptualized here as conditioning materiality rather than as constituting the substance or content of matter, or *hyle*, that subsequently fills in form, or *morphê*), and I would argue that Laruelle's quadripartite diagram structure – cross-referenced with the Simondonian account of the pre-individual – best accounts for the active and autonomous forces of subversion that are the really dominant and virulent powers and which make Nietzsche's thinking unique in the history of western political thought. Will-to-power is the Dionysian pre-individual or latent tendency that resists and subverts the dominating tendency of the Apollonian principle of individuation, and which – in so doing – continuously asserts itself as active rather than reactive. To assert the primacy of the mastering pole over the subversive pole – that is, to see them as dialectically mediated – would be to fall back into a reactive view of will-to-power: will-to-power as the will-to-knowledge. Rather than think of will-to-power as the dialectical relation of a dominating force over a dominated one (especially since we cannot think of the Apollo-Dionysus relation dialectically since the Dionysian, as the pre-individual, is involved on an ongoing basis in modifying the Apollonian principle of individuation at every moment or blink of the eye, cf. Zarathustra's *Augenblick*), Laruelle thinks of individuation as non-mediated duplicity or affirmation of a primarily active subversive tendency modifying a secondary dominating, formalizing/signifying tendency.

> Let us stretch the political subject to the four corners of the chiasmus. It is precisely the categories of Fascism, of Mastery, of Rebellion that will change the political sense in function of this complex machine: the fascistic pole makes sense of an unlimited, planetary use, of negation, and the production of effects of technical, organizational powers and of mastery. The revolutionary or rebel, [makes sense] of a certain use of affirmation and of the production of effects of active resistance to all dominant powers (Laruelle 1977, pp. 10f.).

> Libidinal determination presupposes a matter that 'individuates' or determines Relations of power, contradictory if you like, no longer passing further by a specific form. This materialist determination of Relations of production is made however, at once, short of and beyond species and genre, of form, essence and quality. What then individuates con-

tradition? The determination of contradiction is made no longer from form (transcendental in Althusser, and rationalist in other Marxists), but from what we will call the Other or Difference, and which Nietzsche provided the compositional formula ... within the affinity or correlation of two characteristics at once syntactical and materialist: activity as intrinsic definition of power or rather of Relations of power; affirmation as intrinsic definition of libidinal material or rather of the relation that constitutes all material determination (Laruelle 1977, p. 33).

Laruelle offers a different dynamics from which to diagram will-to-power's mechanism in the form of a chiasmic, X-structure, rather than a dialectical one; this is a superior model because it accounts for the productions of individuations (will-to-power's 'form-giving' capacity) based on the concurrence of two overlapping but unmediated tendencies which could account for the fact that in Nietzsche's thinking, it is the reactive that comes to dominate in the history of western societies. Will-to-power is an internal pre-individual differential immediation, not an external law subjecting organisms as in Darwin's theory of natural selection, nor a dialectical law driven by negation and negativity; in Laruelle's schema, the will-to-life (the primacy of an a-signifying pole) is not propelled by negation and reactivity, but rather by affirmation and activity. The internal structure of will-to-power is already political insofar as it already always tends toward mastery as well as the opposite tendency, subversion. This is why both tendencies are wholly present in Nietzsche's published and unpublished works, and why the question of 'politics' cannot be merely resolved by placing Nietzsche's statements within the context of the right/left spectrum of political ideologies (e.g. yes Nietzsche is fascistic since he supports domination and authoritarianism; no Nietzsche is really democratic because he advocates for rebellion against authority, etc.). This ascription of Nietzsche as either 'fascistic' or 'democratic' misses the point of the inherent and internal political materialism at the heart of will-to-power. One can and must always detect both the tendency towards mastery (reactivity) as well as the tendency to subvert or rebel against mastery (activity).

Although Laruelle's interpretation of Nietzsche was written before the formal exposition of his concept of 'non-philosophy',[5] it does share with non-philosophy the propensity to refuse the philosophical 'decision' (either/or) structure of western thought, in order to articulate how the decision (between fascistic and subversive tendencies for example) comes to be structured in Nietzsche's thinking. And while Deleuze's account would describe the nature of the human subject as the outside folded in (following the logic of the 'fold'),

---

[5] See for example Laruelle 2011, Laruelle 1999, Mullarkey/Smith 2012, Brassier 2003 and Smith 2010.

that is as an immanently political, social, embedded subject, Laruelle uses the concept of the 'chiasmus' to describe the destiny of the human subject, as distended and pulled apart between two non-mediating poles or tendencies of Mastery and Subversion. In qualifying Nietzsche's thinking as political materialism, Laruelle's aim is not to deny that there are both fascistic and subversive tendencies in Nietzsche – mastery and resistance to mastery – but to affirm the double-dealing (duplicity) of both tendencies which produces a text, a thinking that cuts and cleaves rather than conserves and preserves. The political agents are the impulses that vie with one another to produce political effects in human subjects. Force is not fundamentally mediated by representation – it is the active discharging of energetic materials – but from the point of view that sees the will-to-knowledge and mastery as primary (e.g. a dialectical point of view which is necessarily a 'reactive' perspective) force is always subject to representation, be it physico-mathematical or logico-grammatical, and the question of politics becomes secondary to and mediated by the discursive. Thus the thrust of Laruelle's interpretation of Nietzsche's political materialism is to resist and subordinate the ontologico-existential reading in favour of one that is politico-physiological or materialist and which sees in Nietzsche's thinking a mechanism that 'cuts' and cleaves a subject (Laruelle 1977, p. 17). Nietzsche alters the concept of political; the 'political' is no longer an instance, object, or practice (e.g. class struggle grounded on the struggle of economic classes) but rather the internal working of objects: "the task is to produce political agents (partial organs of power) with fascistic or critical functions (properties, uses or effects)" (Laruelle 1977, p. 23). Will-to-power should be conceived as the production, reproduction and destruction of political agents. For Laruelle, it is the internal political definition of will-to-power as pulsions or forces that are the real political agents of/in Nietzsche's thought.

Bibliography

Biswas Mellamphy, Nandita/Mellamphy, Dan (2005): "In 'Descent' Proposal: Pathologies of Embodiment in Nietzsche, Kafka, and Foucault". In: *Foucault Studies* 1(3), pp. 27–48.

Biswas Mellamphy, Nandita/Mellamphy, Dan (2009): "What's the 'Matter' with Materialism? – Walter Benjamin and the New Janitocracy". In: *Janus Head: Journal of Interdisciplinary Studies in Literature, Continental Philosophy, Phenomenological Psychology, and the Arts* 11(1), pp. 162–182.

Brassier, Ray (2003): "Axiomatic Heresy: The Non-Philosophy of François Laruelle". In: *Radical Philosophy* 121, pp. 24–35.

Butler, Judith (1989): "Foucault and the Paradox of Bodily Inscriptions". In: *The Journal of Philosophy* 86(11), pp. 601–607.

Butler, Judith (1997): "Subjection, Resistance, Resignification". In: Judith Butler: *The Psychic Life of Power: Theories in Subjection*. Stanford: Stanford University Press, pp. 83–105.

Cox, Christoph (2006): "Nietzsche, Dionysus and the Ontology of Music". In: Keith Ansell-Pearson (ed.): *A Companion to Nietzsche*. London: Blackwell, pp. 495–513.

Deleuze, Gilles (1983): *Nietzsche and Philosophy*. Hugh Tomlinson (trans.). London: Athlone Press.

Deleuze, Gilles (2004): "Nomadic Thought". In: Gilles Deleuze: *Desert Islands and Other Texts 1953–1974*. David Lapoujade (ed.), Mike Taormina (trans.). New York: Semiotext(e), pp. 252–260.

Haase, Marie-Luise/Salaquarda, Jörg (1980): "Konkordanz. Der Wille zur Macht: Nachlass in chronologischer Ordnung der Kritischen Gesamtausgabe". In: Nietzsche-Studien 9, pp. 446–490.

Laruelle, François (1977): *Nietzsche contre Heidegger: Thèses pour une politique nietzschéenne*. Paris: Éditions Payot.

Laruelle, François (1999): "Summary of Non-Philosophy". In: *Pli: The Warwick Journal of Philosophy* 8, pp. 138–148.

Laruelle, François (2011): *Philosophies of Difference: A Critical Introduction to Non-Philosophy*. Rocco Gangle (trans.). London: Continuum.

Mellamphy, Dan (1998): "Fragmentality: Thinking the Fragment". In: *Dalhousie French Studies* 45, pp. 82–98.

Mullarkey, John/Smith, Anthony Paul (eds.) (2012): *Laruelle and Non-Philosophy*. Edinburgh: Edinburgh University Press.

Nietzsche, Friedrich (1956): *The Birth of Tragedy and the Genealogy of Morals*. Francis Golffing (trans.). New York: Doubleday.

Nietzsche, Friedrich (1966): *Beyond Good and Evil*. Walter Kaufmann (trans.). New York: Random House.

Nietzsche, Friedrich (1974): *The Gay Science*. Walter Kaufmann (trans.). New York: Random House.

Nietzsche, Friedrich (1990): *Twilight of the Idols*. R.J. Hollingdale (trans.). New York: Penguin Books.

Nietzsche, Friedrich (1997): *Untimely Meditations*. Daniel Breazeale (ed.), R. J. Hollingdale (trans.). Cambridge: Cambridge University Press.

Simondon, Gilbert (1992): "The Genesis of the Individual". In: Mark Cohen/Sanford Kwinter (eds.): *Incorporations: Zone 6*. New York: Zone Books, pp. 296–319.

Simondon, Gilbert (2005): *L'individuation à la lumière des notions de forme et d'information*. Grenoble, Editions Jérôme Million.

Simondon, Gilbert (2010): "The Essence of Technicity". In: Ninian Mellamphy, Dan Mellamphy and Nandita Biswas Mellamphy (trans.). In: *Deleuze Studies* 5(3), pp. 406–424.

Smith, Anthony Paul (2010): "The Philosopher and the Heretic: Translator's Introduction". In: *Future Christ: A Lesson in Heresy*. Anthony Paul Smith (trans.). London: Continuum, pp. xi-xxv.

II. Democratic, or Liberal, or Egalitarian Politics in Nietzsche

Paul Patton
Nietzsche on Power and Democracy circa 1876–1881

My aim in this chapter is to elaborate and explore a conception of democratic political organization of society that has its roots in Nietzsche's writings during the late 1870s and early 1880s. These include the three sets of aphorisms that make up the complete version of *Human, All Too Human*, which were published separately between 1878 and 1880, along with *Daybreak* published in 1881.[1] There are several reasons for focusing on this relatively restricted period of Nietzsche's work: first, while it is true that he offered a range of opinions towards democracy over the course of his writing career, many of them critical, his remarks during this period include some of his most favourable judgments on democratic political organization.[2] His attitude is nuanced and includes criticism of existing forms of democracy as well as support for many of its ideals. He viewed the democratic politics that was only beginning to take hold in Germany at this time as an irreversible and irresistible transformation in the political organization of society, with both positive and negative consequences. While he is clearly critical of the demagogic character of party politics and of the political judgment of many of those whom the parties seek to win over, this is criticism of the organizations and of the people who make up the nascent European democracies with which he was familiar. It is not criticism of the principles of democratic political association as such. Nietzsche was well aware that democratic society is a work in progress and happily drew a distinction between its present forms and those of a democracy "yet to come" (HH I 293).

Second and more importantly, in his writings of this period Nietzsche offers conjectures about the origins of justice, rights and other foundational elements of liberal democracy that stand in marked contrast to the standard views of liberal political theory. These suggest the possibility of a novel interpretation

---

[1] The first set of maxims, published under the title *Human, All Too Human*, appeared in 1878; the second set appeared as *Assorted Opinions And Maxims* in 1879, while the third set were first published as *The Wanderer And His Shadow* in 1880.
[2] Thomas H. Brobjer acknowledges that Nietzsche was "fairly positively disposed" towards democracy throughout the works of this period (Brobjer 2008, p. 224). Herman Siemens mentions two characteristics of Nietzsche's writings during this period that stand out in contrast to his overall treatment of democracy: "first, his positive evaluation of democracy and second, his engagement with democracy as a political phenomenon" (Siemens 2009, p. 23).

of the sources and future development of democratic political community, grounded in a historical conception of human nature that develops on the basis of the specifically human forms of expression of the will to power. The novelty of Nietzsche's approach lies in the demonstration that democratic political community is an intelligible and achievable outcome for human beings understood not as subjects of right or interest, but as subjects of power. The interest of his approach, for political philosophy, lies in the manner in which it implies a historical perspective and a dynamic that is largely absent from contemporary liberal political thought.

As an exercise in developing a conception of liberal democratic political organization on Nietzschean foundations, this chapter does not claim to offer a comprehensive account of his views on politics in general or on democracy in particular. I agree with Herman Siemens that Nietzsche's attitude towards democracy changed over the different phases of his work and that "he had no blueprint or univocal political position" (Siemens 2008, p. 232). I do not suggest that Nietzsche was first and foremost a political thinker, much less that he was actively engaged in the political issues of his time. Thomas H. Brobjer criticizes much of the commentary on Nietzsche and politics and argues that Nietzsche was primarily an a-political, anti-political or supra-political thinker and that he was generally not concerned with politics (Brobjer 2008, p. 205).[3] I agree with Brobjer, Siemens and others that the political organization of society was for Nietzsche a secondary concern and that his overriding primary concern was with the future development of human nature, human culture or what he often referred to as the "spirit" of humanity.

In a certain sense, Nietzsche was a perfectionist thinker, although one whose focus was not individual but generic perfection.[4] He was concerned with the future attainment of the highest possible form of the human species as a whole. As he suggests in the Preface to *On the Genealogy of Morals*, the ultimate standard against which all forms of morality must be judged is the attainment of "the highest power and splendor of the human type" (GM Preface 6). Indeed, it is because he approaches political organization in the light of this

---

[3] See also Brobjer 1998 where he also claims that "Nietzsche's perspective was always personal, philosophical and cultural, and never, or very rarely, political in any ordinary sense of that word" (Brobjer 1998, p. 313).

[4] Siemens suggests that what is at stake for Nietzsche "is not a few individuals but, in fact, the future of humankind, a concern that has its sources in a positive ethical impulse that fuels Nietzsche's thought from beginning to end: that is, his perfectionist demand that we overcome ourselves as we are, that we do everything to enhance or elevate the human species by extending the range of human possibilities" (Siemens 2009, p. 30; see also Siemens 2008, p. 235).

overriding concern, and on the basis of his conception of the dynamics of the will to power as this is played out in social interaction and human history, that Nietzsche offers an interesting alternative to the a-historical approach of so much contemporary liberal political thought. Together these provide him with a uniquely historical conception of the evolution of human nature and political institutions. Rather than seeing him as an anti- or a-political thinker, we should see him as a supremely historical political thinker in the sense that he considered all forms of political organization of society in the light of this species perfectionism and the human manifestations of the will to power.

Concern with the future and higher state of human nature and human culture does make him, in a sense, a supra-political thinker, but not necessarily one who "regarded political thinking as contradictory to, incompatible with, and counterproductive for philosophical, cultural and existential thinking" (Brobjer 2008, p. 210). Brobjer relies on a simplistic opposition between political and cultural or existential issues that does not take into account the manner in which cultural and existential changes feed back into political judgments and, eventually, into the laws and public policies based on those judgments. The causal connections between culture and politics run in both directions. This feedback is widely recognized in political theory. It is explicitly theorized in Deleuze and Guattari's concept of a "micropolitics" that involves the subterranean movements of desire and affect that react back onto the macropolitical order of different sexes, races or parties (Deleuze/Guattari 1987, pp. 208–231).[5] William Connolly's concept of the "visceral" dimension of intersubjectivity that is prior to the order of public reasons and rational deliberation expresses a similar idea (Connolly 1999). In Nietzsche's case, concern for the cultural development of humankind is by no means incompatible with political thinking. Quite the reverse: he is fully aware that there is an intimate connection between politics and the cultural development of humanity. For example, consider his comment in *Human, All Too Human* on socialist responses to the unequal distribution of wealth and its origins in primitive accumulation by means of injustice and violence: the problem with proposals for a revolutionary redistribution of property and wealth is that there is no moral superiority on the side of the dispossessed. What is needed, he suggests, "is not a forcible

---

5 Deleuze and Guattari acknowledge that politics operates through "binarized interests" and the choices that these imply, but suggest that "Political decision making necessarily descends into a world of microdeterminations, attractions, and desires, which it must sound out or evaluate in a different fashion" (Deleuze/Guattari 1987, p. 221).

redistribution but a gradual transformation of mind: the sense of justice must grow greater in everyone, the instinct for violence weaker" (HH I 452).[6]

In *Human, All Too Human* and in *Daybreak* Nietzsche presents himself as a supporter of the Enlightenment. He aligns himself with the enemies of superstition and religion by referring to "we children of the Enlightenment" (HH I 55). He refers to the Enlightenment that "we must now carry further forward" and dismisses the German reaction against the Enlightenment as mere "sporting of waves in comparison with the truly great flood which bears us along!" (D 197). He contrasts the Catholic Church as the universal institution of the Middle Ages unfavourably with modern institutions, suggesting that the former was designed to meet "artificial needs reposing on fictions which, where they did not yet exist, it was obliged to invent (need of redemption)," whereas modern institutions provide remedies for "real states of distress" and will soon come to serve "the true needs of all men" (HH I 176). In a paragraph of *The Wanderer And His Shadow* entitled "Reason and the tree of humanity," he describes the goal of enlightenment by means of a metaphor in which humanity appears as a tree bearing "many milliards of blossoms that shall all become fruit one beside the other, and the earth itself shall be prepared for the nourishment of this tree" (WS 189). At the end of this passage he describes the task of preparing the earth for the production of this "greatest and most joyful fruitfulness" as "a task for reason on behalf of reason!" (WS 189).

While political philosophy may not have been Nietzsche's primary concern, Brobjer overstates the case for his lack of interest in politics or in engagement with political thought, especially during the period in which he wrote *Human, All Too Human* and *Daybreak*. He draws attention to the fact that, in both of these books, Nietzsche insisted that some of society's "most gifted spirits" ought to be excused from preoccupation with politics and that it would be short-sighted to suppose that politics should consume all the intellectual energy of a society. Brobjer notes that Nietzsche had limited practical experience of democracy and never voted in any election: the first free elections in Prussia took place in 1867, when Nietzsche was too young to meet the twenty five year minimum age qualification. The next general election took place after the unification of Germany in 1871, by which time Nietzsche had already moved to Switzerland and renounced his citizenship (Brobjer 2008, p. 214). However, Brobjer does not mention his remarks in favour of a more radical conception

---

[6] Similarly, in WS 221 Nietzsche draws a contrast between the dangerousness of Enlightenment ideals as expressed in violent revolutionary events and the manner in which these ideals might work through individuals to slowly transform the customs and institutions of nations (See my comments on his preference for evolution over revolution below p. 106).

of universal suffrage that would demand "the unanimity of all citizens" as a precondition for its implementation (WS 276). The non-participation of even a few citizens amounts to an objection to the system of majority rule in its current form. Brobjer also claims that references to the USA are "absent from his discussions and comments" (Brobjer 2008, p. 215) when Nietzsche explicitly argues that the student of economics and politics should direct his or her eyes "to North America – where one can still see and seek out the inaugural and normal motions of the body politic" (WS 287).

More importantly, Brobjer passes over the many passages in which Nietzsche appears as a keen observer of European society and its politics.[7] These include the passages in the section of *Human, All Too Human* entitled "A Glance at the State" that comment on the emerging forms of democratic government, the relation between religion and government, as well as the challenge posed by socialism and the questions that it raises, such as the compatibility of justice with the institution of private property. They include his comments on war and conscript armies, and on the power of the press. They include his many comments throughout this period on political parties and the dangers that these pose for democracy. In their efforts to appeal to the masses, all political parties are "compelled to transform their principles into great al fresco stupidities" (HH I 438). Nietzsche suggests that this dimension of modern democratic politics is something to which citizens must accommodate themselves, just as they would to a natural disaster such as an earthquake that changes the very contours of the ground and affects the value of their property, but he clearly regards this as one of the negative consequences of the democratic politics of his time. Several passages in *Assorted Opinions And Maxims* are critical of the ethos of political parties and the attitudes they encourage in their members (AOM 301, 305, 308, 314). Others are critical of the demagogic character of party politics and the manner in which they corrupt the democratic ideal:

> Now it is parties who vote: and at every vote there must be hundreds of abashed consciences — those of the ill-informed and incapable of judgement, of those who merely repeat what they have heard, are drawn along and borne away. Nothing debases the dignity of every new law so much as this clinging blush of dishonesty to which every party vote constrains. (AOM 318)

---

[7] In response to Dombowsky, who points out that political commentary may be found in every one of Nietzsche's published works (Dombowsky 2002, p. 388), Brobjer admits that his claim that Nietzsche was not primarily a political thinker does not mean that he did not sometimes say interesting things about politics or that his views did not have political consequences (Brobjer 2001, p. 395; see Brobjer 2008, p. 210).

In *The Wanderer And His Shadow*, Nietzsche lists political parties among the enemies of independence of mind and way of life and suggests that democracy should strive to "prevent everything that seems to have for its objective the organization of parties" (WS 293). In *Daybreak*, too, he is critical of aspects of democratic political culture. At one point, he wonders whether, just as earlier principles of political morality provoke laughter, "there will one day be laughter" at the idea that questions of public wellbeing should be addressed in terms designed to "produce a favourable wind for the party's sails" (D 183).

Power

Human, All Too Human begins with a call for a chemistry of the moral, religious and aesthetic sensations and of "all the agitations we experience within ourselves in cultural and social intercourse, and indeed even when we are alone" (HH I 1). Nietzsche ventures the hypothesis that there are no actions that are either completely egoistic or completely disinterested, there are only sublimations "in which the basic element seems almost to have dispersed and reveals itself only under the most painstaking observation" (HH I 1). He does not immediately tell the reader what he takes to be this "basic element" in all human actions, but the answer becomes apparent in the course of his analyses of human sensations and the many "agitations" that are experienced in the course of social interaction. It is power, or more precisely the awareness of one's power that comes through exercising it, whether over others or over oneself.

Later passages address this chemistry of human agency in terms of enjoyment, excitation of the senses, or self-enjoyment. For example, in "The innocent element in wickedness," Nietzsche suggests that the objective of wicked acts is not so much the suffering of others but rather "our own enjoyment, for example the enjoyment of the feeling of revenge or of a powerful excitation of the nerves" (HH I 103). In the next passage entitled "Self-defence," he argues that there is no difference between a wicked act that causes harm to others and an act of self-defence insofar as the act is accompanied by a pleasure or "feeling of one's own power, of one's own strong excitation" (HH I 104). Finally, under the heading "Unaccountability and innocence," he answers the question raised at the outset concerning the basic element in all human actions:

> It is the individual's sole desire for self-enjoyment (together with the fear of losing it) which gratifies itself in every instance, let a man act as he can, that is to say as he must: whether his deeds be those of vanity, revenge, pleasure, utility, malice, cunning, or those of sacrifice, sympathy, knowledge. (HH I 107)

Some commentators take such passages as evidence that in *Human, All Too Human* Nietzsche embraced a form of psychological hedonism: all human actions are ultimately undertaken in order to achieve a pleasurable psychological state.[8] In fact, even though his terminology at this stage is not yet fixed, all of these formulations amount to early versions of what he later refers to as the "feeling of power." This is not a simple psychological state but a feeling bound up with experience of agency on the part of complex, self-conscious human animals.

At this stage, Nietzsche has not presented in explicit form his cosmological theory that "in all events a will to power is operating" (GM II 12). This doctrine appears in published work for the first time in *Thus Spoke Zarathustra* (Z II On Self-Overcoming). It appears in notebooks from as early as 1880, but especially in 1885, where he asserts that "This world is the will to power – and nothing besides!" (NL 1885, KSA 11, 38[12]; see also KSA 11, 36[31] and KSA 8, 6[130][9]). Applied to the organic world, this theory does not claim that all things seek power over their environment, or that they seek self-preservation, but rather that everything seeks to exercise or express its own distinctive capacities. Whether or not that leads to self-preservation or to power over other things will depend not only on the intrinsic capacities of the body concerned, but also on the environment and the capacities of that on which it seeks to exercise its power. As Nietzsche later writes:

> A living thing desires above all to vent its strength – life as such is will to power – self-preservation is only one of the indirect and most frequent consequences of it (BGE 13).

Applied to the human world, this theory takes on a further dimension by virtue of the fact that, to a greater degree than all other living things, human beings are conscious of their actions. They act for particular reasons, in the light of particular ways of understanding the meaning, goals and content of their actions. This implies two things: first, that there is an inescapable interpretative element in all human action; second, that human beings are affected by their own actions. When the action is misdirected or blocked they experience a feeling of impotence or powerlessness; when it succeeds, or is believed to have succeeded, they experience a feeling of power. Nietzsche's mature doctrine of the will to power as it applies to human beings is summed up in a passage from *On The Genealogy of Morals*:

---

8 See, for example, Richardson 1996, p. 19, fn.5.
9 I am grateful to Keith Ansell-Pearson for this last reference.

> Every animal … instinctively strives for an optimum of favourable conditions under which it can express all its strength and achieve its maximal feeling of power (GM III 7).

Even though he only explicitly formulates this principle some years later, it is implicit in many of the analyses of human social interaction undertaken in *Human, All Too Human* and *Daybreak*. For example, his analyses of gratitude and revenge (HH I 44), or of the desire to excite pity in others (HH I 50), all rely on a conception of human beings as subjects endowed with a certain degree of power and striving to achieve or restore the feeling of their own power. So, for example, gratitude is a form of requital for the "intrusion" on an individual's sphere of power by a benefactor. The desire to incite pity in others, on the part of those who suffer, arises because of the affect that accompanies successful incitation. Nietzsche refers here to the feeling of superiority which accompanies the demonstration that, whatever their misfortune, the one arousing pity still has the power to elicit this response from others. This feeling of superiority provides "a sort of pleasure" and it follows that the thirst for pity is "a thirst for self-enjoyment, and that at the expense of one's fellow men" (HH I 50). In a later passage, he refers simply to a "pleasure of gratification in the exercise of power" (HH I 103).

The feeling of power is explicitly invoked in Nietzsche's analyses of a variety of human actions and attitudes in *Daybreak*. For example, the pleasure obtained from practicing or witnessing cruelty to other animals, "one of the oldest festive joys of mankind," can be understand as a form of gratification of the feeling of power (D 18). The phenomenon of blaming others for one's failure can similarly be understood: "for failure brings with it a depression of spirits against which the sole remedy is instinctively applied: a new excitation of the feeling of power" (D 140). The criticism of the preceding generation by a younger generation may be understood in similar terms, since "in criticizing it enjoys the first fruits of the feeling of power" (D 176). He argues that in those moments in history when "grand politics" occupies centre stage and people are ready to stake their lives, their property and their conscience on the success of a particular cause, "the strongest tide which carries them forward is the need for the feeling of power" (D 189). The drive to accumulate wealth that has become such an important feature of modern commercial society may be understood as "that which now gives the highest feeling of power and good conscience" (D 204).

As these examples suggest, the scope of Nietzsche's will to power hypothesis and its far-reaching consequences for our understanding of human nature cannot be underestimated. They are summed up in his suggestion that, because for so much of human history it was believed that natural phenomena were endowed with purpose and the power to frustrate human endeavours, the feeling of impotence has been widely and strongly felt. Moreover,

> Because the feeling of impotence and fear was in a state of almost continuous stimulation so strongly and for so long, the feeling of power has evolved to such a degree of subtlety that in this respect man is now a match for the most delicate gold-balance. It has become his strongest propensity; *the means discovered for creating this feeling almost constitute the history of culture* (D 23, emphasis added).

As Clark and Leiter argue, Nietzsche's analysis of the springs of human action in terms of power and the feeling of power amounts to a form of egoism in the sense that there is a psychological benefit to the individual or group even in apparently unegoistic acts (Clark/Leiter 1997, pp. xx – xxvi). However, this does not mean that such origins do not lead to the positive evaluation of actions that are of genuine benefit to others. The account of the origin of justice is a case in point. The idea of justice in dealing with others originates from circumstances where there is no clearly recognizable superior force on either side and where it makes more sense to recognize and negotiate over the demands of each party. This avoids conflict that would only lead to injury on both sides with no assurance of any decisive outcome. In short: "Justice (fairness) originates between parties of approximately equal power" (HH I 92). In *The Wanderer And His Shadow*, Nietzsche outlines an account along similar lines of the manner in which unselfish dealings with others could have acquired a positive evaluation. Neighbouring chieftains who had long been in conflict with one another come to a peaceful agreement because of the intervention of a third party who threatens to side with whoever is the victim of aggression by the other, thereby convincing both to keep the peace. As a consequence, they enter into peaceful relations of trade and mutual assistance that increase the "prosperity and wellbeing" of all involved (WS 190). On this basis, the virtue of unselfish behaviour became acknowledged. It was not that it had not previously occurred in private or on a small scale, but rather that

> this virtue became truly noticeable only when for the first time it was painted on a wall in large letters legible to the whole community. The moral qualities are recognized as virtues, accorded value and an honoured name, and recommended for acquisition only from the moment when they have visibly determined the fate and fortune of whole societies (WS 190).

Social relations involving fair cooperation and justice, and the value of such relations, can thus be understood to have emerged between individuals and groups seeking to express their own power and to achieve a maximal feeling of power. The same is true of the rights that come to regulate the interaction of individuals and groups within civil or political societies. Already in *Human, All Too Human*, Nietzsche argued that the rights of those conquered or enslaved are a product of the fact that they still possess at least the power to destroy themselves, thereby inflicting a loss on the conqueror or the slave master (HH I 93). In *The Wanderer And His Shadow* he suggests that rights originate in some long forgotten agreement, and also that a right is a kind of power (WS 39, 251). In *Daybreak*, he offers an account of the origin of rights and duties where rights are defined as recognised and guaranteed degrees of power (D 112). This account relies on a conception of the parties involved as subjects of power, where this means not only bodies endowed with certain capacities for action but also bodies capable of experiencing the feeling of power. He qualifies the definition of rights as recognized and guaranteed degrees of power by specifying that the rights of others "constitute a concession on the part of our feeling of power to the feeling of power of those others" (D 112). Human beings are acutely sensible to changes in the relations of power that obtain between themselves and others. That is one of the reasons that rights may come to exist where they did not before, or go out of existence where they had previously existed. Nietzsche argues that my rights "are that part of my power which others have not merely conceded me, but which they wish me to preserve" (D 112). He goes on to canvass reasons why others might wish me to preserve a part of my power to act, offering different reasons according to the nature of the power-relation involved.[10]

Nietzsche's discussion of the origin of rights does not consider the late modern idea of a democratic societies governed by means of laws, where it is assumed not only that all citizens are equal before the law but also that they participate equally in the formation of new law. However, his conception of rights as recognized and guaranteed degrees of power is perfectly applicable to this model: the basic civil and political rights which form the basis of democratic government would amount to the "degrees of power" that all citizens would agree to accord one another. These degrees of power would include those necessary for the conduct of government where this is ultimately a matter of the ways in which citizens collectively exercise coercive power over one another: not only the protection of person and property but freedom of speech and opinion, rights to participation in the political process and so on. As such, these rights provide the framework of a constitutional democracy in which the exercise of the collective power of the citizens is determined by reasoned deliberation. In other words, there must be some form of public justification for the

---

[10] For further discussion of Nietzsche's approach to an immanent historical understanding of the origin of rights, see Patton 2004, pp. 43–61 and Patton 2008.

institutions and policies of government. While he does not consider the giving of reasons in domestic political contexts, Nietzsche does speculate on the future effects of the spread of democracy in Europe. He suggests that this will lead to a European league of nations with reduced powers and revised borders and where decisions will be made by future diplomats, experts in matters of culture, agriculture and communications, who will rely not on armies but on "arguments and questions of utility" (WS 292). If we apply this idea of a nascent European sphere of public reason to the domestic sphere, we arrive at a conception of government similar to that found among late modern theorists of constitutional democracy.

The question then arises whether, on the basis of Nietzsche's conception of individuals as subjects of power, it is possible to conceive of a stable, deliberative democratic society? Can a form of political society based on the equality of citizens qua citizens be more than an accommodation between differential spheres of power? In other words, can we reconstruct a pathway from rights understood as mere modus vivendi between individuals and state institutions, of vastly different degrees and kinds of power, to a situation in which the rights guaranteed for all citizens are not the result of a simple modus vivendi but derive from an overlapping consensus about what is fair and just? Can we envisage a society in which the affirmation of the equal rights of all citizens is a means to the feeling of power for individuals and the community as a whole? For the remainder of this chapter I want to argue that elements of a positive answer to this question can be found in *Human, All Too Human* and *Daybreak*.

Democracy

To demonstrate that it is possible to arrive at the idea of an effectively self-governing society on basis of Nietzsche's conception of individual and collective bodies as subjects of power, we should begin by noting his apparent commitment to democratic institutions and ideals. Paragraph 275 of *The Wanderer And His Shadow*, "The age of cyclopean building," reiterates his view that the democratization of Europe is both irresistible and valuable. It is irresistible because any opposition to it now has to employ "precisely the means which the democratic idea first placed in everyone's hands," namely it has to appeal to the judgment and will of those affected by it (WS 275). It is valuable because of the "cyclopean" institution building that is undertaken by democratic society and that serves to separate European modernity from the Middle Ages. This includes a range of "prophylactic measures" by means of which the foundations of a future, higher form of society are laid "so that the future can safely build upon them" (WS 275). In particular, he suggests that by these measures

> We make it henceforth impossible for the fruitful fields of culture again to be destroyed overnight by wild and senseless torrents! We erect stone dams and protective walls against barbarians, against pestilence, against physical and spiritual enslavement! (WS 275)

Nietzsche does not spell out precisely what form these prophylactic measures take in modern society. However, the experience of those episodes in the course of the twentieth century when they have failed or not been present at all gives us some indication of what is involved, namely the fundamental constitutional and legal architecture of liberal democratic society. The stone dams and protective walls include freedom of conscience and opinion, freedom of association, protection of person and property, and an independent judiciary to guarantee that these protections really do amount to a rule of law. These are the legal, and institutional, expressions of the Enlightenment principles of which Nietzsche declares himself a partisan.

At the same time, Nietzsche's historical perspective allows him to see that the emergence of democratic government implies fundamental changes in the nature, and in the perception, of government. His most elaborate consideration of the consequences of the modern democratic conception of government occurs in a long passage in *Human, All Too Human*, devoted to the relationship between religion and government. Here he argues that "absolute tutelary government" which regards itself as the guardian of the people will always want religion to continue, at least so long as it fully understands the benefits that religion provides. These include calming the populace and helping them to deal with calamities, whether natural or social, but also ensuring civil peace and legitimacy for the state itself:

> the power that lies in unity of popular sentiment, in the fact that everyone holds the same opinions and has the same objectives, is sealed and protected by religion (HH I 472).

By contrast, a very different dynamic takes over once government is no longer considered to stand above and apart from the people, but is regarded merely as an expression of the will of the people. In an earlier passage, Nietzsche noted that historically, the relation of government to the governed was seen as a relation between "two distinct spheres of power" that resembled a range of other hierarchical relations in society: between teachers and pupils, masters and servants, fathers and families and so on (HH I 450). The "more logical" conception of government as "nothing but an organ of the people" implies change in the nature of these other relations as well (HH I 450). Henceforth, too, "the attitude towards religion adopted by the government can only be the same as that adopted towards it by the people" (HH I 472). Once the people come to hold a range of diverse and conflicting attitudes toward religion, as well as a plurality of conflicting religious beliefs, the state will have no option but to treat religion as a private matter. The secularization of the state will in turn unleash a dynamic of increased religious diversity on the one hand, and increasing hostility towards religion on the part of the state and its irreligious supporters on the other. Religious groups will then turn against the state and become hostile towards it. This will further increase conflict between the forces of religion and secularism and, over time, undermine the "attitude of veneration and piety" toward the state that has hitherto prevailed (HH I 472).

Over time, this will undermine the authority of the state and thereby its effectiveness as an institution of government. It will become the site of constant political struggle between contending parties, incapable of embarking on undertakings that require long-term investment or commitment. Nietzsche's diagnosis can only seem extraordinarily prescient to twenty first century readers all too conscious of the effects of an adversarial political culture dominated by electoral and media cycles, short term political calculation and policy gridlock. From the perspective of an age which has seen the proliferation of private enterprises taking over the educational, protective, punitive and even military functions of the state, it is particularly striking that he foresees the decline and eventual death of the state as its essential functions are taken over by private companies:

> Even the most resistant remainder of what was formerly the work of government (for example its activities designed to protect the private person from the private person) will in the long run be taken care of by private contractors. Disregard for and the decline and death of the state, the liberation of the private person (I take care not to say: of the individual), is the consequence of the democratic conception of the state; it is in this that its mission lies. (HH I 472)

Commentators on this passage have a tendency to stop at this point and to suppose that Nietzsche simply welcomes the death of the state. Reading this passage alongside his better known characterizations such as the suggestion that "State is the name for the coldest of all cold monsters" (Z I Idols) leads Lester Hunt to the view that he is an anti-political thinker (Hunt 1985, pp. 454, 458ff.). Leiter takes this passage to indicate that Nietzsche believes humanity to be set on a path towards "a kind of anarchy" (Leiter 2009, p. 2). Siemens suggests that "the argument of this text is that the concept of popular sovereignty has the effect of destroying the religious aura of the state so that 'modern democracy is the historical form of the decay of the state'" (Siemens 2009,

p. 25). In fact, Nietzsche's comments about the decline and death of the state are not his final words on the subject. He presents the state in a longer-term historical perspective as merely one among many "organizing powers" that have held sway for periods in the history of humanity in various parts of the world. Others include the racial clan, the family and the Greek *polis*.[11] How many such organizing powers has humankind not see die out? Far from adopting an anti-political view, his long term historical perspective enables him to envisage a future in which some other form of "organizing power" will emerge that better serves the "prudence and self-interest" of people (HH I 472).

While he appears confident that the prudence and self-interest of people will lead to the invention of new such powers in the future, Nietzsche is reluctant to speculate what form these might take. In this matter, as in all questions of historical change, he considers that "nothing is more desirable than caution and slow evolution" (HH I 450). In keeping with the horticultural metaphors that he uses to describe his version of the Enlightenment, he takes a strong stand in favour of slow, piecemeal social change and against sudden, revolutionary upheaval. Against the partisans of revolution he defends "the spirit of the Enlightenment and of progressive evolution" (HH I 463). Nietzsche's preference for evolution is partly based on the historical evidence that revolutions can lead to the resurrection of "savage energies" and atavistic impulses long submerged in civilized societies (HH I 463). While revolutions can be a source of energy and aid in the overthrow of institutions that have outlived their usefulness, he remains convinced of "the merely half-usefulness or the total uselessness and perilousness of all sudden changes" (HH I 464). His preference for moderation and evolutionary change stems in part from his embrace of a fundamental principle according to which "nature never makes a leap": however abruptly things may appear to change "closer observation will nonetheless discover the dovetailing where the new building grows out of the old" (WS 198). In a paragraph of *The Wanderer And His Shadow* entitled "The perilousness of the Enlightenment," he attributes the dangerous character of contemporary Enlightenment ideals to the fact that they have in the nineteenth century become bound up with the idea of revolution, with all its "semi-insanity, histrionicism, bestial cruelty, voluptuousness, and especially sentimentality and self-intoxication" (WS 221). Left to itself, he argues, the spirit of the Enlightenment would have pursued a much quieter path, addressing itself to indi-

---

[11] Nietzsche describes the Greek *polis* as mistrustful of the growth of culture, like every 'organizing political power' (HH I 474).

viduals rather than crowds or parties, "so that it would have transformed the customs and institutions of nations only very slowly" (WS 221).[12]

Nietzsche's historical speculation about the consequences of democratic institutions leave us with two key elements for the problem of accounting for a more thoroughgoing and deliberative democracy on the basis of his conception of the will to power and the dynamics that it unleashed in human history: first, a distinction between the state, understood as a distinct sphere of power over and above the power of those governed, and government, understood as the means by which citizens collectively exercise power over one another; second, a recognition that the evolution of modern society will inevitably entail a plurality of religious, philosophical and moral views. In other words, effective and stable democratic government will no longer be able to expect that everyone will have the same opinions and objectives but will have to take into account a plurality of conceptions of the good.

A fundamental principle of late modern liberal conceptions of democracy is what we might call an egalitarianism of conceptions of the good. This is often expressed in terms of the idea that individual lives should be lived from the inside. People should not be beholden to external authorities to tell them how to live. Individuals have the right to their own conception of the good and the right to live in accordance with their own conception of what makes a life worthwhile or at least endurable. Nietzsche endorses the core of this principle when he writes:

> Moreover, if the purpose of all politics really is to make life endurable for as many as possible, then these as-many-as-possible are entitled to determine what they understand by an endurable life; if they trust to their intellect also to discover the right means of attaining this goal, what good is there in doubting it? They _want_ for once to forge for themselves their own fortunes and misfortunes; and if this feeling of self-determination, pride in the five or six ideas their head contains and brings forth, in fact renders their life so pleasant to them they are happy to bear the calamitous consequences of their narrow-mindedness, there is little to be objected to, always presupposing that this narrow-mindedness does not go so far as to demand that _everything_ should become politics in this sense, that _everyone_ should live and work according to such a standard. (HH I 438)

This qualified endorsement of the egalitarian principle assumes that the antecedent of the conditional in the opening sentence of this passage is false: it is

---

[12] Nietzsche's concern to separate the progress of enlightenment from revolution echoes Kant's view in _Conflict of the Faculties_ that what was important about the French revolution was not the uprising itself but the widespread sympathy for enlightenment ideals that it aroused. See Foucault's discussion of this text in Nietzschean terms in his lecture of 5 January 1983 (Foucault 2010, pp. 15–19).

not the purpose of all politics to make life endurable for as many as possible. Nietzsche's own conception of "grand politics" aims at something altogether different, namely the higher power and splendor of humanity as a whole. In *Daybreak*, he argues that many political and economic affairs "are not worthy of being the enforced concern of society's most gifted spirits" (D 179). He readily acknowledges that the idea and the pursuit of such grand politics are not for everyone, but this does not make him an enemy of democracy. The egalitarian principle that all should be allowed to live in accordance with their own conception of the good, subject to this not causing harm to others, can readily accommodate the requirement that some more enlightened spirits ought to be allowed to abstain from those forms of politics aimed only at making life endurable for as many as possible.

It is the task of the enlightened few to question the prevailing conceptions of the good and to ask whether these serve or hinder the progressive evolution of humankind. Nietzsche was always critical of the idea that the highest good should stop at the desire to create a comfortable life for as many as possible. He attributes this idea to socialists, who "desire to create a comfortable life for as many as possible" (HH I 235). A similar idea is expressed in the twentieth century liberal egalitarian ideal of maximizing the growth of the middle class. For Nietzsche, however, the attainment of this comfortable life for as many as possible would

> destroy the soil out of which great intellect and the powerful individual in general grows ... the state is a prudent institution for the protection of individuals against one another: if it is completed and perfected too far it will in the end enfeeble the individual and, indeed, dissolve him – that is to say, thwart the original purpose of the state in the most thorough way possible (HH I 235).

Nietzsche is therefore opposed to the perfection of the state as a prudential institution, but not to the liberal ideal of a democratic society of autonomous and self-determining individuals. Nothing in his commitment to grand politics prevents him from recognizing the value of the basic democratic right of self-determination for all citizens, including those focused on species perfection.

Democracy to come

In a passage towards the end of *The Wanderer And His Shadow*, Nietzsche defines democracy as that form of political organization that "wants to create and guarantee as much independence as possible: independence of opinion, of mode of life and of employment" (WS 293). This complex ideal of independence goes beyond the basic architecture of negative liberties and protections mentioned above. Independence of opinion and mode of life implies a plurality of conceptions of the good and the ability of individuals not only to choose but also to live in accordance with their chosen mode of life. Independence of employment implies the capacity to freely choose one's mode of employment. In the view of contemporary liberals as diverse as Rawls and Hayek, this implies a free market in labour. This threefold sense of independence is an ideal that calls for the right of individual self-determination mentioned above. As such, it not only serves the interest of those socialists and egalitarians concerned to create a comfortable life for as many as possible, but also serves the interest of those concerned with species perfection, since it provides the conditions under which they can best pursue their intellectual and cultural pursuits. Nietzsche distinguishes this ideal from the currently existing forms of democratic society by specifying that here he is speaking of democracy

> as of something yet to come. That which now calls itself democracy differs from older forms of government solely in that it drives with new horses: the streets are still the same old streets, and the wheels are likewise the same old wheels. — Have things really got less perilous because the wellbeing of the nations now rides in this vehicle? (WS 293)

There are, on Nietzsche's view, "three great enemies of independence in the above-named threefold sense ... the indigent, the rich and parties" (WS 293). One of the points at issue here is the same as that identified in *Human, All Too Human* I 452: it is not simply the relatively early stage of development attained by the democratic political institutions of his day but the relative lack of independence among the mass of citizens. This is hardly surprising when we consider the social circumstances in Europe at this time. There were many who lacked the means to genuine independence of opinion and mode of life, including servants, women and all those who possessed no property. We should not hasten to conclude that Nietzsche would prefer to exclude such dependent persons from full citizenship. On the contrary, his commitment to a conception of a democracy to come that "wants to create and guarantee as much independence as possible" might be taken as justification for providing all with access to sufficient wealth and education to ensure such independence.[13] By the same token, we might argue for limitations to the degree to which those who already possess the means to independence – the genuinely rich but also the rulers of political parties – can use their power to deny independence to

---

[13] Rawls argues that measures of this kind to establish a "property owning democracy" are required by liberal principles of justice (Rawls 2001, pp. 135–140).

others. This might lead, for example, to the public financing of elections and limits to campaign contributions on the part of individuals, corporations and other vested interests. It might lead to restrictions on the degree to which political parties control the votes of their members.

Nietzsche's writings around 1880 show that he is well aware of the ways in which modern democratic society generates the conditions for genuine independence, on the part of individuals. For example, he laments the disappearance of subordination, which becomes increasingly impossible as a consequence of the disappearance of belief in unconditional authority and definitive truth. But he also draws attention to the fact that the same conditions mean that "people subordinate themselves only under conditions, as the result of a mutual compact, thus without prejudice to their own interests" (HH I 441). He also recognizes that modern democratic society would lead to the flourishing of a plurality of conceptions of good. This is one of the implications of the independence of mind that he associates with genuine democracy. Together, these suggest that he could well have supported a conception of democratic government that citizens might endorse on the basis of their own moral or political points of view, as though by mutual compact. We can find an intimation of such a conception of government as an expression of the collective power of citizens in the suggestion in *Daybreak* that it is not unthinkable to imagine a future state of affairs in which a criminal

> calls himself to account and publicly dictates his own punishment, in the proud feeling that he is thus honouring the law which he himself has made, that by punishing himself he is exercising his power, the power of the lawgiver (D 187).

Given the inevitable diversity of moral, religious and philosophical views, such a conception of democratic government would require an overlapping consensus on fundamental principles of justice and constitutional association. It would also require a commitment to public reason as the ultimate locus of decision-making. In addition to conceiving of him or herself as a lawgiver, the citizen of such a democracy to come would also have to recognize his or her differences from others and accept that they do not necessarily share a common conception of the good. This implies that what are compelling reasons for one are not necessarily compelling for others. It obliges citizens to argue for or against particular proposals in terms that they can reasonably expect others to endorse. In so doing, citizens would honour themselves by honouring the independence and feeling of power of others. In a democracy dedicated to creating and guaranteeing as much democracy as possible, citizens might achieve their own feeling of power by respecting the independence of others. In this manner, a conception of citizens as subjects of power, as well as reasonable subjects with a capacity for justice and a conception of the good, allows us to imagine a democracy in which the fundamental political relation of citizens to one another is a means to the feeling of power for all.

Bibliography

Brobjer, Thomas H. (1998): "The Absence of Political Ideals In Nietzsche's Writings: The Case of the Laws of Manu and the Associated Caste Society". In: *Nietzsche-Studien* 27, pp. 300–318.
Brobjer, Thomas H. (2001): "Nietzsche as Political Thinker. A Response to Don Dombrowsky". In: *Nietzsche-Studien* 30, pp. 394–396.
Brobjer, Thomas H. (2008): "Critical Aspects of Nietzsche's Relation to Politics and Democracy". In: Herman W. Siemens/Vasti Roodt (eds.): *Nietzsche, Power and Politics: Rethinking Nietzsche's Legacy for Political Thought*. Berlin, New York: de Gruyter, pp. 205–227.
Clark, Maudemarie/Leiter, Brian (1997): "Introduction". In: Friedrich Nietzsche: *Daybreak*. Cambridge: Cambridge University Press, pp. vii-xxxiv.
Connolly, W. E. (1999): *Why I Am Not A Secularist*. Minneapolis, London: University of Minnesota Press.
Deleuze, Gilles/Guattari, Felix (1987): *A Thousand Plateaus: Capitalism and Schizophrenia*. Brian Massumi (trans.). Minneapolis: University of Minnesota Press.
Dombrowsky, Don (2001): "A Response to Thomas H. Brobjer's 'The Absence of Political Ideals In Nietzsche's Writings'". In: *Nietzsche-Studien* 30, pp. 387–393.
Foucault, Michel (2010): *The Government of Self and Others: Lectures at the Collège de France 1982–1983*. F. Gros (ed.), G. Burchell (trans.). Houndmills, Basingstoke: Palgrave Macmillan.
Hunt, Lester H. (1985): "Politics and Anti-Politics: Nietzsche's View of the State". In: *History of Philosophy Quarterly* 2(4), pp. 453–468.
Leiter, Brian (2009): "Tamsin Shaw, Nietzsche's Political Skepticism (Princeton University Press, 2007)". In: *Notre Dame Philosophical Reviews*. http://ndpr.nd.edu/news/23891-nietzsche-s-political-skepticism/, visited January 30th 2014.
Patton, Paul (2004): "Power and Right in Nietzsche and Foucault". In: *International Studies in Philosophy* 36(3), pp. 43–61.
Patton, Paul (2008): "Nietzsche on Rights, Power and the Feeling of Power". In: Herman W. Siemens/Vasti Roodt (eds.): *Nietzsche, Power and Politics: Rethinking Nietzsche's Legacy for Political Thought*. Berlin, New York: de Gruyter, pp. 471–490.
Rawls, John (2001): *Justice as Fairness: A Restatement*. Cambridge: Harvard University Press.
Siemens, Herman W. (2008): "Yes, No, Maybe So ... Nietzsche's Equivocations on the Relation between Democracy and 'Grosse Politik'". In: Herman W. Siemens/Vasti Roodt (eds.): *Nietzsche, Power and Politics: Rethinking Nietzsche's Legacy for Political Thought*. Berlin, New York: de Gruyter, pp. 231–268.
Siemens, Herman W. (2009): "Nietzsche's Critique of Democracy (1870–1886)". In: *Journal of Nietzsche Studies* 38, pp. 20–37.

Lawrence J. Hatab
Nietzsche's Will to Power and Politics

In this essay I want to explore Nietzsche's concept of will to power (*Wille zur Macht*) and its bearing on political philosophy. First I present an overview of will to power and its centrality in Nietzsche's thought, where power involves a structure of reciprocal tensions rather than destructive force. After disposing of the idea that Nietzsche is an apolitical or anti-political thinker, I argue that Nietzsche's approach to social structures departs from traditional political theories, especially the modern liberal contract theory of government. Then I revisit an argument marking my previous work, namely that Nietzsche's espousal of the agonistic structure of social life offers a robust alternative for political philosophy, especially with regard to legal institutions and democratic politics.[1]

Will to Power

"The world viewed from inside ... would be 'will to power' and nothing else" (BGE 36).[2] The world, for Nietzsche, is never in a fixed condition but always in process of becoming. Moreover, all movements of becoming are related to other movements, and the relational structure is not simply expressive of differences, but primarily resistances and tensional conflicts (NL, KSA 13, 14[93]). Will to power depicts in dynamic terms the idea that any affirmation is also a negation, that any condition or assertion of meaning must overcome some "Other," some obstacle or counterforce. An 1888 note states:

> A quantum of power is characterized by the effect it exercises and by what resists it. [...] it is essentially a will to violation and resisting violation. [...] every atom's effect works out to the whole of existence — if one thinks away this radiation of power-will, the atom itself is thought away. For this reason I name it a quantum of "will to power". [...] (NL, KSA 13, 14[79])

An "atom" is a quantum *of* will to power, so the latter must refer to the radiating "whole." Indeed an atom is not a "thing" but a *dynamic* quantum "in a tensional relation (*Spannungverhältnis*) with all other dynamic quanta." And

---

1 Portions of this essay are drawn from earlier work of mine (Hatab 1995 and Hatab 2008).
2 I have occasionally modified published translations.

we are told in another 1888 note that will to power is not a metaphysical unity manifesting particular forms, because with that "one has struck out the character of will by subtracting from its content, its Wohin, its 'Where to?'" (NL, KSA 13, 14[121]).³

Nietzsche draws out the implications of will to power even further: "will to power can manifest itself only against resistances; therefore it seeks that which resists it" (NL, KSA 12, 9[151]). A similar formation is declared in *Ecce Homo* in reference to a warlike nature: "It needs objects of resistance; hence it looks for what resists" (EH Wise 7). What is crucial here is the following: Since power can *only* involve resistance, then one's power to overcome is essentially related to a counter-power; if resistance were eliminated, if one's counter-power were destroyed or even neutralized by sheer domination, one's power would evaporate, it would no longer *be* power. The will "is never satisfied unless it has limits and resistance" (NL, KSA 13, 11[75]). Power is *overcoming* something, not annihilating it: "there is no annihilation in the sphere of spirit" (NL, KSA 12, 7[53]). Will to power, therefore, cannot be understood in terms of individual states alone, even successful states, because it names a tensional force-field, *within which* individual states shape themselves by seeking to overcome other sites of power. Individual events are understood in terms of *degrees* of overcoming and resistance (NL, KSA 13, 14[79]). An achieved state or goal cannot suffice for explaining will to power, because that would leave out its essential character as a "driving force" (NL, KSA 13, 14[121]).

> The "development" of a thing, a tradition, an organ is certainly not its progressus towards a goal […], instead it is a succession of […] processes of subjugation exacted on the thing, added to this the resistances against these processes expended every time, the attempted transformations for the purpose of defense and reaction, and the results, too, of successful counter-actions. (GM II 12)

Power cannot be construed as "instrumental" for any resultant state, whether it is knowledge, pleasure, purpose, even survival, since such conditions are epiphenomena of power, of a drive to overcome something (GM II 12, 18). Will to power as a drive is not goal-directed but activity-directed; its "aim" is the *perpetuation* of overcoming, not a completed state.⁴ For this reason, Nietzsche

---

3 Another note refers to "the absolute momentariness of the will to power" (NL, KSA 11, 40[55]). And we should note a passage wherein the idea of the will "is a unity only as a word" (BGE 19).

4 On this point see Katsafanas 2011, which presents a very cogent account of drives, which do not "end" with the attainment of a goal. This helps make sense out of Nietzsche's requirement of ongoing resistance, even with the achievement of a particular goal. Katsafanas also cites contemporary research that supports Nietzsche's position: happiness is better realized with *activities* that are built around challenges and the execution of skills.

depicts life as "that which must always overcome itself" (Z II Self-Overcoming). This accounts for Nietzsche's objections to measuring life by "happiness," because the structure of will to power shows that *dissatisfaction* and *displeasure* are intrinsic to movements of overcoming (NL, KSA 13, 11[111]), and so conditions of sheer satisfaction would dry up the energies of life. Pleasure "is only a symptom of the feeling of power achieved, a consciousness of difference" (NL, KSA 13, 14[121]). Indeed, "unpleasure" is a *stimulant* to will to power, the experience of a resistance that is to be overcome, a resistance presupposed by any achieved pleasure. That is why "man seeks resistance, needs something to oppose him" (NL, KSA 13, 14[174]).

According to Nietzsche, any doctrine that would reject will to power as he depicts it would undermine the conditions of its own historical emergence as a contention with conflicting forces. Any scientific, religious, moral, or intellectual development began with elements of dissatisfaction and impulses to overcome something, whether it was ignorance, worldliness, brutality, confusion, or competing cultural models. Even pacifism – understood as an impulse to overcome human violence and an exalted way of life taken as an advance over our brutish nature – can be understood as an instance of will to power. Power, Nietzsche tells us, includes human mastery "over his own savagery" (NL, KSA 13, 11[111]).

A prefiguration of will to power can be found in an early text, *Homer's Contest* (HC, KSA 1, pp. 783–792). Arguing against the idea that culture is something antithetical to brutal forces of nature, Nietzsche spotlights the pervasiveness in ancient Greece of the *agōn*, or contest, which operated in all cultural pursuits (in athletics, the arts, oratory, politics, and philosophy). The *agōn* can be seen as a ritualized expression of a world-view expressed in so much of Greek myth, poetry, and philosophy: the world as an arena for the struggle of opposing (but related) forces. Agonistic relations are depicted in Hesiod's *Theogony*, Homer's *Iliad*, Greek tragedy, and philosophers such as Anaximander and Heraclitus.[5] In *Homer's Contest*, Nietzsche argues that the *agōn* emerged as a *cultivation* of more brutal natural drives in not striving for the annihilation of the Other, but arranging contests that would test skill and performance in a competition. Accordingly, agonistic strife produced excellence, not obliteration, since talent unfolded in a struggle with competitors. As a result, the Greeks did not succumb to a false ideal of sheer harmony and order, and thus they ensured a proliferation of excellence by preventing stagnation, dissimulation, and uniform control. The *agōn*, Nietzsche claims, expressed the

---

5 See my discussion in Hatab 1990, chs. 2–6.

general resistance of the Greeks to "domination by one" (*Alleinherrschaft*) and the danger of unchallenged or unchallengeable power – hence the practice of ostracizing someone too powerful, someone who would ruin the reciprocal structure of agonistic competition.

The Greek *agōn* is a historical source of what Nietzsche later generalized into the dynamic, reciprocal structure of will to power. And it is important to recognize that such a structure undermines the idea that power could or should run unchecked, either in the sense of sheer domination or chaotic indeterminacy. Will to power, especially in the cultural sphere, implies a certain "measure" of contending energies, even though such a measure could not imply an overarching order or a stable principle of balance. Nevertheless there *is* a capacity for measure in agonistic power relations. Nietzsche tells us in an early note (KSA 8, 5[146]) that Greek institutions were healthy in not separating culture from nature in the manner of a good-evil scheme. Yet they overcame sheer natural forces of destruction by selectively ordering them in their practices, cults, and festival days. The Greek "freedom of mind" (*Freisinnigkeit*) was a "measured release" of natural forces, not their negation. Likewise in a published work:

> Perhaps nothing astonishes the observer of the Greek world more than when he discovers that from time to time the Greeks made as it were a festival of all their passions and evil inclinations and even instituted a kind of official order of proceedings in the celebration of what was all-too-human in them. [...] They do not repudiate the natural drive that finds expression in the evil qualities but regulate it and, as soon as they have discovered sufficient prescriptive measures to provide these wild waters with the least harmful means of channeling and outflow, confine them to definite cults and days. This is the root of all the moral free-mindedness of antiquity. One granted to the evil and suspicious, to the animal and backward, [...] a moderate discharge, and did not strive for their total annihilation. (AOM 220)

In line with this Greek precedent, Nietzsche's concept of agonistic will to power should not be construed as a measureless threat to culture but a naturalistic re-description of cultural measures. Will to power allows a kind of *structured* dynamic rather than an amorphous disarray of forces. Each overcoming and resistance shapes a counter-acting *form* of differentiation rather than sheer repulsion. Agonistic measure cannot be stable, uniform, or universal; it emerges only out of and within episodes of conflict. Yet there are "laws and measures immanent in the contest" (*dem kampfe immanenten Gesetzen und Maassen*) (PTAG, KSA 1, p. 826).[6] The reciprocal structure of agonistic relations means

---

[6] Nietzsche even calls the capacity to dwell with negative limits a measure (NL, KSA 11, 25[515] and 35[69]; NL, KSA 12, 2[97] and 9[41]). Conversely, the ascetic ideal's contempt for life is characterized as lacking a kind of measure (GM III 22; TI Morality 2; NL, KSA 11, 26[167]); the

that competing life forces productively delimit each other and thus generate dynamic formations rather than sheer dissipation or indeterminacy.[7]

Nietzsche's celebration of power is often taken to mean a repudiation of moral and political conceptions of justice; and his emphasis on creativity and free spirits seems incompatible with social norms and institutions; and of course his critique of equality seems to undermine democratic politics. Yet Nietzsche's philosophy does not amount to a repudiation of social norms and political institutions. I want to argue that from a Nietzschean standpoint the state is neither a conventional construct (as in modern political theory) nor strictly "natural" (as in ancient thought), because "nature" and "culture" are not incommensurate spheres for Nietzsche; rather, culture arises out of, and modifies, natural forces, as in the case of the Greek institution of the *agōn*. Nietzsche did recognize the political purposes of the *agōn* (HC, KSA 1, p. 789), but he clearly took it to be an aristocratic activity, where the few talented types would compete for cultural and political status. He did not seem to recognize a connection between an agonistic culture and the emergence and practice of Greek democracy. The philosophical development of a questioning spirit and challenges to traditional warrants helped nurture the practices of open debate and public contests of speeches that came to characterize democratic procedures.[8]

Nietzsche and the Political

Before exploring these questions and confronting Nietzsche's attitude toward democracy, it is important to set the stage by considering the matter of institutions, without which political philosophy could not get off the ground. It is foolish to think that modern societies could function without institutions and

---

same is said of Christianity's attack upon nature (HH I 114) and of modern aesthetic sensibilities (HH I 221; BGE 224). Moreover, a higher nature is marked by a gathered measure that is fashioned out of a plurality of competing drives (NL, KSA 11, 26[119] and 27[59]).

[7] For important discussions of this idea, see van Tongeren 2002 and Siemens 2002. See also Acampora 2002. Agonistic measure can be ascertained in the example of athletic games. Particular rules and layouts stem from a more general sense of conditions that must be met for a competitive game: A field of play must carve out scenarios of performance that require skill – in a manner that is neither too easy nor too difficult; and competitors must all be *able* to perform in the game, which rules out actions that disable opponents.

[8] For a discussion of the connections between Greek democracy and contests, see Vernant 1980, pp. 19–44. On the open atmosphere of uncertainty and interrogation see Castoriadis 1991.

the coercive force of law. Fredrick Appel, like many interpreters, construes Nietzsche's "political" thought as advancing more an "aesthetic" activity than institutional governance (Appel 1999, pp. 160ff.). Nietzsche supposedly envisions elites who compete with each other for creative results in isolation from the mass public; indeed the elite simply use the masses as material for their creative work, without regard for the fate or welfare of the general citizenry. Appel maintains that such a political aesthetics is problematic because it is incompatible with the maintenance of stable institutions. And Nietzsche is also presumed to eschew the rule of law in favor of the hubris of self-policing. If this were true, one would be hard pressed to find Nietzsche relevant for any political philosophy, much less a democratic one.

It is a mistake, however, to read Nietzsche in simple terms as being against institutions and the rule of law on behalf of self-creation. Those who take Nietzsche to be an anti-institutional transgressor and creator should take heed of a passage from *Twilight of the Idols* that clearly diagnoses a repudiation of institutions as a form of decadence. Because of our modern faith in a foundational individual freedom, we no longer have the instincts for forming and sustaining the traditions and modes of authority that healthy institutions require.

> The whole of the West no longer possesses the instincts out of which institutions grow, out of which a future grows: perhaps nothing antagonizes its "modern spirit" so much. [...] That which makes an institution an institution is despised, hated, repudiated: one fears the danger of a new slavery the moment the word "authority" is even spoken out loud. (TI Skirmishes 39)

Modern political philosophy, beginning with Hobbes, advances the social contract theory of government, primarily stemming from a baseline notion of free, individual selves in the "state of nature." The collective, coercive character of the state is therefore not "natural" and requires justification. Warrant is found in the "contract" between individuals who agree to limit their freedom with legal constraints that will bring peace and order to the strife intrinsic to the state of nature. In comparison, a Nietzschean emphasis on power and agonistics offers significant advantages for political philosophy, in that we can be freed from the modern project of "justifying" the force of social institutions because of a stipulated freedom from constraint in the state of nature. With Nietzsche's primal conception of power(s), the forces of law need not be seen as alien to the self, but as modulations of a ubiquitous array of forces *within which* human beings can locate relative spheres of freedom. Indeed, for Nietzsche, freedom is a relational term – *not* an individual faculty or possession – that fits the agonistic structure of will to power. Our sense of freedom arises from the delight in overcoming obstacles (BGE 19), and the measure of freedom can only be gauged "according to the resistance that must be overcome" (TI Skirmishes 38). With human competition understood as a *reciprocal* striving and resistance, freedom can be construed as a *social* phenomenon, and so agonistic political practices need not be shunned as a degradation of an idealized political order or the collapse of social virtues.

Justice and Law in the *Genealogy*

Nietzsche's remarks about justice and law in the *Genealogy* have not received a lot of attention. In GM II 10, Nietzsche says that when a community grows in power and confidence, "its penal law becomes more lenient." We can even imagine a society "so conscious of its power, that it could allow itself the noblest luxury available to it--that of letting its malefactors go unpunished." (GM II 10)[9] This would be consistent with the agonistic structure of will to power, in that an overly superior power can and even should alter its disposition toward an underling, especially when resistance is significantly diminished or absent.[10] Justice, Nietzsche tells us, can "sublimate itself" and move from punishment toward *mercy*. The idea that justice and law are not grounded simply in retribution for injury is articulated further in the next section of the *Genealogy*.

In Section 11, Nietzsche challenges attempts to find the origin of justice (*Gerechtigkeit*) in revenge (*Rache*), which he connects with resentment (of the type indicated in slave morality). In such accounts, justice is based in "reactive affects," in feelings of being wronged; yet these accounts themselves are said to be based in resentment, owing to their animosity toward "active affects" such as the lust for mastery, which Nietzsche takes to have more value than reactive feelings. We are told that justice does not arise from reactive sentiments because such feelings are "the last territory to be conquered by the spirit of justice." Echoing section 10, Nietzsche then talks about a heightened development of justice, where a just man remains just toward someone who harms him--a "positive attitude" to be distinguished from indifference,

---

[9] In many respects, Nietzsche associates power with a fulfilling sense of achievement and actualization rather than the force of violence. In fact, an impulse to hurt people is a sign of lacking power and frustration over this lack (GS 13), or dissatisfaction over blocked development (GS 290).

[10] Here we can note familiar objections to a dominant position overdoing its mastery, as in running up the score in sports.

a "clear objectivity both penetrating and merciful" that does not diminish even in the face of injury or scorn. Nietzsche calls this attitude "a piece of perfection, the highest form of mastery to be had on earth," which is more likely to emerge in active types: "The active, aggressive, over-reaching man is still a hundred paces nearer to justice than the man who reacts." The active type has "a <u>clearer</u> eye, a better conscience on his side," as opposed to the "false and prejudiced assessment" and the "bad conscience" of reactive sentiments (GM II 11).

Nietzsche maintains that a historical consideration of justice shows that it did not originate in reactive feelings against injury, but rather "with the active, the strong, the spontaneous, and the aggressive." Justice emerged as a battle waged by active forces "<u>against</u> reactive feelings," by types who "expended part of their strength in trying to put a stop to the spread of reactive pathos, to keep it in check and within bounds, and to force a compromise." Wherever justice is "practiced and maintained," the *stronger* power aims to end "the senseless ravages" of resentment among inferior individuals or groups. It seems that one of the main elements in Sections 10 and 11 is that a strong person is not motivated by resentment and revenge, and that Nietzsche is here augmenting his genealogy of values (GM I 10–12) by claiming that just as in the sphere of morality, the *political* value of justice emerged first not from the interests of weak types but from the active power of strong types. Impulses toward revenge among the people prompted a response from the ruling order, in terms of multifaceted experiments with justice that aimed to remove the *target* of resentment from "the hands of revenge" (GM II 11). These experiments included substituting for revenge "a struggle against the enemies of peace and order," creating compensations for injury, and "elevating certain equivalences of harms into a norm," a reciprocal order that resentment would now have to accept as the rectification of offenses.

Then Nietzsche announces a culmination of this process, its most "decisive" development, which occurred when the ruling authorities were strong enough to counter "the stronger power of hostile and sympathetic feelings" by instituting a legal system (*Gesetz*). Nietzsche's point seems to be that political justice has a genealogical history comparable to his treatment of morality. The establishment of law is not grounded in some metaphysical warrant of "right" (whether divine, natural, or human) because it arises as a *modification* of prior conditions of social power for the purpose of addressing the *problem* of vengeful dispositions (which thus are not the *origin* of justice). With a legal system, Nietzsche says, the ruling authorities create an "imperative declaration" of what counts as just and unjust in *their* eyes. Laws, especially in written form, provide a more formal reference for justice and injustice than the more immediate settings of harmful behavior and effects. Nietzsche claims that in a legal system--when human offences are now "crimes," or violations of the law set up by the ruling authority--what is "offensive" about injury can be modulated beyond the injured parties themselves toward the broader sphere of the legal order. Now the vengeful feelings of subordinate, reactive types can be "distracted" (*abgelenkt*) from the immediate damage done to them. Nietzsche judges that such distraction is able to counter the force of revenge by shifting the estimation of injuries away from the narrow perspective of the injured party toward an "evermore impersonal assessment of the action." It should be noted that the impersonal force of law here is very much in keeping with modern legal conceptions, but Nietzsche situates this idea in more natural forces of power relations, rather than in any grander rubric of "natural law" or universal principles of justice. We could say that for Nietzsche the law aims for an impersonal *effect*, but it is not based in any exalted formula of "impersonal reason."

Nietzsche continues (GM II 11) that "justice" and "injustice" only arise when a legal system is in place rather than in any pre-legal settings of human injury. Moreover, he says that any concept of justice *as such* is meaningless, because natural life "functions essentially in an injurious, violent, exploitative, and destructive manner." From the standpoint of natural forces, legal conceptions of justice are "exceptional conditions," in being exceptions to brute nature. Yet given Nietzsche's analysis, this would not "falsify" legal conditions, any more than other valuable cultural forms that emerge from and modify natural forces. Indeed, Nietzsche goes on to describe the law in ways that resonate with his treatment of the agonistic structure of Greek culture in *Homer's Contest*. Legal conditions are "partial restrictions" of natural forces of power, yet not on this account something "other" or even "lesser" than natural power (GM II 11). Legal provisions are called "particular means" serving life-powers, and Nietzsche adds: "as a means toward creating greater units of power." In other words, legal culture *adds* dimensions of power that nature alone does not exhibit. He concludes by counter-posing this agonistic conception of *legal culture in the midst of nature* against the conception of law as "sovereign and general"--as something secured in its own rational sphere apart from natural life, and especially as a means "against conflict in general" and toward egalitarian equanimity, which Nietzsche calls something "hostile to life" and "a secret path toward nothingness." For Nietzsche, the law is not a force that strictly speaking secures an end to power and conflict, because it serves and participates *in* an ongoing "conflict of power-complexes." In other words, justice, for Nietzsche, is not a displacement of power but the cultivated orchestration of power(s).

Democratic Politics

It seems that Nietzsche's analysis of justice and law insists on their aristocratic origins. It also seems evident that his own political vision sustains an elitist character, and that he would deem democratic politics to be a consequence of slave morality. But in my work I have tried to identify elements of democratic politics that might disrupt Nietzsche's account, particularly by considering agonistic features in democratic political practice. How can we begin to apply the notion of agonistics to politics in general and democracy in particular? First of all, contestation and competition can be seen as fundamental to self-development, but also as socially structured, rather than based in individual drives alone. Agonistics therefore helps us articulate the social and political ramifications of Nietzsche's concept of will to power. We have seen that will to power is essentially related to resistances. For Nietzsche, every advance in life is an overcoming of some obstacle or counterforce, so that conflict is a mutual co-constitution of contending forces. Opposition generates development. This is why the modern conception of autonomous selfhood is displaced in Nietzsche's philosophy. The human self is not formed in some internal sphere and then secondarily exposed to external relations and conflicts. The self is formed in and through what it opposes and what opposes it; in other words, the self is *constituted* by agonistic relations. Therefore, any annulment of one's Other would be an annulment of one's self in this sense. Competition can be understood as a *shared* activity for the sake of fostering high achievement and self-development, and therefore as an intrinsically social activity.[11]

In light of the difference between a cultural *agōn* and natural destruction, it is necessary to distinguish between agonistic conflict and sheer violence. A radical agonistics rules out violence, because violence is actually an impulse to *eliminate* conflict by annihilating or incapacitating an opponent, bringing the *agōn* to an end. In a notebook passage (NL, KSA 12, 10[117]), Nietzsche says that he fights the Christian ideal "not with the aim of destroying it but only of putting an end to its tyranny and clearing the way for new ideals," and that for these ideals, "the continuance of the Christian ideal is one of the most desirable things there are." Such new ideals must have "strong opponents, if they are to become strong." In TI Morality 3 Nietzsche discusses the "spiritualization of hostility [*Feindschaft*]," wherein one must affirm both the presence and the power of one's opponents as implicated in one's own posture. And in this passage Nietzsche specifically applies such a notion to the political realm:

---

11 It is significant that the etymology of the word "compete" is "to seek together."

"almost every party understands how it is in the interest of its own self-preservation that the opposition should not lose all strength." The structure of competition requires the sustained maintenance of opposing sides, rather than a zero-sum game of individual ambitions. The implication here is that the category of the social need not be restricted to something like peace or harmony. Agonistic relations need not connote a deterioration of a social disposition, and they can thereby be extended to political affairs.

How can democracy in general terms be understood as an agonistic activity? Allow me to quote from my previous work.

> Political judgments are not preordained or dictated; outcomes depend upon a contest of speeches where one view *wins* and other views *lose* in a tabulation of votes; since the results are binding and backed by the coercive power of the government, democratic elections and procedures establish temporary control and subordination — which, however, can always be altered or reversed because of the succession of periodic political contests. [...] Democratic elections allow for, and depend upon, peaceful exchanges and transitions of power. [...] [L]anguage is the weapon in democratic contests. The binding results, however, produce tangible effects of gain and loss that make political exchanges more than just talk or a game ... . The urgency of such political contests is that losers must yield to, and live under, the policies of the winner; we notice, therefore, specific configurations of power, of *domination and submission* in democratic politics. (Hatab 1995, p.63)[12]

The agonistics of democracy shows itself at every level of political practice, from local to national formats, from elections to legislation and jurisprudence. In all cases the contestation of different perspectives seems to be a necessary (if not sufficient) condition for democratic procedures. Even though political exchanges locate and can create degrees of agreement by means of persuasive discourse, nevertheless sheer unanimity would not only seem to be a rarity, but in fact it would suggest the end or irrelevance of democratic practices. The open invitation to all perspectives and the employment of vote tabulations to provide contingent settlement of contested issues seems to presuppose an ineradicable economy of differences and the absence of a globally decisive truth.[13] Accordingly, all the seemingly fractious features of democratic practice – from

---

[12] Here must be mentioned a psychological disposition that is often missed in describing democracy (especially when it is recommended for cultures lacking democratic traditions) but that is essential to the spirit of democratic citizenship: the willingness to *lose* a political contest and not resort to rebellion.

[13] In Greek, voting was associated with the word *diopherō*, to differ or go against; *diaphoros/on* meant distinctive, making a difference, disagreement. Naturally the presumption against a decisive truth, which underwrites the call for open competition, can be linked to Nietzsche's critique of objective truth in favor of perspectivism. See Hatab 1995, ch. 6.

local debates to election campaigns to legislative disputations to judicial arguments – are in fact simply the orchestrated rituals of political life, without which democracy would evaporate. The affirmation of conflict does not entail permitting a kind of political donnybrook; there are better and worse, fair and unfair ways of conducting a political contest – actually dictated by the very structure of competition, in that the different sides must be *capable* of winning, which is why rigging an election is not really an election. The point is simply that democracy should not recoil from the disorder and friction of political dispute; something like sheer harmony or unanimity would spell the end of politics or perhaps amount to nothing more than the silhouette of coercion, suppression, or erasure. Still, it is important not to overdo the model of competition, because there is a notable difference between democratic engagements and more strictly competitive formats, like games, where opponents simply play to win and defeat the other side. In democracy, we do not engage in political speech only to win, but also to persuade, which carries the implicit possibility of changing sides, so to speak. In this way democratic debate goes beyond sheer competition to include the self-formation of citizens.

Legal Agonistics

There are many parallels between the political agonistics of democracy and a democratic legal system, at least in the Anglo-American common law tradition. That tradition is often called an adversarial system, to distinguish it from the so-called inquisitorial system that operates in France and Germany, for example. An adversarial model pits two procedurally equal parties against each other in open court, each competing to persuade a jury of the guilt or innocence of a defendant. Most of the procedural rules and the presumptions about the posture of lawyers are built around the notion that each party in a trial is entitled to have its best possible case presented in court and to vigorously challenge the other side's case; the judge in most respects serves as an impartial, procedural referee; the contest is then decided by the deliberations of a jury. An inquisitorial system is different to the extent that a judge is given much more deliberative and evidentiary power. Proceedings are not restricted to the aggressive advocacy of competing parties; the court is responsible for presenting the arguments and is not confined to the parties' presentations; a judge does most of the questioning of witnesses and can guide the course of a case in ways that are impermissible in an adversarial system.[14] One attraction

---

14 For an overview of the differences between the two systems see Luban 1998, ch. 5.

of the inquisitorial system is that it is simpler, less restricted by procedural rules, and much relieved of the various lawyerly tactics, probings, and challenges that often frustrate observers of the adversarial system, and that may acquit a seemingly guilty defendant on a technicality or because of evidentiary exclusions.[15]

Despite its difficulties, the agonistics of an adversary system can at least be better understood in the context of our discussion of democracy.[16] An inquisitorial system puts much more trust in the performance, integrity, and impartiality of judges and the judicial system. An adversarial system in many ways is animated by suspicions about the competence and possible motives of the government and judicial officials. Adversarial procedures, then, are intended to give competing parties every appropriate means of challenging or subverting possibly unfair, deceptive, fallacious, or discriminatory practices. Cognitive and ethical suspicion are operating here, and this is often forgotten in complaints about legal machinations that clog proceedings or block the government's case against an apparently guilty party. We should at least remember that procedural rules and the so-called presumption of innocence are meant to *contest* the government, to protect citizens from abuses of power – and not, as is often supposed, to express sympathy for the interests of criminals. Accordingly, we should be *willing* to trade the acquittal of guilty persons for protections against the presumably more heinous outcome of convicting innocent persons. Acquitting a guilty person may be morally repugnant, but it upholds the legal *system*, because each case also concerns *any* case that can come before the system. Since the power of government is contested in the system, acquitting a guilty person simply means that the government has failed to prove its case, that the defendant is *legally* not guilty, rather than proven innocent. At a systematic level, the government should affirm such defeats, because the presumption of innocence and the legal tactics afforded the defense constitute the government's own self-imposed *test* of its strength. We might spotlight the dangers of foregoing a more adversarial system by considering the case of Japan. In the Japanese legal system a suspect can be interro-

---

15 The adversarial system did not exist in England until the late 18th Century, and even then only in a minority of cases. There was a slow evolution, with little legal or philosophical debate about principles or justification. Changes were introduced by Parliament or judges in the face of particular cases' perceived injustices or unfairness. So the system emerged as immanent, contextual, and pragmatic modifications that gradually became common practice. See Langbein 2003.
16 Note that in Greek democracy trials were called *agones* and litigants *agonistai*. *Agōn* also meant "assembly" and "gathering place" (related to *agora*).

gated without a lawyer for up to 23 days. The confession rate of suspects is 92%. Of those suspects brought to trial, the conviction rate is 99.9%[17] We could admire such a system only if the actual rate of guilt and innocence roughly matches these percentages. Yet even a God's-eye view of true guilt and innocence would have to be surprised at the success rate in the Japanese system.

In this way, an adversarial legal system mirrors the separation of powers that marks the American form of government: Legal and political structures are organized around the contestation of power sites, rather than the termination of conflict, and this can accord with Nietzsche's formulation that a legal order is "a means in the conflict between power-complexes," rather than a means of preventing conflict (GM II 11). James Madison (in *Federalist* 51) argued that the division and separation of powers in government provides an internal structure that prevents tyranny by simply *multiplying* the number of potentially tyrannical units and permitting them to check each other by mutual ambition and distrust. This touches on a main reason why I think Nietzsche's philosophy is important for democracy: An agonistic framework is not a "new" model for democratic political thought but a genealogical critique of traditional political *theories*. In its inception and practice, democracy has *always been* agonistic, and political philosophy has tended to suppress or resist this agonistic structure because its radically tensional character disturbs certain principles presumed to be the bedrock foundation of democracy.

The Question of Equality

Needless to say, appropriating Nietzsche for democratic politics faces significant difficulties. Appel, in *Nietzsche Contra Democracy*, has offered a vigorous criticism of attempts to employ Nietzsche for democratic politics, particularly with respect to agonistics. Appel maintains that Nietzsche's thought is radically aristocratic throughout and it cannot be selectively employed for democratic purposes (Appel 1999, pp. 5f.). He also assumes that there is an egalitarian consensus in contemporary political philosophy: that all human beings are of equal moral worth, and they equally bear basic rights that need defending and promoting (Appel 1999, pp. 7f.) – a defense that Appel's book, however, does not provide. He insists that Nietzsche is anti-democratic to the core, and that we cannot succeed in preserving democratic ideals by selective interpretations or by sanitizing Nietzsche with a reading of his elitism as an apolitical call for

---

17 *Harper's*: July 2007, p. 15.

self-creation. In my own work I do not argue that Nietzsche was an overt or covert democrat, but that in the spirit of his own thought he could have, or should have been, an advocate for democracy, but not in terms of traditional political frameworks. For example, I agree that Nietzsche's thought is indeed anti-egalitarian, but I also argue that egalitarianism may not be a necessary condition for democratic politics, and that many elements of democratic practice and performance are more Nietzschean than he suspected (or we have suspected).

Appel concedes that a political agon can be healthy and prevent the establishment of entrenched, permanent hierarchies (Appel 1999, p.162). But he poses an important question: Might not a radical agon all the way down in political life debunk important democratic "verities" such as universal suffrage, equal respect, and human rights? This is indeed a pressing question; yet Appel simply assumes the truth and necessity of these traditional democratic notions, without much articulation of how agonistics threatens these notions, and without any defense of the viability of these notions in the wake of Nietzschean genealogical criticisms. Such criticisms have been effectively advanced by Foucauldian appropriations of Nietzsche that reveal how modern "reason" cannot help being caught up in what it presumes to overcome – namely regimes of power – and consequently cannot help producing exclusionary effects and constraints that belie the modern rhetoric of emancipation.

Nietzsche's philosophy has helped shape familiar critiques of the "dark side" of the Enlightenment and modernity. We have become alert to ways in which self-definition has historically required a demoted or displaced "Other" for its articulation and social placement (Eze 2001). This might give us bearings for decoding the promotion of equality and its decidedly non-ideal history. Universal egalitarianism has been rare in practice and indeed absent until recent periods. Political equality was not universalized in Greek democracy, of course, given the exclusion of slaves, women, and resident aliens. And the modern conception of the "universal rights of man" was dishonest and myopic owing to a host of exclusions and the subordination of "barbaric" peoples in the name of political progress. It seems that the professed confidence in egalitarian ideals was originally based on in-group allegiance (e.g., white male property owners). *Actual* universal equality was absent and even resisted when proposed. Why? Not simply because of an interest in protecting power and privilege; a "positive" sense of equality may not have been conceivable apart from differentiating a "we" from a "they" ("We are all equal" translates as "We are equally not *them*"). Now we might be less surprised by certain racist tendencies in such "enlightened" thinkers as Hume and Kant, among others. Indeed it has been argued that the very idea of "race" was a construction of Modern philosophy, and that the emerging science of "anthropology" was racially tinged in coming to terms with non-European peoples (Eze 2001, chs. 1–3). A Nietzschean analysis can help unmask concealed forms of power in political ideals that presume universality and emancipation but that have not owned up to their exclusionary effects. In fact, the very idea of universalism underwrites the *demotion* of other cultures that do not share or measure up to "rational" principles – otherwise other cultures would simply be *different* rather than falling short of what "any rational being" would or should believe.

An Enlightenment narrative can also give cover to more overt, practical forms of supremacism. Here a few remarks about the social contract theory are pertinent. The state of nature story in modern political thought emerged in a historical setting that can show it in a different light. The story pictures the formation of political society as an act of will on the part of rational individuals to quit the state of nature, as opposed to the ancient idea that the state emerges out of a "natural" social condition. The "artificial" construction of the state accorded with and bolstered the ideal of individual autonomy; it could also help make sense out of the apparent contingency of political forms in the face of encountering new lands in the Age of Discovery. Political "naturalism" could be haunted by contingency when familiar formats were not evident in Asia, Africa, and America. The state as a willed artifice would not suffer from the same difficulty. Yet another consequence of the contractarian alternative was its complicity with colonialism. The artificial willful construction of the political order could underwrite the willful *imposition* of European models upon the supposed pre-political, "natural" condition of native peoples, especially when their forms of life were deemed "backward," not to mention exploitable.

A glance at Locke can be illuminating here. In his *Second Treatise* (Locke 1980, pp.18–28), Locke framed the social contract in terms of property rights. Each individual is rightfully his own "property," his own self-possession. When, through artifice, individuals mix their labor with nature, they are entitled to the resulting product as their own property. Locke connects this idea with the divine command to subdue and cultivate the earth, and modern forms of production seem to be the highest expression of following this command. Locke at times mentions American Indians (the "merciless savages" mentioned in the *Declaration of Independence*) and their primitive production in the midst of vast stretches of uncultivated land. He says that even the smallest parcel of cultivated land in England is superior in value to the largest area of untapped land in America. Revealingly, Locke calls this uncultivated land "waste." Who could fail to notice here the hints of colonialist rhetoric? The "state of nature" in discovered lands not only lacks proper political conditions that can be imposed, it also lacks legally protected property that can *by right* be claimed by productive settlers – because nature is *wasted* by the natives (besides, as Eddie Izzard puts it, the natives had no flags). One advantage of a Nietzschean genealogy is its capacity to put a critical spotlight on such philosophical moments in the contract theory that otherwise might be only dimly seen, if at all.

I am suggesting that traditional egalitarianism was structurally "alteric" in simultaneously *bringing*-down an aristocratic elite and *keeping*-down existing "others" (women, the poor, savages). The Nietzschean take on this is that the force of such an alteric structure was the fuel for actual egalitarian movements emerging in history (despite their professed metaphysical warrants). And if traditional egalitarianism was fueled by power relations, then equality-talk can be unmasked and shown the dangers of exclusionary effects inimical to its professed rhetoric. Accordingly, it could follow that an agonistic deconstruction of equality is more *inclusive* politically, by foregoing any typological criteria for citizenship and simply inviting all competitors to the contest.

Meritocratic Democracy

A question remains: Can a Nietzschean agonistics be viably democratic? Any democratic appropriation of Nietzsche's philosophy of openness and difference must confront his elitism and affirmation of cultural excellence. Excellence is a form of difference that implies gradations and judgments concerning superior and inferior, better and worse performances. Many have embraced a Nietzschean openness to difference on behalf of a generalized liberation of diverse life styles and modes of self-creation. Such a generalized emancipation, however, would repulse Nietzsche. He was interested in fostering special individuals and high achievements. I wonder whether certain postmodern celebrations of difference conceal a kind of egalitarianism in their avoidance or suppression of Nietzsche's clear comfort with social stratification. And it is important, in my view, to sustain a sense of excellence that is vital for both democratic politics and cultural production. Excellence and democracy are compatible as long as excellence is understood in a contextual and performative sense, rather than a substantive sense of permanent, pervasive, or essential superiority.

I have argued for a meritocratic sense of proportional justice modeled on Aristotle's conception of justice in the *Politics* 1280a10–15 (Hatab 1995, pp. 111–119). What is usually missed in Aristotle's formulation is that sometimes it is just to treat people unequally, if they are unequal in a certain attribute relevant to a certain context. For example: it is just to deny children the right to vote since they do not have the maturity to engage in political practice; it is just for teachers to treat students unequally when they assign different grades to their work. Similarly, we can grant praise, status, even privilege to certain performances in social and political life as long as they exhibit appropriate levels of distinction that fit the circumstances. We can still be "democratic" in opening opportunity for all to prove themselves, without assuming fixed or protected locations of excellence. Yet we can be "aristocratic" in apportioning appropriate judgments of superiority and inferiority, depending on the context, and thus we can avoid what Nietzsche took to be the most insidious feature of egalitarianism, resentment in the face of excellence. We can also borrow from Nietzsche's denial of a substantive self on behalf of a pluralized sphere of actions (BGE 19–21) in order to keep the contextual apportionment of excellence open both between and within selves, so as not to slip into any essentialistic aristocratic confidences about superior selves per se.

What is helpful to democratic political philosophy in appropriating a Nietzschean comfort with stratification is that we are no longer bedeviled by puzzles surrounding so-called "democratic elitism." Whenever democratic practice has exhibited unequal distributions of power, authority, function, or influence, it has seemed to be incompatible with democratic ideals because equality has usually been the baseline principle defining democratic life. But as long as opportunities are open in a democratic society, a meritocratic, contextual apportionment of different roles and performances need not be undemocratic. Such phenomena as representative government, executive and judicial powers, opinion leaders, and expertise can be understood as appropriate arrangements in political practice. One way to ascertain this is to realize that the only way to guarantee purely egalitarian practices would be to have all political decisions produced by a direct tally of all citizens, or to have political offices distributed by lot. Any reservations about such prospects will open space for a non-oxymoronic conception of democratic elitism.

A Nietzschean promotion of agonistics and non-foundational openness can go a long way toward articulating and defending democratic practices without the problems attaching to traditional principles of equality. My earlier suggestion that traditional equality was alterically structured can account for the fact that contemporary egalitarianism generally operates with non-substantive conceptions of equal treatment or procedural equality. The reason for this may be that the greater inclusiveness of contemporary politics inevitably chipped away at substantive conceptions so that equality would no longer have much descriptive force or would be harder and harder to identify. The now vague and questionable character of equality may be due to the *loss* of its alteric structure owing to genuine inclusiveness. The source of the alteric character of equality can be described as follows: Evident differences among humans and no evidence of substantive sameness in the natural sphere meant (absent any transcendent warrant) that the only possible version of equality was a differentiated "we" who are equally not "them." With no alteric "Other" in inclusive politics, the equal "we" loses its specific, positive contours. An *agonistic* model of political practice need not track any positive quality of sameness and can simply be construed as non-exclusionary, in the sense that no citizens capable of thinking about their political fate can be excluded from the contest to decide that fate.

Along these lines, I offer some final reflections on power and politics. We can distinguish between *power-for* and *power-over*, the former suggesting individual freedom for self-development, the latter suggesting domination or control of other selves. Advocates of democracy obviously stress power-for, not power-over, and they would likely read Nietzsche's will to power as power-over and thus incompatible with democratic politics. This is why some who try to find room for Nietzsche's thinking in liberal politics want to take his promotion of self-creation as the primary meaning of will to power, even to the point of reading Nietzsche's rhetoric of domination as a mask for self-creation; in other words, that power for Nietzsche is not power-over but power-for.[18]

There is much to be said for locating in will to power forms of power-for and self-creation. First of all, *Macht* can be associated with capability and potency. And certainly self-development is an important theme in Nietzsche's writings (see, for instance, GS 290). As noted earlier, Nietzsche traces human abuse not to a flagrant expression of power but to a *lack* of power and frustration over this lack (GS 13), and to self-dissatisfaction (GS 290). Nevertheless, the neutralizing of Nietzsche's references to political power and domination is dubious. Will to power certainly includes social force, although we must remember the ongoing reciprocal structure of such forces (which is distinct from raw destructive powers in nature). Moreover, I do not think that power-for can be separated from power-over in Nietzsche's thought. With his agonistic model of selfhood and his rejection of atomistic individuality, it follows that self-development never leaves the world untouched; some "Other" will always be affected. Any form of self-assertion will produce some kind of diminishment or differentiation in the social field of play, a certain "pathos of distance" (TI Skirmishes 37). Finally, power-over need not refer only to crude control and domination; it can include both informal and institutional forms of *authority*, which is another connotation of the word *Macht*. Usually authority is a form of warranted, even granted, power, in milieus such as governance and educa-

---

[18] See, for example, Warren 1988, pp. 157–58 and ch. 7. This approach would accord with common interpretations of Nietzsche as an anti-political, or at least apolitical, thinker (which I think is mistaken).

tion. I think that Nietzsche's account of power (which he never took to be exclusively a matter of overt force) helps us understand the complex permutations of social relations and roles, which cannot be properly understood by way of binary opposites such as individual freedom and political coercion. The *limits* of freedom and force mark the ongoing debates in political philosophy, and the negotiated orchestration of these reciprocal limits marks the perennial deliberations of democratic politics.

Bibliography

Acampora, Christa Davis (2002): "Of Dangerous Games and Dastardly Deeds: A Typology of Nietzsche's Contests". In: *International Studies in Philosophy* 34(3), pp. 135–151.

Appel, Frederick (1999): *Nietzsche Contra Democracy*. Ithaca, NY: Cornell University Press.

Castoriadis, Cornelius (1991): "The Greek *Polis* and the Creation of Democracy". In: David Ames Curtis (ed.): *Philosophy, Politics, Autonomy: Essays in Political Philosophy*. New York: Oxford University Press, pp. 81–123.

Eze, Emmanuel Chukwudi (2001): *Achieving Our Humanity: The Idea of the Postracial Future*. New York: Routledge.

Hatab, Lawrence (1990): *Myth and Philosophy: A Contest of Truths*. Chicago: Open Court.

Hatab, Lawrence (1995): *A Nietzschean Defense of Democracy: An Experiment in Postmodern Politics*. Chicago: Open Court.

Hatab, Lawrence (2008): *Nietzsche's* On The Genealogy of Morality: *An Introduction*. New York: Cambridge University Press.

Katsafanas, Paul (2011): "Deriving Ethics From Action: A Nietzschean Version of Constitutivism". In: *Philosophy and Phenomenological Research* 83(3), pp. 620–660.

Langbein, John H. (2003): *The Origins of Adversary Criminal Trial*. New York: Oxford University Press.

Locke, John (1980): *Two Treatises of Government*, ed. C.B. Macpherson. Indianapolis, IN: Hackett Publishing.

Luban, David (1988): *Lawyers and Justice: An Ethical Study*. Princeton, NJ: Princeton University Press.

Nietzsche, Friedrich (1954): "Thus Spoke Zarathustra". In: Friedrich Nietzsche: *The Portable Nietzsche*. Walter Kaufmann (ed./trans.). New York: Viking Press, pp. 103–439.

Nietzsche, Friedrich (1954): "Twilight of the Idols". In: Friedrich Nietzsche: *The Portable Nietzsche*. Walter Kaufmann (ed./trans.). New York: Viking Press, pp. 463–563.

Nietzsche, Friedrich (1966): "Beyond Good and Evil". In: Friedrich Nietzsche: *Basic Writings of Nietzsche*. Walter Kaufmann (ed./trans.). New York: Random House, pp. 181–435.

Nietzsche, Friedrich (1966): "Ecce Homo". In: Friedrich Nietzsche: *Basic Writings of Nietzsche*. Walter Kaufmann (ed./trans.). New York: Random House, pp. 658–791.

Nietzsche, Friedrich (1974): *The Gay Science*. Walter Kaufmann (trans.). New York: Random House.

Nietzsche, Friedrich (1986*)*: *Human, All Too Human*. R.J. Hollingdale (trans.). New York: Cambridge University Press.

Nietzsche, Friedrich (2007): *On the Genealogy of Morality*. Keith Ansell-Pearson (ed.), Carol Diethe (trans.). Cambridge: Cambridge University Press.

Siemens, H.W. (2002): "Agonal Communities of Taste: Law and Community in Nietzsche's Philosophy of Transvaluation". In: *Journal of Nietzsche Studies* 24, pp. 83–112.
van Tongeren, Paul (2002): "Nietzsche's Greek Measure". In: *Journal of Nietzsche Studies* 24, pp. 5–24.
Vernant, Jean-Pierre (1980): *Myth and Society in Ancient Greece*. Janet Lloyd (trans.). Sussex, UK: Harvester Press.
Warren, Mark (1988): *Nietzsche and Political Thought*. Cambridge, MA: MIT Press.

Barry Stocker
A Comparison of Friedrich Nietzsche and Wilhelm von Humboldt as Products of Classical Liberalism

1 Nietzsche and Classical Liberalism

While there is no explicit political theory in Nietzsche to be correct about, there are many political moments in Nietzsche's texts, and many political aspects of his philosophy. Any political reading must take account of the liaisons between the political aspects of Nietzsche's thought and classical liberal political thought. There are more anti-liberal readings of Nietzsche, but not a real consensus in the anti-liberal readings, which include Caesarist-Bonapartist readings (Dombowsky 2004), radical aristocracy (Detwiler 1990), aristocratic power (Cristi 1998) and post-modern left anti-humanism (Mellamphy 2011, Lemm 2009). The last option overlaps with some post-modern pluralist egalitarian liberal accounts of Nietzsche (Connolly 2002), and so leads us in the direction of a liberal reading of Nietzsche, if we think of liberalism as the political thought of changing and interacting identities.

The part of liberalism that is most widely mentioned in attempts to define that concept is to do with individual rights, property rights and a state which is based on consent is under law. However, the context in which these ideas emerged is of the very broad changes associated with the growth of individualistic and commercial society in the seventeenth, eighteenth and nineteenth centuries. The broad changes include: rebellion against traditional political and church authority; major changes in art, science and philosophy; the consolidation of the state and its legal codes. The effect of these forces interacting with the growth of commercial society and economic individualism, is that individuals think much more of social existence as including change and as taking place in a historically evolving society. More people moving to towns means more people experiencing social change and moving to places where varied interaction with different kinds of people is normal. More commercial life means more trade between different parts of a country and between different countries, so greater individual experience of dealing with different kinds of people, as well as greater individual experience of variety and newness in traded goods. The increasing strength of state institution and national legal codes at the time reinforces that greater knowledge of different parts of the same country, while also reinforcing political change since a more integrated state and legal system creates a national public opinion, and therefore more national politics, in a world where assumptions about the permanence and unity of political and religious institutions are increasingly under challenge. The spread of printing and literary means that more and more people have access to more and more news and ideas, and make up their minds on these topics without the guidance of local lords, priests, and other authority figures. The colonisation of the Americas, Africa and large parts of Asia encourages interest in different parts of the world and the idea that people have different ways of living and thinking which can be usefully compared. The printing press encourages the growth of high literature in the language of the common people, so that a critical imaginative engagement with the cultured world becomes an increasingly widespread experience. Liberalism comes out of a world of these changes in individual experience and relation to society, the ideas about individual rights, property, law and consent are ways of trying to shape and perfect the structure of those experiences. We can see all these issues discussed in Montesquieu, Hume, Smith, Kant, Alexis de Tocqueville, as well as Humboldt and many others. In the twentieth century Max Weber (1978), Friedrich Hayek (1960), and Michel Foucault (2003) have engaged with these historical aspects of liberalism. At present Deirdre McCoskey (2006), Daron Acemoglu and James Robinson (2012), amongst many others, are exploring liberalism as something that thrives now, and in the past, in relation to the kind of social and historical context discussed above.

Both Humboldt and Nietzsche were products the early, or classical, version of liberalism concerned as it was with the evolutionary, changeable and interactive nature of individuals, which was becoming more apparent in the development of civil and commercial society from the seventeenth century onwards. Cristi's very anti-democratic reading of Nietzsche places him somewhere in the same sphere as the conservative and authoritarian liberals he writes about from a very critical perspective (Cristi 1998). In a less critical examination of liberalism, Villa's work places Nietzsche in the same range of political argument as the last great classical liberal, John Stuart Mill (Villa 2001). Lester Hunt (1993) has argued in a positive way for a libertarian reading of Nietzsche, and that certainly leads us back to the classical liberal type of political philosophy which libertarianism tries to revive.

Classical liberalism can be defined as the liberal tradition in its development from a beginning in the late seventeenth century, signified by John Locke, ending in the mid nineteenth century in the work of John Stuart Mill, who provided important liberal arguments, but was also ambiguous between liberalism and socialism. At about the same time Gustave de Molinari, Benjamin Tucker and others took the anti-statist elements of liberalism to an anarchist conclusion. The Mill leanings towards socialism anticipated a major shift of liberal thinking in the English speaking world towards compromise with socialism expressed as new liberalism, constructive liberalism, or progressivism, and a weakening of liberalism in other parts of the world. The more anti-statist individualist free market aspects of liberalism continued to have notable adherents like Herbert Spencer and Carl Menger, but did not really express itself so much as an influential political current and intellectual option in political thought until the work of the Austrian Liberal school, inaugurated by Menger, became more influential through its influence on post-war German economics. That is through the *Ordoliberalismus* of the Freiburg School, as described by Michel Foucault under the name of Neoliberalism (Foucault 2010). That influence became more internationalised through Friedrich Hayek (a major object of criticism for Cristi), along with Joseph Schumpeter and Ludwig von Mises. It then converged with the influence of various innovative forms of Neoclassical economics at the University of Chicago, along with Virginia Public Choice theory and so on, in a great revival of limited government ideas in economics. That process had a more populist aspect, most famously in the bombastic novels of Ayn Rand, who was a reader of Nietzsche. Internationally there are other expressions of the revival of classical liberalism and new discussion of libertarianism, as in the French historiographical and political theory rediscovery of its liberal heritage, a sharp upturn internationally in scholarly work on Adam Smith and the Scottish Enlightenment, increasing attention within Normative theory to Libertarianism as an option in discussions of justice, and various other areas of growth. That is the background for the Lester Hunt reading of Nietzsche. It is also the background for Taylor's account of culture, state and education in early Nietzsche (Taylor 1997), which brings in Wilhelm von Humboldt as a point of reference for the role of culture in Nietzsche, with regard to Enlightenment and Romantic ideas of culture and education, but not his political theory. It is the political theory of Humboldt in comparison with Nietzsche that is the main concern here, but that cultural aspect is inseparable from the political thought of Humboldt and of its relevance to Nietzsche.

One factor that has concealed the ways that Nietzsche draws on classical liberalism is the influence of the belief that Karl Marx almost single handedly invented a 'materialist' view of history and society, in which broad economic, social and political factors are given more weight than great men or dominant ideas of the time. However, even Marx and Friedrich Engels conceded that much of this 'materialist' work drew on earlier thought, and it would be hard to appreciate their efforts properly without locating its origins in that preceding work. That is the work of classical political economy, Enlightenment history of civil society, and slightly later on a rich vein of historical and social French liberalism, particularly in Alexis de Tocqueville and Hyppolite Taine. If we avoid the temptation to believe that 'materialist' views of history, society and politics began with Marx, we can have a much better understanding of how Nietzsche's own anti-idealism connects with classical liberal thought. We should also avoid the temptation to believe that classical liberalism is about the isolated, self-contained, and complete individual, because while there is an element of that, as there is in Nietzsche, there is a deep engagement with the contingency of individuality defined by historical and social change, and the complications of living through and in communities. Wilhelm von Humboldt provides a good 'romantic' understanding of those aspects of liberal 'individualism'.

> The true end of man, or that which is prescribed by the eternal and immutable dictates of reason, and not suggested by vague and transient desires, is the highest and most harmonious development of his powers to a complete and consistent whole. Freedom is the first and indispensable condition which the possibility of such a development presupposes [...]. (Humboldt 1993, p. 10)

There are many possible entry points for understanding Nietzsche's relationship with classical liberalism, but we can start with Tocqueville and Taine for the reasons mentioned above. For Tocqueville, that is particularly regarding his wish to preserve aristocracy of some kind (Tocqueville 1988, vol. I, part II, ch. 8) and the dangers of a culture of mediocrity in democracy (Tocqueville 1988, vol. II, part III). We can extend that to John Stuart Mill, even if Nietzsche mainly takes him as an object of derision (D 51, 132; BGE 253). Tocqueville did influence Mill personally, and through *Democracy in America* (Tocqueville 1988, vol. I, part II, ch. 7), as in the discussion of 'tyranny of the majority' in On Liberty (Mill 1991, p. 8). There are also leanings towards a cognitive aristocracy in chapters VI to VIII of *Considerations on Representative Government* (in Mill 1991). If we consider liberals that Nietzsche singled out for derision, we should also include Herbert Spencer (BGE 253; GM I 3, GM II 12; EH Destiny 4; TI Skirmishes 37), an original social Darwinian, though not with the eugenic and racial overtones the phrase has acquired through racist social Darwinians. Spencer's appeal to Darwinism brings him into conflict with Nietzsche (GM II 12), in part, because Nietzsche regarded Darwin as too inclined towards a passive reactive theory of evolutionary change in living species. It should be remembered in this context, that what is now called Darwinism is really Neo-Darwinism (Lennox 2010), a view developed after Darwin's death, which combines evolutionary adaptation with genetic hereditariness and genetic mutation. The idea that human history, human institutions and human types, should be understood on a natural basis, including competition between individuals, is common to Darwin, Spencer and Nietzsche, despite Nietzsche's scornful attacks.

Another point of comparison introduced above is with the historian and social thinker Taine with whom Nietzsche corresponded. There is some debate about classifying Taine politically, but he is certainly appreciated by many of classical liberal inclination. For example, some of his works can be found at the *Online Library of Liberty*, a comprehensive collection of online versions of classical liberal, and related, thought. It is the social and historical way of thinking in Taine, which particularly attracts the attention of Nietzsche, in any case, rather than political arguments.

Nietzsche's friends included Jacob Burckhardt, the German historian who was a colleague at the University of Basel, and who is occasionally referred to favourably in Nietzsche's books. Burckhardt's most relevant books in this context are *The Civilisation of the Renaissance in Italy* (1944) and *History of Greek Culture* (most readily obtainable in English as Burckhardt 2008). Again Burckhardt is not so easy to classify, there is a case to be made for defining him as conservative rather than liberal. Nevertheless, his emphasis on the individual, and on the human cost of establishing antique institutions, gives his thought a critical liberal edge, as well as a conservative traditionalist element.

2 Nietzsche and Humboldt

The last one to add to the list of classical and nineteenth century liberals who can fruitfully be compared with Nietzsche, and the one who will be compared in some detail here is Wilhelm von Humboldt, particularly with regard to *The Limits of State Action* (*Ideen zu einem Versuch, die Grenzen der Wirksamkeit des Staates zu Besitemmen*; Humboldt 1993), a text which had a major influence on Mill's *On Liberty*, as can be seen from Mill's own direct references in the Introduction, along with Chapters III and V. The J.W. Burrow edition of Humboldt referred to here contains a table of parallel topics in *On Liberty* and *The Limits of State Action* (Humboldt 1993, pp. 148–151). Humboldt's career in some way distances him from Nietzsche. His links with the German War of Liberation, and administrative reforms of Prussia at that time, is removed from Nietzsche's criticism of statism, or of nationalism, and of German nationalism in particular, along with his praise for Napoleon. *The Limits of State Action* is in itself in some respects at odds with Humboldt's own political career though. In the book, Humboldt denies any role to the state other than that of providing law and order, and the defence of national frontiers. This is in harmony with

Nietzsche's condemnation of the state in "On the New Idols" in *Thus Spoke Zarathustra* (Z I Idols), *Human, All Too Human* (HH I 8), and elsewhere.

> State is the name of the coldest of all cold monsters. Coldly it lies too; and this lie crawls out of its mouth. 'I, the state, am the people.' That is a lie! It was creators who created peoples and hung a faith and a love over them: thus they served life. It is annihilators who set traps for the many and call them 'state': they hang a sword and a hundred appetites over them. Where there is still a people, it does not understand the state and hates it as the evil eye and the sin against customs and rights. (Z I Idols)

Humboldt praises the role of war in keeping alive the spirit of human individuality, though he recognises that war is not entirely beneficial (Humboldt 1993, pp. 41ff.):

> [...] war seems to be one of the most salutary phenomena for the culture of human nature; and it is not without regret that I see it disappearing more and more from the scene. It is the fearful extremity through which all that active courage – all that endurance and fortitude – are steeled and tested, which afterwards achieve such varied results in the ordinary conduct of life, and alone give it that strength and diversity, without which facility is weakness, and unity is inanity. (Humboldt 1993, p. 41)

The points on which Humboldt and Nietzsche particularly bear comparison are on: criticism of the state, scepticism about democracy, an interest in ancient virtues, the goal of many sided but unified self-development, the value of custom and law based on custom. As mentioned above, Humboldt's public career was not entirely in line with *The Limits of State Action*, and his public career was in itself very influential. For example, in his classic of cultural and social theory, *Culture and Anarchy* (Humboldt 1932), Matthew Arnold refers to Humboldt's example in the use of the state to promote education, and therefore prepare citizens for liberty (Arnold 1932, pp. 126f.). This refers to the single, but very important, year that Humboldt spent as Prussian Minister of Education in the crisis and reform period stimulated by military defeat at the hands of Napoleon. Humboldt reformed school education to provide free and compulsory primary and secondary education, and founded the first university in Berlin, now known as the Humboldt University. In *The Limits of State Action*, written in 1792, but not published in full until after Humboldt's death, all forms of national education are criticised as imposing conformity, stifling human creativity, and overextending the role of the state (Humboldt 1993, ch. VI). Since Nietzsche did not have a political or high administrative career of any kind, these kind of contradictions are not an issue, but we can compare them with the tensions in Nietzsche's writing.

Some aspects of Humboldt's thought that he has in common with Nietzsche, are often taken to be at odds with liberalism. That is the respect for war and the lack of concern for equality of economic outcomes between individuals. A lot of commentary on Tocqueville exhibits similar tendencies, according to which Tocqueville was not 'really' a liberal because of aristocratic and antiegalitarian impulses (Wolin 2003). This mode of commentary, however, is assuming that liberalism is defined by John Rawls, or maybe by Mill as represented in Nietzsche's jibes. We can think of Mill as Nietzsche describes him in Dawn 132, as purely concerned with sympathy and the utility of the greatest number. As Nietzsche also suggests here, there is also a more unsettling relation with the French Revolution and the principles of socialism. Beyond this, we should note that in *On Liberty* and *Considerations on Representative Government*, Mill favoured colonial rule for 'backward' peoples, cognitive elitism apparent in the defence of liberty of speech for the purposes of truth, and the inclination towards extra voting rights for the more educated. Mill also admired antique republics and virtues, as we see for example in *Considerations on Representative Government*, Chapter III. He was strongly affected by the favourable picture of Athens in George Grote's *History of Greece* (2001), which he reviewed twice (Mill 1846, 1853). His admiration for Athenian democracy is compatible with elitist tendencies, because of the slave basis of Ancient Athenian society, which Mill thought was justified in ancient times, and his perfectionist view of democracy in which an elite, at least for a while, dominates in an attempt to raise the level of the mass of the population.

The early history of liberalism is just as much one of suspicion of mass democracy as a welcome, and as we have seen that goes on up to Mill who marks the end of the history of classical liberalism. It is only in the early 19th century that the idea takes root that all adults should have full political rights. Locke's *Essay on Civil Government* might appear to endorse the political rights of all, but in practice Locke went along with the prevailing idea that only men of substantial property could have full political rights, and Locke believed that slavery was a justified outcome of war. Even for the most radical of the time, the idea that those 'dependent' on others as servants or employees should have political rights was unusual. We can see this explicitly up to the late 18th and early 19th centuries in Benjamin Constant and Immanuel Kant. The dominant liberal political figure in Europe of the 1830s and 40s, François Guizot, was strongly associated with the rule of the top 100 000 during the Orléanist monarchy in France. The emphasis begins to change with the American and French Revolutions of 1776 and 1789, though the abolition of the property qualification extended from 1812 to 1860 in America, a universal male suffrage has only existed continuously in France since 1848, and in conditions of political freedom only since 1870. A mass electorate was not instituted in Britain until 1867, and the principle of universal suffrage was only put into law in 1918.

The British Prime Minister, William Ewart Gladstone, who took over from Guizot as the leading liberal politician in Europe, rejected the title of democrat, regarding the 1867 Reform, expanding voting rights to a large part of the working class, he presided over as a rebalancing between people and aristocracy, though over time he became more and more opposed to the conservative aristocracy, showing the direction of liberal evolution. Questions of race and gender in voting have been left aside here, to concentrate purely on the idea of universal suffrage regardless of property for some substantial section of the population, which was the prelude to equal political rights across ethnicity and gender. If we take those factors into account, we have to go up to the Civil Rights legislation of 1960s America for the completion of the movement towards effective universal suffrage in Britain, France and America, the first three major states to move in the direction of political liberalism. We can also note that there is still an unelected second chamber in Britain and that the American President is elected by an electoral college, not directly by the people, both persistent remnants of the late eighteenth century liberal belief that democracy should be limited by institutionalised forms of aristocracy.

It should also be noted here that the word "liberal" as a political concept dates from Spain of the 1820s, and only became widely used in Britain (and presumably other countries) in that sense from the 1840s. Before then, "liberalism" was referred to as "republicanism", belief in liberty, or belief in a constitution, or maybe a liberal system of political economy as in Adam Smith. What we might now call liberalism was up to, and including, the late eighteenth century revolutions in America and France, very largely looking back to antique republics in Rome and Greece, and sometimes the government of the ancient Jews, and seeing how far these could be applied to the present. Not much direct doubt was expressed about the applicability of the ancient models in the Early Modern period, though some like Hobbes and Spinoza rejected the moralising distinctions between good and bad forms of government. In the eighteenth century, concerns about lack of individual liberty in ancient republics appear as a central theme of political thought.

That eighteenth century concern is discussed in Constant as the liberty of the ancients compared with that of the moderns (in Constant 1988 and Constant 2003, book VI) and by Humboldt, as the nature of positive and negative welfare amongst the ancients and the moderns (Humboldt 1993). One superficial way of understanding this has been as the emergence of modern liberalism, distinguishing itself from antique liberty, itself giving rise to the idea that a clear distinction can be made between liberalism and republicanism in political theory. The issues also overlap with the discussion of positive and negative ethical duties in Kant (1996, p. 166), merging in the more recent discussion of negative and positive liberty (Berlin 1969). This is reductive as we can see when looking at classical liberal texts, like those of Humboldt, in detail. Focusing on the issues that concern Humboldt and Nietzsche, we will look at what Humboldt says about welfare.

The state can promote positive welfare (in its own active intervention) or negative welfare (allowing liberty) for its citizens (Humboldt 1993, chs. III and IV). It is negative welfare that Humboldt endorses, and it is the positive welfare that he regards in a more critical light. Negative welfare is a constant concept in relation to historical variation (Humboldt 1993, ch. III); positive welfare is more variable over history (Humboldt 1993, ch. IV). The key variation is the one between the ancients and the moderns. Positive welfare in the ancient world takes the form of state intervention in the soul, since the state concerns itself with the religion, civic spirit, and morality of individuals, trying to promote homogeneity in all these aspects. Positive welfare in the modern world refers to state action to relieve poverty and to protect industry (Humboldt 1993, p. 17). Humboldt regards modern positive welfare as undermining the independence of individuals, the capacity of individuals to freely co-operate. These are barriers to the achievement of economic, and other benefits through free individual initiative, and co-operation between individuals. Such interventions lessen the sphere of individual action, and the consequent development of individuals. It also results in a state bureaucracy, which has an interest in constant expansion of itself. The result is a shrinking sphere of individual initiative, and the creation of an expanding class of people who are dependent on the state (Humboldt 1993, p. 18), and are guided by the ambition of a state pension on retirement. Such people become similar in personality, reducing the possibilities of individual diversity.

> A spirit of governing predominates in every institution of this kind [promoting positive welfare]; and however wise and salutary such a spirit may be, it inevitably produces national uniformity, and a constrained and unnatural manner of acting. Instead of men grouping themselves into communities in order to discipline and develop their powers, even though, to secure these benefits, they may have to forego a part of their exclusive possessions and enjoyments, they actually sacrifice their powers to their possessions. The very variety arising from the union of numbers of individuals is the highest good which social life can confer, and this variety is undoubtedly lost in proportion to the degree of State interference. Under such a system, we have not so much the individual members of a nation living united in the bonds of a civil compact; but isolated subjects living in relation to the State, or rather to the spirit which prevails in its government — a relation in which the undue preponderance of the State or rather to the spirit which prevails in its government — a relation in which the undue preponderance of the State already tends to fetter the free play of individual energies. (Humboldt 1993, p. 18)

The contrast between a self restraining state and an interventionist state is explained as the lifeless mechanical (Humboldt 1993, p. 30) opposed to the developmental organic (Humboldt 1993, p. 32).

Positive welfare in the modern world, in itself, may be less dangerous than positive welfare in the ancient world, because it does not propose to capture the inner life of individuals (Humboldt 1993, p. 7). However, the ancient world had counter-forces that promoted the development of individual strengths, that we can call antique virtues. That is virtues developed in frequent war with neighbouring states, and in the struggle with nature of farmers trying to produce the means of life. The qualities of bravery in battle, self-sacrifice, endurance over time, and the toleration of pain as necessary to reaching a goal, are strong in antiquity. The struggle with nature, and with other humans, enhances individual strength and the independence of the individual.

These counter-forces are more lacking in the modern world, which is why the positive welfare of the solicitude of the state with regard to economic conditions becomes dangerous. Greater prosperity and security in the modern world means a decline in the struggle for survival at the margins (Humboldt 1993, p. 41), and reduction in war between states lessens the chances, or obligations, for citizens to become soldiers defending a frontier. We can see one reason why Humboldt, in principle, opposes 'national' education (Humboldt 1993, p. 48), which he appears to think means state education, though he sometimes distinguishes between what is national and the sphere of the state (Humboldt 1993, p. 35). For national education, there must be education which is the same everywhere and consequent increased conformity across the nation concerned, as opposed to the variations which private education provides. The contrast between principle and practice with regard to Humboldt's attitude to education is maybe explained by the last chapter of *The Limits of State Action*, where he suggests that he is writing something which we can take as an ideal point of reference, rather than a guide to political action.

The apparent dangers of positive welfare for the moderns leads Humboldt towards a critical attitude towards democracy (Humboldt 1993, p. 36). He defends a monarchist constitution (Humboldt 1993, pp. 39f.), though not in the sense of defending the Prussian monarchy as it existed at that time, and since he refers to the earliest forms of monarchy, he may be allowing for elective monarchy. *The Limits of State Action*, remained unpublished in Humboldt's own lifetime, because though it argues that state sovereignty should inhere in the monarchy, the state should have very few powers compared with those enjoyed by the Hohenzollern dynasty at any time. The reasons for preferring monarchy to democracy appear in an account, towards the end of Chapter III, of the impossibility of obtaining the consent of all citizens, and the injustice of an expanding state forcing the will of the majority only on everyone (Humboldt 1993, p. 36). Such a system is structured to undermine the long term benefits of individual initiative, free co-operation, and free trade. Humboldt's argument is not that we should disregard the interests of the majority, but that democracy is not the best structured polity with regard to the interests of the majority, and that therefore it is a form of polity which undermines polity, a government of laws. There is still a way in which Humboldt thinks of popular sovereignty entering into monarchy. He refers back to the earliest forms of monarchy, when a people felt no loss of liberty in assenting to the most suitable candidate becoming monarch, they would have felt insulted at the very suggestion of a loss of liberty (Humboldt 1993, pp. 39f.). Humboldt, with possibly deliberate distance, romanticises early human history to suggest a form of government resting on universal assent. This is part of Humboldt's variation on contract theory, which limits the original contract to protection of negative welfare (Humboldt 1993, pp. 35f.). The nature of the political contract is something discussed by Humboldt only in passing, and not as a fully developed theory.

In this rather romantic looking account of ancient kingship, Humboldt draws on the Homeric image of kings who rule by virtue of their military prowess and innate capacities, along with the ways that later antique writers looked on barbarians as retaining lost freedoms, as in Tacitus's account of the Germans. Apart from Humboldt's own direct acquaintance with such material, he was a classical scholar and translator himself, there is the likely influence of various Enlightenment writers including Vico, Hume, Smith and Adam Ferguson who in different ways were fascinated by 'barbaric' and 'savage' communities, with reference to a violent kind of lawless freedom in contrast to the law governed freedom of modern commercial and civil societies. Ferguson seems particularly important here, as *An Essay on the History of Civil Society* was widely read in Germany (Ferguson 1995). Ferguson, and the other Enlightenment thinkers mentioned, also provide background and context to Nietzsche's thoughts on history, culture and the state, though in his case it's likely that the influence is refracted by intervening thinkers. However indirect the influence, a reading of *An Essay on the History of Civil Society* in conjunction with Nietzsche is a very revealing exercise. Foucault's discussion in Lecture Nine of *Society Must be Defended* of the savage man, and of *homo economicus* in the eighteenth century, puts forward a good argument for the importance of that subject area for the political and social thought of the time (Foucault 2003).

Humboldt and Nietzsche share with Ferguson an unstable movement between: valuing the liberty of the ancients or of 'savages'/'barbarians', and devaluing the corruption of that simple liberty by the modern state, modern complexity, and modern luxury; valuing the openness and progress of the modern world, freed from the customary shackles of early stages of human society, and devaluing the violent narrow minded poverty stricken and tradition bound nature of ancient/barbaric/savage society. The differences between barbarian, savage and civilised ancient are sometimes eroded by the sense that ancient states were not far removed from the lives of stateless peoples, particularly when compared with modern civilisation.

For Humboldt, even in the modern world the customary life of rural peoples is to be admired.

> How striking, to take an illustration, is the historical picture of the character fostered in a people by the undisturbed cultivation of the soil. The labour they devote to the land, and the harvest with which it repays their industry, bind them with sweet fetters to their fields and firesides. Their participation in beneficent toil, and the common enjoyment of its fruits, entwine each family with bonds of love, from which even the ox, the partner of their work, is not wholly excluded. The seed which must be sown, the fruit which must be gathered annually, occasionally with disappointed hopes, make them patient, trusting and frugal. The fact of their receiving everything immediately from the hand of nature, the ever-deepening consciousness that, although the hand of man must first scatter the seed, it is not from human agency that growth and increase come, the constant dependence on favourable and unfavourable weather, awaken presentiments, sometimes fearful, sometimes joyful, of the existence of higher beings — in the rapid alternations of fear and hope — and dispose them to prayer and thanksgiving. The visible image of the simplest sublimity, the most perfect order, and the gentlest beneficence mould their lives into forms of simple grandeur and tenderness, and dispose their hearts to custom and law. (Humboldt 1993, pp. 22f.)

This might be in tension with his admiration for the variety and constant reinvention of the world of commerce, and of free interaction between individuals. Customary life is admired beyond the reasons Humboldt offers, which are familiar from Montesquieu's comments on ancient democratic republics, though the fact he does implicitly bring that in creates a tension with his critique of democracy. The implicit reasons are the return to the ancient struggle with the environment, and the solidity of a timeless present in which the community never changes, but only reconfirms its structure, habits, customs, and reproduction. There is an implied dissatisfaction with modern societies which also emerges in his desire to retain war, and his fears of positive welfare eroding liberty, because modern societies offer less barriers to weak looking threats to liberty.

3 Politics and Law

In Nietzsche we see frequent admiration and respect for the simplicity and unity of Ancient Greek polities, in a wish to see a repetition of such unity, even in the complexity of modern nations. As part of that, we see considerable respect for societies governed by the law of custom rather than civil law.

> Popular codes of law, for example the Germanic have been crude, superstitious and illogical and in part stupid, but they correspond to quite definite, inherited and indigenous customs and feelings. — Where, however, law is no longer tradition, as is the case with us, it can only be commanded, imposed by constraint; none of us any longer possesses a traditional sense of law, so we have to put up with arbitrary law, which is the expression of the necessity of the fact that there has to be law. The most logical is in the event the most acceptable, because it is the most impartial even admitting that in every case the smallest unit of measurement in the relationship between crime and punishment is fixed arbitrarily. (HH I 459)

> Such a law-book as that of Manu originates as does every good law-book: it summarises the experience, policy and experimental morality of long centuries, it settles accounts, it creates nothing new. The precondition for a codification of this sort is the insight that the means of endowing with authority a truth slowly and expensively acquired are fundamentally different those by which one would demonstrate it. (A 57)

It would not be correct to see this as Nietzsche's final view, and the same could be said for Humboldt's views on customary communities, as idealised agricultural societies (Humboldt 1993, pp. 22f.), or his account of the benefits of the earliest forms of monarchy (Humboldt 1993, pp. 39f.). In Nietzsche we see a discussion of custom as the sacrifice of the individual in *Assorted Opinions and Maxims* 89, for example, which has echoes throughout *On the Genealogy of Morality* I and II. Nietzsche gives a sharper version of the general unease Humboldt has with the law giving modern state, the state that does not claim to be just writing down laws which come from the unwritten codes of ancestors, deities, God, or nature, but keeps making more and more laws. The reason, in Humboldt's terms, is that the demands for government intervention, what he calls positive welfare, continued to intensify, so that government is constantly meeting the demands of sections of the population, and expanding in order to meet demands, thereby creating further expectations (Humboldt 1993, chs. III, VI). There is something recognisable about the history of state welfarism and democracy since Humboldt's own time here, even if we place a less negative value on them than Humboldt does. Democracy has grown, the state has grown bigger, and the field of intervention has grown bigger. Ferguson traces democratic intrusion on individual property rights, and associated liberties, back to the birth of democracy in Athens (Ferguson 1995, pp. 151, 177f.), though he also associates democracy with the Cretans, Spartans and Israelites. For Ferguson, democracy is only workable at all in conditions of the equality of conditions, and must have very negative consequences if applied in other circumstances, which he sees as increasingly the case in Athens. Though this is not entirely in line with Humboldt's contrast between the ancients and the moderns, it does add to the reasons to suppose that Humboldt was affected by the ideas of *History of Civil Society*.

What Humboldt does not say directly, and may not have thought about, is that the increasing complexity of commercial society, and its constant self reinvention itself requires constant legal innovation. The comments of Machiavelli in the Preface to Book One of *The Discourses* (Machiavelli 2003, pp. 97ff.) and then Grotius in the first paragraph of *The Rights of War and Peace* (Grotius 2005, p. 75), on the newness of legal codification, and constructing the history of law, are an implicit recognition of the consequences of the rise of commercial society in the Italian city states and the merchant cities of the low countries in late Medieval and early modern Europe. We can say the same about the early version of legal positivism in Hobbes, though none of these people had an explicit jurisprudence with regard to constant legal innovation. Hume has a view about how state institutions arise from the economic interests of the elite, and the increasing legality of modern civil society. As with Smith, there is a critical view of law and institutions which go beyond natural evolution of society, and they are seen as serving the interests of those who seek advantages from the state. We see a partial transition towards seeing the law as an evolving and increasingly complex instrument of civil society. That is close to Humboldt, though his direct references are to Rousseau and the Physiocrats rather than the Scottish Enlightenment. Nietzsche carries on an unease with newness in law which goes back to the ancients, and this is another aspect of how Nietzsche's thought is conditioned by admiration for the liberties of the ancients. His wish for re-evaluation is combined with this anxiety about eroding custom, which may seem inconsistent, but rests on the thought that law that cannot maintain itself, needs to be overthrown.

There does not seem to be a point at which a legal theorist advocated constant innovation in law, but the legal positivism most closely associated with such a view continues its preformation in Bentham, and is articulated with the name of positivism in the work of John Austin. The right way to explain this is that the emergence of positivism is necessary to understanding how it became possible to see law as constantly increasing and changing, at the will of the political sovereign, even where restrained by constitutionalism. It simply becomes a presupposition of most legal theory, whether referring to natural law, realism, naturalism or positivism, and it is only really noticed when subject to criticism. The point is that legal thought has evolved since then to assume huge detailed and ever expanding legal codes.

Nietzsche's thought about custom and law are not a simple demand to go back from civil law to customary law. His description of antique Germanic codes is not entirely favourable and we should not regard his description of the law of Manu, in India, as highly favourable either. Nietzsche does praise Manu's code, including its most notorious aspect, the caste system, but in terms which should alert the reader. The relish with which Nietzsche describes the condition of the 'untouchable' castes is repellent and that should be seen as a rhetorical strategy, since Nietzsche does have a clear belief that the wish to see others suffer is repellent, even if he does not think virtue begins in concern for others, or in egalitarianism. Nietzsche likes to confront the reader with the evidence of the suffering and extremes of subordination behind human culture, but what he sees as negative comes just as much from the upper class as the lower class, as in his analysis of the priest in *On the Genealogy of Morality* I. The exemplary individual in Nietzsche, unlike the priest, does not need to engage in cruelty and does not need to engage in its moralising justification. From this we can conclude that the exemplary political figure in Nietzsche is concerned with self-growth and greatness, but not with the enjoyment of the suffering of others, or the wish for a vengeful pleasure in seeing any disliked group, or individual, suffering.

4 The Heroic Self

In Nietzsche's references to political figures, many of his exemplary figures are liberal, democratic or republican: Pericles (GM I 11) Mirabeau the Younger (GM I 10), Kaiser Friedrich III, the liberal Hohenzollern Emperor who reigned for a few months in 1889 (EH Z I), Lazare Carnot (D 167), in addition to frequent mentions of Goethe and Voltaire. If we consider the two figures he sometimes highlights as the greatest of the modern age, Goethe was a liberal or an aristocratic elitist kind, while Napoleon was a modern Caesar, both are compared to Pericles by Theodor Mommsen, in his monumental *History of Rome*, published from 1854 to 1856, that is someone who justified autocracy through some form of popular will, which in Napoleon's case meant a claim to continue the principles of the French Revolution and to rest his power on the will of the French nation, rather than obedience to a monarch. In both Napoleon and Goethe, there is a heroic individualism trying to mould the future, along with a wish for continuity with antique and feudal Europe, that connects with the more traditionalist and antique virtue oriented aspects of classical liberalism. Both aspects can be seen in Humboldt. The idea of Europe was important for both, and can be found as a major theme in Nietzsche, particularly in *Beyond Good and Evil*.

The liberal aspects of Nietzsche are distinctly constrained by a strong and consistent streak of aristocratic, and self-contained neo-Stoic disdain for commercial culture in Nietzsche, which is embedded in his criticisms of an ethics of sympathy (D 174), which means that his criticisms of commercial culture are not exactly those of the standard rejections of capitalism. For Nietzsche, the problem with commerce is that it leads us to be concerned with satisfying the needs of the other party to the transaction. Commercial life means providing things that other people want so that we can enter into a financial transaction. In this respect, Nietzsche is reacting to commercial society as understood by Adam Smith, something that is particularly clear if we take *An Inquiry into the Nature and Causes of the Wealth of Nations* and *The Theory of Moral Sentiments* together, though it is unlikely that Nietzsche had studied them. Again the general influence of Hume, Smith and Ferguson on German Enlightenment leaves traces that Nietzsche incorporates very readily. Nietzsche fears a loss of self if it becomes dominated by a fellow feeling or suffering (*Mitleid*), in a life oriented to commerce. Alternative values include the gift giving of the *Zarathustra* Prologue (Z I Prologue), the ground virtue of selfishness in 'On The Gift Giving Virtue' section in *Zarathustra* (Z I Virtue), and the discussion of hospitality in *Daybreak* 174, where he recommends the merits of inviting others to share the comfort of an isolated home, clearly a metaphor for the self.

> In the meantime, the question itself remains unanswered whether one is of more use to another [*dem Anderen*] by immediately leaping to his side and helping him – which help can in any case be only superficial where it does not become a tyrannical seizing and transforming – or by creating something out of oneself that the other can behold with pleasure [*Genuss*]: a beautiful, restful, self-enclosed garden perhaps, with high walls against storms and the dust of the roadway but also a hospitable gate. (D 174)

Selfishness is not supposed to be taken as economic enrichment, but is the cultivation of the self in a new version of antique virtue ethics. The ways Nietzsche thinks about the self, giving, and hospitality are ways of getting away from the expected reciprocity expected in the exchanges of commercial life. It could also be argued that Nietzsche's values provide a grounding for commercial society and civil society, or could do so with some reframing of the kind that is inevitable in any attempt to determine the political uses of a writer. Few have argued that commercial society can do without an ethical basis which goes beyond expectations of reciprocity and self-advancement, important as these may be in commercial society. For the defenders of commercial society, like Hume and Smith, commercial society is the best way of mitigating extreme egotism, through the constraints of law and satisfying the preferences of others. Nietzsche's disdain for commercial society and anxiety that a ruling class has emerged in the bourgeoisie that is not culturally superior to the lower classes, and is seem as no better by members of the lower classes than themselves, is shared with some liberal thinkers. Tocqueville is a good example though we see that anxiety itself constrained by enthusiasm for a world of moral egalitarianism and economic flourishing in the commercial sphere.

As we have seen, there is some tension in Humboldt about how far the virtues of commercial society are to be preferred to heroic virtues of antiquity. This is a common aspect of the classical liberal thinkers who were largely trying to think about how political, social, ethical and cultural communities can exist with shared values and interests, to replace the seemingly dominant shared values and actions of ancient republics. Nietzsche even offers an answer himself of the expansion of the Aristotelian polity through written communication in *The Wanderer and His Shadow* 87, which he shares with Tocqueville to some degree, when the latter suggests in the sixth chapter of the second volume of *Democracy in America* (Tocqueville 1988), that it is newspapers, which create a substitute to antique republican solidarity in modern democracies with free political institutions. That is in tension with *Assorted Opinions and Maxims* 321, and other places where Nietzsche condemns newspaper reading, but tension is a constant factor in Nietzsche. The cultural interaction, and the growth of human culture that Humboldt sees in the liberty of the moderns is an earlier version of that. Those aspects of Humboldt and Tocqueville are at the basis of a great deal of current cultural and social thinking, via Matthew Arnold, Émile Durkheim and others.

We might think there is a tension within Humboldt, and all classical liberal thinking, between the value of the autonomous individual, the value of cooperation between individuals, the design and enforcement of laws and institutions which make both of those possible. Tension is not contradiction, or refutation, it is the source of inquiry and creative solutions, so this is not a knock down refutation of Humboldt or classical liberalism, which is no more full of interesting tensions other broad traditions of political thought. We can understand Nietzsche as someone both conditioned by, and reacting to, classical liberalism, of the kind favoured by Humboldt. He takes the elements of Humboldt which are most dissatisfied with modern commercial life, its tendencies towards homogenisation and averaging out, the loss of heroic self in co-operative, commercial and civil self. He also follows Humboldt, in a way more familiar from an average understanding of classical liberalism, in the fear of the state, and ways in which the growth of democracy tends to foster the growth of the state. The phenomenon Nietzsche refers to in *Twilight of the Idols*, of liberal institutions betraying liberal principles (TI Skirmishes 38). Where Nietzsche most obviously differs is in the stronger tendency to reject commercial society, the stronger and even shocking rhetoric directed at egalitarianism, and the clearer wish for a more isolated kind of individual life without the 'neighbour'. None of that should detract from what Nietzsche shares with a classical liberal commitment to the individual, even heroic individualism, and the cultivation of virtues which both provide a basis for commercial democratic society, and something more than the vulgar utilitarianism and complacent egalitarian conformity, they risk.

Bibliography

Arnold, Matthew (1932): *Culture and Anarchy*. J. Dover Wilson (ed.). Cambridge: Cambridge University Press.
Berlin, Isaiah (1969): "Two Concepts of Liberty". In: Isaiah Berlin: *Four Essays on Liberty*. Oxford: Oxford University Press.
Burckhardt, Jacob (1944): *The Civilization of the Renaissance in Italy*. S.G.C. Middlemore (trans.). London: Allen & Unwin.
Burckhardt, Jacob (2008): *The Greeks and Greek Civilization*. Oswyn Murray (ed.), Sheila Stern (trans.). New York, NY: St Martin's Griffin.
Connolly, William E. (2002): *Identity/Difference: Democratic Negotiations of Political Paradox*. Minneapolis, MN: University of Minnesota Press.
Constant, Benjamin (1988): *Political Writings*. Biancamaria Fontana (trans./ed.). Cambridge: Cambridge University Press.
Constant, Benjamin (2003): *Principles of Politics Applicable to All Governments*. Etienne Hofmann (ed.), Dennis O'Keeffe (trans.). Indianapolis, IN: Liberty Fund.
Cristi, Renato (1998): *Carl Schmitt and Authoritarian Liberalism: Strong State, Free Economy*. Cardiff: University of Wales Press.
Detwiler, Bruce (1990) *Nietzsche and the Politics of Aristocratic Radicalism*. Chicago IL: University of Chicago Press
Dombowsky, Don (2004): *Nietzsche's Machiavellian Politics*. Basingstoke: Palgrave Macmillan.
Ferguson, Adam (1995): *An Essay on the History of Civil Society*. Fania Oz-Salzberger (ed.). Cambridge: Cambridge University Press.
Foucault, Michel (2003): *Society Must be Defended*. Mauro Bertani and Alessandro Fontana (eds.), David Macey (trans.). New York, NY: Picador.
Foucault, Michel (2010): *The Birth of Biopolitics*. Michel Senellart (ed.), Graham Burchell (trans.). New York, NY: Plagrave Macmillan.
Grote, George (2001): *A History of Greece: From the Time of Solon to 403 B.C.* J.M. Mitchell and M.O.B. Caspari (eds.). London: Routledge.
Grotius, Hugo (2005): *The Rights of War and Peace* (3 vols.). Richard Tuck (ed.). Indianapolis, IN: Liberty Fund.
Hayek, Friedrich (1960): *The Constitution of Liberty*. London: Routledge.
Humboldt, Wilhelm von (1993): *The Limits of State Action*. J.W. Burrow (ed.). Indianapolis, IN: Liberty Fund.
Hunt, Lester (1993): *Nietzsche and the Origin of Virtue*. London: Routledge.

Kant, Immanuel (1996): *Practical Philosophy*. Mary J. Gregor (ed./trans.). Cambridge: Cambridge University Press.
Lemm, Vanessa (2009): *Nietzsche's Animal Philosophy: Culture, Politics, and the Animality of the Human Being*. New York, NY: Fordham University Press.
Lennox, James (2010): "Darwinism". In: *Stanford Encyclopedia of Philosophy*. http://plato.stanford.edu/entries/darwinism/, visited on March 6th 2012.
Machiavelli, Niccolò (2003):*The Discourses*. Bernard Crick (ed.), Leslie J. Walker and Brian Richardson (trans.). London: Penguin.
McCloskey, Deirdre N. (2006): *The Bourgeois Virtues: Ethics for an Age of Commerce*. Chicago, IL: University of Chicago Press.
Mellamphy, Nandita Biswas (2011):*The Three Stigmata of Friedrich Nietzsche: Political Physiology in the Age of Nihilism*. Basingstoke: Palgrave Macmillan
Mill, John Stuart (1846): "*A History of Greece* by George Grote, Esq". In: *Edinburgh Review* LXXXXIV, pp. 343–377.
Mill, John Stuart (1853): "*A History of Greece* by George Grote, Esq. Vols. IX, X, XI". In: *Edinburgh Review* XCVIII, pp. 425–447.
Mill, John Stuart (1991): *On Liberty and Other Essays*. John Gray (ed.). Oxford: Oxford University Press.
Nietzsche, Friedrich (1954): "Thus Spoke Zarathustra". In: *The Portable Nietzsche*. Walter Kaufmann (ed./trans.). New York, NY: Viking Press, pp. 103–439.
Nietzsche, Friedrich (1968): *Twilight of the Idols/The Anti-Christ*. R.J. Hollingdale (ed./trans.). Harmondsworth: Penguin Books.
Nietzsche, Friedrich (1989): *On the Genealogy of Morals/Ecce Homo*. Walter Kaufmann (ed./trans.) R.J. Hollingdale (trans.). New York, NY: Vintage Books.
Nietzsche, Friedrich (1990): *Beyond Good and Evil: Prelude to a Philosophy of the Future*. R.J. Hollingdale (trans.). London: Penguin Books.
Nietzsche, Friedrich (1996): *Human, All Too Human: A Book for free Spirit*. R.J. Hollingdale (trans.). Cambridge: Cambridge University Press.
Nietzsche, Friedrich (1997): *Daybreak*. Maudmarie Clark and Brian Leiter (eds.), R.J. Hollingdale (trans.). Cambridge: Cambridge University Press.
Taylor, Quentin P. (1997): *The Republic of Genius: A Reconstruction of Nietzsche's Early Thought*. Rochester, NY: University of Rochester Press.
Tocqueville, Alexis de (1988): *Democracy in America*. J.P. Mayer (ed.), George Lawrence (trans.). New York, NY: Harper Perennial [first published Harper & Row 1966].
Villa, Dana (2001): *Socratic Citizenship*. Princeton, NJ: Princeton University Press.
Weber, Max (1978) *Economy and Society*. 2 vols. Guenther Roth/Claus Wittich (eds.). Berkeley, CA: University of California Press.
Wolin, Sheldon (1993): *Tocqueville between Two Worlds: The Making of a Political and Theoretical Life*. Princeton, NJ: Princeton University Press.

Donovan Miyasaki
A Nietzschean Case for Illiberal Egalitarianism

Introduction

Nietzsche's hostility to moral and political egalitarianism is well known. However, I would like to argue that we can find resources in his work to defend a noble egalitarianism: a unique, non-liberal form of political egalitarianism that is independent of classical liberal views from Locke to Rawls about essential human equality of worth and right. My argument will be based in a critical reconstruction of Nietzsche's own distinction of noble and slavish forms of egalitarianism, a reconstruction grounded in Nietzsche's moral psychology of the will to power as affect and feeling of power. A noble, Nietzschean form of egalitarianism would be a strong, non-formal kind, promoting general proportionality of power, grounded in a relative equality of welfare, resources, and capabilities.

As a partially critical endeavor, my purpose is not to offer a case for egalitarianism that Nietzsche would accept, nor one that is compatible with any and every philosophical and normative position Nietzsche in fact holds. Rather, my goal is to use Nietzsche *contra* Nietzsche, to redirect his best ideas – the most plausible, original, and fruitful for further development – against the weaker elements of his philosophical work, particularly those views – such as his arguments against egalitarianism – that are less distinctive, less convincingly argued and, often, more deeply grounded in his own character and prejudices than in his philosophical commitments.[1]

Of course, since Nietzsche's particular views – even those that are not logically bound to his key philosophical claims – do not exist in isolation from the whole of his life and thought, my aim cannot be accomplished without departing substantially from Nietzsche's own claims in both letter and spirit: I propose a Nietzsch*ean* defense of egalitarianism, not Nietzsche's. Although my argument will have its foundation in what I consider to be a core philosophical commitment in Nietzsche's thought, the moral psychology of the will to power,

---

[1] I share Mark Warren's view that "one might choose the philosophical Nietzsche while excluding his politics, but do so without eclecticism – that is, without fragmenting the internal necessities of his thinking [...] Nietzsche's own politics [...] violates the intellectual integrity of his philosophical project" (Warren 1988, p. 208).

his views are only a departure point; the rest is reconstruction and development beyond that foundation. I claim only that from a central Nietzschean view we *can* move to a novel case for egalitarianism – not that we must, and certainly not that Nietzsche would do so.

1 Noble and Slavish forms of Morality and Egalitarianism

The idea of a distinctly noble form of egalitarianism is part of Nietzsche's conception of the noble form of evaluation, in which moral values are created through "self-glorification" (*Selbstverherrlichung*) grounded in a primary self-evaluation as good (BGE 260, KSA 5, p. 209). Nietzsche believes that in an aristocratic culture, the elite not only determine moral values using their own condition and character as the criterion of goodness, but also that they uphold the "severity" (*Strenge*) of a "principle [*Grundsatz*] that one has duties [*Pflichten*] only to one's peers [*Seinesgleichen*]," including a duty to treat each other as what they, in fact, are: social equals (BGE 260, KSA 5, p. 210).[2] Because they view their own character type as the measure of goodness, they are kept "strictly [*Streng*] within limits [*Schranken*] *inter pares*" by an elitist variant of egalitarianism: equal respect, promoted by "mores" (*Sitte*, which Nietzsche will later insist in GM I 11, KSA 5, p. 274 are incompatible with autonomy) of "consideration, self-control, tact, loyalty, pride, and friendship" for their peers (GM I 11, KSA 5, p. 274).

This element of customary respect and dutiful self-restraint toward others – an aspect shared with noble morality's opposite, "slave morality" – is an often forgotten aspect of noble morality, easily overlooked in Nietzsche's provocative account of its origins in violence and conquest, his vivid descrip-

---

2 Warren emphasizes this element of equality in noble morality, arguing that Nietzsche's position is compatible with equality of political rights, provided that equality is founded in equality of capacity to act (Warren 1988, p. 73). Lawrence Hatab (1995), Maudemarie Clark (1999), David Owen (2002), and Herman Siemens (2009) also interpret Nietzsche's anti-egalitarianism as one consistent with formal equality of rights, but all within a liberal democratic framework, while Daniel W. Conway argues that Nietzsche endorses the political inequality of "political perfectionism" only as a means to the more primary goal of individual moral perfectionism, which does not require political inequality (Conway 1997, p. 55). My position differs from these readings, because I claim that Nietzsche's moral psychology of power supports a strong, and not merely formal, egalitarianism of economic and social power, as well as of the resources and capabilities that such equality might depend on, rather than democratic liberal egalitarianism.

tions of the brutal behavior of aristocratic societies toward their perceived inferiors. Noble morality is, he would have us believe, the work of "uncaged beasts of prey [*losgelassne Raubthiere*]," "barbarians in every terrible sense of the word" who "do not know what guilt, what responsibility, what consideration [*Rücksicht*, a characteristic of noble morality in GM I 11, KSA 5, p. 274] is" and whose actions are "instinctive," "involuntary," and "unconscious" (GM I 11, KSA 5, p. 274; GM II 17, KSA 5, p. 324; BGE 257, KSA 5, p. 205f.).

It is surprising that such "beasts" should – or could – be "so strictly" bound by custom and principle, dutifully observing a moral obligation to respect even their equals. It is perhaps more surprising that Nietzsche unhesitatingly admires noble egalitarianism, insisting that the "true voice of justice [*Gerechtigkeit*]" commands, "Equality for equals, inequality for unequals" (TI Skirmishes 48, KSA 6, p. 150). Nietzsche's contrast of noble and slave morality is a critical one, intended to call into question the origin and aim of slavish values, particularly those of pity and selflessness, in *ressentiment* and revenge, exposing such other-regarding ideals as "anti-natural" values engineered to protect "the herd" at the expense of higher individuals, undermining, through self-destructive guilt, the healthy warrior ethos of noble peoples (GM I 7, KSA 5, pp. 266–28; BGE 260, KSA 5, pp. 208–12; BGE 201–02, KSA 5, pp. 121–26). Why, then, does he believe that respect for equality entirely loses its unnaturalness and harmfulness when limited to an elite?

The form of egalitarianism that Nietzsche rejects is a development of the "slavish" form of moral evaluation, supposedly characteristic of a politically oppressed people. Slave morality begins, in contrast to noble self-affirmation, in an envy-motivated negation of the privileged that defines noble characteristics and values as "evil," in contrast to the slave's characteristics as "good" (GM I 10, KSA 5, p. 270). Slave values are, then, reducible to a condemnation of privilege. Slavish egalitarianism is a political extension of this value system, identifying inequality – the existence of any kind of spiritual or political superiority – with intrinsic evil and its elimination with moral goodness.

This characterization of slavish egalitarianism as normative envy is surely unflattering, but it does not demonstrate that equality is undesirable, nor that inequality is morally acceptable. Ugly origins aside, why is equality objectionable? Why take seriously Nietzsche's claim that justice demands we "never make equal what is unequal"? (TI Skirmishes 48, KSA 6, p. 150). His case against slave egalitarianism is grounded in the view that it promotes the wellbeing of society at the expense of the highest, rarest, and culturally most valuable individuals, and that this amounts to harm to humanity as a whole, since the flourishing of humanity is measured by its "highest exemplars" (HL 9, KSA 1, p. 317).

This harm supposedly takes three primary forms. First, the belief in the equal worth of all persons undermines the individual will to self-development (BGE 257, KSA 5, p. 205). Second, the attempt to achieve equality produces cultural leveling in the form of damage to superior powers, talents, and abilities (TI Skirmishes 37, KSA 6, p. 138).[3] Third, by destroying the belief in orders of rank, equality produces cultural assimilation. By eliminating hierarchical orders of rank, equality undermines the desire for "self-overcoming," destroying the "will to stand out" that promotes a "multiplicity of types" and values (*Vielheit der Typen* and *Werthverschiedenheit*), eventually dissolving distinctive forms of identity, value, and life (TI Skirmishes 38, KSA 6, p. 139).

2 Reconceiving noble egalitarianism

My purpose is to reconstruct a *positive* Nietzschean case for egalitarianism, so I will not extensively discuss his arguments against egalitarianism.[4] However, his critique is not incompatible with the defense of some forms, since he attributes harm not to equality as such, but to the belief in equality and only to some methods of achieving it. His arguments are aimed only at slavish forms of egalitarianism, where the moral good is equated with the eradication of spiritual, qualitative, or evaluative superiority, entailing the rejection of belief in any kind of superiority, as well as of any qualitative differences that could support such belief.

However, this overlooks the possibility that a noble form of egalitarianism could be extended to all, rather than limited to members of a political elite. Nietzsche even explicitly acknowledges this possibility, only to ignore it in his later critique: "The thirst for equality can express itself either as a desire to draw everyone down to oneself (through diminishing them, spying on them, tripping them up) or to raise oneself and everyone else up (through recognizing their virtues, helping them, rejoicing in their success)" (HH 1 300, KSA 2, p. 240).

A noble but *universal* egalitarianism of this form must, if is to be consistent with Nietzsche's critique of slavish egalitarianism, have three key characteris-

---

[3] In the contemporary literature, this has come to be known as the "leveling down objection." See Larry Temkin (1993).

[4] I have argued elsewhere that Nietzsche's criticisms of egalitarianism succeed only on a narrow and inconsistent interpretation of power as purely quantitative, and not on his more primary conception of power as qualitative, where he emphasizes that human flourishing is grounded in the *feeling* of power rather than power simply. See Miyasaki (2013).

tics. First, it must not assume that human beings are equal in moral or cultural worth. It is, then, *normative* without *descriptive* egalitarianism: although humans are not qualitatively equal in value, they should be equal in social, political, and economic power.[5]

Second, such equality must be achieved through positive means, through proportional empowerment and complementary enhancements of status, rights, wealth, and abilities, rather than through the direct diminishment or "leveling down" of forms of superiority. Put differently, political institutions may prevent or alleviate social inequalities only if all parties, including the most privileged, benefit.

We might contrast this to John Rawls' "difference principle," according to which social and economic inequality is acceptable only if it is "improves the expectations of the least advantaged members of society" (Rawls 1971, p. 75). The difference principle reflects the "maximin" rule of choice in Rawls' hypothetical original position, where, given ignorance of our individual fortune under a given system of justice, we "adopt the alternative the worst outcome of which is superior" (Rawls 1971, p. 153). Because Rawls' difference principle of justice reflects the aim of maximizing the wellbeing of the least advantaged, it tolerates inequality only as a means to that end. Nietzschean egalitarianism, in contrast, follows what I will call a maxi*max* rule of choice: its aim is to maximize human wellbeing, and so it tolerates *equality* only where equality also benefits the *most* advantaged.[6]

---

[5] In answer to Amartya Sen's question, "Equality of what?" (Sen 1980), Nietzschean egalitarianism aims for a relative equality of individual power. However, Nietzsche's understanding of power is, as I explain in more detail below, a unique one in which power is measured qualitatively as the feeling of capability in the face of resistance rather than as quantitatively superior ability. Consequently, the egalitarian promotion of power in this sense does not directly entail any specific form of quantitative distributive equality, and cannot easily be fitted to the usual categories of egalitarianism, such as equality of welfare (Arneson 1989), resources (Dworkin 1981), or capabilities (Sen 1980, Nussbaum 1992). However, because Nietzsche suggests that the principal conditions of the feeling of power are resistance to action and an ability to act that is proportional to resistance, it is likely that equality of power is promoted through a high degree of equality in all three respects – welfare, resources, and capability – insofar as they are compatible. This would be necessary to promote equality of particular kinds of abilities and a generally equal ability to develop particular abilities to an equal degree.

[6] This should be distinguished from John Richardson's description of Nietzsche's moral and political values as "maximax," according to which Nietzsche "aims not at the greatest sum of all wills but at the greatest concentrations of power in individual wills" (Richardson 1996, p. 150). While I agree that this is Nietzsche's explicit view, I will argue that the priority of the qualitative feeling of power in his psychological theory implies that power is maximized precisely through equality of power rather than quantitative superiority, whether that of the sum of all wills or the concentration of power in individual wills.

Yet, in such cases, equality is not only tolerated but may also be imposed, in contrast to Rawlsian liberalism. Rawls' difference principle is moderated by the priority of the first principle of liberty: egalitarian measures are permitted only if they do not violate equally distributed individual rights (Rawls 1971, p. 61). In contrast, because noble egalitarianism denies descriptive egalitarianism, it is only limited by the maximax rule. Measures to promote equality are not constrained by a liberal principle of equal rights. Instead, the liberal principle of *equality of rights* is constrained by an illiberal principle of *right to equality* within the maximax rule. Rights are justified only insofar they serve such greater overall equality, which in turn is justified only if it is compatible with the wellbeing of the most advantaged.

So, the third key characteristic of a universal noble egalitarianism is the *illiberal rights principle*: rights are guaranteed only within the limits of equality of distribution allowed by the maximax rule. In conflicts between rights and equalizing measures beneficial to all, equality overrides rights. By rejecting descriptive egalitarianism, the noble form also rejects any claim of a moral obligation to protect equality of rights at the expense of shared advantage – particularly those rights of the privileged that might preserve or promote unequal distributions of power and wealth – but conceivably any individual rights that prevent universally beneficial equalizing measures.

The three characteristics I have sketched – descriptive anti-egalitarianism, the maximax rule of distribution, and the illiberal rights principle – ensure that this view is not subject to Nietzsche's first two objections. Because my reconstructed, universal form of noble egalitarianism does not endorse belief in the essential equal worth and rights of all persons, it evades his worries about harm to the individual incentive toward self-improvement and development. And because the maximax principle disallows direct harm to the advantaged for the sake of equality, it avoids the consequence of cultural leveling.

But how can I answer the third criticism that egalitarianism promotes the assimilation of qualitatively different forms of life, that it is, in effect, anti-pluralistic and anti-individualistic? Of course, egalitarianism need not have such assimilation as its aim. So, Nietzsche's argument might depend upon a false conflation of quantitative equality of power with qualitative equality of types, of equality (*Gleichheit*) with "sameness" or "likeness."[7]

---

[7] Martha Nussbaum's wholesale dismissal of Nietzsche as a political philosopher on the topic of liberty depends in part on this questionable interpretation, attributing to Nietzsche the belief that liberal egalitarians "deny that differences among people exist in abundance, including differences of achievement" (Nussbaum 1997, p. 10). Nietzsche does not, of course, believe this. Instead, he objects to the liberal egalitarian's beliefs about equal moral desert, the view, in Nussbaum's words, that "humanity itself has dignity and gives its bearer a claim to the goods

However, Nietzsche's criticism is not directed at the goal of equality, but rather at its consequences. He believes assimilation is the unintended but inevitable consequence of equality. My answer to this third criticism depends on my positive argument in favor of egalitarianism. So, I will first argue that distributive equality is beneficial to all, because it establishes the optimal conditions for maintaining and enhancing the abilities of all individuals, including – in accordance with the maximax rule – those of superior economic and political power. Then, in response to Nietzsche's final criticism, I will argue that noble egalitarianism, extended universally, also establishes the optimal conditions for cultural pluralism, for the promotion and preservation of qualitative differences in human types, values, and forms of life, and so does not promote cultural assimilation.

3 Making the case: the will to power as feeling-able in relation to proportional resistance

My argument begins with two assumptions that I consider to be Nietzsche's, as well. His views on these points are, of course, a matter of controversy, but I need not insist on them as interpretive claims. The Nietzschean foundation of my argument is the conception of noble egalitarianism and the moral psychology of the will to power, so these claims do not require his support, even though I believe they have it. My foundational assumptions are: 1) moral anti-realism, according to which moral and political *normative* claims cannot be justified on strictly epistemic grounds, and so must be argued on the basis of true descriptive claims about *general desirability*, not claims about obligation and 2) moral naturalism, according to which *descriptive* claims about the desirability of moral or political principles must be grounded in claims about human nature and psychology, and so are not claims about *perceived* interest or merely *subjective* desirability.

Consequently, my approach will be to argue for the general objective desirability of a nobly achieved, universal equality of social, political, and economic power, including its desirability to the advantaged, while grounding this claim

---

distributed by politics" (Nussbaum 1997, p. 11). His objection is that distribution should be based on the real enhancement (*Erhöhung*) of humanity, upon the actual value of any given individual, rather than on moral considerations of merit or desert – particularly ones based on potential value (essential humanity) or counterfactual value where "today's differences in merit reflect yesterday's differences in power" (moral luck).

in Nietzsche's views about moral and social psychology. By arguing that equality is *objectively* desirable, I am granting that the "maximax" rule may permit egalitarian institutions and laws that are not initially subjectively desirable to all. The privileged in societies marked by substantial inequality will likely interpret such measures as harmful to their current level of wellbeing. However, my approach assumes the possibility that there are objective truths about subjective conditions of desirability – that subjects can predictably desire differently under different social conditions, so that their given desires do not necessarily track which social conditions would, if realized, best promote their own subjectively evaluated happiness. Subjective judgments about the desirability of equality can be mistaken, based in a failure to accurately compare current happiness to potential happiness in an egalitarian society.[8] The maximax rule would apply in precisely such cases of mistaken subjective judgments about desirability.

So, the desirability of equality is to be found in Nietzsche's psychology, which, as is well known, gives a central place to the concept of power. However, Nietzsche's psychology is not, as often thought, a theory of a central desire, drive, or instinct for the accumulation of power. In its most developed form, the "will to power" is not brute instinct, but self-conscious affectivity. The primary drive is not toward the quantitative increase of power, but the qualitative increase of the *feeling* of power.[9] Accordingly, Nietzsche defines the human good as "all that heightens the feeling of power [*Gefühl der Macht*], the will to power, power itself" (A 2, KSA 6, p. 170). Priority is given to feeling, while the desire for power and its attainment come second, precisely because they are a mere means to the former. Likewise, Nietzsche identifies human flourishing or happiness, not with the possession or accumulation of power, but with "the feeling that power increases [*wächst*], that a resistance [*Widerstand*] is overcome" (A 2, KSA 6, p. 170). Notice that for happiness, in contrast to the good, there is no further qualification: the feeling of power and the feeling of overcoming resist-

---

[8] Nietzsche's will to power is a mix of speculative and common sense psychology, based in generalizations about the inseparability of resistance and proportionality from the feeling of power, so the legitimacy of a noble egalitarianism ultimately depends upon the possibility of empirically verifying Nietzsche's psychological claims generally and the ability to demonstrate the falseness of mistaken subjective judgements about desirability. However, there is growing empirical support for some of Nietzsche's psychological views (Knobe/Leiter 2006), and some studies provide support for key suggestions I will draw from Nietzsche's psychology: that happiness as affect (emotional wellbeing in contrast to reflective self-evaluations of happiness) is not strongly related to wealth or directly related to relative superiority in wealth (Kahneman/Deaton 2010) and that wellbeing depends on relative rather than absolute quantity of wealth (Easterlin 1974 and Easterlin et. al. 2010).
[9] I develop this interpretation in more detail in Miyasaki (2014).

ance are alone the condition of happiness – a will to power and the attainment of power are unnecessary. So, the objective psychological good of a human being includes power and the desire to increase power, but only as a precondition for the subjective psychological good of happiness, which is reducible to feeling, to qualitative rather than quantitative states of power.

This distinction between quantitative power and the qualitative experience of one's state of power is easily confused – indeed, Nietzsche conflates them frequently – so I will try to capture it in slightly different terms. Let us say that happiness, a better or more flourishing life, depends solely on the feeling of power as *ability*, including both the feeling of power that comes from an ability's successful exercise (the feeling of active power), and the feeling *that* one is capable of exercising an ability (the feeling of potential power). In contrast, the preservation of the human good as *general wellbeing* includes additional conditions: the will to power as *incentive to exercise and develop abilities*, and power itself, understood as *effective active and potential ability*.

Because the conditions of happiness are weaker than the conditions of wellbeing, happy states do not directly track states of wellbeing. There are two striking consequences. First, happiness (the feeling of ability) can be increased relatively, without a corresponding absolute increase in wellbeing (absolute ability and the desire for its increase). For example, a chess player who consecutively defeats increasingly talented opponents may experience a feeling of increasing ability or power ("the feeling that power is growing, that resistance is overcome"), despite achieving no absolute change in her skill level.

Second, an absolute decrease in wellbeing need not result in a decrease in happiness. For example, our chess player might grow bored with the game and allow her skills to deteriorate from lack of practice. However if, when she returns to the game, she chooses less skillful but still challenging opponents, she may feel no less accomplished in her gameplay than she did before.

At this point, we might wonder: if wellbeing is not necessary to happiness, then in what sense is it a human "good"? This question highlights the deeply relational nature of Nietzsche's view of human psychology. The "feeling of power," of ability and its exercise, is precisely the feeling of proportionally, if not absolutely, equal resistance – specifically, the feeling that my activity is resisted and I am able to act despite this resistance. In excess, of course, resistance produces the opposite feeling of impotence. However, the complete absence of any resistance would produce no feeling at all, for it is the tension of action and counter-action that produces the feeling of ability.[10]

---

10 Nietzsche's psychology of power is, consequently, a fitting accompaniment to Bernard Suits' definition of a game as "a voluntary attempt to overcome unnecessary obstacles" (Suits 2005, p. 55). Compare Suits' explanation of the gamewright's craft: "The gamewright must

Moreover, our ability to qualitatively distinguish higher states of wellbeing, higher degrees of happiness, is also based in the feeling of resistance: the greater the resistance, the more intense the feeling of power experienced in its equaling or overcoming. As Nietzsche suggests, happiness, a form of positive freedom, is not found in the absence of interference, but in its proportional intensity:

> How is freedom measured, in individuals as in nations? By the resistance [*Widerstand*] which has to be overcome, by the effort [*Mühe*] it costs to stay aloft. One would have to seek the highest type of free man where the greatest resistance [*Widerstand*] is constantly being overcome: five steps from tyranny, near the threshold of the danger of servitude. (TI Skirmishes 38, KSA 6, p. 140)

Consider, for example, the different intensities of power experienced by a professional weight lifter compared to an amateur, or the intensity of power felt in winning an arm-wrestling match with someone of equal strength compared to winning against someone much weaker.

Because the feeling of ability is based in qualitative states determined by relations, not by property or individually possessed goods, happiness is both social and agonistic; it is based in contests of power. It requires others to resist us; it needs proportionally equal counter-powers and counter-actions. However, happiness also requires a degree of wellbeing in the form of absolute quantitative ability, since resistance without the power to act is felt as impotence. And this is why both "power itself" (effective ability) and "the will to power" (a desire to exercise and increase ability) are beneficial to happiness, though not direct conditions for it: happiness requires the exercise of power, and thus its possibility is preserved by a desire to put our abilities to use and, in so doing, to enhance them.

4 The intrinsic good of equal distribution vs. the instrumental worth of distributed goods

If Nietzsche's conception of happiness is right, it provides us with a novel way of arguing for the general desirability of substantial social and political equali-

---

avoid two extremes. If he draws his lines too loosely the game will be dull because winning will be too easy [...] On the other hand, rules are lines that can be drawn too tightly, so that the game becomes too difficult" (Suits 2005, p. 45).

ty. The goal of minimizing inequality is misleadingly conceived as the equal distribution of intrinsic "goods," of simple, direct components of happiness. Consequently, egalitarian methods of distribution or redistribution are misconstrued as simple subtractions of intrinsic goods, as the direct diminishment of the wellbeing of the privileged. Rightly understood, however, the goods of distribution are relative ones – necessary in some amount for wellbeing, but only minimally and indirectly conditions for happiness. Such goods only increase happiness given broader social conditions that promote the increased *feeling* of power, rather than mere accumulation of power. Just as the chess player's ability is, taken as an absolute measure of power, not itself the source of her happiness, so the goods of political distribution are not themselves the principal basis of human happiness.

On the contrary, if Nietzsche's psychology is correct, the most desirable human good – and the only *intrinsic* one – to be distributed by a just political system is not quantitative but qualitative, not possession but feeling, not power but *relations that promote the feeling of power*. In other words, the primary good is the form of distribution rather than its contents. The primary good to be distributed is equality of distribution itself.

For if happiness is the feeling that ability is growing in relation to a resistance, its key foundation is the proportionality of that resistance relative to our abilities; it is found, as Nietzsche says, in "mighty" opponents against whom we must "stake all our strength," opponents "who are our equals [*gleiche Gegner*]" (EH Wise 7, KSA 6, p. 274).[11] Happiness requires the presence of resistances to our abilities that are neither too strong to produce any feeling of power, nor too weak to produce any feeling of resistance. Admittedly, this is a relation of only relative equality, since some differences in ability are required for the feeling of increasing power or overcoming a resistance. However, it is a relative equality that is absolutely incompatible with substantial, permanent social and

---

11 Nietzsche calls this demand for equality the "first presupposition of an honest dual," a claim that introduces a four-proposition summary of his "practice of war" – a "just war theory" of sorts (EH Wise 7, KSA 6, p. 274). But rather than an abstract duty, as implied by his claim that "the voice of justice" commands us to "never make equal what is unequal" (TI Skirmishes 48, KSA 6, p. 150), this principle is grounded in the noble nature: "Being able to be an enemy [...] belongs to a strong nature. It needs objects of resistance; hence it looks for what resists." It is a curious contrast: if it is in the nature of the noble personality to seek and invite resistance, then why do not "honest" (*rechtschaffen*, righteous or upright) warfare and "justice" (*Gerechtigkeit*) also permit the cultivation of worthy opponents? Why not "make equal what is unequal" as a means to righteous warfare?

political inequality, since such inequalities destroy the resistance to ability and action upon which the feelings of power and happiness depend.[12]

We can refine this condition by suggesting that human happiness requires stability of equality over time, but only proportional, variable degrees of equality at any given time. We can further define the *proportional equality* at stake as a relation in which inequalities do not endanger stability of equality over time. In such relations, inequalities of ability, advantage, and opportunity are limited to those that are 1) non-debilitating, allowing all to act with *some* degree of success, 2) non-dominating, allowing all to *sometimes* act with a high degree of success, and 3) non-demoralizing, allowing everyone the possibility of *feeling* powerful in the relation, even in the absence of successful action.

This, in turn, suggests a novel view of the relationship between equality and happiness. Equality is not desirable as an equal opportunity to obtain intrinsic goods that comprise happiness; rather, the relative goods of distribution contribute to happiness only when possessed in relationships of relative equality. Equality is itself the good to be distributed as the basic ground of any form of wellbeing, and as the necessary condition for any degree of happiness at all.[13] This is a dramatic conclusion, since it means that not just some, but *everyone's*, happiness is directly endangered by the toleration of disproportional degrees of inequality: those with substantially superior powers and abilities lack sufficient resistance to their exercise to produce or enhance their feeling of power, while those with substantially inferior powers and abilities experi-

---

[12] Because Nietzschean noble egalitarianism aims for equality of power in a sense related to one's ability to act, it has similarities to the capabilities approach (Sen 1980, Nussbaum 1992). However, the Nietzschean question is not Sen's "equality of what," but equal *how*? Power is not measured quantitatively but qualitatively, not by functionality or freedom but by feeling, which depends upon the proportionately equal capabilities of others as limited *resistance to* functional capability. Consequently, the equal distribution of basic abilities would not be sufficient to achieve noble egalitarianism. A substantial degree of equality of wealth and economic opportunity would likely be necessary to ensure not merely that basic capabilities are equal, but that non-basic, more developed capabilities find resistance and competition, that a sufficient number of individuals are economically capable of developing their capabilities to a relatively proportional level.

[13] Elizabeth S. Anderson also emphasizes equality of relations rather than holdings when she criticizes those who assume egalitarianism is about compensation, restitution, or desert, arguing instead that it is the creation of a certain form of human relation, a kind of community (Anderson 1999, p. 289). However, she shifts the aim of equality from desert to freedom, to the elimination of oppression (Anderson 1999, p. 288), which for noble egalitarianism is a consequence, but not the aim, of equality. The aim of noble egalitarianism is, on the contrary, the maximization of human happiness as the feeling of power, which happens to coincide with proportional equality of power and thus with conditions of non-domination.

ence their exercise only as impotence, due to disproportional resistance to action.

So, our key conclusion for the objective desirability of egalitarianism is that any social good contributes to happiness only to the degree that it promotes the exercise of abilities in conditions of proportional equality. A noble egalitarianism of proportional equality is beneficial to the happiness of everyone, including those currently advantaged by present inequalities. In contrast, substantial permanent inequalities are not accidentally, but intrinsically, harmful to the happiness of all, including the most advantaged. Inequality promotes relations of *conquest* – the overcoming of competition in the form of disproportional resistance – rather than relations of *contest* – the preservation of proportional resistance and competition.[14] In doing so, inequality destroys the primary social conditions of happiness for anyone.

5 The maximization of happiness and assimilation objections

This is the core of my argument; however, it leaves two unresolved issues. First, Nietzsche's argument against egalitarian leveling may still be raised in a more modest form. It may be argued that although proportional equality preserves the possibility of happiness for all, it is incompatible with the *maximization* of happiness, which requires the feeling of the *increase* of power. Moreover, the feeling of increasing power requires the feeling of overcoming increasingly greater resistances and, consequently, requires increasingly greater degrees of inequality. However, this argument fails for two reasons.

First, even if egalitarianism limits the maximal degree of happiness by limiting the increase of power inequalities, anti-egalitarianism fares worse since, by allowing expanding inequalities, it reduces the proportional resistance that is the condition of *any* degree of happiness – temporary increases in the feeling of power gained in this way must eventually undermine any capacity for the feeling of power at all. Where unequal societies produce increases in happiness, it is in localized relations of proportional equality. For example, a power-

---

14 In this respect Nietzschean noble egalitarianism resembles what Suits calls an "open game": "a system of mutually enabling moves whose purpose is the continued operation of the system" (Suits 2005, p. 124). Compare also Nietzsche's early, admiring account of the ancient *agon*, in which the most accomplished competitors were expelled: "Why should no one be the best? Because with that the contest would dry up" (HC).

ful CEO is able to fully experience the power of her position only by falling short of a total monopoly over her own company and the industry in which it operates: her power is felt in relation to proportionally equal competing employees in her own company and CEOs in competing companies. To whatever degree she is successful in *continually* expanding her power *disproportionally* to her competition, she will destroy her own happiness. At the ideal limit of such development, she would conquer all competitors, attain total relative power, and reduce her feeling of resistance, her happiness, to zero.

Consequently, the maximization of happiness through the feeling of increasing power depends not on expanding inequalities, but upon expansions of proportional power: the feeling of increased power comes, not from conquest, not from the absolute overcoming of resistance, but through the overcoming of increasingly greater resistances. For my feeling of power to increase, power must indeed increase, but it must do so in proportional equality with that of others, in order to preserve the resistance that grounds any feeling of power. For example, a tennis player increases her feeling of power through the defeat of ever-stronger opponents. Her heightened happiness does not come from the absolute increase of her ability, nor from the degree of inequality between her abilities and those of her opponents. Instead, it comes from the proportionally increased abilities of the sport as a whole, from contest rather than conquest: her potential competitors must improve their abilities to a relatively equal degree if she is to continue to feel powerful in relation to them.

So, by preserving, through the maximax rule, the possibility of temporary, proportional inequalities in power or ability, noble egalitarianism allows for increases of power. And by requiring proportional equality over time, it also ensures that such increases preserve the resistance necessary to experience the feeling and happiness of increased power. Therefore, noble egalitarianism protects basic happiness while maximizing the happiness of the most talented, able, and powerful.

We are now in a position to decisively reject a second objection: Nietzsche's claim that egalitarianism harms cultural pluralism, leading to the assimilation of qualitatively different human types, values, and ways of life. By promoting equality in the form of proportional, oppositional resistances, noble egalitarianism also protects and promotes a diversity of human types and values, since proportional power enables differing individuals and groups to resist domination and coercion by one another. By protecting contest from the undermining effects of conquest, noble egalitarianism preserves power relations that are non-debilitating, non-dominating, and non-demoralizing.

Such relationships promote cultural pluralism in two ways. First they protect what Nietzsche calls the "pathos of distance": the "will to be oneself, to stand out" (TI Skirmishes 37, KSA 6, p. 138). They protect the *subjective incentive* to maintain differences of identity, value, and type, by reducing the risk of feelings of impotence in the face of overwhelming resistance. Second, they protect the *objective foundation* of pluralism by minimizing dominating social relationships that undermine the real ability of different groups and types to maintain the distinctiveness of their forms of life.[15] Unlike liberal egalitarianism and anti-egalitarianism, noble egalitarianism protects individuals' real ability – rather than their abstract right – to preserve a distinct identity against the coercive social and economic power of the majority. Consequently, a Nietzschean form of noble egalitarianism, far from leading to assimilation, would provide the only strong foundation for lasting, stable, and happy pluralistic societies.

Bibliography

Anderson, Elizabeth S. (1999): "What is the Point of Equality?". In: *Ethics* 109, pp. 287–337.
Arneson, Richard J. (2000): "Welfare Should Be the Currency of Justice". In: *Canadian Journal of Philosophy* 30, pp. 477–524.
Clark, Maudemarie (1999): "Nietzsche's Antidemocratic Rhetoric". In: *Southern Journal of Philosophy* 37 (Suppl.), pp. 119–41.
Conway, Daniel W. (1997): *Nietzsche and the Political*. London: Routledge.
Deaton, Angus/Kahneman, Daniel (2010): "High Income Improves Evaluation of Life but not Emotional Well-Being". In: *Proceedings of the National Academy of Sciences* 107(38), pp. 16489–16493.
Dworkin, Ronald (1981): "What is Equality? Part 2: Equality of Resources". In: *Philosophy and Public Affairs* 10, pp. 283–345.
Easterlin, Richard (1974): "Does Economic Growth Improve the Human Lot? Some Empirical Evidence". In: Paul A. David/Melvin W. Reder (eds.): *Nations and Households in Economic Growth: Essays in Honor of Moses Abramovitz*. New York: Academy Press, Inc., pp. 89–125.
Easterlin, Richard/Angelescu McVey, Laura/Switek, Malgorzata/Sawangfa, Onnicha/Smith Zweig, Jacqueline (2010): "The Happiness-Income Paradox Revisited". In: *Proceedings of the National Academy of Sciences* 107(52), pp. 22463–22468.
Hatab, Lawrence (1995): *A Nietzschean Defense of Democracy: An Experiment in Postmodern Politics*. Chicago: Open Court Press.

---

15 As Vanessa Lemm points out, "While equality based on recognition of universality [...] forecloses the possibility of struggle and, hence, freedom as responsibility, equality based on the recognition of difference [...] generates freedom as responsibility" (Lemm 2009, p. 43). However, to this must be added Nietzsche's psychological insight that equality based in the formal recognition of difference has real, if relative, power equality as its precondition.

Knobe, Joshua/Leiter, Brian (2007): "The Case for Nietzschean Moral Psychology". In: Brian Leiter/Neil Sinhababu (eds.): *Nietzsche and Morality*. Oxford: Oxford University Press, pp. 83–109.
Lemm, Vanessa (2009): *Nietzsche's Animal Philosophy: Culture, Politics, and the Animality of the Human Being*. New York: Fordham University Press.
Miyasaki, Donovan (2014): "The Equivocal Use of Power in Nietzsche's Failed Anti-Egalitarianism". In: *Journal of Moral Philosophy*. Forthcoming, DOI: 10.1163/17455243-4681016.
Nietzsche, Friedrich (1966): *Beyond Good and Evil*. W. Kaufmann (trans.). New York: Vintage Books.
Nietzsche, Friedrich (1967): *Ecce Homo*. Walter Kaufmann (trans.). New York: Vintage Books.
Nietzsche, Friedrich (1968a): *The Anti-Christ*. R. J. Hollingdale (trans.). London: Penguin Books.
Nietzsche, Friedrich (1968b): *Twilight of the Idols*. R. J. Hollingdale (trans.). London: Penguin Books.
Nietzsche, Friedrich (1986): *Human, All Too Human*. R. J. Hollingdale (trans.). Cambridge: Cambridge University Press.
Nietzsche, Friedrich (1995): "Homer's Contest". C. Davis Acampora (trans.). In: *Nietzscheana* 5, pp. 1–8.
Nietzsche, Friedrich (1997): *Untimely Meditations*. R. J. Hollingdale (trans.). Cambridge: Cambridge University Press.
Nietzsche, Friedrich (1998): *On the Genealogy of Morality*. Maudemarie Clark and A. J. Swanson (trans.). Indianapolis: Hackett.
Nussbaum, Martha (1992): "Human Functioning and Social Justice: In Defense of Aristotelian Essentialism". In: *Political Theory* 20(2), pp. 202–246.
Nussbaum, Martha (1997): "Is Nietzsche a Political Thinker?". In: *International Journal of Philosophical Studies* 5(1), pp. 1–13.
Owen, David (2002): "Equality, Democracy, and Self-Respect: Reflections on Nietzsche's Agonal Perfectionism". In: *Journal of Nietzsche Studies* 24, pp. 113–31.
Rawls, John (1971): *A Theory of Justice*. Boston: Harvard University Press.
Richardson, John (1996): *Nietzsche's System*. Oxford: Oxford University Press.
Sen, Amartya (1980): "Equality of What?". In: S. M. McMurrin (ed.): *The Tanner Lectures on Human Values*. Salt Lake City: University of Utah Press.
Siemens, Herman (2009): "Nietzsche's Critique of Democracy". In: *Journal of Nietzsche Studies* 38, pp. 20–37.
Sinhababu, Neil/Leiter, Brian (eds.) (2007): *Nietzsche and Morality*. Oxford: Oxford University Press.
Suits, Bernard (2005): *The Grasshopper: Games, Life and Utopia*. Toronto: Broadview Press.
Temkin, Larry (1993): *Inequality*. Oxford: Oxford University Press.
Warren, Mark (1988): *Nietzsche and Political Thought*. Cambridge, Mass.: MIT Press.

III. Aristocratic, or Anti-Liberal, or Non-Egalitarian Politics in Nietzsche

Renato Cristi
Nietzsche, Theognis and Aristocratic Radicalism*

> Kyrnos, this polis is pregnant, and
> I fear it will give birth to a man who
> will take revenge of our bad hubris
> (Theognis 1962, pp. 39f.)

The hegemony attained by democratic legitimacy in the modern world makes it difficult to conceive of non-democratic political regimes. It doesn't make much sense for us to dismiss democracy and defend monarchical or aristocratic legitimacy. But this is precisely what Nietzsche does, as he so acknowledges in his response to a letter sent to him on 26 November 1887 by Georg Brandes, a well-known Copenhagen intellectual. Brandes points out that there is much in Nietzsche's writings that accords with his own contempt for ascetic ideals and profound dislike "with respect to democratic mediocrity." He also notes that he converges with his "aristocratic radicalism" (KGB III/6, Bf. 500). Nietzsche responds from Nice on 2 December: "The expression 'aristocratic radicalism' that you employ is very clever. If you allow me, it is the shrewdest description that I have read about my person" (KGB III/5, Bf. 960). A few weeks later, on 20 December, he writes to Heinrich Köselitz and comments that Brandes has used the expression "aristocratic radicalism" to characterize his writings. He then comments: "This is well-said and meaningful" (KGB III/5, Bf. 964).

Nietzsche readily accepts Brandes's verdict, an indication of the centrality of aristocratism in his writings. There is no novelty in this.[1] Novel is the enthusiasm with which Nietzsche recognizes his own radicalism. Alfred von Martin observes that both Nietzsche and Burckhardt defend aristocratic conservative positions. But while Burckhardt is a conservative Whig, who admires Burke

---

* I would like to thank Don Dombowsky, Manuel Knoll, Vanessa Lemm and Barry Stocker for their valuable comments. I would also like to thank Robert Kerr for translating for me Nietzsche's dissertation *De Theognide Megarensi*.
1 As early as 1901, Aloys Riehl noted Nietzsche's "aristocratic, individualist tendencies" (Riehl 1901, p. 158). In agreement with Riehl, Bruno Bauch, a neo-Kantian philosopher, articulated in 1921 Nietzsche's aristocratic convictions and contempt for democratic equality (Bauch 1921, p. 15). Bauch shared the conservative views defended by conservative Nietzscheans like Thomas Mann, Ernst Bertram, Hugo von Hoffmanstahl, Richard Oehler, Friedrich Würzbach and other aristocratizing literary figures (cf. Oehler 1921).

and detests revolution, Nietzsche is a revolutionary conservative "who needs a *tabula rasa* to imprint the image of his own spiritual power over the ruins of present culture" (von Martin 1941, p. 54; cf. Martin 1941, pp. 58–60, 97). His radicalism distances him from conventional politics, and for this reason he adopts an openly anti-political attitude. Nietzsche intends to undermine the culture that supports modern democracy. His anti-political radicalism rejects democratic ends and means defined, at best, by parliamentary competition and political compromise, and at worse, by chicanery and wheeler dealing. Anthony Jensen sees this as Nietzsche's "immeasurable" contribution to European politics. This contribution is "paradoxically but fundamentally anti-political: Nietzsche saw himself variously as herald, critic, and advisor with regard to the political, without participating directly in politics itself" (Jensen 2007, p. 319).

Nietzsche's aristocratic radicalism accords with his individualism. In "Uses and Disadvantages of History for Life," his second *Untimely Meditation*, he maintains that humanity's aim is the production of its "highest exemplars" (HL 9). According to Walter Kaufmann, there is perhaps "no more basic statement of Nietzsche's philosophy in all his writings than this statement. Here is [...] the clue to his 'aristocratic' ethics and his opposition to socialism and democracy" (Kaufmann 1950, p. 149; cf. Kaufmann 1950, p. 319). As von Martin writes, his individualism marks another difference with Burckhardt. While Burckhardt writes about nobility as a social group, Nietzsche's only concern is the "aristocratic individual" (von Martin 1941, p. 222, note 96).

When Nietzsche beholds his own epoch he notices the hegemony of democracy and socialism, and also the triumph of what he perceives as decadent Christian morality. Faced with this bleak spectacle he seeks consolation in the classical past. There he contemplates the aristocratic splendour described by Homer, but also the decline of this blissful world as seen through the resentful eyes of Theognis, the hypochondriac aristocrat described by Goethe (BAW 3, p. 36). When Nietzsche surveys the future, as he does in his notebooks of 1885–86, he announces a new aristocracy that will last for millennia. Nietzsche's aristocratic radicalism is observable throughout the entirety of his writings and constitutes the core of his thought. As Fredrick Appel rightly observes, "Nietzsche's radical aristocratic commitments pervade every aspect of his project" (Appel 1999, p. 5; cf. Detwiler 1990, Dombowsky 2004).

The origins of the aristocratic restoration aspired by Nietzsche can be traced to his acquaintance with Homer and Theognis, poets of the Dorian nobility. From the former he derives his aristocratism, from the latter his radicalism. In this essay I examine, first of all, Nietzsche's early encounter with the elegies of Theognis, whom he sees as the prime witness of the defeat of the Megarian aristocracy at the hands of a rising commercial class. The poet laments that the Megarian plebs has amassed new wealth and imposed democratic institutions.[2] In Theognis's bitter and lacerating reaction one finds the roots of Nietzsche's radicalism. Later, in the *Birth of Tragedy*, Nietzsche expands the political theology that sustains Theognis's reaction. Nietzsche studies the aristocratic type represented by Apollo and contrasts it to the plebeian and secularized image of Socrates.

Second, Nietzsche's interest in the tragic fate of the Dorian aristocracy is not purely contemplative. To invoke Apollo, distant and reserved, is not enough to revert aristocratic decline. For this reason Nietzsche appeals to Dionysian intoxication as a way to arouse counter-revolutionary enthusiasm. Like Theognis, Nietzsche looks to the future for ways to restore aristocracy to its seat of honour. He gives up on the possibility of political action and embraces Theognis's deployment of a culture war against democrats. His aim is the formation of a new aristocracy. Nietzsche toys with the idea of recruiting and training these new aristocrats, and instilling in them a counter-morality to displace the ethos that sustains democracy, namely Judeo-Christian morality. Because of his individualism, he is more comfortable with assigning that task to heroic superhuman figures, like Napoleon and Bismarck. Nietzsche wants men like these to be the leaders of the aristocratic re-constitution he yearns for.

I conclude this essay by showing the futility of recent attempts to place Nietzsche's political thought at the service of democracy (Ottmann 1999, pp. 462–466). These attempts do not take to heart Nietzsche's radicalism by which he seeks to subvert the very foundation of the democratic ethos and restore aristocratic cultural hegemony. I examine critically the position defended by Lawrence Hatab for whom Nietzsche's anti-essentialism, his attack on rationalism and his adoption of epistemological perspectivism, help to overcome the levelling practices and certain exclusions imposed by the modern democratic experience.

I

One should not underestimate the effect of Nietzsche's early Theognidean studies on his later ethical and political reflections. It is true that, in his published work, we only find Theognis mentioned in *On the Genealogy of Morality*. It is also true that the overt aim of Nietzsche's Theognidean research is philological

---

[2] This historical development takes place principally in Corinth, Megara and Sykion between 650 and 600 BCE (Grote 1869, Arnheim 1975, Morris 1996).

in nature, and not ethical or political. He seeks to decipher the enigma surrounding the fragmentation and multiple interpolations endured by the Theognidean corpus (BAW 3, p. 15; cf. Janz 1978, vol. I, p. 123). In a letter to Gustav Krug and Wilhelm Pinder (12 June 1864, KGB I, 1, Br. 426), Nietzsche states that he intends to write up his dissertation, titled *De Theognide Megarensi*, "with the right philological grounding and in the most scientific way possible" (KGB I/1, Bf. 426). But, as Antimo Negri intimates, what in fact guides his dissertation "is not the same philological interest that will essentially determine his next work, *Zur Geschichte der Theogneidischen Spruchsammlung*" (Negri 1985, pp. 6f.).[3] In TM, he uses Theognis's elegies as a "critical observatory" (Negri 1985, p. 27) from which he contemplates the birth and proclamation of aristocratic ideals at a time when the Megarian aristocracy had been mortally wounded. Theognis appears to him as "a grand feudal lord [*Junker*], sophisticated and run-down, full of mortal hate against an aspiring people." Nietzsche defines him as a "contorted Janus head" who contemplates a splendorous past with nostalgia and envisions a repugnant future defined by a demand for "equal entitlements." He sees Theognis as representative of "somewhat corrupted and no longer firmly established blood aristocracy," as the "characteristic head of those noble figures that represent an aristocracy on the eve of a popular revolution [*Volksrevolution*], an aristocracy that sees its privileges threatened forever and is ready to fight with the same passion for its own existence and that of its caste" (BAW 3, p. 74; cf. Porter 2000, pp. 231f.).

In the first part of his dissertation, Nietzsche traces the socio-historical roots of that popular revolution. He writes: "due to the colonies founded by the Megarians in fertile regions, from which riches and luxuries flowed back to the metropolis, dissension arose between the optimates and the plebs" (BAW 3, p. 23). Historical material conditions determined the fate of the Megarian aristocracy (Cancik 2000, p. 10).[4] In light of this background, the second part

---

[3] Nietzsche manifests his dissatisfaction with the whole philological enterprise in a letter to Carl von Gersdorff (6 April 1867): "I honestly do not want to write again so woodenly and drily, in such a logical corset, as I did for example, in my Theognis essay, at whose cradle no Graces sat [...] For we would not deny that most philologists lack that elevating total view of antiquity, because they stand too close to the picture and investigate a patch of paint, instead of gazing at the big, bold brush strokes of the whole painting and – what is more – enjoying them" (KGB I/2, Bf. 540; cf. Negri 1985, pp. 40ff.).

[4] A footnote is missing. The footnote reads: As historical evidence to support his argument in TM, Nietzsche refers to Rochette (1815), Müller (1824; cf. 1839), Plaß (1852), Duncker (1856) and Grote (1869). When Nietzsche mentions Theognis again in GM, in connection with the social and political status of the nobility, one should assume that those are the sources of the historical evidence that backs his argument. Failure to take TM into account explains why Peter Berkowitz writes that GM is, in that respect, a "...freewheeling reconstruction, devoid of reference to

of TM examines the reception of the Theognidean writings which were "transmitted to us in a most deplorable condition, disjecta et interrupta, and mixed together with parodistic verses of other poets" (BAW 3, p. 35). Assuming this, Theodor Bergk claimed "that nothing of Theognis still exists except a disparate succession of disjunct aphorisms" (BAW 3, p. 54). This also led Friedrich Gottlieb Welcker to assume that Theognis was a gnomic poet (Welcker 1826, pp. lxxi). Welcker held this view because he neglected to see that certain events, "mentioned in the poems, needed to be interconnected and placed in precise order" (BAW 3, p. 29). Once this was done, it became possible for him to reconstruct the trajectory of Theognis' life and sketch a coherent biographical account. Nietzsche was able to determine the unity of Theognis's work and rise above Welcker's and Bergk's philological woodcutting. Leaving behind the analysis of separate trees he took an overview of the forest.[5] The forest he discovered was the fate of Megara's aristocratic faction and of Theognis' lifelong devotion to its ideals. Finally, the third part of the dissertation, titled *Theognidis de deis, de moribus, de rebus publicis opiniones examinantur*, describes the traditional role of the Dorian aristocracy. Nietzsche examines Theognis's "opinions with regard to matters human and divine" in order to illuminate how Megarian aristocrats were able traditionally to assert their "dignity and authority" and discern "how much aristocrats were valued at that time, and how superior they were to the plebs" (BAW 3, pp. 55f.). He acknowledges a close connection between Theognis' conception of the gods and morals, and his judgment on political matters. Since Megarian society was strictly divided along class lines, when a "bitter class struggle [*certamen acerrimum inter has classes*]" broke out, and Theognis rose as a champion of the aristocracy, he was able to pronounce one class, the aristocrats, as good (ἀγαθός), and the other class as bad (κακός or δειλός), for among the latter "among whom every moral depravity, irreverence and ungodliness was said to exist" (BAW 3, p. 56).

Nietzsche outlines five criteria that define an aristocrat as opposed to a *homo plebeius*: pure lineage, monopoly of war, supervision of the religious cult (*sacrorum administratio*), devotion towards luxury and splendour,[6] and the

---

specific historical situation" (Berkowitz 1995, p. 74). More generally, Lawrence Hatab also refers to Nietzsche's genealogical investigations in GM as "quasi-historical" (Hatab 2008, p. 29).
5 In his letter to Hermann Mushacke (March 14, 1866), Nietzsche used the expression "philological woodcutting" to describe the work he was engaged in at that moment at Leipzig (KGB I/2, Bf. 498)
6 In connection with Sappho, who wrote: "I love luxury" (Sappho, fr. 58,25), Ian Morris comments: "luxury bridged the gulf between mortals and gods [...] Lavish display made the aristocracy something more that human" (Morris 1996, p. 32).

cultivation of art. According to Frank Schweitzer, the third criterion, the one that presents aristocrats as a "bridge or link between gods and humans", is crucial (Schweitzer 2007, p. 360). The gods do not communicate with the common people, but prefer to do so with aristocrats with whom they maintain a certain degree of proximity. There is a compact (*foedus*) between gods and humans by which these receive goods and beneficence in exchange for a sacred cult (*honores sacraque*). This cult remains a monopoly held by the aristocracy (BAW 3, p. 57). The elevated presence of the aristocracy allows them to transcend the separation between the human and the divine. Since times immemorial the subordinated masses had been inculcated with the belief "that the aristocracy were superior beings endowed with qualities which set them off from lesser mortals" (Arnheim 1975, p. 183). Nietzsche's reading of verses 105–108,[7] hints at the deteriorated social relations between the declining aristocracy and the now enriched plebs. This is the reason why Theognis recommends aristocrats to take an amiable and friendly approach when seeking to employ the services of plebeians, knowing they will face the inextinguishable hate (*odio inexstincto*) that consumes plebeians (BAW 3, p. 60).

In this conflict Nietzsche sides with the Megarian aristocrats as is evident from his characterization of the *homo plebeius* as corrupt and ungrateful. This is a preview to his later affirmation of a pathos of distance and absolute rejection of a morality of slaves, key elements of his aristocratic radicalism. According to Jensen, Nietzsche shares Theognis's radicalism, but this manifests itself only when he positions himself inside the political agon. In such circumstances, he most definitely asserts the pathos of distance and a drastic subjugation of those who must live as slaves. At the same time, Jensen believes that Nietzsche is able intellectually to place himself outside and above the agon. From this external point of view, Nietzsche affirms "the necessity of the competition between Theognis' aristocrats and the opposed δειλοί as precondition of real flourishing. Theognis' *Vernichtungskampf* is rejected; Theognis as the mouthpiece of one side of the early Greek *Wettkampf* is preserved" (Jensen 2007, pp. 328f.). Jensen believes that this marks Nietzsche's distance from Theognis' political position. Nietzsche "could not accept Theognis' unwillingness to permit entry to the newly ascendant cultural class," because he thought that "only through the productive Eris of which Hesiod spoke can cultural enhancement follow political upheaval" (Jensen 2007, p. 327).

---

7 There is no glory in helping the δειλούς,
   Just like sowing the grey, salty sea,
   Sowing the sea brings not a rich harvest,
   Nor will doing good to the κακούς return good.

Jensen's interpretation misses the mark. First, he does not take into account that Nietzsche first touched upon the notion of agon in 1867, in his Leipzig lecture titled "Der Sängerkrieg auf Euböa" (Vogt 1962, p. 105; cf. Pâdurean 2008, pp. 83ff.). Moreover, Nietzsche owes to Burckhardt the idea that the agon is the essential trait of Greek culture. Burckhardt first presented this idea in 1872, in the course of his lectures on Greek civilization, which Nietzsche attended (Young 2010, p. 205). It is therefore anachronistic to interpret his early reading of Theognis in terms of the agon; at that time he was unaware of the full import of that notion. Second, even if one were to take the agon into account, in no case did Nietzsche envisage the possibility of political competition with the subordinate classes. He was deeply convinced that aristocrats would suffer defeat at the hands of democrats were they to compete in the political arena. For this reason Nietzsche sought the 'cultural' annihilation of democrats, a key feature of the uncompromising radicalism he shared with Theognis. Jensen does not take into account that Theognis's own radicalism was the result of the 'political' weakness of the Megarian aristocracy, which was no longer the dominant rank but a minority party with no hope of regaining its former status. This explains why Theognis renounced the political agon which he anticipated as irremediably lost. At the same time, he engaged in a *Vernichtungskampf* with his enemies and aimed at defeating them on a different battlefield – the realm of culture.[8] The comparison advanced by Nietzsche between Theognis and a character of Schiller, the Marquis of Posa, proves, according to Jensen, that "Nietzsche found in Theognis a way to influence culture on a grand scale without resorting to governmental politicking" (Jensen 2007, p. 326; cf. BAW 3, p. 41). By emphasizing the advisory role in politics exemplified by Theognis and Posa, Jensen correctly identifies the root of Nietzsche's anti-politicality. But it is a mistake to conclude from this that Nietzsche abandoned a radical *Vernichtungskampf* against the democratic rabble, the δειλοί. Nietzsche rejected democracy because he wanted to shun the possibility of competing politically with the subordinate classes. Experience showed

---

8 This view is advanced by Werner Jaeger who interprets the "aristocratic theory [*Adelslehre*]" offered by Theognis as a "cultural [*geistige*] struggle against the social revolution," a struggle that "should not be understood narrowly as a strict political activity" (Jaeger 1958, pp. 263, 266). The reason for this is that Theognis saw that Megara's aristocratic minority could not prevail politically given the new social situation. It is true that he advised his disciple "to adapt externally to existing circumstances [...] to act like a polyp that takes on the colour of the rock to which it adheres, and constantly changes its coloration" (Jaeger 1958, p. 266; cf. Theognis 1962, pp. 213–218). But it seems to me that this pliability should not be read as a willingness to reach a democratic compromise, but as a way to disguise the political intentions of his *Kulturkampf* against it.

him that in that kind of war democrats were invincible. A culture war was, therefore, his ultimate resort.

Nietzsche's inchoate political theology, drawn up on the basis of Theognis's aristocratism, is further developed in BT inspired this time by Homer. In the *Twilight of the Idols*, Nietzsche acknowledges that BT was his "first revaluation of all values" and also the "ground [*Boden*]" from which his will and his abilities grew (TI Ancients 5). The aim of BT is to vouch for the intrinsic value of aristocratic culture – the value to which all other values ought to be subordinated. Nietzsche intends to trace the origins of aristocratic culture to Homeric times, then chronicle its extinction in 5th century Greece and announce its imminent contemporary re-birth with Wagner.

The aristocratic order of primitive Greece, mirroring the order and hierarchy of the Olympian regime, is the theme of Homer's political theology. Nietzsche personifies this aristocratic order by means of Apollo, the commanding divinity within the Olympic pantheon. The Apolline figure is the source of the many features that define the aristocratic way of life at its zenith. First, aristocratic distance is best symbolized by Apollo's luminous bow. Homer presents him as the god that shoots from a distance, who rejects proximity and familiarity, and opts for the objectivity of a remote vision. The aristocratic world of Homer, where culture defeats wild nature, constitutes an intelligible and secure order. This is consistent with the view that Apollo shows his splendour as the god of light and the sun (DW, KSA 1, p. 554; cf. Buffiere 1956, pp. 187f.).

Second, Apollo also presides over the world of dreams. Dreams reveal actions and figures profiled to perfection as opposed to the incomplete and not entirely intelligible everyday reality. The Apolline defines the measurable, the determinable and intelligible. Apollo is more contemplative than active, more prone to leisure than practice. In *Human All Too Human* (HH I), Nietzsche focuses on what he calls 'the aristocrats of the spirit' to define the Apollinean disposition.

> Quiet fruitfulness. The born aristocrats of the spirit are not too zealous: their creations appear and fall on a quiet autumn evening unprecipitately, in due time, not quickly pushed aside by something new. The desire to create continually is vulgar and betrays jealousy, envy, ambition. If one is something one really does not need to make anything – and one nonetheless does very much. There exists above the 'productive' man a yet higher species (HH I 210).

Apollo, in the third place, is the deity who, on maintaining separation and distance, affirms independent individuality. In BT, Nietzsche presents him as the "deification of the principium individuationis" (BT 4). In his notebooks, he also presents Apollo as the paradigmatic individual. "The term 'Apolline' expresses: the tendency to be perfectly for oneself, to be the typical 'individual', the impulse that simplifies, defines, strengthens, clarifies, renders precise and typical: liberty under the law" (NL, KSA 13, 14[14]). Apollo typifies individual freedom – a legislated, ordained and authorized freedom nonetheless. In sum, for Nietzsche Apollo is the "aristocratic legislation that declares: "So it must always be!" (NL, KSA 12, 2[106]). This is not the empire of law, of the abstract rule of law. Apollo represents the figure of the individual legislator who can command and demand universal obedience.

The appearance of Apollo in the Homeric scenario coincides with the apex of the hegemony of the Dorian aristocracy. Nietzsche presents it as a moment of great stability that allows for the peaceful fecundity of the aristocrats of the spirit. He believes that the Apolline "naive magnificence" was preceded in time by an "iron age with its Titanic struggles and bitter popular philosophy" (BT 4). Apolline serenity is only possible after its triumph over the Dionysian tumult. Nietzsche then detects the re-emergence of Dionysian intoxication, followed by Apollo's resurgence. "Confronted with this new power,[Apollo] rose up again in the rigid majesty of Doric art and view of the world" (BT 4). In this manner, the first section of BT is structured around these two hostile impulses and the conflict which inevitably ensues. This same conflict ends up uniting them in the fecund embrace that gives birth to Attic tragedy:

> These two very different drives exist side by side, mostly in open conflict, stimulating and provoking one another to give birth to ever-new, more vigorous offspring in whom they perpetuate the conflict [*Kampf*] inherent in the opposition between them [...] until eventually, by a metaphysical miracle of the Hellenic Will, they appear paired and, in this pairing, finally engender a work of art which is Dionysian and Apolline in equal measure: Attic tragedy (BT 1).

Nietzsche tracks the birth of Attic tragedy by sketching a genealogy of the Olympian gods. These are relatively new deities who rise together with the supremacy attained by Apollo over the chthonic divinities represented by Dionysus. The cult of Dionysus, immediately tied to nature, had arisen out of the celebration of ancestral rural myths. With Dionysus we enter the realm of the imprecise, of what is vague and intuitive. This deity presides over the night where the orgiastic reigns. "Dionysiac nature desiderates intoxication, and hence proximity; Apollonian desiderates clarity and form; and hence distance" (Otto 1954, p. 78). Dionysus comes alive together with the anarchic *populus* that shun the *principium individuationis*. Under its ascendancy "all the established separations among castes disappear, be they necessary or arbitrary. The slave is now a free person, the aristocrat and the person of obscure birth are united in the same Bacchic choir" (DW, KSA 1, p. 555). Apollo and aristocratic culture rise against this savage instinct and impose form and order over intoxication and ecstasy. Nietzsche understands that the Dionysian is the basis and condition for the possibility of the Apolline and aristocratic spirit. This understanding is mediated by the adoption of a philosophical point of view: "The philosophical temper prefigures that beneath our everyday reality lies hidden a second reality that is completely different" (DW, KSA 1, p. 555).

The Apolline/Diosysian fusion breaks apart when Socrates appears on the Athenian cultural scene. In BT, Nietzsche acknowledges that Socrates is the "archetype of a form of existence unknown before him, the archetype of theoretical man" (BT 15). Socrates, as a theoretical man, has repressed and forgotten the Dionysian. Socratic dialectics lacks a substantive core and reduces to a purely mechanical logicism. This is the same enlightened tendency that will later determine the rise of Alexandrian culture. Socrates, in Nietzsche's view, is "the opponent of Dionysus" who forces its retreat from Athenian culture and the subsequent disintegration of tragedy (BT 12). Socratic reason is plebeian and deviates decisively from the Apolline wisdom that now "has disguised itself as logical schematism" (BT 14). Nietzsche thinks that originally that intuitive and instinctive form of knowledge was not infiltrated by dialectics. When Socrates starts his pedagogical mission he seeks to formalize knowledge to make it universally transmissible. In contrast, the knowledge claimed by Apollo is not easy to acquire and remains the innate and exclusive property of a few noble individuals. Later in TI, Nietzsche confirms this view:

> With Socrates, Greek taste suddenly changed in favour of dialectics: what really happened here? Above all, an aristocratic [*vornehmer*] taste was defeated; with dialectics, the rabble [*der Pöbel*], rises to the top. Before Socrates, dialectical manners were rejected in good society: they were seen as bad manners, they humiliated people. The young were warned against them. People were generally distrustful of reasons being displayed like this. <u>Honette</u> things, like <u>honette</u> people, do not go around with their reasons in their hand. It is indecent to show all five fingers. Nothing with real value needs to be proved first. Where authority is still part of the social fabric, wherever people give commands rather than reasons, the dialectician is a type of clown: he is laughed at and not taken seriously. — Socrates was the clown who made himself be taken seriously: what really happened here? (TI Socrates 5)

In *Beyond Good and Evil*, Nietzsche presents a similar conception of the aristocratic way of life:

> Socrates of course had initially sided with reason, given the taste of his talent — that of a superior dialectician. And in point of fact, didn't he spend his whole life laughing at the shortcomings of his clumsy, noble Athenians, who like all noble people, were men of instinct and could never really account for why they acted the way they did? (BGE 191)

Athenian aristocrats, unable to deal with dialectical sleights of hand, appear obtuse and incompetent. Socrates ignores the fact that the aristocratic talent does not arise from reason, but from instinct. Reason makes us deliberate indefinitely; instinct forces a decision. Aristocrats, exasperated by Socrates eminently utilitarian and plebeian disposition, allow themselves to be guided by instinct. In this noble decisionism lie the roots of aristocratic radicalism. In the *Gay Science*, Nietzsche writes: "the higher nature is more unreasonable – the noble, magnanimous and self-sacrificing person does in fact succumb to his drives" (GS 3). Higher natures can "risk health and honour for the sake of passion for knowledge" (GS 3).

The virtue of aristocratic decisionism lies in "the art of commanding and the art of proud obedience" (HH I 440). The instinctive capacity to command is further needed to ensure the leisure required for intellectual creativity. Aristocratic leisure presupposes a regime that authoritatively assigns productive labour to slaves. This is the theme of Nietzsche's essay titled "The Greek State" which was originally to appear as a section of BT. Nietzsche is aware of the political meaning that attaches to Homeric theology. The social basis that sustains the aristocratic superstructure is made of men of obscure birth who toil as slaves. "The misery of workers must even be increased in order to make the production of the world of art possible to a small number of Olympian men" (GSt, KSA 1, p. 767). The aristocratic state envisaged by Homer is supposed to secure "an Olympian existence and ever-renewed breeding and preparation of the genius" (GSt, KSA 1, p. 776). In his late notebooks of 1887, Nietzsche insists on the need of a social basis to secure the existence of an aristocratic regime. Leisure and other aristocratic dispositions cannot be extended universally because the "industrial masses" require virtues that are exclusive to them.

> Main point of view: that one not consider the task of the superior species as guide for that of the inferior (as Comte does), but that the inferior species serve as the basis on which the superior one rest in order to dedicate itself to its proper task, on which it may elevate itself. The conditions under which a strong and aristocratic species may preserve itself (with respect to spiritual discipline) are the reverse of the ones required by the 'industrial masses', by small shopkeepers in the style of Spencer. That which is available to stronger and more fertile natures, and is the condition for their existence — leisure, adventure, incredulity, and even dissipation –, if it were ready at hand for mediocre natures would necessarily and effectively destroy them. For these what is appropriate is industriousness [*Arbeitsamkeit*], rules, moderation and firm conviction — in sum, the virtues of the herd; by means of them, mediocre persons attain their perfection (NL, KSA 12, 9[44]).

An "Olympian existence," the aristocratic way of life existence defined by Apollo, is not possible without Apollo's prolific espousal with Dionysus. Nietzsche laments modern culture cannot constitute itself as aristocratic. This is due to the prevalence of two ideas: the dignity of the human being and the dignity of labour. These ideas interfere with the decisionist ethics of command and obedience. If the Greeks were able to develop a superior culture they did so by means of the exploitation of slave work. Democratic states, based on popular consent, are incapable of generating an elevated culture.

The formation of the aristocratic ethos assigns capital importance to competition, emulation, and also envy. In "Homer's Competition" he observes that "the greater and more noble the Greek, the more intense burns the fire of ambition, devouring anyone who runs with him on the same lane" (HC, KSA 1, pp. 787f.). He notes that in Greek popular pedagogy "all talent must develop by means of a struggle [*muß sich kämpfend entfalten*]" (HC, KSA 1, p. 789). It is not desirable that the genius overcome his competitors absolutely and consolidate his hegemony. The struggle cannot end with the annihilation of the adversary. *Wettkampf* that leads to *Vernichtungskampf* eliminates competition. Nietzsche observes that in the natural order one witnesses "numerous geniuses that incite themselves mutually towards action." And he sees the "abomination of autocracy" and the practice of ostracism as the core of Hellenic pedagogy.

Many have interpreted this recognition of agonism as Nietzsche's affirmation of equality and democratic balance. According to Hatab and Appel, those who adopt this point of view do not take into account that the universe defined by Nietzsche's essay is the closed circle of the Homeric aristocracy. Agonism does not involve the large subordinate mass explicitly excluded by Homer, even after its gained political predominance as witnessed by Theognis. *Pace* Jensen, Niezsche joins Theognis in rejecting competition between the aristocracy and the plebs (Jensen 2007, p. 327). The agon is essentially "an aristocratic activity, where the few talented types would compete for cultural and political status" (Hatab 2008, p. 258; cf. Appel 1999, pp. 140f.). It cannot be waged against inferior men as it makes no sense to compete with those who do not share one's status – "you cannot wage war against things you hold in contempt" (EH Wise 7; cf. Appel 1999, p. 157).

Theognis, whom Nietzsche regards as the "mouthpiece of the Greek aristocracy", fired the first volley in the "millenium-long battle" fought between the opposed values 'good' and 'evil' (GM I 5).[9] Nietzsche admits that the second value "has had the upper hand for a long time," though he also recognizes that the outcome of this culture war is still "undecided" in some places. The battle is for sure no longer fought in Greek terms. He concedes that aristocratic

---

9 In Curt Paul Janz's opinion, Nietzsche did not take sides and did not identify with Theognis's aristocratic apology (Janz 1987, p. 109; cf. Jensen 2007). But, undoubtedly, when Nietzsche mentions him again in GM, it is clear that he has fully embraced Theognis's point of view.

values were better preserved in Rome, where they became identified with the Roman spirit, in spite of the ascendancy of Jewish values. "Just consider before whom one bows today in Rome as before the quintessential of all the highest values" (GM I 16). The Roman aristocratic spirit is re-ignited in the Italian cities of the Renaissance, and in seventeenth and eighteenth century France, the "last European aristocracy" that would thereafter suffer defeat at the hands of French revolutionaries (GM I 16). Napoleon rises to counteract this revolutionary triumph and saves the aristocratic spirit from that historical debacle. Napoleon appears as "the incarnate problem of the noble ideal in itself [...] Napoleon, this synthesis of an inhuman and a superhuman" (GM I 16; cf. Dombowsky 2007). Hope for the future revival of the aristocratic ideal must be placed in the hands of a Napoleon-like figure.

II

Like Theognis, Nietzsche looks to the future for ways to restore a seat of honour to aristocratic values. And again, like Theognis, he senses the futility of direct political action to reach this end and opts instead for the attainment of cultural hegemony. The new aristocrats must retreat from active politics and abandon the public square. They will cultivate a sense of solidarity working in common to produce the highest human exemplars. An institutional framework to reinforce aristocratic solidarity was already visible in Theognis. He encouraged the formation of closed aristocratic circles gathered around symposia and exclusive clubs (Morris 2003, p. 21). His advice to Kyrnos was the following: "don't ever join the κακοισι, keep a distance from them, and only get together with the ἀγαθων; eat and drink only in their company" (Theognis 1962, pp. 31ff.). Nietzsche went one step further. In the cultural institutions he had in mind, his radicalism demanded of its members "suppression of all ridiculous claims to independent judgment, and the inculcation upon young men of a strict obedience [*strenge Gehorsam*] under the sceptre of genius" (FEI, KSA 1, p. 680). Suppression of subjective individuality went together with the exaltation of the individuality of commanders who demand obedience. In accordance with his individualism, he fixed his attention on heroic super-human figures, like Napoleon and Bismarck, to lead the aristocratic re-constitution he yearned for (Dombowsky 2007).

Following the pioneer work of Walter Kaufmann, the majority of Anglo-American commentators dismiss political readings of Nietzsche's cultural ideals. His preponderant interest was purely cultural and coincided with his own professed anti-politicality. According to these commentators, Nietzsche was not committed to the formation of an aristocratic political regime; his heroes were not "authoritarian, elitist or exploitative" political agents whose aim was to "mobilize the masses;" (NL, KSA 13, 16[39])[10] there is no evidence that he ever took an interest in laying out detailed governmental programs. Those who oppose this interpretation consider it to be an extreme view "that Nietzsche's concern with culture was not also political" (Cameron/Dombowsky 2008, p. 1). I would add that, like Theognis, Nietzsche did not have to engage in overt political struggle, because he was able successfully to hide and disguise it under the culture war he waged against his political adversaries. His task was to prepare the right soil where new commanders would rise as leaders of the aristocratic cultural revival. This meant cultivating exceptional human exemplars whose charismatic authority would overcome the limitations of a bureaucratic authority whose decisions were kept in check by the formal juridical rules demanded by democracy.

In *The Future of our Educational Institutions*, Nietzsche reinforces the idea that a true culture is essentially aristocratic. He thinks that the birthplace of culture, its homeland (*Heimat*), is Greece, and believes it is possible to affirm that the German spirit is "tied to the Greeks by the noblest necessity" (FEI, KSA 1, p. 713). At present, democrats demand a universal expansion of culture and are fanatical opponents of true culture, "one that adheres firmly to the aristocratic nature of the spirit" (FEI, KSA 1, p. 698). Nietzsche explains that the aim of democratic educators is "the emancipation of the masses," a fundamental distortion because what is needed is that they should be put under the "authority of eminent individuals." What democrats intend is the overthrow of "the most sacred order within the realm of the intellect, namely, the serfdom of the masses, their submissive obedience, their instinctive loyalty to the scepter of the genius" (FEI, KSA 1, p. 698). Nietzsche laments also that the enormous advances of popular education have ruined the traditional teaching imparted by the German *Gymnasium*. At present, the *Gymnasium* has become the seat of a spurious *Bildung* (FEI, KSA 1, p. 712). Nietzsche attributes this phenomenon to the fear evoked by "the aristocratic nature of true education" (FEI, KSA 1, p. 710). Democrats reject aristocratic education because they hate what is truly German, and they resent the superiority of individuals in leadership positions, who seek to submit the masses to "a rigid and strict discipline" (FEI, KSA 1,

---

10 In an excellent article, Vanessa Lemm argued that Nietzsche granted to the aristocracy a purely spiritual authority. His aristocrats did not meddle in political affairs because they cared only for the spiritual and cultural elevation of the individual (Lemm 2008, pp. 367f.). In contrast, Manuel Knoll rightly points out that for Nietzsche "the procreation of a higher human type is not primarily to be understood as the concern of an isolated individual, but as a social and political task" (Knoll 2010, p. 21).

p. 710). They think it possible to persuade the masses that they can govern themselves "under the leadership of the state!" (FEI, KSA 1, p. 710)

Nietzsche is not satisfied with acknowledging the flowering of culture in Greece and its decline in the modern world. More than a reform of the *Gymnasium*, and a recommendation that numbers should be drastically reduced, he outlines establishments that will foster the birth of a new aristocracy guided by great leaders. He has precise plans for the functioning of those institutes of high culture, which will become meeting places for his select group of philosophical commanders. They ought to maintain their distance from the large masses to avoid contagion from the decadent culture that encircles them. Similar to the counsel Theognis gives to his disciple Kyrnos, Nietzsche recommends that one ought to prevent the new aristocrats "lose sight of their noble and elevated task due to premature exhaustion, or going astray from the true way" (FEI, KSA 1, p. 729). The institutions he foresees foster a community spirit, and their members must possess a singular disposition – they ought to be "free from the seal of subjectivity, so as to be able to rise above the fluctuating play of the temporal and reflect the eternal and permanent essence of things" (FEI, KSA 1, p. 729). The purposes that assemble the Platonically inspired institutions is the formation of geniuses. It is important to impress on the young who will become part of these institutes that they must leave behind their personal independence because "the most natural and peremptory need of the young is the submission to great leaders and the enthusiastic emulation of their masters" (FEI, KSA 1, pp. 745f.). And he adds:

> All cultural education [*Bildung*] begins with the opposite of what is now celebrated as academic freedom. It begins with obedience, subordination, discipline, and serfdom. And just as a great leader needs followers, also these need of a leader to guide them (FEI, KSA 1, p. 750).

The German spirit, "noble and victorious," and its capacity to lead a cultural restoration, allows Nietzsche to hope for a better future. The triumph of the pseudo-culture espoused by democracy is possible only under the auspices of the state. But the modern state is not the Greek aristocratic state. Greek citizens had "a deep sense of admiration and gratitude, a sentiment that is felt as offensive by modern individuals" (FEI, KSA 1, p. 709). Greeks saw the aristocratic state "not as a border guard, a regulator or supervisor, but as a muscular friend and companion, prepared to go to battle that accompanied it noble, admired and, so to say, celestial friend through harsh reality, and thus deserved gratitude" (FEI, KSA 1, p. 709).

The genesis of a new aristocracy is re-visited by Nietzsche in the works of the middle period when he discusses aristocratic culture and the authority it confers. In HH I, in the section titled "The tyrants of the spirit", he writes: "In the spheres of higher culture there will always have to be a sovereign authority [*Herrschaft*], to be sure – but this sovereign authority will hereafter lie in the hands of the oligarchs of the spirit. Their spatial and political division notwithstanding, they constitute a cohesive society whose members know and recognize each other" (HH I 261). Later, in his notebooks of 1885/86, he again announces a new aristocracy that will be constituted by the possession of philosophical knowledge: "a race of masters, the future rulers of the earth – a new and vast aristocracy founded on a strict self-legislation, in the will of powerful philosophers and tyrant-artists, that will last for millennia" (NL, KSA 12, 2[57]).

In the works of the middle period, Nietzsche considers the search for knowledge as essential to the aristocratic way of life. A contemplative attitude is only possible under one condition: liberation from work. In HH I he writes: "as at all times, so now too, men are divided into the slaves and the free; for he who does not have two-thirds of his day to himself is a slave, let him be what he may be otherwise: statesman, businessman, official, scholar" (HH I 283). This contemplative attitude is incompatible with the speed demanded by modern times. For Nietzsche's aristocratic mind, only the mentality of slaves accords with the urge of being busy all the time: "from lack of repose our civilization is turning into a new barbarism" (HH I 285).

A passage from *Daybreak* shows the Germanic punctiliousness with which he set rules of good behaviour for his new aristocrats. The comportment he demands is reminiscent of Aristotle's description of the *megalopsychos* in the *Nicomachean Ethics*.

> A person of aristocratic habits [*adeliger Sitte*], man or woman, does not like to fall into a chair as if utterly exhausted; where everybody else makes himself comfortable, when travelling on the railway for example, he avoids leaning against his back; he seems not to get tired if he stands for hours on his feet at court; he orders his house, not with a view to comfort, but in a specious and dignified manner, as though it were the home of grander (and taller) beings; he responds to a provocation with restraint and a clear head, not as though horrified, crushed, mortified, breathless, in the manner of the plebeian. Just as he knows to present the appearance of being at all times in possession of high physical strength, so, through maintaining a constant cheerfulness and civility even in painful situations, he also wants to preserve the impression that his soul and spirit are equal to every danger and every surprise (D 201).

The set of habits that Nietzsche wishes to inculcate on the aristocrats of the future do not correspond to virtues that respect the interest of others, or virtues that instill love for one's neighbour. What he has in mind are habits that strengthen the control one can exert over one's actions and that may boost one's self-esteem. Others should be made aware of the excess of the power one possesses. Aristocratic culture "breathes power [*Macht*]." At a minimum, it demands "the semblance of the feeling of power" so as to be able to intimidate others (D 201; cf. D 386). The spectacle offered by the submission of subordinates increases self-esteem and breeds a "feeling of superiority" (D 201). In his notebooks of 1887 one finds the same connection between the aristocratic spirit and the ability to wield power: "A culture of the exception, of experimentation, danger and nuance leads to a wealth of forces [*Kräfte-Reichtums*]: that is the aim of every aristocratic culture [*Cultur*]. Only when a culture has as its disposal excessive force may it, exactly for this reason, generate a culture of luxury [*Luxus-Cultur*]" (NL, KSA 12, 9[139]). To instill an attitude of contempt with regard to the herd and its inertia, is part of the education of the new aristocrats. The herd is to be despised for readily surrendering to the power of the state and sacrificing individual freedom.

> The ideal of the human herd [...] against this I defend aristocratism [*den Aristokratismus*]. A society that preserves consideration, and a délicatesse with respect to freedom, must be seen as an exception and ought to confront a power [*Macht*] from which it must distinguish itself, towards which it must maintain a hostile attitude and consider it its inferior [*herabblickt*] [...] (NL, KSA 13, 11[140]).

Nietzsche believes he is *ad portas* of a new epoch. Free spirits like him have now the opportunity to recruit new aristocrats among those born into noble families and those who have received a noble education. The task is made easier because the new recruits now bring with them virtues unknown to the Dorian aristocrats Theognis had to deal with. Nietzsche acknowledges that the children of noble families who have kept alive the spirit of mediaeval feudalism possess ingrained virtues that far exceed the disposition of the noblest Greeks.

> Loyalty, magnanimity, care for one's reputation: these three united in a single disposition — we call aristocratic [*adelig, vornehm, edel*], and in this quality we excel the Greeks [...] To grasp how, from the viewpoint of our own aristocracy, which is still chivalrous and feudal in nature, the disposition of even the noblest Greeks has to be seen of a lower sort and, indeed, hardly decent (D 199).

In the works of the middle period, Nietzsche assumes that both birth and meritorious behaviour may bestow aristocratic status. Later on, the meritocratic conception of aristocracy recedes to give way to an aristocracy by birth (Abbey 2000, p. 98).[11] In the notebooks of August 1885 one reads:

---

11 Contrary to Abbey, Angela Holzer believes that Nietzsche becomes increasingly skeptical "of the biological foundations of the existing *Adel* as a separate class," and that he therefore "shifts the focus from the biological foundations of a distinguished but powerless class to the

> There exists only the nobility of birth, the nobility of blood. (I do not refer to the prefix 'von' or to the Almanach de Gotha: a parenthesis for asses). When one refers of the 'aristocrats of the spirit' it is not for lack of reason to hide something; as is well-known it is a favourite term among ambitious Jews. Spirit alone does not make noble; there must be something additional to ennoble the spirit. What then is required? Blood (NL, KSA 11, 41[3]; cf. Ottmann 1999, p. 271).

Nietzsche condemns Christianity for its rejection of traditional eugenic practices. Eugenics is now seen as the most adequate means to generate aristocratic elites. He shares Theognis's disappointment when the poet lamented the fact that an impoverished aristocracy caved in to the charm of money and allowed its blood to be mixed with that of the new rich. Theognis writes: "To breed a ram, an ass or a horse, Kyrnos, we select a thoroughbred; but an ἐσθλὸς does not hesitate to marry the κακὴν daughter of a κακου father if he is given lots of goods, and a girl does not scorn the bed of a κακου if he is wealthy" (Theognis 1962, pp. 183–188). This is a lesson that became ingrained in Nietzsche's mind. In his notebooks of 1885-6, Nietzsche indicates that great discipline is required to breed "a new, vast aristocracy" (NL, KSA 12, 2[57]; cf. BGE 203, 211, 212). His radicalism demands the generation of an aristocracy based on blood. This is the radical *tabula rasa*, the pure and absolute point of departure, for the delivery of a new aristocracy.

Conclusion

Lawrence Hatab acknowledges the existence of a political language in Nietzsche, and that this language suggests "an aristocratic, authoritarian political arrangement" (Hatab 2008, p. 249). Nietzsche approves of the domination and exploitation of a mass of workers as the condition for the possibility of aristocratic excellence (cf. BGE 258). Excellence can only be generated through the imposition of a hierarchical order. In contrast, democracy opposes authority and order, and reduces to what Nietzsche calls "misarchism", the terms he coins to indicate the opposition "against everything that rules and desires to rule" (GM II 12). Hatab does not fail to mention Nietzsche's chilling assertion in the *Antichrist* that makes explicit his preference for the elimination of "the weak and the failures" in order to promote superior life (A 2). He can thus categorical-

---

political dimension, that is to political power and agency implied by the term *Aristokratie*" (Holzer 2007, p.381). But in *BGE*, Nietzsche clearly associates the authority of aristocratic values (*der Herrschaft aristokratischer Werte*) with belief in *Herkunft* (*BGE* 32), which has to be read as pointing to biological foundations.

ly conclude that "Nietzsche saw democracy and liberalism as forms of cultural decadence and obstacles to a higher politics" (Hatab 2008, pp. 249f.).

In spite of this conclusion, Hatab re-affirms his aim of using Nietzsche's thought to promote democratic politics. He believes that Nietzsche's critique against essentialism and rationalism, and his perspectivist epistemology, may be used to overcome leveling and also exclusionary practices that result from the modern democratic experience. Principally, Hatab identifies Nietzsche's agonism as a key ingredient to "prepare a 'post-modern' vision of democratic life," that is fully inclusive and affirms life (Hatab 2008, p. 250). In spite of the criticisms leveled against a post-modern Nietzsche, Hatab insists that, though Nietzsche himself was not a democrat, "in the spirit of his own thought he could have or should have been an advocate for democracy, but not in terms of traditional political theories" (Hatab 2008, p. 251).

The argument employed by Hatab to defend his Nietzschean view of democracy assumes, first, that "democratic elitism" is not an oxymoron (Hatab 2008, p. 225). This is possible because, as he himself acknowledges, he operates with a model of democracy derived from Robert Dahl, which is to be distinguished from the more substantive republican model that is visible in classical Athens and the Italian cities of the Renaissance (Hatab 1995, p. 56).[12] This is a model of formal democracy that observes the participation of the people with suspicion and that need not "imply any kind of substantive or intrinsic equality" (Hatab 1995, p. 57). Hatab also maintains that a democratic theory could benefit from Nietzsche's critique of egalitarianism: and he further points out that democratic practice cannot abstain from implementing a representative function. Democracy also assigns merit, discriminates in its rewards and establishes lines of authority. It is thereby impossible to deny that democratic egalitarianism combines with certain aristocratic elements. In this limited sense Schlegel could be right when he wrote: "A perfect republic would have to be more than just democratic, it would have to be at the same time aristocratic" (Friedrich Schlegel, cit. in Conant 2001, p. 186). Thus, Nietzsche's aristocratism, which runs parallel to his acerbic critique of democracy, would paradoxically contribute to strengthen a democratic politics. What Hatab does not take into account is the radicalism of Nietzsche's aristocratism. As I showed above, Nietzsche's radicalism, which seeks to subvert the cultural basis of democracy, makes it unimaginable that Nietzsche could be recruited in the service of democracy. No re-interpretation or re-description will allow it.

---

[12] Dahl coincides with Schumpeter and his economic conception of democracy according to which democracy is only a means and not an intrinsic end (Taylor 2012).

Second, Hatab limits what he perceives as Nietzsche's contribution to the enhancement of democracy to the cultural sphere. He acknowledges that his aristocratism cannot be extended to the political sphere. As a result, Nietzsche has nothing to say with respect to the "formation of institutions, actual political practices, the justification of coercion, and the extent of sovereignty" (Hatab 2008, p. 255). His aristocratism is only defensible with regard to creativity and excellence. Hatab insists that Nietzsche's' conception of culture is "compatible with, and even constitutive of, much of democratic politics and life" (Hatab 1995, p. 256). This presupposes the possibility of separating the realms of the cultural and the political. It also presupposes not taking into account Nietzsche's radicalism. But it is precisely his radicalism that disallows the separation of culture as a sphere absolutely separate from the political. Even though Nietzsche explicitly re-affirms an anti-political posture, he does so adopting the same strategy assumed by Theognis. As noted by Jensen, when confronted to an upheaval that appears imminent and disastrous in political terms, Theognis seeks to produce a cultural change that is sufficiently deep so as to undermine the foundations of the new regime. He believes that this may be attained, not by direct participation in political affairs, but through a cultural revolution that strengthens the aristocratic values, norms and affinities now threatened (Jensen 2007, p. 326). Nietzsche adopts the same strategy. He does not see himself participating politically to bring forth institutional change, something that accords with his genuine and sustained anti-political stand. More generally, he is deeply convinced that radical political interventions can only succeed if one proceeds indirectly through the attainment of cultural hegemony. This is the radical lesson he owes to Theognis.

Bibliography

Abbey, Ruth (2000): *Nietzsche's Middle Period*. Oxford: Oxford University Press.
Appel, Frederick (1999): *Nietzsche Contra Democracy*. Ithaca, London: Cornell University Press.
Arnheim, M. T. W. (1977): *Aristocracy in Greek Society*. Plymouth: Thames & Hudson.
Bauch, Bruno (1921): "Friedrich Nietzsche und das aristokratische Ideal". In: Max Oehler (ed.): *Den Manen Friedrich Nietzsches*. Munich: Musarion Verlag.
Berkowitz, Peter (1995): *Nietzsche. The Ethics of an Immoralist*. Cambridge, Mass.: Harvard University Press.
Buffiere, Félix (1956): *Le Mythes d'Homère et la Pensée Grecque*. Paris: Les Belles Lettres.
Cameron, Frank/Dombowsky, Don (2008): *Political Writings of Nietzsche: An Edited Anthology*. London: Palgrave Macmillan.
Cancik, Hubert (2000): *Nietzsche Antike*. 2nd edition. Stuttgart, Weimar: J. B. Metzler.

Conant, James (2001): "Nietzsche's Perfectionism: A Reading of *Schopenhauer as Educator*". In: Richard Schacht (ed.): *Nietzsche's Postmoralism: Essays on Nietzsche's Prelude to Philosophy's Future*. Cambridge: Cambridge University Press

Detwiler, Bruce (1990): *Nietzsche and the Politics of Aristocratic Radicalism*. Chicago, London: University of Chicago Press.

Dombowsky, Don (2004): *Nietzsche's Machiavellian Politics*. London: Palgrave-Macmillan.

Dombowsky, Don (2007): "Nietzsche as Bonapartist". In Herman W. Siemens/Vasti Roodt (eds.): *Nietzsche, Power and Politics. Rethinking Nietzsche's Legacy for Political Thought*. Berlin, New York, de Gruyter, pp. 347–369.

Duncker, Max (1856): *Die Geschichte der Griechen*. Berlin: Duncker & Humblot.

Grote, George (1869): *A History of Greece*. London: John Murray.

Hatab, Lawrence J. (1995): *A Nietzschean Defense of Democracy: An Experiment in Postmodern Politics*. Chicago: Open Court.

Hatab, Lawrence J. (2008): *Nietzsche's* On the Genealogy of Morality. *An Introduction*. Cambridge: Cambridge University Press.

Holzer, Angela (2007): "'Nietzsche Caesar': The Turn against Dynatic Succession and Caesarism in Nietzsche's Late Works". In: Herman W. Siemens/Vasti Roodt (eds.): *Nietzsche, Power and Politics. Rethinking Nietzsche's Legacy for Political Thought*. Berlin, New York: de Gruyter, pp. 371–391.

Jaeger, Werner (1959): *Paideia. Die Formierung des Griechischen Menschen*. 4th edition. Berlin: de Gruyter.

Janz, Curt Paul (1978): *Friedrich Nietzsche. Biographie*. Munich: Carl Hanser.

Jensen, Anthony K. (2007): "Anti-Politicality and Agon in Nietzsche's Philology.". In: In: Herman W. Siemens/Vasti Roodt (eds.): *Nietzsche, Power and Politics. Rethinking Nietzsche's Legacy for Political Thought*. Berlin, New York: de Gruyter, pp. 319–345.

Kaufmann, Walter (1968): *Nietzsche: Philosopher, Psychologist, Anti-Christ*. 3rd edition. New York: Vintage.

Knoll, Manuel (2010): "Nietzsches 'aristokratischer Radikalismus'. Seine Konzeption des Menschen, der Verteilungsgerechtigkeit und des Staates". In: Hans-Martin Schönherr-Mann (ed.): *Der Wille zur Macht und die 'große Politik' – Friedrich Nietzsches Staatsverständnis, Series Staatsverständnisse*. Rüdiger Voigt (ed.). Baden-Baden: Nomos, pp. 35–67.

Lemm, Vanessa (2008): "Nietzsches Vision einer 'neuen Aristokratie'". In: *Deutsche Zeitschrift für Philosophie* 56, pp. 365–383.

Martin, Alfred von (1941): *Nietzsche und Burckhardt*. Munich: Verlag Ernst Reinhardt.

Morris, Ian (1996): "The Strong Principle of Equality and the Archaic Origins of Greek Democracy". In: Josiah Ober/Charles Hedrick (eds.): *Demokratia: A Conversation on Democracies, Ancient and Modern*. Princeton: Princeton University Press, pp. 19–48.

Müller, Karl Otfried (1824): *Die Dorier*. Breslau: J. Max.

Müller, Karl Otfried (1839): *The History and Antiquities of the Doric Race*. Henry Tufnnel and George Cornewall Lewis (trans.). London: John Murray.

Negri, Antimo (1985): *Friedrich Nietzsche. Teognide di Megara*. Rome: Laterza.

Oehler, Max (1921): *Den Manen Friedrich Nietzsches*. Munich: Musarion Verlag.

Ottmann, Henning (1999): *Philosophie und Politik bei Nietzsche*. 2nd edition. Berlin, New York: de Gruyter.

Otto, Walter (1954): *The Homeric Gods: The Spiritual Significance of the Greek Religion*. London: Thames and Hudson.

Pâdurean, Vasile (2008): *Spiel, Kunst, Schein: Nietzsche als ursprüngliche Denker*. Stuttgart: Kohlhammer.
Plaß, Hermann Gottlob (1852): *Die Tyrannis in ihren beiden Perioden bei den alten Griechen: dargestellt nach Ursachen, Verlauf und Wirkungen*. Leipzig: Gumprecht.
Porter, James I. (2000): *Nietzsche and the Philology of the Future*. Stanford: Stanford University Press.
Riehl, Alois (1901): *Friedrich Nietzsche: Der Kunstler und der Denker*. 4th edition. Stuttgart: Frommanns Verlag.
Rochette, Désiré-Raoul (1815): *Histoire critique de l'établissement des colonies grecques*. Paris: Treuttel et Würtz.
Schweizer, Frank (2007): "Adel und Volk in Nietzsches Lateinischer Schrift *De Theognide Megarensi*". In: *Nietzsche Studien* 36, pp. 355–366.
Taylor, Charles (2012): *Democracia Republicana/Republican Democracy*. Santiago de Chile: LOM Ediciones.
Theognis (1962): *Poèmes Élègiaques*. Jean Carrière (ed.). 2nd edition: Paris: Société d'édition Les Belles Lettres.
Vogt, Ernst (1962): "Nietzsche und der Wettkampf Homers". In: *Antike und Abendland* 11, pp. 103–113.
Welcker, Friedrich Gottlieb (1826): *Theognidis Reliquae. Novo ordine disposuit, commentationem criticam et notas adiecit*. Frankfurt: H.L. Broenner.
Young, Julian (2010): *Friedrich Nietzsche. A Philosophical Biography*. Cambridge: Cambridge University Press.

Don Dombowsky
Aristocratic Radicalism as a Species of Bonapartism: Preliminary Elements

> *Corte is the city of Napoleon's conception.... Does it not seem that a pilgrimage there would be an appropriate preparation for the "Will to Power. Toward a Revaluation of all Values"?* — (BVN – 1886, 734. Brief an Heinrich Köselitz 16/08/1886. www.nietzschesource.org)

The imperial government of Napoleon Bonaparte has been described as a military dictatorship. (Goltz 1887, p. 74). Nietzsche recognises that militarism is a defining structural feature of Bonapartism as a political movement or ideology, ennobling this feature as a "cure" for "decadence": "The cure ... militarism, beginning with Napoleon" (WP 41; NL, 15[31], KSA 13, p. 427). In its origins the Bonapartist state was antiparliamentarian. It was an autocracy supported by popular consent through a plebiscite backed by universal manhood suffrage which spoke for order and social equality against the "chaos" and "anarchy" wrought by the French Revolution. The doctrine of a centralised executive authority legitimated by a plebiscite was "the pillar of Bonapartism". In such a political arrangement parliament operated as a mere façade with "no power to change the constitution or to interfere with the executive" (Fisher 1908, p. 22) as the regime mutated from republic to empire.

Instead of describing Bonapartism as a "military dictatorship", Frédéric Bluche considers it more accurate to define Bonapartism as "democratic absolutism" (Bluche 1980, p. 88), which is to say, as "Caesarism", a term coined during the reign of Napoleon III which denotes a combination of democracy and absolutism. Bonapartism has also been defined as a doctrine in which political power is viewed as a quality necessarily achieved through a *coup d'état* or usurpation as Benjamin Constant was to observe (Constant 1989, pp. 90f.); that it is "synonymous with the seizure of power in a *coup d'état*" (Woloch 2004, p. 29). It is said that Bonapartism derived "its force and vitality" from Napoleon's genius (Fisher 1908, p. 7), which implies that it could not have existed without Napoleon; that it was a political power which legitimated itself through his personal ability, talent or proficiency – or *virtù* in the Renaissance sense – thus legitimation as self-legitimation, based on personal characteristics and qualifications. Napoleon acknowledged this fact when he said: "I found the crown of France in the gutter and I picked it up" (Herold 1955, p. 276).

Yet Bonapartism's underlying dogmas of legitimacy are not merely personal and democratic but also dynastic and religious. Bonapartism is also synonymous with "the formation of an hereditary empire" (Woloch 2004, p. 29) which is consequently consecrated by religion when Napoleon wins the support of the Roman Catholic Church for his imperial reign. The forces of monarchy and religion notably combine when Napoleon is crowned Emperor by Pope Pius VII on 2 December, 1804 in the Notre Dame Cathedral in Paris; as Gregorovius narrates it, "taking the imperial crown from the hands of the pope, and placing it on his head with his own hands". (Gregorovius 1855, p. 385). Thus it can be said that Bonapartism is an illegally constituted, miltaristic, autocratic power that legitimates itself through democratic or plebiscitary consent and the monarchical (hereditary, dynastic), religious "ritual exercise of sovereignty" (Foucault 1979, p. 217).

It demonstrates Nietzsche's structural understanding of Bonapartism that he rightly recognises that Napoleon legitimated his power through his own *virtù* and genius as a "first-rank organising power" (NL, 14[2], KSA 10, p. 476) in governing and military strategy; through criminal illegality (conspiracy and *coup d'état*); through religious dissimulation (HH I 472) and simulation of the symbolic power of the monarchy (NL, 25[110], KSA 11, p. 41); and through plebiscitary affirmation or, more precisely, plebiscitary *belief* or *faith* which is not denigrated by Nietzsche and should be distinguished from "the public" or "public opinion" in Nietzsche's consistently pejorative use of those terms. Nietzsche's recognition of these strategies of legitimation is not simply structurally descriptive but also celebratory and reverential in the face of "the two grave crimes committed against Europe: the formation of the new German Empire and the ruin of Napoleonic thought". (Bianquis 1933, p. 54). The *virtù* which Napoleon possessed was "moraline-free" (*moralinfreie*), the kind of personal "virtue" cultivated by the criminal in "the age of the Renaissance" (WP 740; NL, 10[50], KSA 12, p. 480).[1] Since Napoleon was a "posthumous man" (NL, 9[76], KSA 12, p. 375), a representative of the Renaissance according to Nietzsche (following Stendhal's and Taine's descriptions), he was also, according to Nietzschean codes, criminal, immoralistic and anti-Christian, with his antipathy for "Christian virtues" (NL, 25[175], KSA 11, p. 60),[2] a Dionysian destroyer of boundaries. The "perfection" or "completeness" of a Napoleon, Nietzsche writes, is such that his criminality is accompanied by a "joyful con-

---

[1] See, also, A 2: "Not contentment, but more power; not peace at all, but war; not virtue, but proficiency (virtue in the Renaissance style, virtù, virtue free of moralic acid)."
[2] On a similar wavelength, Germaine de Staël observed: "The duration of the power of Bonaparte was a perpetual lesson of immorality." (De Staël 2008, p. 520)

science" (NL, 6[267], KSA 9, p. 267). "The same with the great Renaissance man! The worm of conscience is for the rabble and a true corruption of noble-mindedness" (NL, 25[259], KSA 11, p. 79). Bonapartism is the invention of criminal genius. The personal sanction[3] or legitimacy it receives as a political movement is the auspicious result of a fateful, "involuntary" overflowing of deeds and "physical accomplishments", an expansion of ecstatic possibilities. Geniuses, great men, such as Napoleon "are explosive material in whom tremendous energy has been accumulated." The "pressure of the energies" they bear is so powerful that it "forbids" them from acting with any "care" or "prudence", or legality. Napoleon was stronger and more mature than his epoch simply because he was "the heir of a... longer, older civilisation than that which was going up in dust and smoke in France"; neither an "heir" of the French Revolution nor of the France of the Bourbon Kings. "And because Napoleon was different... he became master here, he alone was master here" (TI Skirmishes 44).[4]

Napoleon "was a piece of 'return to nature'", as Nietzsche understands it while negating "nature" in its Christian, Romantic or Rousseauian sense: "a going-up... into a high, free, even frightful nature and naturalness, such as plays with great tasks, is permitted to play with them" (TI Skirmishes 48), "a going-up to the naturalness of the Renaissance" (TI Skirmishes 49).[5] As "one of the greatest continuators of the Renaissance" (GS 362), Napoleon must, following Nietzsche's description of the culture of the Renaissance in *The Anti-Christ*, represent the "revaluation of Christian values", the "attempt... to bring about the victory of... noble values" (A 61).[6]

---

3 Friedrich Gundolf stated: "[Napoleon] appears to us as the last ruler of the world based on personal sanction... and only such a world can still conceive true fame in the ancient or Renaissance sense". (Gundolf 1928, p. 301)
4 Nietzsche's theory of the "genius" (e.g. Napoleon) expressed here in *Twilight of the Idols* is at odds with what he states in NL, 26[28], KSA 11, p. 155 and WP 877; NL, 10[31], KSA 12, p. 471 where Napoleon is conceived as unthinkable without the French Revolution.
5 See, also, NL, 9[116], KSA 12, p. 402: "I too speak of a 'return to nature': even though it is not a 'return' but rather an 'elevation' – into the strong, pure as the sun, terrible nature and naturalness of the human being, which may play with great tasks as they would become tired of the small and would feel disgust. – Napoleon was a 'return to nature' in terms of tactics and above all in strategic terms."
6 Lou Salomé comments that "For Nietzsche... it seemed of greatest importance that Napoleon inherited the tyrannical spirit of the Renaissance and transplanted it to Corsica where it could be preserved intact in the wildness and age-old customs derived from its forebears; with its primal energy, it finally emerged to subjugate modern Europe, which provided it with a different kind of space than Italy has offered for the release of energy. To Nietzsche's last phase belongs his admiration for the great Corsican as well as for the Italian Renaissance". (Salomé 2001, p. 109)

Nietzsche follows Goethe's Spinozist interpretation of Napoleon as a product of practical activity and Dostoevsky's psychological testimony on the Siberian convict, the durable criminal type. Goethe "had no greater experience" than his encounter with "that ens realissimum called Napoleon" to whom he felt naturally related as to no one else. Thus Goethe's experience of Napoleon, as Nietzsche elaborates it, was of a

> strong, highly cultured human being, skilled in all physical accomplishments, who keeping himself in check[7] and having reverence for himself dares to allow himself the whole compass and wealth of naturalness, who is strong enough for his freedom; a man of tolerance, not out of weakness, but out of strength, because he knows how to employ to his advantage what would destroy an average nature; a man to whom nothing is forbidden, except it be weakness, whether that weakness be called vice or virtue.... A spirit thus emancipated stands in the midst of the universe with a joyful and trusting fatalism,[8] in the faith that only what is separate and individual may be rejected, that in the totality everything is redeemed and affirmed – he no longer denies.... such a faith is the highest of all possible faiths: I have baptised it with the name Dionysus. (TI Skirmishes 49)[9]

Napoleon is the "most famous case" in which "a human being proves stronger than society". Because he is among "innovators of the spirit" he is "close to the type of which the criminal is the perfection", a perspective which coincides with the well-known view of Raskolnikov in Dostoevsky's *Crime and Punishment*. As both the innovator and the criminal are aberrant forms of existence, "they... feel the terrible chasm which divides them from all that is traditional and held in honour" (TI Skirmishes 45).[10] The personal claim of the "Caesar"

---

[7] For Nietzsche's remarks on Napoleon's self-control and mastery of his passions see, for example, NL, 6[94], KSA 9, p. 218 and NL, 38[20], KSA 11, p. 617.

[8] This characterisation of Napoleon's spirit effectively negates Nietzsche's critique of Napoleon's "belief in himself and in his star", his "almost insane fatalism", made in HH I 164. It is an echo of Nietzsche's own idea of *amor fati*, the love of fate.

[9] Seung interprets this passage from *Twilight of the Idols* in the following manner: "Nietzsche names Napoleon Bonaparte as the greatest naturalist and realist. He portrays the impressive stature of this Dionysian hero by using Goethe's encounter with him.... Napoleon has become the most real being because he is one with Mother Nature.... By virtue of his union with this ultimate reality, Napoleon Bonaparte stands as a Dionysian hero par excellence.... For his Dionysian faith, Nietzsche singles out Napoleon as the only one to be called the superman without any qualifications.... Only Cesare Borgia comes close to this awesome title in Nietzsche's ranking. He refers to Borgia as a 'a kind of superman'." (Seung 2005, p. 348-349) Ernst Bertram explains that for Nietzsche, "Napoleon is nature – ancient nature, living antiquity – thus his unparalleled exceptional status among Nietzsche's historical valuations". (Bertram 2009, pp. 175f.)

[10] On Nietzsche's view of Napoleon and the question of "honour" see, for example, NL, 8[107], KSA 9, p. 405.

to a state of exception and immunity from the law reflects "a personal interest in advocating and even abetting a bolder private morality" which accepts no external, legal or moral restrictions. This is a portrait of Napoleon himself: the criminal author "of the spiritual colonisation and origin of new states and communities" (GS 23).

Nietzsche's visualisation of this great representative type, Napoleon, is a visualisation of the Bonapartist regime itself, a regime which founds itself on criminal illegality (conspiracy and *coup d'état*). As Nietzsche clearly understands, "Catiline"[11] is structurally "the antecedent form of every Caesar", of all Caesarism, of Bonapartism.[12] As Nietzsche expands on this representative criminal typology he writes: "every genius knows as one of the phases of his development the 'Catilinarian existence', a feeling of… revolt against everything which already is, which is no longer becoming" (TI Skirmishes 45). Napoleon knew this Catilinarian existence at the Château de Saint-Cloud where the raucous *coup d'état* of 18 Brumaire transpired on 9 November, 1799.

Nietzsche's recognition of conspiracy as a necessary structural trait of Bonapartism is at the same time an affirmation of a political strategy. A philosopher who argues for exceptional types must also argue for exceptional measures. Thus Pierre Klossowski is correct when he says, "as Nietzsche's thought evolved, it abandoned the strictly speculative realm in order to adopt, if not simulate, the preliminary elements of a conspiracy". (Klossowski 1997, p. xv). As Nietzsche's thought becomes increasingly political he becomes increasingly positive about the transformative role Napoleon played in European history. He even advocates, on the terrain of the revaluation of all values, plainly Napoleonic ideas such as the political and economic union of Europe. If Leo Strauss is right that what "Nietzsche was waiting for was a new Napoleon" (Strauss 1967, p. 5) then it seems reasonable to assume that Nietzsche was both explicitly and implicitly agitating for the emergence of a Bonapartist, Caesaristic regime, agitating for conditions to bring about its constitution, promoting its political tactics (dissimulation), forms of legitimacy, iconography, political ancestry and institutions. Nietzsche's Aristocratic Radicalism is a species of Bonapartism. The two are fundamentally related ideologies. Aristocratic Radicalism walks in the footsteps of Bonapartism with no other model ultimately than what Bonapartism took for itself: the *imperium Romanum*.

---

11 Catiline refers to Lucius Sergius Catilina, the Roman patrician who conspired against the Roman Republic.
12 As Bertram explains, "Catiline, according to Nietzsche, is the preliminary form of existence of every Caesar: all legitimate greatness must first traverse the stage of disreputable and criminal illegality." (Bertram 2009, p. 11)

Nietzsche ceases his criticism of Napoleon between the autumns of 1885 and 1886 in his notebooks and after 1882 in his published writings (NL, 2[101], KSA 12, p. 111 and GS 282). Though before this period as a declared "free spirit" he would violate his own code of independence were he to follow Napoleon,[13] he still expresses admiration and fascination for the Emperor, ambivalence and contradiction, as expressed in the numerous "Napoleonic dicta and psychologica" found in his notebooks (cf. Bertram 2009, p. 182): Napoleon "lacked... greatness of... soul (magnanimity)" (NL, 25[110], KSA 11, p. 40), yet "in words and deeds paid tribute to the nobler drives and thus won for himself their splendour" (NL, 4[301], KSA 9, p. 175). Napoleon possessed the

> mixed, impure character of artists: ambitious and ruthless; in furious rivalry against everything that has a reputation... against everything that is valuable and admirable... slanderously pernicious... but around him it is as if one breathed a purer air, because he knows what he wants and does not fool himself. (NL, 4[66], KSA 9, p. 115)

And while he may have lacked "noblesse of character" (WP 1026; NL, 7[27], KSA 10, p. 251), Napoleon belonged "to another type of being, in which the force to calculate, the power to combine, the ability to work are unspeakably more developed than in us" (NL, 25[110], KSA 11, p. 40). But, more specifically, Nietzsche's criticism that Napoleon was without "inner perfection" (NL, 25[278], KSA 11, p. 83) because self-doubt, or self-scepticism, was not in his character,[14] or because he fanatically and fatalistically succumbed "to belief in his 'star' or 'destiny'",[15] or that he was, like Bismarck, "corrupted by power"

---

13 A sentiment clearly articulated by Nietzsche in NL, 6[71], KSA 9, p. 213 and NL, 6[78], KSA 9, p. 215

14 Tom Stern argues, though it should not be taken as Nietzsche's definitive position and a reason for a complete rejection of the Emperor, that "Nietzsche accuses Napoleon [...] of not seeking out conflict. [Nietzsche's] accusation is that Napoleon did not experience inner conflict... he acts instinctively and without any self-doubt" and thus was not as "'free' as Caesar." (Stern 2009, p. 97)

15 Steven Englund claims that Nietzsche rejected Napoleon for this reason and believed that "Napoleon, to be consistent with himself, should not have attributed his successes to anything other than his talent and will", certainly not to any "star" or "destiny". "It was [this] failure in Napoleon's capacity for self-understanding that thus brought his ruin" (Englund, 2004, p. 535 n. 67). But after 1878 (HH I 164), Nietzsche will never testify that Napoleon was ruled by anything other than his "personal interest" (NL; 25[110], KSA 11, p. 40). Rather, Napoleon is the "legislator" who "obeys his own commandments", who is "above the law", creating "a God for himself, in his own image." Napoleon "acts as if he were the measure of all things, with the inexperience of a lonely shepherd who is surrounded with sheep only. His sore point is that people do not want to believe him, while he believes himself: and thus his imagination becomes cruel and sinister and he creates hell for those who do not believe in him. His lack of education keeps him from imagining how passion comes into being and from seeing himself

(NL, 7[46], KSA 10, p. 257), is mitigated by Nietzsche's Goethean inspired perception of Napoleon as an individual guided by a singularity of purpose (and thus a representative of antiquity), a "representative of great personal goals" (NL, 26[196], KSA 11, p. 201), and revised when he includes Napoleon among "stronger spirits" who are masters of their passions and drives,[16] and revalued when he recognises in the "appearance of Napoleon" the "main event of the last millenium" (NL, 35[65], KSA 11, p. 539). And while Nietzsche does not abandon his fascination for Napoleon as a type (the character and psychology of this type), a "living type" (NL, 7[119], KSA 10, p. 282), the "type of the great ambitious one" (WP 751; NL, 14[97], KSA 13, p. 273),[17] an "inventive, constantly striving" being (NL, 1[99], KSA 9, p. 27), who in certain respects may be compared to that Dionysian monster Zarathustra, he increasingly exhibits interest in and fidelity to the "underlying structures" of the Napoleonic empire; the social, political and institutional features of the empire that may be resuscitated or reborn. Invoking the terminological distinction Hazareesingh makes in his book, *The Legend of Napoleon*, it can be said that Nietzsche makes the transition from "Napoleonism... the sentimental identification with the Emperor" to "Bonapartism... the belief in a political system governed by Napoleonic ideas and institutions." (Hazareesingh 2004, p. 210).

Nietzsche's political philosophy, his Aristocratic Radicalism, is neither fascist nor liberal democratic but is rather a species of Bonapartism. In my view, the link to Napoleon (and by extension to the Renaissance) produces the only truly coherent reading of Nietzsche's political thought. Nietzsche refers to no other political figure – neither Alcibiades, Julius Caesar, Friedrich II, Cesare Borgia nor Bismarck – as frequently as he does to Napoleon. What is significant also is that when Nietzsche refers to these other political figures, with the exception of Bismarck, whom he ultimately opposes in 1888, we are told virtually nothing about their political philosophies. Rather Nietzsche speaks of their admirable levels of self-mastery and self-control. Alcibiades, Caesar and Friedrich II all demonstrate "a real mastery and subtlety in waging war against oneself"

---

once objectively: he never stands above himself... completely egoistical." (NL, 6 [229], KSA 9, p. 257ff.) Napoleon, in part, saw it this way as well as he stated in a letter to his brother Jérôme (King of Westphalia) in 1805: "What I am, I owe to strength of will, character, application and daring." (See Herold 1955, p. 43)

16 See NL, 38[20], KSA 11, p. 617 where Nietzsche writes, "For stronger spirits, however, it is required to be...a passionate person but also the <u>master</u> of one's passions.... Just as Napoleon... let his anger bark and roar at times and then, just as suddenly, silenced it, thus should do the strong spirit with his wild dogs ...." And NL, 7[275], KSA 9, p. 374: "Napoleon, who lusts for <u>power</u>, represents the Stoic type seen from within."

17 See, also, NL, 25[199], KSA 11, p. 66, where Napoleon is placed among "truly great men".

(BGE 200); Caesar, "the maximum of authority and discipline towards oneself" (TI Skirmishes 38), "that subtle machine working at the highest pressure which is called genius" (TI Skirmishes 31). We understand that they are all "active" natures, Borgia even a kind of *Übermensch* (TI Skirmishes 37). Beyond such descriptions we understand that Borgia represents the *healthy immorality* of the Renaissance and the "revaluation of Christian values" (A 61) while the Hohenstaufen Holy Roman Emperor Friedrich II is "an atheist and enemy of the church" (EH Z 4) who advocates "friendship with Islam" (A 60). All of these figures are closely related to and admired by Nietzsche but Napoleon stands out because he represents for Nietzsche more than merely a type or simply another anti-Christian. He is unique among political figures, again with the exception of Bismarck, praised in Nietzsche's writings because when he is discussed by Nietzsche we are provided with a glimpse of his political ideas and of the way he governed and we recognise that Nietzsche typically glorifies him: his imperialistic geopolitical vision of a unified Europe, the way he used religion in ruling, his aristocratic conception of society, his militarism, the fact that he personified power, the will to power.

But not all of Nietzsche's political ideas are transparently embellished with the name of *Napoleon*, but that such a significant number are articulated under the Emperor's sign, in association with his name, in all probability indicate that other aspects of Nietzsche's political thinking are indebted to Napoleon and represent a moral and political conspiracy designed to ignite and nourish a new Bonapartist movement. This may be supposed simply because of Nietzsche's long memorial to the Emperor and to his Napoleonic precursors, especially to Goethe, but also to Stendhal and the "Caesarian" Heine (poet of the dead Emperor who imagines him returning to life "in defiance of Death and the Devil").[18] Why recall this imperial glory, why summon this faith in pure activity, "passion", "vitality", constant striving for power, "raw and hostile" force,[19] why remember Napoleon, his character, his tactics, his institutions, if not for political reasons?

To say that Nietzsche's political philosophy is Bonapartist is to say that Nietzsche has fundamentally no objection to a government founded on a *coup d'état* or usurpation as Napoleon's was on 9 November, 1799 (18 Brumaire on

---

18 Heinrich Heine, "Germany, A Winter's Tale": http://helios.hampshire.edu/~jjwSS/. Describing this poem, Georg Brandes writes, "his faithful, boundless devotion to Napoleon… finds expression… in the dirge of the dead emperor, brought in his coffin from St Helena to Paris." (See Brandes 1905, pp. 113 and 116)

19 Character traits Nietzsche attributes to Napoleon. See NL, 31[3], KSA 7, p. 748; NL, 1[97], KSA 9, p. 27 and NL, 1[99], KSA 9, p. 27.

the French Republican Calendar); that he has no objection to autocratic rule, to the individualisation and centralisation of power in executive authority; to military dictatorship (the Consulate established by the Constitution of the Year VIII, 13 December, 1799) and, consequently, no objection to the "underlying military structures... [which] formed the hard base of Napoleon's power" (Ellis 2003, p. 58); that he must subscribe to the "essential ethic... propagated during the Empire", the *ethos* of "martial valour" (Ellis 1997, p. 93), and to the "total mobilisation" of the French nation which made every citizen a soldier (Hegemann 1931, p. 10), as the Napoleonic regime, as Benjamin Constant pointed out, was a regime of perpetual warfare (Constant 1989, pp. 90f.).

To say that Nietzsche's political philosophy is Bonapartist is to say that he must have no objection to Napoleon becoming First Consul for Life (1802) or hereditary Emperor (1804), which saw him crowned by Pope Pius VII, restoring a dynastic politics of hereditary succession (Constitution of the Year XII); or to charismatic leadership; and that he must subscribe to "Caesarism" since Bonapartism is the "modern counterpart" of "Roman Caesarism" (Treitschke 1963, p. 196). But Bonapartism is also aristocracy under the form of democracy, an authoritarian democracy or authoritarian republicanism; or as Treitschke called it, "democratic despotism" (Treitschke 1963, p. 196). "Napoleon wants to be a tyrant on a democratic footing" (Hegemann 1931, p. 325). Thus we are presented with a paradox, for how can Nietzsche's political philosophy be Bonapartist if it is antidemocratic as is generally recognised? Napoleon also created the Civil Code, passed on 21 March, 1804, renamed the Napoleonic Code in 1807, which "confirmed the great principles of the Declaration of the Rights of Man": "personal freedom, equality among citizens, suppression of privileges attached to title or social class" (Dufraisse 1992, p. 73), the end of feudalism. Yet Nietzsche caustically opposes democratic "rights", "equality" and "suppression of privileges", so how can his political thought be correctly characterised as Bonapartist given Napoleon's implementation of such a Code? Napoleon also supported universal manhood suffrage, a central provision of the Constitution of Year VIII, while Nietzsche declares war on universal suffrage. How can democracy, universal manhood suffrage and the Napoleonic Code, all central institutions and innovations of Bonapartism, be reconciled with Nietzsche's antidemocratic, anti-egalitarian political philosophy?

First of all, it is important to qualify Bonapartist democracy, the use of the plebiscite. The foundation of the legitimacy of the Napoleonic regime was popular consent, "the principle of national sovereignty" (Dufraisse 1992, p. 50), but this was exercised on only four occasions (confirming the Constitution of the Year VIII in 1800, the Consulate for Life in 1802, the hereditary Empire in 1804 and the "Additional Act" in 1815) in the form of plebiscites whose operations were limited to universal manhood suffrage. Thus universal manhood suffrage was recognised by the regime but it was rarely utilised. So "in reality", as it has been vigorously argued, "the Bonapartist system was nothing but an autocracy" with a token plebiscitary foundation (Dufraisse 1992, p. 46). It is often cynically stated that under the Bonapartist regime universal manhood suffrage was a partial illusion and that "Napoleon never had the slightest intention of basing his rule on the people" (Dufraisse 1992, p. 147), even if only the male population of a certain age (in France 21), that universal manhood suffrage was merely a pretense. Gustave Le Bon comments that Napoleon was "suspicious of large and incompetent assemblies of popular origin" (Le Bon 1980, p. 269). "Bonaparte's constitution was designed to put effective control in the hands of relatively few" as Nietzsche bluntly recognises in the *Genealogy of Morals*. Universal manhood suffrage merely paid lip service to popular sovereignty (Holtman 1967, p. 76). The plebiscites were, effectively, "exercises in official manipulation, whose straight choice between 'yes' or 'no' to what were already in effect *faits accomplis* was hardly a free choice at all" (Ellis 2003, p. 24).

Second, with respect to the Napoleonic Code, this was "a unified system of law applicable to all citizens without distinction" (Holtman 1967, p. 98), but it expressed a conservative view of the family, affirming the authority of the husband, and did not grant women political rights. The Code reflected Napoleon's belief in female inferiority (Fisher 1908, p. 40). It also limited worker's rights. Thus while the Code "provided for legal equality in most cases, it did not do so for the relations of workers and employers... [the] worker was legally inferior to the employer" (Fisher 1908, p. 117). The Penal Code of 1810 further exacerbated existing inequalities through fortifying laws against worker's unions. Napoleon also compromised or violated the Code in other ways: first, he "prohibited 'interpretation' of his legal creation on the grounds that this would contravene imperial will" thus reacting against the principle of popular sovereignty. Napoleon revived the "old idea that the will of the prince was the law" (Kelly 2002, pp. 288f.). Second, he undermined the principle of equality when he established the Legion of Honour in 1802, imperial titles (such as "Prince", "Count" or "Knight") in 1804 and a new nobility between 1802 and 1806, an expression Nietzsche mobilises for his own or similar purposes in *Thus Spoke Zarathustra*. The new nobility constituted a "project for a hierarchical reorganisation of the nation" (Bergeron 1981, p. 63). Its members came primarily from the military, demonstrating Napoleon's preference for a society organised along martial lines, but it was open to members of all social classes as it was an order based on merit or talent which associated "the idea of nobility with that of public service" (Markham 1963, p. 132) or services rendered to the State.

The introduction of the these various social orders resuscitated social privilege, order of rank and hierarchy which served to revive to a large extent the institutions of the *ancien régime*, constituting a rupture with the principle of equality. Le Bon expresses a commonly accepted opinion when he writes that Napoleon in "great measure" re-established the *ancien régime* (Le Bon 1980, p. 146), that he re-established a type of monarchy. Thus Napoleon's commitment to the principle of equality is treated with scepticism in the scholarly literature on Napoleon, as certain institutions he introduced betrayed or undermined it. Bonapartism was a plebiscitary democracy opposed to the institution of parliament and party politics. Under Napoleon, representative institutions decayed. He believed that he alone indivisibly represented the people, concentrating sovereignty in his own person, executive and legislative functions in a *single will*. He "legislated more and more by personal and senatorial decree.... Political and administrative centralization became all the more rigorous" (Dufraisse 1992, p. 114). Napoleon declared: "I am the *pouvoir constituant*".[20]

Nietzsche begins to think about Napoleon in more coherently political terms in the period 1883–1885 as he is developing his ideas regarding the "Philosopher as legislator... who experiments with new possibilities", who "uses religion", whose opposite is "the morals of herd animals"; as he conceives the necessity of "new types", "new values", "institutions for the breeding of higher beings", "Great politics", "Earth government"; and among those who have "prepared" him are "the ideal artists, the very offspring of the Napoleonic movement", "the higher Europeans, precursors of great politics", Napoleon himself: "unconscious countermovement" to democracy, who sets the political task for the future, the "Dionysian" (NL, 35[45], KSA 11, p. 532), whereby "the public" (popular representation) and "parliamentarianism" are denounced by Nietzsche as "the most unsuitable organisations".[21]

Nietzsche performs a transition from "Napoleonism" to "Bonapartism", from being a mere sycophant of the Napoleonic cult of personality to supporting the system governed by Bonapartist ideas of social organisation and political institutions, anchored in the disdain for the French Revolution, the Paris Commune, the Marxist International, Saint Simonians, "contemporary socialistic movements" (BT 19), and popular sovereignty; activated towards the subversion of democracy and egalitarianism. The "new possibilities" and "tasks"

---

20 Quoted in Arendt 1990, p. 163.
21 As Nietzsche notes, "[...] the next century will walk in the footsteps of Napoleon, the first and most anticipating human being of modern times. For the tasks of the next centuries, the ways of 'the public' and parliamentarianism are the most unsuitable organisations" (NL, 37[9], KSA 11, p. 584).

Nietzsche speaks about are not so new. They follow the constructive path made by Napoleon, transition-type to the *Übermensch*.[22]

Nietzsche's Aristocratic Radicalism may be aligned with generic structural features of Bonapartism with latitude, however, for consideration of the fact that Nietzsche also performs an immanent critique of the Bonapartist system. In Nietzsche's political thought there are theoretical points of tension with Bonapartism regarding, for example, the censorship of the press; the constraints on the economic liberties of the Jews but not their assimilation; the institution of universal manhood suffrage; the establishment of an hereditary empire; and the precise criteria establishing a new nobility.[23]

Zarathustra's Prologue contains four iconic symbols, three of which are Napoleonic: the star (symbol of destiny), the eagle (symbol of imperial Rome),[24] and the bee (symbol of resurrection and immortality). To this coat of arms Nietzsche adds the serpent, instrument of the Anti-Christ. In his Prologue, Zarathustra, in effect, says he loves Napoleon when he announces:

I love him who makes his virtue his addiction.... whose soul squanders itself.... whose soul is overfull.... I love him who has a free spirit and a free heart: then his head is simply the entrails of his heart, yet his heart drives him to his going-under. (Z Prologue 4)

This passage not only informs descriptions of Napoleon found elsewhere in Nietzsche's writings but also incorporates a variation on a Napoleonic maxim which Nietzsche had recorded earlier in 1882: "'The heart belongs to the entrails' – said Napoleon. The entrails of the head lie in the heart" (NL, 3[1], KSA 10, p. 69). The passage demonstrates that Zarathustra and Napoleon are erotical-

---

[22] Nietzsche's friend, Resa von Schirnhofer states that Napoleon was "the only historical personality which seemed to fascinate [Nietzsche] and whom he characterized with the greatest admiration as a transition-type to the [*Übermensch*]." (See Gilman 1987, p. 151)

[23] However, the following may be identified as shared structural features of Aristocratic Radicalism and Bonapartism: the privileging of executive power (autocracy); the hierarchical reorganization of the state (aristocracy); the opposition to authentic popular sovereignty; anti-egalitarianism; anti-parliamentarianism; the opposition to party politics; controlled factionalism (the preparation to act, if necessary, against any class or estate of society in the name of any other class or estate); the subordination of the worker; the depoliticisation of women; the absolute right of property ownership; the support of slavery; anti-Enlightenment; anti-Rousseau; the opposition to the principles of the French Revolution; anti-Christian; the glorification of the Roman Empire under Julius Caesar; the support for the formation of a European Union; anti-English; the support of Jewish assimilation; dissimulation (maintaining the semblance of democracy, maintaining religious belief in order to conserve the social order), society as spectacle, the state as a work of art; the glorification of war and military culture.

[24] Georges Bataille states: "Politically the eagle is identified with imperialism... with the unconstrained development of individual authoritarian power". (Bataille 1985, p. 34)

ly entangled; as the self of Zarathustra is composed of many souls and thus a social structure, it may be said that Napoleon is one of Zarathustra's many selves. "With Zarathustra's *convalescence*, there is Caesar...." (NL, 16[80], KSA 10, p. 526.) Napoleon is also the lion (*leone*) and the King of Rome is his child.

Nietzsche's philosophy was characterised as "Aristocratic Radicalism" by Georg Brandes and enthusiastically accepted by Nietzsche on the 2nd of December, 1887: anniversary of the coronation of Napoleon I and the victory at Austerlitz; anniversary of the *coup d'état* of Napoleon III and his ascendancy to the throne as Emperor of France. To Brandes Nietzsche posted his gratitude: "The expression Aristocratic Radicalism, which you employ, is very good. It is... the cleverest thing I have yet read about myself." (Brandes 1972, p. 64) But Brandes also wrote to Nietzsche on another occasion intimately exposing that "Caesarism" was one of a few "bridges leading from [his] inner world to [Nietzsche's]", to which Nietzsche expressed no objection. Thus it can be assumed that, for Brandes, Aristocratic Radicalism and Caesarism (i.e. Bonapartism) are either synonymous or related as a species.

Nietzsche's aristocratic radicalism is characterised by Brandes as "an aristocracy of intellect that could seize the dominion of the world." (Brandes 1972, p. 52), "spiritual" without doubt, but not to be separated from "contempt [...] for every kind of democracy" and "the impossibility of the ideals of equality" or "militarism" (Brandes 1972, p. 53).

We should lay to rest the opinion in the Nietzsche scholarship that Nietzsche's view of Napoleon is "highly ambivalent" (Emden 2008, p. 306). Nietzsche makes some 150 explicit remarks about Napoleon in his published and unpublished writings and notes. In my assessment, 15 of them are critical, only 10% (the final critical remark noted between the autumns of 1885–1886; cf. NL, 2[101], KSA 12, p. 111). 9 of these 15 critical remarks are made prior to 1882 (Some of which merely paraphrase the criticisms of Madame de Rémusat.) The other remarks are descriptive (for example, of Napoleon's character or style of governance), some are simply quotations by or on Napoleon; the remainder, about 70, almost 47%, are reverential. No explicit critique of Napoleon occurs in Nietzsche's published writings after 1882.

Bibliography

Arendt, Hannah (1990): *On Revolution*. London: Penguin Books.
Bataille, Georges (1985): "The Old Mole". In: Georges Bataille: *Visions of Excess: Selected Writings, 1927–1939*. Allan Stoekl, Carl R. Lovitt and Donald M. Leslie Jr. (eds.). Vol. 14: *Theory and History of Literature*. Minneapolis: University of Minnesota Press.
Bergeron, Louis (1981): *France Under Napoleon*. R. R. Palmer (trans.). New Jersey: Princeton University Press.

Bertram, Ernst (2009): *Nietzsche: An Attempt at a Mythology*. Robert E. Norton (trans.). Urbana: University of Illinois Press.
Bianquis, Geneviève (1933): *Nietzsche*. Paris: Les Éditions Rieder.
Bluche, Frédéric (1980): *Le Bonapartisme: Aux origines de la droite autoritaire (1800–1850)*. Paris: Nouvelles Editions Latines.
Brandes, Geore (1905): *Main Currents in Nineteenth Century Literature. Vol. VI: Young Germany*. London: William Heinemann.
Brandes, Georg (1972): *Friedrich Nietzsche: An Essay on Aristocratic Radicalism*. New York: Haskell House Publishers.
Constant, Benjamin (1989): *Benjamin Constant: Political Writings*. Biancamaria Fontana (trans.). Cambridge: Cambridge University Press.
Dufraisse, Roger (1992): *Napoleon*. New York: McGraw-Hill.
Ellis, Geoffrey (1997): *Napoleon*. London: Longman.
Ellis, Geoffrey (2003): *The Napoleonic Empire*. Basingstoke: Palgrave Macmillan.
Emden, Christian J. (2008): *Nietzsche and the Politics of History*. Cambridge: Cambridge University Press.
Englund, Steven (2004): *Napoleon: A Political Life*. New York: Scribner.
Fisher, H. A. L. (1908): *Bonapartism: Six Lectures*. Oxford: Oxford Clarendon Press.
Foucault, Michel (1979): *Discipline and Punish: The Birth of the Prison*. Alan Sheridan (trans.). New York: Vintage Books.
Gilman Sandor (ed.) (1987): *Conversations With Nietzsche: A Life in the Words of His Contemporaries*. New York: Oxford University Press.
Goltz, Colmar (1887): *The Nation in Arms*. Philip A. Ashworth (trans.). London: W. H. Allen and Co.
Gregorovius, Ferdinand (1855): *Corsica: Picturesque, Historical and Social With A Sketch of The Early Life of Napoleon*. Edward Joy Morris (trans.). Philadelphia: Parry & M'Millan.
Gundolf, Friedrich (1928): *The Mantle of Caesar*. Jacob Wittmer Hartmann (trans.). London: Grant Richards and Humphrey Tomlin At The Cayme Press Limited.
Hazareesingh, Sudhir (2004): *The Legend of Napoleon*. London: Granta Books.
Hegemann, Werner (1931): *Napoleon or "Prostration Before the Hero"*. Winifred Ray (trans.). London: Constable & Co. Ltd.
Heine, Heinrich: *Germany, A Winter's Tale*. http://helios.hampshire.edu/~jjwSS/
Herold, J. Christopher (ed./trans.) (1955): *The Mind of Napoleon: A Selection from his Written and Spoken Words*. New York: Columbia University Press.
Holtman, Robert B. (1967): *The Napoleonic Revolution*. New York: J. B. Lippincott Co.
Kelly, Donald R. (2002): "What Pleases the Prince: Justinian, Napoleon and the Lawyers". In: *History of Political Thought* XXIII (2), pp. 288–302.
Klossowski, Pierre (1997): *Nietzsche and the Vicious Circle*. Daniel W. Smith (trans.). Chicago: University of Chicago Press.
Le Bon, Gustave (1980): *The French Revolution and the Psychology of Revolution*. New Brunswick: Transaction Inc.
Markham, Felix (1963): *Napoleon*. New York: New American Library.
Nietzsche, Friedrich (1968): *The Will to Power*. Walter Kaufmann (ed.). Walter Kaufmann and R. J. Hollingdale (trans.). New York: Vintage Books.
Salomé, Lou (2001): *Nietzsche*. Siegfried Mandel (trans.). Urbana and Chicago: University of Illinois Press.

Seung, T. K. (2005): *Nietzsche's Epic of the Soul: Thus Spoke Zarathustra*. Lanham: Lexington Books.
Staël, Germaine de (2008): *Considerations on The Principal Events of The French Revolution*. Aurelian Craiutu (ed.). Indianapolis: Liberty Fund.
Stern, Tom (2009): "Nietzsche, Freedom, and Writing Lives". In: *Arion* 17(I), pp. 85–110.
Strauss, Leo (1967): *Seminar on Nietzsche*. Winter Quarter, Department of Political Science, University of Chicago. Unpublished manuscript.
Treitschke, Heinrich von (1963): *Politics*. Hans Kohn (ed.). New York: Harcourt, Brace & World Inc.
Woloch, Isser (2004): "From Consulate to Empire: Impetus and Resistance". In: Peter Baehr/Melvin Richter (eds.): *Dictatorship in History and Theory: Bonapartism, Caesarism and Totalitarianism*. Cambridge: Cambridge University Press, pp. 29–52.

Phillip H. Roth
Political and Psychological Prerequisites for Legislation in the Early Nietzsche*

> *Laws* exist only because of our need to *calculate*. Only *quantities of force* exist.
> (Klossowski 1997, p. 140)

I Introduction

Friedrich Nietzsche famously attempts to reform the idea of philosophy. Already his first published book, *The Birth of Tragedy*, conveys an idea of such an attempt. In this work he tries to view the world from the perspective of art – more precisely: Greek tragedy. In retrospect, Nietzsche thus concluded that it contains a sense of "artists' metaphysics in the background" (BT Attempt, KSA 1, p. 13).[1] Nietzsche's underlying desire is to free philosophy from the practice of pure contemplation and add to it a notion of creativity, a quality he sees as vital for the successful making of politics. Politics, which for Nietzsche goes far beyond the realm of decision-making in public policy, is in the guise of 'great politics' inextricably linked with the role of the legislator and, so I will argue, augmented with a definite sense of aesthetics. Therefore it is no wonder that in 1874, in his third *Untimely Meditation*, he proclaims that he views the task of philosophers "to be legislators to the measure, stamp and weight of things" (SE 3, KSA 1, p. 360). And that he will further keep with this qualification for the rest of his career, when in 1886 he again confirms the early conviction: "Genuine philosophers, however, are commanders and legislators: they say, 'thus it shall be!'" (BGE 211, KSA 5, p.145). But while the traditional view held that law needs to be the closest possible approximation to assessments by science or knowledge, Nietzsche, in contrast, sees law as a work of art.

In this paper, I will outline crucial political and psychological requirements for legislation in Nietzsche's early thought. I will, however, first of all show that, drawing on Plato, he seeks to employ his legislation to secure the

---

* For their helpful comments and valuable suggestions, I am grateful to Harald Bergbauer, Dan Conway, Anthony Jensen, Manuel Knoll, Donovan Myasaki, Werner Stegmaier and Barry Stocker.
1 English renderings are my own.

position of the philosopher *qua* genius, in order to clarify on which grounds he views these requirements as necessary. Disgusted with the state of affairs in his time where the philosopher "has to acknowledge something higher above wisdom, the state" (SE 8, KSA 1, p. 415), and accordingly the state portrays itself to be "the highest goal of humanity" (SE 4, KSA 1, p. 365), Nietzsche seeks to renew the relation between state and philosophy. He precisely sees the end at which the state and society should solely aim as "letting the shining blossom of the genius sprout forth" (GSt, KSA 1, p. 772). To manage this, however, new values are necessary, which would remove the focus from entrenched modern values, such as inalienable natural rights. Accordingly, in this role the philosopher is to Nietzsche primarily a legislator of the "value of being" (SE 3, KSA 1, p. 360).

Secondly, I will develop the claim that Nietzsche, above all, dwells on preliminary observations regarding the specifics of human nature and the institution of law, in order to make the reevaluating end possible. In arguments with astonishing rhetorical similarities to early modern political thinkers, he explains that certain beliefs about human nature radiate their own set of values, like the value of self-preservation so prominent in modern political philosophy. I will show that these values constitute a morality that is a precursor of Nietzsche's later idea of slave morality. On these grounds, and in order to be able to know where he must set up his legislation, Nietzsche learns that aesthetics play a major role in the formation of values in everyday life and thus can take values to be primarily constructed. He states that humans are engaged in the world via aesthetic relations to enable, what Jessica Berry has aptly called "psychological security" (Berry 2011, p. 54). This means, that regarding the perception of the world, humans require having a feeling of sovereignty over their senses. Although Nietzsche is convinced that what we perceive is not reality, but merely our mental construction, he understands that humans need to be deceived into thinking that they are perceiving reality. The question then arises how it comes about that the constructed modern values, i.e. slave morality, are perceived as natural. I will therefore engage into an account of Nietzsche's psychological investigation of the animality in humans and its reflection on law and morality, for which my main source will be Nietzsche's early and unpublished essay 'On Truth and Lies in an Extra-Moral Sense'.[2]

---

[2] Vanessa Lemm has offered a thorough reading of human animality in TL (Lemm 2009, pp. 111–151). Although I share the basic tenor of her arguments regarding the links between animality, truth and morality in Nietzsche's early essay, I will in the following, nevertheless, be addressing issues, which I find problematic in Lemm's interpretation.

I draw on Diego von Vacano's book *The Art of Power* for my definition of aesthetics. The reason for this is that von Vacano rightly keeps with Nietzsche's emphasis on perception in his analysis of aestheticism. He stresses the origin of the term and gives us aesthetics to derive from *aisthesis* in his outline: "In Greek, *aisthesthai* means to perceive as a part of sensory, physical experience. Aesthetics is not the same as philosophy of art, which focuses on the question of beauty, taste and art itself." (von Vacano 2007, p. 143). The importance the feature of perception has to Nietzsche is emphatically illustrated when he defines a common, yet constructed, sensory access to the world as essential to human life. So, as von Vacano points out, Nietzsche is "concerned with the dimension of human experience that allow for purchase on the world through the senses, and how this relates to both political and moral evaluations" (von Vacano 2007, p. 2). Yet, von Vacano moves on to formulate a "politics of taste" in his book, which focuses on a "perception through the senses [...] grounded in both sensory and aesthetic judgment." According to von Vacano, this allows "for us to determine if we approve of a regime based on the way that we experience it in terms of our existence in it." (von Vacano 2007, p. 154). However, a pure politics of taste inspired by Nietzschean aesthetics, in my view, neglects the strong link Nietzsche sees drawn between art and life. The ability to approve of a regime – or of our position within one – is far more dependent on subconscious factors than von Vacano makes apparent. In this paper, I will therefore emphasize the strong connection aesthetics in Nietzsche's eyes has to the psychology of human existence, especially to social existence. I believe taste, as von Vacano suggests, cannot be the criterion on which Nietzsche's aesthetic politics are grounded. Rather I will argue that compatibility with a certain regime is, according to Nietzsche, determined by the perspective from which one is bound to view life.

I will show that Nietzsche's aesthetics are negatively informed by Plato.[3] On the one level, by rejecting the theory of forms, Nietzsche makes subjective sensory access to the world exclusive, in contrast to Plato's conviction that it

---

[3] The positive influence on the aesthetics of the early Nietzsche came primarily from Schopenhauer and Wagner. Schopenhauer, on the one hand, sees the possibility of beholding the eternal forms in nature through what he refers to as the 'objectivation of will', a fact, however, which Nietzsche strongly rejects (Schopenhauer 1998, pp. 241–247). But, on the other, Schopenhauer views art as the primary access to these forms and hence to the world (Schopenhauer 1998, pp. 251–263). Nietzsche and Schopenhauer thus strongly endorse the feature that participation in the world is aesthetic and that through art life finds redemption (Schopenhauer 1998, pp. 265f.). Nietzsche and Schopenhauer also agree on the point that music constitutes the highest form of art (Schopenhauer 1998, p. 339; cf. BT 24, KSA 1, p. 152). For an analysis of the meaning of aesthetics in relation to life in Nietzsche and Schopenhauer cf. Soll 1998.

is possible to objectively behold *eidos*. On another level, Nietzsche takes on the position, which mimetic art holds in Plato's harsh treatment of the arts in the last book of *The Republic*. I want to argue that he in a sense reverses Plato's critique and endorses it as a feature of the human's aesthetic relation to the world.[4] Therefore, as humans, we can only have access to the world in subjective perspective and our perception can be regarded as a sort of *mimesis*.

> The nature of animal conscience [*thierischen Bewusstseins*] brings with it that the world, of which we can become aware, is only a surface and sign-world, a generalized, vulgarized world [*eine verallgemeinerte Welt*]. (GS 354, KSA 3, p. 593)

These premises also enable Nietzsche to use the circumstances of perspective[5] to his advantage, with regard to the reform of values. Because from human perspective the constructed world is necessarily perceived as real, it opens the possibility for Nietzsche to deliberately apply the feature of deception to his legislation. As von Vacano correctly states, already "the idea that reality lies in morality and/or reason is a form of deception" (von Vacano 2007, p. 147). Thus Nietzsche finds that conscious deployment of deceptive measures may entice humans to believe in a form of morality as prevailing. Again his inspiration comes here from Plato and his famous noble lie (cf. Rep. 414d-415d).

In sum, I will portray Nietzsche as a political Platonist, despite his critique of Plato's theoretical philosophy. I will therefore adhere to a certain view of Nietzsche, which has primarily interpreted him as aristocratic. I am well aware that Nietzsche's relation to Plato (and Socrates) is far more complex than what I will develop in this text. I am also aware that Nietzsche refines specifics of Plato's regime, which I will at most be able to glance over in my elaborations. I will therefore be focusing instead on certain aspects of his Platonic politics, especially on those with regard to the relation between the state and philosopher. I will exemplify how Nietzsche's idea of a true philosopher is set apart from Plato's, and that it emerges from Nietzsche's wholehearted rejection of Plato's ontology. Nevertheless, I wish to show that he deploys Platonic political measures to achieve his political and moral ends and that these ends can be stated as instituting and securing a way of life, of which the greatest advocacy

---

4 See on this point Halliwell 2002, p. 367: "Nietzsche feels impelled to reuse […] the classically mimeticist symbol of the artistic mirror […], doing so in a manner that consolidates the romantic turn toward a construal of this idea in terms of natural creativity rather than the production of naturalistic appearances."

5 Nietzsche's famous doctrine of perspectivism is expressed in GM III 12, KSA 5, p. 365; cf. NL 1884, KSA 11, pp. 181f. The most prominent study, which has taken Nietzsche's doctrine of perspectivism as its unifying theme, is Nehamas 1985.

has been recognized as being that of Plato, i.e. a noble and philosophic way of life (SE 3, KSA 1, pp. 350f.).[6]

Why confine oneself to the early Nietzsche? In my opinion, at least two reasons speak for examining the early Nietzsche. Firstly, especially in contrasting *The Birth of Tragedy* and 'The Greek State', we find an obvious contrariety in Nietzsche's attitude toward Plato, which becomes quite subtle in his later writings. On the one hand, Nietzsche rejects Plato's ontology and the contemplative ideals of Socrates' way of life. On the other, he embraces the political ideals of Plato's perfect state.[7] I am not saying that this polar attitude toward Plato merely moves to the background unaltered in his later writing. I am, however, implying that thorough understanding of the Platonism/anti-Platonism, in the younger Nietzsche, enables a better understanding of the modifications his attitude towards the theoretical and practical side of Plato's philosophy undergoes in the mature Nietzsche.

Secondly, Nietzsche explicitly lays out important grounds of his later thought in the early works, when it comes to the socio-psychological import of aestheticism. Valuable insights into his mature thought spring from clarifications of this theme, despite the Schopenhauerian metaphysics with which it is here still tangled. Understanding that humans require a clearly defined and structured world as a means for orientation is a fundamental fact, on which much of his later philosophy hinges. That human beings perform the act of constructing a world is a claim developed in the early texts. Thus the emphasis he lays on a faculty, which can be described as a form of subconscious aestheticism, or that "one is far more an artist than one knows" (BGE 192, KSA 5, p. 114), clearly springs from developments in his early phase. Although Nietzsche will never return to such broad elaborations on aesthetics and art, as he does in *The Birth of Tragedy* and in 'On Truth and Lies in an Extra-Moral Sense', in his later philosophy, the relevance of these themes and their connection to human psychology nevertheless remain crucial.

II The Platonic origins of legislation and the teaching of state and genius

The idea that philosophers represent legislators is certainly not an innovation of Nietzsche's. Already Plato had Socrates present the philosopher as a lawgiv-

---

[6] Scholars, who have also emphasized the strong affinity to Platonic politics in Nietzsche's thought, include Appel 1999, Dombowsky 2004, Knoll 2009, Ottmann 1999 and Rosen 2004 amongst others.
[7] Note that GSt was originally intended as part of BT (cf. NL 1871, KSA 7, pp. 333–349).

er in *The Republic*. He defines philosophers as true legislators, because they have the ability to form a regime according to that which is most just and beautiful by nature (Rep. 501b-c). In harmony with his metaphysical insights about the soul, the regime he lays down, Plato's best *polis*, resembles a three-part structure: a class of producers, a class of guardians and the philosopher-kings. The greater good is strongly tied to the figures of the philosophers, who are the only ones truly capable of just rule, since they have the metaphysical knowledge of the good and just. Since the philosophers need their capacity entirely for contemplation and cannot bother taking care of their bodily needs, the lower classes fulfill their tasks as nurturers and protectors. The underlying anthropological premise is that the single human is not self-sufficient, but requires a form of community to exist (Rep. 369c). Because he is not able to sustain himself, but cares primarily for his own good, he cannot be seen as fit to rule. Therefore Socrates daringly introduces the reign of philosophy in the fifth book (Rep. 473c-e).

We find there are both overlaps with, and differences from, Plato in Nietzsche's view of politics. Nietzsche also wants the philosophers to be exempt from the labor of bodily care. Therefore he, too, prefers a hierarchical structure of society divided into classes pertaining to material well-being and spiritual or cultural well-being. The problem of self-sufficiency is, however, addressed to a far greater extent by Nietzsche. Plato had simply assumed that humans cannot live in solitude, and therefore require a community of ruler and ruled. But since Nietzsche's society is set only toward the legitimization of the ruler, he will painstakingly try to demonstrate why most humans require rule; this, however, primarily with a view to justifying the existence of those who are "solitary and free in spirit" (SE 3, KSA 1, p. 354). Accordingly, he distinguishes between two kinds of humans: the herd-like many and the few solitary philosophers. This distinction is vital to Nietzsche's political philosophy, because it allows him to place the philosopher and the state in a teleological relation. Plato was also convinced of such a teleological connection, which, however, laid greater emphasis on mutuality. In his case only the best regime, ruled by philosophers, allowed for the citizens of that state to become perfect in regard to virtues and therefore happy (Rep. 540d-541b). Nietzsche denies such a mutual relation and endorses a form of slavery on the grounds that slavery is vital for the production of genius and culture, without which humanity would not enjoy any sense of worth (GSt, KSA 1, p. 767).

Due to the qualifications he makes, Nietzsche in his politics simplifies the structure of Plato's regime to represent only two classes: those who are the makers of culture – philosophers and artists – and those who merely act as tools for those makers – the slaves. Therefore Nietzsche takes state and society as means to be directed at a single end. Frederick Appel has argued that we can in fact find a three-parted structure in Nietzsche's regime, just like in Plato, which is owed to an "element of *The Republic* to which Nietzsche is particularly drawn". Appel is referring here to the "martial class of 'guardians' whose function is to insulate the inner circle of nobles from the majority plebeian class." (Appel 1999, p. 137) I do not find that Nietzsche's adoption of an idea of guardians can account for detecting a special class in his regime. Certainly, as Appel points out, in *The Antichrist* the "predominantly muscular and temperamental type" relieves the "predominantly spiritual type" of "everything coarse in the work of ruling." (Appel 1999, p. 137; cf. A 57, KSA 6, p. 243) However, these muscular types are nevertheless under the rule of the spiritual types and the fundamentally defining feature in Nietzsche's regime is the difference between rulers and ruled, masters and slaves.[8] Because Nietzsche's focus is on the rulers, we cannot regard him as having a special interest in the guardian class.

Henning Ottmann has aptly drawn out the dual distinction in Nietzsche. In comparison to Plato, he states that a dualism is far more typical for Nietzsche's political and moral philosophy. Although expressing his regrets at this fact, Ottmann goes on to explain that Nietzsche did not preserve the beautiful architecture, which connected virtues, parts of the soul and ranks in Plato and that instead the division into 'masters' and 'slaves' takes the place of Plato's three classes in Nietzsche's thought (cf. Ottmann 1999, pp. 278 f.). How far this simplification is regrettable can be debated. But Ottmann is certainly right that Plato's three-part structure had a higher philosophical purpose and a metaphysically unifying background to it. But it is exactly this background which Nietzsche rejects. His dualism, therefore, serves observations which he had made in his early years, especially pertaining to the necessity of human collectivity (or the herd) and its foundations in *Schein* (illusions).

Nietzsche is indeed a harsh critique of Plato's idealism, especially with regard to the consequences it had on intellectual history and the history of mankind in general. He asserts that much of the West's thinking and beliefs have been trapped in overarching Platonic architectures (BGE Preface, KSA 5, p. 12; BGE 191, KSA 5, p. 112). Despite his critique, we can, nevertheless, view Nietzsche as a political Platonist with certain reservations. He is first of all

---

[8] Certainly, there exist differences within the masses of the ruled in Nietzsche' thought, which can be grasped as belonging to different classes. However, the possibility to command and the necessity to obey defines the different types of human beings in general, although, drawing the exact lines of this differentiation is very hard to accomplish. Nevertheless, as Manuel Knoll has aptly pointed out, the class of guardians and the class of nurturers are in Nietzsche, in contrast to Plato, entirely instrumental to the ends of the state (Knoll 2009, p. 163).

quite keen on the ambitions that influenced Plato. The idea of a society as such, where the development of philosophers would be actively promoted and their life politically and socially secured, inspired Nietzsche to his conception of legislation. He goes so far as to envision a political order primarily devised to the advantage of philosophers, and the practice of philosophy. In the unpublished treatise on 'The Greek State', Nietzsche defines the aim of the state as "the always anew begetting of and preparation for the genius" (GSt, KSA 1, p. 776). In an early fragment, he asserts again that the "incredible efforts of state and society are in the end only undertaken for a few: the great artists and philosophers." (NL 1870/71, KSA 7, p. 142) For this reason Nietzsche, similar to Plato, favors an understanding of natural hierarchy, a "chemical separation of society" into those who act for the benefit of the higher class and that class itself (GSt, KSA 1, p. 769). Just as in Plato, the order of rank is determined by natural (pre)conditions of individual quality and the best suited regime is therefore an aristocracy.

In the explicit reference to *The Republic* at the end of 'The Greek State', Nietzsche adopts from the

> overall conception of the Platonic state the marvelously great hieroglyph of a profound and ever to be construed secret teaching of the relation between state and genius (GSt, KSA 1 p. 777).

and makes it the core of his conception of legislation. I will explain what Nietzsche took this secret teaching to mean, how his idea of lawgiving is directed towards determining the relationship between state and genius, philosopher and herd, and especially what the indispensable basis for the relationship is.

As has been repeatedly pointed out, we can assert that Nietzsche's philosophy is indeed Platonic in a very specific sense. He especially follows Plato in his politics to restore the prominent and powerful position of philosophers within society. To this end he shapes his model of society after Plato's example. In an infamous note from the early 1870s Nietzsche, however, polemically asserts that his "philosophy [is] reversed Platonism" (NL 1870/71, KSA 7, p. 199). This reversal is due to his highly critical stance towards Plato's ontology, especially toward the idea of the good. I will show how Nietzsche replaces Platonic idealism with a thorough understanding of aestheticism in his early writings. He thereby couches his famous figure of the artist-philosopher in a revised Platonic model of state and society. Ottmann has found that Nietzsche's design, on the political level, reveals a remarkable Platonism which sounds old and familiar, but is strangely modern (Ottmann 1999, p. 276). I agree in part with Ottmann's observation, and therefore will elaborate on how and why

Nietzsche's politics seems both familiarly ancient and peculiarly modern. I believe, however, that Nietzsche's early politics are far more indebted to ancient aspects.

III The primacy of art for life

Reflecting on Plato's ideal society in a note from the early 1870s, Nietzsche detects the, in his eyes, essential flaw regarding the connection of the philosopher to the *polis*. He says that Plato's state "truly is the prototype [*Vorbild*] of a true thinker's state [*Denkerstaat*], with the entirely correct rank for woman and labor." He, however, asserts further that "the mistake only lies in the Socratic conception of the thinker state: philosophical thinking cannot erect, but only destroy." (NL 1870/71, KSA 7, p. 140) The idea of erecting, or creating, is an enduring theme of Nietzsche's philosophy, reflected for example in his ambition to create values. In the early 1870s he aimed at defining a type of human who is indeed a philosopher, but incorporates traits of the artist as well. In his notebook he contemplates the "great perplexity [*Verlegenheit*] whether philosophy is an art or a science." His envisioned definition reads:

> It is an art form in its ends and in its production. But the means, the exposition in concepts [*Begriffen*], it has in common with science. It is a form of poetry [*Dichtkunst*]. – It cannot be situated: therefore we have to invent and characterize a species. (NL 1872/73, KSA 7, p. 439)

To characterize and invent this artistic species, Nietzsche again takes his bearings from Plato. Indeed, Plato's treatment of art in *The Republic* is ruthless at best, tyrannical at worst. He lets Socrates exile most of the poets from the city and practice heavy censorship on the ones allowed to stay (Rep. 378b-79a, 386c-387b). In the last book, productive arts in general are heavily criticized and he has them banished completely.[9] The reason is the mimetic character of these art forms. Such arts merely imitate the appearance of things and therefore are deceptive as to their true nature (Rep. 598a-e). The reason is that such a form of art, like painting, distorts the anyway problematic view of the real

---

9 There has been much debate in regard to Plato's discussion of mimetic arts in book 3 and 10 and the coherence of censoring mimetic art, on the one hand, or banishing it completely on the other. Christopher Janaway offers a reading, in which both accounts are reconciled (Janaway 1995, esp. pp. 106f.). Halliwell 2002 offers a thorough understanding of *mimesis* and of modern reactions to it in his book.

world (the view of *eidos*) and thus gives a false idea of what is real. We cannot find a contribution to an understanding of being in art, because it merely captures one perspective onto the object being portrayed. For that reason the artist, apparently even more than the artisan, does not belong to the group of outstanding people in the ideal city.

With regard to the relation between state and philosopher that, which in Nietzsche's thought must be strikingly different from Plato's, is precisely the conception of a true philosopher. The traditional position holds that philosophers are the highest types of humans, and that contemplation and beholding are the highest forms of human activity. Nietzsche, by contrast, criticizes this position. In his opinion, the contemplative philosopher does not constitute the highest type of human, but rather the artistic philosopher.

The Socratic philosopher is surely closer to a scientist than he is to an artist. His distance from art is what worries Nietzsche the most about this kind of exceptional being. For him, Socrates represented a form of "anti-Greekness", which even threatened to destroy the artistic culture of Greece (BT 12, KSA 1, p. 83; cf. TI Socrates 2, KSA 6, p. 68). Because Socrates distinguished between popular art and philosophy itself as the greatest art form, contemplating and beholding had him refraining from practicing any practical art (Phaedo 60e-61c).[10] But this sort of identification of philosophy with art is not the kind that Nietzsche aims at. He is more interested in combining philosophy with a sense of the popular kind of art. Regarding Socrates' praise of philosophy as the highest art form, Nietzsche mockingly asserts that accordingly the "highest law" of "aesthetic Socratism" has to be that "everything must be comprehensible to be beautiful." (BT 12, KSA 1, p. 85) Nietzsche does not focus on the nature of beauty in his politics, first of all, because he regards beauty as relative to perspective and, secondly, because he precisely wants to break the link existing between comprehension and aesthetics and establish a strong link between art and perception.

Nietzsche therefore specifically makes the artist, next to the saint and the philosopher, part of the genial circle. He exclaims them as "those genuine humans, those no-more-animals, the philosophers, artists and saints" (SE 5, KSA 1,

---

10 That Socrates possessed some artistic skills is revealed in the *Phaedo*, where he is reported to have composed hymns after giving in to a recurring dream, which urged him to make music (Phaedo 60c-61c). Nietzsche questions the strict opposition of Socrates to art in reflecting on this circumstance in BT 14, KSA 1, p. 96. Although Nietzsche sees Socrates as the corruptor of Plato (BGE 190, KSA 5, p. 111; cf. also TI Ancients 2, KSA 6, p. 155) his statements regarding Socrates must nevertheless be carefully weighed out (cf. e.g. Dannhauser 1974).

p. 380). We must disregard the inner relation of this trinity here,[11] but rather focus on the genius as an artistic philosopher. In another journal entry form the same period in the 1870s, Nietzsche emphasizes that he regards art as an essential part to his image of philosophy, whereas "the pure <u>drive for knowledge</u> is not decisive, but the <u>aesthetic</u> one" (NL 1872/73, KSA 7, p. 444). But why favor art over contemplation? Why are aesthetics so immediately important to Nietzsche in regard to philosophy, and thus to his idea of political philosophy in the long run?

That Nietzsche's emphasis lies on aesthetics is owing to a finding connected with the phenomena of the everyday world. He observed crucial premises, during his inquiry into the Apollonian and Dionysian drives of archaic Greece, and during the studies underlying the essay 'On Truth and Lies'.[12] The Apollonian and Dionysian were, according to Nietzsche in *The Birth of Tragedy*, opposed drives and psychological constituents of archaic Greek culture and life. The Dionysian can be said to be approximated in a state of frenzy. It is the experience of nature in its original form: complete oneness, violent and dreadful, but pleasurable at the same time. Yet, life in this state is not sustainable, because it alienates the human from the humane world, throws him back to a state of nature and disables all ordered (inter)action (BT 2, KSA 1, pp. 33f.). To enable human life a balancing drive needs to exist, which ensures that human business can go about in an ordinary fashion. For this, the Apollonian drive, in contrast to the Dionysian, aims at veiling the natural frenzy. It, nevertheless, makes reflections upon the tragedy of life possible, but without having humans give in to the tragic pull.[13] The foremost exposition of the Apollonian drive is then in the form of a work of art, which "as the supplement and completion of

---

[11] Daniel W. Conway has made an effort to single out the specifics of each figure in his book on *Nietzsche and the Political* (Conway 1997, pp. 81–93).

[12] Next to Schopenhauer, whose opposition of the will and representation can be viewed as inspiring to Nietzsche's opposition of the Apollonian and Dionysian, other important sources for Nietzsche at the time include Gerber *Die Sprache als Kunst* (1871) and F. A. Lange *Geschichte des Materialismus* (1866).

[13] According to Nietzsche, the Apollonian is not only representative of art, dream and illusion, but also an essential requirement for the existence of state and society. He calls "the state-building Apollo also the genius of the principii individuationis" and asserts that "state and patriotism [Heimatsinn] cannot live without the affirmation of individual personality." (BT 21, KSA 1, p. 133) Nietzsche, however, claims further that a unifying myth, which controls the Apollonian forces and thereby bans the threat of atomism, holds a culture together. Accordingly, "even the state knows no unwritten laws more powerful than the mythical fundament, which guarantees its connection to religion, its growing out of mythical representations." (BT 23, KSA, p. 145) In the conclusion to this paper, I will discuss means, which Nietzsche most likely viewed as possibilities to erect and sustain such a unifying myth.

being [...] seduces one to continue living" (BT 3, KSA 1, p. 36). Nietzsche primarily views aesthetics as a means to create illusions. By deceiving humans about dreadful nature, distancing them from the tragic and making them believe in illusions as reality, art becomes essential to human life. In the context of 'On Truth and Lies' Nietzsche describes "the human's [...] invincible tendency of letting him be deceived". He is "enchanted with happiness when the rhapsodist tells him tales as if they were true or the actor, in the play, performs the king more royal than reality reveals him to be." (TL 2, KSA 1, p. 888) But it is not art alone, such as the glorious tales of gods and humans in the Homeric epics or the self-destructive deeds in Sophocles' tragedies, that humanity can adhere to and sustain the will to live, but artistry on a far more psychological level. As Ivan Soll has pointed out, for Nietzsche the Apollonian drive itself already represents a "process that brings forth the everyday world." (Soll 2001, p. 14) Art, therefore, is not only present in the artwork (or the dream), but finds its expression already in the illusions of everyday life. The natural state,

> the truly being and primordial oneness [*Wahrhaft-Seiende und Ur-Eine*], as the eternally suffering and contradictory [...], needs the pleasurable illusion for its continuous redemption: this illusion — totally ensnared in it and made up of it — [...] we are compelled to perceive as empirical reality. (BT 4, KSA 1, pp. 38f.)

The need for illusions in everyday life leads Nietzsche, on the one hand, to reject Platonic idealism, and on the other to assert that human beings are necessarily engaged in the world as "artistically creative subjects" (TL, KSA 1 p. 883). In a remarkable statement from 1882, in retrospect on *The Birth of Tragedy* of 1872 – and therewith a decade later emphatically repeating a fundamental insight of his early career – Nietzsche assures that "only as an aesthetic phenomenon the being of the world is justified." (BT Attempt 5, KSA 1, p. 17) Nietzsche underlines the necessity of aesthetics not only for human life, but also as a legitimization of the world in general, a fact that bears the question of legitimization outside the realm of aesthetics. The crux of Nietzsche's statement is an accurate denial of Plato's doctrine of ideas, the denial of the theory of forms, a dissection of the heart of Platonism from its miraculous architecture. Nietzsche achieves this when he in fact declares other doctrines – "true, but deadly" ones – to be fundamental:

> the doctrines of sovereign becoming, of the liquidity of all concepts, types and kinds [*Flüssigkeit aller Begriffe, Typen und Arten*], of the lack of all cardinal differences between human and animal. (HL 9, KSA 1, p. 319)[14]

---

[14] Nietzsche holds on to this early doctrine throughout his career. It underlies many important aspects of his thinking, like the will to power and perspectivism. In GM he restates his

By denying Platonic idealism, he denies objectivity. So for him there are only perspectives. The only thing between the human's view and the real world can be the illusions of order and stability, which humans have formed for themselves. Taking the real world to be the object and humans the subject, we can see that they have no other option but to act in this manner, because

> between two absolutely different spheres, such as between subject and object, there exists no causality, no correctness, no expression, but at the most an aesthetic relation, I mean a hinting transmission, a stammering translation into a totally different language. (TL, KSA 1, p. 884)

The need to veil the flux of reality makes art a psychological prerequisite for life and the perception of the world. At the very end of the short text on 'The Pathos of Truth', Nietzsche draws out this connection: "Art is more powerful than knowledge, because it wants life, and knowledge achieves as its last goal only – destruction. – " (PT, KSA 1, p. 760)

But if the illusions of everyday life are an aesthetic product, the crucial question for Nietzsche lies in asking, which requirements are needed so they can be molded according to the philosopher's will, in order to establish a society that would represent Nietzsche's modified version of the Platonic state. Nietzsche's strict denial of the theory of forms enables him to resituate art at a higher rank within his philosophy. Plato's political critique of the artist's skill of producing the mere appearance of an appearance is, in Nietzsche, thus reversed to become a cardinal skill. Whereas the fact that the artist necessarily takes on a perspective, which in Plato restricts his view towards the nature of being, for Nietzsche perspective is the lynchpin from where he constructs his philosophy. As Soll states, Nietzsche thereby "provocatively reverses Plato's well-entrenched preference for reality over illusion (of *Sein* over *Schein*)." (Soll 2001, p. 15) Having dissected the core from Platonism and understood the world in an aesthetic manner, Nietzsche can view the Philosopher in a more preferable light, with greater liberties for the justification of his lawgiving.

---

doctrine to read "The form is liquid, its 'sense' [*der Sinn*] even more so" (GM II 12, KSA 5, p. 315); a statement which can be considered to be in direct opposition to Plato's theory of forms. Werner Stegmaier has profoundly analyzed the idea of the "liquidity of forms" and the "concept of a concept [*Begriff des Begriffs*]" in GM and its meaning for Nietzsche's philosophy in general (Stegmaier 1994, pp. 60–93).

IV Animality and epistemology

Nietzsche denies that beneath the materialistic layer of the world lies a metaphysical idea of the good. He therefore denies that ideas lend their form to concepts. Taking this for granted, how do concepts then come into existence as an aesthetic creation? More generally, how does the human being as an aesthetic being make sure to secure life and how does this distinguish him from Nietzsche's idea of a genius?

In the unpublished essay 'On Truth and Lies', Nietzsche exemplifies how concepts come into being, and therefore reveals his ontology to be beyond both idealistic and realistic accounts. As Jessica Berry has observed, however, his ontological elaborations can be primarily understood as a reaction to Plato's theory of forms (Berry 2011, pp. 56f.). Nietzsche suggests that "every concept [*Begriff*] originates by equating the unequal [*Gleichsetzen des Nicht-Gleichen*]" and thereby reverses a crucial Platonic premise. In Plato the things were molded after a trans-materialistic archetype [*Urbild*]. Nietzsche, however, contends that in reality it works the other way around. What a thing is, its concept, is established by "dropping those individual differences, through forgetting the distinguishing [elements]" (TL 1, KSA 1, p. 880). In his example, it is not that a primeval leaf is the model after which all leaves in nature are formed, but that only an infinite variety of 'leaves' exist, that none of them are alike, and therefore conceptualizing this infinite variety under the heading of 'leaf' represents an arbitrary equating of things unequal.

However, it is precisely here, when humans perform a forgery with regard to their perception that they act as aesthetic subjects. Nietzsche elaborates on how this act is tied to premises essential for life and therefore reveals great psychological insights into human nature, and the tendency toward politics. He emphasizes the notion of survival to illustrate, what causes the creation of illusions in humans, and therefore explains that human beings are most driven by a desire for self-preservation. In the long run, his illustrations serve to show how the common human differs from the genius.

According to Maudemarie Clark, 'On Truth and Lies' contains a sense of philosophical realism (Clark 1990, p. 85). She finds that Nietzsche's problem with truth lies in the fact that he is convinced that the things we perceive in the world cannot be stated in adequate terms, regarding their nature. Clark sees that "Nietzsche assumes the existence of things themselves, objects that exist independently of consciousness." (Clark 1990, p. 82) But since we are engaged in the world through our senses, we construct in our minds what we perceive solely on the basis of "nerve stimuli" (TL 1, KSA 1, p. 878). The ultimate problem for Nietzsche is then, according to Clark, that "we cannot therefore say anything about what such things are, our linguistic expressions certainly cannot correspond to what they are in themselves." (Clark 1990, p. 83)

As I will argue in the following part of the paper, Nietzsche denies any notion of things independent from consciousness. I will, however, not be offering a critique of this position on epistemological grounds.[15] Rather, my arguments derive from what I consider Nietzsche's primary concern with moral and social phenomena. Precisely because the world for Nietzsche is flux and chaos, the drive for truth is constituted as a need for psychological security. Therefore, what truth is cannot and need not correspond to the world as it is – no matter in what kind of a distorted manner. Nietzsche makes these points clear when he emphasizes that truth is "anthropocentric through and through" (TL 1, KSA 1, p. 883). We must bear in mind that truth for Nietzsche is generated from psychological and social prerequisites. Therefore truth corresponds not to the world as such, but merely to what human beings perceive as being the world. In a critique of Clark and in connection with Nietzsche's treatment of animality, Vanessa Lemm has argued that in the "discourse on truth" in 'On Truth and Lies' Nietzsche seeks

> to unmask power-formations and ideological constructs by exposing how the domination and exploitation of the human being's animality is central to the establishment of a 'truth' that can function as the basis of civil society and is understood as the highest achievement of abstract and conceptual thinking. (Lemm 2009, p. 113)

I strongly agree with Lemm on the point that Nietzsche's focus lies in social conditions, pertaining to truth rather than with sincere epistemological motivations. On this ground, it becomes understandable that Nietzsche expounds his arguments in the rhetoric of modern political philosophy, a tradition known to take its bearings primarily from the human condition. Accordingly, Nietzsche takes his departure in 'On Truth and Lies' from the account of a natural state. However, the famous *bellum omnium contra omnes* for Nietzsche resembles not primarily a physical war, but rather a war of deception and misunderstanding. Since in the state of nature, we must imagine that every individual's representation of the world is unique and singular, there hardly can be a possibility of interaction due to the lack of a way to communicate. To enable community, Nietzsche then sees a consensus on language as necessary. This consensus is reached through a "peace agreement", which defines what language ought to be and incidentally "brings along something that looks like the first step to obtaining the [...] drive for truth." In this agreement

---

15 For a recent position, which argues against the notion of realism and against a correspondence theory of truth in TL, cf. Andresen 2010.

that is fixated, which from now on shall be regarded as 'truth', i.e. a constantly valid and binding designation of things is invented and the linguistic legislation [*Gesetzgebung der Sprache*] also provides the first laws of truth (TL 1, KSA 1, p. 877).

This type of lawgiving, however, is not identical to the philosopher's legislative powers and the political legislation that Nietzsche seeks to employ. But it reveals insights into the level, on which Nietzsche will want to make his legislative approaches, and illustrates important rudiments.

We can derive an insight into the sort of community Nietzsche sees emerging from this agreement. Modern accounts had taken the covenant of one with another to mean a transfer of powers and rights to a sovereign, who ensures the security of the collected individuals, and there with a transition from a natural to a civil state. The transition in Nietzsche's case does not seem to undergo such a great leap. We know that the premodern cases, such as Plato's or Aristotle's, stated that language (or *logos*) is the precondition for a political community (or *polis*) and that the *zoon politikon* would flourish ideally in a 'good' commonwealth. In contrast to premodern accounts, Nietzsche does not see humans inclined to form societies as a result of their natural dispositions toward community (e.g. *logos*). Rather he sees community as a result of animalistic drives. Nevertheless, the creation of sustained communal life is reached by a form of reason. A reason, however, which is a rather primitive faculty compared to premodern *logiké*. Nietzsche's idea of reason resembles animalistic instincts pertaining to self-preservation, rather than a highly developed intellectual faculty. His human beings, in this respect, are thus not far off from animals. The collective living of animals is based on mutual dependence and driven to ensure a higher probability of collective preservation as a whole. In accordance to this animalistic trend, for Nietzsche humans are driven toward community by lack of self-sufficiency. Nietzsche's humans must therefore be seen to represent something close to the political animals in Aristotle, rather than creatures driven to community by their constitution as *zoon logon echon*. On this basis, Paul van Tongeren can conclude that "because the human is an animal and furthermore a weak animal [...], he is dependent on community, develops language and logic, protects himself and sanctions his protection with morality and law." (van Tongeren 2010, p. 67; trans. P.R.). On another account, when he takes reason to mean not much more than a compensation for the lack of certain animal features, Nietzsche also makes the proximity of humans to animals explicit. Just like "horns and predator-jaws" for animals, reason for human beings serves the "preservation of the individual" (TL 1, KSA 1, p. 876).[16] Paul van Tongeren has further elaborated on the issue of the hu-

---

16 On the point that reason primarily serves as a means for self-preservation also cf. Knoll 2012, pp. 258ff.

man animality in Nietzsche's essay. Regarding reason he draws the conclusion that even the artistic manner in which humans secure their existence, i.e. erecting a 'true' reality by means of reason, is not a feature of human beings exclusively (van Tongeren 2010, p. 64). So, in Nietzsche's eyes, humans are driven to community because of their animal constitution.[17] But Nietzsche takes the overcoming of the animal features in humans to be a requirement for the emergence of genius. Therefore he criticizes the primacy of self-preservation[18] in *Schopenhauer as Educator*, which modern political philosophers had made the grounds and end of the state.

> As long one desires life in the same way one desires happiness, he has not lifted his sight beyond the horizon of the animal, only that he wants with greater consciousness what the animal seeks in blind compulsion. (SE 5, KSA 1, p. 378)

I will therefore regard what has been expounded here as the psychological primacy of self-preservation, which has its grounds in human animality. In his later works Nietzsche will stress this characteristic as a crucial source for his philosophy. In accord with his aristocratic affinities, he will take the human primarily to be animal in nature and the philosopher an exceptional being. In *Beyond Good and Evil* he offers an account of such an understanding, proclaiming that generally "the human is the not yet determined animal [*noch nicht festgestellte Thier*]" and that successful exemplars are "the scarce exceptions" (BGE 62, KSA 5, p. 81).

V Deception as the ground for law and morality

Nietzsche takes the convention of truth to serve as a means for the requirements of human animality, in this case to compensate for the lack of self-suffi-

---

17 Lemm has aptly pointed to the "great merits of" TL; that Nietzsche here "shows how the pursuit of 'truth' is inseparably linked with the project of civilization." (Lemm 2009, p. 138). She argues that "[i]n order to gain political control over life it is crucial to gain control over language, that is, to gain control over the animal's drive to bring forth intuited metaphors, pictures, and dreamlike illusions." (Lemm 2009, p. 140). On these grounds, investigating Nietzsche's notion of transcendent truth in TL, as Clark does, becomes rather obsolete. What she regards as "Nietzsche's devaluation of human truth" is, in this respect, linked to psychological and social circumstances, rather than to the impossibility of adequate correspondence between language and truth (Clark 1990, pp. 90–93).
18 Günter Abel very convincingly contrasts the phenomenon of self-preservation with the idea of human enhancement, as an articulation of will to power in Nietzsche (Abel 1982). He thereby reveals Nietzsche's opposition to the modern tradition, which takes self-preservation as a

ciency. Therefore, on this level, he can deny any interest in something which could be regarded as scientific truth. Accordingly, he observes that the human "desires the pleasurable, life sustaining consequences of truth; he is indifferent to purely ineffective knowledge, even set as hostile to the adverse and destructive truths." (TL 1, KSA 1 p. 878) Simply stated, human beings want to know nothing of 'doctrines of sovereign becoming'. Rather the manifestation of "a regular and fixed new world" to which the "needy humans can cling and save themselves" is the crucial issue (TL 2, KSA 1, pp. 887f.). Berry has aptly summarized

> what the drive to 'truth' might in fact be a drive toward: stability, security, control over the world of one's own experience, and even a feeling of importance for oneself and meaningfulness in one's life. (Berry 2011, p. 53)

Therefore Nietzsche can take the agreements reached in a natural state to be a work of art, when what they in fact agree on is a construction pertaining to existential needs. Obviously, the aesthetics that govern the human individual's life also govern the convention making process. As a result, what humans perceive as truth is in fact an artistic creation. Hence morality must be considered as based on such an aesthetic construct. In his famous definition of truth he aptly points out the artistic and even poetic characteristics of the process, and reveals how it conveys a first sense of duty:

> What then is truth? A moveable army of metaphors, metonyms and anthropomorphisms, in short, a sum of human relations, which were poetically and rhetorically enhanced, transmitted, decorated, and which after long use seem fixed, canonical and binding to a people [*einem Volke fest, canonisch und verbindlich dünken*]: truths are illusions, of which one has forgotten that they are such. (TL 1, KSA 1, p. 880)

Nietzsche views truth as a convention, which acts binding, because at the bottom line – although it is a work of art – humans nevertheless regard it as natural.

In an experiment, contrasting the "intuitive human" with the "intelligent human" at the end of 'On Truth and Lies', Nietzsche shows how unbearable life could be, if we fail to comply with the premises of our shared convention, i.e. if we in this regard refrain from acting naturally. Lemm has, nevertheless, argued for the position of the intuitive human. According to Lemm, "Nietzsche

---

leitmotif, and shows how Nietzsche intended to transcend it by breaking the teleological link between life and self-preservation in modern interpretations (Abel 1982, pp. 374f., 386). In my case, Nietzsche's artist-philosopher is someone who has transcended mere self-preservation and therefore resembles a life that lies beyond the animality of human beings.

advocates breaking open conceptual language and releasing its 'fixed' and 'absolute' meanings into the flow of the continuous formation and transformation of intuited metaphors." (Lemm 2009, p. 122) I do not, however, believe that Nietzsche is endorsing such a point. The intuitive human suffers more heavily and more often than the intelligent human of concepts and abstraction, "because he does not understand to learn from experience and again and again falls into the same pit which he once fell into." (TL 2, KSA 1, p. 890) Although his motive might be seen as noble – not regarding as true what is in fact a lie – he is also denying existential requirements of the community. The intuitive human will disregard complying with the communal convention on truth and, due to his individual and intuitive constructions, be hermetically sealed off from the social world. Lemm's assertion comes from Nietzsche's high praise of the philosopher, which she regards as standing

> for a lived singular truth that represents a 'pure and honest drive for truth', which is inseparable from the striving for greater freedom, a freedom that directly conflicts with the objection to conform to a determined set of rules. (Lemm 2009, p. 144)

Certainly, according to Nietzsche the philosopher can live "by his own measure and law" (SE 1, KSA 1, p. 339). He is not existentially bound to conventions. Lemm, however, conflates two distinct views in Nietzsche, which can be seen as represented in the ultimate dualism of the master and slave and accordingly demand different ways of life. The animality of humans makes modes of regulation as his portrait of the intuitive man precisely demonstrates an essential to life. In other words, humans in general require laws and morality to able to exist as human beings, whereas the exceptional beings can transgress and even create them. On these grounds Lemm's opinion that "Nietzsche privileges pictorial thinking over abstract thinking because it affirms the human being's continuity with the totality of life" must be seriously rethought (Lemm 2009, p. 119). The intuitive human is entirely isolated.[19] The philosopher surely has the privilege of being able to retreat from communal life at will, but nevertheless is part of it in the sense that he 'understands' the ordinary humans and even involuntarily functions as their guide at times (SE 3, KSA 1, p. 354). Nietzsche recognizes the influence philosophy has on humans, and we must therefore try to understand his focus on deliberate use of this fact to the advantage of the philosopher. The question then arises, how Nietzsche sees the dictate of

---

[19] Van Tongeren has argued that in TL Nietzsche fails to develop a satisfying account of the philosopher. "Nietzsche seeks for the philosopher who unites the contradictory positions" of the intuitive and intelligent human (van Tongeren 2010, p. 66; trans. P.R.).

law enter into the lives of humans? And how he can make use of the results of his inquiry for philosophical legislation?

We can anticipate that a notion of law is naturally tied to the animality of humans. This becomes evident from the canonical character of truth and is explicitly conveyed when Nietzsche calls humans legislators of language. We must, nevertheless, seek out what Nietzsche more precisely holds laws to be. A classic definition of law by legal philosopher Herbert Hart reads that laws are "orders backed by threats which are generally obeyed". He adds that "it must be generally believed that these threats are likely to be implemented in the event of disobedience." (Hart 1994, p. 25) In Nietzsche's case the mere agreement does not in itself hold such a binding premise. To agree on a common language does not convey a sense of threat. The agreement only becomes binding and ordering, because it derived from essential considerations on human existence, i.e. because it brings the threats to life of the state of nature back into play, whenever an individual does not comply. Therefore, in Nietzsche's natural community existence is connected to a need to be truthful. Conversely, as Clark states, to him "truth telling is mere obedience to convention." (Clark 1990, p. 67) Nietzsche explicitly states this in moral terms to underline the existential requirements of obeying connected to truth-telling. He says that there is a duty to speak the truth, "i.e. to use the familiar [*usuell*] metaphors", for society to be able to exist. "Expressed morally: a duty to lie according to a fixed convention, to lie in hordes in a commonly binding manner [*schaarenweise in einem für alle verbindlichen Stile lügen*]." (TL 1, KSA 1, p. 881) In a journal entry from the time of writing 'On Truth and Lies' Nietzsche stresses the political and moral authority even further:

> In the political community a fixed agreement is necessary; it is based on the familiar [*usuell*] use of metaphors. [...] Thus using every word in the manner the masses use it is political convenience and morality. To be true [*wahr sein*] means just not to deviate from the common meaning [*Sinn*] of things. The true is that which is [*das Seiende*], in contrast to the non-real. The first convention is that on what shall count as 'being' [*'seiende'*]. (NL 1872/73, KSA 7, p. 491)

First of all, we can take from his statements that morality and a notion of law emerge from the agreement itself and not that the agreement generalizes *a priori* existing laws or morality. In this respect Nietzsche is opposed to the Natural Right tradition (Dombowsky 2004, p. 34). But the notion of agreement is dropped, for which reason the laws are perceived by human beings as natural. Secondly, the natural community has means which sanction individual transgressions of its dictates, simply because the animality is bound to the meaning of being and a consensus on being is necessary for existence. Nietzsche illustrates these sanctions through the image of the liar, who reaps reproach from his fellow humans through his untruthful actions. Lying is using the agreed upon metaphors in a distorting manner – or: unnaturally –, i.e. applying them to things and experiences contrary to or different from those they were originally intended for. Individuals practicing such a conduct risk the possibility of being excluded from the society of agreed terms (TL 1, KSA 1, p. 878). Since the human perceives it natural to conform in order to satisfy his animality, liars are seen as acting contrary to nature, i.e. contrary to their natural lack of self-sufficiency and thus their drive towards self-preservation. Concluding, the convention of truth, on the ground of its essential premise, transmits a sense of obedience, a basic definition of 'good' and 'bad', which is, however, meant beyond morality, i.e. a definition of natural and unnatural, of beneficial to survival and not beneficial. This basic definition of law, which Nietzsche applies, is – as the title of his essay suggests – ultimately meant in an extra-moral sense. It merely delivers a dichotomy of to conform and not to conform. Can we thus not view Nietzsche as a Legal Positivist? Hart takes Legal Positivism to mean "that it is in no sense a necessary truth that laws reproduce or satisfy certain demands of morality" (Hart 1994, pp. 185f.). Obviously, Nietzsche's natural community does also not reproduce or satisfy moral demands. It only meets the demands of the human being's animality. So this might satisfy necessary conditions for viewing Nietzsche as a Legal Positivist. But does he not also view law informed by morality in an unorthodox way, i.e. not by moral dictates, but merely by relation?

Next to the feature, which naturally transmits an essential notion of obedience, we must take another psychological aspect of animality into account for a thorough understanding of law in Nietzsche. Right at the beginning of 'On Truth and Lies' Nietzsche asserts that humans are driven by vanity (TL 1, KSA 1, p. 876). For Nietzsche vanity primarily underlies the circumstances of perception. He understands it to be a characteristic, which expresses itself most evidently in the fact that humans take themselves to be "the measure of all things" (TL 1, KSA 1, p. 883). However, since humans are not far from animals, vanity does not only stand out as a feature of humanity. The way Nietzsche takes it, vanity is psychologically tied to subjectivity and perspective in all creatures. Denying the possibility of objectivity, the vain being will deny his subjective perspective and most likely any individual being, even the mosquito, therefore takes itself to be the measure of all things, i.e. to view in him "that flying center of the world" (TL 1, KSA 1, p. 875).[20]

---

[20] Paul van Tongeren also points to the possibility that Nietzsche regarded animals as endowed with aesthetic abilities (van Tongeren 2010, pp. 63f.).

In a revealing passage at the end of the first part of 'On Truth and Lies' Nietzsche draws exactly this connection between subjectivity and the perception of law. Although he is dealing here with laws of nature rather than with political or moral laws, the argument nevertheless generally clarifies Nietzsche's view of the institution of law, especially if we remind ourselves that he is dealing with matters in an extra-moral sense. He says that if we had the possibility to perceive the world in different ways, perhaps as a bird or as a worm or as a plant, "no one would continue to speak of such a regularity of nature [*Gesetzmäßigkeit der Natur*], but conceive it as a highly subjective construction." (TL 1, KSA 1, p. 885) What is regarded as law, and is generally held to convey a sense of universality, is to Nietzsche merely a construction beheld from a subjective perspective. Animality determines this perspective for human beings in modern political philosophy. Thus the relation in this case is set up from the psychological primacy of self-preservation, and sustained by the necessity for community. Self-preservation and self-destruction can thus be regarded as the dichotomy, which this basic definition of law transmits. In other words, since humans regard the preservation of life as the greatest good, but are by themselves not self-sufficient, they accordingly need to transfer their desire to a level on which it is perceived as natural. In an extensive journal entry dealing with skepticism, science and regularity he notes: "'Laws of nature'. Nothing but relations to each other and to the human." (NL 1873, KSA 1, p. 625) For Nietzsche, laws are viewed as binding by people, because they are backed with existential threats, threats, however, those people have constructed for themselves by determining being, i.e. what they see as natural. Laws are then artworks, because they derive from the necessity of humans to justify the being of the world aesthetically. The aesthetic justification again derives from a psychological reaction to the meaningless state of humanity, to deceive oneself into having a worth on the basis of which the dichotomy can be held. The modern kind of justification can be seen to lie in the value regarded as the primacy of self-preservation, which Nietzsche strongly rejects. In *The Gay Science*, Nietzsche will therefore ironically exclaim the psychological invention of law as a great achievement of mankind. "[T]he greatest work of mankind until now was to agree on very many things and to impose a law of agreement – disregarding whether these things are true or false." (GS 76, KSA 3, p. 431) Since the basis, on which being was constituted, has influence even on the level of law and morality, it is here that Nietzsche, above all, views the philosopher as obliged to determine what being is, in order to create moral values. Although Nietzsche fulfills the conditions of Legal Positivism, I propose to regard him as a moral positivist. We can thus infer that, whereas Legal Positivism states the relativity of law to moral grounds, moral positivism means the relativity of morality to the truth of being. Therefore Nietzsche can see master and slave morality as two equally possible options of morality.

In a note from the time of *Schopenhauer as Educator*, Nietzsche makes clear that "there is no *hope* for happiness on earth [*Erdenglück*]" and that the "meaning of life for the individual is always the same, at all times." (NL 1874, KSA 7, p. 794) The only meaning the individual can, according to Nietzsche, acquire for life is by means of "living for the advantage of the rarest and most precious exemplars, but not for the advantage of the many, i.e., taken for themselves, the most worthless exemplars." (SE 6, KSA 1, pp. 384f.). From this position Nietzsche has criticized the agreement on human worth, which has been reached in modernity and endows human beings with "basic rights" (GSt, KSA 1, p. 766). Culture, as the rearing and begetting of geniuses, has a far greater worth to Nietzsche than individual self-preservation.

VII Conclusion

For his project of legislating a philosophy of the future the first question, which forces itself upon us, is on which grounds the early Nietzsche sees his values of culture and the begetting of high kinds of individuals more justified than the prevailing values? How does he legitimize his project? Nietzsche has offered his philosophical lawgiving as a corrective for the indifference of nature regarding high types and taken the creation of culture to mean the fulfillment of nature's end (SE 7, KSA 1, pp. 404f.; cf. SE 5, KSA 1, p. 382). Daniel Conway has correctly detected that this cannot account for a solid legitimization. Accordingly he argues in his study *Nietzsche and the Political* that legislation, as a means for the enhancement of mankind, is only 'justified' "by virtue of their audacious desire to subject to design what naturally falls to chance." (Conway 1997, p. 42) I agree that we find no moral or natural justification in the early Nietzsche, especially considering his encompassing relativism in regard to the world and humanity. I would add, however, that his preference for high types, such as philosophers, and the view of them as being more valuable is primarily informed by his adherence to the philosophic tradition of which he is part, and can particularly be traced back to Plato, who most prominently held a philosophic way of life to be most valuable. This can also explain why Nietzsche holds on to dubious measures in Platonic politics.

Nietzsche sees his philosophy as a reversal of Platonism, precisely because he disregards morality as based in nature. Plato could view morality as coined by the idea of the good and therefore his politics reveal a sympathetic stance toward the lower classes, i.e. grant them an access to happiness under favorable conditions. Nietzsche treats slavish human beings harshly, not because he has a general disposition towards lower kinds of humans, but views their idea of morality as obstructive to his project. The fact that he emphatically states that "to the being of culture belongs slavery" already reveals his thorough reckoning with the lower kinds of humans and his need of them for his project (GSt, KSA 1, p. 767). However, he views any morality, which derives from the slave class, as jeopardizing the possibility of a future philosophy. Nietzsche's envisioned morality, a morality based on the dictum that "force gives the first right" (GSt, KSA 1, p. 770), does indeed not enjoy greater legitimacy than a morality based in the herd. The important fact for him is then not to find a justifying measure, but to view morality in general as a relativistic institution. It has become apparent from my reading of 'On Truth and Lies in an Extra-Moral Sense' that Nietzsche finds morality to be based on deception. Because "being [*Dasein*] has no worth in itself" (GSt, KSA 1, p. 765), it is precisely in this manner that he considers morality to be based on lies, lies about the objective stance of humans in the world, the primacy of self-preservation and consequentially about their self-attributed meaning or value. It also has become clear that he links morality to psychological notions of conformism and collective maintenance. This echoes what Keith Ansell-Pearson has analyzed as the "morality of custom", which is "that the human being is trained to think of itself not as an individual, but as part of a community" (Ansell-Pearson 1991, p. 139). This is a form of morality, which prevents the emergence of geniuses.

The elaborations in 'On Truth and Lies' can therefore be viewed to infer to a precursor of slave or herd morality. The overcoming of slave morality is an important prerequisite for the early and later Nietzsche, which can only be realized by legitimizing certain special individuals; a goal, which, however, can only be achieved by "gain of power" (SE 3, KSA 1, p. 357). We can draw on important aspects of slave morality, which Don Dombowsky has summarized in his study on *Nietzsche's Machiavellian Politics*, to illustrate the parallels in the early Nietzsche and the necessity to overcome that morality. According to Dombowsky, "slave morality has its foundation in an antinatural or transcendental lie and despises the body, and conveys a democratic or egalitarian dispensation." (Dombowsky 2004, p. 50). I believe, however, that Dombowsky's assertion of contempt for the body is misleading. As we can conclude from the results of this paper, slave morality must be understood as highly informed by an ontology developed from sensory perception and thus through the body. I would therefore also add that the human belief in the necessity to preserve life determines slave morality through a sense of utility, which Nietzsche describes in *Beyond Good and Evil*. In the elaboration on the distinction between slave morality and master morality, he asserts that "slave-morality is essentially utility-morality [*Nützlichkeits-Moral*]." (BGE 260, KSA 5, p. 211) So in comparison with Dombowsky's summary, we can see that, first, the early Nietzsche certainly sees deception as the source of morality. Second, the need for deception, however, points to a psychological requirement, which is manifested in viewing the individual as valuable. And third, this notion of value can only be sustained by democratic means, i.e. an agreement on the fact that the individual desire for self-preservation is established as the overarching value of community.

A further and important premise of slave morality is the notion of *ressentiment*. The crucial passage is found in *On the Genealogy of Morality* and reads:

> Whereas all noble morality grows from a triumphant yes-saying to itself, slave-morality from the outset says no to an 'external', to a 'different', to a 'not-self': and this no is its creating act. This reversal of the worth positing view [*werthesetzenden Blicks*] – this necessary direction towards the outside rather than back on itself – precisely belongs to ressentiment: for slave morality to come into existence it always necessarily needs a contrary and external world [...], – its actions are at the bottom reactions. (GM I 10, KSA 5, pp. 270f.)

The sense of *ressentiment* revealed in our case can first of all be located in the denial of perspective and the holding on to humanity as the objective measure of things, which determines morality. Next, it is fundamentally a psychological reaction to the meaningless state of humanity. What the human beings of the natural state are thereby denying, is, in sum, a basic prerequisite of the philosopher as a legislator. The philosopher must acknowledge subjectivity and perspective, he must acknowledge the illusory character of the everyday world and he must acknowledge the intrinsic worthlessness of humanity in the world.

To acknowledge these facts is what Nietzsche calls tragic insight. In *The Birth of Tragedy* he had taken tragedy to arise from "true knowledge, from insight into the horrific truth" of the world (BT 7, KSA 1, p. 57). The denial that there is no worth in the world, that the "ground of metaphysics" has been "pulled away" is a denial of tragic insight. But this sort of insight does not imply a full view of things. Perspective, as we have learned, is inherent in psychological preconditions. Tragic insight can therefore only mean a change of perspective, away from viewing life from the vantage point of self-preservation and to a position from which the wisdom of Silenus can be affirmed (BT 3, KSA 1, p. 35). In the early Nietzsche, this is reflected in the attempt to view life and the world from the perspective of art and culture. Nietzsche notes for himself that the "philosopher of tragic knowledge", i.e. the philosopher after the demise of metaphysics, "restores to art back its rights." So even he needs to "want the illusion – therein lies the tragedy [*das Tragische*]." (NL 1872/73, KSA 7, pp. 427f.) Understanding life "as an inherently artistic process", Lemm, however, argues for Nietzsche's preference for the intuitive position: "intuited metaphors and pictorial thinking are of greater value than universal concepts and abstract thinking." (Lemm 2009, p. 119). But, as I have presented in this paper, such a claim fails to consider the relativity of perspective in Nietzsche.

Nietzsche denies any intrinsic value in humans and on this basis can define law only as a relation, which opens up a simple dualism between conformism and nonconformity. While human beings must adhere to conformity, Nietzsche's philosopher must necessarily be a nonconformist, with respect to prevailing values, to achieve a standpoint that is beyond the exposed legal dualism. It is, however, not enough to be an intuitive human being who rejects the illusions of the everyday world. The philosopher, according to Nietzsche, makes use of illusions to attain his goal, because he knows that "life needs illusions, i.e. untruths taken to be truths." (NL 1872/73, KSA 7, p. 433) As a creator of illusions he necessarily requires great artistic skill.

The later Nietzsche will famously call the nonconformist position a standpoint 'beyond good and evil', from which the value of being can be determined. But how exactly can he determine the value of being? In a note from the 1870s, which offers telling insights into his idea of philosophical legislation, Nietzsche reveals a sense of nominalism[21] as a means for legislation. He is meditating the role of philosophy and its relation to greatness. He states that the "concept of greatness [*Begriff der Größe*]" is a variable one, "partially aesthetic, partially moral." In the face of eliminated metaphysics the task of philosophy thus becomes clearer to him:

> There is a law-giving of greatness [*Gesetzgebung der Größe*], a 'name-giving' connected with philosophy: 'that is great', he says and thereby elevates man. It begins with the lawgiving of morality: 'that is great' (NL 1872/73, KSA 7, pp. 447f.).[22]

Although the early Nietzsche has not yet made up his mind on what political measures to employ exactly to ensure lawgiving of greatness, he does make out an overall important feature that has the ability to bind humans, because it mediates a notion of oldness and familiarity. "If one could create customs [*Sitte*], powerful customs! Thereby one also has morality [*Sittlichkeit*]. / But customs formed through the advancing of single powerful personalities." (NL

---

[21] Knoll also refers to the nominalist tradition, which can be traced back to Ockham, in Nietzsche's TL (Knoll 2012, esp. pp. 259, fn. 9).
[22] Nietzsche used an almost verbatim passage in the Thales chapter of his planned monograph *Philosophy in the Tragic Age of the Greeks* (cf. PTAG 3, KSA 1, p. 816).

1872/73, KSA 7, p. 431) In *Human, All Too Human* he states that it is of no concern where customs derived from, but that it is important that they be "above all as a means to maintain a community, a people" (HH 96, KSA 2, p. 93). Nietzsche's descriptions strongly reflect Platonic means. Plato also saw a necessity that the citizens of his best *polis* believe that they are derived from the same ancestors and have the same customs. Although Plato had taken an adverse stance with regard to art and illusions, he, nevertheless, builds his commonwealth on deceptive illusions. He employs them as emergency measures or necessary evils to secure the rule of philosophy. But because Nietzsche's thought is a fashion of what I dubbed moral positivism, he can take the means of installing illusions without the ignoble overtones Plato had to fight with. Taking lying about the origin of customs is to Nietzsche simply a very powerful tool to ensure political order, whereas Plato persuasively had to legitimize the unjust means in his construction of the just city and thereby risked his moral integrity (cf. Rep. 414b-d). The relativistic grounds, from which Nietzsche constructs his political and moral philosophy, save him from the risk of moral inconsistency. Accordingly, his concentration is on the psychological and social effects of political measures. In *On the Use and Disadvantage of History for Life* Nietzsche thus reflects on the influence of Plato's noble lie in *The Republic* and emphasizes especially its effects: "It is impossible to rebel against the past! It is impossible to resist the work of the gods! It must be held as the indissoluble law of nature" (HL 10, KSA 1, p. 328). Nietzsche views politics as directed at enabling the strongest and longest lasting as its binding effects, even if this includes lying about the past. For him, these effects must secure the emergence and sustaining of noble and powerful kinds of humans, who are no more animals. Therefore, if we take the act of determining being, the qualification of legislation as a lawgiving of greatness and the enduring effects of political measures into consideration, we might be able to glimpse what it means to pursue 'great politics'.

Bibliography

Abel, Günter (1982): "Nietzsche contra 'Selbsterhaltung'. Steigerung der Macht und ewige Wiederkehr". In: *Nietzsche-Studien* 10, pp. 367–407.
Andresen, Joshua (2010): "Truth and Illusion beyond Falsification. Re-reading Nietzsche's 'On Truth and Lie in the Extra-Moral Sense'". In: *Nietzsche-Studien* 39, pp. 255–281.
Ansell-Pearson, Keith (1991): *Nietzsche Contra Rousseau. A Study of Nietzsche's Moral and Political Thought*. Cambridge: Cambridge University Press.
Appel, Fredrick (1999): *Nietzsche Contra Democracy*. Ithaca, London: Cornell University Press.

Berry, Jessica (2011): *Nietzsche and the Ancient Skeptical Tradition*. Oxford, New York: Oxford University Press.

Clark, Maudemarie (1990): *Nietzsche on Truth and Philosophy*. Cambridge: Cambridge University Press.

Conway, Daniel W. (1997): *Nietzsche and the Political*. London, New York: Routledge.

Dannhauser, Werner J. (1974): *Nietzsche's View of Socrates*. Ithaca, London: Cornell University Press.

Dombowsky, Don (2004): *Nietzsche's Machiavellian Politics*. New York: Palgrave MacMillan.

Halliwell, Stephen (2002): *The Aesthetics of Mimesis. Ancient Texts and Modern Problems*. Princton, Oxford: Princeton University Press.

Hart, H. L. A. (1994): *The Concept of Law*. 2nd edition. Oxford: Oxford University Press.

Janaway, Christopher (1995): *Images of Excellence. Plato's Critique of the Arts*. Oxford, New York: Oxford University Press.

Klossowski, Pierre (1997): *Nietzsche and the Vicious Circle*. Daniel W. Smith (trans.). Chicago, London: University of Chicago Press.

Knoll, Manuel (2009): "Nietzsches Begriff der sozialen Gerechtigkeit". In: *Nietzsche-Studien* 38, pp. 156–181.

Knoll, Manuel (2012): "Nietzsches Kritik am wissenschaftlichen Willen zur Wahrheit und seine Tugend der intellektuellen Redlichkeit". In: Helmut Heit/Günter Abel/Marco Brusotti (eds.): *Nietzsches Wissenschaftsphilosophie. Hintergründe, Wirkungen und Aktualität*. Berlin, Boston: De Gruyter. pp. 257–270.

Lemm, Vanessa (2009): *Nietzsche's Animal Philosophy. Culture, Politics, and the Animality of the Human Being*. New York: Fordham University Press.

Nehamas, Alexander (1985): *Nietzsche. Life as Literature*. Cambridge, London: Harvard University Press.

Ottmann, Henning (1999): *Philosophie und Politik bei Nietzsche*. 2nd edition. Berlin, New York: de Gruyter.

Plato (1991): *The Republic*. Allan Bloom (trans.). 2nd edition. Chicago, London: University of Chicago Press.

Plato (1998): *Phaedo*. Eva Brann, Peter Kalkavage, Eric Salem (trans.). Newburyport: Focus Publishing.

Rosen, Stanley (2004): *The Mask of Enlightenment. Nietzsche's Zarathustra*. 2nd edition. New Haven, London: Yale University Press.

Schopenhauer, Arthur (1998): *Die Welt als Wille und Vorstellung*. Vols. I and II. Munich: Deutscher Taschenbuch Verlag.

Soll, Ivan (1998): "Schopenhauer, Nietzsche, and the Redemption of Life Through Art". In: Christopher Janaway (ed.): *Willing and Nothingness. Schopenhauer as Nietzsche's Educator*. Oxford, New York: Oxford University Press, pp. 79–115.

Soll, Ivan (2001): "Nietzsche on the Illusions of Everyday Experience". In: Richard Schacht (ed.): *Nietzsche's Postmoralism. Essays on Nietzsche's Prelude to Philosophy's Future*. Cambridge: Cambridge University Press, pp. 7–33.

Stegmaier, Werner (1994): *Nietzsches 'Genealogie der Moral'*. Darmstadt: Wissenschaftliche Buchgesellschaft.

Van Tongeren, Paul (2010): "'Ein Thier oder ein Gott' oder beides. Nietzsches 'Ueber Wahrheit und Lüge im aussermoralischen Sinne' und Aristoteles' Politik". In: *Nietzsche-Studien* 39, pp. 55–69.

Von Vacano, Diego A. (2007): *The Art of Power. Machiavelli, Nietzsche, and the Making of Aesthetic Political Theory*. Lanham: Lexington Books.

Manuel Knoll
The "Übermensch" as a Social and Political Task: A Study in the Continuity of Nietzsche's Political Thought*

Nietzsche's conception of the "Übermensch" is as famous as it is obscure. The interpretations of the "Overman", or "Superman", found in the literature cover a broad spectrum. While most authors understand the conception of the "Übermensch", for good reasons, as one of Nietzsche's "positive teachings", others resist taking it seriously. According to Alasdair MacIntyre, for example, the *Übermensch* belongs "in the pages of a philosophical bestiary rather than in serious discussion" (MacIntyre 1984, p. 22).[1] The term "Übermensch" first gained notoriety in Nietzsche's writings. Prior to this, however, reference to the term is found, literally or analogously, in the work of many authors, such as Carlyle, Emerson, Herder, Hegel, Goethe and Jean-Paul. The term has connections with Romanticism and Idealism, Darwinism, and the concept of the "genius" in aesthetics.[2] Perhaps the term's original usage can be traced to the Hellenistic Greek word "hyperanthropos", which refers to Greek heroes and divine humans (Ottmann 1999, p. 383).

Nietzsche introduces the conception of the "Übermensch" metaphorically in the first part of *Thus spoke Zarathustra*, which was published in 1883.[3] Zarathustra, the protagonist of Nietzsche's philosophical narrative, is introduced as the teacher of the "Übermensch", and, later in the book, also as the teacher of the "eternal return of the same" (Z I Prologue 3; Z III Convalescent; Z III Riddle). How these two "positive teachings" are connected will be addressed later in this paper.[4] In *Zarathustra*, Nietzsche links the conception of the "Über-

---

* For their astute and helpful comments on this paper, I thank Urs Andreas Sommer, Werner Stegmaier, and the participants of the workshop on "Nietzsche and Political Theory" that Barry Stocker and I organized Sep. 5–7 2012 at the Manchester Workshops in Political Theory (Mancept).
1 According to MacIntyre, Nietzsche saw his "own task" partly in "founding a new morality". MacIntyre criticizes Nietzsche's rhetoric in this context because, for him, it "becomes cloudy and opaque, and metaphorical assertion replaces argument". For MacIntyre, Nietzsche is "philosophically most powerful and cogent in the negative part" of his critique (MacIntyre 1984, p. 22).
2 For the sources of the term "Übermensch" before Nietzsche and for the various connections of the conception see Benz 1961.
3 For an analysis of Nietzsche's metaphors see Stegmaier 2010.
4 For an interpretation of Nietzsche's teachings as anti-teachings see Stegmaier 2000.

mensch" with "the death of God", which according to the fifth book[5] of *The Gay Science* means that "the belief in the Christian God has become unbelievable" (GS 343).[6] The death of God is proclaimed in the prologue of *Zarathustra*, immediately before Zarathustra starts his teaching of the "Übermensch" (Z I Prologue 2). At the end of the first part of the book, Zarathustra solemnly declares: "Dead are all Gods: now we want the Übermensch to live" (Z I Virtue; cf. Z I Hinterworldly). Already in *The Gay Science* Nietzsche states that "perhaps man will rise ever higher as soon as he ceases to flow out into a God" (GS 285).

A central statement of Zarathustra's first teaching, to which he returns throughout the book, is his proclamation that the "Übermensch" is the "meaning of the earth [*Sinn der Erde*]" (Z I Prologue 3).[7] Immediately afterwards he cautions his audience to stay faithful to the earth and to not believe in those who talk about other-worldly hopes. Later he explains that those people, the religious people and especially the priests, created their unhealthy interpretations of the world because they were suffering and their bodies were sick and tired (Z I Prologue 3; Z I Hinterworldly).[8]

What does Nietzsche want to say with his obscure declaration that the "Übermensch" is the "meaning of the earth"? And what does he mean by the term "Übermensch", to which he assigns such an enormous importance in his declaration? What distinguishes the common *man* (*Mensch*), who according to Zarathustra is "something that should be *over*come (*über*wunden)", from the man that is *above* or *over* (*über*) man (Z I Prologue 3, italics by M.K.)? This paper addresses these questions by giving an interpretation of the conception of the "Übermensch" based on Nietzsche's anthropology and by showing how it is connected to his works before and after *Zarathustra*. The first step toward understanding Nietzsche's conception of the Overman is to comprehend his conception of man.

---

[5] Nietzsche added the fifth book of *The Gay Science* only to the second edition, which was published in 1887.

[6] All translations of Nietzsche's writings from German into English are from M.K. based on the text of the KSA.

[7] In the prologue, Nietzsche's Zarathustra proclaims as well: "Uncanny is human existence and still without meaning [...] I want to teach men the meaning of their being: which is the Übermensch, the lightning from the dark cloud man" (Z prologue 7; cf. Z I Virtue 2; Z III Tablets 2).

[8] According to Marie-Luise Haase, Nietzsche uses the word "earth [*Erde*]" instead of "world [*Welt*]" because "earth" excludes the so-called "true world" or "other world [*Hinterwelt*]" (Haase 1984, p. 235).

Though in his late works Nietzsche uses the term "Übermensch" only a few times, his statements are far more clear and informative than the obscure parabolic teachings in his philosophical narrative *Zarathustra*, which should not always be identified with Nietzsche's own views.⁹ In *Ecce Homo* he uses the term "Übermensch" to designate a "type that turned out supremely well", which is opposed to "'modern' men, to 'good' men, to Christians and other nihilists" (EH Books 1). In *The Anti-Christ*, Nietzsche defines the "Übermensch" as a "type of higher value" or as "a higher type" which is "in relation to humankind as a whole a sort of Übermensch" (A 4). These definitions suggest the strong connection of the conception of the "Übermensch" to the themes of Nietzsche's early writings. In the posthumously published essay *The Greek State*, from 1872, Nietzsche claims that the "Olympian existence", the "generation and preparation of the genius", is the "actual goal of the state" (GSt, KSA 1, p. 776). In the third *Untimely Meditation*, *Schopenhauer as Educator*, which appeared in 1874, Nietzsche explains his image of humanity and gives his account of the elevation of man, which culminates in an anthropological imperative: "Mankind must work continually at the production of individual great men – this and nothing else is its task" (SE 6, KSA 1, pp. 383f.).

The above mentioned quotes illustrate and support the first thesis of this paper. In the first thesis the claim is made that *The Greek State* and the third *Untimely Meditation* already contain essential elements of Nietzsche's later conception of the "Übermensch", the meaning of which is better understood by connecting it to arguments articulated in these early writings.¹⁰ The asser-

---

9 *Zarathustra* is a philosophical narrative, not a treatise. Daniel Conway remarks appropriately: "Zarathustra's evolving doctrine of the *Übermensch* often deviates significantly from the account Nietzsche provides in The *Antichrist(ian)*, and we have good reason that Zarathustra did not fully understand the teachings entrusted to him" (Conway 1997, p. 21). According to Conway's convincing proposal, we should distinguish between Zarathustra's and Nietzsche's account of the "Übermensch" (Conway 1997, pp. 21, 25; cf. Conway 1988; cf. a study of the development of Zarathustra's teachings Lampert 1986). In *Ecce Home* Nietzsche distances himself clearly from Darwinist or idealist interpretations of his teaching of the "Übermensch" (EH Books 1; cf. A 3 and 4). Especially the Darwinist misinterpretation, which understands the "Übermensch" as a higher species that should one day progressively evolve out of the species "man", is encouraged by many formulations in the first part of *Zarathustra*. The reason for the Darwinist misinterpretation is in all likelihood a neglect of the context of Zarathustra's teaching: in order to make himself understood amongst his audience, the people, Zarathustra tries to connect his teaching of the "Übermensch" to Darwin's well-know descent theory (Stegmaier 2000, p. 210).
10 Though he doesn't explicitly refer to the above mentioned earlier writings of Nietzsche, Daniel Conway already notices correctly: "the *Übermensch* is best understood within the context of Nietzsche's enduring admiration for heroic individuals and 'higher humanity'" (Conway 1997, p. 20).

tion of the first thesis is that the conception of the "Übermensch" is at the center of Nietzsche's entire philosophical thought. In its substantiation evidence is provided that Nietzsche was concerned mainly with the future or perfection of a few outstanding individuals, and not, as some scholars suppose, with that of the human species as a whole (Siemens 2008, p. 235; Siemens 2009, p. 30; Patton's essay in this volume, p. 94).[11]

According to the second thesis of this paper, Nietzsche conceives the generation of a higher type of man or "Übermensch" not primarily as the affair of an isolated individual but as a social and political task. The individualistic understanding of the "Übermensch" has been especially encouraged by Walter Kaufmann's rehabilitation of Nietzsche's philosophy, which–despite its merits–depoliticized his thought and led to the mistaken view that Nietzsche reflects on the individual detached from social and political contexts (Kaufmann 1950; cf. Ansell-Pearson 1994, pp. 1f.).[12] Since the mid 1970s, in the Anglo-Saxon literature a series of studies on Nietzsche's political philosophy have appeared.[13] However, even in 2008, Thomas H. Brobjer tried to show that Nietzsche was "not interested in or concerned with politics", or that he was an "a-, supra- and anti-political thinker" (Brobjer 2008, p. 205). Along the same lines, already in 1998 Brobjer made an attempt to argue for *The Absence of Political Ideals in Nietzsche's Writings* (Brobjer 1998).[14]

---

11 Herman Siemens speaks of Nietzsche's "generic perfectionism", and declares that Nietzsche's "perfectionist demand" "has a general or generic in orientation, not to the lives of a few select individuals, but to the species as a whole" (Siemens 2008, p. 235). Similar to Siemens, Daniel Conway sees Nietzsche's "commitment to the position known as *perfectionism*" at the center of his political thinking (Conway 1997, p. 6, Conway's italics). For Conway, Nietzsche "locates the sole justification of human existence in the continued perfectibility of the species as a whole, as evidenced by the pioneering accomplishments of its highest exemplars" (Conway 1997, pp. 6f.). Like Siemens, Conway relates perfectionism to the species as a whole. However, his chapter on *Political Perfectionism* shows that he is aware that for Nietzsche only the "few select individuals" truly matter: "The emergence of great human beings contributes to the enhancement of humankind both directly, by advancing the frontiers of human perfectibility, and indirectly, by encouraging (some) others to flourish as well" (Conway 1997, p. 8).
12 Interpretations of Nietzsche's philosophy, which are influenced by Kaufmann, are, for example, Kaulbach 1980, and Hollingdale 1965. Though Hollingdale emphasizes that Kaufmann's book "inaugurated a new epoch in the study of Nietzsche's philosophy", he doesn't interpret the Übermensch exclusively in an individualistic way (Hollingdale 1965, pp. VIII, 196ff., 230). For an extremely individualistic interpretation of the Übermensch influenced by Kaufmann see Nehamas 1985, pp. 7 f., 167, 174, 230.
13 It was mainly Tracy Strong's book, published in 1975, which opened the way for several monographs on Nietzsche's political philosophy (Strong 2000). For an overview and summary of the content of the publications between 1960 and 2000 see Reckermann 2003.
14 For an astute response to this attempt to depoliticize Nietzsche's thought see Dombowsky 2001, cf. Brobjer's reply 2001. Brobjer criticizes Don Dombowsky on the grounds that he

The second thesis can already be substantiated by *The Greek State*, in which Nietzsche declares that "Olympian existence" or "genius" is the "actual goal of the state" (GSt, KSA 1, p. 776). The conception of state and society that Nietzsche explains in his later works *Beyond Good and Evil* and *The Anti-Christ* returns unmistakably to the conception of a good and just political order, which he defends in *The Greek State*: "Every elevation of the type 'man' has so far been the work of an aristocratic society" (BGE 257). While Nietzsche's conception of man and of the elevation of man will be examined in the first part of this paper, the second part investigates his aristocratic conception of a good and just political order and its relation to the generation of a higher type of man or "Übermensch". Another important topic of the second part are the criteria, and standards, that Nietzsche applies to measure the worth or rank of a man, which are as well the criteria for the Overman.

On the whole, this paper aims to show the continuity and unity of Nietzsche's political thought. This might be surprising, because of the aphoristic and anti-systematic way in which Nietzsche presents and sets the scene of his entire philosophy. He even criticizes the "will to a system" as showing a "lack of probity" (TI Arrows 26). However, there are systematic aspects to his political thought. Though the common division of Nietzsche's philosophy in three periods has some good reasons behind it, there are no important changes between the conceptions of a good and just political order he presents in his early and his later works. The same is true for his normative judgment that such an order serves mainly to enable a higher and more valuable type of man. By demonstrating that Zarathustra's doctrine of the "Übermensch" focuses on the generation of this type of man, this paper also shows that Zarathustra's teaching has to be taken seriously, something that has been questioned in the literature (Zittel 2011, pp. 137ff., 199–203; Lampert 1986, p. 258). Zarathustra's doctrine is clearly connected to Nietzsche's early and late concern for the promotion of outstanding individuals, which is an important element in the continuity and unity of his thought. The interpretations in this paper are mainly based on Nietzsche's published works, because it is not clear which parts of the *Nachlass* (the posthumously published notes) were intended for publication, and in which order, and according to which of his plans.[15]

---

doesn't challenge the statements he mentions by Nietzsche in order to substantiate his view that Nietzsche was disinterested with regard to politics and political perspectives. However, the statements Brobjer mentions only suggest that Nietzsche was disinterested in the "politics of the day" and the egoistic politics of the parties and nation states of his time, not in politics in general (Brobjer 2001).

15 The interpretations in this paper are, however, based on Nietzsche's posthumously published essay *The Greek State*. This essay is an almost exact copy of a part of a long fragment

I Nietzsche's anthropology: his conception of man and of the elevation of man

Nietzsche's image of humanity is strongly influenced by Darwinism, which he understands as the "latest great scientific movement" (GS 357). The relation of Nietzsche to Darwin is disputed in the literature, and though Nietzsche criticized Darwin several times, specifically concerning the scientific content of Darwin's theory of evolution, Nietzsche was a Darwinist in all periods of his career (Stegmaier 1987, pp. 264–287, 269).[16] Already in his second *Untimely Meditation*, Nietzsche mentions the "doctrines of sovereign becoming, of the fluidity of all concepts, types and species, of the lack of any cardinal difference between man and animal", which he takes to be "true" (HL 9, KSA 1, p. 319). The conclusions drawn from the descent theory, that man is actually a sort of animal, are of central importance in the way Nietzsche articulates his image of humanity (BGE 202).

Nietzsche uncompromisingly reveals the consequences of the biological sciences for human self-understanding. As a descendent of the monkey, man has to give up his belief that he is a relative of God. Thus, he loses his special position and is to be regarded as any other "natural being [*Naturwesen*]", whose life will ultimately end in death (DS 7, KSA 1, p. 196; D 49). The theory of evolution also has serious consequences for the traditional view of the role of human reason. The intellect of the human animal can no longer be seen as a divine element which inheres in man and allows him to understand the truth about the whole of reality.[17] Confronted with the theory of evolution, the intellect is unable to maintain its vain self-conception and appears in its true function as a "means for the preservation" of "those weaker, less robust individu-

---

Nietzsche had written for an early version of *The Birth of Tragedy* (NL, 10[1], KSA 7, pp. 333–349). *The Greek State* is part of a collection of five short essays entitled *Five Prefaces to Five Unwritten Books* which Nietzsche gave to Cosima Wagner for Christmas 1872. *The Greek State* is a well elaborated text and most of its basic ideas are repeated in *Beyond Good and Evil* and *The Antichrist*. These are the reasons why this essay should not be discarded as a source for Nietzsche's political thought.

16 On the contrary, Andreas Urs Sommer argues that Nietzsche's positive view of Darwin in the middle period of his work since *Human, All Too Human* changes towards a more critical approach in his later works (Sommer 2010, p. 32).

17 See for the divinity of human reason Plato, *The Republic*, 518 a, cf. 490 b, and Aristotle, *The Nicomachean Ethics*, 1177 b 27ff., and Aristotle, *Metaphysics*, 1074 b 15ff. Starting with Plato and Aristotle, and continuing until the thought of German Idealism, the conviction that reason allows man to understand the truth about the whole reality is fundamental for occidental philosophical thought.

als, who are denied horns and sharp fangs of a beast of prey with which to wage the struggle for existence" (TL 1, KSA 1, p. 876).

As a "natural being [*Naturwesen*]" that has not been created by a God, but evolved over time, man has no fixed and unchangeable essence. This is why Nietzsche defines man as the "yet undetermined animal [*noch nicht festgestellte Thier*]" (BGE 62; cf. GM III 13). From an aesthetic perspective, Nietzsche understands man – analogous to the stone of the sculptor – as a material, which can be formed by education and breeding. Culture and especially religion and morals are the means through which the human animal is formed in the course of history (BGE 62; EH Z 7). For Nietzsche, in the flux of becoming, man undergoes significant changes, which can be seen by the fact that in the prehistoric period, and in the ancient world, man had very different characteristics from those he possesses in the modern world. While the world was once dominated by healthy, strong, noble and bellicose men, which were fundamentally predators and beasts, Christianity has managed to largely determine (*feststellen*) the human animal by domesticating it until "a gregarious animal, something benevolent, sick and mediocre has been bread, the European of today" (JGB 62; cf. GM I; NL 1885/86, KSA 12, p. 72). This development goes along with the belief that "the meaning of all culture is to breed a tame and civilized animal, a domestic animal, out of the beast of prey 'man'" (GM I 11).

Nietzsche explains the atrophy and degradation of European man chiefly by the fatal power of Christianity and of the Christian priests. The Christians have devalued this-worldly sensual existence and life by relating it to the imaginary reference point of an other-worldly "higher" existence and life. The Christian interpretation of the world has made the human animal sick, because it understands humans as guilty and sinful and negates their corporeality and sensuality. Religious motives like guilt, sin or original sin, which have been created by the priestly art of interpretation, not only unsettled and discouraged the masses, but created a guilty conscience resulting in a consciousness of guilt. Through the power of such interpretations, which negate life and man, and through the Christian morals, whose ascetic ideal calls for the repression of the drives and instincts, the human animal has become progressively sick and weak (GM II and III). From an aesthetic perspective, Nietzsche understands man as a beautiful stone, which has been "bungled and botched" through Christian sculpture (BGE 62).

For Nietzsche, one important cause for the European man becoming diminished and mediocre is the notion of the equality of all men that had, over the ages, been distributed and enforced by Christianity. This thought, which Nietzsche understands as the "greatest and most malicious assault on noble humanity ever committed" (A 43), has such a harmful effect on man, because it levels the "abysmal disparity in order and gulf of rank between men and man" (BGE 62). The basis of this judgment is Nietzsche's view that men are fundamentally unequal. The thought of the equality of all men has consequences for the political life in Europe, because from it derives the "poison of the teaching 'equal rights for all'" (A 43). The democratic movement "obtains the inheritance of the Christian movement", which promotes the process of the European man becoming diminished and mediocre (BGE 202). In regard to this progressive decay and decline, Nietzsche even considers the possibility of a "collective depravation of man", which could lead to a disdainful type of decay which he illustrates with his conception of the "last man" (BGE 203; cf. Z Prologue 5).[18] However, Nietzsche still has hope for a countermovement, which can cause an increase and elevation of the type "man" through education and "breeding" (cf. Haase 1984, p. 234).

The destiny of humankind, and in particular the creation of individual outstanding men, is one of the most important topics of Nietzsche's entire philosophical thought. This is already evident in the third *Untimely Meditation*, which pronounces Schopenhauer's image of humanity as an ideal. Nietzsche's conception of man is at this time already radically non-egalitarian. He not only conceives of the different men as fundamentally unequal, but attributes to them an extremely unequal value. After the human animal has lost its special position, there is no reason for Nietzsche to attribute to every single man a particular worth or dignity. According to his view, "'man as such', absolute man, possesses neither dignity, nor rights, nor duties" (GSt, KSA 1, p. 776). Analogously, he declares in a fragment of the *Nachlass*, which deals with socialism: "human rights do not exist" (NL 1877, KSA 8, 25[1]). Nietzsche's fundamental anthropological views are oriented towards the Greek thinkers of classical antiquity, who like Plato and Aristotle take as a starting point a fundamental inequality and difference in worth of men and to whom the thought of a general human dignity is alien.[19] In addition, they are a consequence of his turning away from Christianity and of his Darwinism.

In the third *Untimely Meditation*, Nietzsche advocates applying "a teaching to society and its purposes" that one can gain "from the study of all species in the kingdom of animals and plants." According to this teaching, what matters for all species "is only the individual higher exemplar, the more uncommon,

---

18 Laurence Lampert observes shrewdly: "Last man and Superman represent the two extremes made possible by the malleability of man, 'the as yet undetermined animal'" (Lampert 1986, p. 24). According to Werner Stegmaier's convincing interpretation, the "last man" holds himself to be the *last* in the sense that beyond his form of existence man cannot be further enhanced (Stegmaier 2013, p. 163).
19 Cf. Knoll 2009a, subch. 3 of the introduction and ch. VI.1.

more powerful, more complex, more fruitful" (SE 6, KSA 1, p. 384). Nietzsche not only understands the higher exemplars of the species "man", which are the purpose of society and humankind, as the "most valuable exemplars", but holds that the masses of human animals "taken individually, are the least valuable exemplars", which should be regarded as a "failed work of nature" (SE 6, KSA 1, pp. 384f.). In harmony with this, he states in his late philosophy: "Among men, as in every other animal species, there is an excess of failures, of the sick, the degenerate, the fragile, of those who suffer necessarily; the successful cases are, among men too, always the exception" (BGE 62).

On the basis of his image of humanity, in the third *Untimely Meditation* Nietzsche formulates his anthropological imperative: the task of mankind is to work constantly "at the production of individual great men" (SE 6, KSA 1, pp. 384f.). This imperative is in the centre of Nietzsche's entire philosophical thought. Also in his late work he declares that the "higher breeding of mankind" is the "greatest of all tasks" (EH BT 4). Nietzsche understands the higher men as the "genuine men, those who are no longer animal [*Nicht-mehr-Thiere*]", an honoring that only philosophers, artists and saints can achieve (SE 5, KSA 1, p. 380). With them the human animal species "has arrived at its limits and at its transition into a higher species" and thus to the "goal of its development". This evolution, which Nietzsche doesn't conceive of as a linear process of progression, is only possible for a few exceptional men and not, as one could suppose, to humankind as a whole and as a species. The "goal of development" is by no means "the exemplars, which in time are the latest, but rather the apparently scattered and accidental existences, which here and there happen sometimes under favorable conditions" (SE 6, KSA 1, p. 384; cf. HL 9, KSA 1, p. 317)

Analogous to this account in the third *Untimely Meditation*, Nietzsche explains in *The Anti-Christ* and in *Ecce Homo* that his conception of the "Übermensch" should not be understood as a form of Darwinism (EH Books 1). He emphasizes that "humankind does not represent a development towards the better or stronger or higher" and that his problem is not "what should succeed humankind in the sequence of beings". The "type of higher value has often enough occurred, but as a lucky strike [*Glücksfall*], as an exception, never as willed" (A 3; cf. A 4); and thus

> there is a continuous success of single cases at different places of the world coming out from different cultures, which represent a higher type, something which is in relation to humankind as a whole a sort of Übermensch. Such lucky accidents of great success have always been possible and will perhaps always be possible. And even whole families, tribes, or peoples may occasionally represent such a stroke of luck [*Treffer*] (A 4).[20]

---

[20] Contrary to this statement in *The Antichrist*, Zarathustra teaches that there has never existed an "Übermensch" so far (Z II Priests).

These statements clearly show that Nietzsche was mainly concerned with the future of a few outstanding individuals, and not with the perfection of the human species as a whole. They also thereby shed light on similar statements he published in earlier writings that could lead to such a misunderstanding (GM Preface 6).

Nietzsche's account of the elevation of man in the third *Untimely Meditation* links up with his "artists' metaphysics", which he developed two years before in *The Birth of Tragedy* (BT, Attempt 5; cf. BT Attempt 7). A central thought of this metaphysics, which was inspired by Schopenhauer's *The World as Will and Representation*, stays relevant for his later philosophy. The basis of this thought is the view that human life consists of an abundance of suffering and is per se without meaning and value. However, for Nietzsche the world and human existence can be justified through art and culture, because art and culture give life meaning and value, which makes it possible to find redemption from suffering and to affirm life (BT 4; BT Attempt 5). Human life not only gains worth and meaning through art and culture, but through the higher and genuine men, who create art and culture. Nietzsche asserts that the generation and existence of great humans and geniuses is itself the "goal of all culture" and the "last purpose" of humankind (SE 3, KSA 1, p. 358; SE 6, KSA 1, p. 384).

Nietzsche understands the genuine men as the "redeeming men", because through them nature achieves "its redemption from the curse of animal life" and "from itself". Nature longs for this redemption through the "genuine men, those who are no longer animal", and thus it strives to bring out the philosophers, artists and saints in order to complete itself. The higher men are also the goal of nature, because through them nature achieves "enlightenment about itself" and thus "its self knowledge". Through the higher men "being [*Dasein*] holds up before itself a mirror", "in which life appears no longer meaningless but in its metaphysical significance" (SE 5, KSA, p. 378). After the "waters of religion are ebbing away and leaving behind swamps or ponds", the Christian interpretation and meaning-giving of human life, which talks about "other-worldly hopes", loses its credibility (SE 4, KSA 1, p. 366; cf. Z I Prologue 3). On the contrary, the new meaning-giving, which Nietzsche proclaims with his anthropological imperative, and which Zarathustra teaches, is purely terrestrial and secular. It proclaims the "Übermensch" as the "meaning of the earth", as the "meaning" of man's being, and as the "goal of man" (Z I Prologue 3; cf. Z I Prologue 7; Z III Tablets 2). In order to promote this goal, a new morality with new values and value judgments of "good" and "bad" has to be created and established in society through a higher form of politics (BGE 208–212). Nietzsche's Zarathustra teaches that "nobody yet knows what is good and bad – unless it be the creator! But he it is who creates the goal of man and gives the earth its meaning and its future: he it is who <u>achieves that</u> something is good and bad" (Z III Tablets 2).

That the goal of humankind and culture consists in creating great humans and geniuses needs to be made aware to people and to be circulated. So far it has mainly been an unconscious drive of nature, which again and again shaped man. To be sure, most of the artistic experiments nature carries out with the human animal fail. However, Nietzsche concedes that nature "succeeds everywhere in producing the most marvelous beginnings, traits and forms: and thus the people we live among resemble a field of rubble over which are scattered the most precious artistic drafts, where everything shouts towards us: come, help, complete, put together what belongs together, we long immensely to become whole" (SE 6, KSA 1, pp. 385f.; cf. Z II Redemption). In regard of this, Nietzsche considers it necessary "to replace that 'obscure drive' one day with a conscious willing" (SE 6, KSA 1, p. 387). The same thought is expressed in *Zarathustra*. In his first teaching, after he proclaimed that the "Übermensch" is the "meaning of the earth", Zarathustra requests of his audience: "Your will should say: the Übermensch <u>shall be</u> the meaning of the earth!" (Z I prologue 3). In accordance with this request, Nietzsche pronounces in his late philosophy that his problem is "which type of man one should <u>breed</u>, one should <u>will</u>, as more valuable, more worthy of life, more certain of the future" (A 3).

After the belief in the Christian God has become unbelievable, for Nietzsche there is no higher authority left, which could bestow meaning on human life. After the "death of God", man has to create the meaning of his life himself through an autonomous act of will. To be sure, in the third *Untimely Meditation* Nietzsche claims that the endowment of meaning he proposes is linked to the strivings of nature. However, already at this time he is aware that in the end he institutes an autonomous meaning-giving (HL 9, KSA 1, p. 319). In *Daybreak*, which appeared in 1881, Nietzsche extends the thought of the uncircumventable human autonomy to the area of morals. He explains that humankind, which has no "universally recognized <u>goal</u>", equally has no "moral law" that it could "find" somewhere or which it could "<u>receive as a command</u>" from somewhere. But if humankind decides to give itself a goal "at its own discretion", than it can "subsequently impose upon itself a moral law" that corresponds to that goal (D 108).

Nietzsche's thought on the moral autonomy of man, which dissociates itself explicitly from Kant's categorical imperative and Kant's concept of autonomy, has an individualistic, and as well a social and political dimension. It is individualistic, because as the meaning of life, moral values are created by human individuals and because some people are able to live according to their own personal morals. But only those few people are fit for the "creation of new own tablets of values" who can liberate themselves from the ruling "opinions and value judgments" and from the prevailing moral precepts (GS 335). Contrary to the "many" and to the "most", who cling to tradition, the motto of the morally autonomous individuals should be: "We, however, want to become who we are, – the new, the unique, the incomparable, the ones who give themselves the law, who create themselves!" (GS 335; cf. D 107).

Nietzsche's thought on the moral autonomy of man has not only an individualistic, but a social and political dimension. To be sure, in the course of history morals and values are created by a few outstanding individuals. However, they usually want their opinion about good and bad to gain validity among many men. Thus the creators of morals strive to obtain power over the masses, who achieve their cohesion as a people through common value judgments. This is why Nietzsche conceives of morals and values as the expression of "the will to power" of a few (Z I Goals; Z II On Self-Overcoming). Especially in his "polemic" *On the Genealogy of Morals* he tries to shed light on the proceedings and motives of these few. In the *Genealogy*, which appeared in 1887, he develops hypotheses explaining how, in the course of history, the Jewish and Christian priests could succeed in revaluating the once prevailing moral values of the noble warriors and aristocrats, in relation to the morality of the weak and of slaves. Nietzsche holds Jewish-Christian morality not only to be inferior in rank and worth compared to its predecessor but even to be harmful. The reasons for this judgment are that this morality represents an opposition to life, and that its goal is not the elevation of man but its diminishment and mediocrity.

For Nietzsche, the creation of meaning and values is an essential characteristic of man: "Verily, men have given themselves all their good and evil. Verily, they haven't taken it, they haven't found it, it hasn't fallen onto them as a voice from the sky. Values have only been put by man into the things, in order to preserve themselves, – only man has created meaning, a human meaning! This is why he calls himself 'man', this is: the valuator" (Z I Goals). In accordance with this, Nietzsche designates man as "the 'evaluating animal per se'" and as "the being who estimates values, who evaluates and measures" (GM II 8)

According to Nietzsche, the European morality has its essential foundation in the Christian God. After the belief in Him has become unbelievable, for all people with intellectual probity morality loses its fundament and will perish (GS 343; GM III 27). This development, which Nietzsche detects and also forecasts as something that will happen in the next centuries, has enormous consequences for European humanity. In its essence it means that "the highest values devalue themselves", a process he designates in his late philosophy with the term "nihilism" (NL 1887, KSA 12, p. 350). To be sure, as a consequence of nihilism Nietzsche expects a "long abundance and succession of demolition, destruction, downfall, overthrow" and talks about a "tremendous logic of horror". However, he evaluates the expected decline of Christianity as "bliss, relief, amusement, encouragement, dawn" (GS 343). This evaluation can be explained by his hope that this development allows us to revoke the Jewish-Christian revaluation of all noble values and to revaluate once more the prevailing values of Modernity. Nietzsche holds that this important task is something that should be done by the philosophers of the future. Their vocation is to counteract nihilism by creating new values and new morals and thus work on the "elevation" of man. The "new philosophers" should be "commanders and lawgivers" who "teach man the future of man as his will, as dependent on a human will" (BGE 203, 211). They have "to prepare great ventures and collective attempts of breed and breeding": "they say 'thus it shall be!', they determine first the Whereto? and Why? of mankind". As a European nobility ruling over Europe, the "new philosophers" should pursue a "grand politics" of global creation, education and the breeding of man in the tradition of Plato (BGE 203, 208, 211, 212; cf. Z III Tablets 12; SE 3, KSA 1, p. 360).

II Nietzsche's political philosophy: his conception of a just society and the state

Nietzsche conceives the generation of a higher type of man or "Übermensch" not primarily as the affair of an isolated individual, but as a social and political task. His view of the necessary connection between society, state and the creation of higher men is already expressed clearly in his early essay *The Greek State*. This short essay, in which Nietzsche explains for the first time his conception of a good social and political order, can be understood as a complementary work to *The Birth of Tragedy*, which appeared likewise in 1872. The reason for this is that in *The Greek State* Nietzsche reflects on the social and political foundations of the theory of art and culture he laid out in *The Birth of Tragedy*. Nietzsche understands his essay as an interpretation of Plato's perfect state, in whose general conception he recognizes the "marvelously grand hieroglyph of a profound secret teaching of the connection between state and genius, which is to be interpreted eternally" (GSt, KSA 1, p. 777).

For Nietzsche, the state is a means of coercion which initiates and upholds the social process. In his view, this is the true meaning of the state. Through the "iron clamp of the state" the masses of people are squeezed together and are as well separated. This constitutes a social structure that has the form of a pyramid (GSt, KSA 1, p. 769). Analogously, war produces a separation of the estate of the soldiers in military castes, which also constitute an order of rank in the form of a pyramid. In the estate of the soldiers, which for Nietzsche is "the image [*Abbild*], even perhaps the archetype of the state", as well as in society, the lowest stratum is the broadest, while the top of the pyramid is constituted only by one or a few men. As the fundamental goal of the "military proto-state" is the generation of the military genius, the general purpose of every state is for Nietzsche the "Olympian existence and the constantly renewed generation and preparation of the genius". Nietzsche criticizes Plato for putting only "the genius of wisdom and knowledge" on top of his perfect state and for excluding the ingenious artist under the influence of Socrates. In opposition to Plato, Nietzsche proclaims that the purpose and meaning of the state is to generate the genius "in its most general sense" (GSt, KSA 1, pp. 775f.). The problematic in Nietzsche's interpretation is the anachronistic equation of Plato's philosopher-king with a notion of genius that was inspired by the nineteenth century concept of genius, and in particular by Schopenhauer's concept of genius (cf. Schmidt, pp. 129–168; Sommer 2011, pp. 190–219).

The existence of a "small number of Olympian men", who produce the high culture, presupposes slavery, which – according to Nietzsche's provocative and generalizing thesis – belongs "to the essence of a culture" (GSt, KSA 1, p. 767). The estate of the slaves, the lowest stratum of the social pyramid, has to do the additional work, which is necessary in order to exempt the few ingenious producers of culture from the struggle of existence. With the term "slavery" Nietzsche not only means the slaves of the ancient world but the contemporary "anonymous and impersonal" "factory-slavery" (WS 288; cf. D 206). In accordance with his view that man per se has no dignity, Nietzsche does not ascribe any dignity to work. Like the ancient Greeks, he understands work as the "distressful means" to existence and as disgrace (GSt, KSA 1, p. 764). The only dignity that Nietzsche concedes to the working men of the slave estate is "to be dignified as a means for genius". The reason for this is that as a means or tool the estate of the slaves makes possible the genius and his production of the world of art and culture (GSt, KSA 1, p. 776). In accordance with this, Nietzsche explains in the third *Untimely Meditation* that the life of the masses gains only its "highest value" and "deepest meaning" if they live "for the good of the rarest and most valuable exemplars, and not for the good of the many, that is to say for those who are, taken individually, the least valuable exemplars" (SE 6, KSA 1, pp. 384f.).

Nietzsche's interpretation of the outline of a perfectly good city, which Plato develops in his *Politeia* and whose constitution he denominates as a kingship or an aristocracy, is not completely accurate. To be sure, Plato separates the citizens of his best city into three estates, which leads in fact to a social structure that is hierarchical and pyramidal (Rep. 445 d, 544 e, 545 c). The top is constituted by the few philosophers who rule the city, the middle by a military estate that takes care of defense and inner security, and the lowest and broadest estate has to work in order to satisfy the vital needs of everyone. However, Plato does not have a merely instrumental view of the two lower estates as a means for the generation and preservation of the few wise and knowledgeable men and women. He declares explicitly that what matters in a good and just city is not the happiness of a specific estate. Rather, the goal is that the whole city flourishes and becomes happy and that every estate obtains this part of happiness that nature has intended for it (Rep. 420 c–421).

Nevertheless, a strong argument for Nietzsche's interpretation is that Plato's constitutional outline is based on the fundamental inequality of men and of parts of the soul. For Plato, this inequality exists by nature and constitutes the basis for the order of rank and difference in worth, which exists between men. According to his analogy of soul, man and city, the men of the lowest and the highest estate are in such a radical way different as desire, the lowest part of the soul, differs from reason, the highest part of the soul (Rep. 370 a/b, 435 b ff.). Regarding the fundamental anthropological conviction that Plato expresses in the *Politeia*, Nietzsche's view that Plato in the end only cares about the people of the highest estate is not unwarranted. In line with this, the education of the members of the highest estate, which are selected by a multiphase education system, is one of the main topics of the *Politeia*. Opposed to this, Plato has very little to say about the good life of the lowest estate, which he holds to be inferior in rank to the predominantly contemplative life of the few wise and knowledgeable men and women (Rep. 580b ff.).

As some authors have noticed, though Nietzsche rejects Plato's metaphysics from early on, his political philosophy is in many ways influenced by Plato, especially by the *Politeia* (Ottmann 1999, p. 45; Zachriat 2001, pp. 79, 84, 86; Knoll 2009b). The central topic of the *Politeia* is the question of the essence of justice. For Plato, it is just that everyone practices the function in the city for "which his nature made him naturally most fit" (Plato 1991, p. 111, 433 a). As Wolf Gorch Zachriat has observed correctly, in *The Greek State* Nietzsche not only gives an interpretation of Plato's perfect city, but incorporates Plato's conception of justice in his own outline of a just genius-state (Zachriat 2001, p. 79). In line with Zachriat, I have argued in a paper that Nietzsche's conception of social justice is to be understood as a conception of distributive justice and that this conception is central for his early and late political philosophy (Knoll 2009b).

At the basis of Nietzsche's conception of justice is his fundamental anthropological view that men are not only fundamentally unequal but are of extremely unequal value. If rights and duties are distributed in a political community, Nietzsche's conception of justice calls for a distribution according to the formal principle 'to everyone in proportion to his worth or rank'.[21] Like Aristotle, Nietzsche connects this principle with a second formal principle: 'equal shares for equals, unequal shares for unequals' (cf. to both principles HL 6, KSA 1, p. 294; HH I 92, 105, 636; WS 29; Z I Adder; Z II Tarantulas; BGE 211; TI Skirmishes 48). The social order of Nietzsche's just genius-state is, like Plato's just city, formed according to both principles of distributive justice (Knoll 2010). As for Plato, for Nietzsche it is just that people do not have equal rights, duties, positions and activities in a political community, but that these are distributed in proportion to the unequal worth or rank and that only equals should get equal shares. Advocating unequal rights, Nietzsche proclaims that those people who turned out well, the healthy and higher men, the "powerful in body and soul", have a far bigger right to exist than the sickly and lower men: "Their right to exist, the peculiar right of the bell with a full clang compared to the one discordant and cracked is a thousand times greater: they alone are the guarantors of the future, they alone are committed to the future of mankind" (GM III 14).

On the grounds of the above mentioned value judgments, Nietzsche contests all forms of egalitarianism. Egalitarians, who intend to attribute and distribute equal rights to all men, believe in a basic equality of men, which is the fundamental belief of their thought. Nietzsche lets Zarathustra proclaim: "With these preachers of equality I don't want to be mixed and mistaken. Because justice says to me: 'people are not equal'. And they should not become equal! What would be my love to the Übermensch if I talked differently?" (Z II Tarantulas; cf. Z II Scholars). The liberal and egalitarian opinion that all people can claim equal rights and that equality should be politically established is opposed to Nietzsche's conception of social justice. He emphasizes even that the liberal and egalitarian conception of justice is unjust: "Injustice never lies in unequal rights, it lies in the claim to 'equal' rights" (A 57). For Nietzsche, justice forbids that equal rights are distributed to unequal people: "The teaching of equality! [...] But there is no more toxic poison: for it seems to be preached

---

[21] In the literature on Aristotle usually the principle "To each his own" is regarded as the formula for distributive justice (cf. the German literature in Knoll 2009b, p. 167, fn. 28). However, not only for Aristotle, but also for Nietzsche it is more appropriate to rephrase this principle: "To everyone in proportion to his worth [*kat' axian*] or rank" (Aristotle, *The Nicomachean Ethics*, 1131 a 22–29; cf. Knoll 2009a, chs. III.3, IV and V).

by justice itself, while it is the termination of justice...'equal shares for equals, unequal shares for unequals' – this would be the true voice of justice: and, what follows from this, never make equal what is unequal" (TI Skirmishes 48).

Nietzsche's doctrine of the "Übermensch" is not only a consequence of his biological and anthropological views and of his certainty that the Christian interpretation and meaning-giving of the world is declining. It is as well a consequence of his untimely conception of social justice, which is based on his fundamental anthropological views. But if it is just that everyone gets his social position and central activity in life allotted 'in proportion to his worth or rank', the questions arise how the worth and rank of a *man* can be measured, and: which are the criteria for an *over*man? This question amounts to the question: what are the adequate properties for determining and specifying the two formal principles of distributive justice?, or: how to fill these principles with content and make them concrete?

In his texts Nietzsche gives several answers to these questions.[22] Especially in the early 1870's, he holds genius, intellect, wisdom, and creative power that distinguish the few brilliant philosophers and artists to be the decisive criteria for the worth or rank of a man. In the third *Untimely Meditation* he puts the saint as a "genuine man" in the same rank as the philosopher and the artist. In his later thought the question of how to measure the different value of men, and how to determine the order of rank that exists between them, gains more and more importance. His reflections on this question are inextricably linked to the questions of the elevation of man and of the "Übermensch".

At the beginning of his middle period, Nietzsche holds not only intellect, but intellectual freedom to be decisive criteria for the worth or rank of a man. An indication of this is that he chooses for his book *Human, All Too Human* the subtitle *A Book for free Spirits*. In *The Gay Science*, Nietzsche complains that the vast majority of people lack "intellectual conscience". By this he means that the vast majority of people don't hold it "contemptible" to "believe this or that and to live accordingly without being aware of the final and most certain reasons for and against it, and without making an effort to achieve such reasons afterwards". In connection with this critique he emphasizes that it is "the desire for certainty" that "separates the higher men from the lower!" (GS 2).

Nietzsche's account of the "intellectual conscience" and "the desire for certainty" illustrates in all likelihood the virtue of probity, about which he declares in *Beyond Good and Evil*: "Probity [*Redlichkeit*], assuming that this is our virtue, from which we cannot liberate ourselves, we free spirits – well, we want

---

[22] In order to clarify the relation between these answers a separate study would be necessary. This paper only gives an outline of some essential points.

to work on it with all wickedness and love, and will not get tired of "getting perfect" in our virtue, the only one that is left for us" (BGE 227). In *Ecce Homo* Nietzsche announces that Zarathustra is "more truthful [*wahrhaft*] than any other thinker" and that his teaching comprises "truthfulness [*Wahrhaftigkeit*] as the supreme virtue" (EH Destiny 3; cf. Z I Hinterworldly; Z IV Men 8).[23]

Further decisive criteria for the worth and rank of a man, which stay central not only for *Zarathustra* but Nietzsche's late philosophy, are intellectuality (*Geistigkeit*), health, powerfulness (*Mächtigkeit*), strength, and affirmation of life. In retrospect, Nietzsche states that the "great health" represents the "physiological presupposition" of the type man that Zarathustra embodies (EH Z 2). For Nietzsche, the best and most personal explanation of this concept is the account he gives in *The Gay Science*, in which he talks about the "great health" as "a new health that is stronger, craftier, tougher, and more audacious and cheerful than any previous health". This health is "one, which one doesn't only have but acquires and must acquire continually because one gives it up again and again, and must give it up". Those who strive for the "great health" view "contemporary man" as insufficient. Their ideal is "a human, superhuman well-being and benevolence" of a "spirit that plays naively, that is not deliberately, and from overflowing abundance and powerfulness, with everything that was so far called holy, good, untouchable, divine" (GS 382).[24] In his late philosophy, Nietzsche identifies the healthy with the strong and the "powerful in body and soul", and proclaims as a principle for Zarathustra: "The strongest in body and soul are the best". He emphasizes that the strong and powerful, the higher men, have in relation to the weak and low far more rights, for example the "right to happiness" (GM III 14; cf. NL 1884, KSA 11, p. 247).

For Nietzsche, health, powerfulness, and strength are outstanding qualities because they make it possible to affirm life despite all the pain and suffering. The affirmation of life and the overcoming of the life-negating pessimism, which is in particular expressed in the philosophy of his teacher Schopenhauer, are a central theme of Nietzsche's thought. One of the reasons that make

---

23 The above mentioned references suggest that Nietzsche uses the terms "Redlichkeit" and "Wahrhaftigkeit" as synonyms (cf. Clark 1990, p. 241; Lampert 1986, pp. 3, 205; Lampert 1993, pp. 9, 277, 293, 319; different though White 2001, pp. 64f.).
24 With the formulation of the spirit that plays "with everything which so far has been called holy, good, untouchable, divine", Nietzsche anticipates what he calls in *Zarathustra* the transformation of the spirit towards the child. The child symbolizes the "yes" to the "game of creation", to the autonomous human creation of sense and values (Z I Metamorphoses; Z III Tablets; cf. GS 335). As at the beginning of the 1870's, in the middle of the 1880's Nietzsche holds creative power to be a decisive criterion for the rank or worth of a man.

this evident is the fact that he announces "amor fati" to be his "formula for greatness of man". He explains "amor fati" that he strives for in his life through the declarations that "one day he only wants to be someone who says 'yes'", and that he wants to learn to see "what is necessary in things as what is beautiful in them", and to love it. "Amor fati" means as well "that one wants nothing to be different than it is, neither forwards nor backwards, not in all eternity" (GS 276; cf. EH Clever 10). In retrospect, Nietzsche pronounces with regard to *Zarathustra* that the "fundamental thought" of the work is the "thought of eternal return", which he understands as the "highest formula of affirmation that can possibly be attained" (EH Z 1). The essential meaning[25] of this much-debated thought, which Zarathustra teaches together with the "Übermensch", is expressed most clearly in the key aphorism 341 at the end of *The Gay Science*, which is entitled "The greatest weight".[26] Nietzsche introduces the "eternal return of the same" as a thought experiment asking a hypothetical question: "What if some day or night a demon followed you in your loneliest loneliness and said to you: 'This life as you are living it now and have lived it you will have to live once more and countless more times; and there will be nothing new in it, but every pain and every joy and every thought and sigh and everything unspeakably small and great in your life must return to you, all in the same succession and sequence'" (GS 341). Nietzsche assumes that the thought of the eternal return would become for a man over who it "gained power" the "greatest weight". The reason for his assumption is that the imagination that every pain, all the suffering as well as everything small and big of human life returns eternally must be very hard to bear. According to Nietzsche, it is very possible that confronted with this thought most men would fall into desperation and – weary of life – be crushed by its weight (Z III Convalescent 2). The reason for this is that their "amor fati" is not strong enough or, in other words, that they are not strong enough to affirm themselves and life sufficiently. Such an affirmation is especially difficult, because it also has to affirm a world that has in itself no meaning and value, and in which there is no orientation given

---

25 Nietzsche's unpublished notes on the teaching of the "eternal return of the same" indicate that he was reflecting on a cosmological interpretation of it as well. The meaning of the cosmological interpretation and its relation to the interpretation given above will not be discussed in this paper. But the fact that he did not publish these reflections, which start already in the middle of the 1880's, indicates that he was not certain about them and that one should not give them too much weight.
26 The importance of this aphorism is emphasized by the fact that Nietzsche placed it as the penultimate aphorism of the edition of 1882. The text of the last aphorism of this edition, no. 342, is identical with the beginning of *Zarathustra*. Nietzsche added the fifth book of *The Gay Science* only to the second edition, which was published in 1887.

by a God or any other higher authority. In order to bear the thought of the eternal return and to be even transformed by it and to "ask for nothing more than for this ultimate confirmation and seal", one needs strength, the "great health", and highest affirmation of oneself and life (GS 341). In the end Nietzsche holds the thought of the eternal return, which comprises standards like amor fati, strength, and health, to be the central standard for the worth or rank of a man and as the decisive criterion for a higher type of man or overman.[27] Such a man does not break down under the weight of the thought, but welcomes it as the "highest formula of affirmation that can possibly be attained".[28] Because Nietzsche holds the thought of the eternal return to be the decisive criterion for a higher type of man, he makes it together with the "Übermensch" the core of the doctrine, which he lets Zarathustra proclaim (Z III Convalescent 2; Z I prologue 3; cf. GS 285).[29]

In his late works Nietzsche explains again his conception of state and society. In doing this, he returns unmistakably to his early conception of a good and just political order, inspired by Plato. He makes clear that this conception is to be understood as an aristocratic one, and that he holds aristocracy to be the best form of state and society. A key passage of Nietzsche's "aristocratic

---

[27] For Marie-Luise Haase, who investigates the relation of the doctrine of the "Übermensch" and the "eternal return of the same", the Übermensch is the instance that allows us to read off the effect of the "eternal return of the same" (Haase 1984, p. 230). David Owen reflects on "the relationship between *amor fati*, eternal recurrence and the Overman" (Owen 1995, pp. 106f.; italics by D.O.). He quotes Leslie Paul Thiele: "*Amor fati* is the disposition of the Overman" (Owen 1995, p. 110; Thiele 1990, p. 200). For Owen, the figure of the Overman "represents a *perfectionist* ideal of self-mastery" (Owen 1995, p. 111; italics by D.O.). About the relation of *amor fati* and eternal recurrence he states: "Firstly, the thought of eternal recurrence embodies the conceptual structure of *amor fati* [...]. Secondly, the thought of eternal recurrence acts as a test to our *present* capacity to love fate, to embrace necessity of our being what we are, by posing the question 'Do you desire this once more and innumerable times more?'" (Owen 1995, p. 113). According to Owen, the Overman is a "human being who is *amor fati* incarnate" (Owen 1995, p. 113).

[28] In accordance with the interpretation given above, Keith Ansell-Pearson explains: "The Overman is simply the human type which is able to positively experience the eternal return (it does not crush him but changes him)" (Ansell-Pearson 1994, p. 117).

[29] The interpretation that Nietzsche understands the thought of the eternal return to be the decisive criterion for a higher type of man is confirmed by the fact that in the context of "great politics" he views it as a means for breeding and an elevation of man: "My philosophy carries the victorious thought, in relation to which lastly every other way of thinking will perish. It is the grand breeding thought: the races that cannot bear it are condemned; the ones who experience it as a blessing are selected to rule" (NL 1884, KSA 11, p. 250). In his works, Nietzsche mentions additional standards for the worth or rank of man such as courage or bravery (GS 283; Z I War) and benevolence (*Güte*) (Z II Human Prudence; EH Z 6).

radicalism"[30], which also reveals the social dimension of the elevation of man, can be found in *Beyond Good and Evil*, the first book he published after *Zarathustra* in 1886:

> Every elevation of the type 'man' has so far been the work of an aristocratic society — and so it will ever be: a society which believes in a long ladder of order of rank and difference in worth between man and man and that needs slavery in some sense. Without the <u>pathos of distance such as</u> grows out of a deeply entrenched difference of the estates, out of the ruling caste constantly seeing subjects and tools and looking down on them, and out of their equally constant exercise in obeying and commanding, in holding down and holding at a distance, that other, more enigmatic pathos could not have grown, that desire for a constantly increasing expansion of distance within the soul itself, the development of always higher, rarer, farther, more widely stretched, more comprehensive states, in short the elevation of the type 'man', the continuous 'self-overcoming of man', to take a moral formula in a supramoral [*übermoralisch*] sense (BGE 257).

In this aphorism Nietzsche proclaims "an aristocratic society" not only to be the historical, but the future premise for every "elevation" or "enhancement" of man. He conceives of an aristocratic society as a hierarchical society, in which people are distinguished according to their worth and rank in castes and estates, and in which the lowest estate consists of some form of slaves.[31] As he already explained in *The Greek State*, the function of the great masses of the common people is to do the necessary work. A "good and healthy aristocracy" has to defend the "fundamental faith" that the masses of common people and in the end the whole society serves as an "instrument" and "substructure and scaffolding", which allows "a selected kind of being to raise itself to its higher task and generally to a higher <u>existence</u>" (BGE 258).

Nietzsche does not regard society and state as ends in themselves but only as means in order to bring out a higher type of man. He declares that "the essential thing of a good and healthy aristocracy" is "that it does not feel as a

---

30 In a letter sent to Nietzsche November 26 1887, the Danish scholar Georg Brandes talks about Nietzsche's "aristocratic radicalism", which Nietzsche calls in his answer from December 2 as a very good expression and as "the astutest word on him he has so far read" (KGB III/5, Bf. 960; cf. Middleton 1996, p. 279; Brandes 1890). Bruce Detwiler comments on Nietzsche's "aristocratic radicalism": "While aristocratic conservatives and egalitarian radicals have been plentiful in recent times, it is difficult to think of another modern of Nietzsche's stature whose political orientation is both as aristocratic and as radical as his. Among modern philosophers Nietzsche stands virtually alone in his insistence that the goal of society should be the promotion and enhancement of the highest type even at the expense of what has traditionally been thought to be the good of all or of the great number" (Detwiler 1990, p. 189).
31 See for Nietzsche's considerations on different forms of slavery HH I 283; WS 288; D 206; GS 18.

function" of the commonwealth but as its "meaning and supreme justification" (BGE 258). Evidently, for Nietzsche, an aristocracy does not represent the rule of the best for the common best, but "the belief in an elite-humanity and higher caste", which is the meaning and goal of the political community (NL 1884, KSA 11, p. 224). In order to make these few exceptional men or overmen possible, the whole society has to be structured hierarchically in a way that the people on top of the pyramid stand out clearly from the masses of the subjects. The elevated position of the ruling caste and their distance from the subjects is the social presupposition which is necessary that in the course of history the few exceptional men achieve an elevation of their mind and their soul.

Nietzsche explains his last vision of a good social and political order in *The Anti-Christ*, which he wrote in the second half of 1888. He presents his vision as an interpretation of the old Indian legal code of Manu that Nietzsche praises because of its aristocratic and philosophical character (A 56).[32] Nietzsche understands Manu's hierarchical order of the three castes in analogy to the hierarchical order of the three estates, which Plato drafts in his *Politeia*. The top of the social pyramid is constituted by the few "most spiritual human beings" who rule the political community, the middle by the "noble warriors", and the basis of the society by the "mediocre", who have to work (A 57). Like Plato's perfect city, Manu's good social order not only has the fundamental inequality of men as its anthropological basis, but corresponds to this inequality. The inequality of men is produced by nature, which separates three "physiologically" different types:

> The order of castes, order of rank, only formulates the supreme law of life itself; the separation of the three types is necessary for the preservation of society, for making possible higher and highest types, — inequality of rights is the condition for the existence of rights at all. — A right is a privilege [*Vorrecht*]. The privilege of each is determined by his sort of being [*Art Sein*] (A 57).

---

32 For Nietzsche's source and reception of the legal code of Manu see Etter 1987. For a critical analysis of Nietzsche's use of Manu see Sommer 1999, pp. 208–214. Thomas Brobjer's claims, opposed to most commentators, that "the view expressed by Nietzsche in sections 56 to 58 in *The Antichrist* does not constitute Nietzsche's political ideal" (Brobjer 1998, p. 311). For a convincing refutation of Brobjer's claim see Dombowsky 2001. Brobjer argues: "If Manu's society was Nietzsche's ideal society, or akin to it, it is surprising how little interest he shows for such and similar societies" (Brobjer 1998, p. 308). Brobjer asserts that Nietzsche "almost never mentions Plato's political utopia and *The Republic* after the middle of the 1870s. If what Nietzsche describes in sections 58 is his ideal or near to it, this lack of reference to Plato's 'utopia' is highly surprising" (Brobjer 1998, p. 309, cf. p. 310). Brobjer's argument neglects Nietzsche's important text *The Greek State*, published 1872, which is an enthusiastic interpretation of the best city of Plato's *Republic*. Also in later texts Nietzsche refers to *The Republic* (HH I 439).

This quote shows that in *The Anti-Christ*, as in B*eyond Good and Evil*, Nietzsche conceives of the social order primarily as a means for making possible higher and highest men. These highest men are what Nietzsche calls the "Übermenschen".

III Conclusion

In all likelihood, the interpretations and theses of this paper will provoke some objections. Against the second thesis, which stresses the social and political dimension of the conception of the "Übermensch", one could quote the final statements of the aphorism "Of the New Idol" from *Zarathustra*. At the end of this aphorism Zarathustra recommends emigrating from state and civilization and proclaims: "Only there, where the state ceases, does the man who is not superfluous begin". Immediately afterwards he announces that where the state ends one sees "the rainbow and the bridges to the Overman" (Z I Idol). These statements seem to suggest an individualistic interpretation of a type of Overman, who can only develop himself outside or far from the state. But such an interpretation would neglect the meaning and context of the whole aphorism.

In the aphorism Nietzsche criticizes the contemporary nation state, which he calls "the new idol", and the power it has over its citizens. This critique is in part already expressed in the third *Untimely Meditation*, in which Nietzsche remarks that the state wants "men to render it the same idolatry they formerly rendered to the church" (SE 4, KSA 1, p. 368). After the belief in the Christian God has become unbelievable, the modern nation state fills the emptiness that the death of God left behind. With its lies the state is able to lure a lot of people who serve it with devotion and make it the center and goal of their lives. In line with this, the major German historian Friedrich Meinecke explains that all the different understandings of the state in the 19th century shared the view that the state is a moral and living being, and covered it with a golden cloud of comforting feelings (Meinecke 1922, p. 278). For Nietzsche, the esteem and veneration that most people feel for the modern nation state is by no means justified. Zarathustra's teachings have to be understood in the light of this. Zarathustra gives expression to warnings not to live for the state and not to strive for goals such as money and the satisfaction of multiple desires. These bourgeois aspirations are incompatible with the enhancement or elevation of man. Though the artist and the philosopher should beware of the baits that the state uses to lure them, for their form of life they need the division of work and leisure, which only a functioning society can offer. For Nietzsche, the state is justified only as a means for the individual as the "original purpose of the state", not as an end in itself. This is what separates Nietzsche as a modern political philosopher from Plato and what he has in common with liberal political thought, which he usually rejects to a great extent (HH I 235; cf. HH I 473).

In *The Greek State* and the third *Untimely Meditation*, Nietzsche anticipates essential elements of his later conception of the "Übermensch", the meaning of which can be understood by connecting it to the content of these early writings. This thesis, the first thesis of the paper, will in all likelihood provoke the objection that the "higher men" and "great humans" Nietzsche aspires to in his earlier writings are different from the overmen he advocates in *Zarathustra*. To be sure, in his early essay, *The Greek State*, Nietzsche only talks about the "genius", the "Olympian men", and the "Olympian existence", and not about the "Übermensch" (GSt, KSA 1, pp. 767, 772, 776). Admittedly, in his later writings Nietzsche distances himself from his early praise of genius which was in particular inspired by Schopenhauer's concept of genius. However, the definitions of Overman or "Übermensch" as "lucky accidents of great success", who have always been possible, or as "a higher type, something which is in relation to humankind as a whole a sort of Übermensch", have very similar meanings to Nietzsche's early attributes for the "higher men" (A 4). His early terms "*Olympian* men" and "*Olympian* existence" already anticipate his later statements that the "Übermensch" should replace the Christian God and Christianity (Z I Virtue 3; cf. Z II Isles; Z IV Men 2).[33] Especially his anthropological imperative that "mankind must work continually at the production of individual great men", that the "higher man" can be willed and created, anticipates the account of the "Übermensch" he gives in the *Zarathustra*. Though there is some difference in meaning of concepts of "geniuses", "Olympian men", "higher men", "individual great men" etc., they are all variations of Nietzsche's concern for the promotion of outstanding individuals or "Übermenschen", which is an important element of the continuity and unity of his thought.

Some interpreters have tried to precisely pin down Nietzsche's conception of the "Übermensch". The Nietzsche Scholar Wolfgang Müller-Lauter even claims that there are two distinct types of "Übermensch" in Nietzsche's writings. The one is the strong type, who ruthlessly wants to realize his claim to power and his values against all resistance. The other is the wise type, who opens up in a loving way to all the different and opposing values and tries to

---

33 In *The Birth of Tragedy* Nietzsche speaks, referring to Lucretius, of the ancient Gods as "übermenschliche Wesen" (BT 1, KSA 1, 26). Karl Brose remarks that though for Nietzsche the "Übermensch" should replace the Christian God and Christianity, he cannot do without both (Brose 1994, p. 144).

synthesize them (Müller-Lauter 1971, pp. 116–188). The interpretation given by Martin Heidegger is not far from what Müller-Lauter holds to be the first type of "Übermensch". According to Heidegger, the "Übermensch" is the man who is about to start ruling the earth as a whole (Heidegger 1959, p. 106). Such attempts to pin down the "Übermensch" have a vision of Nietzsche's conception that is too narrow. His conception is far more open than these kinds of interpretations suggest. The "Übermensch" can be a gifted artist, a brilliant philosopher, a saint, a courageous free spirit, a renaissance man, a lawgiver, and even an exceptional statesman. Or it can be a mixture of these types.[34] In line with this, it is important to notice that Nietzsche often uses the term "Übermensch" in the plural ("Übermenschen"). Though Nietzsche calls Napoleon a "synthesis of brute [Unmensch] and Übermensch", he recommends to those of his readers, who look for an "Übermensch", to look rather at Cesare Borgia than at Parsifal (GM I 16; cf. EH Books 1). In *Twighlight of the Idols*, Nietzsche gives an enthusiastic characterization of Goethe that suggests the interpretation that this exceptional man is one exemplification of the "Übermensch" (TI Skirmishes 49). The famous definition, that Nietzsche gives in the *Nachlass*, determines the "Übermensch" as "the Roman Cesar with the soul of Christ" (NL 1884, KSA 11, p. 289).

In the end, the "Übermensch" is an open concept, which Nietzsche uses to refer to higher forms of human types and human possibilities. This concept can only be realized by a few individuals, never by mankind as a whole. Some of those higher human types have already been achieved in history; others could potentially be realized in the future under favorable social conditions. Nietzsche is seriously concerned with the destiny of mankind, not mankind as a whole, but the few individuals with the highest rank and value.[35] After the devaluation of Christian values, beliefs, and other-worldly hopes, for Nietzsche, the focus on this world and the enhancement of man are the natural consequences. After the death of God as source of meaning, the collective work of the enhancement of man is humankind's most significant social and political task, which gives value to the world and creates meaning for human life despite all the suffering.

---

34 According to Henning Ottmann, the most extensive definitions of the "Übermensch" are those in which Nietzsche aims at the unity of artist (creator), saint (lover), and philosopher (contemplator) (Ottmann 1999, p. 387; cf. NL 1883, 16[11], KSA 10, p. 501).
35 Maudemarie Clark's interpretation that the conception of the Overman shows Zarathustra's or Nietzsche's desire for revenge is not convincing (Clark 1990, p. 275). On the contrary, Zarathustra proclaims, "that man will be redeemed of revenge: for me this is the bridge to the highest hope and a rainbow after a long thunderstorm" (Z II, 7)

Bibliography

Ansell-Pearson, Keith (1994): *An Introduction to Nietzsche as Political Thinker. The Perfect Nihilist*. Cambridge: Cambridge University Press.
Benz, Ernst (ed.) (1961): *Der Übermensch. Eine Diskussion*. Zürich, Stuttgart: Rhein-Verlag.
Brandes, Georg (1890): "Aristokratischer Radicalismus. Eine Abhandlung über Friedrich Nietzsche". In: *Deutsche Rundschau* LXIII, pp. 67–81 [again in: Guzzoni, Alfredo (ed.) (1979): *90 Jahre philosophische Nietzsche-Rezeption*. Königstein: Anton Hain, pp. 1–15].
Brobjer, Thomas H. (1998): "The Absence of Political Ideals in Nietzsche's Writings. The Case of the Laws of Manu and the Associated Caste-Society". In: *Nietzsche-Studien* 27, pp. 300–318.
Brobjer, Thomas H. (2001): "Nietzsche as Political Thinker. A Response to Don Dombowsky". In: *Nietzsche-Studien* 30, pp. 394–396.
Brobjer, Thomas H. (2008): "Critical Aspects of Nietzsche's Relation to Politics and Democracy". In: Herman W. Siemens/Vasti Roodt (eds.): *Nietzsche, Power and Politics: Rethinking Nietzsche's Legacy for Political Thought*. Berlin, New York: de Gruyter, pp. 205–227.
Brose, Karl (1994): *Nietzsche. Geschichtsphilosoph, Politiker und Soziologe*. Essen: Die Blaue Eule.
Clark, Maudemarie (1990): *Nietzsche on Truth and Philosophy*. New York et. al.: Cambridge University Press.
Conway, Daniel (1988): "Solving the Problem of Socrates: Nietzsche's *Zarathustra* as Political Irony". In: *Political Theory* 16(2), pp. 257–280.
Conway, Daniel (1997): *Nietzsche & the Political*. London, New York: Routledge.
Detwiler, Bruce (1990): *Nietzsche and the Politics of Aristocratic Radicalism*. Chicago, London: University of Chicago Press.
Dombowsky, Don (2001): "A Response to Thomas H. Brobjer's 'The Absence of Political Ideals in Nietzsche's Writings'". In: *Nietzsche-Studien* 30, pp. 387–393.
Etter, Annemarie (1987): "Nietzsche und das Gesetzbuch des Manu". In *Nietzsche-Studien* 16, pp. 340–352.
Haase, Marie-Luise (1984): "Der Übermensch in *Also sprach Zarathustra* und im Zarathustra-Nachlass 1882–1885". In: *Nietzsche-Studien* 13, pp. 228–244.
Heidegger, Martin (1959): "Wer ist Nietzsches Zarathustra?". In: Martin Heidegger: *Vorträge und Aufsätze*. 2nd edition. Pfullingen: Klostermann.
Hollingdale, Reginald J. (1965): *Nietzsche. The Man and His Philosophy*. Baton Rouge: Louisiana State University Press.
Kaufmann, Walter (1950): *Nietzsche: Philosopher, Psychologist, Antichrist*. Princeton, NJ: Princeton University Press.
Kaulbach, Friedrich (1980): *Nietzsches Idee einer Experimentalphilosophie*. Köln, Wien: Böhlau.
Knoll, Manuel (2009a): *Aristokratische oder demokratische Gerechtigkeit? Die politische Philosophie des Aristoteles und Martha Nussbaums egalitaristische Rezeption*. Munich: Fink.
Knoll, Manuel (2009b): "Nietzsches Begriff der sozialen Gerechtigkeit". In: *Nietzsche-Studien* 38, pp. 156–181.
Knoll, Manuel (2010): "Die distributive Gerechtigkeit bei Platon und Aristoteles". In: *Zeitschrift für Politik* 1, pp. 3–30.

Lampert, Laurence (1986): *Nietzsche's Teaching. An Interpretation of "Thus spoke Zarathustra"*. New Haven, London: Yale University Press.
Lampert, Laurence (1993): *Nietzsche and Modern Times. A Study of Bacon, Descartes and Nietzsche*. New Haven, London: Yale University Press.
MacIntyre, Alasdair (1984): *After Virtue*. Notre Dame, IN: Notre Dame University Press.
Meinecke, Friedrich (1922): "Drei Generationen deutscher Gelehrtenpolitik". In: *Historische Zeitschrift* 125, pp. 248–283.
Middleton, Christopher (ed./transl.) (1996): *Selected Letters of Friedrich Nietzsche*. Indianapolis: Hackett.
Müller-Lauter, Wolfgang (1971): *Nietzsche. Seine Philosophie der Gegensätze und die Gegensätze seiner Philosophie*. Berlin, New York: de Gruyter.
Nehamas, Alexander (1985): *Nietzsche. Life as literature*. Cambridge, London: Harvard University Press.
Ottmann, Henning (1999): *Philosophie und Politik bei Nietzsche*. 2nd improved and enlarged edition. Berlin, New York: de Gruyter.
Owen, David (1995): *Nietzsche, Politics and Modernity. A Critique of Liberal Reason*. London, Thousand Oaks, New Delhi: Sage Publications.
Plato (1991): *The Republic*. Allan Bloom (ed./trans.). 2nd edition. New York: Basic Books.
Reckermann, Alfons (2003): *Lesarten der Philosophie Nietzsches. Ihre Rezeption und Diskussion in Frankreich, Italien und der angelsächsischen Welt 1960–2000*. Berlin, New York: de Gruyter.
Schmidt, Jochen (2004): *Die Geschichte des Genie-Gedankens in der deutschen Literatur, Philosophie und Politik 1750–1945*. Vol. 2: *Von der Romantik bis zum Ende des Dritten Reichs*. 3rd edition. Heidelberg: Universitätsverlag Winter.
Siemens, Herman W. (2008): "Yes, No, Maybe So ... Nietzsche's Equivocations on the Relation between Democracy and 'Grosse Politik'". In: Herman W. Siemens/Vasti Roodt (eds.): *Nietzsche, Power and Politics: Rethinking Nietzsche's Legacy for Political Thought*. Berlin, New York: de Gruyter, pp. 231–268.
Siemens, Herman W. (2009). "Nietzsche's Critique of Democracy (1870–1886)". In: *Journal of Nietzsche Studies* 38, pp. 20–37.
Sommer, Andreas Urs (1999): "Ex Oriente Lux? Zur vermeintlichen 'Ostorientierung' in Nietzsches Antichrist". In: *Nietzsche-Studien* 28, pp. 194–214.
Sommer, Andreas Urs (2010): "Nietzsche mit und gegen Darwin in den Schriften von 1888". In: *Nietzscheforschung* 17, pp. 31–44.
Sommer, Andreas Urs (2011): "Nietzsche, das Genie und die Zucht großer Menschen". In: Klaus Wellner (ed.): *Nietzsche – sein Denken und dessen Entwicklungspotentiale*. Neu-Isenburg: Angelika Lenz Verlag.
Stegmaier, Werner (1987): "Darwin, Darwinismus, Nietzsche. Zum Problem der Evolution". In: *Nietzsche-Studien* 16, pp. 264–287.
Stegmaier, Werner (2000): "Anti-Lehren. Szene und Lehre in Nietzsches 'Also sprach Zarathustra'". In: Volker Gerhardt (ed.): *Friedrich Nietzsche, Also sprach Zarathustra*. Berlin: Akademie Verlag, pp. 191–224.
Stegmaier, Werner (2010): "Der See des Menschen, das Meer des Übermenschen und der Brunnen des Geistes. Fluss und Fassung einer Metapher Friedrich Nietzsches". In: *Nietzsche-Studien* 39, pp. 145–179.
Stegmaier, Werner (2013): *Nietzsche zur Einführung*. 2nd corrected edition. Hamburg: Junius.
Strong, Tracy B. (2000): *Friedrich Nietzsche and the Politics of Transfiguration*. 3rd enlarged edition. Urbana, Chicago: University of Illinois Press.

Thiele, Leslie Paul (1990): *Friedrich Nietzsche and the Politics of the Soul*. Princeton: Princeton University Press.
White, Alan (2001): "The Youngest Virtue". In: Schacht, Richard (ed.): *Nietzsche's postmoralism. Essays on Nietzsche's Prelude to Philosophy's Future*. Cambridge: Cambridge University Press, pp. 63–78.
Zachriat, Wolf Gorch (2001): *Die Ambivalenz des Fortschritts. Friedrich Nietzsches Kulturkritik*. Berlin: Akademie.
Zittel, Claus (2011): *Das ästhetische Kalkül von Friedrich Nietzsches Also sprach Zarathustra*. 2nd edition. Würzburg: Königshausen & Neumann.

IV. Ethics, Morality, and Politics in Nietzsche

Keith Ansell-Pearson
Care of Self in *Dawn*: On Nietzsche's Resistance to Bio-political Modernity

The middle period writings (1878–82) are without doubt the most heavily neglected texts in Nietzsche's corpus, especially the two volumes of *Human, all too Human* and *Dawn*. How should they be read? The question is a difficult one to answer given the multifaceted and multi-layered character of the works in question. One can find different philosophical resources in them, including a naturalist agenda and anticipations of phenomenology. I think one especially productive way to read the texts I am referring to is as works of "resistance". In this essay I examine aspects of *Dawn*, from 1881, in the light of this theme of resistance. In these neglected texts we encounter a Nietzsche preoccupied with the care of self and in opposition to the fundamental disciplinary tendencies of bio-political modernity. What intrigues me about the text *Dawn*, for example, are the rarely examined references in the book to "commercial society" and "security". There is a socio-political backdrop to the work and to Nietzsche's attack on the presumptions of morality. This is not to say that Nietzsche is a political thinker in *Dawn*; it would be much more incisive to describe his project at this time as one of an ethics of resistance. "Our age", Nietzsche writes at one point in the text, "no matter how much it talks and talks about economy, is a squanderer: it squanders what is most precious, spirit" (D 179). Nietzsche succinctly articulates his concern in the following manner: "Political and economic affairs are not worthy of being the enforced concern of society's most gifted spirits: such a wasteful use of the spirit is at bottom worse than having none at all" (D 179). Today, he goes on to note, everyone feels obliged to know what is going on every day to the point of neglecting their own work or therapy and in order to feel part of things, and "the whole arrangement has become a great and ludicrous piece of insanity" (D 179). The therapy Nietzsche is proposing in *Dawn* is, then, directed at those solitary free spirits who exist on the margin or fringes of society and seek to cultivate or fashion new ways of thinking and feeling, attempting to do this by taking the time necessary to work through their experiences.

In *Dawn* Nietzsche employs a care of self as a way of taking to task what he identifies as some worrying developments in modern society. We can describe Nietzsche, like Foucault, as a modern-day virtue ethicist who seeks "to liberate the capacity of individual self-choice and personal self-formation from oppressive conformism…" (Ingram 2003, p. 240) This is the set of concerns I wish to explore in this essay.

I

In *Ecce Homo* Nietzsche informs his readers that his "campaign" against morality begins in earnest with *Dawn* and he adds that we should not smell gunpowder at work here but, provided we have the necessary subtlety in our nostrils, more pleasant odours. I think Nietzsche is here drawing the reader's attention to something important, namely, the fact that he wants to open up the possibility of plural ways of being, including plural ways of being moral or ethical. His act is not one of simple wanton destruction.

The "campaign" against morality centres largely on a critique of what Nietzsche sees as the modern tendency, the tendency of his own century, to identify morality with the sympathetic affects, especially *Mitleid*, so as to give us a definition of morality. Nietzsche has specific arguments against the value accorded to these affects, but he also wants to advocate the view that there are several ways of living morally or ethically and the morality he wants to defend is what we can call an ethics of self-cultivation. At one point in *Dawn* he writes: "You say that the morality of being compassionate is a higher morality [*Moral*] than that of Stoicism? Prove it! But remember that what is 'higher' and 'lower' in morality is not, in turn to be measured by a moral yardstick: for there is no absolute morality [*Moral*]. So take your rule from somewhere else – and now beware!" (D 139) With regards to the modern prejudice, which is one of the main foci of his polemic in the book, here there is the presumption that we know what actually constitutes morality: "It seems to do every single person good these days to hear that society is on the road to adapting the individual to fit the needs of the throng and that the individual's happiness as well as his sacrifice consist in feeling himself to be a useful member of the whole…" (D 132) As Nietzsche sees it, then, the modern emphasis is on defining the moral in terms the sympathetic affects and compassion (*Mitleid*). We can, he thinks, explain the modern in terms of a movement towards managing more cheaply, safely, and uniformly individuals in terms of "large bodies and their limbs". This, he says, is "the basic moral current of our age": "Everything that in some way supports both this drive to form bodies and limbs and its abetting drives is felt to be good" (D 132)

Nietzsche's main target in the book is what he sees as the fundamental tendency of modern "commercial society" and its attempt at a "collectivity-building project that aims at disciplining bodies and selves and integrating them into a uniform whole" (Ure 2006, p. 88). Here "morality" denotes the means of adapting the individual to the needs of the whole, making him a useful member of society. This requires that every individual is made to feel, as its primary emotion, a connectedness or bondedness with the whole, with society, in which anything truly individual is regarded as prodigal, costly, inimical, extravagant, and so on. Nietzsche's great worry is that a healthy concern with self-fashioning will be sacrificed and this, in large part, informs his critique of what he sees as the cult of the sympathetic affects within modernity. For Nietzsche it is necessary to contest the idea that there is a single moral-making morality since every code of ethics that affirms itself in an exclusive manner "destroys too much valuable energy and costs humanity much too dearly" (D 164). In the future, Nietzsche hopes, the inventive and fructifying person shall no longer be sacrificed and "numerous novel experiments shall be made in ways of life and modes of society" (D 164). When this takes place we will find that an enormous load of guilty conscience has been purged from the world. Humanity has suffered for too long from teachers of morality who wanted too much all at once and sought to lay down precepts for everyone (D 194). In the future, care will need to be given to the most personal questions and create time for them (D 196). Small individual questions and experiments are no longer to be viewed with contempt and impatience (D 547). In place of what he sees as the ruling ethic of sympathy, which he thinks can assume the form of a "tyrannical encroachment", Nietzsche invites individuals to engage in self-fashioning, cultivating a self that others can look at with pleasure and that still gives vent to the expression, albeit in a subtle and delicate manner, of an altruistic drive:

> Moral fashion of a commercial society — Behind the fundamental principle of the contemporary moral fashion: 'moral actions are generated by sympathy [Sympathie] for others', I see the work of a collective drive toward timidity masquerading behind an intellectual front: this drive desires... that life be rid of all the dangers it once held and that each and every person should help toward this end with all one's might: therefore only actions aimed at the common security and at society's sense of security may be accorded the rating 'good!' — How little pleasure people take in themselves these days, however, when such a tyranny of timidity dictates to them the uppermost moral law [Sittengesetz], when, without so much as a protest, they let themselves be commanded to ignore and look beyond themselves and yet have eagle-eyes for every distress and every suffering existing elsewhere! Are we not, with this prodigious intent to grate off all the rough and sharp edges from life, well on the way to turning humanity into sand? ... In the meantime, the question itself remains open as to whether one is more useful to another by immediately and constantly leaping to his side and helping him — which can, in any case, only transpire very superficially, provided the help doesn't turn into a tyrannical encroachment and transformation — or by fashioning out of oneself something the other will behold with pleasure, a lovely, peaceful, self-enclosed garden, for instance, with high walls to protect against the dangers and dust of the roadway, but with a hospitable gate as well (D 174).

Nietzsche appears to have been exposed to the term "commercial society" from his reading of Taine's history of English literature (Taine 1906, p. 191). As one commentator notes, those who favoured commercial society, such as the French *philosophes*, including thinkers such as Voltaire and Montesquieu, held that by "establishing bonds among people and making life more comfortable, commerce softens and refines people's manners and promotes humaneness and civility" (Rasmussen 2008, p. 18). It is clear that in the aphorism I have just cited Nietzsche is expressing an anxiety that other nineteenth century social analysts, such as Tocqueville, have, namely, that market-driven atomization and de-individuation can readily lead to a form of communitarian tyranny (Ure 2006, p. 82). Unknown to ourselves we live within the effect of general opinions about "the human being", which is a "bloodless abstraction" and "fiction" (D 105). Even the modern glorification of work and talk of its blessings can be interpreted as a fear of everything individual. The subjection to hard industriousness from early until late serves as "the best policeman" since it keeps everyone in bounds and hinders the development of reason, desire, and the craving for independence. It uses vast amounts of nervous energy which could be given over to reflection, brooding, dreaming, loving and hating and working through our experiences: "...a society in which there is continuous hard work will have more security [*Sicherheit*]: and security is currently worshipped as the supreme divinity" (D 173). We are today creating a society of "universal security" but the price being paid of it is, Nietzsche thinks, much too high: "the maddest thing is that what is being effected is the very opposite of universal security" (D 179).

Perhaps Nietzsche's fundamental presupposition in the book is that ours is an age of great uncertainty in which there are emerging individuals who no longer consider themselves to be bound by existing mores and laws and are thus making the first attempts to organize and create for themselves a right. Hitherto such individuals have lived their lives under the jurisdiction of a guilty conscience, being decried as criminals, freethinkers, and immoralists (D 164). Although this development will make the coming century a precarious one (it may mean, Nietzsche notes, that a rifle hangs on each and every shoulder), it is one that Nietzsche thinks we should find fitting and good since it at least ensures the presence of an oppositional power that will admonish that there is any such thing as a single moral-making morality.

Nietzsche's statements on security seem to describe our present-day reality to an uncanny degree. In a recent "critique" of security Mark Neocleous has claimed that today our entire political language and culture is saturated by "security"; indeed, everywhere we look we see being articulated the so-called need for it (Neocleous 2008, p. 3). Moreover, a prevailing assumption is that such security is a good thing, something fundamentally necessary in spite of all interrogations of it. The common assumption is that only security today is able to guarantee our freedom and the good society, and the main issue on the agenda is how to improve the power of the State so it can secure us better. But, then we need to ask some critical questions. As Neocleous bravely puts it, what if at the heart of the logic of security there lays not a vision of emancipation, but rather "a means of modelling the whole of human society around a particular vision of human order? What if security is little more than a semantic and semiotic black hole allowing authority to inscribe itself deeply into human experience?" (Neocleous 2008, p. 4)

The critique of security would see security not as a universal or transcendental value, but rather as an exercise in political technology that shapes and orders individuals, groups, classes, as well as capital. It would contest the "necessity" of security that appears obvious and natural, and that aims to close off all opposition, so remaining "unquestioned, unanalysed and undialectically presupposed, rather like the order which it is expected to secure" (Neocleous 2008, p. 7). Neocleous speaks of resisting the course of a world that continues to hold a gun to the heads of human beings. Although Nietzsche responds to the crisis of security as he saw it in his own time by appealing to the need for everyone to carry their own gun, his point is one largely made in jest. More seriously, he recognizes the fundamental bio-political tendencies of modernity and the way they will impact on individuals, leading ultimately to a political technology of control and discipline and expressed in the name of our welfare and "security".

The morality Nietzsche wants to subject to critique refers to certain ways and habits of thinking, including the morality that is part of our modern self-image of ourselves (as moral agents), and that lacks intellectual conscience and integrity. Morality as we moderns conceive it gives our attempts at self-mastery a bad conscience and infuses our behaviour with guilt. (a) It is supposed that morality must have a universally binding character in which there is a single morality valid for all in all circumstances and for all occasions. Morality expects a person to be dutiful, obedient, self-sacrificing in their core and at all times: this demands ascetic self-denial and is a form of refined cruelty. (b) Ethicists such as Kant and Schopenhauer suppose that it provides us with insight into the true, metaphysical character of the world and existence. For example, in Schopenhauer virtue is "practical mysticism" which is said to spring from the same knowledge that constitutes the essence of all mysticism. For Schopenhauer, therefore, metaphysics is virtue translated into action and proceeds from the immediate and intuitive knowledge of the identity of all beings. (c) It is supposed we have an adequate understanding of moral agency, e.g. that we have properly identified moral motives and located the sources of moral agency. The opposite for Nietzsche is, in fact, the case: we almost entirely lack knowledge in moral matters. (d) It is supposed we can make a clear separation between good virtues and evil vices but for Nietzsche the two are reciprocally conditioning: all good things have arisen out of dark roots through sublimation and spiritualization and they continue to feed off such roots.

It is important we appreciate that Nietzsche is not in *Dawn* advocating the overcoming of all possible forms of morality. Where morality centres on "continually exercised self-mastery and self-overcoming in both large and the smallest of things," he champions it (WS 45). His concern is that "morality" in the forms it has assumed in the greater part of human history, right up to Kant's moral law, has opened up an abundance of sources of displeasure and to the point that one can say that with every "refinement in morality" (*Sittlichkeit*) human beings have grown "more and more dissatisfied with themselves, their neighbour, and their lot…" (D 106) The individual in search of happiness, and who wishes to become its own lawgiver, cannot be treated with prescriptions to the path to happiness simply because individual happiness springs from one's own unknown laws and external prescriptions only serve to obstruct and hinder it: "The so-called 'moral' precepts are, in truth, directed against individuals and are in no way aimed at promoting their happiness" (D 108). Indeed, Nietzsche himself does not intend to lay down precepts for everyone. As he writes, "One should seek out limited circles and seek and promote the morality appropriate to them" (D 194). Here there are links to be made between Nietzsche and Foucault regards an ethics of the care of self.

II

Before turning to an explicit examination of the idea of the care of self in Nietzsche, and to see how he mounts a resistance to disciplinary modernity, let me first outline some salient features of Foucault's account of this task and project.

For Foucault self-cultivation takes the form of an 'art of existence' – a *techne tou biou* – and is guided by the principle that one must 'take care of oneself' (Foucault 1986, p. 43). Foucault claims that care of self (*epimeleia heautou, cura sui*) is a Socratic notion or one that Socrates consecrates (Foucault 1986, p. 44; see also Foucault 2005, pp. 6f.). However, it only becomes a universal philosophical theme in the Hellenistic period, being promoted by the likes of Epicurus, the Cynics, and Stoics such as Seneca. According to Foucault, the Delphic injunction to know one's self was subordinated to self-care. He gives several examples from the literature to vindicate his core thesis, including Epicurus's letter to Menoeceus, a text in which it is stated that it is never too early or too late to occupy oneself with oneself: "Teachings about everyday life were organized around taking care of oneself in order to help every member of the group with the mutual work of salvation" (Foucault 1988, p. 21; see also Foucault 1986, p. 46). For Foucault it is in Epictetus that we find the highest philosophical development of the theme of care of self. For Epictetus the human is destined to care for itself and is where the basic difference between the human and other creatures resides. Moreover, for Epictetus the care of self "is a privilege-duty, a gift-obligation that ensures our freedom while forcing us to take ourselves as the object of all our diligence" (Foucault 1986, p. 47). For Foucault the care of self is not constituted as an exercise in solitude but as a "true social practice" (Foucault 1986, p. 51). He is keen to stress that the "conversion to self" entails the experience of a pleasure that one takes in oneself:

> This pleasure, for which Seneca usually employs the word *gaudium* or *laetitia*, is a state that is neither accompanied nor followed by any form of disturbance in the body or the mind. It is defined by the fact of not being caused by anything that is independent of ourselves and therefore escapes our control. It arises out of ourselves and within ourselves. (Foucault 1986, p. 66)

For Foucault the contrast to be made is with *voluptas* which denotes a pleasure whose origin resides outside us and in objects whose presence we cannot be sure of (a pleasure that is precarious in itself). What Foucault is delineating here resonates, I think, with the "joy of existing" Nietzsche seeks to restore in his middle period as a central concern of a post-metaphysical philosophy and after two centuries of training by morality and religion (see WS 86). However, this tradition has become obscure to us today and we can account for this obscurity in terms of several developments. Foucault notes that there has been a deep transformation in the moral principles of Western society. We find it difficult to base a morality of austere principles on the precept that we should give ourselves more care than anything else in the world. Rather, we are inclined to see taking care of ourselves as an immorality and as a means of escape from all possible rules. We have inherited the tradition of Christian morality which makes self-renunciation the condition for salvation. Here, "to know oneself was paradoxically the way to self-renunciation" (Foucault 1988, p. 22). Such is our assimilation of this morality of self-denial, to the point where we identify it as the domain of morality in and for itself, that the kind of morality pursued by the ancients strikes us today as an exercise in moral dandyism (see Foucault 2005, p. 12). As Foucault notes, we have the paradox of a precept of care of self that signifies for us today either egoism or withdrawal, but which for centuries was a positive principle, serving as the matrix for dedicated moralities. Christianity and the modern world have based the codes of moral strictness on a morality of non-egoism to the point where we forget that such codes originated in an environment marked by the obligation to take care of oneself.

We can note here: Nietzsche, at least in the popular imagination, is taken to be an immoralist in the crude sense identified by Foucault when, on the contrary, he needs to be read as an ethical thinker in the way Foucault thinks we have forgotten ethics. We have developed a bad conscience over an ethics centred on self-care and regard self-renunciation as the basis of morality. We are the inheritors of a secular tradition that sees in external law the basis for morality and this morality is one of asceticism or denial of the self. As Nietzsche astutely points out, if we examine what is often taken to be the summit of the moral in philosophy – the mastery of the affects – we find that there is pleasure to be taken in this mastery. I can impress myself by what I can deny, defer, resist, and so on. It is through this mastery that I grow and develop. And yet morality, as we moderns have come to understand it, would have to give this ethical self-mastery a bad conscience. If we take as our criterion of the moral to be self-sacrificing resolution and self-denial, we would have to say, if being honest, that such acts are not performed strictly for the sake of others; my own fulfilment and pride are at work and the other provides the self with an opportunity to relieve itself through self-denial.

Among the Greeks practices of self-cultivation took the form of a precept, "to take care of self". This precept was a principal rule for social and personal conduct and for the art of life. This is not what we ordinarily think when we think of the ancient Greeks: we imagine that they were ruled by the precept, "Know thyself" (*gnothi seauton*). Why have we moderns forgotten the original precept of take care of the self and why has it been obscured by the Delphic injunction? In modern philosophy from Descartes to Husserl knowledge of the self, or the thinking subject, takes an on an ever-increasing importance as the first key step in the theory of knowledge. Foucault thinks we moderns have thus inverted what was the hierarchy in the two main principles of antiquity: for the Greeks knowledge was subordinated to ethics (centred on self-care) whereas for us knowledge is what is primary. But even the Delphic principle was not an abstract one concerning life; rather, it was technical advice meaning something like, "do not suppose yourself to be a god" or "be aware of what you really ask when you come to consult the oracle".

Two key points are worth making here. First, Foucault insists that taking care of one's self does not simply mean being interested in oneself or having an attachment to or fascination with the self. Rather, "it describes a sort of work, an activity; it implies attention, knowledge, technique" (Foucault 1997, p. 269). Second, regarding the taking care aspect, Foucault stresses that the

Greek word – *epimeleisthai* – designates not simply a mental attitude, a certain form of attention, or a way of not forgetting something. He points out that its etymology refers to a series of words such as *meletan* and *melete*, and "meletan", for example, means to practice and train (often coupled with the verb *gumnazein*). So, the *meletai* are exercises, such as gymnastic and military ones. Thus, the Greek "taking care" refers to a form of vigilant, continuous, and applied activity more than it does to a mental attitude.

III

Foucault contends that in Greek ethics we find a focus on moral conduct, on relations to oneself and others, rather than a focus on religious problems such as what is our fate after death? What are the gods and do they intervene in life or not? For the Greeks, Foucault argues, these were not significant problems and not directly related to conduct. What they were concerned about was to constitute an ethics that was an "aesthetics of existence". Foucault thinks we may in a similar situation to the Greek today "since most of us no longer believe that ethics is founded in religion" (Foucault 1997, p. 255). For him the general Greek problem was not the *tekhne* of the self but that of life, "*tekhne tou biou*, or how to live. It's quite clear from Socrates to Seneca or Pliny, for instance, that they didn't worry about the afterlife, what happened after death, or whether God exists or not. That was not really a great problem for them; the problem was: Which *tekhne* do I have to use in order to live well as I ought to live?" (Foucault, 1997, p. 260) More and more he thinks over time this *tekhne tou biou* became one of the self, so whereas a Greek citizen of say the fifth century would have felt his *tekhne* of life was to take care of the city and his companions, by the time of Seneca the problem is to primarily take care of himself. This taking care of the self for its own sake is something that starts with the Epicureans.

This is remarkably similar to how Nietzsche presents the issue of ethical life in the free spirit period where he suggests we need to cultivate an attitude of indifference with respect to the first and last things. In *Dawn* he explicitly appeals to Epicurus and Epictetus as thinkers who present a model of ethics quite different to what we have inherited through Christianity and modern secularism.

Ruth Abbey is one commentator who has drawn attention to the centrality of an ethics of care of self in Nietzsche's middle period. This centres on a concern for quotidian minutiae, attention to individualized goods, and an awareness of the close connection between psyche and physique (Abbey 2000, p. 102). For Nietzsche, as Abbey notes, the small, daily practices of care of self are undervalued (Abbey 2000, p. 99). In modern culture we can detect, Nietzsche writes, a "feigned contempt for all the things that humans really take to be most important, <u>all the nearest things</u>" (WS 5). As Abbey further notes, in devaluing the small, worldly matters Christian and post-Christian sensibility, "puts people at war with themselves and forbids a close study of which forms of care of the self would be most conducive to individual flourishing" (Abbey 2000, p. 99). As Nietzsche notes, most people see the closest things badly and rarely pay heed to them, whilst "to be <u>ignorant in the smallest and most everyday things</u> and not to have a keen eye – that is what makes the world into a 'pasture of troubles' for so many people" (WS 6). Nietzsche goes on to name Socrates as a key figure in the history of thought who defended himself against this "arrogant neglect" of the human for the benefit of the human race (D 9). Nietzsche argues: "...our continual offences against the simplest laws of the body and spirit bring all of us, young and old, into a shameful dependency and unfreedom...upon doctors, teachers and pastors, whose pressure now lies constantly upon all of society" (WS 5). All the physical and psychical frailties of the individual derive from a lack of knowledge about the smallest and most everyday things, such as what is beneficial to us and what is harmful to us in the institution of our mode of life, in the division of the day, eating, sleeping, and reflecting, and so on.

For Foucault the principle of the care of self allows for variation: in Plato's Alcibiades care of self "refers to an active political and erotic state", but in the Hellenistic and Roman periods the care of self has become a universal principle and politics is left to one side as so to take better care of the self (Foucault 1988, p. 24 and Foucault 1988, p. 31). How does *Dawn* fit into this schema as a nineteenth century work of resistance? It is worth here making a comment on the diagnosis that informs Nietzsche's social critique in *Dawn*. Nietzsche laments the development he sees taking place where old Europe is being infected by the distinctive vice of the new world, the work ethic, which spreads "a lack of spirituality" like a blanket (GS 329). Such is Nietzsche's concern that he thinks that people are becoming frugal with regard to joy, increasingly suspicious of it, and with work enlisting a good conscience on its side to the point where "the desire for joy calls itself a 'need to recuperate'" (GS 329). He wonders whether we shall soon reach a point "where people can no longer give in to the desire for a <u>vita contemplativa</u>...without self-contempt and a bad conscience" (GS 329; see also D 178). Nietzsche notes that the modern culture of a society is the "soul" of commerce, as the personal contest was for the Greeks and war and victory was for the Romans: "The man engaged in commerce understands how to appraise everything without having made it, and to appraise it <u>according to the needs of the consumer</u>... 'who and how many will consume this?' is his question of questions" (D 175). This mode of appraisal then gets applied, Nietzsche notes anxiously, to everything, including the productions of the arts and sciences, of thinkers, scholars, artists, statesmen, etc, so becoming the character of an entire culture.

It is certain that Nietzsche sought to found a philosophical school modelled on Epicurus's garden. In a letter of 26 ^{March} 1879 he asks Peter Gast: "<u>Where</u> are we going to renew the garden of Epicurus?" (KSB 5, p. 399) For commentators such as Horst Hutter, Nietzsche's ultimate goal is the shaping of the future of European humanity and society, and on this conception of his philosophy the retreat into an Epicurean-inspired community of friends is merely a temporary expedient in which free spirits work on themselves so as to become philosophical legislators of a future culture. As Hutter has written, "such fraternities of free spirits would be necessary to traverse the period of nihilism until a future point in time, when direct political action would again become possible" (Hutter 2006, p. 5). One thinks in this regard of what Nietzsche notes in *The Wanderer and his Shadow* when he says that free spirits withdraw into concealment but not out of any kind of personal ill-humour, as though the present social and political situation was not good enough for them; rather, it is that through withdrawal they wish to economize and assemble forces of which culture will one day have great need: "We are accumulating capital and seeking to make it secure: but, as in times of great peril, to do that we have to <u>bury</u> it" (WS 229).

IV

Let me now turn to illuminating the reception of Epicurus and Epictetus we find in *Dawn* and in Nietzsche's middle period in general.

What appeals to Nietzsche about Epicurus is the teaching on mortality and the general attempt to liberate the mind from unjustified fears and anxieties. If, as Pierre Hadot has suggested, philosophical therapeutics is centred on a concern with the healing of our own lives so as to return us to the joy of existing (Hadot 1995, p. 87), then in the texts of his middle period Nietzsche can be seen to be an heir to this ancient tradition. Indeed, if there is one crucial component to Nietzsche's philosophical therapeutics in the texts of his middle period that he keeps returning to again and again it is the need for spiritual joyfulness and the task of cultivating in ourselves, after centuries of training by morality and religion, the joy in existing. In the final aphorism of *The Wanderer and his Shadow* Nietzsche writes, for example:

> Only to the ennobled human being may the freedom of spirit be given; to him alone does alleviation of life draw nigh and salve his wounds; he is the first who may say that he lives for the sake of joyfulness [*Freudigkeit*] and for the sake of no further goal... (WS 350)

In the middle period, then, Epicurus is an attractive figure for Nietzsche because of the attention given to the care of self, and also because he conceives philosophy not as a theoretical discourse but one that, first and foremost, is a kind of practical activity aimed at the attainment of eudemonia or the flourishing life (Young 2010, pp. 279ff.). Nietzsche wants free spirits to take pleasure in existence, involving taking pleasure in themselves and in friendship. Nietzsche is keen to encourage human beings to cultivate an attitude towards existence in which they accept their mortality and attain serenity about their dwelling on the earth, to conquer unjustified fears, and to reinstitute the role played by chance and chance events in the world and in human existence (see D 13, 33, 36; see also Hadot 1995, pp. 87, 223, 252).

At this time Nietzsche is committed to a philosophical therapeutics in which the chief aim is to temper emotional and mental excess. One might contend that there is an Epicurean inspiration informing Nietzsche's actual philosophical practice at this time. According to one commentator, Epicurean arguments "have a clear therapeutic intent: by removing false beliefs concerning the universe and the ways in which the gods might be involved in its workings, they eliminate a major source of mental trouble and lead us towards a correct and beneficial conception of these matters" (Tsouna 2009, pp. 257f.). In part, Nietzsche conceived the art of the maxim in therapeutic terms. The modern age has forgotten the art of reflection or observation, in which it is possible to gather maxims "from the thorniest and least gratifying stretches of our lives" so as to make ourselves feel better, to give ourselves a lift and a tonic. We can return to life revivified rather than depressed from our encounter with thorny problems, and with "presence of mind in difficult situations and amusement in tedious surroundings" (HH I: 38). There is a need, therefore, for modern spirits to learn how to derive pleasure from the art of the maxim, from its construction to its tasting. Nietzsche notes that it is virtually impossible to say whether the inquiry into the "human, all too human" will work more as a blessing than a curse to the welfare of humanity; at any rate, and for the time being, the issue is undecided. He further notes that because science, like nature, does not aim at final ends, any fruitfulness in the way of promoting the welfare of humanity will be the result of science's attaining something purposeful without having willed it. But where science is needed now, as part of a general therapeutic practice of reflection and observation, is in tempering the human mind: "shouldn't we, the more spiritual human beings of an age that is visibly catching fire in more and more places, have to grasp all available means for quenching and cooling, so that we will remain at least as steady... and moderate as we are now..." (HH I: 38) The illnesses and neuroses we encounter in humanity require that "ice-packs" be placed on them (HH I: 38). Nietzsche speaks of the "over-excitation" of our "nervous and thinking powers" reaching a dangerous critical point in our present and notes that "the cultivated classes of Europe have in fact become thoroughly neurotic" (HH I: 244). This concern with a cooling down of the human mind continues in *Dawn* where Nietzsche's makes even more explicit his concern with the spread of fanaticism in moral and religious thinking (see D 50).

In the middle period, then, Epicurus is one of Nietzsche's chief inspirations in his effort to liberate himself from the metaphysical need, to find serenity within his own existence, and to aid humanity in its need to now cure its neuroses. Epicureanism, along with science in general, serves to make us "colder and more sceptical," helping to cool down "the fiery stream of belief in ultimate definitive truths," a stream that has grown so turbulent through Christianity (HH I: 244). The task, Nietzsche says, is to live in terms of "a constant spiritual joyfulness [*Freudigkeit*]" (HH I: 292) and to prize "the three good things": grandeur, repose or peace, and sunlight, in which these things answer to thoughts that elevate, thoughts that quieten, thoughts that enlighten, and, finally, "to thoughts that share in all three of these qualities, in which everything earthly comes to be transfigured: that is the realm where the great trinity of joy rules [*Freude*]" (WS 332).

I have mentioned Nietzsche's concern with religious and moral fanaticism in *Dawn*. Nietzsche's search for a non-fanatical (*nicht fanatisch*) mode of living leads him to the Stoic Epictetus. Although this ancient thinker was a slave, the exemplar he invokes is without class and is possible in every class. He serves as a counterweight to modern idealists who are greedy for expansion. Epictetus's ideal human being, lacking all fear of God and believing rigorously in reason, "is not a preacher of penitence" (D 546). He has a pride in himself that does not wish to trouble and encroach on others: "he admits a certain mild rapprochement and does not wish to spoil anyone's good mood – Yes, he can smile! There is a great deal of ancient humanity in this ideal!" (D 546) The Epictetean is self-sufficient, "defends himself against the outside world" and "lives in a state of highest valor" (D 546). Nietzsche offers this portrait of the Epictetean as a point of contrast to the Christian. The Christian lives in hope (and in the consolation of "unspeakable glories" to come) and allows himself to be given gifts, expecting the best of life not to come from himself and his own resources but from divine love and grace. By contrast Epictetus "does not hope and does allow his best to be given him – he possesses it, he holds it valiantly in his hand, and he would take on the whole world if it tries to rob him of it" (D 546). This portrait of Epictetus contra the Christian provides us with a set of invaluable insights into how Nietzsche conceives the difference between fanatical and non-fanatical modes of living: one way of life is self-sufficient and finds its pride in this, renouncing hope and living in the present; the other devotes itself to living through and for others, its attention is focused on the future (as that which is to come), and it lacks the quiet and calm dignity of self-sufficiency that is the Epictetean ideal.

Epictetus is also admired by Nietzsche on account of his dedication to his own ego and for resisting the glorification of thinking and living for others (D 131). Of course, this is a partial and selective appropriation of Epictetus on Nietzsche's part. Although his chief concerns are with integrity and self-command, Epictetus is also known for his Stoic cosmopolitanism in which individuals have an obligation to care for their fellow human beings, and Nietzsche is silent about this aspect of Stoic teaching. Nevertheless, it is true that the ethical outlook of Epictetus does invite people "to value their individual selves over everything else," (Long 2002, p. 3) and for Nietzsche he serves as a useful contrast to Christian thinkers such as Pascal, who considered the ego to be something hateful:

> If, as Pascal and Christianity claim, our ego [Ich] is always hateful, how might we possibly ever allow or assume that someone else could love it — be it God or a human being! It would go against all decency to let oneself be loved knowing full well that one only deserves hate — not to mention other feelings of repulsion. — 'But this is precisely the kingdom of mercy'. — So is your love-thy-neighbour mercy? Your compassion mercy? Well, if these things are possible for you, go still one step further: love yourselves out of mercy — then you won't need your God any more at all, and the whole drama of original sin and redemption will play itself out to the end in you yourselves (D 79).

Nietzsche wishes to replace morality, including the morality of compassion, with a care of self. We go wrong when we fail to attend to the needs of the "ego" and flee from it. We can stick to the idea that benevolence and beneficence are what constitute a good person, but such a person must first be benevolently and beneficently disposed towards themselves. A "bad" person is one that runs from himself and hates himself, causing injury to himself. Such a person is rescuing himself from himself in others, and this running from the ego (*ego*) living in others, for others "has, heretofore, been called, just as unreflectedly as assuredly, "unegotistical" *and consequently* "good"! (D 516) Such passages clearly indicate, I think, that Nietzsche has what I am crediting him with in *Dawn*, namely, an intimate concern with the care of self.

V

In the interview entitled "On the Genealogy of Ethics" Foucault says:

> What strikes me is the fact that, in our society, art has become something that is related only to objects and not to individuals or to life. That art is something which is specialized or done by experts who are artists. But couldn't everyone's life become a work of art? Why should the lamp or the house be an art object but not our life? (Foucault 1997, p. 261)

Foucault is keen to say that what he's advocating here is not the Californian cult of the self and neither is the heroic freedom of Sartrean existentialism. Both have major flaws for him. He likes to give the example of the Stoics as an alternative: "the experience of the self is not a discovering of a truth hidden inside the self but an attempt to determine what one can and cannot do with one's available freedom" (Foucault 1997, p. 276). He tells us that he's suspicious of the notion of "liberation" since it suggests a self that is repressed and waiting to be liberated beneath the layers of social and historical determination. He makes clear his conception of freedom as ethos in his account of how the Greeks problematized the freedom of the individual as an ethical problem. Here the word "ethical" denotes a way of being and behaviour. Somebody's ethos is evident in their clothing, appearance, gait, and in the calm with which they respond to every event. Thus, a human being possessed of a splendid ethos, who could be admired and put forward as an example, was someone who practised freedom in a certain way. However, extensive work by the self on the self is required for this practice of freedom to take shape in an ethos that can be said to be beautiful, honourable, estimable, memorable, and exemplary.

For Foucault the elaboration of one's own life as a personal work of art was at the centre of moral experiences in antiquity (even if it conformed to certain collective canons or practices). In Christianity by contrast, with the religion of the text, the idea of the will of God, and the principle of obedience, morality increasingly took on the form of a code of rules. From antiquity to Christianity we pass from a morality that was primarily the search for a personal ethics to a morality as obedience to a system of rules. Foucault holds that for a whole series of reasons the idea of morality as obedience to a code of rules is now disappearing and this absence of morality is to be replaced with the search for an aesthetics of existence (Foucault 1990, p. 49).

With respect to this idea of an "aesthetics of existence", this is one area where Foucault's work has invited much criticism. He has been accused of retreating in his late work into an amoral aesthetics, privileging an elitist notion of self-centred stylization, and undermining possibilities of emancipatory politics. Johanna Oksala is a recent defender of Foucault: she argues that his ethics-as-aesthetics needs to be understood first and foremost as a continuation of his permanent questioning of the limits of subjectivity and the possibilities of crossing them. Foucault's ethics thus represent an attempt to seek ways of living and thinking that are transgressive and, like a work of art, are not simply the product of normalizing power. For Oksala one way to contest normalizing power is by shaping one's self and one's lifestyle creatively and the exploration of possibilities for new forms of subjectivity, new fields of experiences, pleasures, modes of living and thinking. She thus argues that the quest for freedom which characterises Foucault's late work is a question of developing forms of subjectivity that are capable of functioning as resistance to normalizing power. This concern on his part can even enable us to understand better the importance of the ancient practices of the self for Foucault. As he stresses, we cannot find in Stoic ethics the attempt to normalize and there is no attempt to normalize the population. Rather, it was, says Foucault, a matter of personal choice, making the choice to live a beautiful life and to leave to others memories of a beautiful existence (Foucault 1997, p. 254). Oksala maintains, then, that Foucault's aesthetics of existence should not be understood as a narcissistic enterprise nor as aesthetic in a narrow visual sense of the word as in looking stylish. It is an aesthetics not because it calls on us to make ourselves beautiful, but because it calls on us to relate to ourselves and our lives in terms of a material, a bios, that can be formed and transformed (Oksala 2005, p. 169). It is Nietzsche who perhaps best revives this conception of ethics for us moderns:

> It is a myth to believe that we will find our true or authentic self once we have left out or forgotten this and that. That way we pick ourselves apart in an infinite regression: instead, the task is to make ourselves, to shape a form from all the elements! The task is always that of a sculptor! A productive human being! Not through knowledge but through practice and an exemplar do we become ourselves! Knowledge has, at best, the value of a means! (NL, KSA 9, 7[213])

VI

Neither Nietzsche nor Foucault advocates an ahistorical return to the ancients. In the case of *Dawn* Nietzsche highlights the teaching of Epictetus, for example, as a way of indicating that what we take to be morality today, where it is taken to be coextensive with the sympathetic affects, is not a paradigm of some universal and metahistorical truth. If we look at history we find that there have been different ways of being ethical, and this in itself is sufficient, Nietzsche thinks, to derail the idea that there is a single moral-making morality. Both thinkers seek to work against the construction of moral necessities out of historical contingencies. A key difference from the ancients is that Nietzsche is developing a therapy for the sicknesses of the soul under specifically modern conditions of social control and discipline.

I think we find in *Dawn* and the resistance to modernity it mounts a clear rebuttal of what Roberto Esposito construes as the guiding idea of modern political thought, namely, the idea of preserving life through the abolition of conflict, difference, and heterogeneity:

> One could say that the heart of Nietzsche's philosophy will be found in his rebuttal of such a conception, which is to say in the extreme attempt to bring again to the surface that harsh and profound relation that holds together politics and life in the unending form of struggle. (Esposito 2008, p. 85)

Esposito goes so far as to claim that although Nietzsche did not formulate the term he nevertheless "anticipated the entire biopolitical course that Foucault then defined and developed...One can say that all the Foucauldian categories are present in a nutshell in Nietzsche's conceptual language" (Esposito 2008, p. 85). As Esposito rightly notes, Nietzsche challenges the idea that the human species is ever given once and for all; rather, it is susceptible, "in good and evil, to being moulded in forms for which we do not have exact knowledge, but which nevertheless constitute for us both an absolute risk and an inalienable challenge" (Esposito 2008, p. 83). He quotes Nietzsche from 1881 on the "selection" of the human: "why should we not realize in the human being what the Chinese are able to do with the tree, producing roses on the one side and on the other side pears?" (NL, KSA 9, 11[276]) Nietzsche's ambition in *Dawn* is clear, I think, from the following note, and it centres on the experiment of cultivating what we can call human pluralization and working against the closure of the human:

> My morality [*Moral*] would be to take the general character of man more and more away from him [...] to make him to a degree non-understandable to others (and with it an object of experiences, of astonishment, of instruction for them)... Should not each individual [*Individuum*] be an attempt to achieve a higher species than man through its most individual things? (NL, KSA 9, 6[158])

Bibliography

Abbey, Ruth (2000): *Nietzsche's Middle Period*. Oxford: Oxford University Press.
Esposito, Roberto (2008): *Bios: Biopolitics and Philosophy*. Timothy Campbell (trans.). Minneapolis: University of Minnesota Press.
Foucault, Michel (1986): *The Care of the Self: The History of Sexuality 3*. Robert Hurley (trans.). Harmondsworth, Penguin.

Foucault, Michel (1988): "Technologies of the Self". In: Luther H. Martin et al (eds.): *Technologies of the Self: A Seminar with Michel Foucault*. London: Tavistock, pp. 16–50.

Foucault, Michel (1990): "An Aesthetics of Existence". In: Michel Foucault: *Politics, Philosophy, Culture: Interviews and Writings 1977–84*. Alan Sheridan et al. (trans.). London: Routledge.

Foucault, Michel (1997): *Ethics: The Essential Works 1*. Paul Rabinow (ed.). Harmondsworth: Penguin.

Foucault, Michel (2005): *The Hermeneutics of the Self: Lectures at the College de France 1981–82*. Graham Burchell (trans.). New York, Palgrave Macmillan.

Hadot, Pierre (1995): *Philosophy as a Way of Life*. Michael Chase (trans.). Oxford: Basil Blackwell.

Hutter, Horst (2006): *Shaping the Future: Nietzsche's New Regime of the Soul and its Ascetic Practices*. Lanham, MD: Lexington Books.

Ingram, David (2003): "Foucault and Habermas". In: Gary Gutting (ed.): *The Cambridge Companion to Foucault*. 2nd edition. Cambridge: Cambridge University Press, pp. 240–284.

Long, A. A. (2002): *Epictetus*. Oxford: Clarendon Press.

Neocleous, Mark (2008): *Critique of Security*. Edinburgh: Edinburgh University Press.

Nietzsche, Friedrich (1974): *The Gay Science*. Walter Kaufmann (trans.). New York: Random House.

Nietzsche, Friedrich (1995): *Human, all too Human: volume one*. Gary Handwerk (trans.). Stanford: Stanford University Press.

Nietzsche, Friedrich (2011): *Dawn: Thoughts on the Presumptions of Morality*. Brittain Smith (trans.). Stanford: Stanford University Press.

Nietzsche, Friedrich (2013): *Human, all too Human: volume two*. Gary Handwerk (trans.). Stanford: Stanford University Press.

Oksala, Johanna (2005): *Foucault on Freedom*. Cambridge: Cambridge University Press.

Rasmussen, Dennis C. (2008): *The Problems and Promise of Commercial Society: Adam Smith's Response to Rousseau*. University Park, PA: Penn State University Press.

Taine, H. A. (1906): *History of English Literature*. Vol. IV. H. Van Laun (trans.). London: Chatto & Windus.

Tsouna, Voula (2009): "Epicurean Therapeutic Strategies". In: James Warren (ed.): *The Cambridge Companion to Epicureanism*. Cambridge: Cambridge University Press, pp. 249–66.

Ure, Michael (2006): "The Irony of Pity: Nietzsche contra Schopenhauer and Rousseau". In: *Journal of Nietzsche Studies* 32, pp. 68–92.

Young, Julian (2010): *Nietzsche: A Philosophical Biography*. Cambridge: Cambridge University Press.

Daniel Conway
"We who are different, we immoralists..."

> We who are different, we immoralists, on the contrary, have opened our hearts to all kinds of understanding, comprehending, and <u>approving</u>. We do not readily deny; we seek our honor in being <u>affirmative</u>. More and more, our eyes have been opened to that economy which still needs and can exploit all that is rejected by the holy madness of the priest, of the priest's <u>sick</u> reason; to that economy in the law of life which can gain advantage even from the repulsive species of the miseryguts, the priest, the virtuous man — <u>what</u> advantage? — But we ourselves, we immoralists, are the answer here... – *Twilight of the Idols*, "Morality", Section 6

> Let us open our eyes and keep our hand firm on the helm! We sail right <u>over</u> morality, we crush, we destroy perhaps the remains of our own morality by daring to make our voyage there — but what matter are <u>we</u>! – *Beyond Good and Evil* 23

My objective in this chapter is to isolate and retrieve the specific meaning that Nietzsche attaches to his immoralism in the writings from 1888. Toward this end, I endeavor to place his immoralism, especially as this position is described and enacted in *Twilight of the Idols*, in the larger context of his envisioned contribution to the endgame sequence in the history of Christian morality. The particular claim I wish to demonstrate is that Nietzsche fully intended his immoralism to deliver a moral critique of morality. The immoralist whom he meant to illuminate in *Twilight of the Idols* (and *Ecce Homo*) thus aims not simply to express his contempt for the norms and values of contemporary Christian morality, but also to demonstrate that Christian morality is untruthful *and*, therefore, immoral. I thus wish to present Nietzsche as intending, *qua* immoralist, to deliver the final, self-consuming judgment on behalf of morality itself.

The irony of Nietzsche's infamous *denial* (*Verneinung*) of Christian morality, which he presents as fundamental to his immoralism (EH Destiny 4), is that it presupposes his prior *affirmation* of Christian morality. He is uniquely entitled to guide Christian morality to a fitting conclusion, that is, because he alone appreciates the *positive* value it may yet contribute to the larger economy of Life itself. When morality finally perishes, he promises, it will have exhausted its last remaining quantum of value. It will have done so, moreover, at the hands of an expert harvester, identified for us in *Twilight of the Idols* as the *last* disciple of Dionysus (TI Ancients 5).

Section I

Nietzsche is often thought or said to have *rejected* morality. This rejection is often cited in turn as ingredient to his *immoralism*, which is a position that sympathetic scholars have generally struggled to define and defend (Clark 1994, pp. 15ff.; Hunt 1991, pp. 7f., 23f.). While some scholars regard Nietzsche as unwittingly complicit in a moral enterprise that he both claims and means to reject,[1] others applaud him for renouncing conventional morality in favor of a "higher" (or more stringent) morality (Jaspers 1979, pp. 155–159; Hunt 1991, pp. 145f.; Berkowitz 1995, pp. 48f., 279f.; May 1999, pp. 177–180; van Tongeren 2000, pp. 228–246; Solomon 2003, pp. 49–50, 132–136; Hatab 2008, pp. 233–240; see also Clark 1994, p. 17). Still others are convinced that Nietzsche's immoralism is motivated by primarily aesthetic commitments (Kaufmann 1974, pp. 321–326; Foot 1994, pp. 3–7; Nehamas 1985, pp. 193–196, 205–218; see also Clark 1994, p. 18–19), which need not be understood to entail his endorsement of the patently immoral (or amoral) activity that is popularly associated with his name and this particular position (Jaspers 1979, pp. 450–458; May 1999, pp. 130–133; and Detwiler 1990, p. 53).

While these interpretive strategies faithfully capture the spirit of what Nietzsche identified as the "antimoral propensity" of his thinking (BT Attempt 5), they also tend to treat his immoralism as if it were emblematic more generally of his critical stance toward morality. As such, these strategies tend to misplace or discount the very specific focus of his immoralism in the writings of 1888. As a result, moreover, these interpretive strategies also tend to ignore or downplay the wondrous transformation that Nietzsche claims to have undergone in the post-Zarathustran period of his career. As his writings from 1888 confirm, in fact, he understands his immoralism as indicative of a relatively recent achievement of self-overcoming on his part. And although this achievement is continuous with the "antimoral propensity" that shapes his earlier writings, it is also sufficiently novel as to oblige him to introduce himself anew (EH Preface 1–2). As an immoralist, as we shall see, Nietzsche intensifies his critical challenge to the contemporary incarnation of Christian morality, such that *he* may lay claim to the mantle and authority of morality itself.

To be sure, Nietzsche is largely responsible for encouraging his readers to draw these divergent conclusions about him. Having exposed morality as trad-

---

[1] This is the gist of Heidegger's influential interpretation of Nietzsche as committed, contrary to his intentions, to "*a metaphysics of the absolute subjectivity of will to power*" (Heidegger, p. 147). See also Benson 2008, pp. 211–216.

ing on a cluster of unacknowledged "prejudices," and having traced contemporary Christian morality to its roots in an archaic slave morality, he often (and passionately) expressed his distrust of morality, his enmity for morality, and his hopes for an extra-moral future. At one time, moreover, he may have believed that the rejection of morality was a viable, worthwhile project, either for himself or for those who were likely to profit from his preparatory labors. Were he free to reject morality, we might conjecture with some confidence, he certainly would have done so.

But he was not free to reject morality, and he knew as much. In light of the broadly genealogical orientation of his post-Zarathustran writings, moreover, it is difficult to imagine how he might have conceived of the rejection of morality as a coherent, much less viable, philosophical project. His genealogical disclosures may have sullied the reputation of morality and tarnished its luster, but they also confirmed the tenacity of its grip on him and his late modern readers.

While his earlier writings may betray some genuine confusion on this point (Hunt 1991, pp. 7–10), his writings from 1888 document a more mature and focused confrontation with morality. Not coincidentally, these are also the writings in which we find the majority of his published references to himself as an *immoralist*. In his writings from 1888, moreover, we find that he prefers the language of *opposition, resistance,* and *denial* to express the nature of his critical engagement with morality. Indeed, although the language of *rejection* conveys a general appreciation of Nietzsche's immoralism, it also contributes to the currency of various misconceptions of what he intended his challenge to morality to involve. The language of *rejection* may imply, for example, that Nietzsche was (or believed himself to be) *free* to discontinue his participation in the basic practices of morality and to divest himself of the fundamental, i.e., "egoistic," values of morality. The language of *rejection* may thus suggest, erroneously, that Nietzsche conceived of our ongoing participation in morality as a matter of our volition, such that we might elect at any moment to cancel our subscription to its guiding principles. Indeed, the language of *rejection* would seem to indicate that a genuinely extra-moral or amoral existence is potentially available to anyone who resolutely elects to pursue it.

In particular, the language of *rejection* may encourage us to underestimate the role of morality in shaping our historical identities (cf. GM II 21).[2] Nietzsche insisted, after all, that our ongoing participation in morality is not simply a matter of our conscious choices and decisions. As his naturalistic (or genealog-

---

[2] As Leiter observes (Leiter 2002, pp. 85f.), *Ecce Homo* in particular emphasizes the fatality (or fatalism) that governs Nietzsche's relationship to the various forces that have shaped him.

ical) approach to history is meant to reveal, in fact, morality exerts a powerful, formative claim upon us, antecedent to and independent of any choices we make regarding its value. He furthermore presented morality as having burdened us with an acquired "second" nature that is bent on extirpating our native endowment of animal vitality and instincts. Our participation in morality, he disclosed, is largely and fundamentally a matter of habituation and acculturation, which we are not free to unlearn or undo simply by dint of an act of will.

He thus acknowledged that certain moral "prejudices" and value judgments – including, most notably, our inherited predilection toward pre-reflective acts of "selflessness" (GM Preface 5) – have become constitutive of our identity as subjects and agents (Leiter 2002, pp. 133ff.; Janaway 2007, pp. 251–254; Acampora 2013, pp. 128ff.). We do not choose, for example, to redirect our natural instinct for cruelty toward ourselves. Nor do we choose to resent those whose achievements dwarf our own. Nor do we choose to feel remorse for what we have done and guilt for what we have not done. And so on. In short, Nietzsche's genealogical approach to morality reveals that we are not free to reject morality, even if we arrive at the determination that it is in our best interests to do so. What is more, Nietzsche draws a similar conclusion about himself and his unknown mates (Ridley 1999, pp. 120–126; Leiter 2002, pp. 279ff.; Janaway 2007, pp. 236–239; Owen 2007, pp. 128ff.; Loeb 2010, pp. 234–237; and Acampora 2013, pp. 192–197). He and they, too, are creatures of virtue and conscience (BGE 214); paragons of piety (GS 344); heirs to the ascetic ideal (GS 344); exemplars of Christian truthfulness (GS 344); "too good" for the job of conducting a proper psychological investigation (GM III 20); not-so-free spirits (GM III 24); and so on.

An example drawn from Essay II of GM may prove instructive here. When Nietzsche finally weighs the merits of a plan for what might be judged to involve the *rejection* of morality, he acknowledges its possibility, urgency, and value, but he despairs nonetheless:

> Humankind has all too long had an 'evil eye' for his natural inclinations, so that they have finally become inseparable from his 'bad conscience.' An attempt at the reverse would in itself be possible — but who is strong enough for it?... To whom should one turn today with such hopes and demands? (GM II 24).

He concludes that his plan for rejecting (or undoing) morality could be carried out only by "a different kind of spirit from that likely to appear in this present age" (GM II 24). He consequently pins his hopes for "redemption" on the emergence of a shadowy "man of the future," whose stores of strength and health will eclipse our own (GM II 24). The lesson of this particular story, or so it would appear, is that any credible plan to reject morality would outstrip the volitional resources available to Nietzsche and his late modern readers.

Taking this lesson to heart, we may conclude that it would be possible for Nietzsche to oppose, resist, deny, and even condemn morality while remaining very much within its thrall. (If these expressions of opposition, resistance, denial, and condemnation are to gain any purchase, as we shall see, they must be understood to trade on the moral authority they seek to discredit.) If morality has become constitutive of our historical identity – bred in the bone, as it were – then it may be the case that we can rid ourselves of morality only if we place our identities and ourselves at mortal risk. Indeed, Nietzsche occasionally signals his understanding that a complete and final liberation from morality, including the invalidation of its involuntary claims upon us, awaits us only in or near death itself (BGE 23; see also Loeb 2010, pp. 234–240).

This is not to suggest, of course, that nothing we do will relax the claim of morality on our lives (Janaway 2007, pp. 249–254; Owen 2007, pp. 63–65, 126–129). Nor should we conclude that Nietzsche's efforts to establish his oft-asserted superiority to his late modern contemporaries were for naught. As we shall see, in fact, a primary attraction of the language of *opposition, resistance*, and *denial* is that it accommodates his understanding of our relationship to morality. Especially in his post-Zarathustran writings, in fact, he was precisely concerned to develop and recommend a regimen of "self-discipline" that would enable him and those like him to establish a critical distance from the formative influences of morality (CW Preface). We thus see, for example, that he recommends the program of self-directed opposition that allowed him to oppose morality even as it exerted its claim upon him:

> What does a philosopher demand of himself first and last? To overcome his time in himself, to become 'timeless.' With what must he therefore engage in the hardest combat? With whatever marks him as a child of his time. Well, then! I am, no less than Wagner, a child of this time; that is, a decadent: but I comprehended this, I resisted it [*ich mich dagegen wehrte*]. The philosopher in me resisted. (CW Preface)

Although "the philosopher in him" (supposedly) does not care for the term, Nietzsche identifies this program of self-directed opposition as catalyzing a process of *self-overcoming* (*Selbstüberwindung*) (CW Preface). It was on the strength of this program, in fact, that he attained the critical distance that informed and enabled his immoralism.

As Nietzsche makes clear, the goal of this program of self-directed aversion is *not* liberation, which remains beyond the ken of his and our volitional resources, but the creation within oneself of internal distance and the potentially fruitful tensions it can engender.³ While explaining the importance of the *pathos of distance*, for example, he points to its role in stimulating "that other, more mysterious pathos," which he associates with the

> craving for an ever new widening of distances *within the soul itself*, the development of ever higher, rarer, more remote, further-stretching, more comprehensive states – in brief, simply the enhancement of the 'human' type, the continual 'self-overcoming [*Selbst-Überwindung*] of humankind,' to use a moral formula in a supra-moral sense. (BGE 257, emphasis added)

Linking this program of self-directed opposition to the general method of "spiritualization" (described in Section II), he subsequently reveals the *value* of such a program:

> Our behavior towards our 'inner enemy' is no different: here, too, we have spiritualized enmity; here, too, we have grasped its value. One is fruitful only at the price of being rich in opposites; one stays young only on condition that the soul does not have a stretch and desire peace... (TI Morality 3)

In an age grown old, decrepit, and infertile, that is, Nietzsche and his mates may remain fruitful by creating within themselves the internal distance and tension that their culture no longer stimulates within them. As such, they may prolong the afterglow of the noble worldview to which they anachronistically pledge their allegiance.

In sum: although Nietzsche is not free to *reject* morality, he and his unnamed mates are free to *oppose, resist,* and *deny* morality, even as they continue, involuntarily, to take their bearings from morality. According to Nietzsche, moreover, his involuntary participation in morality is neither a handicap nor a limitation, but a strategic advantage that he aims to exploit (Ridley 1999, pp. 72–77; and Janaway 2007, pp. 236–239). As we shall see, in fact, the threefold goal of his opposition to morality, through which he will accomplish his promised denial of morality, is to hijack morality, to determine its final historical shape, and, ultimately, to steer it toward an appropriate, self-consuming conclusion. Ultimately, that is, his denial of morality will be meaningful and authoritative only if it issues forth from the seat of morality itself.

---

3 While it is true that Nietzsche renews his provocative challenge to philosophers – namely, to set up shop "beyond good and evil" – he does not mean for this challenge to authorize his best readers to declare themselves beyond the reach of morality (TI Improving 1). Rather, this challenge is meant to remind aspiring philosophers to "move...morality into the realm of appearance" (BT Attempt 5), i.e., to treat moral judgments as symptoms of the creatures who issue them and, therefore, as lacking any independent epistemic or probative value (TI Improving 1; cf. TI Morality 5).

Section II

As described by Nietzsche in *Twilight of the Idols*, his "immoralism" would appear to involve him in a fairly straightforward opposition to (and subsequent denial of) the anti-natural, anti-affective animus that motivates the forms and expressions of morality that are most familiar to his readers:

> Morality, insofar as it <u>condemns</u> — in itself, and <u>not</u> in view of life's concerns, considerations, intentions — is a specific error on which we should not take pity, a <u>degenerate's idiosyncrasy</u> which has wrought untold damage!... We who are different, we immoralists, on the contrary, have opened our hearts to all kinds of understanding, comprehending, <u>approving</u>. (TI Morality 6)

We will return in due course to consider this claim in detail. First, however, let us examine the larger context in which this claim is asserted. Building up to this point, Nietzsche offers the following preliminary observations:

1) The history of morality reveals two prevalent methods for treating the passions during the fateful, "stupid" period of their development: *eradication* and *spiritualization* (TI Morality 1);

2) The former method, eradication, is implemented by those who are "too weak-willed, too degenerate" to undertake with respect to themselves the labor that would be needed to prepare themselves (and the "stupid" passion(s) in question) to undergo the spiritualizing process (TI Morality 2). To say that they *prefer* this method, as they invariably will claim about themselves, thus presupposes their access to stores of strength and vitality that they simply do not possess;

3) Nietzsche's distinction between these two methods authorizes his distinction between two basic kinds or types of morality. Hence the "formula" he proposes:

> All naturalism in morality, i.e., every <u>healthy</u> morality, is governed by a vital instinct — one or another of life's decrees is fulfilled through a specific canon of 'shalls' and 'shall not'... <u>Anti-natural morality</u>, i.e., almost every morality which has hitherto been taught, revered, and preached, turns on the contrary precisely <u>against</u> the vital instincts — it is at times secret, at times loud and brazen in <u>condemning</u> these instincts. (TI Morality 4)

As Nietzsche makes clear in these preliminary observations, he does not mean to oppose himself to every known form or expression of morality. On the contrary, he acknowledges the possibility of *healthy* forms of morality and proposes a useful basis on which his readers might distinguish, as he does, between *healthy* and *unhealthy* (i.e., "anti-natural") forms of morality (May 1999, pp. 107–126; Leiter 2002, pp. 115–125, pp. 156–163; and Janaway 2007, pp. 252–254). As an immoralist, that is, he understands himself to be mounting a restricted challenge, targeting morality only in its most familiar "anti-natural" forms and modes of expression (Leiter 2002, pp. 74–77). If this is his intention, however, then why does he not advert more regularly and consistently, as he does here, to this distinction between *healthy* and *unhealthy* (i.e., antinatural) forms of morality? That is, why does he occasionally speak as if his immoralism places him at odds with *all* forms and expressions of morality? In doing so, as we have seen, he has contributed to the persistence of misunderstandings like those surveyed above.

While there may be various answers to this question, one in particular stands out: Nietzsche means to identify the target of his critique *by the title and name that it prefers for itself*. Nietzsche's readers may be confused or distracted by his incautious, seemingly indiscriminate attacks on *morality*, but the moralists whom he targets will understand that he means to address them and only them. Indeed, the practice of conferring the proprietary title of "morality" upon one among many possible and actual forms of morality originated not with him, but with the moralists to whom he now opposes himself. As he observes, contemporary Christian morality is uniquely identifiable on the strength and audacity of its insistence that it alone qualifies as a genuine morality.

In asserting this claim, moreover, the moralists in question may point to a preponderance of evidence in support of the monopoly they have consolidated. Credible alternatives to Christian morality are few and far between; once discovered, moreover, they quickly become ripe targets for co-optation and assimilation. One would need to be a genealogist of morality, or a (natural) historian of morality, to appreciate the impressive diversity of moralities – and the human types they have served – that have flourished on earth. In proceeding as if *all* of morality were in his cross-hairs, that is, Nietzsche is simply agreeing to address – and provoke – contemporary Christian morality by the proprietary title it has claimed for itself.

A similar explanation accounts for the *nom de guerre* that he awards himself in *Twilight* and *Ecce Homo*. As we have seen, he does not really consider himself immoral (Solomon 2003, pp. 50), especially inasmuch as he presumes to speak *for* morality in its emerging (and, he hopes, final) incarnation. If anything, in fact, he considers himself an exemplary moralist, especially if the regime of "Christian truthfulness" accedes, as anticipated, to a position of moral authority (GM III 27) (Conway 2013, pp. 205–207; May 1999, pp. 137f., 177–180; Ridley 1998, pp. 115–126; Owen 1995, pp. 89–93; and Hatab 2008, pp. 166ff.). In that event, he believes, even the most devastating consequences of his challenge to morality will bear the *imprimatur* of morality. In his own estimation, that is, he is poised to become both the highest and the final arbiter of morality. That he prefers to be known as an (or the) *immoralist* is therefore a provocative concession – perhaps also an homage – to the moralists whom he challenges for the mantle of morality. Simply by dint of his opposition to their authority, he reveals himself to them as an immoralist (Lampert 2001, p. 219).

But why would he wish to address the targets of his opposition on their preferred terms? Does this gambit not place him at a considerable disadvantage? He elects this risky strategy, apparently, because the preferred terms of his opponents *also* belong to him. As an immoralist, as we have seen, he is a variant kind or species of moralist. As such, he speaks the language, knows the routines, and wields the tools of the moralists. According to him, that is, he is optimally situated to capitalize on his involuntary training and acquired expertise in morality. For this reason, in fact, he is comfortable accosting the moralists on their terms and turf. His "war on morality" is best understood, that is, as an intramural, internecine dispute. He has no intention of challenging the validity of every known form of morality. The focus of his challenge is restricted to the particular form of morality that has declared itself alone worthy of the name (Hunt 1991, pp. 21–24; May 1999, pp. 104–107; Leiter 2002, pp. 78-ff., 127–136; Owen 2007, pp. 67–70; 129f.; and Hatab 2008, pp. 233–242).

A useful template for Nietzsche's "immoral" challenge to morality may be found in Essay III of GM. While explaining there how the ascetic priest might have succeeded in prompting the knightly-aristocratic nobles to doubt themselves and question their predatory avocations, Nietzsche reveals that the priest

> will under certain circumstances need to evolve a virtually new type of preying animal out of himself, or at least he will need to represent it – a new kind of animal ferocity in which the polar bear, the supple, cold, and patient tiger, and not least the fox seem to be joined in a unity at once enticing and terrifying. If need compels him, [the priest] will walk among the other beasts of prey with bearlike seriousness and feigned superiority, venerable, prudent, and cold, as the herald and mouthpiece of more mysterious powers, determined to sow this soil with misery, discord, and self-contradiction where he can and, only too certain of his art, to dominate the suffering at all times. (GM III 15)

Several points of comparison bear noting here. First of all, the priest is described in this passage as boldly infiltrating the lair of the beasts of prey. Pledged to "defend his herd…against the healthy, and also against envy of the healthy" (GM III 15), the priest resolves to intercede with the knightly-aristocratic nobles on behalf of the herd. Seizing the element of surprise, he encounters the beasts of prey where they are at their most relaxed, unguarded, and vulnerable: in their (and his) native wilderness. Wary of being drawn into a war of "force" (*Gewalt*) that he cannot win, he surreptitiously initiates a war of "cunning [*List*] (or of the 'spirit')" (GM III 15). Immersed in the depravations of their wilderness sabbatical, the beasts of prey are not prepared for the war of "cunning" that he silently wages against them. As Nietzsche helpfully reminds us, the *contempt* (*Verachtung*) in which the knightly-aristocratic nobles hold the lower orders of society places them at risk of precisely this sort of reprisal (GM I 10).

Second, the priest is able to access and manifest his beastly aspect only in the presence of other predators. Prior to this encounter, or so we apparently are meant to understand, the priest has not permitted himself to express his deeply repressed predatory instincts. He is, after all, "the natural opponent and despiser of all rude, stormy, unbridled, hard, violent beast-of-prey health and might" (GM III 15), *including* the "health and might" that resides, deeply buried, in him. In an irony that Nietzsche detects at the very core of the process of self-overcoming, the beasts of prey are thus responsible for catalyzing in the priest the transformation that eventually proves fatal to them. (As a noble in his own right, the priest is in fact one of them, even if he requires their propinquity – and the harrowing prospect of war – to retrieve his long-estranged predatory instincts.) Exploiting this irony to his own advantage, as we shall see, Nietzsche foretells the downfall of the priest at the hands of those whom the priest has nurtured and raised as his own (GM III 10), those whom we now know to comprise the vanguard generation of immoralists.

Third, the priest himself is vulnerable to the "misery, discord, and self-contradiction" that he suborns in the beasts of prey. As a noble predator in his own right, albeit self-estranged in this respect, he is as dependent as they on the wilderness he aims to befoul. He may put on a brave face, perhaps even fooling himself on occasion, but his is a strategy that can deliver at best a Pyrrhic victory. Although his identity and status are not directly dependent upon his predatory nature – as determined by the rigor of his self-imposed regimen of priestly hygiene – he too will suffer, if only indirectly, from the toxic effects of his cunning. In essence, that is, he has poisoned the well from which he, too, must draw his sustenance. Such is his thirst for revenge against the knightly-aristocratic nobles who humiliated him and assigned him to manage the lower orders of society. (More irony: It was this original assignment that provided the priest with the occasion and motivation to develop his "cunning" to such frightful proportions.)

In short, the moral of the story is this: Because the priest need not survive the assault he masterminds, valuing sweet revenge more highly than his own life, he may attack the beasts of prey in their own home, with their own weapons, and on their own terms. Because he is one of them, moreover, his plan has a reasonable chance of success.

In mounting an internal challenge to the validity of contemporary Christian morality, Nietzsche effectively reprises the strategy he ascribes to the ascetic priest. He too infiltrates the lair of his opponents, which he may do, in part, because he is of their ilk. He speaks their language, wields their weapons, and honors the authority to which they lay claim. Even as he assumes the aspect of the immoralist, as we have seen, he remains a moralist to the end. As in the case of the ascetic priest, that is, Nietzsche derives a strategic advantage from his unsuspected (or unacknowledged) membership in the group he aims to subvert. Moreover, he too attains his most lethal incarnation only in the company of his opponents, who bring out in him the predatory instincts from which he is ordinarily estranged. Like the ascetic priest, that is, Nietzsche is a product or outgrowth – what I elsewhere have called an *excession* – of that which he now seeks to challenge. This means, of course, that he too is vulnerable to the strategy he pursues, for he too relies on the historical authority of morality. Unlike his brethren among the moralists, moreover, he fully intends to hear and heed the call – *patere legem* – to submit to the laws he has imposed on others (GM III 27). As a result, any measure of success on his part, *qua* immoralist, will spell defeat for him, *qua* moralist. Like the priest, however, he neither needs nor expects to survive the assault he initiates.

Inasmuch as he follows in the footsteps of the priest, finally, Nietzsche intimates that he, *qua* immoralist, is the new "philosopher" who, having emerged from the shadow of the priest, will prevail over him (GM III 10). Much as this new "philosopher" is prophesied to exploit his placement within the priestly lineage, so will Nietzsche turn to his advantage the training in morality that he has involuntarily (but not ungratefully) received. Like the priest, in short, Nietzsche has come to realize "that Christian morality [is] his means to power..." (EH Destiny 7). As we shall see, in fact, his training in morality is particularly useful to him in performing the specific acts of denial (*Verneinungen*) that are required of him *qua* immoralist (EH Destiny 4). As strange as it may sound, that is, he aims to arrange for morality a fittingly moral end.

Section III

Nietzsche's introduction of himself in the Foreword to *Ecce Homo* confirms the continuity of this book with *Twilight of the Idols*, which he dedicated on the very same day – September 30, 1888 – that he completed *The Antichrist(ian)*, the book for which *Ecce Homo* was meant to secure a receptive readership. In these books, he both acknowledges and addresses the urgent need to introduce himself in his final incarnation – comprising the combustible trinity of *immor-*

alist, *Antichrist*, and *disciple of Dionysus* – to the readers who will carry forward and complete his critique of Christian morality. Along with the *Dionysus-Dithyrambs*, in fact, these three books constitute what might be called the "Dionysus Quartet," which Nietzsche may have meant as a self-parodic counterpart to Wagner's *Ring* tetralogy.

Several elements contributing to this continuity are worth noting here. For example, *Twilight of the Idols* introduces Nietzsche's readers to the general critical method that he also claims to employ in *Ecce Homo*. As presented in the Preface to *Twilight*, this method authorizes him to sound out venerable ideals and expose them as hollow idols. In his hands, the hammer he inherited from Zarathustra, whose unsentimental "hardness" he recommends to his readers (EH Z 8), thus turns out to be an instrument of auscultation, e.g., a tuning-fork. Before he may wield this hammer as an instrument of destruction, that is, he first must use it to identify the appropriate targets of his selective wrath. As tempting as it may be to swing this hammer wildly and indiscriminately, he must reserve its power for those forms and creatures whom Life itself has marked for destruction. With his tuning-fork, moreover, he must determine the optimal timing of his eventual acts of destruction, so that he might harvest from these hollow idols all that remains viable and productive within them.

As we shall see, in fact, the Nietzsche who wields a tuning-fork stands very much at the forefront of the scientific (or scholarly) investigation of the phenomenon of cultural decay. Rather than deny all forms of life that manifest symptoms of decay, he attempts to isolate the primary agents of pathogenic contagion (EH Destiny 7). Indeed, the Nietzsche of 1888 prides himself on denying as infrequently as possible, as selectively as possible, as precisely as possible, and only when obliged to do so in order to further the deepest interests of Life itself (TI Morality 6). Like *Ecce Homo*, moreover, *Twilight of the Idols* is presented as a *cheerful* expression of Nietzsche's convalescence, of his renewed strength and his resurgent health. After all, only a "psychologist" who has recovered from a debilitating illness could afford to indulge himself in the rambling "idleness" on display in *Twilight of the Idols*.

Twilight of the Idols also offers an instructive preview of the words that Nietzsche famously borrows from Pilate: *ecce homo* (John 19:5). Prior to fixing these words on the title page of his autobiography, that is, Nietzsche places them in the mouth of an unnamed "moralist," who immodestly enshrines himself as the ideal and measure of human flourishing:

> Let us finally consider how naïve it is in general to say: 'Humankind <u>ought</u> to be such and such!' Reality shows us a delightful abundance of types, the richness that comes from an extravagant play and alternation of forms — to which some wretched loafer of a moralist says: 'No! Humankind ought to be <u>different</u>'?... He even knows what humankind

should be like, this maundering miseryguts: he paints himself on the wall and says 'ecce homo!'... (TI Morality 6)

What's going on here? Is Nietzsche's reprise of *ecce homo* intended as an homage to the imperial governor Pilate, as is commonly thought (A 46), or to the wretched moralist whom Nietzsche ostensibly means to challenge?

We know from his Foreword to *Ecce Homo* that he meant for that book to illuminate the decisive contrast that obtains, supposedly, between who he is and who he is not (EH Preface 1). Among the various illustrations he provides of this contrast, we also know, is the opposition between himself, *qua* immoralist, and the moralists whose authority he means to challenge (EH Destiny 3–5). In the passage cited above, however, he designates the signature activity of the moralist with the very words that he *also* selects for the title of his autobiography. Does he mean to suggest that he, too, is a moralist? If so, then how are we to understand the challenge he ostensibly forwards, *qua* immoralist, to the purveyors and champions of morality?

As we know, his writings from 1888 emphasize, and are meant to display, those affects and virtues – e.g., cheerfulness, playfulness, prankishness, audacity, probity, and bravery – that Nietzsche believes will further his campaign to attract (and educate) the readers whom he claims to deserve – viz., those possessed of heightened senses, keened powers of discernment, and an expanded complement of refined sensibilities. Toward this end, he has been particularly concerned to correct and improve the (metaphorical) vision of his best readers, diverting their gaze from the cartoonish dichotomies – e.g., good vs. evil – that are preferred by rival scholars and most moralists. In pursuit of such readers, he apparently wishes to introduce himself by issuing something like the following, pre-emptive note of caution: *Precisely insofar as I am an immoralist, I am and will remain a kind of moralist.*

In other words: The contrast that Nietzsche wishes to illuminate in *Twilight* and *Ecce Homo*, as designated by the opposition between the immoralists and the moralists, does not countenance the kind of diametric, binary oppositions on which the moralists typically rely (EH Destiny 3). The contrast he means to illuminate is far more evanescent and elusive, which is why he must cultivate readers who possess a sharp eye for the subtle nuances, slight differences, and minute variations that are characteristic of the flux of self-overcoming. By identifying himself from the outset as a kind of moralist, that is, Nietzsche not only insulates himself from the kinds of readers who need to fix their coordinates on a grid of binary oppositions, but also attracts the kinds of readers who will appreciate any such cheerful display of honesty as refreshingly emblematic of his resurgent strength and renascent health. Having noted the family resemblance that obtains between Nietzsche and his opponents among the moralists, this latter group of readers may be prepared to recalibrate their sense of the relevant differences involved.

In order to evaluate the supposed differences between Nietzsche (*qua* immoralist) and the moralists, let us interpret *painting oneself on the wall* as his shorthand designation for the natural activity of self-expression on the model of self-exteriorization. In painting himself on the wall, that is, the moralist presents himself as an external other and second self, to be appreciated and admired by various spectators (including himself). As I understand Nietzsche's point here, he does not wish to quarrel with the moralist's activity of self-exteriorization. Nothing could be more natural for the kind of creatures we are and have become, especially inasmuch as we seek recognition within the various social and cultural settings in which we find ourselves. (As he explains elsewhere, creating the world in one's own image is the very essence of the philosophical expression of the will to power (BGE 9).) Nor do I believe that he means to object to the moralist's habit of recommending himself as the ideal model of human flourishing, worthy of general emulation. After all, Nietzsche has cultivated a similar habit, which he openly (and unapologetically) displays in *Ecce Homo*. In any event, as we shall see, the moralist has been authorized to cultivate this habit by no less an authority than Life itself.

In the extracted passage under consideration, Nietzsche presents the difference between these two forms of self-expression as twofold: First, *his* graffito is apparently meant to capture and affirm the "delightful abundance of types" that reality itself actually manifests (Shapiro 1989, pp. 124–133). The moralist is "naïve," that is, inasmuch as he reflexively says *No* to the abundance of diverse human types. Only then, and perhaps as an afterthought, does he say *Yes* to himself and, on the basis of this affirmation, recommend himself as the ideal of human flourishing. Here we may detect the telltale pathology of the slave revolt, which originates in a blanket condemnation of what one is not – the nobles, after all, were pronounced *evil* (*böse*) by the slaves – and follows with a reactive affirmation of what one is, even if the specific content of one's identity – in terms, e.g., of virtues, passions, habits, powers, abilities, capacities, etc. – remains as yet unknown or undeveloped. Thus we should not be surprised to discover that the contemporary moralist is also the current heir to the slave revolt in morality.

But how is it possible to paint oneself on the wall in such a way that conveys and celebrates the "delightful abundance of [human] types"? In recommending oneself, even if one is demonstrably worthier of emulation than the moralist, does one not honor a *particular* human type? And even if one thereby honors a human being who is "as manifold as full, as ample as full" (BGE 212), how might this exemplar be understood to reflect "the delightful abundance" of human types? To be sure, Nietzsche's graffito may be more fully representative of a rich diversity, especially inasmuch as he bodies forth a wider range of human experiences and aspirations. But this would be a matter of comparison, of relative difference, between his graffito and the moralist's. Neither self-portrait would provide a completely faithful depiction of the lavish wealth of human types, even if we concede that Nietzsche's graffito is more comprehensive than the moralist's.

Still, the difference between the moralist and the immoralist is significant, especially inasmuch as the latter's graffito incorporates – and, therefore, tacitly affirms – the former's graffito. (Despite his claim to affirm a diversity of perspectives, Nietzsche more typically demonstrates his fluency in *two* perspectives: that of his opponents (e.g., the priests, moralists, or decadents) and the "physiological" perspective that confirms his superiority to his opponents.) When Nietzsche paints himself on the wall, that is, we should be able to discern in his graffito the moralist's self-portrait as well – hence the significance of his otherwise surprising association of the words *ecce homo* with the signature activity of the moralist. As we have seen, moreover, Nietzsche regards the family resemblance between himself and the moralist not as a limitation of his "immoral" challenge to morality, but as the basis for his most promising strategic advantage.

In fact, the moralist is the single most prominent of the human types whom Nietzsche honors when painting himself on the wall. That he is able to do so, of course, is the most significant difference between him (*qua* immoralist) and the moralists whom he challenges. Whereas his graffito essays a just depiction of the moralists, affirming them in their yeoman service to Life, their graffiti neither acknowledge nor depict him *qua* immoralist. As we are now in a position to understand, in fact, the moralist's "naïveté" is in fact a product of his cramped, limited perspective. He says *No* to the "delightful abundance" of human types because he has no direct experience or perception of this abundance. All he sees and knows is the monochrome world that he has come to dominate, having created it in his own image.

Unable to tolerate difference, ambiguity, anomaly, multiplicity, and the prospect of alternative expressions of human flourishing, the moralist delivers a graffito that bears witness to the limitations of his perspective. As a moralist in his own right, Nietzsche is similarly restricted; he may paint on the wall only what he knows and affirms from personal experience. His graffito offers a flattering portrait of the moralist, that is, because he too is a moralist, even if he is also more than that. Indeed, the diversity of types represented by his graffito faithfully reflects the diversity he has managed to cultivate within himself, by dint of his regimen of self-directed opposition. He thus reaps the full advantage of his bifocal perspective, which allows him to behold the world from the standpoints, respectively, of sickness and health, decadence and growth, seriousness and cheerfulness, *and*, finally, morality and its other (EH Wise 2–3).

Section IV

Still, beholding existence in its diverse abundance is not Nietzsche's signal triumph. What makes him an *immoralist*, especially in the specific sense that he attaches to this term in his writings from 1888, is the capacity for *affirmation* that he derives from his bifocal perspective. In a related passage extracted from the section cited above, for example, he attempts to clarify the contrast he wishes to draw between *moralists* and *immoralists*:

> Morality, insofar as it condemns for its own sake, and not out of regard for the concerns, considerations, and intentions of life, is a specific error on which we should not take pity – a degenerate's idiosyncrasy which has wrought untold damage!… We who are different, we immoralists, on the contrary, have opened our hearts to all kinds of understanding, comprehending, and approving. We do not readily deny; we seek our honor in being affirmative. More and more, our eyes have been opened to that economy which still needs and can exploit all that is rejected by the holy madness of the priest, of the priest's sick reason; to that economy in the law of life which can gain advantage even from the repulsive species of the miseryguts, the priest, the virtuous man – what advantage? – But we ourselves, we immoralists, are the answer here… (TI Morality 6)

Although his reasoning here is compressed, he apparently wishes to make two points in support of the contrast he proposes to elucidate between *moralists* and *immoralists*. First of all, he identifies morality as a "specific error on which we should not take pity" and as "a degenerate's idiosyncrasy which has wrought untold damage" (TI Morality 6). His aim here is to illuminate the limitations of the authority that accrues to the perspective of those who reflexively avail themselves of moral judgments and condemnations. Diminished by their besetting illness, they instinctively strive to inhabit a similarly diminished world, in which the exploits of others neither threaten their feeling of power nor compromise their sense of their own worth. The world they create in their own image thus affords them a relatively narrow and uncomplicated perspective, wherein diametric oppositions are both useful and appropriate.

According to Nietzsche, that is, morality expresses the interests only of the sick and infirm among us. Over time, he concedes, they have managed to infect most of their fellow human beings, gradually drawing them/us within the cramped horizon of their self-serving judgments. The conviction they invest in the moral judgments they render is but a symptom of their degeneration, and it should not be allowed to influence those who are not yet (or no longer) similarly afflicted (EH Destiny 7). So it is, he allows, that an enervated physiological condition, which, by all rights, should be considered idiopathic, has been suffered to assert itself as "normal." As Nietzsche sees it, of course, the alleged normality (or universality) of contemporary Christian morality has been achieved at the expense of the future of humankind (EH Destiny 4), through a degradation of the diversity of human types and a leveling assault on the singular, exotic exploits of the highest human beings.

Nietzsche's caution against showing *pity* for these degenerates serves as a bridge to his second point, for he means thereby to distinguish himself from the *priest*, who exploits pity to sustain his vampiric relationship with the most wretched of the sufferers entrusted to his care. (For his part, Nietzsche apparently believes that these degenerates should be allowed – perhaps even required – to suffer and die in peace (TI Skirmishes 36).)

This is not to say, however, that Nietzsche plans to go easy on these degenerates. Precisely because they cannot help themselves, their influence must be contained (and ultimately eradicated) through measures that are forceful, decisive, and comprehensive. At the same time, however, they are not the primary targets of his destructive wrath. As an immoralist, he is concerned to challenge and discredit the authority of the regnant cadre of moralists, those whom he holds currently responsible for the pandemic spread of sickness and decay. Hoping to reinforce his anticipated victory over the moralists, and thereby provide for the regeneration of a rich diversity of exotic human types, he recommends that the priestly class be banished in its entirety. Helping himself to the wisdom that he discerns in the precepts of the Hindu lawgiver Manu (TI Improving 3), he proposes to designate the priests as *chandalas* (or outcasts), whose enforced exclusion will ensure the structural integrity of the post-Christian polities of the future (TI Skirmishes 45).

In challenging the regnant cadre of moralists, moreover, Nietzsche and his fellow immoralists will draw productively and creatively on their training in morality. The destructive measures they employ will be intimately familiar to their opponents, who have used them effectively to secure their own status and privilege. More precisely, as we have seen, he means to turn the destructive power of morality against its remaining practitioners, a group of dwindling membership that eventually will include only him and his fellow immoralists. After deposing the regnant cadre of moralists, that is, he and his mates will continue to escalate their attack on morality, leading them, eventually, to target themselves. Although Nietzsche too is perched on the limb that he proposes to saw off, he claims not to be personally invested in the morality he seeks to unseat. As an immoralist, he has achieved a healthy measure of critical distance from the morality that he now espouses. This means, according to him, that he will not allow considerations of his own authority and well being to temper his (self-directed) assault on morality. In the words of Zarathustra, Nietzsche is prepared to *go under*. Whether that means that he is ready to die or, less melodramatically, ready to expend his remaining quantum of moral authority, remains to be seen (Loeb 2010, pp. 74–84, 200–206, 240–242).

Second, Nietzsche wishes to draw attention here to the basic insight or epiphany that is emblematic of his most recently attained incarnation. He and his fellow immoralists are distinguished by their enhanced capacity to "understand, comprehend, and approve" of forms of life alien to their own. Slow to judge, and slower still to deny, they now "open their hearts" to forms of life they formerly believed to be inimical to the interests of Life. It is for this reason, in fact, that the immoralists do not simply turn the tables on their brethren among the moralists. While the moralists cannot abide the challenge posed to their authority by the immoralists, the immoralists are not similarly frozen in a posture of reciprocal antagonism. They affirm the role of the moralists within the larger economy of Life, even as they oppose the moralists and seek to exhaust their residual stores of moral authority.

The proof of their expanded capacity for affirmation lies in the specific use that they have determined for Christian morality. Although Nietzsche's rhetoric occasionally suggests otherwise, he and his fellow immoralists have neither renounced Christian morality nor pronounced it useless.[4] As we have seen, they propose to employ Christian morality for the purpose of guiding the enterprise of morality toward a timely, self-consuming conclusion (Staten 1990, pp. 143ff.; Ridley 1998, pp. 124ff.; Loeb 2010, pp. 238ff.). Nietzsche is able to formulate this proposal, moreover, because he has come to appreciate the indispensable role of the moralists in creating the conditions of his emergence as an immoralist. While it may be true that the moralists have unwittingly contributed to the production of their own gravediggers, as Marx wishfully predicted of the bourgeoisie, the moralists nonetheless merit Nietzsche's affirmation. As evidence of his "open heart," in fact, he promises to prepare a gravesite alongside theirs for himself and his unknown mates.

---

[4] Alternative Nietzschean strategies for repurposing morality are instructively explored by Schacht 2001, pp. 156–173; Janaway 2007, pp. 252–260; Loeb 2010, pp. 234–240 and Acampora 2013, pp. 131–139.

Section V

In lauding himself and his fellow immoralists for their expanded capacity for affirmation, Nietzsche builds on an earlier insight. In Essay III of *On the Genealogy of Morality*, we recall, he revealed that the seemingly villainous ascetic priest actually serves the deepest interests of Life itself:

> This ascetic priest, this apparent enemy of life, this denier [*dieser Verneinende*] — precisely he is among the greatest conserving and yes-creating [*Ja-schaffenden*] forces of life. (GM III 13)

This is true of the ascetic priest, moreover, even as he endeavors to degrade the formerly rich diversity of human types, which involves him an assault that could not possibly accord with Life's interests – or so one might have thought. As it turns out, however, the ascetic priest serves Life much as Nietzsche does. For this reason, in fact, Nietzsche declines the opportunity to return the ascetic priest's fire, refusing more generally to be drawn into a retaliatory contest with the ascetic priest (GM III 11). Indeed, the target of his attack in GM is the ascetic ideal itself; the ascetic priest is merely an occasion for this attack.

As Nietzsche explains in GM, the key to appreciating the priest's role lies in adopting a broader, more comprehensive perspective, by virtue of which one might gain a clearer understanding of the complex, sprawling economy of Life. Within the context of this economy, the machinations of the priest are revealed to serve the interests of Life. Not content simply to say as much, Nietzsche proceeds to demonstrate what he has in mind. Immediately after conducting a sympathetic evaluation of the priest from the priest's own perspective, Nietzsche displays the ease of his access to a superior, "physiological" perspective (GM III 17), from which he derives his influential diagnosis of the priest as a *faux* physician (GM III 21). This latter perspective, or so he indicates in GM, is funded by his acquired familiarity with the "instincts" and "interests" of Life itself. From this superior perspective, moreover, he is able to account for both the explanatory power *and* the limitations of the priest's perspective. In other words, the "physiological" perspective that he commands in GM both incorporates and surpasses the priest's perspective (Conway 2008, pp. 116–126). This is possible, as we have seen, because Nietzsche has acceded to his "physiological" perspective from his placement within the priestly lineage.

But Nietzsche's appreciation for the ascetic priest does not end there. In addition to acknowledging the priest's efforts to conserve the sick and infirm, he also hints at the priest's indispensable, if unwitting, role in the emergence and individuation of his *other* – namely, the new "philosopher," who someday soon will deliver the priest's comeuppance (GM III 10). Likening this new "philosopher" to a skittering butterfly, which he describes as due to emerge from the ugly, earthbound caterpillar form of the ascetic priest, Nietzsche places the new "philosopher" squarely within the lineage of the ascetic priest. This new "philosopher" is thus introduced as a kind of priest in his own right, notwithstanding the role reserved for him in deposing the priest. Once this new "philosopher" gains his full independence from the priest, or so Nietzsche suggests, he will turn his ascetic nurture and training against the ascetic ideal itself.

At this point, presumably, the stories that Nietzsche relates about himself and the new "philosopher" are meant to converge. He is or will become the new "philosopher" who will prevail over the ascetic priest as a prelude to his self-consuming assault on the ascetic ideal (Staten 1990, pp. 47–60; Ridley 1998, pp. 61ff.). As we are now in a position to understand, moreover, he will depose the ascetic priest by actually supplanting him as the chief arbiter of, and spokesman for, Christian morality. His intention to exploit his placement in the priestly lineage is confirmed by his designation of himself as a kindred *denier*. Having already identified the priest as such (GM III 13), Nietzsche allows that his standing as an "immoralist" authorizes him to perform two "denials" (*Verneinungen*), which he directs, respectively, toward the "highest type" enshrined by Christian morality – viz., the "good man" – and toward Christian morality itself (EH Destiny 4).

As he makes clear, moreover, he does not mean for these two "denials" to be limited to mere utterances. They are meant to eventuate in the destruction of that which he denies (as well as in the "joy" (*Lust*) that attends destruction) (TI Ancients 5). As he elaborates in *Ecce Homo*, "denying *and destroying* [*Verneinen und Vernichten*] are the preconditions for yes-saying" (EH Destiny 4). This means, in short, that his No-sayings somehow must comprise or touch off a corresponding series of No-doings (or perlocutionary effects) (White 1997, pp. 154–162; Janaway 2007, pp. 245–252). This is possible, however, only if he is in a position to speak *for* morality, even as he works against it. This is why it is so important to Nietzsche that his immoralism is understood to confirm his placement *within* the final generation of practicing moralists, those who cheerfully turn the residual power and authority of Christian morality against themselves.

My point in recalling this earlier insight is to draw from it an instructive template for understanding the relationship, as envisioned in *Twilight of the Idols* and *Ecce Homo*, between the moralists and the immoralists. In both cases, Life is said to derive a distinct advantage from the activities of those – viz., the ascetic priest and moralists, respectively – who are determined to eliminate the rarest and most exotic of its human specimens. In both cases, in fact, the advantage supposedly lies in the eventual emergence of those – viz., the new "philosopher" and the immoralists, respectively – whom Life has authorized to steer morality toward a self-consuming conclusion. In other words, Nietzsche and his fellow immoralists have come to understand that their antagonists – viz., the moralists – continue to thrive, just as *they* do, at the behest of Life itself.

Finally, as Nietzsche makes clear in his parable of metamorphosis, he tends to envision this final, epoch-ending clash as resolving itself into an internecine struggle between exemplary representatives of the two poles that have emerged within a single family or lineage. At this point, we may move productively from the passage extracted above to a similar discussion in *Ecce Homo*. Although Nietzsche speaks in *Twilight* of opposing hosts or pluralities, of moralists vs. immoralists, he narrows his focus in *Ecce Homo* to the destructive prowess of a single immoralist: *himself*. And although it might be tempting to imagine Nietzsche facing off, *mano a mano*, against a formidable world-historical foe, his final opponent among the moralists must be none other than himself. To be sure, his polemics against Socrates, St. Paul, Luther, Darwin, Rée, Strauss, Wagner, *et al.* are instrumental to his growth and development (Acampora 2013, pp. 43–49, 198–207). At the same time, however, these dialogical polemics are also *preliminary* to his final contest, which must be inwardly directed. He will succeed in besting his various nemeses, that is, only in the event that he, *qua* immoralist, vanquishes the moralist resident within himself. Only then will the will to truth, having become "conscious of itself as a problem" (GM III27), finally declare itself *untruthful* and put morality out of business for good (Ridley 1998, pp. 124ff.; May 1999, pp. 90ff.; and Owen 2007, pp. 126–129).

Conclusion

As we have seen, Nietzsche is different from the moralists inasmuch as he manifests an orientation to life that is broadly and generously affirmative. Thus, as he proceeds to explain, even his rare acts of denial are predicated on prior (and sincere) acts of affirmation. Although he too performs selective acts of denial, that is, he does so only after harvesting all that is vital and worthwhile from the designated targets of his denials. The most famous statement of this orientation to Life is found in his interleaf epigraph to *Ecce Homo*, where he insists that he is "entitled" to bury his forty-fourth year, having saved and immortalized "all the life that was in it" (EH Epigraph).

With this in mind, we are now in a position to understand why Nietzsche offers the otherwise gnomic observation, in the passage extracted above, that "we ourselves, we immoralists" are the advantage reaped by Life "from the repulsive species of the miseryguts, the priest, the virtuous man" (TI Morality 6). He apparently regards the emergence of the vanguard generation of immoralists – and his own "rebirth" in particular – as the epochal development toward which the degradations wrought by morality have been pointing all along. These degradations warrant our affirmation, he thus suggests, on the strength of the necessity of their contributions to the production of the immoralists. The signal advantage that Life has reaped from the long, grisly history of morality is the emergence of a variant strain of moralist (viz., the immoralist), which has been bred to consume itself in the process of bringing the enterprise of morality to a timely and fitting conclusion. In short, that is, Nietzsche immodestly presents himself (*qua* immoralist) as the underlying meaning and ultimate justification of the uniquely moral period in human history. If, in the near future, humankind is delivered yet again from the threat of extinction, it will have Nietzsche and his fellow immoralists to thank for its reprieve.

A preposterous hypothesis? Of course. An expression of unchained narcissism? Unquestionably. Before we dismiss this story out of hand, however, two points bear noting. First of all, some such account, though not necessarily so flattering to Nietzsche, would seem to be authorized by his teaching of *amor fati*. If the long history of morality, including the serial mischief of the ascetic priest, is considered necessary, then it also merits our affirmation. As related by Nietzsche, however, the history of morality may strike us as difficult to endorse, especially if we are inclined to accept his account of the downward, extinction-bound arc it describes. Indeed, how would it be possible for creatures like us to behold the history of morality without "wanting anything to be different, not forwards, not backwards, not for all eternity" (EH Clever 10)? One way for us to affirm the chain of fatalities arrayed before us would be to focus our attention on its most recently forged links, which Nietzsche credibly (if melodramatically) associates with himself. Doing so may allow us to see (and affirm) morality on the basis of its role in producing its other, in whom we may glimpse the promise of an extra-moral epoch in human history and a return to past standards of human excellence.

Second, Nietzsche (or his champions) might protest that he comes honestly by the narcissism he expresses in his writings from 1888. Indeed, he (or they) might applaud his creative appropriation of the narcissism that has been bred in us over the course of two millennia of Christian acculturation. No less an authority than Christianity itself has encouraged him to place his debts and misdeeds at the center of the cosmos, where they are deemed sufficiently heinous as to warrant the compensatory sacrifice of God's own Son (GM II 21). If the sins of nameless, faceless mortals are judged to require divine recompense, that is, why should we be surprised if Nietzsche attempts to justify the history of morality on the strength of the unique role that *he* will play, as a result, in its demise? What other, better use might this disciple of Dionysus make of his all-too-human narcissism? Indeed, here we might appreciate Nietzsche's expression of narcissism as a healthy alternative to the narcissism of the Madman (GS 125), who (fatuously) believed himself capable of murdering God (Pippin 2010, pp. 47–59; Conway 2009, pp. 108–124).

In his efforts to orchestrate the destruction of his own moral authority, finally, Nietzsche proves himself as a disciple of Dionysus (Benson 2008, pp. 202–216). Here we recall his parting words in *Twilight of the Idols*, where he establishes the standard to which he now claims to hold himself:

> Saying Yes to life, even in its strangest and hardest problems; the will to life rejoicing in the sacrifice of its highest types to its own inexhaustibility... being oneself the eternal joy of becoming – that joy which also encompasses the joy of destruction... (TI Ancients 5)

The "strangest and hardest problems" of life might very well include the problem – which Nietzsche affirms in *Twilight* – of delivering, and acting on, a moral critique of morality. The "highest types" slated for sacrifice might very well include Nietzsche himself, especially in his most recent incarnation as an immoralist. Finally, the "joy of destruction" is evident throughout *Twilight*, and it is especially notable with respect to the self-referential implications of Nietzsche's destruction of morality.[5]

Bibliography

Acampora, Christa Davis (2013): *Contesting Nietzsche*. Chicago: University of Chicago Press.
Benson, Bruce (2008): *Pious Nietzsche: Decadence and Dionysian Faith*. Bloomington, IN: Indiana University Press.
Berkowitz, Peter (1995). *Nietzsche: The Ethics of an Immoralist*. Cambridge: Harvard University Press.

---

[5] An earlier version of this chapter was prepared for the 2012 MANCEPT workshop. I am grateful to Barry Stocker and Manuel Knoll for organizing the workshop and for providing me with helpful editorial suggestions. I am grateful as well to the other workshop participants for their insights and generous comments. I also wish to thank Paul Loeb for his unpublished paper on Nietzsche's immoralism and for an illuminating conversation on the topic. A companion piece to this chapter appeared under the title "Nietzsche's Immoralism and the Advent of 'Great Politics'," in: Keith Ansell Pearson (ed.): *Nietzsche and Political Thought*. London: Bloomsbury Academic, 2013, pp. 197–217.

Clark, Maudemarie (1994): "Nietzsche's Immoralism and the Concept of Morality". In: Richard Schacht (ed.): *Nietzsche, Genealogy, Morality: Essays on* Nietzsche's Genealogy of Morals. Berkeley and Los Angeles: University of California Press, pp. 15–34.

Conway, Daniel (2008): *Nietzsche's* On the Genealogy of Morals*: A Reader's Guide*. London: Continuum Books.

Conway, Daniel (2009): "Revisiting the Death of God: On the Madness of Nietzsche's Madman". In: *Acta Kierkegaardiana* 4, pp. 105–132.

Conway, Daniel (2013): "Nietzsche's Immoralism and the Advent of 'Great Politics'". In: Keith Ansell Pearson (ed.): *Nietzsche and Political Thought*. London: Bloomsbury Academic, 2013, pp. 197–217.

Detwiler, Bruce (1990): *Nietzsche and the Politics of Aristocratic Radicalism*. Chicago: University of Chicago Press.

Foot, Philippa (1994): "Nietzsche's Immoralism". In: Richard Schacht (ed.): *Nietzsche, Genealogy, Morality: Essays on* Nietzsche's Genealogy of Morals. Berkeley and Los Angeles: University of California Press, pp. 3–14.

Heidegger, Martin (1982): *Nietzsche. Volume IV: Nihilism*. Frank Capuzzi (trans.), David F. Krell (ed.). New York: Harper & Row.

Hatab, Lawrence J. (2008). *Nietzsche's* On the Genealogy of Morality: *An Introduction*. Cambridge: Cambridge University Press.

Hunt, Lester H. (1991): *Nietzsche and the Origin of Virtue*. London: Routledge.

Janaway Christopher (2007). *Beyond Selflessness: Reading Nietzsche's* Genealogy. Oxford: Oxford University Press.

Jaspers, Karl (1979). *Nietzsche: An Introduction to the Understanding of his Philosophical Activity*, trans. Charles F. Wallraff and Frederick J. Schmitz. South Bend, IN: Regnery/Gateway.

Kaufmann, Walter. *Nietzsche: Philosopher, Psychologist, Antichrist*, 4th Edition. Princeton, NJ: Princeton University Press, 1974.

Leiter, Brian. *Nietzsche on Morality*. London: Routledge, 2002

Lampert, Laurence (2001): *Nietzsche's Task: An Interpretation of* Beyond Good and Evil. New Haven: Yale University Press.

Loeb, Paul S. (2010): *The Death of Nietzsche's Zarathustra*. Cambridge: Cambridge University Press.

Loeb, Paul S: "Zarathustra's Immoralism," unpublished manuscript.

Nehamas, Alexander (1985): *Nietzsche: Life as Literature*. Cambridge, MA: Harvard University Press.

May, Simon (1999). *Nietzsche's Ethics and his War on "Morality."* Oxford: Oxford University Press.

Nietzsche, Friedrich (1974): *The Gay Science*. Walter Kaufmann (trans.). New York: Random House/Vintage Books.

Nietzsche, Friedrich (1982): "The Antichrist". In: Walter Kaufmann (ed./trans.): *The Portable Nietzsche*. New York: Viking Penguin, pp. 565–656.

Nietzsche, Friedrich (1982): "Twilight of the Idols". In: Walter Kaufmann (ed./trans.): *The Portable Nietzsche*. New York: Viking Penguin, pp. 463–563.

Nietzsche, Friedrich (1989): *Beyond Good and Evil: Prelude to a Philosophy of the Future*. Walter Kaufmann (trans.). New York: Random House/Vintage Books.

Nietzsche, Friedrich (1989): *On the Genealogy of Morals*. Walter Kaufmann and R.J. Hollingdale (trans.) New York: Random House/Vintage Books.

Nietzsche, Friedrich (1989): *Ecce Homo*. Walter Kaufmann (trans.). New York: Random House/Vintage Books.
Nietzsche, Friedrich (2007): *Ecce Homo*. Duncan Large (trans.). Oxford: Oxford University Press.
Owen, David (2007). *Nietzsche's* Genealogy of Morality. Stocksfield: Acumen.
Pippin, Robert B. (2010): *Nietzsche, Psychology, and First Philosophy*. Chicago: University of Chicago Press.
Ridley, Aaron (1998): *Nietzsche's Conscience: Six Character Studies from the* Genealogy. Ithaca, NY: Cornell University Press.
Schacht, Richard (2001): "Nietzschean Normativity". In: Richard Schacht (ed.): *Nietzsche's Postmoralism*. Cambridge: Cambridge University Press, pp. 149–180.
Shapiro, Gary (1989): *Nietzschean Narratives*. Bloomington, IN: Indiana University Press.
Solomon, Robert C. (2003): *Living With Nietzsche: What the Great "Immoralist" Has to Teach Us*. Oxford: Oxford University Press.
Staten, Henry (1990): *Nietzsche's Voice*. Ithaca, NY: Cornell University Press.
van Tongeren, Paul J.M. (2000): *Reinterpreting Modern Culture: An Introduction to Friedrich Nietzsche's Philosophy*. West Lafayette, IN: Purdue University Press.
White, Richard J. (1997): *Nietzsche and the Problem of Sovereignty*. Urbana, IL: University of Illinois Press.

Christian J. Emden
Political Realism Naturalized: Nietzsche on the State, Morality, and Human Nature

Political realism today is often understood in terms of a theory of international relations, as it came to the fore in the work of E. H. Carr and Hans J. Morgenthau. Even though political realism, most recently, has been brought into a more serious conversation with cosmopolitan theories of international justice and global governance, the central commitments of political realism, including its emphasis on power over universalist claims of justice, have remained surprisingly stable.[1] Within this broader field, political realism is seen as describing the competitive and conflictual relationships among relatively sovereign states with specific self-interests and prerogatives that, even against a given state's declared intentions, will invariably favor power over cooperation. Not surprisingly, political realism does not always have the best of reputations. There is no reason, however, to limit political realism to the field of international relations; there is equally no reason to reduce political realism to *Realpolitik* or *Machtpolitik* in the pejorative sense of these terms. In his famous Munich lecture of 1919, *The Profession and Vocation of Politics*, Max Weber, for instance, explicitly noted that "politics" in general might be best characterized as the "striving for a share of power or for influence on the distribution of power, whether it be between states or between groups of people contained within a single state" (Weber 1994c, p. 311). A realist understanding of the nature of politics, then, requires us to accept that the striving for power is primary to moral motivations. This does not mean, however, that the political is devoid of normative claims. It is merely that such claims need to be grounded in something other than a Kantian understanding of the moral law or the ideals of Judeo-Christian virtue ethics. Niccolò Machiavelli aptly described this view within the framework of what he regarded as politically expedient advice:

> But because I want to write what will be useful to anyone who understands, it seems to me better to concentrate on what really happens rather then on theories or speculations. For many have imagined republics and principalities that have never been seen or known to exist. However, how men live is so different from how they should live that a ruler who does not do what is generally done, but persist in doing what ought to be done, will undermine his power rather than maintain it. (Machiavelli 1988, pp. 54f.)

---

[1] See, of course, Carr 2000 and Morgenthau 1978. For the recent convergence of realist and cosmopolitan theory, see Scheuerman 2011, pp. 98–125.

Political realism, on this account, views political life not against normative standards that precede political life itself, but it takes as its starting point the way in which institutions and people act in specific historical and social contexts. In a more modern version, this stance was recently repeated by Raymond Geuss when he argued for a shift in political philosophy from "how people ought ideally (or ought 'rationally') to act" to "the way the social, economic, political, etc., institutions actually operate in some society at some given time, and what really does move human beings to act in given circumstances" (Geuss 2008, p. 9). Political realism's normative force, then, cannot be derived from a standard outside political action. Rather, it must be seen as co-emerging with real politics; it comes into existence in the way in which people and institutions act.[2]

It is against this background that political realism also entails claims of a more anthropological nature, such as the basic assumption that, in one way or another, the striving for power, whatever form it might take, constitutes an integral part of what it means to be human. Moreover, and more interestingly, such claims invariably imply that behind political realism stands a form of philosophical naturalism: whatever their reasons for acting, human beings are no special case vis-à-vis the rest of nature. If political realism seeks to make claims about human nature, such claims, in other words, must be embedded in an account of philosophical naturalism. Neither Max Weber, nor Machiavelli, however, were able to provide such an account. Indeed, it is Nietzsche who first, and perhaps most fully, made the link between political realism and philosophical naturalism.

This chapter makes three claims. First, the general outlook of Nietzsche's political realism becomes particularly obvious in his discussion of the modern state as a moral community and of the inherently violent nature of moral communities in general. In this context Nietzsche proposes a broad range of reasons as to how and why human beings, even without any direct coercion, act in normatively binding ways. As such, and this is the second central claim of this chapter, Nietzsche's political realism requires a naturalized conception of human actions and, more importantly, a naturalized conception of the values that motivate such actions and of the conditions that render them possible in the first place. Such a naturalized account of what it means to be human finally leads to a wider set of implications for the current debate about Nietzsche's metaethical stance. Given its specific naturalistic commitments, political realism, as I will show, should not be equated with moral realism. In fact, political

---

[2] The claim I make here with regard to the emergence of normativity has been discussed in more detail by Rouse 2007 and Rouse 2002.

realism, at least at first sight, seems to entail an anti-realism about moral values. But in contrast to current debates, which seek to distinguish neatly between moral realism and an anti-realism about values, I shall conclude that such distinctions are less relevant for Nietzsche's political realism than commonly assumed.

1 The Modern State as a Moral Community

Nietzsche is occasionally portrayed as an essentially unpolitical and even antipolitical thinker.[3] His views of political life, whichever direction they might take throughout his intellectual career, remain influenced by an early aestheticism, a tendency to emphasize the primacy of art and aesthetic experience over real social and political concerns. Not surprisingly, Nietzsche's political views, as much as the political implications of his philosophical thought as a whole, have thus been presented as akin to a myth-making exercise that, given the general historical trajectory of German politics from the early nineteenth to the mid-twentieth centuries, at the very least bears dangerous overtones.[4] Nietzsche's politics, as it were, are of a foggy kind. Alternatively, and perhaps with greater awareness for the historical contexts within which his reflections on political life gain momentum, his position continues to be described, in one way or another, as supporting a more conservative and authoritarian agenda, occasionally with a somewhat violent streak, as it comes to the fore in his short essay on *The Greek State* (1871/72) as well as in his many enthusiastic remarks about the cruel Renaissance ruler.[5] At best, Nietzsche seems to remind us about the limits of the democratic ideals we hold, but a properly coherent political theory, in any event, is not to be found in his writings, as Martha Nussbaum famously remarked: on the questions of liberty, justice, and material need, Nietzsche, in short, has nothing to offer, and his contribution to political thinking rather lies in his examination of moral psychology.[6]

On the other hand, and with greater sympathy for Nietzsche's apparent incoherence, his refusal to deliver a systematic theory of politics was also seen

---

[3] Bergmann 1987 goes even so far as to suggest that Nietzsche had little interest in politics and that his views of political life are predominantly based on his aestheticism. A similarly antipolitical account can be found in Thiele 1990, which presents a solitary Nietzsche detached from wider social and political concerns.
[4] See, for instance, Williamson 2004, pp. 234–284.
[5] See Ruehl 2004, Dombowsky 2004, Detwiler 1990.
[6] See Nussbaum 1997.

in a positive vein as supporting a pluralism of values and normative claim. The latter, in a sense, made his more polemical and uncomfortable reflections about the nature of politics palatable within a discourse of politial theory shaped, to a considerable degree, by the broadly liberal commitments of the Anglo-American tradition. In the same way as Nietzsche's views could be presented as expressing the prerogatives of an essentially elitist project, they could also be interpreted as having quasi-democratizing implications.[7] What both interpretations have in common, however, is that they tend to remove Nietzsche's position from the way in which people, groups, as much as entire institutions, act in a political context shaped by conditions that have emerged historically.

Presenting Nietzsche as an inherently political thinker, and assimilating him to specific positions in political theory, had the unintentional effect of distancing his reflections on the nature of politics from the practice of politics. If Nietzsche provides us neither with a theory of government, nor with a theory of justice, as Nussbaum pointed out, we are left, as it were, with his contributions to moral psychology. As a consequence, Nussbaum's own emphasis on moral psychology, needless to say, precisely outlines the area in which Nietzsche's political thought has been discussed, from Bernard Williams and Brian Leiter to Robert Pippin.[8] While there is much to be said for such an approach, Nietzsche does seem to hold certain ideals that are related to actual political practices.[9] Furthermore, Nietzsche's writings are indeed marked by direct interventions in the specific historical contexts within which the political questions of modernity come to the fore: democracy and its discontents, revolution, laws, and rights, power and the state.[10]

While there is indeed little actual evidence, then, for Nietzsche's presumed antipolitical attitude, it is in his reflections on power and the state that he most directly addresses the nature of real political practices. These reflections, to be sure, always need to be linked back to his moral psychology as much as to his broader understanding of power, and it is also important to accept that his views of the state continue to be a matter of debate. But did Nietzsche view the state simply as a predominantly problematic political institution?[11] His

---

[7] See, exemplary, Warren 1988 and Hatab 1995. From a different perspective, see also Lemm 2009.
[8] See, representative of a much broader field, Pippin 2010, Leiter/Sinhababu 2007, Leiter 2002, May 1999; Williams 1993.
[9] See Brobjer 1998.
[10] See, for instance, the contributions in Siemens/Roodt 2009. See also Shaw 2007, Emden 2008, Krulic 2002, Ansell-Pearson 1996, Owen 1995, Marti 1993, Ottmann 1987.
[11] See Appel 1999, p. 141, and Hunt 1985.

seemingly aestheticist glorification of the state in the early essay on *The Greek State*, focusing on "the connection between state and genius," certainly stands in some contrast to his apparent rejection of the state as a religious construct, a decade later, in *Thus Spoke Zarathustra* (1883–85), and it also seems that his critical reflections on the nature of politics in the first volume of *Human, All Too Human*, published in 1878, invariably prepare much of the ground for his later views (GSt; Z I Idols; MA I 438–482). Against this background, it is not entirely surprising that his remarks in *Thus Spoke Zarathustra* – itself perhaps not the high point of his political thought – are often presented as indicative of Nietzsche's anti-political stance: criticizing the presumed identity of "the state" and "the people," which plays a central role in Kant's *Metaphysics of Morals* (1797) and is often seen as the cornerstone of modern democratic theory, Nietzsche suggested that the state was merely a barely secularized version of an illusory divine order; as a consequence, the philosopher of the future can only exist beyond the realm of the state (Z I Idols).[12]

To some extent, Nietzsche's later rejection of the state continues a theme he already addressed in the first volume of *Human, All Too Human*, when he emphasized – in surprising agreement with Marx – that the modern nation state's legitimacy was to a large extent dependent on its use of religion in the public realm, that is, on its self-presentation as a secular version of divine order: considering the public self-perception of the authoritatian nation state in the nineteenth century, it was difficult to overlook that "civil peace and continuity of development" were dependent on the prevalent illusion that political life as a whole is dependent exclusively on "instructions from above." The fusion of "divine and human government" in the authoritarian nation state – in Napoleonic France as much as in Imperial Germany – rendered it more than obvious that "absolute tutelary government and the careful preservation of religion necessarily go together" (HH I 472).[13] In contrast, the democratization of the political landscape, in particular the rise of mass democracy, ran parallel to a shift of religion from the public into the private realm, thus undermining the very legitimacy of the nineteenth-century nation state as a relatively authoritarian polity: as soon as the belief in "a sacred mystery in the existence of the state" was lost, the very structure of the nineteenth-century nation state became questionable, and this is precisely what he had in mind when he spoke, polemically, of "democracy" as "the historical form of the decay of the state."

---

12 See Kant 1996a, pp. 455–461, and HH 450.
13 I am adopting the concept of Imperial Germany as an authoritarian nation state from Mommsen 1995.

The nation state that Nietzsche had in mind in this passage, of course, was modeled on the example of both Napoleonic France and Imperial Germany. By the time Nietzsche wrote these passages in *Human, All Too Human*, it was, moreover, a central characteristic of the German public sphere that Imperial Germany's historical legitimacy was rooted in a quasi-Hegelian narrative that stressed the close connection between the cunning of reason and the unfolding of consciousness, on the one hand, and Prussia's Protestant heritage, on the other. Hegel, without doubt, did not have the intention, in his *Lectures on the Philosophy of History* (1827–31), to glorify the Prussian political system in theological fashion as the logical outcome, and endpoint, of world history, even though a number of prominent passages in the *Elements of the Philosophy of Right* (1821) could be read in this vein.[14] On the other hand, and in response to the 1830 revolutions, his successors, from Karl Rosenkranz to the Protestant Right Hegelians, drew together fundamentalist theology and the philosophy of history in a way that emphasized Prussia's superiority and the legitimacy of a new German Empire.[15] Although these developments take their course already in the 1830s and 1840s, their effect broadened by the 1870s, when it was indeed necessary to find some form of historical legitimacy for Imperial Germany – and this was especially the case during the later 1870s, when economic difficulties, social disparity, and constitutional conflict threatened to undermine the integrity of a newly unified German nation state.

In his assessment of contemporary German politics, Nietzsche largely ignores the long-standing parliamentary tradition that also shaped the constitutional outlook, as much as the constitutional tensions, of Imperial Germany. German liberalism is, in *Human, All Too Human*, merely seen as a variant of those revolutionary political demands that he often tends to attribute to the rise of socialism and social democracy (HH I 446, 451, 463, and 473).[16] Nevertheless, his argument that the modern nation state in the nineteenth century had to present itself publicly as a secularized version of religious order is a case in point for his own realism: political justification requires an appeal to emotional attachment. The crucial point here is not that the nation state was a secularized religious order, but rather that it had to be seen as such. Nietzsche, in other words, did not opt for the kind of political theology Carl Schmitt

---

[14] See, for instance, Hegel 1999b, pp. 222ff., and Hegel 1991, p. 379.
[15] See, for instance, Rosenkranz 1870, and the broader discussion in Toews 1980, pp. 155–164 and pp. 243–254.
[16] Apart from the still relevant standard accounts by Sheehan 1978 and Langewiesche 1988, see also the concise overviews in Nipperdey 1983, pp. 286–300, as well as Gall 1996a and Gall 1996b. For an interesting regional case study, see Palmowski 1999.

proposed at the very moment when the authoritarian nation state in Germany had already been replaced by a mass democracy properly speaking: the concepts that governed the realm of political life in the authoritarian nation state were not in fact secularized theological concepts, but they had to be publicly regarded along these lines in order to safeguard the legitimacy of the state's institutional order.[17] Nietzsche, thus, anticipated Max Weber's argument that the legitimacy of the modern state, for better or worse, could not solely rest on rational legal order alone, but also required appeals to charisma and tradition.[18]

It would be a grave mistake to simply assume that Nietzsche's account of what he regarded as the decay of the modern state is based on an aestheticist version of the political or one driven by existentialist concerns. It is, in this respect, crucial to understand that Nietzsche's critique of the modern state, from *Human, All to Human* to *On the Genealogy of Morality* (1887), is concerned with a very specific notion of the state as a sacred entity and, moreover, as a moral community. In view of this, the problem of political realism in Nietzsche's writings does not emerge solely within a philosophical context, but it is concerned with the problem of policy making in the modern nation state of the nineteenth century.

Nietzsche is certainly aware that modern nation states, such as Imperial Germany, require a rationalization of their political structures, especially on an administrative level. But as far as the actual foundations of the modern state as a nation were concerned, the deep structures of the political imagination continue to be marked by the importance of quasi-religious mentalities that, in the service of public policy, then as now, are able to mobilize large sectors of society. Consider, for instance, the following passage which links the formulation of German foreign policy objectives to European confessional divides that have relatively little to do with the actual strategic interests at stake:

> The statesman excites public passions so as to profit from the counter-passions thereby aroused. To take an example: any German statesman knows well that the Catholic Church will never form an alliance with Russia, but would indeed rather form one even with the Turks; he likewise knows that an alliance between France and Russia would spell nothing but danger for Germany. If, therefore, he is able to make of France the hearth and home of the Catholic Church he will have abolished this danger for a long time to come. Consequently he has an interest in exhibiting hatred towards the Catholics and, through hostile acts of all kinds, transforming those who acknowledge the authority of the Pope into a passionate political power which, hostile to German policy, will naturally ally itself with

---

17 See, in contrast, Schmitt 2005, p. 36.
18 See Weber 1978, pp. 215f.

France as the opponent of Germany: his goal is just as necessary the Catholicization of France as Mirabeau's was its decatholicization. (HH I 453)

Turning France, in the public mind on both sides of the Rhine, into a haven of Catholicism, and thus making it more Catholic than it is, ultimately stands in the service of German foreign policy vis-à-vis Russia. Undercutting a workable strategic alliance between France and Russia, and achieving the isolation of Russia, would prove more difficult without the confessional polarization outlined in this passage. Indeed, Nietzsche's example is neither far-fetched nor counterfactual, since the mere possibility of a military alliance between France and Russia was a central concern of Bismarck's foreign policy from 1878 onward, that is, the year Nietzsche published the first volume of *Human, All Too Human*.[19]

Because of its appeal to emotional investment, religion, coupled with the myths of the nation, allows for the translation of rational policy interests into the wider public imagination, itself guided in no small part by emotional attachment. This, to be sure, is a phenomenon particular, albeit not exclusively, to the large European nation state of the nineteenth century in which authoritarian structures run parallel to increasing demands for the public justification of political decisions. From Hegel through Nietzsche to Max Weber, the political emancipation of citizens within increasingly democratic societies leads to the "demagogic character" of political discourse, since the necessary "intention to appeal to the masses" is common to any form of political representation based on "parties" (HH I 438). On the one hand, Hegel was able to argue that public opinion, despite the fact that "it contains no criterion for discrimination," still expressed "the essence and inner content of the age," thus indirectly contributing to the formation of civil society within the modern state (Hegel 1991, p. 355). On the other hand, Weber, contemplating the conditions of a new parliamentary Germany after the end of empire, laconically concluded: "The *danger* which mass democracy presents to national politics consists principally in the possibility that *emotional* elements will become dominant in politics" (Weber 1994b, p. 230). Seen from this perspective, and sandwiched between Hegel's and Weber's hopes for a proper constitutional order, Nietzsche's remarks appear less radical or unrealistic than commonly assumed: the modern nation state constitutes, among many other things, a moral community with a specific set of normative commitments that are able to be perpetuated to a considerable extent by the emotional attachment they generate. Any political theory which fails to take the irrational dimension of the political into account

---

19 See, in more detail, Emden 2008, pp. 202–216.

also fails to properly recognize how political power is articulated in actuality. To put it more sharply, the practical interests of the state as a moral community, always tied to emotion, highlight the limits of those models of deliberative democracy that aim at rational consensus.[20] From the point of view of Nietzsche's political realism, the business of politics remains linked to the exploitation of emotionally charged concerns.

Against this background, Nietzsche begins to examine in more detail the social function of religion as a political institution within the state, that is, as a way of both mobilizing and controlling political participation for strategic means. Religion, thus, serves a specific function within the evolution of the modern state that, in an ironic turn, ultimately secularizes the state:

> As long as the state, or, more clearly, the government knows itself appointed as guardian for the benefit of the masses not yet of age, and on their behalf considers the question whether religion is to be preserved or abolished, it is very highly probable that it will always decide for the preservation of religion. For religion quietens the heart of the individual in times of loss, deprivation, fear, distrust, in those instances, that is to say, in which the government feels unable to do anything towards alleviating the psychical sufferings of the private person: even in the case of universal, unavoidable and in the immediate prospect inevitable evils (famines, financial crises, wars), indeed, religion guarantees a calm, patient, trusting disposition among the masses. Wherever the chance or inevitable shortcomings of the state government or the perilous consequences of dynastic interests force themselves upon the attention of the knowledgeable man and put him into a refractory mood, the unknowledgeable will think they see the hand of God and patiently submit to instructions from <u>above</u> (in which concept divine and human government are usually fused): thus internal civil peace and continuity of development is ensured. (HH I 472)

It is precisely the appeal to the realm of religion that renders the sovereignty of the state both unlimited and indivisible, which is the reason why Nietzsche remarks that "absolute tutelary government and the careful preservation of religion necessarily go together" (HH 472).

The social function of religion in the realm of the political consists in safeguarding the unity of the state. Or, in Weber's terms, the emotional tendency of the masses and the bureaucratic concerns of administrative rule go hand in hand. For Nietzsche, moreover, the central problem of broader political participation was not simply the inevitably unequal distribution of power (HH I 439 and 440), but rather citizens who are "unknowledgeable." Nietzsche's emphasis on the educational aspect is surprisingly close to Kant's criticism, in his essay *Answer to the Question: What is Enlightenment?* (1784), of the "self-in-

---

20 On this problem, see Mouffe 2005, p. 6 and pp. 24–34.

curred immaturity" that hinders the development of "the public use of one's own reason" (Kant 1991, pp. 54f.). What Nietzsche believed to be lacking in the modern nation state of the nineteenth century, then, was what Weber regarded as political education, or political maturity, and which he defined, already in his inaugural lecture at Freiburg in 1895, as a "grasp of the nation's economic and political *power* interests" (Weber 1994a, pp. 20f.). Such political maturity required, for Weber, an understanding of the nature of rule or *Herrschaft*, and such an understanding was also the subject of Nietzsche's observations about the internal logic of moral communities, including the modern nation state.

2 Hypocrisy and the Common Good

Moral norms do not exist outside moral communities. If such moral communities strive for internal homogeneity – regardless as to whether they are committed to rational liberalism or more authoritarian ways of life – they require absolutes that allow them to exclude that which is seen as threatening such homogeneity. There are, of course, different kinds of moral communities, some more open than others. Moral communities can be porous and open to change, but the normative force of the underlying commitments invariably stands in some contrast to such openness. As with all communities, self-perception often does not accurately reflect the actual practices that shape such communities. Nevertheless, Nietzsche is quite correct that the moral communities which dominate political and social life in the nineteenth century – the nation, a particular confession, the Church, a professional ethos – require precisely those absolutes that, during the 1880s, are the subject of his genealogy. Indeed, the political relevance of Nietzsche's genealogy, leaving aside its philosophical dimension as an immanent critique of the metaphysical tradition, consists in exploring the historical formation of moral communities. Asking why normatively binding commitments that contradict a given individual's concrete interests are able to emerge and proliferate, genealogy renders obvious that such commitments are not in fact absolute but are made to be absolute. This does not simply entail that the norms that govern moral communities are constructed, or that they are arbitrary. Rather, it highlights that they perform a specific function that exceeds the interests of any given individual. Moral norms, on this account, are thus neither arbitrary nor are they natural kinds. They are, in short, co-emergent with the practices that can be found in any given community, practices that the community in question cannot admit to be open to change. This becomes particularly obvious in the context of *On the Genealogy of Morality*.

Focusing on the distinction between "good" and "bad," Nietzsche argues in the first essay that a value neutral notion of "bad" – in the sense of being "inferior" without the burden of blame – has been transformed into the notion of "evil" (GM I 11). While pre-moral societies are based on a hierarchy between "good," in the sense of "virtuous"/"noble," and "bad," in the sense of "inferior"/"common," modern societies have reversed this order by attributing social status to a specific order of moral sentiments.[21] By doing so, Nietzsche argues, "common" individuals ("slaves," in his colorful words) begin to feel hatred toward the "nobility," thus creating the *ressentiment* he locates at the center of the Judeo-Christian tradition, triggering the "slave revolt of morality" (GM I 10 and 7): "evil" becomes that which does not adhere to the order of the "slaves'" moral sentiments merely by its very existence and which therefore is seen as the "other" of any given moral community.

Any moral notion of "evil," however, does not merely refer to an individual's actions, but always to this individual's existence as primordially sinful.[22] Seen from this perspective, even a fully secularized notion of moral evil bears clear theological overtones. Indeed, without such an at least implicitly theological, or religious, framework it seems that the notion of evil would not hold much water as a moral category; it could easily be replaced by the notion of an unexpected and excessive wrongdoing that is more normal, and therefore ethically also more worrying, than the idea of evil.[23]

As Nietzsche already noted in the early 1880s, this is also the reason why moral and political communities, once an existential distinction between "good" and "evil" has become the central value claim of a sizable majority, easily sacrifice the individual for a presumed greater common good that, in reality, is a product of custom:

> The origin of custom lies in two ideas: 'the community [*Gemeinde*] is worth more than the individual' and 'an enduring advantage is to be preferred to a transient one'; from which it follows that the enduring advantage of the community is to take unconditional precedence over the advantage of the individual, especially over his momentary wellbeing, but also over his enduring advantage and even over his survival. Even if the individual suffers

---

[21] Consider, for instance, the distinction in Roman law between *honestiores* ("more honorable men") and *humiliores* ("more humble men"). See *Fontes Iuris Romani Antejustiani* 1941/43, vol. III, p. 405.

[22] As Leiter 2002, pp. 235–242, argued, conscience has thus become moralized through religion, the latter increasingly providing the foundation for moral values.

[23] See Morton 2004, pp. 1–33. The idea that evil is not a deviation from normality, or from normal moral order, also underlies the argument of Kekes 2005. Cole 2006 rightly asks whether a secular notion of evil holds much water. In contrast to the normality of evil, see, however, Card 2010, pp. 1–119, who argues for a distinctively "post-Nietzschean" understanding of evil.

from an arrangement which benefits the whole, even if he languishes under it, perishes by it — the custom must be maintained, the sacrifice offered up. (AOM 89)

Moral righteousness and physical violence are closely linked and come together in an ethic of conviction that guides political ideals. Max Weber, as much a political realist as Nietzsche, points to the political consequences of such an ethic of conviction in his Munich lecture of 1919 with regard to the cultural authority of Protestantism:

> Because the world was corrupted by original sin, it was possible to build violence relatively easily into ethics as a means of chastising sin and heretics who endangered the soul. [...] Normal Protestantism [...] legitimated the state absolutely (and thus its means, violence) as a divine institution, and gave its blessing to the legitimate authoritarian state in particular. (Weber 1994c, p. 364)

The politics of the greater common good — regardless as to whether the latter is seen in religious, social or political terms — entails a necessarily lopsided power relationship: of course, the willingness to sacrifice the individual, as Nietzsche pointedly remarks, invariably "originates [...] only in those who are not the sacrifice" (AOM 89). A Christian ethics of selflessness, which, for Nietzsche, remains in the background of modern liberalism but also socialism and nationalism, emerges as an inherently self-contradictory and dangerous position: "The 'neighbour' praises selflessness because it brings him advantages," not because such selflessness is the realization of a greater common good (GS 21). Most importantly, however, the appeal to a greater common good is based on the misunderstanding that the latter is independent of the actual practices in any given moral community. While the Judeo-Christian tradition, not unlike the Kantian discourse of political philosophy, has to assume that basic norms are decoupled from social and political practices, Nietzsche's political realism postulates that such basic norms are the outcome of social and political practices with historical depth:

> To be moral, to act in accordance with custom, to be ethical means to practice obedience towards a law or tradition established from of old. [...] To be evil is 'not to act in accordance with custom,' to practise things not sanctioned by custom, to resist tradition, however rational or stupid that tradition may be [...] How the tradition has arisen is here a matter of indifference, and has in any event nothing to do with good and evil or with any kind of immanent categorical imperative; it is above all directed at the preservation of a community [Gemeinde], a people (HH I 96)[24]

---

[24] The term *Gemeinde* not only refers to an abstract "community" but also to a religious community in the sense of "congregation" and "parish." Nietzsche here points to the structural equivalence of religious, moral and political communities. What they have in common is a relatively closed structure as it is discussed in Tönnies 2001, pp. 22–51.

In view of the crucial importance of traditions for the preservation of moral and political communities, and taking into account that such traditions essentially naturalize moral and political values for a society, Nietzsche increasingly focuses on the need to unravel the historical evolution of such moral and political communities, which is, of course, one of the central themes of both *Human, All Too Human* and *On the Genealogy of Morality* (AOM 223).

The inherently historical perspective of Nietzsche's political realism, to be sure, is also one of the reasons why he positions himself outside, or beyond, the traditional fault lines of political discourse in modernity. This is already the case in *Human, All Too Human*, when he criticizes, and rejects, the central tenets of liberalism, socialism, and conservative nationalism in equal measure: the real focus of politics, he repeatedly suggests, is neither "compromise," nor social justice in terms of an "equality of rights," nor "artificial nationalism"; rather, it remains the "question of power" (HH I 446, 450–51, and 475).[25] This realist stance, which can all too easily be misunderstood as an apolitical or antipolitical attitude, is also repeated, a few years later, in *The Gay Science* (1882/87), when he seeks to disentangle the future persona of the philosopher from the dominant camps in the history of modern political thought:[26]

> We 'conserve' nothing; neither do we want to return to any past; we are by no means 'liberal'; we are not working for 'progress'; we don't need to plug our ears to the marketplace's sirens of the future: what they sing — 'equal rights,' 'free society,' 'no more masters and no servants' — has no allure for us. We hold it absolutely undesirable that a realm of justice and concord should be established on earth (because it would certainly be the realm of the most profound leveling down to mediocrity and chinoiserie); we are delighted by all who love, as we do, danger, war, and adventure; who refuse to compromise, to be captured, to reconcile, to be castrated; we consider ourselves conquerors; we contemplate the necessity for new orders as well as for new slavery — for every strengthening and enhancement of the human type also involves a new kind of enslavement — doesn't it? (GS 377)

While passages such as these, with their polemical tone and seemingly literal endorsement of "war" and "slavery," can easily be misread as a justification of

---

25 See also Nietzsche's remarks at HH I 452, 454, 463, and 473.
26 Nietzsche's "free spirit," much like his "sovereign individual," implies a specific understanding of the role and self-perception of the philosopher that has rarely been discussed in any great detail. Questions concerning the persona of the philosopher have largely focused on the period between the sixteenth and eighteenth centuries. See, for instance, Hunter 2007 and Condren/Hunter 2008 as well as the contributions in Condren/Gaukroger/Hunter 2010. It would be worthwhile, indeed, to extend this genealogy of the persona of the philosopher into the nineteenth century.

authoritarian politics and as an invitation to tyranny, Nietzsche's central focus remains the "homeless" European philosophers. The latter are "the rich heirs of millennia of European spirit, with too many provisions but also too many obligations" (GS 377). The historical consciousness, and historical understanding, that marks these new philosophers not only means that they are "too well-informed" and "too 'well-travelled'," but as such they are critically disposed toward the comforting myths of progress and "humanity" that characterize the dominant strands of European political thought, from the French Saint-Simonists and British liberalism to German nationalism and imperialism, "the mendacious racial self-admiration and obscenity that parades in Germany today" (GS 377). Behind such critical commentary on contemporary politics, however, also stands the demand of Nietzsche's political realist for a political discourse that rethinks the origins and functions of its own normatively binding commitments beyond standard claims for the moral superiority of specific party political programs.

Nietzsche's disparaging comments about the appeals to humanity and sense for community that is a hallmark of political discourse in the modern nineteenth-century nation state is not without reason. French Saint-Simonists as much as German nationalists view the modern polity, at its very core, as a moral community. Moral communities, needless to say, rely on trust. Although it seems only apt to emphasize trust as the central point of reference for moral action, trust itself is more ambivalent that commonly assumed, since not everything that is the outcome of situations of trust, such as the exploitation of others, should really be accepted.[27] Indeed, the exploitation of others, especially in modern mass democracies, tends to be more efficient in a context of trust than if it is based on violent coercion, and it is therefore not surprising that the question of trust has emerged as a central issue in debates about the current state and future of liberal democracy beyond closed moral communities.[28] Whatever hopes we might have, the exploitation of trust, it seems, is more normal than commonly perceived also in closely knit moral communities. Nietzsche's sovereign individual is able to recognize this more so than, say, the Kantian philosopher, precisely because the sovereign individual is able to recognize that trust is a problem of social practices, not norms. Nietzsche's sovereign individual is able to adopt a notion of trust that excludes moral absolutes: mutual trust can only be acceptable and ethically justified, if each party is critically aware, and not only assumes to be aware, of the other's reasons

---

[27] See Baier 1994, p. 95. For Kant, in contrast, such a position is almost impossible to hold, since he does not even allow for the possibility of lying out of moral duty. See Kant 1996b.
[28] See Hardin 2006 and the contributions in Warren 1999.

for trusting and for continuing to rely on mutual trust.[29] But since such knowledge tends to be quite rare, especially in the realm of the political, it is, for Nietzsche, above all, the "free spirit" and the "sovereign individual" as they emerge in the context of his genealogical enterprise – from *The Gay Science* to *Beyond Good and Evil* (1886) and *On the Genealogy of Morality* – who are able to consider the possible consequences of trust.

What is at stake for Nietzsche's political realist is not simply the question of lying, or hypocrisy, in order to exploit other people's trust, or to persuade them to behave in ways that are, in one way or another, contrary to their immediate interests. Straight-forward hypocrisy – saying, for instance, that I am selfless in helping my neighbor while I only do so because I expect the neighbor to eventually return the favor – is largely unproblematic from Nietzsche's perspective. It is, indeed, expected in the realm of politics and morality. The problem that Nietzsche's political realism deals with, rather, is what David Runciman described as the "move from the first-order hypocrisy of faking virtue to the second-order hypocrisy of trying to find a way to make that fake virtue appear real" (Runciman 2008, p. 70). Moral communities, as the ones that Nietzsche has in mind, do not simply engage in hypocrisy in order to exploit trust, but their emphasis on the primacy of the good, together with their appeal to a greater common good, presents itself as a stance against hypocrisy and in favor of virtue. The moralization of the political, as it emerged in the course of the later seventeenth century and took center stage in the Kantian project of Enlightenment, is marked by an appeal to moral authenticity and moral conviction that, against better judgment, ignores that the emergence of normative order is bound up with the social and political practices in which we engage as natural beings.[30] Second-order hypocrisy, in effect, requires the assumption that moral norms stand outside politics and outside nature, serving as quasi-transcendental points of reference.

It is against this background that Nietzsche's sovereign individual and his free spirit have to become what they really are, that is, natural beings aware of their own history and, thus, willing to face the reality of the normative order within which we live. This is the reason why, in *Beyond Good and Evil*, he demands of his future philosophers to be "curious to a fault," even "to the point of cruelty," in the sense of a "genuine honesty" (BGE 44 and 227). On the one hand, such individuals are able to perceive "<u>reality itself</u>" (EH Destiny 5), and on the other, their actions would be marked by "the extraordinary privi-

---

[29] See Baier 1994, p. 128.
[30] On the history of this philosophical moralization of the political, see Kittsteiner 1991, pp. 254–286.

lege of responsibility," that is, by their choice to accept accountability (GM II 2). Although this sovereign individual is presented, in *On the Genealogy of Morality*, as the ultimate outcome of the same long-term process of social evolution that gives rise to moral communities (GM II 20), the sovereign individual is able to reach beyond its own past and to gain an independence from this past. In other words, the sovereign individual, "having freed itself from the morality of custom," constitutes "an autonomous, supra-ethical individual," who has recognized both the weakness and the dangers of moral communities (GM II 2).

Such a sovereign individual, to be sure, is often seen as representing an authoritarian tendency in Nietzsche's political thought.[31] This is especially the case, when the sovereign individual, like the free spirit, is related to other remarks in *Beyond Good and Evil* in which Nietzsche seems to advocate for a Hobbesian notion of political life: "What I'm trying to say is: the democratization of Europe is at the same time an involuntary exercise in the breeding of tyrants – understanding that word in every sense, including the most intellectual [*im geistigsten*]" (BGE 242).[32] The "breeding of tyrants" out of a highly industrialized mass democracy seems one of the preconditions for a new elitist political order that Nietzsche had in mind.[33] In contrast, I would rather like to suggest that when he speaks of a "tyrant," what he has in mind is not necessarily a "despot," but he merely points to the inevitability of rule that even mass democracies cannot avoid. It is in this respect that Nietzsche's "tyrant" shares much common ground with Machiavelli's "ruler" or "prince": since the reality of political life is not to be found in the way "one should live," and since "what ought to be done" is rarely in accord with "what is generally done," any "ruler who wishes to maintain his power must be prepared to act immorally when this becomes necessary" (Machiavelli 1988, pp. 54f.). Machiavelli, though, did not wish the ruler to act without any ethical considerations; given the central importance of political order for Machiavelli, it would have simply been counterproductive for him to argue that ethical considerations need to be entirely ignored, since the political can only be realized successfully in a *res*

---

[31] See Detwiler 1990, pp. 4f.; Schutte 1985, p. 161; Wolin 2004, pp. 28ff. and 54–58. While Schutte and Wolin present a literal reading with little contextualization and attention to the complexity of Nietzsche's political thought, only Detwiler's argument is philosophically convincing.
[32] Judith Norman translates the German *im geistigsten Sinne* as "in the most spiritual sense." The German *geistig* is, of course, notoriously difficult to render in English, but in Nietzsche's context the term "spiritual" seems too metaphysical. There is no indication that Nietzsche did not simply refer to intellectual ability. See also BGE 203.
[33] See, for instance, Detwiler 1990, pp. 117–143.

publica.³⁴ Rather, he sought to acknowledge that the nature of the political does not correspond to Christian virtue ethics.³⁵ The latter would inevitably lead to the kind of second-order hypocrisy in politics which rulers, as much as citizens, have to resist: using the moralization of politics in order to achieve specific gains is one thing; believing in this moralization as representing the normative order of reality is quite another.

Nietzsche's sovereign individual, like his tyrant, represent what Max Weber, many years later, was to describe as the responsible politician. The essential requirements for such a politician in many ways bear Nietzschean overtones: a concern for *Sachlichkeit*, coupled with the demand for responsibility and for what Weber termed "judgement," that is, "the ability to maintain one's inner composure and calm while being receptive to realities, in other words *distance* from things and people" (Weber 1994c, pp. 352f.). As such, it is of no surprise that Weber's politician should also be a political realist, "acting by the maxim of the ethic of responsibility, which means that one must answer for the (foreseeable) *consequences* of one's actions" (Weber 1994c, p. 360). It is here that we can find Nietzsche's political realism, and toward the end of his intellectual career he begins to situate himself, rightly, in a tradition of political thought that specifically excludes any reference to the dominant political fault lines of his own time: "Thucydides, and perhaps Machiavelli's *Principe*, are most closely related to me in terms of their unconditional will not to be fooled and to see reason in *reality*, – *not* in 'reason,' and even less in 'morality'" (TI Ancients 2). Nietzsche's inconspicuous and almost fleeting remark that, for the political realist, it is necessary to see "reason in reality" entails an appeal to the normative nature of the factual. The sources of normativity, to use Christine Korsgaard's phrase, are not to be found in a transcendental standard, or in the presumed autonomy of human individuals, but they are inherently bound up with our practical engagement with a world of which we are already a part as natural beings.³⁶ Not surprisingly, the political realist of the Nietzschean kind has to naturalize, as it were, his position.

3 "Naturalism in Morality"

It is not difficult to see that political realism, irrespective of any ideological commitments it may have, often appeals to human nature. Machiavelli as

---

34 See Viroli 1992, pp. 126–177.
35 See Machiavelli 1988, p. 62.
36 See, in contrast, Korsgaard 1996, pp. 7–47.

much as Thomas Hobbes, to be sure, paint a rather pessimistic picture of such human nature, characterized by violence, self-interest, by inevitable quarrels over access to power and resources, and by hypocrisy and dissimulation.[37] While it was possible to reign in such excesses through law and the organization of power within the polity, as Machiavelli showed in *The Discourses* (1517) and Hobbes in his account of natural law, neither seriously assumed that it would be feasible to overcome, in principle, the central inclinations of human nature, as Samuel Pufendorf did, for instance, through the "recognition of men's natural equality," or Kant through right grounded in the moral law.[38] Likewise, classical realists such as Hans Morgenthau, despite their repeated claim that there are objective laws of politics and thus the possibility of a "rational theory" of political action, invariably noted that the norms of political action "have their roots in human nature."[39] Political realism, then, cannot only be concerned with the motivation of human actions but it tends to embed the latter in an anthropological understanding of nature which, at times explicitly, denies that human individuals constitute a special case vis-à-vis the rest of nature. As such, political realism's emphasis on the primacy of power over the primacy of the good, and over the primacy of the moral law in the Kantian sense of the term, ultimately requires a concept of human action that might be best described in terms of philosophical naturalism.

While this is not the place for a properly detailed account of Nietzsche's naturalism, it is crucial to recognize how his political realism, as it comes to the fore in the pages of *Human, All Too Human* and elsewhere, is connected to his demand, from the early 1880s onward, "to naturalize humanity with a pure, newly discovered, newly redeemed nature," as he notes in *The Gay Science* (GS 109). Nietzsche's naturalism, in other words, is an inherently normative project, not only in the sense that he wishes to advance specific values that contribute, in one way or another, to the flourishing of human life, but also in the sense that our normatively binding commitments are themselves co-emer-

---

37 See Machiavelli 1988, pp. 54–72, and Hobbes 1994, pp. 74–78.
38 See Machiavelli 2003, pp. 104–111, and Hobbes 1997, pp. 32–42. In contrast, see Pufendorf 1991, pp. 61ff., and Kant 1996a, pp. 455f.
39 Morgenthau 1978, p. 4. Morgenthau's account of human nature is heavily influenced both by his early reading of Nietzsche but also by the psychology of drives as it had emerged, around 1900, in the context of psychoanalysis. Morgenthau's psychologizing, for want of a better term, separates his positon, however, from that of Nietzsche, who grounds his political realism in a more sophisticated version of philosophical naturalism that, in many ways, is closer to Hobbes and Spinoza. On Morgenthau's reading of Nietzsche, see Frei 2001, pp. 94–130 and pp. 187f., as well as Petersen 1999. On Morgenthau's understanding of human nature and its context, see Schuett 2007, and Koskenniemi 2001, pp. 445–455.

gent with our actions as natural beings. In the same way in which Nietzsche's political realist claims that our norms are always bound up with our actions, and do not originate elsewhere, Nietzsche's naturalist claims that these actions are always bound up with our existence as natural beings. It is in this respect that Nietzsche's naturalism is fundamentally different from that of Quine and much closer to that of Joseph Rouse, who noted that scientific practice, much like any other human activity, "discloses not objects or laws independent of us and our concerns, but phenomena that we are part of" (Rouse 2002, p. 331).[40] What Rouse notes here with regard to scientific practices, however, might also be the case in the realm of the political, which equally "involves material intervention that transforms the world and is also simultaneously a conceptual articulation" (Rouse 2002, p. 310).

Much of the discussion of Nietzsche's naturalism, as it pertains to his rejection of traditional conceptions of morality, continues to be filtered, however, through the lens of Quine's project of naturalizing epistemology by turning to psychology.[41] As such, it is not surprising that many recent contributions have emphasized not only the primacy of psychological interpretation but also suggested that Nietzsche's normative commitments are of an individualistic and aesthetic kind.[42] To some extent at least, the implication of this account is that Nietzsche's normative project is concerned with affect and taste rather than with an understanding of the social and political world. It is quite ironic, indeed, to recognize that the attention to Nietzsche's philosophical naturalism had the effect of depoliticizing his project, or at least of consistently underplaying the political dimension of his thought. This is particularly surprising since at the center of Nietzsche's project certainly stands a profound interest in the emergence of normative order. That his account of the emergence and function of morality has political implications becomes particularly obvious in *Beyond Good and Evil*, but these implications are less concerned with the endorsement of a particular normative order than with recognizing that any normative order is best served with a healthy dose of skepticism. Greek tragedy looms large in the background of Nietzsche's political realism as it is part of his philosophical naturalism. In the same manner in which political realism, because of its consequentialist stance, ascribes a tragic dimension to the outcomes of human action that invariably fall short of any normative ideal, translating humanity

---

40 See, in contrast, Quine 1961 and Quine 1969.
41 See, for instance, Leiter 2002, pp. 3–12. This is even the case among those that do not explicitly address Quine's legacy at any length. See Pippin 2010, pp. 1–21, and Reginster 2006, pp. 139–147.
42 See, for instance, Railton 2012 and Poellner 2012.

back into nature forces us to accept that such an approach entails tragedy, especially if measured against the Kantian tradition of human autonomy:

> To translate humanity back into nature; to gain control of the many vain and fanciful interpretations and incidental meanings that have been scribbled and drawn over that eternal basic text of <u>homo natura</u>, hardened by the discipline of science, — with courageous Oedipus eyes and sealed up Odysseus ears, deaf to the lures of the old metaphysical bird catchers who have been whistling to him for far too long: 'You are more! You are higher! You have a different origin!' (BGE 230)

Nietzsche's reference to Oedipus, in this passage, clearly implies that philosophical naturalism, if it is to hold much water, demands of us to accept our own fate and position in a world in which there cannot be any poetic justice – a world whose conflicts and paradoxes cannot easily be dissolved, neither on epistemological grounds, nor in the realm of politics. Nietzsche's account of tragedy is of a different kind than, say, Hegel's, which ultimately aims at the reconciliation of difference in the idea of an ethical whole.[43] Such an ethical whole, however, would constitute, from Nietzsche's perspective, an external normative standard that is not itself bound up with human, and in particular political, action. Human reason and the construction of complex normative forms of order through moral values as much as through political institutions do not allow the human individual to escape from its existence as a part of nature.

Nietzsche's philosophical naturalism certainly seems to imply, at least at first sight, that he adopts the position of a moral anti-realist: moral values and political commitments do not exist outside human consciousness, even though the latter has to be seen as part of the natural world. Moral categories, on this account, are projected onto nature in order to produce normativity but the, as it were, need to produce such normativity is itself a phenomenon of the natural world. Moral values, then, as much as our political commitments, interests and actions, do not overcome nature, and moral consciousness does not merely run parallel to natural conditions. Rather, they constitute an intervention in nature that paradoxically is itself already part of the natural world.

Moral anti-realism, once taken seriously, entails precisely that kind of political realism that takes center stage in Nietzsche's political thought and that views with great skepticism the primacy of the good as it appears in both the Judeo-Christian tradition and the tradition of idealism from Plato to Kant and beyond:

---

[43] See, for instance, Hegel, 1999a, pp. 151f. On Hegel's notion of tragedy, see especially Schulte 1992.

> Whether I regard human beings with a good or with an evil eye, I always find them engaged in a single task, each and every one of them: to do what benefits the preservation of the human race. Not from a feeling of love for the race, but simply because within them nothing is older, stronger, more inexorable and invincible than this instinct — because this instinct constitutes the essence of our species and herd. [...] Hatred, delight in the misfortunes of others, the lust to rob and rule, and whatever else is called evil: all belong to the amazing economy of the preservation of the species, an economy which is certainly costly, wasteful, and on the whole most foolish — but still proven to have preserved our race so far. (GS 1)

> The strongest and most evil spirits have so far done the most to advance humanity: time and again they rekindled the dozing passions — every ordered society puts the passions to sleep –, time and again they reawakened the sense of comparison, of concentration, of delight in what is new, daring, unattempted [...] Mostly by force of arms, by toppling boundary stones, by violating pieties — but also by means of new religions and moralities! (GS 4)

The traditional assumption of a primacy of the good disappears as soon as we are concerned not with single individuals and their actions but with the natural history of normative order as a whole. Even those individuals who exemplify what Nietzsche calls "the lust to rob and rule," such as Cesare Borgia or Napoleon Bonaparte, belong to this natural history, for better or worse.

Although it will still be necessary to cast a critical eye on the distinction between moral realism and moral anti-realism, it appears reasonable to argue that Nietzsche views power as an internal standard against which to measure our normative commitments.[44] Nietzsche himself left no doubt that there must be some kind of standard, which can especially be seen with regard to the nature of our moral commitments. In *The Gay Science*, for instance, he suggests that moral universalism and moral relativism were "equally childish": it is certainly not reasonable to present the normative commitments of a specific historical and social context as universal, but it is also wrong to argue that differences in "moral valuations" necessarily mean "that no morality is binding" (GS 345). He had no intention of denying the evolutionary value of normative order. He also advanced an understanding of such normative order along the lines of political realism, emphasizing the central role of power and domination for any form of order, social and otherwise. This becomes particularly clear in a central passage of *Beyond Good and Evil*:

> For as long as there have been people, there have been herds of people as well (racial groups, communities, tribes, folk, states, churches), and a very large number of people

---

[44] See also the discussion in Wilcox 1974, pp. 194ff.

who obey compared to relatively few who command. So, considering the fact that humanity has been the best and most long-standing breeding ground for the cultivation of obedience so far, it is reasonable to suppose that the average person has an innate need to obey as a type of <u>formal conscience</u> that commands: 'Thou shalt unconditionally do something, unconditionally not do something,' in short: 'Thou shalt.' (BGE 199)

Nietzsche's reference, in this passage, to "breeding" and "innate needs" certainly suggests that the normative order he described, that is, the normative order of Judeo-Christian morality, was the outcome of a natural history. It is important to point out, however, that even the "new philosophers" and "free spirits" did not undercut normative order. Rather, Nietzsche regarded them in the position of "a new type of [...] commander," who would still partake in the natural history of normativity (BGE 203).⁴⁵ While the morality of the herd invariably translated power and domination into "public spirit, goodwill, consideration, industry, moderation, modesty, clemency, and pity," the new philosophers were not supposed to take part in this kind of "moral hypocrisy" (BGE 199). Instead, Nietzsche argued, their political realism made them "severe spirits": "these philosophers admit to taking <u>pleasure</u> in saying no, in dissecting, and in a certain level-headed cruelty that knows how to guide a knife with assurance and subtlety, even when the heart is bleeding" (BGE 210).

From the perspective of political realism, as much as from the perspective of Nietzsche's naturalism, normative order is not a question of justice, but it is a question of power. An appeal to the will to power would be able to decide whether or not holding certain moral commitments contributed to the flourishing of human life.⁴⁶ It is also only in this respect that clearly negative and life-denying phenomena, such as suffering and guilt, are able to retain their value as ascetic ideals: within the natural history of our normative commitments, they allowed for a domestication of our natural cruelty, rendering it possible for human beings both to exist and to flourish.⁴⁷ As Nietzsche noted in *Twilight of the Idols* (1888), a "naturalism in morality" has to emphasize that the practices with which we conceptually articulate our historically contingent interventions in the world are "governed by an instinct of life." This, needless to say,

---

45 Compare also Nietzsche's remarks at BGE 211.
46 A similar point is also made by Janaway 2007, p. 29. Janaway, however, speaks in this context of the "healthy psychological flourishing of human beings," whereas I would argue that from Nietzsche's perspective such flourishing belongs, first and foremost, to the realm of organic life. Psychology is secondary. Hussain 2011, pp. 150–157, also argues that Nietzsche's notion of life should best be understood along the lines of growth and flourishing.
47 For a more detailed discussion of this point, see Reginster 2006, pp. 229–235, and Janaway 2007, pp. 141f.

also extends to the normative commitments we subscribe to, unwittingly or consciously. Nietzsche, thus, does not deny the role of normative commitments, but he seeks to reconceptualize them: commitments that govern what we "should" or "should not" do cannot reasonably be based on a supernatural understanding of normativity that denied life, but they need to be seen as deriving from a naturalized understanding of normativity (TI Morality 4).

The naturalistic dimension of Nietzsche's political realism inevitably triggers the question of freedom. The existence of the latter, at least at first sight, seems thoroughly denied in his attempt to translate humanity back into nature as the basis for political realism. At the end of his genealogical project, there is no such thing as "free will" anymore:

> People were once endowed with 'free will' as their dowry from a higher order of things: today we have taken even their will away, in the sense that we do not see it as a faculty any more. The old word 'will' only serves to describe a result, a type of individual reaction that necessarily follows from a quantity of partly contradictory, partly harmonious stimuli: — the will does not 'affect' anything, does not 'move' anything any more ... (A 14)

The consequence of naturalizing human agency and political institutions is the destruction of free will, or so it seems. Free will might have been a useful illusion to have, but it contradicts central tenets of Nietzsche's naturalism.[48] Unsurprisingly, he puts "free will" in quotation marks.

Nietzsche does not deny, however, the notion of freedom; indeed, he could not have done so, given the hope he placed in the "free spirits" throughout the 1880s (GS 343 and 347; BGE 24–44 and 227; A 13). While he might have occasionally demanded a "freedom from [...] the sum of commanding value judgements that have become part of our flesh and blood," as in the fifth book of *The Gay Science* (GS 380), he seems to have been fully aware that such freedom could only exist as a thought experiment, as a counterfactual perspective itself conditioned by our existence as natural beings. As a consequence, he remarks in *Twilight of the Idols* that freedom can only be "measured by the resistance that needs to be overcome," and the latter is a reference to the will to power as an expression of the processes of organic life (TI Skirmishes 38).

If the growth of organic life is dependent on overcoming environmental resistance, Nietzsche clearly seeks to advance a naturalized notion of freedom.

---

48 See also BGE 18–19 and 21. On Nietzsche's critique of the free will, see the discussions in Richardson 2009, pp. 138–141, and Leiter 2002, pp. 87–101. While Richardson regards Nietzsche's account as part of a more emancipatory project, arguing that the freedom of human agency comes to the fore in the individual's recognition of her own natural limitations, Leiter, on the other hand, opts for a deterministic account that ultimately has to deny the role of freedom in Richardson's sense. My own reading is closer to that of Richardson.

While the tension between freedom and necessity remains perhaps the central problem of metaphysics, Nietzsche's account is able to chip away at this tension by arguing that freedom is part of the necessity of organic life. There is no such thing as radical autonomy, but the futural openness of our own natural history allows for a space of possibilities. The latter, to be sure, are always limited by the natural history of our normative commitments, a history even Nietzsche's free spirit cannot really escape.

Such a notion of freedom ties in well with a specific kind of philosophical naturalism, which should shift our attention from substantive claims to an understanding of normativity as inherently bound up with the practices that define us as natural beings. Changes in the "normative configuration" within which we live are neither causally determined in a narrow sense of causation, nor are they the result of some autonomous choice. Rather, changes in the normative configuration of the world are the consequences of changes both in the wider environment and with regard to our situatedness in this environment, which taken together "reconfigure what are intelligible and binding possible choices" (Rouse 2002, pp. 346f.). For Nietzsche's political realism, the choices we have in political life are inherently limited by the natural history that stands in the background of these choices and that renders these choices possible in the first place.

The notion of freedom Nietzsche accepts remains the freedom of the "sovereign individual" as it appears in *On the Genealogy of Morality*. This sovereign individual is a paradoxical figure, to be sure. On the one hand, it is the outcome of that "long history of the origins of *responsibility*," which made human beings "reliable, regular, automatic [*notwendig*]" and which thus fundamentally denies any sovereign actions properly speaking (GM II 1 and 2). Human beings are animals "able to make promises," but at the end of this history stands their transformation into beings who have "the right to make a promise." Being able to do X and having a right to do X are, of course, two different things. The latter implies, from Nietzsche's perspective, that the individual has "freed itself from the morality of custom," endorsing a morality grounded in its own drives, biological conditions, and environmental circumstances. Such a morality is inherently open toward the future, but it is also conditioned by its very own past. The right to make a promise, in other words, entails normative commitments the individual gives to itself, albeit with the insight that these normative commitments are inherently limited by their natural history. The "sovereign individual," after all, does not transcend the natural history of our normative commitments, but it is "the ripest fruit on its tree" (GM II 2). Human autonomy is based on the insight into the limits of this autonomy. This is precisely what makes this individual "strong enough to remain upright in the face of mishap or even 'in the face of fate'," as Nietzsche noted in a seemingly innocuous turn of phrase that evokes a long tradition ranging from the *rhathymía* he detects in Thucydides to Epicurean *ataraxía* and Machiavelli's *virtù*.[49] From the perspective of the political realist, fate demands emotional equanimity: "Thucydides has self-control, and consequently he has control over things as well" (TI Ancients 2).

4 Beyond Metaethics

If Nietzsche's political realism is grounded in a philosophical naturalism, and if this should be a reasonable position to hold, he cannot assume that we have an external point of view on organic life: as natural beings we are certainly shaped by organic life, but by conceptually articulating the way in which we are shaped by organic life, we already transform what we regard as organic life. If this should be a general feature of both Nietzsche's political realism and his philosophical naturalism, it also affects the metaethical questions raised in his later work. What is at stake is the condition under which our commitments, values, and judgments gain normative force. At first sight, it seems that he has to claim that there truly are objective facts with regard to what is morally "good" and "bad," what we should do and should not do. Such moral realism, which always has to appeal to some kind of objective standard, would have to regard normative commitments and values as independent of those human agents that hold them. In the sense that Nietzsche naturalizes our normative commitments, arguing that values only have normative force because they defer to organic life, it is certainly possible to suggest that he is a moral realist or at least that he eventually became one.[50] Such an account, however, has to assume that Nietzsche gave up the epistemological skepticism of his early work, trading in such skepticism for an increasingly empiricist position.

On the other hand, it is also possible to argue that Nietzsche adopted the role of a moral anti-realist, when he described morality as a myth in the opening pages of *Daybreak*, when he claimed, in *Thus Spoke Zarathustra*, that "good" and "evil" do not exist, or when he noted, in *Twilight of the Idols*, that "there are absolutely no moral facts" (D 3; Z II Self-Overcoming; TI Improv-

---

[49] See also the remarks at GM I 11 and TI Ancients 2.
[50] See, for instance, Schacht 1983, pp. 348f., and Clark/Dudrick 2007, pp. 193–201 and pp. 216–225.

ing 1).⁵¹ The question is, however, what the term "moral" refers to in such statements. It cannot refer to the idea that values are detached from organic life and that our moral practices have to be situated outside nature. Rather, when he contends that there are "no moral facts," he seems to have in mind what is regarded as factual in the metaphysical tradition, such as the *a priori* structure of Kant's moral law. Nietzsche, thus, also uses the term "facts" in this context rather loosely. To be sure, it is not entirely unlikely that he oscillated between moral realism and moral anti-realism, depending on the themes he addressed in his writings.⁵² It seems, then, that his position is more complex.

Bernard Reginster has pointed in this direction, when he rightly distinguished between two different claims that moral realism has to make: the first claim is that there are objective values, in terms of facts, and the second that the value of values depends on their objective standing.⁵³ It is entirely possible to subscribe to the latter claim without accepting the first. Any moral realism, however, that subscribes to both claims constitutes the kind of nihilism that Nietzsche saw as the fundamental condition of modernity, which was the outcome of the ascetic ideal's long natural history as a life-denying principle. Nietzsche, undoubtedly, rejected the idea that there are objective values independent of the natural beings that hold them. Therefore he also has to be regarded as a moral anti-realist, but given his continued insistence on the value of having values throughout most of his writings, he does seem to have accepted that the usefulness of such values actually depends on their objective standing as a kind of regulative fiction. Human beings create values that they hold to be objective.⁵⁴ Nietzsche thus seems willing to entertain moral realism's second claim as outlined above. The principal difference between the members of Nietzsche's "herd morality" and his "free spirits" would be that the latter, as Nadeem Hussain argued, "engage in a simulacrum of valuing by regarding things as valuable in themselves while knowing that they are not."⁵⁵ Needless to say, most individuals will lack this kind of insight. This is, however, the crucial insight of political realism, which should not be confused with moral realism.

While there is much to be said for such an approach to Nietzsche's metaethics, it does not resolve one of the underlying issues of his naturalism. To

---

51 For standard accounts of Nietzsche's moral anti-realism, see Leiter 2002, pp. 136–161, and Richardson 2004, pp. 104–132.
52 This is the view of Shaw 2007, pp. 78–136.
53 Reginster 2006, pp. 9f. and pp. 56–69, calls these different claims "descriptive objectivism" and "normative objectivism," respectively.
54 See Reginster 2006, pp. 85–97. Reginster refers back to Vaihinger 1924, pp. 341–362.
55 Hussain 2007, p. 178.

accept, in terms of a normative fiction, that we hold values to be objective and factual which, ultimately, are neither, still requires an objective standard, an epistemically privileged position able to distinguish between fictional norms and objective facts. Nietzsche's understanding of human agents as natural beings denied that such a distinction was reasonably possible. It seems, then, that the neat distinction between realism and anti-realism in Nietzsche's moral thought is inherently problematic. On the one hand, claiming that normative commitments are natural kinds, or properties of nature, cannot give any compelling reasons why these commitments, as much as our conceptual articulation of nature, should undergo change. On the other hand, claiming that nature is anormative is not sufficient to provide compelling reasons why anything should have normative force in the first place.

Both moral realism and moral anti-realism implicitly require that we are able to make an objectively valid distinction between us, as human beings, and the rest of nature. In other words, both moral realism and moral anti-realism are based on the assumption of a privileged epistemic position, even though anti-realism in particular claims to reject such a position.[56] The attempt to describe Nietzsche's metaethics along the lines of a tidy distinction between moral realism and moral anti-realism is largely unable to recognize its own metaphysical presuppositions and, as such, it fails to naturalize these presuppositions.

In the fall of 1887, Nietzsche seems to have attained a certain, and rare, autumnal contentment while spending a month in Venice, where he worked on the final corrections of *On the Genealogy of Morality*. Upon his return to Nice in late October, he began to change his reading material, turning mostly to French literature and culture, from Montaigne to the *Journal des Goncourt* – both offering examples of realistic descriptions of human moral psychology in all its shades of gray. It is in this context that he somewhat suddenly began to present an unusually positive assessment of modernity itself, praising what he described as the "naturalization of man in the 19th century" (NL, KGW VIII/2, 10[53]). It almost seemed, albeit only for a moment, that modernity was able to overcome the moral predicaments and cultural authorities of the ascetic ideal: the public criticism of traditional spiritual authorities, in particular the dogmas of the Judeo-Christian tradition, was as much as sign of this development as a surprisingly hedonistic emphasis on the human body in art and the growing recognition that the world of politics, at its very core, was not so much concerned with virtue as with the realization of power.

---

[56] This is the central problem of Leiter's rejection of moral realism as adopting a privileged epistemic position. In order to carry through this criticism, his argument ulimately has to rely on the very assumption that he seeks to reject. See Leiter 2000.

While many of his more conservative contemporaries, in academic circles as much as among the ranks of the German *Bildungsbürgertum*, saw such developments as a sign of increasing cultural "corruption," Nietzsche, for that brief moment in 1887, regarded them as symptoms of a new realism about life that was grounded in an understanding of nature, in particular human nature, very different from that of the metaphysical tradition: "In summa: there is evidence that the European of the nineteenth century is less ashamed of his instincts; he has made a great step toward admitting, finally, his unconditional naturalness, i.e., his amorality, without exacerbation: on the contrary, with sufficient strength to cope with this view alone" (NL, KGW VIII/2, 10[53]). Such optimism, however, did not last long and, perhaps, continues to be misplaced today.

Bibliography

Ansell-Pearson, Keith (1996): *Nietzsche contra Rousseau: A Study of Nietzsche's Moral and Political Thought*. Cambridge: Cambridge University Press.
Appel, Fredrick (1999): *Nietzsche contra Democracy*. Ithaca, N.Y.: Cornell University Press.
Baier, Annette C. (1994): "Trust and Antitrust". In: Annette C. Baier: *Moral Prejudices: Essays on Ethics*. Cambridge, Mass.: Harvard University Press, pp. 95–129.
Bergmann, Peter (1987): *Nietzsche, the Last Antipolitical German*. Bloomington, Ind.: Indiana University Press.
Brobjer, Thomas (1998): "The Absence of Political Ideals in Nietzsche's Writings: The Case of the Laws of Manu". In: *Nietzsche-Studien* 27, pp. 300–318.
Card, Claudia (2010): *Confronting Evils: Terrorism, Torture, Genocide*. Cambridge: Cambridge University Press.
Carr, E. H. (2001): *The Twenty Years' Crisis, 1919–1939: An Introduction to the Study of International Relations*. 5th corrected edition. New York: Palgrave.
Clark, Maudemarie/Dudrick, Dave (2007): "Nietzsche and Moral Objectivity: The Development of Nietzsche's Metaethics". In: Brian Leiter/Neil Sinhababu (eds.): *Nietzsche and Morality*. Oxford: Clarendon Press, pp. 192–226.
Cole, Phillip (2006): *The Myth of Evil: Demonizing the Enemy*. Edinburgh: Edinburgh University Press.
Condren, Conal/Gaugroker, Stephen/Hunter, Ian (eds.) (2010): *The Philosopher in Early Modern Europe: The Nature of a Contested Identity*. Cambridge: Cambridge University Press.
Condren, Conan/Hunter, Ian (2008): "The Persona of the Philosopher in the Eighteenth Century". In: *Intellectual History Review* 18, p. 315–317.
Detwiler, Bruce (1990): *Nietzsche and the Politics of Aristocratic Radicalism*. Chicago: University of Chicago Press.
Dombowsky, Don (2004): *Nietzsche's Machiavellian Politics*. New York: Palgrave Macmillan.
Emden, Christian J. (2008): *Friedrich Nietzsche and the Politics of History*. Cambridge: Cambridge University Press.
Fontes Iuris Romani Antejustiani (1941–1943). S. Riccobono, J. Baviera, C. Ferrini, J. Furlani, V. Arangio-Ruiz (eds.). Corrected edition. Florence: Barbèra.

Frei, Christoph (2001): *Hans J. Morgenthau: An Intellectual Biography*. Baton Rouge, LA.: Louisiana State University Press.
Gall, Lothar (1996a): "Liberalismus und 'bürgerliche Gesellschaft': Zu Charakter und Entwicklung der liberalen Bewegung in Deutschland". In: Lothar Gall: *Bürgertum, liberale Bewegung und Nation: Ausgewählte Aufsätze*. Munich: Oldenbourg, pp. 99–125.
Gall, Lothar (1996b): "Liberalismus und Nationalstaat: Der deutsche Liberalismus und die Reichsgründung". In: Lothar Gall: *Bürgertum, liberale Bewegung und Nation: Ausgewählte Aufsätze*. Munich: Oldenbourg, pp. 190–202.
Geuss, Raymond (2008): *Philosophy and Real Politics*. Cambridge: Cambridge University Press.
Hardin, Russell (2006): *Trust*. Cambridge: Polity Press.
Hatab, Lawrence J. (1995): *A Nietzschean Defense of Democracy: An Experiment in Postmodern Politics*. Chicago: Open Court.
Hegel, Georg Wilhelm Friedrich (1991): *Elements of the Philosophy of Right*. Allen W. Wood (ed.), H. B. Nisbet (trans.). Cambridge: Cambridge University Press.
Hegel, Georg Wilhelm Friedrich (1999a): "On the Scientific Ways of Treating Natural Law, on its Place in Practical Philosophy, and its Relation to the Positive Sciences of Right". In: G.W.F. Hegel: *Political Writings*. Laurence Dickey (eds.), H. B. Nisbet (eds./trans.). Cambridge: Cambridge University Press, pp. 102–180.
Hegel, Georg Wilhelm Friedrich (1999b): "Lectures on the Philosophy of History". In: G.W.F. Hegel: *Political Writings*. Laurence Dickey (eds.), H. B. Nisbet (eds./trans.). Cambridge: Cambridge University Press, pp. 197–224.
Hobbes, Thomas (1994): *Leviathan, with Selected Variants from the Latin Edition of 1668*. Edwin Curley (ed.). Indianapolis, Ind.: Hackett.
Hobbes, Thomas (1997): *On the Citizen*. Richard Tuck, Michael Silverthorne (eds./trans.). Cambridge: Cambridge University Press.
Hunt, Lester H. (1985): "Politics and Anti-Politics: Nietzsche's View of the State". In: *History of Philosophy Quarterly* 2, pp. 453–468.
Hunter, Ian (2007): "The History of Philosophy and the Persona of the Philosopher". In: *Modern Intellectual History* 4, pp. 571–600.
Hussain, Nadeem J. Z. (2007): "Honest Illusion: Valuing for Nietzsche's Free Spirits". In: Brian Leiter/Neil Sinhababu (eds.): *Nietzsche and Morality*. Oxford: Clarendon Press, pp. 157–191.
Hussain, Nadeem J. Z. (2011): "The Role of Life in the *Genealogy*". In: Simon May (ed.): *The Cambridge Critical Companion to Nietzsche's* On the Genealogy of Morality. Cambridge: Cambridge University Press, pp. 142–169.
Janaway, Christopher (2007): *Beyond Selflessness: Readin Nietzsche's Genealogy*. Oxford: Oxford University Press.
Kant, Immanuel (1991): "Answer to the Question: What is Enlightenment?" In: Immanuel Kant: *Political Writings*. Hans Reis (ed.). H. B. Nisbet (trans.). 2nd enlarged edition. Cambridge: Cambridge University Press.
Kant, Immanuel (1996a): "The Metaphysics of Morals". In: Immanuel Kant: *Practical Philosophy*. Mary J. Gregor (ed./trans.), Allen Wood (Introd.). Cambridge: Cambridge University Press, pp. 353–603.
Kant, Immanuel (1996b): "On a Supposed Right to Lie from Philanthropy". In: Immanuel Kant: *Practical Philosophy*. Mary J. Gregor (ed./trans.), Allen Wood (intro.). Cambridge: Cambridge University Press, pp. 605–615.
Kekes, John (2005): *The Roots of Evil*. Ithaca, NY: Cornell University Press.

Kittsteiner, Heinz D. (1991): *Die Entstehung des modernen Gewissens*. Frankfurt: Insel.
Korsgaard, Christine M. (1996): *The Sources of Normativity*. Cambridge: Cambridge University Press.
Koskenniemi, Martti (2001): *The Gentle Civilizer of Nations: The Rise and Fall of International Law, 1870–1960*. Cambridge: Cambridge University Press.
Krulic, Brigitte (2002): *Nietzsche, penseur de la hiérarchie: Pour une lecture "tocquevillienne" de Nietzsche*. Paris: L'Harmattan.
Langewiesche, Dieter (1988): *Liberalismus in Deutschland*. Frankfurt: Suhrkamp.
Leiter, Brian (2000): "Nietzsche's Metaethics: Against the Privilege Readings". In: *European Journal of Philosophy* 8, pp. 277–297.
Leiter, Brian (2002): *Nietzsche on Morality*. London: Routledge.
Leiter, Brian/Sinhababu, Neil (eds.) (2007): *Nietzsche and Morality*. Oxford: Clarendon Press.
Lemm, Vanessa (2009): *Nietzsche's Animal Philosophy: Culture, Politics, and the Animality of the Human Being*. New York: Fordham University Press.
Machiavelli, Niccolò (1988): *The Prince*. Quentin Skinner (ed.). Cambridge: Cambridge University Press.
Machiavelli, Niccolò (2003): *The Discourses*. Bernard Crick (ed.), Leslie J. Walker, Brian Richardson (trans.). London: Penguin.
Marti, Urs (1993): *"Der grosse Pöbel- und Sklavenaufstand": Nietzsches Auseinandersetzung mit Revolution und Demokratie*. Stuttgart: J. B. Metzler.
May, Simon (1999): *Nietzsche's Ethics and His "War on Morality"*. Oxford: Clarendon Press.
Mommsen, Wolfgang J. (1995): *Imperial Germany, 1867–1918: Politics, Culture, and Society in an Authoritarian State*. Richard Deveson (trans.). London: Arnold.
Morgenthau, Hans J. (1978): *Politics Among Nations: The Struggle for Power and Peace*. 5th corrected edition. New York: Knopf.
Morton, Adam (2004): *On Evil*. London: Routledge.
Mouffe, Chantal (2005): *On the Political*. London: Routledge.
Nietzsche, Friedrich (1994): *On the Genealogy of Morality*. Keith Ansell-Pearson (ed.), Carol Diethe (trans.). Cambridge: Cambridge University Press.
Nietzsche, Friedrich (1994): "The Greek State". In: Friedrich Nietzsche: *On the Genealogy of Morality*. Keith Ansell-Pearson (ed.), Carol Diethe (trans.). Cambridge: Cambridge University Press, pp. 176–816.
Nietzsche, Friedrich (1996): *Human, All Too Human*. R. J. Hollingdale (trans.), Richard Schacht (intro.). Cambridge: Cambridge University Press.
Nietzsche, Friedrich (1997): *Daybreak: Thoughts on the Prejudices of Morality*. Maudemarie Clark and Brian Leiter (eds.), R. J. Hollingdale (trans.). Cambridge: Cambridge University Press.
Nietzsche, Friedrich (2001): *The Gay Science*. Bernard Williams (ed), Josefine Nauckhoff (trans.). Cambridge: Cambridge University Press.
Nietzsche, Friedrich (2002): *Beyond Good and Evil*. Rolf-Peter Horstmann and Judith Norman (eds.), Judith Norman (trans.). Cambridge: Cambridge University Press.
Nietzsche, Friedrich (2005): *The Anti-Christ*. In: Friedrich Nietzsche: *The Anti-Christ, Ecce Homo, Twilight of the Idols, and Other Writings*. Aaron Ridley and Judith Norman (eds.), Norman (trans.). Cambridge: Cambridge University Press, pp. 1–68.
Nietzsche, Friedrich (2005): *Ecce Homo: How to Become What You Are*. In: Friedrich Nietzsche: *The Anti-Christ, Ecce Homo, Twilight of the Idols, and Other Writings*. Aaron Ridley and Judith Norman (eds.), Norman (trans.). Cambridge: Cambridge University Press, pp. 69–151.

Nietzsche, Friedrich (2005): *Thus Spoke Zarathustra: A Book for Everyone and Nobody*. Graham Parkes (ed./trans.). Oxford: Oxford University Press.
Nipperdey, Thomas (1983): *Deutsche Geschichte, 1800–1866: Bürgerwelt und starker Staat*. Munich: C. H. Beck.
Nussbaum, Martha (1997): "Is Nietzsche a Political Thinker?". In: *International Journal of Philosophical Studies* 5, pp. 1–13.
Ottmann, Henning (1987): *Philosophie und Politik bei Nietzsche*. Berlin, New York: de Gruyter.
Owen, David (1995): *Nietzsche, Politics and Modernity: A Critique of Liberal Reason*. London: Sage.
Palmowski, Jan (1999): *Urban Liberalism in Imperial Germany: Frankfurt am Main, 1866–1914*. Oxford: Oxford University Press.
Petersen, Ulrik Enemark (1999): "Breathing Nietzsche's Air: New Reflections on Morgenthau's Concepts of Power and Human Nature". In: *Alternatives* 24, pp. 83–113.
Pippin, Robert B. (2010): *Nietzsche, Psychology, and First Philosophy*. Chicago: University of Chicago Press.
Poellner, Peter (2012): "Aestheticist Ethics". In: Christopher Janaway/Simon Robertson (eds.): *Nietzsche, Naturalism, and Normativity*. Oxford: Oxford University Press, pp. 52–80.
Pufendorf, Samuel (1991). *On the Duty of Man and Citizen*. James Tully (ed.), Michael Silverthorne (trans.). Cambridge: Cambridge University Press.
Quine, Willard Van Orman (1961): "Two Dogmas of Empiricism". In: W.V.O. Quine: *From a Logical Point of View: Nine Logico-Philosophical Essays*. 2nd revised edition. Cambridge, Mass.: Harvard University Press, pp. 20–46.
Quine, Willard Van Orman (1969): "Epistemology Naturalized". In: W.V.O. Quine: *Ontological Relativity and Other Essays*. New York: Columbia University Press, pp. 69–90.
Railton, Peter (2012): "Nietzsche's Normative Theory? The Art and Skill of Living Well". In: Christopher Janaway/Simon Robertson (eds.): *Nietzsche, Naturalism, and Normativity*. Oxford: Oxford University Press, pp. 20–51.
Reginster, Bernard (2006): *The Affirmation of Life: Nietzsche on Overcoming Nihilism*. Cambridge, Mass.: Harvard University Press.
Richardson, John (2004): *Nietzsche's New Darwinism*. Oxford: Oxford University Press.
Richardson, John (2009): "Nietzsche's Freedoms". In: Ken Gemes/Simon May (eds.): *Nietzsche on Freedom and Autonomy*. Oxford: Oxford University Press, pp. 127–149.
Rosenkranz, Karl (1870): *Hegel als deutscher Nationalphilosoph*. Berlin: Duncker & Humblot.
Rouse, Joseph (2002): *How Scientific Practices Matter: Reclaiming Philosophical Naturalism*. Chicago: University of Chicago Press.
Rouse, Joseph (2007): "Social Practices and Normativity". In: *Philosophy of the Social Sciences* 37, pp. 46–56.
Ruehl, Martin A. (2004): "Politeia 1871: Young Nietzsche and the Greek State". In: Paul Bishop (ed.): *Nietzsche and Antiquity: His Reaction and Response to the Classical Tradition*. Rochester, NY: Camden House.
Runciman, David (2008): *Political Hypocrisy: The Mask of Power from Hobbes to Orwell*. Princeton, NJ: Princeton University Press.
Schacht, Richard (1983): *Nietzsche*. London: Routledge & Kegan Paul.
Scheuermann, William E. (2011): *The Realist Case for Global Reform*. Cambridge: Polity Press.
Schmitt, Carl (2005): *Political Theology: Four Chapters on the Concept of Sovereignty*. George Schwab (trans.), Tracy B. Strong (Foreword). Chicago: University of Chicago Press.

Schuett, Robert (2007): "Freudian Roots of Political Realism: The Importance of Sigmund Freud to Hans J. Morgenthau's Theory of International Power Politics". In: *History of the Human Sciences* 20(4), pp. 53–78.

Schulte, Michael (1992): *Die "Tragödie im Sittlichen": Zur Dramentheorie Hegels*. Munich: Wilhelm Fink.

Schutte, Ofelia (1985): *Beyond Nihilism: Nietzsche Without Masks*. Chicago: University of Chicago Press.

Shaw, Tamsin (2007): *Nietzsche's Political Skepticism*. Princeton, NJ: Princeton University Press.

Sheehan, James J. (1978): *German Liberalism in the Nineteenth Century*. Chicago: University of Chicago Press.

Siemens, Herman/Roodt, Vasti (eds.) (2009): *Nietzsche, Power and Politics: Rethinking Nietzsche's Legacy for Political Thought*. Berlin, New York: de Gruyter.

Thiele, Leslie Paul (1990): *Friedrich Nietzsche and the Politics of the Soul: A Sudy of Heroic Individualism*. Princeton, NJ: Princeton University Press.

Toews, John Edward (1980): *Hegelianism: The Path Toward Dialectical Humanism, 1805–1841*. Cambridge: Cambridge University Press.

Tönnies, Ferdinand (2001): *Community and Civil Society*. Jose Harris (ed.), Jose Harris, Margaret Hollis (trans.). Cambridge: Cambridge University Press.

Vaihinger, Hans (1924): *The Philosophy of "As If": A System of Theoretical, Practical and Religious Fictions of Mankind*. C. K. Ogden (trans.). London: Kegan Paul, Trench, Trubner & Co.

Viroli, Maurizio (1992): *From Politics to Reason of State: The Acquisition and Transformation of the Langiage of Politics, 1250–1600*. Cambridge: Cambridge University Press.

Warren, Mark (1988): *Nietzsche and Political Thought*. Cambridge, Mass.: MIT Press.

Warren, Mark (ed.) (1999): *Democracy and Trust*. Cambridge: Cambridge University Press.

Weber, Max (1978): *Economy and Society: An Outline of Interpretive Sociology*. Guenther Roth/Claus Wittich (eds.). Berkeley, CA: University of California Press.

Weber, Max (1994a): "The Nation State and Economic Policy". In: *Max Weber: Political Writings*. Peter Lassmann, Ronald Speirs (eds.). Cambridge: Cambridge University Press, pp. 1–28.

Weber, Max (1994b): "Parliament and Government in Germany under a New Political Order: Towards a Political Critique of Officialdom and the Party System". In: *Max Weber: Political Writings*. Peter Lassmann, Ronald Speirs (eds.). Cambridge: Cambridge University Press, pp. 130–271.

Weber, Max (1994c): "The Profession and Vocation of Politics". In: *Max Weber: Political Writings*. Peter Lassmann, Ronald Speirs (eds.). Cambridge: Cambridge University Press, pp. 309–369.

Wilcox, John T. (1974): *Truth and Value in Nietzsche: A Study of His Metaethics and Epistemology*. Ann Arbor, Mich.: University of Michigan Press.

Williams, Bernard (1993): "Nietzsche's Minimalist Moral Psychology". In: *European Journal of Philosophy* 1, pp. 4–14.

Williamson, George S. (2004): *The Longing for Myth in Germany: Religion and Aesthetic Culture from Romanticism to Nietzsche*. Chicago: University of Chicago Press.

Wolin, Richard (2004): *The Seduction of Unreason: The Intellectual Romance with Fascism from Nietzsche to Postmodernism*. Princeton, N.J.: Princeton University Press.

Tamsin Shaw
The "Last Man" Problem: Nietzsche and Weber on Political Attitudes to Suffering

Introduction

Modern European ways of thinking about political authority and legitimacy have evolved over hundreds of years, largely in the context of different religious, predominantly Christian, world views. It is only relatively recently that the question of how they might need to be adapted in largely secular societies has arisen. One set of relevant questions will be entirely theoretical, concerning the adaptations that will have to be made to normative notions such as legitimacy, if they are to be reconceived on the basis of entirely secular assumptions. Another set of questions must have more sociological content: which forms of political authority are likely to be accepted as legitimate in secular societies, and which are likely to be ruled out as requiring some religious justification? No thinker has paid greater attention to this constellation of problems than Max Weber. With regard to the latter, especially, he provides us with an incomparably rich analysis of the potential effects of secularization.

One striking and unique feature of this analysis is its focus on the problem of how human beings deal with suffering. For Weber, this question is deeply relevant to the justification of political power, since that power is necessarily coercive and its means are those of force or violence. The problem of political legitimacy is that of justifying violence, or the infliction of non-voluntary suffering. Such justifications of course take place in an overall context of justification and for two millennia this context has incorporated theodicies, which have made overall sense of both voluntary and non-voluntary suffering for human beings. Weber therefore sets out to examine the potential effects of doing without any such theodicy. His conclusions, I shall claim in this paper, are pessimistic ones for secular political thought, and I want consider whether they are unduly pessimistic.

I shall argue that underlying Weber's view of secularism is a deeply Nietzschean set of assumptions concerning our attitudes to suffering and, in particular, our need for suffering to have meaning.[1] In Weber's evocative conclusion

---

[1] Helpful general discussions of Nietzsche's influence on Weber may be found in Eden 1983, Hennis 1998, Fleischmann 1964, pp. 190–237, and Hartung 1994, pp. 302–318. Many interesting insights into the relationship between these thinkers may also be found in Mitzman 1969 and

to *The Protestant Ethic and the Spirit of Capitalism*, he laments a process of secularization that dissolves a spiritually meaningful form of worldly asceticism into "pure utilitarianism" (PE, p. 125; GARS I, p. 205). He claims that this cultural development culminates in the arrogance of those "last men" (*letzte Menschen*) who imagine themselves to be the apex of civilization, whilst being merely "specialists without spirit, sensualists without heart" (PE, p. 125; GARS I, p. 204). In his final published lecture on *Science as a Vocation*, he again recalls Nietzsche's "devastating criticism of those 'last men'" who 'invented happiness'" (FMW, p. 143; GAW, p. 598). The problem to which he is referring with these references to the "last man" is a complex and interesting one.

The image derives from Nietzsche's *Thus Spoke Zarathustra*. Here Nietzsche describes a being who seeks only a comfortable life, entertainment, distraction, and an agreeable enough death. He writes:

> The earth has become small, and on it hops the last man, who makes everything small. His race is as ineradicable as the flea-beetle; the last man lives longest.
> 'We have invented happiness,' say the last men, and they blink. They have left the regions where it was hard to live, for one needs warmth. One still loves one's neighbor and rubs against him, for one needs warmth.
> Becoming sick and harboring suspicion are sinful to them: one proceeds carefully. A fool, whoever still stumbles over stones or human beings! A little poison now and then: that makes for agreeable dreams. And much poison in the end, for an agreeable death.
> One still works, for work is a form of entertainment. But one is careful lest the entertainment be too harrowing. One no longer becomes poor or rich: both require too much exertion. Who still wants to rule? Who obey? Both require too much exertion.
> No shepherd and one herd! Everybody wants the same, everybody is the same: whoever feels differently goes into a madhouse.
> 'Formerly all the world was mad', say the most refined, and they blink.
> One is clever and knows everything that has ever happened: so there is no end of derision.
> One still quarrels, but one is soon reconciled — else it might spoil the digestion.
> One has one's little pleasure for the day and one's little pleasure for the night: but one has a regard for health.
> 'We have invented happiness,' say the last men, and they blink. (Z I Prologue 5)[2]

In other words, the last man views suffering always as something that should simply be eradicated, never as something meaningful. This exclusive hedonism, on Nietzsche's view, generates a form of human life that is contemptible. Many subsequent thinkers have found in this image a gripping and apparently

---

Scaff 1989. Articles on more specific aspects of Nietzsche's influence on Weber are discussed in footnotes below.

[2] In each Nietzsche citation I have adopted the translation cited, with some modifications, based on the KGW.

simple illustration of what is wrong with secular cultures, or, more recently, with the secularism of liberal democratic politics (cf. e.g. Strauss 1989 and Fukuyama 1992, pp. 303–312). But an examination of the rhetorical force of the image reveals that the underlying assumptions are in fact complex.

The rhetorical force is supposed to derive from the fact that we recognize in ourselves the "last man" and yet at the same time find such a being contemptible. This evaluation presupposes what we might call an ideal of the dignity of humanity, according to which humans should pursue ends other than the merely animalistic ones of maximizing pleasure and minimizing pain. We will refer to this as the anti-hedonistic ideal. But at the same time the image of the "last man" draws our attention to the fact that, insofar as we recognize ourselves in this being, we are subject to a failure of commitment to non-hedonistic values. We seem unable to reconcile ourselves to simple hedonism or to live up to the anti-hedonistic ideal.

So the threat to the dignity of humanity derives, for Nietzsche, from our unwillingness to suffer or to make others suffer for the sake of great human goals, even as we acknowledge such goals to be what makes the spectacle of human life on this planet something worthwhile and valuable. This is in part, for Nietzsche, a political problem, since secular political ideals, be they liberal, democratic or socialist, seem to him to be exclusively hedonistic; they encourage us to view suffering, he claims, as something that is simply to be abolished (BGE 44).

Subsequent critics of secularism have followed Nietzsche in associating cultural concerns, about secularization with a critique of liberal and democratic political ideas.[3] But it is still only Max Weber who has engaged in the kind of detailed analysis of religion that would yield a precise account of what secularism is supposed to deprive us of, how this deprivation occurs, or how we should understand its potential political effects.

The "last man" problem raises an immediate question about how we could have arrived at such a predicament. In his writings on the sociology of religion, Weber offers us a uniquely detailed explanation of how this could have come about. The anti-hedonistic ideal may be seen to arise from the need for an overall meaning or purpose for human suffering, or what I shall call the *theodicy-demand*. He sees this demand as an ineliminable feature of human psychology, even under secular conditions. So under such conditions we are presented with the theodicy-demand minus a theodicy. We then find ourselves simultaneously committed to an anti-hedonistic ideal and unable to sustain our com-

---

[3] Cf. e.g. Schmitt 1996, Morgenthau 1946 and 1974, Strauss 1995 and Fukuyama 1992).

mitment to non-hedonistic values (cf. e.g. Schmitt 1996, Morgenthau 1946 and 1974, Strauss 1995 and Fukuyama 1992).

The "last man" problem, then, does not simply betray an anti-egalitarian fear of social leveling that is peripheral to Weber's core concerns.[4] It in fact unites what have been identified as two of the two central issues in Weber's work. Wilhelm Hennis (1988a, 1988b) has argued that the question of the type of human being fostered by a given form of society is Weber's "central concern." Friedrich Tenbruck (1980, pp. 316–351), on the other hand, has identified the central theme in his work as the fundamental role of theodicies in impelling rationalization. Properly understood, the "last man" problem allows us to see the essential unity of these two themes. It brings together the issues that are of most importance to Weber.

I shall claim that Weber, following Nietzsche, hopes to resolve the dilemma that the "last man" problem presents to us in the direction of the anti-hedonistic ideal, rather than a capitulation to hedonism. This position is expressed in his early, explicit anti-eudaimonism but it persists in the later writings in a more sophisticated form.[5] Not only does Weber come to see the theodicy-demand as basic to human cultures, he also comes to hold the view that the maintenance of stable forms of political authority demands that it be met.

Modern states, Weber insists, must have rulers. Power cannot be distributed equally within them. Some people will have to obey others. This means that rulers must be accepted as legitimate by those over whom they rule. In order for this to be the case, people must accept that there are ends that can be legitimately coerced. And the problem of legitimate coercion or violence, Weber sees, is precisely the problem of what meaning suffering (and in particular non-voluntary suffering) has for us.[6] He views an encroaching hedonism as a

---

4 Regina Titunik (1997, pp. 680–80) repudiates the view that Weber fears a "future of equalized and diminished 'last men,'" but she views the "last man" image as an expression of a fear of the social leveling promoted by democratization.

5 The values of the "last man" have been described by Nietzsche and his followers as being either eudaimonistic, utilitarian, or hedonistic. I will refer to the basic idea of minimizing suffering as "hedonistic" and will take eudaimonism and utilitarianism to be more complex views which might incorporate hedonism. For both Nietzsche and Weber, I shall claim, the fundamental issue is the hedonistic aspect of those larger views.

6 Others who have the problem of meaningful existence as one of Weber's central concerns have taken his views on political legitimacy to be relatively detached from this concern (cf. e.g. Shafir 1985, pp. 516–530). Shafir follows Jeffrey Alexander (1983, pp. 77–83) in claiming that Weber, in his explicitly political studies, views obedience to political authorities "as a matter of formal obligation, entirely uninspired by the problem of meaning." However, as we shall see, in one of the key texts where Weber outlines his typology of legitimacy, his *Politics as a Vocation* address, his argument culminates in a discussion of the central importance of

threat to political legitimacy. It shrinks the sphere of possible ends for which coercion will seem justified.

So Weber sees secularism as generating a general cultural problem: that of a psychologically ineliminable theodicy-demand minus a theodicy. But he also identifies a specifically political component to this problem: that of a politically ineliminable legitimacy-demand minus political ends that can be accepted as legitimate. His later espousal of charismatic leadership is intended, I shall claim, to fill the gap left by religion in these two areas and it does so in a way that mimics quite precisely the kind of religious solution to the theodicy-demand that he views as most successful.

If we do not wish to accept Weber's political recommendations, and they have been widely derided, an exposition of the way in which they are motivated by his Nietzschean critique of secularism will allow us to assess where we might want to depart from this critique. I shall argue, in particular, that his claims about the theodicy-demand, or the problem of the meaning of suffering, are controversial, even as extrapolations from his own sociology of religion. They impel him to entertain a range of political attitudes to suffering that might otherwise be narrowed in a more humane direction.

Making Sense of Suffering

I shall claim that Weber's affinity with Nietzsche so far as the "last man" problem is concerned arises from his adopting a key Nietzschean claim concerning our psychological need for an overall justification of human suffering. They both adopt what I shall call a holistic view of justifying suffering. It is a psychological, rather than a normative claim, and it concerns the amount of justification that will satisfy us sufficiently to support motivations of certain kinds, more specifically, our motivation to act in accordance with non-hedonistic values.

On Nietzsche's view, the main problem confronting human beings is not that we suffer, but rather that most of our suffering is meaningless. He claims that "what actually arouses indignation over suffering is not the suffering itself, but the senselessness of suffering" (GM II 7).[7] Unlike pleasure, Nietzsche

---

the theodicy problem to the way in which "legitimate violence" is justified. And his emphasis on the religious origins of political values also indicates the interrelatedness of these issues in his thought.

7 Cf. also TI Arrows 12: "If you have your 'why?' in life, you can get along with almost any 'how?' People don't strive for happiness, only the English do."

insists, suffering always provokes the question "why?" Whereas the pursuit of pleasure might be an end in itself, requiring no further justifications, enduring suffering ordinarily requires some further justification.

When human beings act in the world they will bring upon themselves many forms of frustration and pain, small and great. On Nietzsche's view, action that entails suffering gives rise to a demand for justifications. We will inevitably ask "suffering for what?" and the kind of answer we are looking for will posit an end that seems sufficiently to justify our suffering (GM III 28). If that justifying end is a hedonistic one, that is, if we expect some hedonic compensation, a relatively simple calculation will tell us how much suffering we ought to endure. If we are pursuing some non-hedonistic value, there may be no fixed amount of suffering that human beings will universally find acceptable as the cost of achieving it, but within any human culture we will be operating with some set of norms for how much suffering is justified for what ends. However, our motivation to pursue non-hedonistic ends is, on Nietzsche's view, a fragile affair and one that is vulnerable to a particular form of debilitating skepticism or despair.

This despair arises from awareness of the following set of facts about the world. Following Schopenhauer, Nietzsche holds, first, that whatever we do to try to diminish it, suffering will always outweigh pleasure for any of earth's creatures, including us. Second, most of our suffering will not seem justified in relation to any purposes that are realizable by human beings. Schopenhauer himself says: "If suffering is not the first and immediate object of our life, then our existence is the most inexpedient and inappropriate thing in the world (Schopenhauer 2001, vol. I, ch. XII)." Disease and mortality are ineliminable features of any creature's life. Unlike the other animals, we inevitably suffer psychologically as well as physically, owing to our reflective awareness of mortality. And if our sense of loss at the thought of our own death seems mitigated by our attachment to others, we need only remember that everyone we love is going to die too.[8] Besides these natural and ineliminable features of the human condition, we impose all sorts of gratuitous suffering on one another as a result of either base cruelty or stupidity. Ultimately, most of the suffering that we

---

[8] Joshua Foa Dienstag 2006 emphasizes the central role that these pessimistic insights of Schopenhauer's play. David Owen, like Dienstag, stresses Nietzsche's awareness of the ineliminability of "intensional" forms of suffering, that is, those that depend of self-consciousness, such as knowledge of our dependence on chance and of our own mortality (cf. Owen 2000, pp. 258f.). As we shall see, both Nietzsche and Weber certainly share a preoccupation with these psychological forms of suffering, but the overall range of varieties of suffering with which they are concerned is very broad.

experience will have to seem unjustified, at least if we are limited to all available natural explanations or narratives.

On Nietzsche's view, this raises a problem for non-hedonistic human motivations. The insight into the inevitability of meaningless suffering, he insists, paralyses the will. In *The Birth of Tragedy*, he sees this view of human life as a distinctively Dionysian one and says of it:

> Dionysian man is similar to Hamlet: both have gazed into the true essence of things, they have <u>acquired knowledge</u> and they find action repulsive, for their actions can do nothing to change the eternal essence of things; they regard it as laughable or shameful that they should be expected to set to rights a world so out of joint' (BT 7).

And Nietzsche continues to insist, throughout his work, that knowledge of the truth about the human condition presents a motivational danger to us. Restating the central message of *The Birth of Tragedy* in *The Gay Science*, he writes: "<u>Honesty</u> would lead to nausea and suicide. But now there is a counterforce against our honesty that helps us to avoid such consequences: art as the <u>good</u> will to appearance. [...] As an aesthetic phenomenon existence is still <u>bearable</u> for us" (GS 107). Our motivation to act can only be sustained by delusion.

What Nietzsche seems to suggest is that acknowledgement of the truth will lead to a sense of ultimate futility that is motivationally debilitating. This is not the more familiar anxiety about futility that is generated by the question "What is the point of it all?"; i.e. the worry that we have no reason to act unless some end is intrinsically motivating, but in fact no human ends are; we would need some authoritative end given by God to get the whole process of justification off the ground. Nietzsche seems to have no problem with merely human ends being intrinsically motivating. His concern derives instead from the more specific Schopenhauerean problem with suffering. I think we can reconstruct it in the following way.

When we act in accordance with our values, we are adopting a picture of the way the world should be and aiming to shape the world to fit this picture. And in doing so, since predicted pain and pleasure have to be factored into our practical reasoning, we are necessarily operating with a sense of how much suffering is justified by what ends. Once our sense of these norms for justified suffering is engaged, we are bound to acknowledge that we are suffering too much, that no ends we are likely to achieve can possibly justify the misery that most people experience in the course of a human life. And this thought is a paralyzing one so far as our practical calculations are concerned.

Nietzsche's concern about the meaning of suffering, then, seems to presuppose a holistic view of the way in which suffering can be made to seem justified. Insofar as we must engage in action in the world, and this action is liable to entail suffering and sacrifice of various sorts, an overall theodicy has to be the necessary psychological anchor for all our motivations. I shall refer to this holistic requirement as the theodicy-demand. The most important role of religion in human life has been its fulfillment. The ascetic ideal espoused in the Judaeo-Christian tradition has, for reasons that we shall explore, played this role most successfully:

> Except for the ascetic ideal: man, the animal man, had no meaning up to now. His 'existence' on earth had no purpose; 'What is man for, actually?' — was a question without an answer; there was no will for man and earth; behind every great human destiny sounded the even louder refrain 'in vain!' This is what the ascetic ideal meant: something was missing, there was an immense lacuna around man, — he himself could think of no justification or explanation or affirmation, he suffered from the problem of what he meant. Other things made him suffer too, in the main he was a sickly animal: but suffering itself was not his problem, but the fact that there was no answer to the question he screamed, 'Suffering for what?' Man, the bravest animal and most prone to suffer, does not deny suffering as such: he wills it, he even seeks it out, provided he is shown a meaning for it, a purpose of suffering. The meaninglessness of suffering, not the suffering, was the curse which has so far blanketed mankind [...] (GM III 28)

The theodicy-demand is presented as a fundamental feature of human psychology and much of Nietzsche's work addresses the question of how this basic psychological need can be met once the religious solutions that we have evolved have been discredited.

Weber seems to share with Nietzsche these two important premises: first, the claim that suffering inevitably outweighs pleasure in human life; and second, the distinctively Nietzschean holistic view of justifications for suffering. And it is on the basis of these two premises that he sees the theodicy-demand as a persistent feature of human psychology. The first can be found throughout his work, going as far back as his inaugural lecture of 1895. Here he criticizes the "vulgar conception of political economy" which "consists in devising recipes for universal happiness," and sees its justification as that of "adding to the 'balance of pleasure' [*Lustbilanz*] in human existence." He insists that "[a]s far as the dream of peace and human happiness is concerned, the words written over the portal into the unknown future of human history are: '*lasciate ogni speranza*' [abandon all hope...]" (PW, pp. 14f.; GPS, p. 12).

In Weber's later work, most famously in the *Politics as a Vocation* lecture, he stresses the extent to which meaningless suffering is the inevitable outcome of even the most carefully planned purposive action. The problem of unintended consequences constantly mocks the pretensions of instrumental reason. The perpetual possibility of unpredictable bad effects in any human action, but particularly the large-scale, collective forms of action in which politics engages us, make rational calculations about the justifications of means by ends impossible (PW, p. 360; GPS, p. 552). Weber calls this the "ethical irrationality of the world" (PW, pp. 361f.; GPS, p. 533). Not only do we experience unjustified suffering as a result of our natural condition in the world, the very pursuit of the ends that we feel would justify our suffering generates a further, meaningless excess of it.

Like Nietzsche, Weber holds that meaningless suffering is psychologically unacceptable to us, and that the demand for a justification of particular instances of suffering that we experience will inevitably generate a demand for justification *tout court*. In *The Economic Ethic of the World Religions* he discusses the variety of beliefs that have evolved in response to this problem, saying: "Behind them always lies a stand towards something in the actual world which is experienced as specifically 'senseless' [*sinnlos*]. Thus, the demand has been implied: that the world order in its totality is, could, and should somehow be a meaningful 'cosmos'" (FMW, p. 281; GARS I, p. 253). Religious rationalization has resulted, he tells us, from this "metaphysical need for a meaningful cosmos" (FMW, p. 281; GARS I, p.253). This essay, intended as an introduction to Weber's series of detailed studies of world religions (written in 1913), is, as Friedrich Tenbruck has pointed out, the place where Weber first clearly articulates his general claims about the way in which practical reasoning evokes the theodicy-demand.[9] He then reiterates the view in the *Zwischenbetrachtung* essay of 1915, known in English as *Religious Rejections of the World and their Directions*.[10] On the basis of his researches into the development of religious beliefs, he concludes that their role is not primarily explanatory but rather

---

9 Cf. Tenbruck 1980, p. 337, where he summarizes the position of the essay thus: "[H]uman action is not sufficiently successful. In the encounter with the world there occur surplus experiences that demand elucidation. These experiences originate from the experience of suffering that derive directly from deprivation or social injustice. The original solution to this was the search for charisma [...] – that is, a magic-based superiority over the insecurities of a world full of suffering."
Also Tenbruck 1980, p. 337f.: "For Weber, the purposive-rational orientation encloses a perpetual need, a search for charisma that lies beyond the everyday; charisma promises an immediate deliverance from the uncertainty of action, and the desire that action should result in success goes hand in hand with the reality of the uncertainty of action."
He continues: "every charismatic explanation reaches out beyond itself so long as a unified and comprehensive elucidation of the lack of meaning in the world has not been attained, as is sought by articulated theodicies." (Tenbruck 1980, p. 338)
10 Cf. FMW, p. 353; GARS I, p. 567: "all religions have demanded as a specific presupposition that the course of the world be somehow *meaningful* [*sinnvoll*], at least in so far as it touches on the interests of men. As we have seen, this claim naturally emerged first as the problem of unjust suffering..."

justificatory. As such, they are responses to a need that is an ineradicable feature of human psychology.[11]

Weber does not state quite as boldly as Nietzsche that the meaning of suffering, rather than suffering itself, is the problem for us. Unlike Nietzsche, in examining the ways in which religions have responded to the problem of suffering, he stresses the extent to which a hedonistic desire for the cessation of suffering, or for some future hedonic compensation, has found expression in them. At the same time he insists that this compensation-demand is characteristically a demand of the "mass" and not of the intellectual strata from whom prophets have emerged and hence whose ideas have been the primary forces in shaping religious doctrines.[12] It is also a demand which, since it cannot be fulfilled in this world, can only exacerbate the need for a theodicy. Weber tells us in the *Religious Rejections* essay that,

> In so far as appearances show, the actual course of the world has been little concerned with this postulate of compensation. The ethically unmotivated inequality in the distribution of happiness and misery, for which a compensation has seemed conceivable, has remained irrational; and so has the brute fact that suffering exists (FMW, p. 354; cf. GARS I, p. 567).

We should not infer from Weber's claims about the hedonic compensation-demands of the mass that the non-hedonistic theodicy-demand is restricted to the class of intellectuals. He does hold that intellectuals are the ones who have generally supplied the narratives which attempt to satisfy it. But for Weber, as for Nietzsche, reflection on our justifications for action tends, for anyone, to raise the problem of whether any ends can justify suffering overall. In the religion section of *Economy and Society*, he makes clear that the working classes, too, insist on a satisfactory solution to the theodicy problem and that their increasing disbelief in religion stems from their awareness that it has in fact offered no stable solution. He writes:

> a recent questionnaire submitted to thousands of German workers disclosed the fact that their rejection of the god-idea was motivated, not by scientific arguments, but by their difficulty in reconciling the idea of providence with the injustice and imperfection of the social order (ES I, p. 519; cf. WG, p. 315).

We might suspect that underlying both Nietzsche and Weber's attribution to humans of this universal psychological tendency, or "metaphysical need",

---

[11] Cf. FMW, p. 275; GARS I, p. 246, on the "metaphysical conception of God and the world, which the ineradicable demand [*das unausrottbare Bedürfnis*] for a theodicy called forth."

[12] Also, ES, pp. 490ff.; GW, p. 299. On this distinction between the typical demands of different social classes, cf. Shafir 1985.

there is really a normative claim about our justifications for suffering. The theodicy-demand would then be seen as one that any rational person ought to raise. As we shall see though, neither is committed to such a normative claim and in fact both of them offer suggestions as to how our world-view might be rationally reoriented in order to dispense with the psychological need. But neither of them fully follows through on the strain in their work that would permit such a resolution.

Instead, they both remain convinced that the theodicy-demand will persist in secular cultures and therefore continue to be preoccupied with the question of how the theodicy-demand can be met. Religions have developed various non-rational means of addressing the theodicy-demand. When Weber imports conceptions (such as "charisma" and "vocation") from his sociology of religion to fill the gaps that he perceives in secular political thought, he is presupposing a specific, Nietzschean picture of these non-rational means and how they might be adapted.

Addressing the theodicy-demand

On the interpretation of the theodicy-demand that I have set out, meeting it requires an overall interpretation of the meaning of suffering. This does not mean that the particular justification for every instance of suffering has to be transparent to us, only that we can have faith that there is some justification. On Weber's view, there can be no a priori answer to the question of what will count as a satisfactory overall justification for us. But human cultures do exhibit common tendencies, which he describes in a schematic fashion in his later writings on the sociology of religion, particularly the sections on religion published in *Economy and Society* (written 1911–1913), the introductory essay on *The Economic Ethic of the World Religions* (written in 1913), the *Zwischenbetrachtung* essay, (1915), and the two lectures, *Politics as a Vocation, and Science as a Vocation* (delivered in 1918). I shall claim that we can still detect Nietzsche's influence in these writings, where Weber sets out the constraints that must govern any possible solutions.

Nietzsche's own studies of religions, and specifically of the various ways in which they have addressed the theodicy-demand, begin in *The Birth of Tragedy* (1871). Although Nietzsche's philosophical views on many topics undergo considerable development and change across his career, we find significant continuity in his later writings with the framework laid out here for understanding the problem of the meaning of suffering. In his famous dichotomy of the Dionysian and the Apolline, he lays out two ways in which the theodicy-demand can be met. The first is to achieve obliviousness to the demand, though this is not a strategy that can be incorporated into our practical lives. The second is to develop some narrative that might supply us with a satisfactory solution, one that can be integrated into our ordinary motivations to act.

The obliviousness strategy was, on Nietzsche's view, successfully adopted in the orgiastic cults of Dionysus and the art-forms to which they gave rise. In the Dionysian experience, the Greeks felt themselves to be "absorbed, elevated, and extinguished" (BT 7). They felt a sense of oneness with the rest of existence which gave them solace, for in such a state life is experienced not as a state of suffering but as something "indestructibly mighty and pleasurable" (BT 7). However, this kind of experience can only be available to humans as an extraordinary and transient state. It is not compatible with their functioning in the world. For that, what is required is not simply some way of halting the demand for justifications for suffering, but a narrative that satisfactorily meets this demand.

The role of Apolline art, Nietzsche claims, was precisely to facilitate action by providing some form of theodicy, that is, a satisfaction of our demand for justifications. Thus he interprets the image of the Sophoclean hero. The figure of the suffering Oedipus, on Nietzsche's interpretation, shows his audience that as a suffering being the hero achieves a state of passivity in which he becomes a vessel of the gods. He thereby exerts on the world "a magical, beneficent force which remains effective even after his death" (BT 9). Aeschylus's Prometheus, on the other hand, provides us with an example of suffering as a punishment from the gods, though one that must be endured by any human being who strives for noble ends (BT 9). On both of these views, suffering that is senseless from the point of view of merely human purposes may be seem justified in relation to supra-human purposes that we find authoritative.[13]

Although we can escape the grip of the theodicy-demand temporarily through the attainment of certain extraordinary psychological states, if we are to be able to act in the world, we will need suffering to make sense in relation to purposes. Most non-voluntary suffering cannot be justified by any human purpose, but it may still seem justified to us in the light of a purpose that is authoritative for us.[14] Religions have therefore addressed the theodicy-demand by justifying suffering in relation to supra-human purposes.

---

[13] Nietzsche tells us that Promethean virtue gives us an insight into "the ethical foundation of pessimistic tragedy, justification of the evil in human life, both in the sense of human guilt and in the sense of the suffering brought about by it." (BT 9)

[14] This distinction is made by Bernard Williams, who sees it as central to Nietzsche's approach to the problem of suffering (Williams (2006, p. 333).

The supra-human purposes of the Greek gods could serve as justifying ends, thereby ending the regress of justifications, because they had inherent authority by virtue of issuing from an authoritative source. The aesthetic perfection of the gods conferred on them such authority, for life viewed in this aesthetically perfected form seemed to be worth living.[15] In his *On the Genealogy of Morality*, Nietzsche describes the way in which the purposes of these gods justified human suffering. The Greeks, he says, imputed to these ideal beings the same delight in cruelty that they felt themselves.[16] So for the Greeks, although most human suffering had to seem futile from the point of view of any merely human purposes, the supra-human purposes of the gods who delighted in it could provide it with a meaning.

At the end of the *Genealogy*, however, Nietzsche claims that it is only the ascetic ideal, promoted by Christianity, which first succeeds fully in addressing the theodicy-demand. Up to now, he tells us, suffering had no meaning and man was "like a leaf in the breeze, the plaything of the absurd, of 'non-sense'", but on the basis of the interpretation permitted by the ascetic ideal "he could will something, no matter what, why, and how he did it at first, the will itself was saved" (GM III 28). So why should Nietzsche, having claimed that the Greeks had a theodicy of their own, nevertheless go on to state that it was the ascetic ideal that first saved the human will from the debilitating effects of meaningless suffering?

The underlying view seems to be that the polytheistic religious beliefs of the Greeks could not fully meet the theodicy-demand, as they could not supply the faith that suffering is, overall, normatively intelligible. They did meet the bare demand that non-voluntary suffering, which makes sense in relation to no human purposes, seem meaningful in relation to some authoritative purposes. They thereby conferred the sense of meaningfulness that is minimally required to prevent the debilitating consequences of perceived meaninglessness. But the pantheon of Greek gods did not otherwise support practical reasoning, since it could not provide a coherent set of purposes that might be continuous and consistent with human purposes in the world. In such a polytheistic universe, there are many gods with unpredictable wills and often clashing purposes, so there can be no overall normative coherence. Hence the fact that rationalism is taken by Nietzsche to be so profoundly antagonistic to such a culture.

---

15 Cf. BT 3: "gods justify the life of men by living it themselves – the only satisfactory theodicy! Under the bright sunshine of such gods existence is felt to be worth attaining."
16 GM II 7: The Greeks "could certainly think of offering their gods no more acceptable a side-dish to their happiness than the joys of cruelty."

The ascetic ideal, on the other hand, supplies the faith that all human suffering is, in principle normatively intelligible. Suffering is meaningful in relation to a single god's coherent and consistent will.[17] So even if this will cannot be fully comprehended by limited human intelligences, it still makes sense for us to aim, insofar as we do understand God's purposes, for rational integration of our own purposes with them. Any apparently antinomian suffering can be taken to reveal simply the limits of our understanding.

The *Genealogy*, described by Weber as Nietzsche's "brilliant essay," is an important touchstone for his own account of religious development (FMW, p. 270; GARS I, p. 241).[18] He defends Nietzsche's view that it is only a version of the ascetic ideal that has succeeded in meeting the theodicy-demand, by providing a solution that is satisfactory from the point of view of our practical reasoning. Like Nietzsche, Weber sees in the history of religion two distinct ways of addressing the theodicy-demand. One attempts to extinguish the demand, or render us oblivious to it; the other attempts to provide a solution. The first gives rise to mysticism. The second achieves its most refined form in an ascetic tradition. In Weber's analyses of these traditions, particularly of the latter, he extends and deepens Nietzsche's insights into the way in which fulfillment of the theodicy-demand has supported our commitment to non-hedonistic ends.

The obliviousness strategy must either be temporary or, if prolonged, will be incompatible with any purposeful functioning in the world. In his essay on *The Economic Ethic of the World Religions*, Weber tells us that primitive religious experience consists in the attainment of extraordinary psychological states that are sought as a temporary refuge from the ordinary human experiences of distress, hunger, sickness and suffering. The alcoholic intoxication of the Dionysian is one of the examples that he provides, along with totemic meat-orgies, cannibalistic feasts, and intoxication by hashish, opium, and nic-

---

17 Cf. GM III 23: "The ascetic ideal expresses one will. [...] The ascetic ideal has a goal, – which is so general, that all the interests of human existence appear petty and narrow when measured against it; it inexorably interprets epochs, peoples, man, all with reference to this one goal, it permits of no other interpretation, no other goal, and rejects, denies, affirms, confirms only with reference to its interpretation (- and was there ever a system of interpretation more fully thought through?); it does not subject itself to any power, in fact, it believes in its superiority over any power, in its unconditional superiority of rank over any other power, – it believes there is nothing on earth of any power which does not first have to receive a meaning, a right to existence, a value from it, as a tool to its work, as a way and means to its goal, to one goal ..."
18 The strong affinities between Nietzsche's *Genealogy* and Weber's essay on *The Economic Ethic of the World Religions* are discussed by Tracy Strong 1992, pp. 9–18.

otine (FMW, pp. 278ff.; GARS I, p. 249ff.). In striving to make this form of redemption permanent, intellectuals have made the "inexpressible contents" of such experiences the focus of more sustained contemplation (FMW, p. 282; GARS I, p. 254). They have attempted to live in such a way that their entire lives are pervaded by mystic experience. But the religious mystic's attempt to sustain this sense of charismatic illumination requires withdrawal from the world and is only available as a way of life to those who can live off the labor of others (ES, p. 547; WG, p. 331). For those in a position to live such a life, reasoning may be stilled by the force of non-rational psychological experiences. But this requires removing oneself from the realm of action that provokes the demand for justifications.[19]

The strategy of devising a solution, on the other hand, through the articulation of a theodicy, has generated attempts to integrate entirely our purposes in the world with the theodicy narrative in which justifications come to a satisfactory end. Weber in fact sees this aspiration to rational integration as the primary motor of rationalization in the West (cf. Tenbruck 1980). The demands that it makes, however, are complex, and stable solutions have seldom been found.

The theodicy-demand is raised, because our norms for how much suffering is justified by what ends reveal an inevitable surplus of suffering, so far as merely human purposes are concerned. This surplus might be rendered meaningful in relation to supra-human purposes, if those are taken to be justifying ends for us. This raises the demand for normative coherence: we will want our own ends in the world and these ultimately authoritative, justifying ends to be consistent and continuous with one another. Ethical religions of salvation have aimed for such consistency and continuity. But it is no easy task to generate a seamless web of justifications.

Weber sees that the fundamental problem facing such an aspiration is the ubiquitous "incongruity between destiny and merit [*der Inkongruenz zwischen Schicksal und Verdienst*]" (FMW, p. 275; GARS I, pp. 246f.). Practical rationality requires that we ask not simply "Why suffering?" but also "Why me?" If suffering is to be explained, for example, by reference to the purposes of an ethical

---

[19] Both Nietzsche's and Weber's understandings of the obliviousness strategy as manifested, respectively, in the Dionysian and mystical worldviews, are indebted to Schopenhauer. Nietzsche's conception of the Dionysian, in The Birth of Tragedy, is directly derived from Schopenhauer's conception of the Will and of music as an immediate expression of it. Weber's conception of mysticism is shaped by his reading of Tolstoy, who himself adopted a Schopenhauerean worldview. Neither finds satisfactory the withdrawal from the world that Schopenhauer's philosophy of resignation entails.

deity who rewards and punishes, we will want the relationship between action and reward to be intelligible to us. But it is very difficult to make sense of the distribution of suffering in the world, and few theodicies have proved satisfactory from this point of view.[20] In fact, Weber tells us:

> The metaphysical conception of God and of the world, which the ineradicable demand for a theodicy called forth, could produce only a few systems of ideas on the whole – as we shall see, only three. These three gave rationally satisfactory answers to the questioning for the basis of the incongruity between destiny and merit: the Indian doctrine of Kharma, Zoroastrian dualism, and the predestination decree of the *deus absconditus*. These solutions are rationally closed; in pure form, they are found only as exceptions (FMW, p. 275; cf. GARS I, p. 247).

A "rationally closed" solution must be one which supports practical reasoning, insofar as it presupposes the faith that suffering is justified and also allows us to explore the nature of the justifications, but which nevertheless brings the demand for rational justifications to a halt at some acceptable point.

This kind of "rational closure" must involve acceptance of the limits of merely human reason. The demand for justifications is not satisfied rationally; it comes to a halt before some non-rational faith. But this faith must be such that it preserves our sense that our reasons in principle form a complete and coherent system, even where ultimate justifications remain inaccessible to our limited intelligence. Our human inability to explain suffering in a way that seems compatible with the existence of a benevolent and omnipotent God has been met, for example, by hypothesizing "an unimaginably great ethical chasm between the transcendental god and the human being continuously enmeshed in the toils of new sin." This view, which Weber claims is initially formulated in the Book of Job, makes God's justice ultimately incomprehensible to men. (ES I, p. 522; WG, p. 317). But it preserves their faith that suffering is justified in ways unknown to them.

The admission of incomprehensibility turns out to be an enabling one so far as human action is concerned. For this non-transparent sense of justification can support a commitment to a thoroughly non-hedonistic mode of living: the rational and methodical patterns of action engaged in by the ascetic. The

---

[20] In discussing the need to solve this distribution problem, Weber again displays his indebtedness to Nietzsche's *Genealogy*, invoking Nietzsche's distinction between "slave morality" and the values of the "masters": "Und keineswegs nur nach einer 'Sklavenmoral', sondern auch an den eigenen Maßstäben der Herrenschicht gemessen, waren es allzu oft nicht die Besten, sondern die "Schlechten", denen es am besten geriet." (FMW, p. 275; GARS I, p. 246) Weber then goes on to borrow Nietzsche's term "*Ressentiment*" and discuss the extent to which it has influenced theodicies of suffering.

inner-worldly ascetic, for Weber, is the man of vocation: "it suffices for him that through his rational actions in this world he is personally executing the will of god, which is unsearchable in its ultimate significance" (ES I, pp. 547f.; cf. WG, pp. 331f.).[21] The ascetic may take on voluntary suffering in the faith that some justifying end, however inscrutable, is being served. Calvinism represents, for Weber, the perfection of this fostering of non-hedonistic ends under the aegis of a non-transparent but presumed rational theodicy. It supports, for example, the forms of economic behavior described in *The Protestant Ethic and the Spirit of Capitalism* as being "so irrational from the standpoint of merely eudaimonistic self-interest" (PE, p. 38; cf. GARS I, p. 62).

Successful theodicies of this kind provide us with justifications for the natural and inevitable forms of suffering that any human beings must endure. But more essentially, they support human motivations that require us to add to the overall balance of suffering in the world, whether this means individuals taking on voluntary suffering themselves or inflicting non-voluntary suffering on others. Faith in the existence of some authoritative, supra-human justifying end makes it possible for us to tolerate an overall extent of suffering that would seem utterly excessive from the point of view of any merely human ends.

One important feature of this expansion of our capacity to tolerate suffering is the way in which it expands the range of politically permissible ends and obligations. It makes tolerable a distribution of suffering in a society that might otherwise be seen to require some political remedy. Weber claims that religions have devised various means of reconciling people to vast discrepancies in their standard of living and have sanctified different orders of life with different ethics, including differential degrees of political power. He sees here a parallel between the Hindu caste system and the Catholic ethic that differentiates between the modes of life permitted for the monk, the knight, and the burgher (PW, p. 363; GPS, p. 555).

But more importantly, theodicies may render acceptable state-inflicted violence that is necessary in the maintenance of political power or the pursuit of political ends. As Weber repeatedly stresses, "the specific means of *legitimate violence per se* in the hands of human associations is what gives all the ethical

---

[21] Cf. also PE 38, GARS I, p.62: "The ascetic, when he wishes to act within the world, that is, to practice inner-worldly asceticism, must become afflicted with a sort of happy stupidity regarding any questions about the meaning of the world, for he must not worry about such questions. Hence, it is no accident that inner-worldly asceticism reached its most consistent development on the foundation of the Calvinist god's absolute inexplicability, utter remoteness from every human criterion, and unsearchableness as to his motives."

problems of politics their particular character" (PW, p. 364; cf. GPS, p. 556).[22] If the state finds it necessary to employ violent means, that is, to inflict non-voluntary suffering, a theodicy that simply convinces people that the extent of suffering in their world is not excessive will already be playing an important justificatory role. And a theodicy that promotes attachment to non-hedonistic ends will help to legitimize the use of force in pursuit of those ends; it will expand the range of ends that can acceptably be pursued through coercive means. But theodicies have gone even further than this in justifying state power. As Weber points out, "Normal Protestantism [...] legitimated the state absolutely (and thus its means, violence) as a divine institution, and gave its blessing to the legitimate authoritarian state in particular" (PW, p. 364; cf. GPS, pp. 555f.). Calvinism and Islam, similarly, he claims, have sanctified the use of state violence where the state is understood as the essential means of defending the faith (PW, p. 364; GPS, p. 556).

The modern state, then, has had to justify both the distribution of suffering, within the society that it rules, and also its own infliction of non-voluntary suffering on its subjects and others. It has hitherto done so in an overall context of justifications for suffering that has been shaped by theodicies. To be sure, there have been tensions between religious ethics and the pragmatic demands of politics, but these have frequently collapsed into compromises, motivated, Weber tells us, "by the usefulness and the use of religious organizations for the political taming of the masses and, especially, by the need of the powers-that-be for the religious consecration of legitimacy" (MW, pp. 337f.; cf. GARS I, p. 551).

Since the modern state has evolved in this justificatory context, the question must arise of what impact secularization will have on the perception of its legitimacy. In particular, if justification of the pursuit of non-hedonistic ends requires belief in supra-human purposes, will there still be ends that can be commonly accepted as justifying force or violence once such purposes are discredited?

We shall see that Weber's response to this question involves an attempt to provide some substitute for meaning-conferring supra-human purposes. This

---

22 Cf. also *Religious Rejections* in FMW, p. 334; GARS I, p. 547: "it is absolutely essential for every political association to appeal to the naked violence of coercive means in the face of outsiders as well as in the face of internal enemies. It is only this very appeal to violence that constitutes a political association in our terminology. The state is an association that claims the monopoly of the *legitimate use of violence*, and cannot be defined in any other manner." Bryan Turner takes this emphasis on politics as violence to be derived from Nietzsche (cf. Turner 1982, p. 372).

attempted solution reveals the dangers that lie within the theodicy-demand thesis. If we accept the ineliminability of such a demand we will be vulnerable to a specific set of concerns about political life, that is, to anxieties about the affront to human dignity that is constituted by the politics of the "last man." And as we shall see, the attempt to address these concerns by way of fulfilling the theodicy-demand leads to an expansion of the permissible range of attitudes to suffering in politics. This expansion will appear unnecessary and inhumane if the underlying concerns are ill-founded, which I shall suggest they are.

The Politics of the Last Man

Nietzsche himself condemns liberal and socialist political values as crudely hedonistic. He tells us that in Europe and America we now find "narrow, restricted, chained-up" types of spirit, who

> are un-free and ridiculously superficial, particularly given their basic tendency to think that all human misery and wrongdoing is caused by traditional social structures: which lands truth happily on its head! What they want to strive for with all their might is the universal, green pasture happiness of the herd, with security, safety, contentment, and an easier life for all. Their two most well-sung songs and doctrines are called: 'equal rights' and 'sympathy for all that suffers' — and they view suffering itself as something that needs to be abolished. (BGE 44)

This exclusive hedonism naturally follows, for Nietzsche, from the loss of the supra-human purposes that supplied a justificatory context in which suffering for the sake of non-hedonistic goals made sense to us. Weber's approach to modern politics is clearly more nuanced, but he shares with Nietzsche the worry that secularism will entail unmitigated hedonism in our political values.

On the view shared by Nietzsche and Weber, in the absence of a solution to the theodicy-demand our commitment to non-hedonistic ends will be endangered, for our suffering will already seem excessive and our primary aim will be to diminish it. For Nietzsche, it is this very general claim that seems to lie behind his concerns about secular political values. Weber, on the other hand, supplies a more detailed account of the kind of justifications, besides the overall, holistic one, that theodicies have supplied. He traces in detail relationships between specific theodicy narratives and forms of political legitimation. And he is therefore able to state a more precise view of what is lacking in secular political values.

For Weber, theodicies have provided answers not just to the question, "Why suffer?" but also to the question "Why me?" They have justified unequal distributions of suffering in the societies where they have been accepted. This kind of justification has reconciled people to their roles in articulated, hierarchical societies.[23] In its absence, we might then expect the evident "incongruity between destiny and merit" to promote a questioning of social roles and to motivate demands for political change oriented around the redistribution of social goods. It would be crude, however, to take this to imply simply a demand for "social leveling" or for an equal distribution of material goods. Unlike Nietzsche, Weber resists such an interpretation of progressive political movements. He sees that the ethical motivations underlying the socialist movement, for example, are complex. He understands the basic problem that socialism seeks to address not as that of inequality *simpliciter,* but as that of alienation, or "the rule of things over men," where the fault lies in a system which fails to address the real needs of human beings and in which no particular individuals can be held accountable.[24] What socialism demands, therefore, is a more fully human form of social, economic, and political organization, one which places the basic conditions of life in the hands of real human beings, to be shaped by real human needs.

However, Weber also sees a discrepancy between this political ideal and the actual motivations of fallible human creatures. Here we do find in his work a strongly Nietzschean tendency. The motivational structure that in fact drives the socialist movement is described in unmistakably Nietzschean terms. The actual socialist leader, he tells us, needs a human "apparatus":

> He must promise these people the necessary inner and outward prizes — rewards in heaven or on earth — because the apparatus will not function otherwise. Under the conditions of modern class-warfare the inner rewards are the satisfaction of hatred and revenge, of *ressentiment* and the need for the pseudo-ethical feeling of being in the right, the desire to slander one's opponents and make heretics of them. The outward rewards are adventure, victory, booty, power and prebends. The success of the leader is entirely dependent on the functioning of his apparatus. He is therefore dependent on *its* motives, not his own. He is dependent also on the possibility of providing those prizes *permanently* to his following, the Red Guard, the informers, the agitators he needs. Given these conditions of his activity, what he actually achieves does not, therefore, lie in his own hands but is, rather, prescribed for him by the, in ethical terms, predominantly base or common [*gemein*] motives prompting the actions of his following (PW, pp. 364f.; cf. GPS, p. 556).

---

[23] Cf. ES, pp. 490–492; WG, pp. 298ff., where Weber tells us that the privileged classes have achieved, through belief in salvation religions, confidence in their own worthiness, whilst the unprivileged classes have acquired the hope of some future compensation.
[24] *Socialism*, in: PW, p. 284.

The demand for compensation that salvation religions once addressed is here seen to have degenerated into a purely egoistic demand for personal reward and an unmitigated resentment of the privileged.

Neither is this egoistic self-concern confined to the unprivileged strata of society. The intellectual classes too, on Weber's view, display both egoism and hedonism in their pursuit of purely private and individualistic forms of secular salvation. In his *Religious Rejections* essay Weber describes the way in which aesthetic experience comes to serve this function, with music in particular constituting "an irresponsible *Ersatz* for primary religious experience" (FMW, pp. 342f.; cf. GARS I, p. 556). The erotic life too, and particularly extramarital sexual life, Weber tells us, provides a means of escape from the ultimately futile cultural existence of human beings, a flight into animality and reunion with nature. (FMW, p. 346; GARS I, p. 560). Like the mystic's strategy of dealing with the theodicy-demand by generating temporary obliviousness to it, these forms of secular salvation require detachment from the realm of practical judgment and action.

This retreat from the ultimate meaninglessness of human endeavors manifests itself directly, Weber claims, in the intellectual's retreat from political responsibility. The conflict between the need for meaningfulness and the experience of the actual, empirical realities of our existence prompts the intellectual's disengagement from the real political and institutional conditions that structure life in this world:

> This may be an escape into loneliness, or in its more modern form, e.g., in the case of Rousseau, to a nature unspoiled by human institutions. Again, it may be a world-fleeing romanticism, like the flight to the "people", untouched by social conventions, characteristic of the Russian *narodnichestvo*. It may be more contemplative, or more actively ascetic; it may primarily seek individual salvation or collective revolutionary transformation of the world in the direction of a more ethical status. All these doctrines are equally appropriate to apolitical intellectualism (ES, p. 506; cf. WG, p. 308).

It seems, then, that the loss of the theodicies, which reconciled human social beings to their inherited social orders, must lead to fragmentation and individualism. In the face of a new dissatisfaction with their social world, neither the privileged nor the unprivileged classes seem able to retain the kind of motivations that would permit them to reshape that world in accordance with higher human values. Weber tells us that "the ultimate and most sublime values have retreated from public life either into the transcendent realm of mystic life or into the brotherliness of direct and personal human relations" (FMW, p. 155; cf. GAW, p. 612).

As we have seen, on Weber's account theodicies have also played a further, more direct role, in political legitimation. They have assisted states in justifying the infliction of non-voluntary suffering on human beings, which is a necessary feature of states qua entities that are defined precisely by their coercive powers. Under secular conditions, the general preparedness to suffer and to inflict non-voluntary suffering must be diminished simply by the insight that the balance of human suffering already exceeds what can be justified by any merely human ends. But also the specific justifications for inflicting suffering that states have hitherto invoked, for example pursuit of the non-hedonistic ends of defending the true faith or realizing God's glory through earthly greatness, must be discredited. Throughout his work, Weber displays concern that the narrow hedonism and utilitarianism of secular subjects will rule out their finding any common, non-hedonistic ends legitimate. They will refuse to acknowledge any non-hedonistic ends as justifications for political coercion.

In his 1895 inaugural address, Weber exhorts Germans to embrace the goals of honor and greatness in world politics. He fears that economic developments are threatening the "political instincts" with decay, and warns his fellow political economists: "It would be a great misfortune if economic science were also to strive towards the same goal by breeding a soft, eudaimonistic outlook, in however spiritualized a form, behind the illusion of independent 'socio-political' ideals" (PW, p. 27; cf. GPS, p. 24). He speaks of "that unspeakably philistine softening of sensibility, however much it may command affection and respect in human terms, which believes it is possible to replace political with 'ethical' ideals, and ingenuously to identify these in turn with optimistic hopes of happiness" (PW, p. 27; cf. GPS, p. 24). In his earliest work he is already decrying the politics of the "last man." And these sentiments are echoed in 1916, when he berates the "pacifism of American 'ladies' (of both sexes)" as well as Swiss anti-militarism as displaying a failure to comprehend the "tragic historical obligations incumbent on any nation organized as a Machtstaat" (PW, p. 77; cf. GPS, p. 144). The basic tendency of these pacifists, he claims, is to object not just to war, but to "each and every law of the social world" insofar as the constitution of that world necessarily involves the infliction of suffering for the sake of common goals.

So does Weber fear that states, as inherently coercive forms of political organization, will no longer be accepted as legitimate, that they will be subject to the disintegrative forces of an incipient anarchism? Far from it. His concern is rather that states and their actions will be accepted on the basis of deeply entrenched structures of legitimation comprised by an inflexible grid of utilitarian calculations and pragmatic reasons of state. The process of legitimation will have become entirely impervious to any other substantive values.[25]

---

[25] Cf. *Religious Rejections* in: FMW, p. 334; GARS I, p. 547: "By virtue of its depersonalization, the bureaucratic state, in important points, is less accessible to substantive moralization than were the patriarchal orders of the past."

In Economy and Society, Weber charts the way in which the last attempt to make legitimation a genuinely moral form of assessment, the natural law tradition, inevitably degenerated, in its secular form, into a non-moral form of practical calculation. In this tradition, during the seventeenth and eighteenth centuries, Weber tells us, "nature" and "reason" became the substantive criteria by which legitimacy should be judged. The voluntary rational contract, and on the basis of it the establishment of legitimately acquired rights, specified the way in which they were to shape political life (ES, p. 869; WG, p. 498). But when brought into relation with existing political realities, compromise became necessary. Weber tells us that many institutions in the prevailing system "could not be legitimated except on practical utilitarian grounds. By 'justifying' them, natural law "reason easily slipped into utilitarian thinking" (ES, p. 870; cf. WG, p. 499).

The shift from a substantive moral doctrine to a form of politically expedient calculation can be traced, Weber claims, by examining the shifting meaning of the term "reasonableness" (Vernünftigkeit). He tells us that:

> in purely formal natural law, the reasonable is that which is derivable from the eternal order of nature and logic, both being readily blended with one another. But from the beginning, the English concept of "reasonable" contained by implication the meaning of "rational" in the sense of "practically appropriate." From this it could be concluded that what would lead in practice to absurd consequences cannot constitute the law desired by nature and reason. This signified the express introduction of substantive presuppositions into the concept of reason which had in fact always been implicit in it (ES, p. 870; cf. WG, p. 499).

Formal natural law doctrines were thereby transformed in technically substantive ones, which were taken up, Weber tells us, by the socialist movement. But before they could achieve any practical influence over the administration of justice, he claims, they were already "being disintegrated by the rapidly growing positivistic and relativistic-evolutionistic skepticism" that was spreading amongst the intellectual strata (ES, p. 874; WG, p. 502). Legal positivism, he claims, has since advanced irresistibly.

Weber's sociological observations concerning modern politics therefore seem to bear out the view underlying his account of theodicies and their justificatory role. Absent such theodicies, non-hedonistic ends will fail to find support as legitimate bases for political coercion, except insofar as they are justified by the raw pragmatism of reasons of state. The more controversial aspects of Weber's later political thought are intended, I shall argue, to address precisely this problem.

The aristocratic solution

It is natural that both Nietzsche and Weber should want to resolve the "last man" problem in the direction of the anti-hedonistic ideal since, given the overall extent of inevitable suffering that they perceive in human life, it is bound to seem unsatisfactory from a narrowly hedonistic point of view. What we need are purposes or ends that can justify that suffering. Nietzsche and Weber both find that no merely human purposes are adequate to this task. In the absence of belief in supra-human purposes, Nietzsche suggests that we posit *super*-human goals that can take their place. Many of the more inhumane aspects of his thought follow from this proposal, so it is worth examining the extent to which Weber himself endorses such a solution.

In his *Thus Spoke Zarathustra*, Nietzsche has Zarathustra proclaim: "It is time mankind set himself a goal. It is time that mankind plant the seed of his highest hope" (Z I Prologue 5) In relation to this goal, the suffering of humanity might have a meaning. The goal, of course, is that of the over-man, or superman. Zarathustra says: "I teach you the *Übermensch*. The *Übermensch* is the meaning of the earth" (Z I Hinterwordly). The self-overcoming of humanity is the meaning-generating end for the sake of which we may not only tolerate but actually will suffering. Rather than the contemptible spectacle of the "last man" we can aspire to promote a higher being. The evolution of just a few specimens of humanity to a new stage of greatness will justify the whole dismal spectacle of human baseness and misery.[26]

Nietzsche makes clear that he does not just hold that voluntary suffering is justified in pursuit of this goal. Rather, non-voluntary suffering may be inflicted on others for its sake. For it is a means of overcoming the whole attitude to suffering embraced by the secular moralist, who desires only that suffering be diminished. He states this forcefully in *Beyond Good and Evil*:

> Whether it is hedonism or pessimism, utilitarianism or eudaimonism — all these ways of thinking that measure the value if things in accordance with pleasure and pain, which are mere epiphenomena and wholly secondary, are ways of thinking that stay in the foreground and naïvetés on which everyone conscious of creative powers will look down not without derision, nor without pity. [...] You want, if possible — and there is no more insane

---

[26] Cf. BGE 258: "the essential feature of a good, healthy aristocracy is that it does not feel that it is a function (whether of the kingdom or of the community) but instead feels itself to be the meaning and highest justification (of the kingdom or community),- and, consequently, that it accepts in good conscience the sacrifice of countless people who have to be pushed down and shrunk into incomplete human beings, into slaves, into tools, all for the sake of the aristocracy."

'if possible' — to abolish suffering. And we? It really seems that we would rather have it higher and worse than ever. Well-being as you understand it — that is no goal, that seems to us as an end, a state that soon makes man ridiculous and contemptible — that makes his destruction desirable.

The discipline of suffering, of great suffering — do you not know that only this discipline had created all enhancements of man so far? That tension of the soul in unhappiness which cultivates its strength, its shudders face to face with great ruin, its inventiveness and courage in enduring, preserving, interpreting, and exploiting suffering, and whatever has been granted to it of profundity, secret, mask, spirit, cunning, greatness — was it not granted to it through suffering, through the discipline of great suffering? (BGE 225)

Nietzsche clearly holds that we must be prepared to will the suffering of others and to accept the "sacrifice of countless people who have to be pushed down and shrunk into incomplete human beings, into slaves, into tools," for the sake of his goal (BGE 258). The advent of a new aristocracy, the emergence of superhuman beings, becomes the justifying end which, if we embrace it, will provide the kind of holistic justification that we need for human suffering. All of the apparently futile misery suffered by mere humans will turn out to be worthwhile, if it provides the conditions for the emergence of these beings. Since even greater suffering than we naturally experience may be justified by this purpose, its embrace will support an attachment to a variety of non-hedonistic ends.

If human beings are to aspire to overcome their limited human state and achieve this higher state of being, we might expect such a goal to foster a rich array of non-hedonistic values. Humanity will be guided in its aspirations by whatever qualities the *Übermensch* is supposed to embody. But Nietzsche's vision of these qualities remains relatively opaque. He offers us no concrete vision of precisely what kind of achievements would provide sufficient justification for present human suffering. In effect, he asks us to adopt the faith that there are such goals and that our suffering will be justified by some future, inscrutable state of affairs. In this sense, his solution mirrors the solutions of the successful theodicies that Weber has described. So does Weber himself adopt the same strategy?

Weber seems to share with Nietzsche the view that the "last man" dilemma should be resolved in the direction of the anti-hedonistic ideal, rather than a capitulation to hedonism. In his inaugural address on *The Nation State and Economic Policy*, Weber says:

The question which stirs us as we think beyond the grave of our own generation is not the *well-being* human beings will enjoy in the future but what kind of people they will *be* [...]. We do not want to breed well-being in people but rather those characteristics which we think of as constituting the human greatness and nobility of our nature (PW, p. 15; cf. GPS, pp. 12f.).[27]

He suggests, in other words, that rather than simply seeking a diminishment of suffering, we should adopt a purpose, human greatness, which serves as a justifying end for it.

This view is reiterated in 1916 in a brief address now entitled *Between Two Laws*. Weber here excoriates the American pacifists, defending the war not by maintaining that it will lead to any overall diminishment of human suffering, but by claiming that the suffering that it entails is meaningful insofar as it is justified by a non-hedonistic end. He contrasts this with the meaningless suffering entailed by the division of labor, which is tolerated by the pacifists and which is a greater evil insofar as it is for the most part meaningless in terms of any higher human goals:

> This is just another form of man's struggle with man, one in which not millions but hundreds of millions of people, year after year, waste away in body and soul, sink without trace, or lead an existence truly much more bereft of any recognizable 'meaning' [*Sinn*] than the commitment of everybody ...to the cause of honor [*Ehre*], which means, simply, commitment to the historical obligations imposed on one's nation by fate (PW, p. 78; cf. GPS, p. 145).

For Weber, as for Nietzsche, the problem is not suffering *per* se, but meaningless suffering. He goes on to claim that the pacifists "are in opposition not just to war [...] but ultimately to each and every law of the social world, if this seeks to be a *place of worldly 'culture'*, one devoted to the beauty, dignity, honor and greatness of man as a creature on this earth" (PW, p. 78; cf. GPS, p. 145). Weber does, then, seem to adopt the view that human greatness is a value which trumps hedonism and which justifies extensive human suffering, both voluntary and non-voluntary.

So the problem faced by both Nietzsche and Weber is how human beings who are in the grip of the "last man" predicament can be made to embrace the higher, redemptive goals that would give life meaning. Nietzsche struggles with this problem throughout his career. In spite of grandiose claims in *Ecce Homo* about the world-transformative impact that his philosophy would have, he never identified any mechanism by which he might secure the needed transformation, or revaluation of values (cf. Shaw 2007). Weber, on the other hand,

---

[27] David Owen draws attention to the striking similarity of this passage to Nietzsche's own statements of concern with the kind of human being which future generations must breed (cf. Owen 1992, pp. 79–91).

claims to have discovered in his analyses of religion the kind of mechanism that can play this transformative role. It is of course charisma.

In *Politics as a Vocation*, Weber famously recommends charismatic leadership as the only means by which the mechanisms of modern politics can be made permeable by substantive human values.[28] In his earlier writings on charismatic authority, Weber has identified it as a means of galvanizing popular support without simply deferring to the popular will, but rather transforming that will through a display of extraordinary and compelling qualities. He writes:

> the power of charisma rests upon the belief in revelation and in heroes, upon the conviction that certain manifestations — whether they be of a religious, ethical, artistic, scientific, political or other kind — are important and valuable; it rests upon "heroism" of an ascetic, military, judicial, magical or whichever kind. Charismatic belief revolutionizes men "from within" and shapes material and social conditions according to its revolutionary will (ES, p. 1116; cf. WG, pp. 657f.).

Unlike the socialist leaders who, we have seen, he describes as being subservient to the base motivations of their followers, the charismatic leader is able to co-opt the will of his followers to support his own values.[29]

This galvanizing of the popular will in the service of common values is necessary, on Weber's view, if a people is to have agency in world history and not simply be shaped passively by the machinery of modern bureaucratic, capitalist societies. In his essay on *Parliament and Government in Germany*, Weber employs the concept of a *Herrenvolk*, a "nation of masters" which controls its own affairs, to express this kind of political dignity (PW, p. 269; GPS, p. 442). Charisma is the means through which a leader can form such a people.

In *Economy and Society*, the raw, primitive power of charisma is described in Nietzschean terms as the power of the "blond beast" (ES, p. 1112; WG, p. 654). Nietzsche himself employs the blond beast metaphor, in his *Genealogy*, to describe such a brute, people-forming power.[30] But the kind of charismatic

---

28 PW, p. 351; GPS, p. 544: "the only choice lies between a leadership democracy with a 'machine' and democracy without a leader, which means rule by the 'professional politician' who has no vocation, the type of man who lacks those inner, charismatic qualities which make a leader."
29 Cf. ES, p. 1113; WG, p. 655: the charismatic leader "does not derive his claims from the will of his followers, in the manner of an election; rather, it is their *duty* to recognize his charisma."
30 Cf. GM II 17: "I used the word 'state': it is obvious what is meant by this – some pack of blond beasts of prey, a conqueror and master race, which, organized on a war footing, and with the power to organize, unscrupulously lays its dreadful paws on a populace which, though it might be vastly greater in number, is still shapeless and shifting."

leadership which Weber ultimately recommends, though it employs this form of power, is ethically complex. The inner qualities of the charismatic leader envisaged by Weber are to constrain the use of this power, so that it is exercised out of a sense of responsibility to the people and not contempt for them.[31] Weber, seeing such contempt exhibited by contemporary "Nietzscheans," explicitly warns against a superficial appropriation of Nietzsche's idea of an aristocracy based on the "pathos of distance."[32]

After experiencing the horrors of World War I, Weber is especially concerned to specify that political judgment must be constrained by an ethic of responsibility. The endorsement of such an ethic seems to place some distance between Weber and Nietzsche, so far as their preparedness to inflict suffering for the sake of their higher, meaning-giving ends is concerned. It is therefore worth examining precisely what kind of constraints this ethic implies and whether it exempts Weber from the concerns about inhumanity that Nietzsche's work raises.

Weber distinguishes, in *Politics as a Vocation*, between the ethic of conviction and the ethic of responsibility. The former is typified by the Christian who "does what is right and places the outcome in God's hands," whereas the latter weighs ends carefully against the necessary means, that is, where this includes all of the foreseeable consequences of acting to promote those ends (PW, pp. 359f.; GPS, pp. 551f.). The proponent of the ethic of responsibility, then, tries to take into account what Weber calls the "ethical irrationality of the world," that is, the dangerous and violent means often required to achieve political ends, the inevitable shortcomings of men in pursuing them, and the unintended consequences which so often follow (PW, p. 360; GPS, p. 552).

---

31 Cf. ES, p. 1114; WG, p. 656, on the religious model of the charismatic leader: "his divine mission must prove itself by *bringing well-being* to his faithful followers; if they do not fare well, he obviously is not the god-sent master. It is clear that this very serious meaning of genuine charisma is radically different from the convenient pretensions of the present 'divine right of kings,' which harks back to the 'inscrutable' will of the Lord, 'to whom alone the monarch is responsible.' The very opposite is true of the genuinely charismatic ruler, who is responsible to the ruled – responsible, that is, to prove that he himself is indeed the master willed by God."

32 On the "pathos of distance", cf. BGE 257. Weber writes in *Suffrage and Democracy in Germany*, PW, pp. 122f.: "Various 'prophecies' produced under the influence of Nietzsche are based on a misconception, for 'distance' is certainly not to be achieved by standing on a pedestal of some 'aristocratic' contrast between oneself and the 'all too many'; indeed, on the contrary, distance is always inauthentic if it needs this inner support nowadays."
David Owen has argued that we can find in Weber a much deeper and more genuinely Nietzschean account of and commitment to the pathos of distance (cf. Owen 1991).

The ethic of responsibility seems to indicate a humane desire to diminish human suffering. But it seeks to do so only along one specific dimension. It aims to eliminate *futile* suffering. It follows from Weber's conviction that suffering should be meaningful, that is, justified by intrinsically valuable ends. The necessary means of politics is violence, or the infliction of suffering. But the ends to be achieved by such violence often cannot, owing to the problem of unintended consequences, be assured. So even political actors with good motivations can generate a great deal of futile suffering. The leader who adopts the ethic of responsibility strives to limit such futile suffering and to ensure that suffering is, as far as possible, meaningful in relation to their goals.

This preoccupation with minimizing futile suffering does seem to distinguish Weber from Nietzsche, even though it ought logically to follow from Nietzsche's own conception of meaning-generating goals. But it remains the case that Weber, like Nietzsche, believes that political life should be shaped not by an overall desire to diminish suffering *per se*, but rather by the aim of making suffering as meaningful as possible. Charismatic, meaning-conferring leaders should be prepared to encourage voluntary suffering and inflict non-voluntary suffering for the sake of the non-hedonistic goals that make the spectacle of human life on this planet worthwhile.[33]

In Weber's work as in Nietzsche's the content of these goals remains inscrutable. We are only told that the charismatic leader must have a passionate devotion to a cause, "to the god or demon who commands that cause" (PW, p. 353; cf. GPS, p. 545). Weber lapses here into irrationalism and obscurity. True to his own understanding of what constitutes a successful theodicy, he brings to a halt the demand for justifications before the bare faith that there is some justification that will make human existence in all its suffering worthwhile. From there he asks us to follow blindly whichever charismatic leader succeeds in commanding our devotion. His surrogate religious solution, like the solution of the Calvinist, is "rationally closed."

Disenchantment and the demise of the theodicy-demand

Weber's political thought, in aiming to resolve the "last man" problem in the direction of the anti-hedonistic ideal, seems to make permissible a broad range

---

[33] Tracy Strong views Weber's conception of charismatic leadership as a secularized religious ethics, which aims to fulfill our need for redemption. He claims that since Weber, unlike Nietzsche, does not explicitly repudiate the moral point of view, his own vision may be more insidi-

of political attitudes to suffering, whether it is voluntary or non-voluntary, natural and inevitable, or deliberately inflicted. He preserves the rich array of attitudes and meanings that belief in supra-human purposes once permitted us. I want to suggest, however, that insofar as this is justified, on his view, by our need to satisfy the theodicy-demand, its basis is questionable. His own insights into secularization, and particularly his account of disenchantment, seem to deny the inevitable persistence of such a demand. And if we do not take that demand to be psychologically basic, we do not, I shall argue, need to fear that all of our non-hedonistic motivations are under threat. Disenchantment itself ought to solve the "last man" problem for us.

The Schopenhauerean assumption that I have attributed to both Nietzsche and Weber consists in the following claim: suffering will always outweigh pleasure in human life and this extent of suffering will always seem unjustified by any merely human ends. According to this kind of holistic calculus, we will always, if we are confined to merely naturalistic narratives, be suffering too much. This insight will inhibit our motivation to take on even more suffering as a means to non-hedonistic ends and we will slide into the exclusive hedonism of the last man. But the holistic calculus seems to me to be flawed. It adopts a notion of justification derived from suffering which results from intentional human actions and illegitimately extends it to all suffering. Even on Nietzsche's and Weber's own views, I shall claim, this is an error. Much of the suffering that we undergo (illnesses, the deaths of loved ones, the fear of one's own death etc. etc.) should not raise any demand for justification and although it will inevitably be burdensome to us, even unbearably so, it should not weigh on us as being unjustified. If it does, we are still operating with an essentially theistic view of the world.

Suffering is often clearly justification-apt. The way in which it becomes so is through interaction with intentions. We might intentionally take on suffering for the sake of some end and will wonder whether the amount of suffering is justified by the end. Or non-voluntary suffering might be intentionally inflicted on us for the sake of ends that we hold to be justified or unjustified, and to an extent that we find justified or unjustified by those ends. Or we might undergo non-voluntary suffering that could have been avoided through some intentional action of a third party; if suffering is intentionally allowed the question of whether it is justified by some end again arises. But the justification-aptness of suffering always relies on some such intentional relation of means to ends.

---

ous, more permissive, and more dangerous (cf. Strong 1992, p. 15 and Strong 2002, pp. 15–41; at p. 41).

In the absence of this intentional structure (for example in the case of unavoidable natural occurrences) it is simply not justification-apt.

We have to distinguish, then, between suffering that is not justification-apt and unjustified suffering. Suffering will be unjustified if it is inflicted to no just end, or if it outweighs the ends that it is intended to serve. But suffering that is not intentionally caused or allowed is not unjustified; it is justification-inapt.

In a world invested with interfering gods and spirits, many kinds of suffering, including being struck by lightning or getting cancer, might seem to be the product of intentional actions and hence be deemed justification-apt; they will provoke the questions "Why?" or "Why me?" or "Why so much?". In a monotheistic universe in which an omnipotent and omniscient God is ultimately responsible for everything that happens, all forms of suffering are justification-apt; it is all either intentionally caused or allowed by God. It makes sense for the theist to demand an overall justification for everything that happens and to want to account for the precise extent of suffering in the world.

The Schopenhauerean calculus adopted by Nietzsche and Weber treats all suffering implicitly in this theistic way. The entirety of human suffering is treated as justification-apt, but in the absence of a theodicy the demand for justifications cannot for the most part be met; most of our suffering appears unjustified. "Only as an aesthetic phenomenon," Nietzsche tells us, "can the world seem justified." But the mistake here is to hold that all the suffering in the world requires justification.

If we make that mistake it will always seem that our suffering outweighs any human ends, so no merely human ends that we adopt can possibly justify an increase in it; hence the apparent threat to non-hedonistic motivations. Once we acknowledge that much of our suffering is not unjustified but normatively insignificant that threat should disappear. Suffering that is not intentionally caused should not be weighed against our ends or purposes.

If Weber had followed through consistently on his own insights he would have come to this conclusion and the "last man" problem would have lost its traction for him. For on Weber's construal, disenchantment involves precisely the replacement of belief in intentional causes by mechanical causes. Intellectualization, he tells us:

> means principally that there are no mysterious incalculable forces that come into play, but rather that one can, in principle, master all things by calculation. This means that the world is disenchanted. One need no longer have recourse to magical means in order to master or implore the spirits, as did the savage, for whom such mysterious powers existed. Technical means and calculations perform the service (FMW, p. 139; cf. GAW, p. 594).

And Weber remarks at several points that this essentially mechanistic worldview not only robs the world of meaning, it erodes the very demand for meaning. He goes as far as to say:

> Who — aside from certain big children who are indeed found in the natural sciences — still believes that the findings of astronomy, biology, physics, or chemistry could teach us anything about the *meaning* of the world? If there is any such "meaning," along what road could one come upon its tracks? If these natural sciences lead to anything in this way, they are apt to make the belief that there is such a thing as the "meaning" of the universe die out in its very roots (FMW, p. 142; cf. GAW, p. 597).

In other words, the mechanistic worldview in no way relates events or states of affairs in the world to supra-human purposes, so the very belief in such purposes becomes irrelevant to us. But it also follows that this worldview cancels the demand for justifications since this demand only arises in relation to intentions or purposes.[34] Weber comes tantalizing close, then, to acknowledging that on a secular worldview the theodicy-demand disappears. It no longer makes sense to demand a holistic justification for suffering *tout court*. But Weber refrains, perhaps on account of his persisting religious sensibilities, from drawing this conclusion.[35] The "last man" problem appears to be a vestige of a religious worldview, the product not of secularization but of incomplete secularization.

Conclusion

If the "last man" problem is deflated, our commitment to taking on voluntary suffering for the sake of non-hedonistic ends, such as art or human under-

---

34 Nietzsche himself acknowledges this is GS 109, where he writes: "let us beware of thinking that the world is a living being. [...]. How could we reproach or praise the universe! Let us beware of attributing to it heartlessness or unreason or their opposites: it is neither perfect, nor beautiful, nor noble, nor does it want to become any of these things; in no way does it strive to imitate man! In no way do our aesthetic and moral judgments apply to it! [...] Once you know that there are no purposes, you also know that there is no accident, for only against a world of purposes does the word 'accident' have a meaning."
But he does not follow through on this claim when it comes to assessing the demand for an overall meaning for suffering, which he apparently continues to see as a basic feature of human psychology."
35 Cf. ES, p. 506; WG, p. 308: "As intellectualism suppresses belief in magic, the world's processes become disenchanted, lose their magical significance, and henceforth simply 'are' and 'happen' but no longer signify anything." However, Weber sees this development not as diminishing the demand for meaning, but rather exacerbating it: "As a consequence, there is

standing, no longer appears to be threatened. But might Weber nevertheless be justifiably concerned about secular politics? Politics, on Weber's view, has to involve the infliction (or threat of infliction) of non-voluntary suffering. Secularism in politics deprives us of the justifying role of theodicies that, as Weber points out, have previously supported the infliction and toleration of non-voluntary suffering. And if we deny the persistence of the theodicy-demand, we will also be deprived of the secular theodicy-substitutes proposed by Nietzsche and Weber. Secularism, then, necessarily narrows the realm of legitimate coercion. Does this mean that secularism commits us to political hedonism, or that no non-hedonistic ends will be held to justify coercion?

It may still be the case that secular leaders can galvanize populations around non-hedonistic ends for the sake of which coercion is held to be legitimate. But Weber's basic intuition about the implications of secularism for politics may be correct: it seems plausible that it will be much harder to generate agreement on such ends in the absence of the kind of ultimate justifications that theodicies provide. If that is the case, it might turn out that secularism is less conducive to legitimating political coercion for any end other than the hedonistic one of promoting an overall reduction in suffering. And secularism does not just place restrictions on the deliberate infliction of suffering; it also constrains our interpretations of the suffering that results from natural, non-intentional causes. Disease, for example, cannot be regarded as a punishment, devastating hurricanes as a test, or famine as a purge of the sinful. If no such "meanings" for non-voluntary suffering are permissible, we lack any justification for tolerating it where it is avoidable. Secularism would then seem to commit us to the eradication of natural, non-voluntary suffering where this is possible. This would seem to imply, then, an implicit aspiration to eradicate non-voluntary suffering, and hence to delegitimate any coercion for non-hedonistic ends.

So Weber's work does seem to raise interesting questions about the implications of secularism for politics. These will apply to polities that are secular by virtue of deep change in popular belief and also to those liberal polities that are secular by virtue of excluding religious arguments from the public realm. I doubt that these questions can be answered a priori. But if it did turn out that secular polities were peculiarly susceptible to the hedonism that Nietzsche and Weber describe, the question would be whether we should view this outcome as a threat to human dignity, or as the attainment of a distinctively humane form of politics. If Weber does give us reason to believe that secularism tends

---

a growing demand that the world and the total pattern of life be subject to an order that is significant and meaningful."

to promote the political ideal of eliminating non-voluntary suffering, this will indeed be a victory for the ideal of those who, as Nietzsche puts it, proclaim "'sympathy for all that suffers' – and [who] view suffering itself as something that needs to be abolished." But this ideal need not be viewed as a threat to human dignity, even if we hold that our dignity does indeed require the attainment of non-hedonistic ends. Rather, it might reasonably be understood as a necessary precondition for the existence of the kind of society in which our highest dignity can be realized through the voluntary pursuit of those ends. If modern secular polities are in fact oriented by that ideal, as contemporary proponents of the "last man" thesis have claimed, we might, against Nietzsche and Weber, consider it an unrivalled achievement in the long, bloody history of human politics.[36]

Bibliography

Max Weber – Abbreviations and works

FMW = *From Max Weber* (1946/1958). H.H. Gerth and C. Wright Mills (eds./trans.). New York: Oxford University Press.

WG = Weber, Max (1972): *Wirtschaft und Gesellschaft: Grundriss der Verstehenden Soziologie*. Johannes Wincklemann (ed.). 5th edition. Tübingen: J.C.B. Mohr [Paul Siebeck].

ES = Weber, Max (1978): *Economy and Society*. Guenther Roth and Claus Wittich, (eds.). Berekely, Los Angeles, London: University of California Press.

GARS = Weber, Max (1988): *Gesammelte Aufsätze zur Religionssoziologie*. Tübingen: J.C.B. Mohr [Paul Siebeck].

GAW = Weber, Max (1988): *Gesammelte Aufsätze zur Wissenschaftslehre*. Tübingen: J.C.B. Mohr [Paul Siebeck].

GPS = Weber, Max (1988): *Gesammelte Politische Schriften*. Tübingen: J.C.B. Mohr [Paul Siebeck].

PE = Weber, Max (1992): *The Protestant Ethic and the Spirit of Capitalism*. Talcott Parsons (trans.). London and New York: Routledge.

---

36 In writing this essay I have benefited greatly from comments made by audiences at NYU's Remarque Institute, the Chicago Political Theory Workshop, the Yale Political Theory Workshop, the Harvard Political Theory Colloquium, and the Stanford Political Theory Workshop. Special thanks to Paul Boghossian, Joshua Cohen, Brian Leiter and Michael Rosen for their insightful comments, and to the editors of this volume, Manuel Knoll and Barry Stocker for their very helpful feedback and advice.

PW = Weber, Max (1994): Political Writings. Peter Lassman and Ronald Speirs (eds.). Cambridge: Cambridge University Press

Other works cited

Alexander, Jeffrey (1983): Theoretical Logic in Sociology: Vol. 3. The Classical Attempt at Theoretical Synthesis: Max Weber. Berkeley: University of California Press.
Dienstag, Joshua Foa (2006): Pessimism: Philosophy, Ethic, Spirit. Princeton, Oxford: Princeton University Press.
Eden, Robert (1983): Political Leadership and Nihilism: A Study of Weber and Nietzsche. Gainseville: University Press of Florida.
Fleischmann, Eugene (1964): "De Weber á Nietzsche". In: Archives Européens de Sociologie 1, pp. 190–237.
Fukuyama, Francis (1992): The End of History and the Last Man. New York: The Free Press.
Hartung, Gerald (1994): "Zur Genealogie der Schuldbegriffs: Friedrich Nietzsche und Max Weber im Vergleich". In: Archiv für Geschichte der Philosophie 76, pp. 302–318.
Hennis, Wilhelm (1998): Max Weber: Essays in Reconstruction. Keith Tribe (trans.). London: Unwin Hyman.
Mitzman, Arthur (1969): The Iron Cage: An Historical Interpretation of Max Weber. New Brunswick and Oxford: Transaction Books.
Morgenthau, Hans (1946, 1974): Scientific Man Versus Power Politics. Chicago, London: University of Chicago Press.
Nietzsche, Friedrich (1997): On the Genealogy of Morality. Keith Ansell-Pearson (ed.), Carol Diethe (trans.). Cambridge: Cambridge University Press.
Nietzsche, Friedrich (1999): The Birth of Tragedy and Other Writings. Raymond Geuss (ed.) and Ronald Speirs (ed./trans.). Cambridge: Cambridge University Press.
Nietzsche, Friedrich (2001): The Gay Science. Bernard Williams (ed), Adrian Del Caro (trans.). Cambridge: Cambridge University Press.
Nietzsche, Friedrich (2002): Beyond Good and Evil. Rolf-Peter Horstmann and Judith Norman (eds.), Judith Norman (trans.). Cambridge: Cambridge University Press.
Nietzsche, Friedrich (2005): The Anti-Christ, Ecce Homo, Twilight of the Idols, and Other Writings. Aaron Ridley and Judith Norman (eds.), Judith Norman (trans.). Cambridge: Cambridge University Press.
Nietzsche, Friedrich (2006): Thus Spoke Zarathustra: A Book for Everyone and Nobody. Adrian Del Caro (trans.). Cambridge: Cambridge University Press.
Owen, David (1992): "Autonomy and 'inner distance': a trace of Nietzsche in Weber". In: History of the Human Sciences 4(1), pp. 79–91.
Owen, David (2000): "Of Overgrown Children and Last Men: Nietzsche's Critique and Max Weber's Cultural Science". In: Nietzsche-Studien 29, pp. 252–265.
Scaff, Lawrence (1989): Fleeing the Iron Cage: Culture, Politics, and Modernity in the Thought of Max Weber. Berkeley, Los Angeles and London: University of California Press.
Schmitt, Carl (1996): The Concept of the Political. George Schwab (trans.). Chicago: University of Chicago Press.
Schopenhauer, Arthur (2001): Parerga and Paralipomena. E.F.J. Payne (trans.). Oxford: Oxford University Press.

Shafir, Gershon (1985): "The Incongruity between Destiny and Merit: Max Weber on Meaningful Existence and Modernity". In: The British Journal of Sociology 36(4), pp. 516–530.
Strauss, Leo (1989): "Relativism". In: Pangle, Thomas (ed.): The Rebirth of Classical Political Rationalism. Chicago: University of Chicago Press.
Strauss, Leo (1995): "Preface to Spinoza's Critique of Religion". In: Leo Strauss: Liberalism Ancient and Modern. Chicago, London: University of Chicago Press.
Strong, Tracy (1992): "'What have we to do with morals?' Nietzsche and Weber on history and ethics". In: History of the Human Sciences 5, pp. 9–18.
Strong, Tracy (2002): "Love, Passion, and Maturity: Nietzsche and Weber on Science, Morality, and Politics". In: McCormick, John (ed.): Confronting Mass Democracy and Industrial Technology. Durham: Duke University Press, pp. 15–41.
Tenbruck, Friedrich (1980): "The Problem of Thematic Unity in the Works of Max Weber". In: The British Journal of Sociology 31(3), pp. 316–351.
Titunik, Regina (1997): "The Continuation of History: Max Weber on the Advent of a New Aristocracy". In: The Journal of Politics 59(3), pp. 680–700.
Williams, Bernard (2006): "Unbearable Suffering". In: The Sense of the Past. Princeton, Oxford: Princeton University Press.

V. **Physiology, Genealogy, and Politics in Nietzsche**

Razvan Ioan
The Politics of Physiology

The task of this paper is an inquiry into Nietzsche's political thought in relation to his understanding of physiology. This project will require two stages of analysis. The first step will be dedicated to outlining the characteristics of the relation between politics and physiology. The main argument in this section of the paper will be that Nietzsche's originality can be found in his treatment of political events as symptoms of physiological processes and, in return, seeing physiological processes as symptoms of political tastes or models. Given that there is no complete and explicit outline of Nietzsche's views on politics in his writings, we may look for the reflection of his political views in physiology in order to obtain clues for understanding his political thought. This section sets the framework for the second step of the inquiry. The onus of the second stage will be on analysing the changes in Nietzsche's physiology from the *Genealogy of Morality* onwards, changes that mirror an important shift in political views. In the *Genealogy* and the unpublished material of the period, Nietzsche criticizes democratic taste as the corrupting factor in, among others, the science of physiology. He uses this critique as a stepping stone for giving his own account of what physiology should look like and we can see that his view of the way the human body is structured is compatible with a hierarchical system. Towards the end of his philosophical career, in the very last unpublished notes, as well as in *Ecce Homo*, there is a trend towards a more radical approach to physiology. This not only stands in marked contrast with his earlier arguments, but offers a much less palatable political view even for the advocates of hierarchy and is, arguably, of a more unelaborated and simplistic nature. If the latter is indeed the case then it will be argued that it is in the spirit of Nietzsche's philosophical project to prefer the political model of the *Genealogy*. We must remember that Nietzsche's criticism of both physiology and politics is motivated by his concern with what he perceives to be the "decadence" of the culture and of the society he lived in. The critical task of showing where mistakes have been made is accompanied by Nietzsche's project of strengthening the human species. Even if the project for enhancing the human species is not clearly defined and formulated, its presence in Nietzsche's writings cannot be questioned. Therefore, the arguments of the second stage of this paper will have to take into consideration Nietzsche's attempts at offering solutions to the crisis he perceives in modernity just as much as his criticism of modernity. The thesis is that we can catch a glimpse of Nietzsche's political views not only from his criticism of the degeneration of physiological structures but also from his suggestions for enhancement.

I The framework of the politics-physiology relation

Thomas Brobjer (B2008, p. 213), in making his case for the assumed lack of interest on Nietzsche's part in the question of politics, uses a note from the *Nachlass* in which Nietzsche advocates "The dominance of physiology over theology, morality, economy and politics" (NL 1887, KGW VIII/2, 9[165]) as part of his proposed remedies for "Modernity".[1] No reader of Nietzsche's work can fail to observe his constant concern with and criticism of modernity or rather of the decadence (*Entartung*) he believes is at the heart of contemporary European society and culture.[2] In this context it is not surprising that Nietzsche thinks physiological remedies might help overcome the sickliness endemic in modernity. In the same note, Nietzsche talks about improved diet or "increasing cleanliness and health"[3] as appropriate responses to contemporary decadence. In the interest of exactness it must be mentioned that this note is by no means one of a kind. Nietzsche is a fervent advocate, especially in his later works, of the importance of physiology, especially in contrast with morality or religion.

> Moral value as apparent value, by comparison with the physiological (NL 1888, KGW VIII/3, 14[104]).[4]

> this entire praxis of spiritual restoration must be deferred to a physiological foundation (NL 1888, KGW VIII/3, 14[155]).[5]

---

[1] "die Vorherrschaft der Physiologie über Theologie, Moralistik, Ökonomie und Politik". – The translation of the quotes from the published works is taken from Carol Diethe's translation for the *Genealogy of Morality* and from Judith Norman's translation for *Ecce Homo* and *Twilight of the Idols* while the translation of the fragments from the unpublished material belongs to the author.
The example used here, from the work of Thomas Brobjer, is not singular. In the Introduction to his book on "Nietzsche as Political Thinker" Keith Ansell-Pearson starts by pointing to an entire tradition of interpreting Nietzsche as the thinker of the "solitary, isolated individuals, far removed from the cares and concerns of the social world" (Ansell-Pearson 1994 pp.1f.). This way of viewing Nietzsche, inaugurated by Kaufman, is the result of the attempts to distance his writings from the abuse they suffered at the hands of the Nazis. Also relevant is Martha Nussbaum's argument in Nussbaum, 1997 that serious political philosophy needs to forget about Nietzsche.
[2] See the upcoming *Nietzsche-Wörterbuch* entry on "Entartung" for a comprehensive survey of this concept in Nietzsche's work
[3] "zunehmende Reinlichkeit and Gesundheit".
[4] "Die Moralwerthe als Scheinwerthe, verglichen mit den physiologischen".
[5] "diese ganze Praxis der seelischen Wiederherstellung muß auf eine physiologische Grundlage zurückgestellt werden".
For similar texts see: NL 1886, KGW VIII/1, 7[6]; KSA 12, p. 273, GM I 17 or GM III 13.

Given this body of text it might seem at first that the issue of the relation between physiology and politics (as well as art or morality for that matter) can have only one solution for Nietzsche: the "Vorherrschaft" of physiology over all these other disciplines and fields of activity. It seems this way until we realise that this selection of texts is arbitrary and that the content of the notion of supremacy or hegemony "Vorherrschaft" is by no means simple to elucidate.

First, the claims in favour of a privileged status for physiology among all other sciences and disciplines are tempered by notes in the *Nachlass* in which Nietzsche considers the possibility that physiology does not give definite or definitive explanations for morality, aesthetics or for what a human being is: "The human as a multiplicity: physiology gives only an indication of the wonderful traffic within this multiplicity" (NL 1884, KGW VII/2, 27[8]; cf. also NL 1884, KGW VII/2, 26[432] or NL 1888, KGW VIII/3, 15[41]).[6]

The second problematic aspect of a quick dismissal of Nietzsche's understanding of politics is the question of what exactly he meant by hegemony or "Vorherrschaft". The first question we can ask is whether the supremacy of physiology implies that any account of society, even of events that would commonly be referred to as political in nature, should be done in physiological terms. Does it make sense to stop talking about democracy, aristocracy or human rights, to choose only a few examples, and instead to speak about hygiene, nutrition or physical growth of individuals and of societies i.e. to resort to reductionism? Since such an approach is completely unsatisfactory for describing Nietzsche's position on the issue of politics, we must look for a more refined and multi-faceted way of describing the link between politics and physiology. The second question is what is the best way to describe such a complex relation, what methodological tools should be used. A rather traditional procedure would be to argue that physiological processes are the cause of political events and perhaps, in turn, political events cause changes in the physiological structure of societies and individuals. This is not a path that Nietzsche neglects, although this method finds its use mainly in describing the relation between physiology and morality. Nietzsche's originality, however, finds its expression in the development of a new conceptual device deployed in this context, a device that can best be labelled symptomatology.

If the arguments in favour of a more balanced view of the relation between physiology and politics do indeed prove to be solid, we have not yet proven that Brobjer's main point becomes invalid – Nietzsche had little to say about politics compared to philosophers like Aristotle, Hobbes, Spinoza or Rousseau.

---

6 "Der Mensch als Vielheit: die Physiologie giebt nur die Andeutung eines wunderbaren Verkehrs zwischen dieser Vielheit".

He did not offer any systematic treatment of different forms of government, or of political institutions or of specific political events that occurred during his lifetime. There are numerous places where Nietzsche offers nuggets of his insights into the workings of aristocracy or of democracy (see for instance the detailed account of Nietzsche's views on democracy in Siemens 2008), but it can be safely stated that there is no worked out political theory in Nietzsche's writings. Nevertheless, despite arguments by Brobjer and many others, it does not follow that he is not a political thinker. The aim of this paper is to take an indirect route in uncovering Nietzsche's views on politics. It does not aim to look directly at notions belonging to political theory, but to look through the prism of Nietzsche's account of physiology. As much as Nietzsche believes that physiological processes and developments affect politics, it is also the case that political or moral events affect society's and an individual's physiological constitution and Nietzsche not only applies physiological models and interpretations to political events, but also uses political vocabulary in order to make sense of physiology. Nietzsche's views on politics can surface not only from his direct take on politics, but from the political models and language he uses to account for physiological multiplicities.

II How should we understand "Vorherrschaft"?

In the discussions of politics with respect to physiology that were published, Nietzsche either leaves the question of the relation open (such as BGE 242 when he simply talks about physiological processes being behind moral and political foregrounds – "hinter all den moralischen und politischen Vordergründen") or he uses words that indicate quite clearly he does not have a reductionist account in mind (BT Preface 4 – the relation is qualified by the word "Symptom" or GM I 5 – political events signify (*bedeuten*) physiological processes). In the case of BGE 242 the political language runs parallel to the physiological vocabulary and is never abandoned. In the argument of BGE 242, when Nietzsche jumps from political to physiological language, he explicitly mentions that it is just a manner of speaking (*physiologisch geredet*). The main benefit of not endorsing reductionism is that the language of politics (and morality or religion) can be kept, while being invested with new meanings. Nietzsche attempts to imbue the language of politics with physiological nuances that open up novel ways of answering existing questions. The way Nietzsche goes about this task is by opening up the question of the relation between the vocabulary of physiology and the vocabulary of politics. The relation, to be precise, is one between the situations described in political terms and the situations or processes described in physiological terms. The analysis of the relation between these two languages or descriptions is governed by the notion of metaphor, and so a study of it would benefit from looking at Blondel's book: *Nietzsche, le corps et la culture*. Nevertheless, in this paper, the relation between the two languages will be analysed first and foremost not from a linguistic but from a medical/physiological perspective. This means the events described in the language of politics will be considered symptoms of the processes described in physiological language. This choice stems from the fact that Nietzsche himself seemed to have a marked preference for physiological language.

Blondel, in his book on Nietzsche, and especially in chapter 9, is correct to emphasize the various vocabularies (physiological, moral, political or religious) that constitute Nietzsche's understanding of reality (cf. Blondel 2001). He argues that the connection between these vocabularies is governed by the notion of metaphor: language is a device used to construct interpretations and also to give coherence to this multi-layered world-view. The argument here is not that the link between these layers or vocabularies is not governed by language, but it is about the exact type of language that Nietzsche has in mind for connecting these various layers. Blondel's argument focuses on metaphors, on philological devices. However, the conjecture of this paper is that medical language is at least as important. To give Blondel's argument its due, we can indicate a number of passages where Nietzsche writes that affects or moral judgments and valuations are symbols or signs of physiological processes (NL 1883, KGW VII/1, 7[87]; NL 1884, KGW VII/2, 27[8]; M 119, KSA 3, p. 113). Nevertheless, the term symptom is a constant occurrence whenever morality or Christianity, for instance, need to be interpreted physiologically (NL 1885, KGW VIII/1, 2[165]; NL 1885, KGW VIII/1, 2[190]; BGE 202; NL 1888, KGW VIII/3, 14[13]). In this case, physiology not only acts as the interpretative layer that offers the vocabulary into which other layers should be translated, but it also offers the means by which that translation is accomplished. In the somewhat rarer cases where physiology does not play this role, Nietzsche is vaguer about how physiological vocabulary should be interpreted, translated: "The human as a multiplicity: physiology gives only an indication of the wonderful traffic within this multiplicity" (NL 1884, KGW VII/2, 27[8]).

It must be said that the relation between political and physiological processes, or events, is not conceptualised by Nietzsche only in the manner shown above. Next to the vocabulary of symptomatology we can place that of causality. This means that sometimes physiological processes are seen as causes and moral or political situations as effects. We can find examples of this at NL 1880, KGW V/1, 3[61], GM III 15 or NL 1888, KGW VIII/3, 15[12]. A critic might immediately point out that the fragments mentioned so far have given a picture in which morality is only the effect of physiological processes. Morality and resentment do not seem to be efficacious elements in the causal chain. This picture would, however, distort Nietzsche's thinking and take away from the impact of morality on physiology (for better or for worse): "The growth of physiological and moral evil in the human species is, conversely, the result of a sick and unnatural Morality" (NL 1888, KGW VIII/3, 15[41]; cf. NL 1888, KGW VIII/3, 14[210]).[7]

Considering physiological and political or moral processes as causes and effects is something Nietzsche does regularly, but not as often as considering these processes symptoms of one-another. As section 6 of the Preface (*Vorrede*) to the *Genealogy* shows, an explanation in terms of causality can very well exist alongside an interpretation of morality, politics or of any other field as a symptom of physiological states and processes ("morality as result, as symptom, as mask [...] but also morality as cause, remedy, stimulant"; GM Preface 6). In discussing the relation between physiology and politics, Nietzsche appealed consistently to symptomatology and so we must now focus on the way physiological language can influence political language and on the way political language has found its way into physiological descriptions. It is precisely here that this paper must find its niche in the study of Nietzsche's politics, namely in the role political language plays in physiology, the way political thinking comes to influence Nietzsche's physiology and from there on play a central role in his philosophy. The first step is to see what Nietzsche finds wrong in the physiology of his time and then how he suggests we can improve on the state of this science.

III The Genealogy of Morality: Political Prejudices in Physiology

Nietzsche does not take the science of physiology for granted – he is very critical of the errors that have crept in this discipline:

> How feeble has all physiological knowledge been so far (NL 1881, KGW V/2, 11[173]).[8]

> Physiological misconceptions: 1) sickness as higher form of misunderstanding life 2) Intoxication 3) Impassibility (NL 1888, KGW VIII/3, 14[69]).[9]

---

[7] "das Wachsthum der physiologischen und moralischen Übel im menschlichen Geschlecht ist umgekehrt die Folge einer krankhaften und unnatürlichen Moral"
[8] "Wie unkräftig war bisher alle physiologische Erkenntniß!"
[9] "Die physiologischen Mißverständnisse. / 1. die Krankheit als höhere Form des Lebens mißverstanden / 2. der Rausch / 3. die Impassibilität".

However, far more interesting for our purposes are two passages from the *Genealogy of Morality* that link errors in physiology to political notions i.e. democratic prejudices. Both these fragments engage with the issue of "democratic prejudice" or "modern misarchism" as Nietzsche calls it. The conjecture of this paper is that the errors he is referring to are from Wilhelm Roux's book *Der Kampf der Theile im Organismus*: Nietzsche deals with Roux's notion of physiology by spelling out his assumptions and criticizing what he sees as mistaken in those assumptions. The improvement he suggests is based on the work of another scientist of his time, William Rolph. Before looking at their contributions to physiology and Nietzsche's take on them we need to identify the relevant texts in Nietzsche's work:

> To me, this[10] seems an essential insight into moral genealogy; that it has been discovered so late is due to the obstructing influence which the democratic bias within the modern world exercises over all questions of descent. And this is the case in the apparently most objective of fields, natural science and physiology, as I shall just mention here (GM I 4).[11]

> The democratic idiosyncrasy of being against everything that dominates and wants to dominate, the modern misarchism (to coin a bad word for a bad thing) has gradually shaped and dressed itself up as intellectual, most intellectual, so much so that it already, today, little by little penetrates the strictest, seemingly most objective sciences, and is allowed to do so; indeed, I think it has already become master of the whole of physiology and biology, to their detriment, naturally, by spiriting away their basic concept, that of actual activity (GM II 12).[12]

In section 4 of the first essay of the *Genealogy*, from which the first text is taken, Nietzsche is busy outlining the history of the notions good and bad. He accuses the democratic prejudice characteristic of the modern world of having hidden the origin of these two terms and, in his words, "only hints" at the fact

---

10 "This ... insight" refers to the investigation into the etymological origin of the notions of "good" and "bad" that Nietzsche presents previously in this section
11 "Dies scheint mir in Betreff der Moral-Genealogie eine wesentliche Einsicht; dass sie so spät erst gefunden wird, liegt an dem hemmenden Einfluss, den das demokratische Vorurtheil innerhalb der modernen Welt in Hinsicht auf alle Fragen der Herkunft ausübt. Und dies bis in das anscheinend objektivste Gebiet der Naturwissenschaft und Physiologie hinein, wie hier nur angedeutet werden soll."
12 "Die demokratische Idiosynkrasie gegen Alles, was herrscht und herrschen will, der moderne Misarchismus (um ein schlechtes Wort für eine schlechte Sache zu bilden) hat sich allmählich dermaassen in's Geistige, Geistigste umgesetzt und verkleidet, dass er heute Schritt für Schritt bereits in die strengsten, anscheinend objektivsten Wissenschaften eindringt, eindringen darf; ja er scheint mir schon über die ganze Physiologie und Lehre vom Leben Herr geworden zu sein, zu ihrem Schaden, wie sich von selbst versteht, indem er ihr einen Grundbegriff, den der eigentlichen Aktivität, eskamotirt hat."

that physiology and natural science are under the spell of the same prejudice. Because Nietzsche is not explicit about what he means we are restricted to guess work regarding how exactly he thinks physiology is corrupted. What we can do is try to understand what Nietzsche means by "questions of origin" (*Fragen der Herkunft*) and then apply that to the field of physiology. In the context of section 4 the question of origin is the question of how the words good and bad have changed their initial meanings to the ones that we are familiar with today. The pair originally referred to the opposition between "aristocratic soul", "noble" on the one hand and "common", "plain", "simple" on the other before they came to refer to moral notions and gained inculpatory implication. In other words, democratic prejudice did not allow "historians of morality" (GM I 2) to see that good and bad referred to a distinction within a hierarchy and not to moral notions. What Nietzsche is getting at here is the opposition he sets up between the democratic way of thinking, consisting in the levelling of all differences of rank, (visible in the science of physiology in the work of Roux, as it will be argued later) and a way of thinking that acknowledges the importance of hierarchies.

Historical/genealogical research and the notion of hierarchy are just as important to the physiology Nietzsche is trying to build as they are to understanding morality and politics, and section 12 of the second essay of the *Genealogy* shows how. The main topic of this section is Nietzsche's analysis of the notion and of the history of punishment. Nevertheless, he is a bit more generous than before with his remarks regarding contemporary physiology, the kind he wants to criticize and improve. A central role in this account of physiology is played by the notion of "activity". However, before it can become clear why "activity" plays such an important role, it is crucial to grasp what Nietzsche is trying to argue for at this stage of the *Genealogy*. The main argument of section 12 of the second essay is that there should be a distinction between the origin and the purpose of a custom or of an institution: in this particular case the institution studied is that of "punishment". Nietzsche argues that a researcher of human customs, institutions etc. must realize that the purpose or meaning of the custom has nothing to do with its origin, but with the interpretation it is given at a specific time and place by a "will to power" that is strong enough to become master and give meaning to customs. What is peculiar about this analysis is that at every step of the argumentation Nietzsche draws parallels between the re-interpretation of the institution of "punishment" and physiological processes. To begin with, Nietzsche applies the distinction between origin and purpose to any and every event in the "organic world". Furthermore, when enumerating the different "things" for which this distinction is valid Nietzsche chooses to start with "physiological organ"(s). Only after mentioning the term "physiological organ" do other examples appear, and only in parenthesis (the examples are "legal institution, a social custom, a political usage, a form in art or in a religious cult"). Later on we can see that the examples Nietzsche chooses, in order to show how the mistake of conflating origin and purpose manifests itself, are from the world of biology: "the eye being made for seeing, the hand being made for grasping". This trend continues when Nietzsche mentions the terms "organ" and "custom" side-by-side. They are mentioned together because a) histories of both organs and customs are long chains of interpretations and re-interpretations and b) the "evolution" of both of them is by no means a progress toward a goal but a succession of processes of mastering. Later, Nietzsche goes even further in focusing on physiology, by dropping the notion of "customs" altogether and giving an analysis of the fluidity of "meaning" at the level of both organs within an organism and of individuals within a species. In the last part of the section Nietzsche decides to make a point not about the study of customs, the concept he started off with, but about the science of physiology. He considers it worth his time to criticize the insidious influence of democratic taste on the "strictest, apparently most objective sciences". The conflation of origin and purpose does not allow us to see the importance of the "will to power" as the giver, the creator of meaning. We should see the "will to power", not the origin of a custom or of an organ, as the determining factor in establishing meaning or function. Because we do not understand that meaning is created by the "will to power" that masters a "thing", we do not have a proper understanding of the difference in rank, of the hierarchy between the functions or meanings of organs and customs. If this understanding is lacking (we might even hate the idea of hierarchy and of domination – this is what Nietzsche means by "misarchism") then we cannot have an adequate science of physiology and therefore we cannot strengthen (*stärkeren*) the species man, but instead contribute to the corruption of life. Nietzsche, as he makes it very clear in this context, is concerned with the project of advancing the species man, of creating a stronger species – this he considers an actual progress (*wirklichen progressus*). In order to see precisely why Nietzsche builds the parallel between the study of social customs and political institutions on the one hand, and physiological organs on the other hand, we must address the following questions: who is he referring to when he deplores the state of the science of physiology (1) and what exactly is wrong with this science and how can it be set right (2)?

1) The use of the term "Evolution" (*Entwicklung*) in GM II 12 cannot escape the notice of someone familiar with 19th century science. Nietzsche gives us his own view on evolution, arguing against understanding evolution as progress, i.e. being directed towards a goal. His view on evolution is that it is the sum

of processes of mastering and subduing in which a "will to power" becomes master and gives purpose, i.e. a function, to an organ, within the organism. The history of evolution is the history of various "wills to power" that succeed each-other in determining the purpose of an organ.

The comparison that Nietzsche draws out is that between the different meanings or purposes a custom can have and the functions of organs of a body. In the same way that multiple purposes of a custom can co-exist even if some are more prominent than others, different functions of organs of the body can and should co-exist even if one organ masters others and uses them for its own purposes, therefore imposing on them functions that are dominant (GM II 12). The process of mastering is, of course, nothing else but the sign that a "will to power" has become dominant. In order to understand what this co-existing and mastering mean in the case of organs, this paper will argue that it is highly informative to turn to Nietzsche's reading of the physiologist Wilhelm Roux and his *Der Kampf der Theile im Organismus*.[13] In order to understand Roux's view on the organism, and on the relation between organs, it is to the second section of Roux's book that we must turn. This section is dedicated to explaining the different types of struggle that occur between elements of the body. Parts of the body may fight for space or for access to nutrients, given that both resources are insufficient for all the parts of the body to thrive. The fight between cells or organs, as far as Roux is concerned, is motivated by the scarcity of resources available. Roux distinguishes between four types of elements that engage in combat – molecules, cells, tissues and organs but, more importantly, he differentiates between the conflict occurring at the level of molecules and cells and the conflict at the level of tissues and organs. The difference consists mainly in the outcome of the fight: molecules and cells, if they lose in the struggle for survival, perish, but tissues and organs must endure and find some sort of balance (*Gleichgewicht*) if the organism as a whole is to survive. At the level of cells and molecules the outcome of the fight is decided by the ability of molecules or cells to respond, react to outside stimuli and to grow as much as possible. The greater the intake of nutrients compared to expenditure the greater the space will be that cells occupy and the better chance they have to outlive their competitors. (Roux 1881, pp. 75f.) In this way the cells that are the strongest, i.e. have the best properties for the stimuli they are subject to, will survive and give the body as a whole the best building blocks it could have. The cells that do not make it in this struggle will die, but the organism does not need them and therefore is not affected by their destruc-

---

[13] See Müller-Lauter's (1978) classical study of Nietzsche's reading of Roux.

tion. The cells that survive and the ones that die in the struggle are supposed to fulfill similar functions, so the organism only needs the cells that are best equipped to handle the specific task a group of cells must perform. The situation is radically different in the case of tissues and organs, because an organism needs all of its tissues and organs in order to survive. Therefore, no tissue or organ can monopolize all the resources available and all the space within a body, if the organism as a whole is to survive. (Roux 1881, p. 97) The point is that the properties of tissues and organs are heterogeneous, as opposed to cells, where the difference is mainly one of degree of strength. Because different organs have different tasks, the failure of any one of them will be fatal to the entire system. Of course, we might have a case in which one organ or one tissue becomes stronger than the rest and uses more resources, but the organs and tissues that are being dominated never disappear or die. (Roux 1881, pp. 104f.) The dominant organ can only grow more powerful through dependency on the activity of other organs and their ability, even if diminished, to perform their function. Organs, even if diminished by their neighbours in size, still have the ability to defend themselves and not be over-run completely. This picture should not give the impression that Roux's account of the organism is teleological. The balance/equilibrium existing in the organism is not the result of any intelligent design, or pre-established harmony, and the individual components of the body do not somehow act with the benefit of the entire organism in mind. The organs and tissues do not destroy each other not because they somehow do not wish to do it, but because the other organs have the ability to defend themselves, an ability which defeated cells to not possess. Roux gives a fully mechanistic account of the inner-working of the body and the balance resulting from the fight of the components is just the result of a contingent process. Roux, in fact, is careful to state (Roux 1881, p. 98) that harmony is possible only for a certain period of time, while all the necessary conditions happen to be met.

This short account of Roux shows how it is possible to imagine a hierarchy, a relation based on mastering and subduing that does not require that the defeated or dominated organ be annihilated or destroyed. An organ can keep existing and in fact it can be very useful for the dominating element since it can be imprinted with the function that the dominating "will to power" assigns to it.

2) It is now time to turn to Nietzsche's critique of Roux. In section 12 of the *Genealogy,* Nietzsche argues that in all events, whether at the level of physiology or of customs in a society, the "will to power" operates. This essay does not include an attempt to elucidate the notion of "will to power" in Nietzsche's philosophy, but it looks at the way it operates in this specific context. In Nietzsche's words:

> [T]hat everything that occurs in the organic world consists of overpowering, dominating, and in their turn, overpowering and dominating consist of re-interpretation, adjustment, in the process of which their former 'meaning' and 'purpose' must necessarily be obscured or completely obliterated (GM II 12).[14]

It might seem that Roux's account is perfectly consistent with Nietzsche's view since, after all, Roux fully believed that in the struggle between parts of the body some will gain the upper hand and will subdue the others (especially in the case of tissues and organs where destroying the other participants to the contest is not an outcome to be desired). Nevertheless, it seems that Nietzsche takes issue with Roux's stance on two issues: he attacks the mechanistic way of understanding events (a) and he argues that death, even in the case of organs, is among the conditions of "actual progress/*wirklichen progressus*" (b). The argument will be that Nietzsche does indeed depart from Roux's understanding of physiology regarding point (a), but that their disagreement on point (b) is only an illusion, a matter of semantics rather than of content. Nietzsche will disagree with Roux about (b) only in the latter part of his work, as will be argued for later.

a) Nietzsche makes it very clear that his theory of the "will to power" is opposed to complete fortuitousness or mechanistic senselessness. The doctrine of the "will to power" has the idea of hierarchy, of becoming master at its core and Nietzsche believes mechanistic explanations are a symptom of the modern, democratic taste which is in favour of the abolition of hierarchy. Mechanistic explanations have the notion of "adaptation" at their core. Nietzsche, of course, together with the whole scientific establishment of the time, had no idea about how genetics worked, so he believed that any theory of adaptation is based on the notion of "reactivity". In the course of their development, animals would react to external stimuli and thus adapt, change their form to one that would suit them better. If we remember that Lamarckism was by no means a defeated theory at the time, and that the idea of inherited acquired traits had not been dismissed, this picture of how evolution works seems entirely plausible. In order to contrast this understanding of evolution with contemporary accounts, we must begin by arguing that "adaptation" as it is conceived now does not have the notion of "reactivity" at its core. It is true that the accidental genetic mutations that occur in DNA are tested by the way the organism that suffered the mutation can survive in its environment – the genetic mutations must help the organism adapt. However, the mutations are not the result of the

---

[14] "alles Geschehen in der organischen Welt ein Überwältigen, Herrwerden und dass wiederum alles Überwältigen und Herrwerden ein Neu-Interpretieren, ein Zurechtmachen ist, bei dem der bisherige 'Sinn' und 'Zweck' nothwendig verdunkelt oder ganz ausgelöscht werden muss"

environment's influence on the organism or on its parents. They are random processes and by no means a response to external stimuli. This, of course, was not available to Roux so his theory explains evolution and adaptation through external stimuli (*Reize*), since the response to these stimuli decides whether cells or tissues grow. (Roux 1881, p. 78) The emphasis on the environment, on the importance of external factors (*die Lehre vom Milieu*), is a usual target for criticism on Nietzsche's part, in this period and even later:

> The fact that people in present-day France think about this much differently (and in Germany too, but this does not matter), the fact that the theory of the milieu, a true neurotics' theory, has become sacrosanct and almost scientific, that it has even caught on with physiologists, all this 'smells bad', this is a bad train of thought (TI Skirmishes).[15]

> NB NB The doctrine of Millieu a decadence-theory, but infiltrated and become master in physiology (NL 1888, KGW VIII/3, 15[105]).[16]

To this reactive understanding of organisms, Nietzsche opposes a different view of life, one based on "activity". In virtue of an organ's, or a custom's "will to power", it establishes relations with its environment in which it is the dominant force. The "will to power" is, according to Nietzsche, the essence of life and it consists in the priority of the "spontaneous, aggressive, expansive, form-giving forces". In spite of Nietzsche's protests that mistaken concepts have taken over all physiology, the importance of expansive forces within an individual is a theory he read about in the work of the English biologist William Rolph (Nietzsche probably read him around 1884 – Moore 2006, p. 47). Rolph was a theoretician of evolution who was not in agreement with Darwin's explanation of evolution. Rolph rejected self-preservation as the fundamental principle of life and, instead posited appetite, insatiable desire for assimilation as the guiding principle of organisms. When organisms are weak they may, of course, aim at working together, at co-operation, but when organisms are strong then they dominate, they wish to exercise their power and keep their distance and independence from other living beings. Rolph criticizes Darwin and, together with him, Malthus, for believing that scarcity (key issue for Roux as well, as has been mentioned) is the motor of evolution, whereas he argued life is based on abundance and consists in expressions of power. Rolph is anti-

---

[15] "Dass man hierüber in Frankreich heute sehr anders denkt (in Deutschland auch: aber daran liegt nichts), dass dort die Theorie vom milieu, eine wahre Neurotiker-Theorie, sakrosankt und beinahe wissenschaftlich geworden ist und bis unter die Physiologen Glauben findet, das 'riecht nicht gut', das macht Einem traurige Gedanken".
[16] "NB NB die Lehre vom Milieu eine décadence-Theorie, aber eingedrungen und Herr geworden in der Physiologie".

Darwinian in that he sees the fight for expansion as the principle of life (instead of the fight for the conservation of life). He bases his arguments on the case of the first organisms that developed and became more complex, even if they had an abundance of food and an absolute lack of competition. Rolph argues that only prosperity induces diversity and gives as proof the diversity of domesticated animals, as opposed to that of their wild counterparts. (Rolph 1884, pp. 72, 77, 124) Therefore, regarding the first objection, there is a good case to be made that by the time the *Genealogy* was written, Nietzsche's commitment to the doctrine of the "will to power" was backed up by his choice of biological theories. The notion of activity is paramount to his philosophy and to his critique of Roux, i.e. Nietzsche now believes that the fight between cells or organs is not motivated by the scarcity of resources, but by their own spontaneous activity, their drive to expand. The issue is how far this critique goes and how much it changes in the Roux-inspired picture of the organism as a harmonious collectivity, i.e. can the active expansion of an organ lead to another's destruction?

b) The fact that Nietzsche mentions the death of organs, among the conditions for an actual progress (GM II 12) in the species man, flies in the face of Roux's arguments in favour of the balance between organs. Nietzsche's interest in physiology and genealogical research was not purely historical, of course, but it was to be used in the project of creating a "stronger species of man" ("stärkeren Species Mensch"; GM II 12). If genealogical research showed that sacrifice was necessary for progress (not just reduction in number or strength but actual death of an organ), then our democratic prejudices should not obscure that fact. Death might not be welcome if an organism is to persevere in existence. Nevertheless, Nietzsche's goal is not to find ways of preserving anything, but to strengthen man. Organisms or even mankind in the mass (*die Menschheit als Masse*) might have to be destroyed in the process and that is a sacrifice we must accept. If we also look at a later passage such as EH M 2: "The physiologist demands that the degenerate part be cut out, he refuses solidarity with anything degenerate, pity is the last thing on his mind"[17] then Nietzsche's position seems to be quite radical and we might be tempted in believing that this was a permanent trait of Nietzsche's thinking. One could argue that in the *Genealogy*, as well as in *Ecce Homo*, Nietzsche appeals to the model of struggle for annihilation we found at the level of cells or molecules. Nevertheless, there are good reasons not to accept this thesis. The pertinent question in this context is: is this a reading of Nietzsche that holds up to scruti-

---

[17] "Der Physiologe verlangt Ausschneidung des entarteten Theils, er verneint jede Solidarität mit dem Entartenden, er ist am fernsten vom Mitleiden mit ihm".

ny, is there enough textual evidence and is there agreement with the rest of his thought? There are serious philosophical reasons for Nietzsche not wishing to commit to such an extreme view. The obvious objection to any desire to annihilate those that are, in Nietzsche's view, dominated by resentment, is the fact that he could also be charged with resentment in this case. If the goal is to fight against the very existence of a specific species or type of man (e.g. the ascetic priest) then we would only replicate the priest's desire to annihilate the noble type and our actions would be borne out of the same hatred and resentment. We would also lose access to everything that the ascetic priest and slave morality have developed and worked on throughout their existence (man acquired depth, became evil and in these respects is superior to other beasts) and that is exactly what makes man the most interesting animal (GM I 6).

In GM II 12 we could be tricked into thinking that death means the same thing as annihilation or destruction. However, if we look carefully at the elements that make up what Nietzsche calls, "in short, death" we will be surprised. Death implies "diminution of utility, atrophying and degeneration, a loss of meaning and of purposiveness". None of these imply the disappearance of the organ, but they mean its subordination within the hierarchy that is the human body and their dependence on whatever element is dominant. The degenerated organs, lacking in their original purpose, are reduced to the role of subjects of the element strong enough to give them direction. The "loss of meaning" is not absolute; rather the organs are invested with a new function given by the ruling element. In a note from the *Nachlass* dating from 1885, Nietzsche goes one step further and makes it explicit that the dominant element, the higher type as he calls it on that occasion, is possible only through the reduction of the lower to a function. In other words the higher type can dominate, can manifest its aggressive "will to power" only against something that obeys: "Slavery and the division of labour-the higher type possible only through the reduction of a lower to a function" (NL 1885, KGW VIII/1, 2[76]).[18] Earlier in the same note Nietzsche makes it clear that he is thinking about a collection of dominant elements in the body that form an aristocracy: "Aristocracy in the body, the plurality of the regents (Struggle of the tissues?".[19] In the parenthesis he goes so far as to ask if aristocracy is not similar to a fight between tissues (question reminiscent of Roux, of course). The conjecture here is that the question mark at the end of this fragment stands for an element of uncertainty on Nietzsche's part that will find its solution in section 12 of the

---

[18] "Die Sklaverei und die Arbeitstheilung: der höhere Typus nur möglich durch Herunterdrückung eines niederen auf eine Funktion". See also BGE 258 for a similar argument.
[19] "Die Aristokratie im Leibe, die Mehrheit der Herrschenden (Kampf der Gewebe)?"

second essay of the *Genealogy*. Judging by the *Nachlass* note, in conjunction with section II 12 of the *Genealogy*, we can develop the following picture of Nietzsche's physiology: the history of a custom is constituted by numerous instances in which a "will to power" took over the custom and gave it a purpose, a meaning. This takeover implies that there is a hierarchy in which a dominant "will to power" governs. The relation between the various "wills to power" and the various meanings that they impose is built by Nietzsche on the model of the struggle within the organism. A "will to power" may be dominant at some point, but it can also become dominated and subdued by another "will to power". The function is, however, never destroyed, annihilated and we can see that in the fact that the different meanings with which the institution of "punishment" has been invested with do not disappear. Instead, they co-exist in the range of purposes we can identify in punishment (Nietzsche offers a list at GM II 13). The different meanings do not exclude each other, but can co-exist, even if there is a hierarchy governed by the "will to power" that created each of them. What Nietzsche got from Roux was the understanding that, in a body, multiple organs can co-exist and dominate each-other without annihilating each-other, but by being given new functions. An organ never really loses all function in this case (that would lead to atrophying and to death), it is simply invested with a new one. Nietzsche then applied the model of this type of struggle, which leads to balance, in which there is no final victor, to the conflict existing between the different purposes or meaning of a custom. Where he differs from Roux is in placing the concept of "activity" or "spontaneity" at the heart of the conflict that exists between organs. The development of an organ or of any other "thing" in the organic world is not the result of external influence, but of its own drive for expansion. After these considerations we can conclude that Nietzsche definitely moves away from Roux regarding the issue presented under (a), but that, regarding the problem presented under (b), he is not yet ready to take a radical stand point, to commit himself to advocating the elimination of the subdued element. This sharp stance will become manifest only later in Nietzsche's writings, after the *Genealogy of Morality*.

In the last part of his philosophical career, Nietzsche's physiology seems to move in a very clearly defined direction. He becomes much more adamant that the degenerate elements in a body require excision (EH M 2), that there can be no solidarity in a society that includes unproductive, unfruitful elements (NL 1888, KGW VIII/3, 15[41]) and that the degenerate should be separated from the healthy organs lest the whole body be destroyed. (NL 1888, KGW VIII/3, 23[1]) The question that arises is what kind of hierarchy we can have, if anything that is less than healthy must be destroyed, and not made better nor dominated by the healthy. Can it be the case that Nietzsche is willing to part with the notion of "Rangordnung" as he understood it in the *Genealogy* in favour of a radical solution against the sickly? There are very solid arguments against such a radical view, (see for instance Ridley 1998 or Fossen 2008), but they are based mainly on texts from the *Genealogy* or from *Beyond Good and Evil* that come earlier than the texts just mentioned: in *Ecce Homo* and in the late *Nachlass*. For the purposes of this paper the key fragment that must be considered is the note entitled Great Politics at NL, KGW VIII/3, 25[1] in which Nietzsche's thoughts on the relation between politics and physiology are outlined.

IIIa Drives as the fundamental elements of the science of physiology

It is necessary to stop for a moment here and emphasize the fact that Nietzsche's physiology does not have the notion of organ at its centre in most cases, but that of drive (*Trieb*) and sometimes that of instinct (*Instinkt*). Nietzsche's rhetoric of higher and lower forms of life is grounded in the different configurations of instincts these different types of life possess. The distinction between higher and lower, commanding and subduing, plays a crucial role, as we have already seen, in Nietzsche's critique of contemporary physiology. Not only does it contradict the democratic prejudice, the "misarchism" Nietzsche identifies in physiology, but the recognition of the existence of hierarchies turns out to be indispensible for what Nietzsche called in the *Genealogy* the "prosperity of one single stronger species of man"[20] (GM II 12). This key role played by drives in this discussion of hierarchy is the reason why the notion of drive needs clarification. The vocabulary of "Trieb" or "Instinkt" was part of Nietzsche's physiological language from his earliest writings (NL 1872, KGW III/4, 19[117]). Later on he starts associating the concept of hierarchy with that of drives (NL 1884, KGW VII/2, 25[411]) and to distinguish between higher and lower instincts. This, of course, implies that Nietzsche has in mind a plurality of instincts or drives (for instance TI Skirmishes 39 when he speaks of "Geschlechtstrieb"/"sex drive", "Eigenthumstrieb"/"drive for property" or "Herrschafts-Trieb"/"drive to dominate"). The diversity of drives in Nietzsche's work is the result of what Assoun (2006, p. 54) argues is a propensity to postulate an instinct for every human activity. This multiplicity is kept together in a unity, but the instincts are never blended together.

The impact of the drives is not restricted to persons or human beings, it extends to all possible types of interaction between human beings: art, morali-

---

20 "Gedeihen einer einzelnen stärkeren Species Mensch".

ty, science and, of course, politics. Since any human being's actions are governed by his or her specific drives, any interaction between humans will ultimately come down to their drives. The greater the interaction, the more complicated the inter-play between drives is, but even in dealing with great complexity Nietzsche has a few favourites among drives in explaining different cultural and social phenomena (*Herrschafts-Trieb* or *Heerdeninstinkt* for instance). This explains why Nietzsche is never truly preoccupied with an account of institutions or political systems in the classical fashion of political theory. It also means that physiology could be perfectly suited to an analysis of politics and of the drives that contribute to it. We have already seen, in GM II 12, the parallel Nietzsche draws between the impact of the "will to power" on customs and on organs. Now we can see that the parallel can also be drawn with the way drives behave in Nietzsche's view: they form a multiplicity in which one (or some) become dominant for a period of time and then they are subdued by stronger drives.[21]

This line of reasoning has, of course, an important consequence: if Nietzsche is to take his project of strengthening the human species seriously then he needs to give an account of how physiology impacts on politics and consider the possibility that politics can help strengthen or bring about a progress in man. An example of this account can be found in Nietzsche's account of "Great Politics".

IIIb Great Politics

Nietzsche's philosophical activity cannot be reduced to a comprehensive critique of modern instincts, institutions and scientific disciplines. As we have already seen in GM II 12, Nietzsche also has a project of enhancing man: he claims that creating a single stronger species of man would be an advance (GM II 12). This project is pursued by Nietzsche up to the last moments of his creative life. One of the last fragments (NL, 25[1], KSA 13, p. 637) that Nietzsche ever wrote, bearing the title of "Die große Politik", offers important insights into the way he came to regard the relation between physiology and his project of Great Politics. Nietzsche starts the argument of this passage by distinguishing between the war (*Krieg*) he advocates and war as usually understood, war between peoples (*zwischen Volk und Volk*). The war he advocates is one between the will to life (*Willen zum Leben*) and vengefulness toward life (*Rach-*

---

21 For an analysis of the way the multiplicity of drives is structured in Nietzsche's philosophy see Parkes 1996.

sucht gegen das Leben). The war is between what affirms life and what is degenerate. His criterion for distinguishing the camps in this war is a physiological one. Those that are characterised by vengefulness are physiologically doomed (*physiologisch verurtheilt*), they are impoverished in their instincts (*in seinen Instinkten so verarmt*). The distinction between the higher and the lower forms of life does not coincide with the distinction between classes or levels (*Stände*) in society. As a matter of fact, Nietzsche criticizes the higher (*obenauf*) level of society (*Gesellschaft*) for being physiologically doomed. He is also careful to emphasize that belonging to one of the sides in this combat is not a question of choice, of free will. One is determined by what one is ("was man ist"). We affirm or deny what we are, not what we choose arbitrarily. It becomes immediately apparent that physiology's role in this argument is essential since it allows us to distinguish between the two sides in the war Nietzsche claims he brings. As a consequence, Nietzsche characterizes physiology as "Herrin über alle anderen Fragen", a characterisation repeated twice in KSA 13.368. What matters are the reasons for this high regard of physiology and they are twofold: physiology detects what is parasitic or degenerate in life (a) and it breeds a new type of humans (b).

a) The first task, critical in essence, must be performed relentlessly (*unerbittlich, schonungloser*) and it must be aimed at what poisons (*verdirbt, vergiftet*) life. It is crucial to identify this type of decadent life because its overcoming, its destruction will bring about a higher type of souls (*einer höheren Art Seelen*). The higher type of life that can survive the test of Nietzsche's physiological critique will bear a sign, a guarantee (*Bürgschaft*) for life. The subjects of Nietzsche's physiological critique are races, peoples or individuals and they are judged according to their future, according to the sign, the guarantee that they have within them and that indicate the coming of a new type of man.

b) This new type, the second aspect of Nietzsche's project here, is characterised as being complete, whole and higher (*Ganzes und Höheres*) and Higher Politics is responsible for the creation or breeding (*züchten*) of this type (a project already hinted at in *Zarathustra*; cf. Z II Redemption). Some of the issues that require solving in order to create this new humanity are outlined by Nietzsche in the preceding paragraph of the same text, accompanied by his surprise that only recently had these questions come to the fore of research:

> Is it not a consideration that makes one shiver that only in the last 20 years or so have the important questions of nutrition, clothing, board, health, reproduction been attended to with rigour, seriousness and honesty? (NL, 25[1], KSA 13, p. 638)[22]

---

[22] "Ist es nicht, eine Erwägung, die Einem Schauder macht, daß erst ungefähr seit 20 Jahren alle nächstwichtigen Fragen, in der Ernährung, der Kleidung, der Kost, der Gesundheit, der Fortpflanzung mit Strenge, mit Ernst, mit Rechtschaffenheit behandelt werden".

This picks up on a train of thought already present in BGE 234, where Nietzsche deplores the lack of knowledge of physiological matters by women who, as cooks, have missed acquiring the art of healing (*Heilkunst*). This, Nietzsche claims, is responsible for the impairment of the development of the human species, an impairment existing for millennia.

The entire project of physiology, of distinguishing between *Aufgang* and *Niedergang*, will to life and desire for revenge against life, gains meaning within the context of Nietzsche's notion of war. The Great Politics is a war-like practice, occurring not between nations or dynasties but between two types of life. Physiology is necessary insofar as the lower, resentful type of life is the result of bad instincts (*schlechte Instinkte*). The emergence of these bad instincts is the result of the physiological nonsense (*Widersinn*) with which mankind has been treated during the last two thousand years. Nietzsche claims that we have come to a point where the contradiction in instincts brings about the corruption of life: we have reached a moment of profound crisis. Nietzsche advocates an elimination of the degenerate, of the parasitical: ("It (physiology) implacably does away with all that is degenerate and parasitical"[23]; NL, 25[1] KSA 13, p. 638). Much has been made of the influence of Gobineau or Goethe on Nietzsche and of Nietzsche's refusal to consider the decadent as something that should simply be excluded, but instead as something to be integrated in the process of human development. (Moore 2006, p. 174) This very last fragment, however, combined with EH M 2, indicates quite clearly that in the last stage of his career Nietzsche is much more decisive regarding what he considers the lower type of life. The sick, the degenerate must be dealt with by being eliminated from the state, from culture and also from the organism. After this process of selection the healthy instincts find themselves in a competition similar to that between tissues and organs (inter pares) – they reach a balance in order to create humans that are "Ganzes und Höheres". The therapeutic practice required for this development consists in encouraging the development of life-affirming drives to the detriment of drives (such as the one behind moral, ascetic practices) that are contrary to human nature and that lead to a contradiction between instincts (*Instinkt-Widersprüchlichkeit*). Judging by the reflection of political models in physiology, there is a shift from the *Genealogy* and the notion of *Rangordnung* we can encounter there and the late understanding of the concept of hierarchy. The concept keeps being highly important to Nietzsche even in the later texts, but advocating excision of the degenerate, i.e. lower, sickly element, undermines the possibility of having a highly diverse

---

[23] "sie (Physiologie) macht unerbittlich mit allem Entarteten und Parasitischen ein Ende".

hierarchy. If Nietzsche's project were successful, we would have a multiplicity of healthy instincts, healthy organisms. However, we would miss out on what Nietzsche claimed, in the *Genealogy*, made man an interesting animal. And, as has already been argued, Nietzsche himself would be liable to the charge of being dominated by resentment if he advocated the excision of the instincts he considers sick.

This radical solution would probably find little favour with any advocate of democracy: after all, it is built on the most extreme of measures, namely the excision of whatever element does not manage to affirm itself in a way that would live up to Nietzsche's ideal (whatever the details of that ideal might be). The argument of this paper is that this stance is not something that is in agreement with Nietzsche's philosophy either, or at least with what he thought on the issue at the time of the *Genealogy*.

Conclusion

In the course of this paper, we have seen the importance of physiology for Nietzsche when dealing with political questions. It has been argued that Nietzsche aims to preserve the vocabulary of politics and to invest it with new meanings. This allows him find a use for political language in describing the physiological structure of an organism. It has also been argued that Nietzsche is influenced in his understanding of politics by his readings in biology. In the *Genealogy* he models his understanding of the various purposes of a custom or institution on the relation between the various functions of organs. Later, he will shape his project of Great Politics on the way he believes we need to deal with degenerate instincts. This indicates that Nietzsche abandons a hierarchical and yet relatively tolerant model of the organism in favour of a more intransigent hierarchical system based on the exclusion of the degenerate elements. This shift means that he no longer subscribes to Roux's understanding of struggle between organs within the organism, struggle that leads to balance. He now models his physiology and therefore his politics on the way Roux describes the fight between cells: an elimination process in which only the healthy survive.

Bibliography

Ansell-Pearson, Keith (1994): *An Introduction to Nietzsche as Political Thinker: The Perfect Nihilist*. Cambridge: Cambridge University Press.
Assoun, Paul-Laurent (2006): *Freud and Nietzsche*. London: Continuum.

Blondel, Eric (1986): *Nietzsche, le corps et la culture: La philosophie comme généalogie philologique*. Paris: Presses Universitaires de France [Translated into English by Sean Hand as Eric Blondel (2001): *Nietzsche: the Body and Culture*. London: Continuum].

Brobjer, Thomas H. (2008): "Critical Aspects of Nietzsche's Relation to Politics and Democracy". In: Herman W. Siemens/Vasti Roodt (eds.): *Nietzsche, Power and Politics. Rethinking Nietzsche's Legacy for Political Thought*. Berlin, New York: de Gruyter, pp. 205–230.

Fossen, Thomas (2008) "Nietzsche's Aristocratism Revisited". In: Herman W. Siemens/Vasti Roodt (eds.): *Nietzsche, Power and Politics. Rethinking Nietzsche's Legacy for Political Thought*. Berlin, New York: de Gruyter, pp. 299–318.

Moore, Gregory (2006): *Nietzsche, Biology and Metaphor*. New York: Cambridge University Press.

Müller-Lauter, Wolfgang (1978): "Der Organismus als innerer Kampf: Der Einfluss von Wilhelm Roux auf Friedrich Nietzsche". In *Nietzsche-Studien* 7, pp. 189–223.

Nietzsche, Friedrich (1997): *On the Genealogy of Morality*. Keith Ansell-Pearson (ed.). Carol Diethe (trans.). New York: Cambridge University Press.

Nietzsche, Friedrich (2005) *The Anti-Christ, Ecce Homo, Twilight of the idols, and Other Writings*. Aaron Ridley, Judith Norman (eds.), Judith Norman (trans.). New York: Cambridge University Press.

Nussbaum, Martha (1997): "Is Nietzsche a Political Thinker?". In: *International Journal of Philosophical Studies* 5, pp. 1–13.

Parkes, Graham (1996): *Composing the Soul: Reaches of Nietzsche's Psychology*. Chicago: University of Chicago Press.

Ridley, Aaron (1998): *Nietzsche's Conscience. Six Character Studies from the Genealogy*. Ithaca, London: Cornell University Press.

Rolph, William (1884): *Biologische Probleme, zugleich als Versuch zur Entwicklung einer rationellen Ethik*. Leipzig: Engelmann.

Roux, Wilhelm (2011): *Der Kampf der Theile Im Organismus*. Bertrams Print on Demand, printed in the USA: Nabu Press.

Siemens, Herman (2008): "Yes, No, Maybe So... Nietzsche's Equivocations on the Relation between Democracy and 'Grosse Politik'". In: Herman W. Siemens/Vasti Roodt (eds.): *Nietzsche, Power and Politics. Rethinking Nietzsche's Legacy for Political Thought*. Berlin, New York: de Gruyter, pp. 231–268.

Tongeren, Paul J.M./Schank, G./Siemens, H. (eds.) (2004): *Nietzsche-Wörterbuch*. Berlin, New York: de Gruyter.

Tom Angier
On the Genealogy of Nietzsche's Values

The notion of "genealogy" has had a chequered history since its seminal use in Nietzsche's *On the Genealogy of Morality*. On the one hand, since Foucault's *Discipline and Punish* (Foucault 1975) it has gained a largely favourable reception among philosophers in the continental tradition, along with those social scientists and literary critics influenced by Foucault. On the other hand, it has largely been shunned by analytic philosophers, who – with the qualified exception of Bernard Williams[1] – have found little to recommend it. As I shall document, when analytic philosophers[2] turn to Nietzsche's text, all that most of them find is the notion that the value of "moral" practices, and the truth of "moral" claims are determined by the social and psychological conditions that originally gave rise to them. And, accordingly, they judge Nietzsche guilty – or somehow have to get him off the hook – of committing the "genetic fallacy": i.e. of inferring, illegitimately, from the origins of x to the value or truth of x. Given that the notion of "genealogy" is central to Nietzsche's most widely read work, GM, this hardly bodes well for the cogency of its argument. What are we to make of this analytic critique?

My answer to this falls into two parts, the first being preparatory to the second. In Part One, I acknowledge that the analytic critique of Nietzsche's method in the *Genealogy* has *prima facie* plausibility. There are problems with Nietzsche's argument from history, especially since he himself appears to repudiate the inference from historical origins to current value or truth. But on closer inspection, the evidence that Nietzsche either uses history improperly, or repudiates genetic reasoning altogether, does not stand up. On the contrary, he carves out a logical space in which appeals to history can be made to do critical, evaluative work in the present, and moreover without falling into fallacy. Having said this, it does not follow that Nietzsche's actual deployment of genealogical argument – in the context of Jewish and Christian history – is convincing; in fact, there is strong evidence against this. And this motivates the second part of my argument. In Part Two, I maintain that although Nietzsche's use of genealogy lacks cogency, genealogy *per se* remains a powerful argumentative tool. To demonstrate this, I apply Nietzsche's method to the *Genealogy* itself, asking what we can learn about its evaluative claims and

---

[1] See especially his *Truth and Truthfulness: An Essay in Genealogy* (Williams 2002).
[2] These include Brian Leiter, Ken Gemes, Raymond Geuss, Peter Kail, Lawrence Hatab and Robert Solomon.

commitments once these are put in the context of Nietzsche's own social and class background in nineteenth century Germany. And the scholar who helps us most in this task of genetic understanding is, as I will elaborate, the great German Jewish sociologist, Norbert Elias.[3]

Part One

Nietzsche and the "genetic fallacy"

To start, then, what exactly is the "genetic fallacy"? Understood strictly – as a relation between propositions, that is, rather than as one between (say) practices – it is classed as an informal fallacy, specifically as a fallacy of relevance. Those who commit it cite supposedly irrelevant information, viz. the origin, cause or function of a claim, in order to infer its truth or falsity. In this way, it essentially involves bypassing reasons *for* holding true in favour of reasons *behind* holding true. Perhaps the most straightforward species of genetic fallacy is that of the *ad hominem*, where the falsity of someone's belief is inferred from who or what he or she is. For instance, it seems fallacious to infer that Nietzsche's claims in *Ecce Homo* concerning his own genius are false merely because they were made when he was on the verge of madness. Maybe, despite his incipient derangement, those claims are in fact true. Likewise, *ad hominem*'s mirror-image, the argument from authority, also seems fallacious: Aristotle's renown, for example, does not entail the truth of any one of his claims. At an historical level,[4] although philosophical interest in the genetic fallacy goes back to late nineteenth century attacks on psychologism in logic, the term itself gained common currency only in the late 1930s, in reaction to the notion (common among *Wissenssoziologen*, sociologists of knowledge) that knowledge-claims can be evaluated in virtue of their source. Crucially, a key inspiration behind *Wissenssoziologie* was none other than Nietzsche, and especially his GM[5] – so it is time we turned to why that text, in particular, incurred (and still incurs) the accusation of committing the genetic fallacy.

---

[3] Norbert Elias (1897–1990) was born in Breslau, worked for many years at the University of Leicester, and died in Amsterdam. He is best known for his monumental work, *The Civilising Process* (Elias 2000), but I shall be drawing, instead, on his *Studien über die Deutschen*, published in English as *The Germans* (Elias 1996).
[4] See Loeb 2008, pp. 4f.
[5] According to Loeb 2008, p. 5, n. 15, the link between GM and the sociology of knowledge is Karl Mannheim, a sociologist who had read Nietzsche and whose *Ideology and Utopia* (1936)

GM incurs this accusation because it invites it directly. For example, Nietzsche maintains in the *Preface* that "we need a critique of moral values, the value of these values should itself, for once, be examined – and so we need to know about the conditions and circumstances under which the values grew up, developed and changed" (GM Preface 6). This inference appears fallacious because there seems no reason to think that the motives and conditions that originally lay behind the affirmation of, say, *Mitleid* [pity, compassion] – to take one of Nietzsche's main examples – still do. Perhaps, to take up the theme of GM I, *ressentiment* did play a large part in conditioning Jewish, Christian and subsequent secular attitudes towards *Mitleid* – but why should it now? Why couldn't other, less suspect motives – such as genuine generosity and concern – be at work? Nonetheless, Nietzsche reiterates his historicising inference without conceding anything to the opposition. In order to arrive at a proper assessment of values like pity, selflessness and humility, he argues, we have to uncover "morality as it really existed and was really lived", "to focus [a] sharp, unbiased eye in ... the direction of a real history of morality" (GM Preface 7). For although the so-called "English psychologists"[6] are "to be thanked for having made the only attempts so far to write a history of the emergence of morality" (GM I 1), they merely project current moral valuations – centrally, the equation of goodness with "unegoism" – into the past. Hence "they all think in a way that is essentially unhistorical" (GM I 2). Nietzsche will, by contrast, reverse this ahistoricism, thereby supposedly coming to an accurate evaluation of *current* moral values.

This apparently fallacious mode of argumentation occurs not only at the beginning of GM, but also at that of GM's parent-text, *Beyond Good and Evil*. Here Nietzsche suggests that "things of the highest value" may "originate in [their] antithesis ... [e.g.] will to truth in will to deception ... Or the unselfish act in self-interest ..." (BGE 2). This echoes GM's disparagement of current morality as originating in the devious self-interest of the weak, implying that an inference from bad origins to present disvalue is made also in BGE. And yet those who both condemn the "genetic fallacy", and want to defend Nietzsche's overall argument, cannot acknowledge this. Instead, they try to circumvent the above evidence, and this in two main ways. First, they try to sideline the argumentative relevance of GM's genealogy, and even try to deny its status as

---

was accused of the genetic fallacy by Maurice Mandelbaum (among others). For more on the history of the genetic fallacy, see Klement 2002, p. 384.
6 These include Nietzsche's one-time German Jewish friend, Paul Rée. For more on Rée, and the way GM is targeted directly at his *The Origin of the Moral Sensations*, see Janaway 2007, ch. 5.

history altogether. Brian Leiter, for example, holds that "the critique of morality does not depend on the genealogy of morality, though the genealogy may help us arrive at it" (Leiter 2002, p. 177), citing the following passage in support: "[Genealogy] concerned me only for one end, to which it is one of many means [...] [viz. deciding] the value of morality" (GM Preface 5). And Ken Gemes observes that despite Nietzsche's genuflections to historical veracity, GM lacks historical apparatus and specificity, contains "sweeping" narratives, and is subtitled "A Polemic" – the upshot being that Nietzsche is "not really [interested in] telling us about the historical origins of our morality" (Gemes 2006, p. 205), only about the moral psychological present.[7] If, then, as Leiter and Gemes suggest, history is merely tangential – or even irrelevant – to Nietzsche's project of revaluation, the genetic fallacy clearly no longer poses a threat: genealogy becomes wholly oblique to his main purpose.

Secondly, as several commentators point out,[8] Nietzsche appears explicitly to repudiate genetic-type reasoning. In GM itself, for instance, he declares that "the origin of the emergence of a thing and its ultimate usefulness, its practical application and incorporation into a system of ends, are toto coelo separate ... [its] former 'meaning' [*Sinn*] and 'purpose' must necessarily be obscured or completely obliterated" (GM II 12). In other words, past "meanings" or *Sinne* need have nothing to do with present ones, and only "naïve moral and legal genealogists" (GM II 13) would assume otherwise. To illustrate this, Nietzsche shows how punishment has had many purposes over time, rendering any attempt to criticise its present form on the basis of past forms empty. And this view is bolstered at *Gay Science* 345, where he remarks that "I have hardly detected a few meagre preliminary efforts to explore the history of origins of ... [moral] feelings and valuations (which is something quite different from a critique ...)" And this seemingly uncompromising dissociation of genealogy from evaluative critique recurs in the *Nachlass* (NL 1886, KSA 12, 2[189]; WP 254),[9] where Nietzsche maintains that "The enquiry into the origin of our evaluations ... is in absolutely no way identical with a critique of them ... even though the insight into some pudenda origo [shameful origin] certainly ... prepares the way to a critical mood and attitude toward [them]".

---

[7] Christopher Janaway gestures in a similar direction: "Nietzsche's procedure", he claims, "involves a projected or imagined generic psychology" (Janaway 2007, p. 11). György Lukács goes so far as to say that Nietzsche engages in "mythicising" history (see Lukács 1995, p. 253). Cf. Kail 2011, p. 217.
[8] See (e.g.) Schacht 1994b, pp. 428–432; Geuss 2001, p. 338; Leiter 2002, pp. 169–179; Kail 2011, pp. 214f.
[9] The entry is dated 1885/86, i.e. a year or two before the publication of GM.

In light of these passages, and the purportedly merely ancillary role of genealogy within Nietzsche's argument, many scholars have concluded that genealogy *per se* can have little (if any) evaluative force. Raymond Geuss, for example, claims that "Nietzsche asserts very clearly that nothing about the history of the emergence or development of a set of valuations could have direct bearing on its value" (Geuss 2001, p. 338). Peter Kail argues that "no genealogy has normative consequences simply in virtue of its being a genealogy" (Kail 2011, p. 215); at most, he holds, genealogy is capable of "destabilising" moral beliefs (Kail 2011, p. 215) – *contributing* to revaluation, that is, without *constituting* it (Kail 2011, p. 221).[10] And this view finds favour also with Lawrence Hatab, who maintains that Nietzsche's "quasi-historical, genealogical discussions" subvert confidence in "traditional belief systems", without refuting them (Hatab 2008, p. 29). As Robert Solomon puts matters, Nietzsche "did not so much refute the doctrines of religion and morality as undermine them, by exposing the sometimes pathetic motives and emotions that motivated them" (Solomon 1996, p. 181). In Robert Guay's words, genealogy is "merely preparatory to the 'real' doctrines" found in the Nietzschean corpus, which centre on the deleterious *effects* of "moral" evaluation, rather than its psychological *origins* (see Guay 2006, pp. 353f.). For Leiter, meanwhile, although "The point of origin of a morality has a special *evidential* status as to the *effects* (or causal powers) of that morality" (Leiter 2002, p. 177), it can have no more than this: origins *per se* are of little or no interest.

Can genealogy constitute critique?

Clearly, the idea that genealogy has no genuine, autonomous force as critique is widespread in the analytic literature. But is it justified? I will argue it is not, starting with the notion that genealogy is inessential to the evaluation of the moral *status quo*. While Nietzsche does claim at GM Preface 5 that "hypotheses ... on the origin of morality" are "one of many means" to determining "the value of morality", the context here is that of his mid-period works *Human, All Too Human* (1878) and *Daybreak* (1881), in which his "hypotheses ... on the origin of morality" were less developed.[11] Furthermore, even if genealogy is

---

10 Cf. Gemes and Schuringa 2012, pp. 228ff. To bolster his view, Kail cites *Ecce Homo*, where Nietzsche describes the three essays of GM as "A psychologist's three crucial preparatory works for a revaluation of all values" (EH GM).
11 N.B. his use of the past tense: "just then I was preoccupied", "the latter concerned me only for one end". The implication is that whereas genealogy was sidelined in his earlier works, it is now his paramount concern (and rightly so).

"one of many means", it remains a means nonetheless, and one that is centre-stage in Nietzsche's most systematic work, GM. Critics are on stronger ground when they point out that GM lacks historical specificity, and contains "almost no confirming evidence (other than ... etymological ...)" (Leiter 2002, p. 180), presenting instead a "conjectural" account (Kail 2011, pp. 232f.) or "projective reconstruction" of the past (Janaway 2009, p. 344). But even if true, these claims do not mean that GM is eschewing historical accuracy. For GM's lack of scholarly documentation is deliberate, a refusal of the dry, lifeless history-writing decried in *On the Uses and Disadvantages of History for Life* (1874).[12] And it would anyhow be very difficult to document the kind of psychological mechanisms at issue in GM: viz. *ressentiment* (GM I), the inward redirection of cruelty (GM II), and the will to power of priests (GM III). In each case, Nietzsche simply takes his naturalistic explanations of moral phenomena to be far more plausible than any of the (especially theological) alternatives.[13]

Taking these points on board, it might still be objected that GM does too little to corroborate the "slave revolt", i.e. to supply it with a rich texture of actions and events. As Edward Craig adjures, "the 'fact pressure' is pretty low around here" (Craig 2007, p. 189), something embarrassing in a supposedly historical work. And this makes it difficult to agree with Alexander Nehamas' notion that for Nietzsche, "genealogy simply *is* history, correctly practised" (Nehamas 1985, p. 246, n. 1). But I would respond, in turn, that the kind of history relevant to Nietzsche's project *must* be non-specific. For although he focuses on the first and most influential rebellion of the "weak" – that in Ancient Israel – its explanatory power lies precisely in the psychological (and physiological) template it supplies *throughout* history. After all, the Jewish revolt against Rome is the paradigm, but not the sole instance of a "slave revolt": Nietzsche refers, for example, to "the last great slave revolt which began with the French Revolution" (BGE 46). And he claims that "In a tour of many finer and coarser moralities which have ruled [...] on earth [...] two basic types were revealed [...] There is master morality and slave morality" (BGE 260). In other words, the historical non-specificity of Nietzsche's genealogy is both intentional and suits his purposes well: the typology it supplies is, in virtue of being generic, of maximally wide explanatory scope.[14]

---

12 On this, see Brobjer 2004, pp. 303f., 314.
13 As Solomon puts matters, in face of the mystifying pretensions of "philosophical, theological, and metaphysical dogma", Nietzsche takes his "simple appeals to motives and emotion" to have far greater explanatory power (see Solomon 1996, p. 186).
14 I will elaborate below how this typology, rather than floating free of its origins, is inextricably indebted to them, so that invoking them in order to understand current morality is not otiose.

What, then, of the passages that supposedly repudiate genetic reasoning?[15] At GM II 12, Nietzsche does indeed distinguish a thing's origin from its "ultimate usefulness", "meaning" or "purpose". But it does not follow that he denies common and essential properties that bind, say, punishment as practised now to punishment as practised long ago. For he explicitly acknowledges that "anything in existence, *having somehow come about*, is continually interpreted anew, requisitioned anew, transformed and redirected to a new purpose" (my italics). That is, while interpretations and purposes change in manifold ways, they presuppose an unchanging ontological core. And this is confirmed in GM II 13, where Nietzsche contrasts two "aspects" of punishment: "one is its relative permanence, the custom, the act, the 'drama' ... the other is its fluidity, its meaning, purpose ... the [former] will be something older ... the latter [being] ... interpreted into the procedure". As applied to morality as a whole, this leaves room for certain core "acts" – such as recoiling from a more powerful enemy, or failing to retaliate out of weakness – which are subsequently interpreted "morally" (in the cases just mentioned, as "humble" and "forgiving" respectively).[16] It is the job of the genealogist, according to Nietzsche, to peel away these moralised *Sinne*, revealing how they came about, and hence what ontological core they obscure.

As to GS 345 and NL 1885/86, KSA 12, 2[189] (WP 254), these draw a strong contrast between enquiring into the *origin* of evaluations, and mounting a genuine *critique* of them – and this seems to rule out genealogy as a vehicle of critique itself. But taken in context, this can be seen not to be the case. For Nietzsche here clearly has in mind not genealogy *per se*, but the superficial moral histories offered by "English psychologists", who condemn the Christian origins of current morality, without criticising that morality itself. As he writes, "they uncover and criticise the possibly foolish opinions of a people about their morality ... opinions about its origin, its religious sanction ... and then think they have criticised the morality itself" (GS 345). But far from criticising it, they "serve as its shield-bearers", upholding the values of "selflessness, self-denial, self-sacrifice, or sympathy and compassion" (GS 345). Nietzsche is arguing, in other words, that it is pointless to criticise the religious origins of morality if one fails to criticise its normative content[17] – for it is the latter, according to

---

15 In what follows, I am indebted to Loeb 2008, pp. 6f.
16 N.B. "When stepped on, the worm curls up. That is a clever thing to do. Thus it reduces its chances of being stepped on again. In the language of morality: humility" (TI Arrows 31). Cf. the "moral" interpretation of involuntary suffering and deprivation as "piety" (see GM I 7).
17 Besides Rée, Nietzsche's main target here is George Eliot, who having "got rid of the Christian God ... feel[s] obliged to cling all the more firmly to Christian morality" (TI Skirmishes 5).

him, which constitutes its pernicious core. It is in this sense, then, that he draws a line between "the history of origins" and "critique": without tackling the normative core of a phenomenon, the former will yield only superficial and ineffective criticism. But Nietzsche evidently also believes that genealogy *need not* be superficial, and can be genuinely challenging – announcing at the end of GS 345, "Precisely that is our task".

In sum, I have argued that nothing in Nietzsche's texts rules genealogy out as either a genuine species of history, or a form of challenging evaluative critique. His historical account is admittedly polemical and broad-brush, but both these features suit his purposes well, especially in a context where probative evidence is difficult (perhaps impossible) to assemble. Furthermore, none of the passages cited by interpreters to demonstrate Nietzsche's supposed divorce between genealogy and critique are in fact demonstrative. Neither his analysis of punishment (GM II 12–13), nor his subtle distinction between the origin of evaluations and a critique of them (GS 345; NL 1885/86, KSA 12, 2[189] (WP 254)) institute the kind of principled divorce that such interpreters allege. And all this is fortunate, I think, since otherwise we would be left in the awkward position of those who admit that genealogy is central to GM's methodology, but sideline it as (at best) a peripheral strategy for "destabilising"[18] what Leiter calls "morality in the pejorative sense" (Leiter 2002, pp. 74f.)

It might still be objected, however, that even if Nietzsche leaves logical room for genealogical critique, it remains unclear why we should take seriously – let alone believe – his version of it. For why believe that current moral values embody the kind of psychological traits he alleges they did over two thousand years ago?[19] Why not simply hold, once again, that motivations like *ressentiment* and inner-directed cruelty have lapsed, or are at least far less common, now that we live under radically different social and psychological conditions?

Nietzsche's genealogical critique

To answer this, we need to know why Nietzsche believes that psychological (and in particular, moral psychological) traits are inherited, in such a way that

---

18 The term is Kail's. Indeed, Kail goes so far as to characterise Nietzsche's genealogy as a merely "rhetorical attack" on Christian-derived values (see Kail 2011, p. 223, n. 18).

19 Craig makes an important distinction between moral principles "arising out of", as opposed to being "expressions of" emotions and attitudes (see Craig 2007, p. 183). Only if current moral values express, rather than merely arise out of *ressentiment*, etc., will genealogical critique gain traction and avoid the genetic fallacy.

providing a genealogy of current morality reveals "the actuality of the past in the present" (Strong 2006, p. 94). Leiter, for one, responds to this by arguing that Nietzsche is heavily influenced by nineteenth century German materialism (Leiter 2002, pp. 63–71), leading him to believe in a "Doctrine of Types", according to which each person inherits a "fixed psycho-physical constitution, which defines him as a particular type of person" (Leiter 2002, p. 8). And indeed, there is evidence that Nietzsche affirms some form of psycho-physical determinism. "Answers to the questions about the <u>value</u> of existence", he claims, "may always be considered first of all as the symptoms of certain bodies" (GS Preface 2). At BGE 262, he holds that "A <u>species</u> arises, a type becomes fixed and strong, through protracted struggle against essentially constant <u>unfavourable</u> conditions". Nietzsche goes on to talk about "breeding" here, something that preoccupies him also elsewhere. For instance, at *The Anti-Christ* 3 he writes: "The problem I raise ... is ... what type of human being one ought to <u>breed</u>". And at GM I 17, he maintains that "every table of values ... needs first and foremost a <u>physiological</u> elucidation and interpretation ... and all of them await critical study from medical science". Evidently he is impressed by the burgeoning sciences of biology and physiology, and is keen to acknowledge their explanatory potential, even in GM.

Notwithstanding Nietzsche's liberal use (here and elsewhere) of the language of the life sciences,[20] I think it can be shown they are not central to his conception of genealogy. For a start, although human types may, on Nietzsche's view, display distinct, largely determined sets of physical and psychological traits, as yet this does not account for his insistence that we cannot evaluate those sets without discovering their distant origins. (One can, after all, see the disvalue of someone's sickly, weak constitution or attitude to life without reference to his ancestry.) Furthermore, although *we* may be familiar with the notion that someone's genetic history can be traced using scientific methods, such methods were in their infancy in Nietzsche's day. So even though authors like Brian Leiter and Joshua Knobe are keen to supply Nietzsche with a proto-geneticist account of inherited traits[21] – according to which genetic inheritance is (purportedly) explanatorily more fundamental than upbringing or cultural difference – Nietzsche could not plausibly have imagined such an account himself. Last but not least, even if physical traits are strictly heritable, and thereby constitutive of physical types, it is far more controversial that psychological traits are likewise heritable. So notwithstanding Nietzsche's

---

[20] For more on Nietzsche's indebtedness to contemporary German science, see Moore and Brobjer 2004.
[21] See Knobe/Leiter 2007.

apparent optimism about the prospects for psychology as a genuine (or "hard") science, I think interpretative charity demands we not attribute such a controversial idea to him without further evidence.[22]

Given all this, it seems reasonable to conclude that Nietzsche's conception of psychological inheritance is not of the strict, scientific form implicit in Leiter's notion of human types with "fixed psycho-physical constitution[s]". So what conception of psychological inheritance plausibly informs Nietzsche's notion of genealogy? I suggest the most promising answer to this is: a sociocultural conception, as seen paradigmatically in the way noble or aristocratic families pass on traditions of behaviour, and norms of psychological response. This aristocratic model accords not only with Nietzsche's choice of the term "Genealogie", but also with his invocation of "Herkunft" [social origin or descent] – terms both found in the rhetoric of upper class self-legitimation.[23] Of course, *contra* the use of "Genealogie" or "Herkunft" in aristocratic circles, Nietzsche is deliberately inverting the value ascribed to "morality", by showing its distinctly plebeian (or "slavish") descent.[24] But in line with their aristocratic usage, Nietzsche is pointing to the absolute evaluative salience of origins: for just as an aristocrat typically gestures towards his ancestors in order to indicate his *own* indelible nobility, so Nietzsche delineates the psychological origins of "morality" in order to establish *its* irrevocable "shamefulness". It is in light of this (paradigmatically upper class) set of cultural assumptions, I want to argue, that Nietzsche affirms an "unalterable innate order of rank" (BGE 263), and claims that "That which his ancestors … most constantly did cannot be erased from a man's soul" (BGE 264). Such assumptions were not only common among the nobility of the time, supplying Nietzsche with a social (rather than rarefied, scientific) model for his genealogical investigations; they also afford a reading of "genealogy" that is continuous with his interest in all things aristocratic,[25] and, crucially, which manages to make sense of his genealogical mode of argument.

---

[22] For Nietzsche as a weak naturalist, as opposed to Leiter's reading of him as a strong naturalist, see Janaway 2007, ch. 3 and Janaway 2009, pp. 340, 346, 350. Weak, or "methodological" naturalism requires that "explanations in philosophy be compatible with our best science", whereas strong naturalism requires that they be *"justified or supported by* … science" (Janaway 2007, p. 37).

[23] For "Herkunft", see, for example, GM I 2, 5; GM II 23; BGE 200, 242, 244, 260; GS 135, 348–349.

[24] He refers to the plebeian origins of compassion, selflessness, sympathy, etc., at (e.g.) GM I 9, 10, 13, 14, 16; GM II 22; BGE 264; GS 3.

[25] Besides GM I, see, for example, BGE part nine ("What is Noble?"); GS 3, 40, 55; *The Will to Power* (ed. Walter Kaufmann) book four, part one, section three ("The Noble Man"). Nietzsche

Does this conception of genealogy *qua* evaluatively inverted aristocratic pedigree stand up? Raymond Geuss, for one, thinks not – and on three main grounds. He argues, first, that because Nietzsche devalues morality's origins, his is the "exact reverse" of a noble pedigree or genuine genealogy (see Geuss 2001, pp. 322f.). But this is a *non sequitur*: Nietzsche is clearly ironising only one *aspect* of a noble genealogy – namely, its positive evaluative force – and to deliberate, striking effect. Geuss goes on to argue that Nietzsche's genealogy lacks a "singular origin" (Geuss 2001, p. 325) – because it locates morality's origins in *ressentiment*, inner-directed cruelty and priestly will to power – thereby further disqualifying it as *bona fide*. But as Christopher Janaway points out, German *Stammbäume* (family trees) or *Ahnentafeln* (ancestor tables) tend to have a singular *terminus*, rather than a singular point of origin (see Janaway 2009, p. 347) – thus fitting the narrative of Nietzsche's *Genealogie* perfectly. And Geuss is wide of the mark a third time when he argues that a pedigree's "unbroken succession" is not reflected in the "overwhelming contingency" of Nietzsche's genealogical account (Janaway 2009, p. 326; cf. Ansell-Pearson 2012, p. 206). But even if the events recounted in GM are "contingent" in the obvious sense of being historical, Geuss here is simply bypassing Nietzsche's widespread allegiance to what Paul S. Loeb calls "aristocratic determinism" (Loeb 2008, p. 7). That is, he is bypassing Nietzsche's conviction that "It is quite impossible that a man should not have ... the qualities and preferences of his parents and forefathers: whatever appearances may say to the contrary" (BGE 264).

And this is precisely the locus, I take it, of the real problem: for the cogency of Nietzsche's genealogical critique depends, ultimately, on our sharing his allegiance to aristocratic determinism. Yet how cogent is the latter? As we've already seen, the psycho-physical determinism elaborated by Leiter is implausible enough. For there do not appear to be higher and lower physical types, sporting correlative kinds of psychological trait over time. As Nietzsche himself admits, over two thousand years there has been "the mixing of blood of masters and slaves" (BGE 261), and "even within the same man, within one soul" (BGE 260), master and slave moralities can coexist. What this points to is that morality and moral psychology are not matters of biology, but of variable and often highly local social-cultural formation. And once this is acknowledged, the outlook for aristocratic determinism looks bleak. For there seem very few classes or groups that have, over the centuries, embodied an unchanging, stable set of moral-cum-moral psychological features. Indeed, ruling-class groups

---

develops the notion of "rank order" at BGE 219, 221, 228, 257. And his anti-egalitarianism is evident at (e.g.) BGE 202, 212; A 48, 62; TI Skirmishes 48; GS 377.

have (to take one example) adhered to warrior-like ideals at one time, but comparatively pacific and commercial ideals at another.[26] And, as I will expound below, the German middle classes found themselves shifting their moral and cultural ideals markedly over the course of the nineteenth century. Is this unravelling of Nietzsche's aristocratic determinism – which can find a basis neither in biology, nor in cultural history – genealogy's death-knell?

On the one hand, I think that if genealogical critique is wedded to Nietzsche's notion of ineluctable *Herkunft*, it is in serious trouble. For that notion escapes the genetic fallacy at the cost of affirming an implausibly rigid, and strongly contraindicated theory of moral psychological inheritance, which even Nietzsche's texts themselves suggest is unsalvageable. There simply seems no good reason to believe that human groups cannot change their moral or moral psychological patterns and structures over time: something Nietzsche effectively admits, I take it, by acknowledging that the "nobles" came to adopt slave morality (for which the mixing of blood hardly provides a convincing explanation). On the other hand, it does not follow that *all* forms of genealogical critique have to fail. In the remainder of this chapter, I want to explore one instance where genealogy can, when suitably adjusted, shed very interesting (and I hope persuasive) light on evaluative practices and claims. But instead of the values Nietzsche takes as the object of his genealogy – namely, those of Judaeo-Christian *Moral* – the values to which I will apply the genealogical method are Nietzsche's *own*.

Part Two

Nietzsche on Art and Power

Although Nietzsche's positive axiology is rich and variegated, two sets of values dominate his work, and receive particularly detailed and sophisticated treatment: first, a set that centres on art, creativity and aesthetic appreciation, and second, a set that centres on power, dominance and victory. The first set is expounded at length in *The Birth of Tragedy*, where Nietzsche makes his well-known claim that "only as an aesthetic phenomenon can existence and the world be eternally justified" (BT 5; cf. BT 24, GS 107). But even after this early, Schopenhauerian text, Nietzsche continues to privilege art and creativity.

---

[26] For an excellent illustration of this, see Arthur Adkins' fascinating account of the cultural transition from Homeric to post-Homeric Greece (Adkins 1960).

For example, although art may be in some sense an "unnatural", because convention-laden activity, he says it remains "the expression of a lofty, heroic unnaturalness and convention" (GS 80). According to Nietzsche, "aesthetic activity" is valuable as expressing "intoxication" (TI *Skirmishes* 8; cf. GS 85), and stands in contrast to the "moral", Christian-derived affects, which constrain instinct and exuberance (TI *Skirmishes* 9). As he puts things at NL 1887, KSA 12, 10[24] (WP 823), we can view "Art as freedom from moral narrowness and corner-perspectives; or as mockery of them". Many of Nietzsche's heroes are artists – men such as Wagner, Goethe and Beethoven – and in general he associates them with an irrepressible vitality and authenticity. About Wagner, for instance, he writes: "Let us remain faithful to Wagner in what is true and authentic in him ... justice and patience are not for him. Enough that his life is justified before itself and remains justified" (GS 99).

Nietzsche's attraction to power and domination finds paradigm expression in his description of the "nobles" (those "beasts of prey") in GM I – but this attraction is evident also elsewhere in GM. For example, he writes:

> No cruelty, no feast: that is what the oldest and longest period in human history teaches us – and punishment, too, has such very strong festive aspects! [...] I expressly want to place on record that at the time when mankind felt no shame towards its cruelty, life on earth was more cheerful than it is today [...] At all events, the Greeks could certainly think of offering their gods no more acceptable a side-dish to their happiness than the joys cruelty (GM II 6–7).

Though one might be tempted to bracket these sorts of passage as merely rhetorical, or as wholly atypical, such "tyrannophilia" (Staten 1998, pp. 239f.) can be found far beyond GM. At GS 325, for example, Nietzsche asks: "Who will attain anything great if he does not find in himself the strength and the will to inflict great suffering?" And at A 2, he poses a similar question: "What is good? – All that heightens the feeling of power, the will to power ... Not contentment, but more power; not peace at all, but war ... The weak and ill-constituted shall perish ... And one shall help them to do so".[27] Indeed, this warlike tone punctuates Nietzsche's writings all the way from his earliest works to his late fragments. In *The Greek State* (1871/72), for instance, he maintains that "The only counter-measure" to "a self-seeking, stateless money-aristocracy" is "war and war again" (GM p. 171), and at NL 1888, KSA 13, 14[40] (WP 53) he judges that "The herd instinct ... assigns a higher value to peace than to war:

---

[27] At BGE 259, Nietzsche goes so far as to say: "life itself is essentially appropriation, injury, overpowering of the strange and weaker, suppression, severity, imposition of one's own forms, incorporation and, at the least and mildest, exploitation".

but this judgment is anti-biological ... Life is a consequence of war, society itself a means to war".

How should we interpret these two sets of values, and their interrelation? One approach, which is prevalent in the analytic philosophical literature, is to concentrate on the first, art-based set, either ignoring the second, power-based set, or interpreting it very emolliently. Lawrence Hatab, for instance, highlights some isolated passages[28] where Nietzsche speaks of the desire to hurt and dominate others as arising merely from a lack of self-development and style. He then proceeds to construct his own, purportedly optimal – yet highly eirenic – interpretation of Nietzsche's texts on this basis (see Hatab 2008, p. 267). But while this is intriguing *per se*, it comes at the price of sidelining other, incompatible passages, which are more numerous[29] – thereby failing to offer an interpretation of Nietzsche's texts in the round.[30] The opposite approach is to focus on the morally repugnant nature of the second, power-based set of values, castigating Nietzsche for having even countenanced these (see, for example Ferry/Renaut 1997). The trouble with this approach is that it tends to reiterate the claims of "morality", but without properly engaging Nietzsche's critique of those claims. In this way, it not only courts the accusation of moralism, but also fails to accrue any theoretical advantage. Furthermore, and crucially, it ignores the vital fact – as does the first approach – that Nietzsche tries continually to integrate the first and second sets of values within a unified, theoretical whole. How so, exactly?

Nietzsche's attempt at a systematic synthesis between the values of art and power goes back to his earliest writings. In *The Greek State*, for instance, he proclaims that "Culture [*Bildung*], which is first and foremost a real hunger for art, rests on one terrible premise ... the overwhelming majority has to be slav-

---

[28] E.g. "The state in which we hurt others is ... a sign that we are still lacking power, or it betrays a frustration in the face of this poverty" (GS 13); "And if we learn better to enjoy ourselves, we best unlearn how to do harm to others and to contrive harm" (Z II *Pitying*).

[29] And even in close proximity to those he cites. GS 13, for instance, continually lauds the pursuit of power as a good *per se*, especially when sought at the expense of one's equals, and depreciates compassion. Z II *Pitying* condemns compassion and forgiveness, and although two lines advise against harm (as militating against self-enjoyment – perhaps only because of the consequences of harm), the bulk of the section suggests "pettiness" is far worse.

[30] On the dangers of instrumentalising Nietzsche's work for one's own theoretical purposes, see *Domesticating Nietzsche* (Abbey/Appel 1999). As these authors show, such instrumentalisation is especially prominent in political philosophy, where Nietzsche has been used even in support of egalitarian democracy. See, e.g., Hatab's notion of "agonistic democracy" (Hatab 2008, pp. 256, 270).

ishly subjected to ... the minority" (GM p. 166).³¹ Much later, in passages like GM I 11, he recapitulates this idea, talking of the "nobles" as "instruments of culture". Elsewhere, art appears not as *dependent* on ruthless force, but rather as its *expression*. For example, after identifying "intoxication" as essential to the "psychology of the artist", Nietzsche places it on a continuum with "the intoxication of ... contest, of the brave deed, of victory ... of cruelty ... destruction" (TI *Skirmishes* 8; cf. NL 1887, KSA 12, 9[102] (WP 801)). Elsewhere again, he presents artistic skill as somehow warlike in form: "Good prose", he avers, "... is an uninterrupted, courteous war with poetry ... War is the father of all good things; war is also the father of good prose!" (GS 92). And the Kaufmann edition of *The Will to Power* contains a lengthy section entitled "The Will to Power as Art" (book three, part four), in which Nietzsche, at the end of his authorship, can be seen still trying to effect a symbiosis between art and power. To take one representative example: "The greatness of an artist cannot be measured", he contends, "by the 'beautiful feelings' he arouses ... the grand style ... disdains to please ... it commands ... It repels; such men of force are no longer loved" (NL 1888, KSA 13, 14[61] (WP 842)).

Despite the rhetorical élan that characterises these and similar passages, overall they hardly convey a sense of theoretical trenchancy or coherence. To begin with, Nietzsche does little to substantiate the notion that great art relies inextricably on state coercion, let alone slavery. The link between artistic "intoxication" and the more martial concepts he adduces seems tenuous, suggestive more of thought-association than careful analysis of the "psychology of the artist". Indeed, despite Nietzsche's occasional acknowledgement that art requires production according to various norms and rules,³² his tendency to emphasise artists' supposedly all-conquering energy – which goes back to BT's notion of Dionysian art – obscures rather than illuminates art's necessarily tradition-bound and institutional context.³³ And when it comes to his notion that prose and poetry are related by means of an "uninterrupted, courteous war" (GS 92), it really does seem he is struggling to conjoin two sets of values

---

31 In this way, he maintains, there is a "mysterious connection ... between the state and art, political greed and artistic creation, battlefield and work of art" (GM p. 170).
32 See, for example, GS 290; NL 1887/1888,KSA 13, 11[312] (WP 849) and especially Nietzsche's extended paean to "Apollonian" form-giving in BT. Even here, however, Nietzsche conceives of the constraints on artists as largely self-imposed, rather than as deriving from cultural norms.
33 Cf. Henry Staten's brilliant critique of Nietzsche on art, in which he emphasises Nietzsche's insensitivity to the way in which artistic excellence and success is necessarily mediated by craft-traditions. As he puts it, "I can have ... all the energy in the world ... [but] in the absence of the appropriate *techne* [craft] never succeed in so much as tying my shoelaces" (Staten 2009, p. 576).

that are fundamentally disjoint. Perhaps the most plausible interpretation here is that, having pitted morality and art against each other as early as BT, Nietzsche has simply lighted upon conquest and war as the most "anti-moral" practices available, and hence associated them, according to the logic of his initial antithesis, with art. Is this the best we can do to rescue Nietzsche's attempt to synthesise the values of art and power?

Three attempts at synthesis

Three scholars have made better, but what I will argue are, nevertheless, ultimately unconvincing attempts at such a synthesis. Bernard Reginster argues that we should understand artistic creativity as a "paradigmatic manifestation" of the will to power (Reginster 2007, p. 34). This is because the latter, on his view, involves a desire for the "overcoming of resistance", and hence for "perpetual striving", since without new challenges the will is left idle and unfulfilled (Reginster 2007, pp. 39ff.). Artistic creation is at the centre of Nietzsche's vision of fulfilment, then, because (according to Reginster) it requires manifold overcoming of resistance: the artist has to overcome not only his own suffering (Reginster 2007, p. 45), but also the resistance put up by his own drives (Reginster 2007, p. 48) in the process of creation. While this is an attractive reading of "the will to power as art", and one responsive to many of Nietzsche's texts,[34] it remains dubious whether Reginster has effected a stable *modus vivendi* between Nietzsche's two basic sets of values. For surely one could question whether artistic creation provides a "paradigmatic manifestation" of overcoming resistance and perpetual striving. If these are the *desiderata*, then why not engage in war and conquest, rather than in their etiolated, not to say merely metaphorical equivalents in the realm of the arts? Wouldn't these afford more full-blooded challenges, and thus greater fulfilment? Reginster admits many Nietzsche-interpreters have felt embarrassment at this possibility (Reginster 2007, p. 35)[35] – but it is not clear that Nietzsche would have felt the same way himself.

---

[34] See GS 56, 310, 363; GM I 13; Z II *Self-Overcoming*; NL 1887, KSA 12, 9[151]; NL 1887/88, KSA 13, 11[75]; NL 1887/88, KSA 13, 11[111] (WP 656, 696, 704 respectively). Mention should also be made here of Nietzsche's favourable attitude towards the Greek *agôn* or contest: see (e.g.) D 38, TI *Socrates* 8, TI *Skirmishes* 23, and note 39 below.

[35] N.B. Reginster's strained reading of NL 1883, KSA 10, 8[14] (WP 417), where Nietzsche lauds "Dionysian wisdom. Joy in the destruction of the most noble and at the sight of its progressive ruin". Reginster reads this as an encouragement to surpass one's creative achievements, maintaining that "to destroy here might plausibly mean to surpass, supplant, or make obsolete"

Salim Kemal offers a similar resolution to the art/power *contretemps*, drawing on Nietzsche's long-standing association between beauty, life and health on the one hand, and between ugliness, degeneration and sickness on the other.[36] "For Nietzsche", he maintains, "the aesthetic need for beauty is the need for us to continue life ... art gives us a sense of the order and power that are available to us. It allows us to believe that we can construct and create, that we can make an order that suits us. This is the aesthetic need, the need to continue to live, that beauty satisfies" (Kemal 1998, p. 283). This reading certainly captures Nietzsche's early notion – one central to BT – that art can save us from despair, a notion repeated at GS 107: "As an aesthetic phenomenon", Nietzsche holds, "existence is still bearable to us, and art furnishes us with the eye and hand and above all the good conscience to be able to make such a phenomenon of ourselves". While this is an affirmation of art, it remains a rather minimal one, since beauty is confined to extricating us from a negative condition. But even if Nietzsche ascribes a more positive and ambitious role to art in his later, post-Schopenhauerian works, one can still raise the question of whether the creation and/or experience of artistic beauty is the most (or even a paradigmatic) life-enhancing form of activity. Again, why not opt for the order, power and life-enhancement afforded by a skilfully conducted battle? Wouldn't this be a more direct, more vital, and "healthier" activity in which to engage?

Henry Staten is more willing than either Reginster or Kemal to concede there is a real problem in marrying Nietzsche's artistic values with his power-based ones. As Staten puts matters, Nietzsche's admiration for figures like Caesar and Napoleon makes it difficult to "liberate the concepts of noble values and active force from their genesis in concepts of political domination and class distinction" (Staten 1998, p. 241). Indeed, he goes so far as to say that only in Z is the will to power "developed in a way that does not remain in disturbing proximity to [Nietzsche's] tyrannophilia and his apologia for cruelty" (Staten 1998, pp. 241f.).[37] Nonetheless, Staten thinks Nietzsche does manage to give coherent shape to the "will to power as art": namely, through tragic drama. Staten cites the example of Macbeth, who, according to Nietzsche, exerts a "'demonic' attraction" on audiences, or at least those audience-members

---

(Reginster 2007, p. 52). But this is not what Nietzsche says, either here or in the rest of the passage.
36 In corroboration of these groupings, Kemal cites GS 78, BGE 223, TI *Skirmishes* 19–20 and A 1–2.
37 For examples of Z's (occasionally) more critical attitude towards the infliction of harm, see note 28 above.

who are "really possessed by raging ambition [and] behold[...] its image with joy" (D 240). For according to Nietzsche, the tragic poets – especially Shakespeare and the Ancient Greek dramatists – were "half-drunk and stupefied by [an] excess of blood and energy" (D 240), conveying this intoxication to those who appreciate their tragic art. And in BT 9 he illustrates this with the example of Aeschylus' Prometheus, a "titanically striving individual", who demonstrates the "sublime view that <u>active sin</u> is [... his] true [...] virtue".

This is arguably the most successful attempt so far to synthesise Nietzsche's two sets of values. What we are being told, in effect, is that Nietzsche, while retaining his allegiance to an ideal of power or force, is placing that ideal within an artistic (and specifically a dramatic) context. And the vehicle for his doing so is the tragic hero or villain, the apogee of the powerful man, only one now located not in history (such as Napoleon) but on stage (Macbeth, for example). The trouble with this reading, however, is that it brings art and power together in a basically adventitious way. Granted, Nietzsche does revere the assertion of power, as well as the arts, so the notion that his greatest reverence is reserved for power-as-expressed-through-art – particularly through Greek music-drama, which is his paradigm of artistic expression – makes sense. But what is lacking here, still, is an account of how art and power form an essential, unified whole. After all, art needn't convey the exploits of the powerful and heroic,[38] and powerful heroes needn't be represented or experienced though art. So we are left once more, I suggest, with the juxtaposition of two value-commitments of fundamentally different provenance. Nietzsche's values of art and power, although capable of coexistence in certain contexts, have not been shown to share any deep affinity – despite his continual efforts at showing they do. And hence the impression remains of two tectonic plates, as it were, within Nietzsche's thought, which although continually colliding with each other, are incapable of systematic and genuine synthesis.

In sum, I have argued that none of the three attempts at synthesis outlined above is fully convincing. Reginster exaggerates when he claims that artistic creativity, in virtue of its (supposed) perpetual "overcoming of resistance", is

---

[38] Staten lays particular emphasis on this point: "even when Nietzsche does not press it in the direction of the great man", he maintains, "the image of the hero remains in a fundamental way allergic to the ordinariness of the ordinary individual" (Staten 1998, p. 248). As an example of art that celebrates "the ordinariness of the ordinary individual", Staten cites Joyce's *Ulysses*, and more widely the realistic novel, which, as he points out, Nietzsche completely ignores. I would add that a similar point could be made about music, which Nietzsche prizes far above the other arts. For although we hear a lot about Beethoven and Wagner in his work, less "titanic" musical artists – such as Bach, Schumann or Haydn – hardly get a mention.

a "paradigmatic manifestation" of the will to power. Kemal's notion that (what he dubs) "the aesthetic need" optimally embodies the will to power *qua* the will to "continue life" appears forced, and to underestimate other "seductive lure[s] to life" (GM II 7). Finally, Staten's view that the tragic hero or villain is the apotheosis of the "will to power as art", although promising, still fails to show why power is best expressed through art, or why art has any marked affinity with power. Having exhausted these three sophisticated accounts of the relation between art and power in Nietzsche's work,[39] it is time to move on to my own account of that relation. This account is grounded in Nietzsche's genealogy, in the sense of his family and historical background, and draws extensively on the sociological research of Norbert Elias. Clearly, in having recourse to Nietzsche's biography, which lies "beyond" his texts – or at least, beyond what is explicitly in those texts – I am assuming such information can afford genuine appreciation and understanding of claims and arguments that lie "within" those texts. And in this way, I am running the risk of committing the genetic fallacy myself. But in what follows, I hope the value of this approach – viz. of applying Nietzsche's methodology to his own work – will become clear. Indeed, I hope that the application of genealogy *to* Nietzsche's work will be seen to bear greater fruit than the application of genealogy *within* Nietzsche's work ever does.

A genealogy of Nietzsche's values

According to Norbert Elias, the German middle classes – to which Nietzsche's family belonged – had been largely excluded from political power prior to the second half of the nineteenth century, and more particularly prior to the Franco-Prussian War of 1870/71. As Elias puts it, "the middle class had hardly any access to those government positions where decisions were made regarding the political, military, economic and many other affairs of the various [German] states. These were almost exclusively in the hands of the princes and their court-civilised public servants" (Elias 1996, p. 113). This aristocratic dominance

---

[39] Here one should also mention Nietzsche's early work, *Homer's Contest* (see GM pp. 174–181), in which he elaborates how Ancient Greek dramatists competed for prizes, thereby saturating the artistic world of the time with the spirit of the *agôn*, or contest. As he puts things, the *agôn* was the "permanent basis of life in the Hellenic state", a "tournament of forces" that required a never-ending competition between "geniuses", thereby contributing to the good of the state (GM p. 178). As these quotations suggest, however, the kind of "contest" adverted to here remains external to art, rather than essentially informing it; moreover, the value of contest extends far beyond the bounds of merely artistic competition.

of the power structures of the German states was generally resented by the middle classes, but they coped with their subordinate political position by developing a basically counter-political, and counter-militaristic sense of self-worth. This sense of self-worth centred on an ideal of *Kultur*, or "culture", which had strong artistic and aesthetic components. As Elias writes, "cultural achievements, especially in the areas of literature, philosophy and science, had a very high rating in the German upper middle-class scale of values" (Elias 1996, p. 113). Indeed, these areas – "such as religion, science, architecture, philosophy and poetry" – "provided the politically excluded German middle classes with the main basis for their self-legitimisation and the justification of their pride" (Elias 1996, p. 126).

Given this, we can see Nietzsche's admiration for and devotion to the arts as typical of his class background.[40] Where he clearly departs from that background is in his disdain for a key element of middle class *Kultur* – namely, "morality". As Elias relates, in the "code of behaviour and feeling" typical of the German middle classes before the second half of the nineteenth century, "questions of morality played the same role that questions of courtesy, manners and good form played in convivial social life in the [nobility] ... the ideals of equality and humanity were ... central to the code of the upwardly mobile German middle classes – Schiller wrote 'You millions I embrace you' and Beethoven took up the theme – whereas the idea of human *in*equality was embedded at least implicitly in the court-aristocratic code" (Elias 1996, p. 114). In this respect, then, Nietzsche is strongly out of tune with his class background, at least as that background was structured before the later nineteenth century. For right from the start of his authorship, he shows marked disaffection with and disdain for the values of egalitarian democracy, the kind of "moral" values to which Kant (a member, it is worth noting, of the late eighteenth century German middle class) gives paradigm philosophical expression.

We can now better appreciate Nietzsche's sociological position before the appearance of his first major work, BT, in 1872. Essentially, he is allied to his middle class origins insofar as he places immense value on the arts, ascribing to them (and especially music) something close to redemptive power. But he is sharply at odds with his origins insofar as he contemns the moral aspect of *Kultur* – a contempt rooted in his pietistic Lutheran family and education. It is at this juncture that a crucial event takes place – the Franco-Prussian War

---

40 As Christian Emden notes, Nietzsche's early work, *Über die Zukunft unserer Bildungsanstalten* – "On the Future of Our Institutions of Cultural Education" (1872) – is essentially a "hymn" to the *Bildungsbürgertum*, viz. the culturally educated German middle classes. See Emden 2008, p. 114.

(1870/71) – which fundamentally alters the direction of middle class moral and cultural aspiration (Nietzsche's included). As Elias contends: "At the beginning of the nineteenth century, the German states were weak; even warlike Prussia was overrun by Napoleon's revolutionary armies without much difficulty ... However, in the second half of the century, Germany rose relatively quickly to become a great power itself: indeed, Germany ... became the leading power in continental Europe within a few decades" (Elias 1996, p. 117). The effects of this political transformation were marked, particularly on the middle classes. For with the rapid rise of Germany to great power status – a rise Nietzsche would have experienced at first hand, having volunteered in the war[41] – the temptation to abandon the traditionally anti-political, anti-militaristic attitudes of the middle classes became ever greater. In short, the values of strength, domination and victory gradually unseated those of *Kultur*.

Elias charts this axiological development with skill: "Certainly there were still sections of the German middle class", he argues, "who continued after 1871 to justify themselves in terms of the concept of culture ... But large parts of the middle class ... adopted the upper-class code of honour as their own. And in the rank-order of values represented by this code, especially in its Prussian version, cultural achievements ... were ranked lower, if not positively despised" (Elias 1996, p. 114). Thus on the one hand, Germany's rise to power spelled the demise, or at least the demoting of the arts as a middle class value. As Elias holds, "The musical interests of the court-aristocratic society ... were minimal, and the same was true of the model-setting circle of officers in the *Kaiserreich*" (Elias 1996, p. 114). On the other hand, the traditional commitment of the middle classes to moral universalism and equality came more and more to be sidelined. In Elias' words: "It is not surprising that for many [...] the experience of this astonishing [...] swing [...] from weakness to strength [...] led to a glorification of strength, and to the idea that upholding consideration towards others, love and readiness to help others were mere hypocrisy" (Elias 1996, p. 117). Moreover, this turn to the political and the militaristic – away from the anti-political, anti-militaristic confines of the realm of *Kultur* – was made all the more attractive to the middle classes by the fact that, as the second half of the nineteenth century unfolded, they were given steadily greater chances to enter the German – now newly national – power élite (see Elias 1996, pp. 139f.)

---

[41] It is controversial to what degree Nietzsche actually participated in the war. Emden maintains that "he enrolled late, did not face any combat, and by the time he had reached the frontline, the war was virtually over" (Emden 2008, p. 121).

What can we learn from this historical and class narrative, a narrative that intimately informs Nietzsche's own? Most saliently, I think it sheds significant light on Nietzsche's struggle to reconcile his two basic value commitments: viz. those to art and power. For Elias' analysis shows that that struggle is also one that Nietzsche's class – in particular the intellectuals within it[42] – faced, as nineteenth century German history moved through the upheaval of the Franco-Prussian War. Just as the middle classes confronted a situation in which it was more and more tempting to bracket, if not dispose of their artistic and aesthetic values and pursuits, so Nietzsche was confronted by the same temptation: something seen in the move from BT, in 1872, where art-based values predominate, to GM in 1887, where power-based values are to the fore. Where Nietzsche stands out from his class background, I take it, is in the *intensity* with which he is drawn to both value-sets, and hence also that with which he experiences the tension between them. On the one hand, he is drawn strongly to the power-set, since he had always been attracted to the anti-"moral" aspects of aristocratic militarism, in a way not true of his class as a whole. But on the other hand, the cost of abandoning the artistic ideals of middle class *Kultur* was particularly galling for Nietzsche, given his (Schopenhauer- and Wagner-mediated) attraction to those ideals. In fine, I think it is fair to conclude that the axiological conflict affecting the German middle classes was fundamentally Nietzsche's own: it is just that he felt it more keenly, more excruciatingly – hence his unflagging (though ultimately unsuccessful) attempts to solve it, by reconciling the disparate value-sets he had inherited from his culture and class.

Some conclusions

If my argument is cogent,[43] what are its implications for theory, and in particular for genealogy and the status of the "genetic fallacy"? I will answer this question in two stages: first, by unpacking what I think the foregoing exercise in genetic understanding does not and cannot achieve; second, by outlining

---

[42] See Elias 1996, pp. 123–134, which documents the way in which "cultural history" and "political history" became mutually hostile disciplines within the nineteenth century German university.

[43] I.e. not on the level of many of Nietzsche's own *ad hominem* attacks, which succeed merely in explaining certain evaluative commitments and arguments away. See, for example, the following passages, which fail to establish much of philosophical or cultural substance: TI *Socrates* 3 (on Socrates), A 11 (on Kant), and TI *Germans* 2 (on representatives of German culture).

what I believe it can and does achieve, thereby pointing up the real and lasting value of Nietzsche's methodology.

First, a knowledge of Nietzsche's own national, cultural and class background does not and cannot help us identify the core value-commitments, and thus the core value-conflict at the heart of his work: these must be gleaned from his writings alone. Nor does such knowledge assist us in judging the success with which he overcomes that conflict. For it is sufficiently plain – both from Nietzsche's repeated, and sometimes strained attempts at doing this, together with the impressive efforts of recent scholars – that that project faces an uphill battle. Furthermore, and crucially, applying the genealogical method to Nietzsche's values of art and power serves in no way to undermine them. Whereas Nietzsche's genealogy of "morality" *does* seek seriously to undermine (at least Judaeo-Christian) moral practices and claims – on the basis of their supposed grounding in a "life-denying", "slavish" moral psychology – my genealogy does not, and could not have the same aim vis-à-vis Nietzsche's values. And this because the fact that Nietzsche's values derive largely from his German middle class cultural milieu is not, in and of itself, grounds for criticising those values.[44]

Secondly, a grasp of Nietzsche's historical background does, nevertheless – as I hope I have shown – enable us to appreciate far better the cultural force and ramifications of terms like "art" and "power" in his vocabulary. And with this appreciation, there comes a deeper understanding of why the conflict he faces is, despite his best efforts, insuperable: namely, because it is grounded in a deep contemporary social conflict, of which his writings are, in many respects, an artefact. In affirming this, I want to make clear, however, that I am not endorsing either of two false alternatives. First, Nietzsche's axiology does not reduce to the cultural conflict or fissure I have outlined, as if a more thorough examination of his word-usage, or structure of argument, could reveal his value-commitments simply as a veiled reproduction of that fissure. After all, Nietzsche prized Ancient Greek over contemporary German music-drama, and found the power-politics of the new *Reich* in many ways distasteful. Equally, though, Nietzsche's texts are not wholly autonomous or insulated from their historical environment. What these false alternatives point to, then, is that genealogy supplies a genuine, well-founded methodological middle way: rather than confining our attention either to Nietzsche's historical back-

---

44 Unless, of course, one takes there to be good (perhaps Nietzsche-inspired?) reason to impugn wholesale the values of the nineteenth century German *bourgeoisie*. By contrast, if "moral" values are grounded in the way Nietzsche alleges, there *would* be incontrovertible reason to criticise them (given the logic of the relation between such values and moral psychology).

ground, or to his texts *"per se"*, it alerts us to the essential fructification between these, which – although it does not have a unique, delimited locus – is of vital importance for understanding and assessing his overall argument.

In conclusion, even if Nietzsche's application of genealogy to "moral" values fails, in virtue of the failure of genealogy *qua* aristocratic determinism, I hope I have made a good case for the claim that genealogy *qua* sociological conditioning proves very fruitful – and even interpretatively essential – when applied to Nietzsche's own values.[45]

Bibliography

Abbey, R./Appel, F. (1999): "Domesticating Nietzsche: A Response to Mark Warren". In: *Political Theory* 27(1), pp. 121–125.
Acampora, C.D. (ed.) (2006): *Nietzsche's* On the Genealogy of Morals: *Critical Essays*. Lanham, MD: Rowman and Littlefield.
Adkins, A. W. H. (1960): *Merit and Responsibility: A Study in Greek Values*. Oxford: Clarendon Press.
Angier, T. (ed.) (2012): *Ethics: The Key Thinkers*. London: Bloomsbury Academic.
Ansell-Pearson, K. (ed.) (2009): *A Companion to Nietzsche*. Oxford: Wiley-Blackwell.
Ansell-Pearson, K. (2012): "Nietzsche: *On the Genealogy of Morality*". In: R.B. Pippin (ed.) (2012): *Introductions to Nietzsche*. Cambridge: Cambridge University Press, pp. 199–214.
Brobjer, T.H. (2004): "Nietzsche's View of the Value of Historical Studies and Methods". In: *Journal of the History of Ideas* 65(2), pp. 301–322.
Craig, E. (2007): "Genealogies and the State of Nature". In: A. Thomas (ed.) (2007): *Bernard Williams*. Cambridge: Cambridge University Press, pp. 181–200.
Elias, N. (1996): *The Germans: Power Struggles and the Development of Habitus in the Nineteenth and Twentieth Centuries*. Cambridge: Polity Press.
Elias, N. (2000): *The Civilising Process*. Revised edition. Oxford: Blackwell Publishers Ltd.
Emden, C.J. (2008): *Friedrich Nietzsche and the Politics of History*. Cambridge: Cambridge University Press.
Ferry, L./Renaut, A. (eds.) (1997): *Why We Are Not Nietzscheans*. Chicago: Chicago University Press.
Foucault, M. (1975): *Surveiller et Punir: Naissance de la Prison*. Paris: Gallimard.
Gemes, K. (2006): "'We remain of necessity strangers to ourselves': The Key Message of Nietzsche's *Genealogy*". In: C.D. Acampora (ed.) (2006): *Nietzsche's* On the Genealogy of Morals: *Critical Essays*. Lanham, MD: Rowman and Littlefield, pp. 191–208.
Gemes, K. /Schuringa, C. (2012): "Nietzsche". In: T. Angier (ed.) (2012): *Ethics: The Key Thinkers*. London: Bloomsbury Academic, pp. 217–238.

---

[45] That Nietzsche seems wholly unaware of the sociological conditioning of his own values is striking, and gives the lie to Solomon's view that he refuses to cut philosophy from its "moorings in the soul of the individual and his or her culture" (Solomon 1996, p. 217).

Geuss, R. (2001): "Nietzsche and Genealogy". In: J. Richardson/B. Leiter (eds.) (2001): *Nietzsche*. Oxford: Oxford University Press, pp. 322–340.
Guay, R. (2009): "The Philosophical Function of Genealogy". In: K. Ansell-Pearson (ed.) (2009): *A Companion to Nietzsche*. Oxford: Wiley-Blackwell, pp. 353–370.
Hatab, L.J. (2008): *Nietzsche's* On the Genealogy of Morality: *An Introduction*. Cambridge: Cambridge University Press.
Janaway, C. (2007): *Beyond Selflessness: Reading Nietzsche's* Genealogy. Oxford: Oxford University Press.
Janaway, C. (2009): "Naturalism and Genealogy". In: K. Ansell-Pearson (ed.) (2009): *A Companion to Nietzsche*. Oxford: Wiley-Blackwell, pp. 337–352.
Kadarkay, A. (ed.) (1995): *The Lukács Reader*. Oxford: Blackwell Publishers Ltd.
Kail, P.J.E. (2011): "'Genealogy' and the Genealogy". In: S. May (ed.) (2011): *Nietzsche's* On the Genealogy of Morality: *A Critical Guide*. Cambridge: Cambridge University Press, pp. 214–233.
Kemal, S. (1998): "Nietzsche's Politics of Aesthetic Genius". In: S. Kemal/I. Gaskell/ D.W. Conway (eds.) (1998): *Nietzsche, Philosophy and the Arts*. Cambridge: Cambridge University Press, pp. 257–286.
Kemal, S./Gaskell, I./Conway, D.W. (eds.) (1998): *Nietzsche, Philosophy and the Arts*. Cambridge: Cambridge University Press.
Klement, K.C. (2002): "When Is Genetic Reasoning Not Fallacious?" In: *Argumentation* 16, pp. 383–400.
Knobe, J. and Leiter, B. (2007): "The Case for Nietzschean Moral Psychology". In: B. Leiter/ N. Sinhababu (eds.) (2007): *Nietzsche and Morality*. Oxford: Oxford University Press, pp. 83–109.
Leiter, B. (2002): *Nietzsche on Morality*. London: Routledge.
Leiter, B./Sinhababu, N. (eds.) (2007): *Nietzsche and Morality*. Oxford: Oxford University Press.
Loeb, P.S. (2008): "Is There a Genetic Fallacy in Nietzsche's Genealogy of Morals?" In: *The Agonist* I/II, pp. 1–14. [http://www.nietzschecircle.com/AGONIST/2008_12/PDFs/ AgonistDEC2008LoebEssaySECURE.pdf].
Lukács, G. (1995): "Friedrich Nietzsche". In: A. Kadarkay (ed.) (1995): *The Lukács Reader*. Oxford: Blackwell Publishers Ltd, pp. 246–265.
Magnus, B./Higgins, K.M. (eds.) (1996): *The Cambridge Companion to Nietzsche*. Cambridge: Cambridge University Press.
May, S. (ed.) (2011): *Nietzsche's* On the Genealogy of Morality: *A Critical Guide*. Cambridge: Cambridge University Press.
Moore, G. /Brobjer, T.H. (eds.) (2004): *Nietzsche and Science*. Aldershot: Ashgate Publishing Ltd.
Nehamas, A. (1985): *Nietzsche: Life as Literature*. Cambridge, MA: Harvard University Press.
Nietzsche, Friedrich (1968), *The Will to Power*. W. Kaufmann and R.J. Hollingdale (trans.). New York: Vintage Books.
Nietzsche, Friedrich (1982), *Daybreak: Thoughts on the Prejudices of Morality*. R.J. Hollingdale (trans.) Cambridge: Cambridge University Press.
Nietzsche, Friedrich (1990), *Beyond Good and Evil: Prelude to a Philosophy of the Future*. R.J. Hollingdale (trans.) Harmondsworth: Penguin Books.
Nietzsche, Friedrich (1999), *The Birth of Tragedy and Other Writings*. R. Speirs (trans.) Cambridge: Cambridge University Press.

Nietzsche, Friedrich (2001), *The Gay Science: With a Prelude in German Rhymes and an Appendix of Songs*. J. Nauckhoff, A. del Caro (trans.) Cambridge: Cambridge University Press.

Nietzsche, Friedrich (2005), *The Anti-Christ, Ecce Homo, Twilight of the Idols and Other Writings*. J. Norman (trans.) Cambridge: Cambridge University Press.

Nietzsche, Friedrich (2006), *Thus Spoke Zarathustra*. A. del Caro (trans.) Cambridge: Cambridge University Press.

Nietzsche, Friedrich (2007), *On the Genealogy of Morality*. C. Diethe (trans.) Cambridge: Cambridge University Press.

Pippin, R.B. (ed.) (2012): *Introductions to Nietzsche*. Cambridge: Cambridge University Press.

Reginster, B. (2007): "The Will to Power and the Ethics of Creativity". In: B. Leiter/N. Sinhababu (eds.) (2007): *Nietzsche and Morality*. Oxford: Oxford University Press, pp. 32–56.

Richardson, J./Leiter, B. (eds.) (2001): *Nietzsche*. Oxford: Oxford University Press.

Schacht, R. (ed.) (1994a): *Nietzsche, Genealogy, Morality: Essays on Nietzsche's* On the Genealogy of Morals. Berkeley: University of California Press.

Schacht, R. (1994b): "Of Morals and *Menschen*". In: R. Schacht (ed.) (1994a): *Nietzsche, Genealogy, Morality: Essays on Nietzsche's* On the Genealogy of Morals. Berkeley: University of California Press, pp. 427–448.

Solomon, R.C. (1996): "*Nietzsche* ad hominem: *Perspectivism, personality and* ressentiment *revisited*". In: B. Magnus/K.M. Higgins (eds.) (1996): *The Cambridge Companion to Nietzsche*. Cambridge: Cambridge University Press, pp. 180–222.

Staten, H. (1998): "Dionysus Lost and Found: Literary Genres in the Political Thought of Nietzsche and Lukács". In: S. Kemal/I. Gaskell/D.W. Conway (eds.) (1998): *Nietzsche, Philosophy and the Arts*. Cambridge: Cambridge University Press, pp. 239–256.

Staten, H. (2009): "A Critique of the Will to Power". In: K. Ansell-Pearson (ed.) (2009): *A Companion to Nietzsche*. Oxford: Wiley-Blackwell, pp. 565–582.

Strong, T.B. (2006): "Genealogy, the Will to Power, and the Problem of a Past". In: C.D. Acampora (ed.) (2006): *Nietzsche's* On the Genealogy of Morals: *Critical Essays*. Lanham, MD: Rowman and Littlefield, pp. 93–108.

Thomas, A. (ed.) (2007): *Bernard Williams*. Cambridge: Cambridge University Press.

Williams, B. (2002): *Truth and Truthfulness: An Essay in Genealogy*. Princeton: Princeton University Press.

Evangelia Sembou
Foucault's use of Nietzsche*

Nietzsche is the philosopher of power, a philosopher who managed to think of power without having to confine himself within a political theory in order to do so.... For myself, I prefer to utilise the writers I like. The only valid tribute to thought such as Nietzsche's is precisely to use it, to deform it, to make it groan and protest. And if commentators then say that I am being faithful or unfaithful to Nietzsche, that is of absolutely no interest. (Foucault 1980a, pp. 53f.)

Foucault once said that "...reading Nietzsche was the point of rupture" for him (Foucault 2000, p. 438), while in his last interview he claimed: "[...] I am simply Nietzschean [...]" (Foucault 1990a, p. 251). In his genealogical work Foucault consciously followed in the footsteps of Nietzsche. In his famous essay "Nietzsche, Genealogy, History" (Foucault 1984a), where he lays out his genealogical approach, Foucault makes explicit his debt to Nietzsche, while the title of the first volume of *The History of Sexuality*, "The Will to Know" (La Volonté de Savoir), is inspired by Nietzsche's work (Foucault 2000, p. 445).

In this paper I shall argue that, despite the commonalities between Nietzsche's and Foucault's genealogies, there are several differences. Ultimately, beneath the layer of similarities, facilitated by Foucault's use of Nietzschean terminology, Foucault employs Nietzsche's categories differently. Therefore, his genealogical method turned out to be very different from Nietzsche's 'genealogy of morals'. I will first look at Foucault's reading of Nietzsche. Then I will proceed to explore the points at which Nietzsche's and Foucault's genealogies differ.

I[1]

In his well-known essay "Nietzsche, Genealogy, History" Foucault characterizes genealogy as "gray"; its task is to decipher the hieroglyphic script of humans' past, a past that is neither black (i.e. totally unknown) nor white (i.e.

---

* I am grateful to Kimberly Hutchings for discussing with me several of the issues raised in this paper. An earlier version of this paper was presented at a Workshop entitled "Nietzsche and Political Theory", in the context of the MANCEPT Workshops in Political Theory 2012. The Workshop was convened by the editors of this volume.
1 In this section I draw on Sembou 2011a.

transparent), but something in between (gray), namely, ambiguous and uncertain. Thus, a rigorous investigation is needed, if the meaning of the past is to be uncovered: "Genealogy, consequently, requires patience and a knowledge of details, and it depends on a vast accumulation of source material." (Foucault 1984a, pp. 76f.) Due to its minuteness, genealogy may initially give us the impression that it deals with trivial, everyday things, rather than with important developments. However, genealogy acquires its character from recording "what we tend to feel is without history", instances such as "sentiments, love, conscience, instincts" (Foucault 1984a, p. 76).

Crucially, the writing of the human past by the genealogist is necessarily an interpretation, which itself is neither true nor false. For Foucault, the genealogist is an interpreter but not an hermeneutician. The genealogist as interpreter recognizes that the meaning he/she gives to history is doubtful (hence "gray"), "acknowledges its system of injustice" (Foucault 1984a, p. 90) and the fact that his/her interpretation is open to revision. The genealogist-interpreter has a sense of where he/she stands in history and does not ignore the fact that he/she is the product of historic and social circumstances; nevertheless, he/she is simultaneously able to distance him-/herself from his/her situation in order to examine things from afar. In so doing, the genealogist-interpreter ignores the actors' own interpretation(s) of the meaning of their actions. Therefore, the genealogical approach is one of detachment. By contrast, the approach of the hermeneutician is one of engagement, as he/she attempts to grasp the significance of things from within them. As opposed to the interpreter-hermeneutician, the genealogist-interpreter "finds that the questions which are traditionally held to be the deepest and murkiest are truly and literally the most superficial". It follows that "their meaning is to be discovered in surface practices, not in mysterious depths" (Dreyfus/Rabinow 1982, p. 107). Consequently, a genealogical interpretation[2] is distinctly different from an hermeneutical approach.

The claim that interpretation is not the uncovering of a hidden meaning has revolutionary implications for philosophy; or better, it is a direct attack against philosophy as it traditionally has been understood. For Foucault's genealogy undermines the belief in the existence of unchanging essences and truths. In his genealogical writings Foucault engaged in a deconstructive exercise. Continuing Nietzsche's tradition of "philosophizing with the hammer"

---

[2] For a textualist interpretation of Nietzsche's Genealogy of Morality see Larry Hatab and Dan Conway, while Chris Janaway and David Owen offer contextualist accounts of the same text: Owen 2008, p. 141. See also Hatab 2008, Conway 2008, Janaway 2007, Owen 2007.

(EH, "Twilight of the Idols"), Foucault sought to destroy all the metaphysical ideas that have dominated Western philosophy since Plato.

Foucault was more conscious of genealogy as a method than Nietzsche was (GM). Therefore, he set forth its objectives. To begin with, Foucault was more careful to define what genealogy as an history concerned with tracing origins meant. In examining Nietzsche's genealogy, Foucault noted that Nietzsche used *"Ursprung"*, *"Entstehung"* and *"Herkunft"* interchangeably. Foucault argues that the problem of the term *"Ursprung"* is that it refers to "something that was already there" – viz. a deeper reality – before the search began.

> However, if the genealogist refuses to extend his faith in metaphysics, if he listens to history, he finds that there is "something altogether different" behind things: not a timeless and essential secret, but the secret that they have no essence or that their essence was fabricated in a piecemeal fashion from alien forms. (Foucault 1984a, p. 78)

Put differently, for Foucault, the idea of the "origin" is just a metaphysical truth that has dominated European thought for two thousand years. In Nietzschean terms, genealogy questions the "will to truth": "...devotion to truth and the precision of scientific methods arose from the passion of scholars, their reciprocal hatred, their fanatical and ending discussions, and their spirit of competition – the personal conflicts that slowly forged the weapons of reason" (Foucault 1984a, p. 78).

According to Foucault, *"Herkunft"* and *"Entstehung"* characterize the task of genealogy better.

> Herkunft is the equivalent of stock or descent; it is the ancient affiliation to a group, sustained by the bonds of blood, tradition, or social class. The analysis of Herkunft often involves a consideration of race or social type. But the traits it attempts to identify are not the exclusive generic characteristics of an individual, a sentiment, or an idea, which permit us to qualify them as 'Greek' or 'English'; rather, it seeks the subtle, singular, and subindividual marks that might possibly intersect in them to form a network that is difficult to unravel. (Foucault 1984a, pp. 80f.)

Genealogy engages in deconstruction,[3] for the analysis of *"Herkunft"* fragments what was considered unified; it does not merely challenge the linear conception of history but also identifies an underlying continuity, which is the product of "the accidents, the minute deviations – or conversely, the complete reversals – the errors, the false appraisals, and the faulty calculations that gave

---

[3] In using the term 'deconstruction' I do not mean it in the sense of Derrida, who made of deconstruction a method.

birth to those things that continue to exist and have value for us" (Foucault 1984a, p. 81).

"*Entstehung*", on the other hand, denotes emergence, that is, "the moment of arising". So it is different from "origin" in the usual sense of the word; for "origin" usually has metaphysical connotations – it implies an as yet unknown purpose that seeks its realization the moment it arises. However, genealogy does not seek to uncover substantial entities; rather, it studies the emergence of a battle which defines and clears a space (Foucault 1984a, pp. 83f.). Instead of origins or deeper meanings Foucault, the genealogist, finds force relations operating in particular events[4] and historical developments. This is where Foucault's genealogical analysis is reminiscent of Nietzsche's. There is an important difference, however; whereas Nietzsche grounds morality as well as social and political institutions in the tactics ("will to power") of individual actors or groups of actors, Foucault sees social and political practices as the result of strategies without strategists: "...no one is responsible for an emergence; no one can glory in it, since it always occurs in the *interstice*" (Foucault 1984a, p. 85; my italics). Foucault's use of the term "interstice" should be emphasized; the play of forces in a particular historical context is conditioned – to a lesser or greater extent – by the space which defines them. For Foucault, human actors do not first exist and then enter into combat or harmony; rather, they emerge on a field of battle. Subjects are caught in networks of power – what Foucault calls "rituals of power" (Foucault 1991, p. 186 and Foucault 1975, p. 188)[5] ("dispositifs") (Foucault 1976, p. 99; Foucault 1980d, p. 138) – that lie beyond their control. These "rituals of power" are neither the conscious creation of actors nor simply a set of relationships; they are not located in specific places; and it is not easy to identify the moment of their emergence. It is the task of Foucault's genealogy to identify and analyze these "rituals of power".

In *Discipline and Punish* and the first volume of *The History of Sexuality*, Foucault isolates specific sites (not places) of "rituals of power", to wit, Bentham's Panopticon and the confessional (Foucault 1991, pp. 200–209 and Foucault 1998, pp. 61f., respectively).[6] As genealogist, Foucault then tries to specify how power works, when, how and what its effects are. The rules that emerge from "rituals of power" are passed into civil law or moral conventions, which – supposedly – prevent the violence that would otherwise ensue. But, as a genealogical analysis shows, these rules and conventions only perpetuate power and facilitate its diffusion within the body politic as a whole (Foucault 1984a,

---

[4] For the idea of "eventalization" see Foucault 2002a, pp. 226–229.
[5] "Dispositifs" is translated as "apparatuses" elsewhere, e.g. in Foucault 1980d, p. 138.
[6] On Bentham's Panopticon see also Foucault 1980e, pp. 146–165.

p. 85). For Foucault, "Power is war, the continuation of war by other means." (Foucault 2004, p. 15) Thus, he inverts Clausewitz's dictum that "War is a mere continuation of policy by other means" (Clausewitz 1982, p. 119); instead, he argues that "politics is the continuation of war by other means" (Foucault 2004, p. 15).[7]

Rules "are impersonal and can be bent to any purpose" (Foucault 1984a, p. 86), says Foucault following Nietzsche. A traditional historical analysis of the 'purpose' of social and political institutions cannot unearth their "*Entstehung*", because "The successes of history belong to those who are capable of seizing these rules, to replace those who had used them, to disguise themselves so as to pervert them, invert their meaning, and redirect them against those who had initially imposed them" (Foucault 1984a, p. 86). Therefore, genealogy demonstrates that interpretations are dependent on specific configurations of power. And the more the genealogist-interpreter uncovers an interpretation, the more he finds not a fixed meaning but only another interpretation. In this way the arbitrariness of all interpretation is revealed. Since there is no 'original' essence, there is nothing to interpret; and, if there is nothing to interpret, everything is open to interpretation. This is the insight we gain by practising genealogy.

For Foucault, genealogy is an "effective history" (*wirkliche Historie*); this differs, he says, from traditional history. Firstly, "effective history" puts everything into motion; that is to say, it relativizes all ideals of truth, firmness and solidity. In Foucault's words, "...it places within a process of development everything considered immortal in man" (Foucault 1984a, p. 87). According to Foucault, history "can evade metaphysics and become a privileged instrument of genealogy if it refuses the certainty of absolutes" (Foucault 1984a, p. 87). Secondly, having dispensed with metaphysics, genealogy as "effective history" eschews a supra-historical perspective. This is done by reversing the relationship between proximity and distance (Foucault 1984a, p. 89). Whereas traditional history examines the distant past, "Effective history studies what is closest, but in an abrupt dispossession, so as to seize it at a distance..." (Foucault 1984a, p. 89). Moreover, genealogy recognizes its interested character (Fou-

---

[7] According to Foucault, this implies: First, that power relations "are essentially anchored in a certain relationship of force that was established in and through war at a given historical moment that can be historically specified" (Foucault 2004, p. 15); second, political power constitutes a "silent war", as it reinscribes that relationship of force "in institutions, economic inequalities, language, and even the bodies of individuals"; third, "...the last battle would put an end to politics...would at last...suspend the exercise of power as continuous warfare" (Foucault 2004, p. 16).

cault 1984a, p. 90). In addition, unlike traditional history which is past-oriented, genealogy is an "history of the present". Foucault says in *Discipline and Punish*:

> I would like to write the history of this prison, with all the political investments of the body that it gathers together in its closed architecture. Why? Simply because I am interested in the past? No, if one means by that writing a history of the past in terms of the present. Yes, if one means writing the history of the present. (Foucault 1991, pp. 30f.)

According to Foucault, "a history of the past in terms of the present" commits the "presentist fallacy"; that is, the historian takes "a model or a concept, an institution, a feeling, or a symbol from his present" and attempts to "find that it had a parallel meaning in the past" (Dreyfus/Rabinow 1982, p. 118). A genealogical history also avoids finalism by refusing to embark on an attempt to discover the underlying laws of history. In particular, finalism holds that the present is the accomplishment of some latent goal in the past. However, contra finalism, a genealogical history begins with a diagnosis of the present. The genealogist-historian locates the manifestations of a given "meticulous ritual of power" to see where it arose and how it developed. Accordingly, *Discipline and Punish* explores the emergence (Entstehung) of the human sciences (which Foucault calls "pseudo-sciences") and their relation to the emergence (Entstehung) of the prison. A genealogical enquiry shows that "…power produces knowledge…that power and knowledge directly imply one another" (Foucault 1991, p. 27). It seems that Foucault does not clearly differentiate between the *Entstehungsgeschichten* of the prison and the human sciences, despite the fact that he did not wish to reduce the one to the other. (Foucault 1991, p. 305) Foucault's use of an hyphen between the terms "power" and "knowledge" is meant to show the constitutive (or productive) aspect of knowledge (Foucault 1980b, p. 102). Power (relations) and knowledge (or truth) implicate each other (Foucault 1980c, pp. 131ff.; Foucault 1980b, p. 93; Foucault 1991, pp. 27f.; Foucault 1998, p. 60), hence Foucault's term "power-knowledge" (pouvoir-savoir; Foucault 1991, p. 28; Foucault 1975, p. 32).

For Foucault, as indeed for Nietzsche, genealogy is a critical enterprise. The aim of Nietzsche's 'genealogy of morals' was to de-construct the past in order to create the future. I agree with White when he says that genealogy is a "performative critique"; that is to say, "Nietzsche uses his reading of the past in order to direct us towards a particular vision of the future" (White 1988, p. 685). So Nietzsche's "re-valuation" of values has a critical bent. The vision of the future toward which Nietzsche wants to guide us is the 'sovereign' individual who orders and overcomes all the brutal accidents of his/her past. The *Übermensch* will be the master of his own future; he will be able "to transform every 'It was', until the will says: 'But I willed it thus! So shall I will it-'" (Z III Tablets). Likewise, according to Foucault, "A critique is not a matter of saying that things are not right as they are"; rather, "It is a matter of pointing out on what kinds of assumptions, what kinds of familiar, unchallenged modes of thought the practices that we accept rest." (Foucault 1990c, p. 154)[8] The starting-point of critique is the "principle of reversal" (Foucault 1981, pp. 67, 70); that is, critique turns our deep-rooted conceptions upside-down – hence its radicalism. The task of Foucault's genealogy is to provide us with a different interpretation, to make a different perspective known, in order to allow for the possibility of our becoming otherwise than we are. Genealogy as critique aims to isolate the constraints immanent in a particular society and the possibilities of transformation (given those constraints or impediments); "the important question" is "whether the system of constraints in which a society functions leaves individuals the liberty to transform the system" (Foucault 1990b, p. 294). Having identified the practices that restrain us, we will be able to resist them in order to create ourselves in our autonomy. So, for Foucault, power presupposes resistance and vice versa (Foucault 1998, pp. 95f.; Foucault 1980d, p. 142; Foucault 1982, pp. 211f., 221f., 225f.; reprinted in Foucault 2002a, pp. 329ff., 340, 342, 346ff.). However, Foucault insisted that the intellectual should not tell others what they should do (Foucault 1990c, p. 155; cf. Foucault 1990d, p. 265). On the contrary, he/she ought to confine him-/herself to a critique formulated by way of an historical analysis, whose purpose is to show that many postulates, évidences, institutions and ideas we take for granted are historical constructs, and that "we are much more recent than we think" (Foucault 1990c, p. 156). So, like Nietzsche, Foucault refused to legislate for others. Similarly, like Nietzsche, Foucault wished to use genealogy as an argument against particular possibilities that had become realities. He followed Nietzsche in carrying out a performative critique.

Finally – what is crucial –, Foucault contrasted the "universal" to the "specific" intellectual. Whereas the former is concerned with positing universal norms, the latter offers specific analyses and engages in "local" criticism and/or struggle (Foucault 1980c, p. 132).[9] By practising "local" criticism, genealogy allows "an insurrection of subjugated knowledges" (Foucault 1980b, p. 81).

---

8 This interview was published in *Libération* under the title "Est-il Donc Important de Penser?" on 30–31 May 1981. An English translation under the title "So Is It Important to Think?" appears in Foucault (2002b, pp. 454–458).
9 On the "*local* character of criticism" see also Foucault 1980b, p. 81. Instances of local critique include the anti-psychiatric movement, challenges to morality and sexual ethics, as well as protests against the judiciary and the penal system; see Foucault 2004, pp. 5f.

By "subjugated knowledges" Foucault means two things; first, "historical contents" or "historical knowledges" that "have been buried or masked" by "functional arrangements or systematic organizations" and, second, "a whole series of knowledges that have been disqualified as nonconceptual knowledges, as insufficiently elaborated knowledges: naïve knowledges, hierarchically inferior knowledges, knowledges that are below the required level of erudition or scientificity" (Foucault 2004, p. 7). Genealogy consists in

> a way of playing local, discontinuous, disqualified, or nonlegitimized knowledges off against the unitary theoretical instance that claims to be able to filter them, organize them into a hierarchy, organize them in the name of a true body of knowledge, in the name of the rights of a science that is in the hands of a few. (Foucault 2004, p. 9)

II

According to Foucault, Nietzsche's intention was to criticize *"Ursprung"*, where this meant an ἀρχή, i.e. a deeper reality from which everything derives. On the contrary, Foucault argued, genealogy attempts to construct a *"Herkunft"* (descent) by fragmenting what has hitherto been regarded as unified. *"Herkunft"*, according to Foucault's reading of Nietzsche, abandons the search for original or primordial entities. This is where the radicalism of Nietzsche's genealogical history lies, for Foucault. For, as a challenge to the metaphysics of the origin, genealogy defined itself in terms of an historical anti-essentialism (anti-Ursprung). Not only is genealogy concerned with *"Herkunft"*, it also studies the *"Entstehung"* (emergence) of a battle between historical forces of domination (Foucault 1984a, pp. 83f.). However, Foucault failed to grasp the nature of *"Ursprung"*, *"Herkunft"* and *"Entstehung"*. Pizer has shown that, contrary to Foucault's understanding, in the German philosophical tradition *"Ursprung"* is used to denote a struggle or confrontation, while *"Entstehung"* refers to an original unity which gives rise to an uninterrupted continuity (Pizer 1990, pp. 462–478).[10] For instance, Pizer notes that in the *Birth of Tragedy* the *"Ursprung"* of tragedy is the struggle between Apollo and Dionysus (Pizer 1990,

---

10 See also Ansell-Pearson 1991, pp. 120–122; Ansell-Pearson also provides a useful list of all the references to "origin" in *On the Genealogy of Morals* (Ansell-Pearson 1991, pp. 252–253, note 51). According to Langenscheidt Standard German Dictionary, "Entstehung" means "(a) coming into being, development, emergence, (b) origin, beginning", (c) creation" (Messinger/ Türck/Willman 1993, p. 182), whereas "Ursprung" means "origin" (Messinger/Türck/Willman 1993, p. 603).

p. 469). Therefore, it is *"Ursprung"*, not *"Entstehung"* as Foucault thought, which delineates the struggle of forces whence social and political institutions emerge. In point of fact, in the first essay of the *On the Genealogy of Morals* Nietzsche uses the term *"Ursprung"* to denote the conflict between master and slave moralities (Pizer 1990, p. 473). Furthermore, as Keith Ansell-Pearson has remarked, in section 12 of the second essay of *On the Genealogy of Morals*, where the crucial distinction between "origin" and "purpose" is made, Nietzsche uses the term *"Ursprung"* for "origin". Consequently, the English psychologists whom Nietzsche attacks are the utilitarians who, in carrying out *Entstehungsgeschichten*, think they are engaging in a genealogy of morals (Ansell-Pearson 1991, p. 123). This section of *On the Genealogy of Morality* is important for our understanding of the nature of Nietzsche's genealogical history. According to Nietzsche, an historical analysis in the traditional sense (what Nietzsche terms *Entstehungsgeschichte*) is unable to unearth the "origin" (Ursprung) of punishment, because it tends to confound "Ursprung" (origin) with "Zweck" ("purpose"). However,

> [...] every purpose and use is just a <u>sign</u> that the will to power has achieved mastery over something less powerful, and has impressed upon it its own idea [Sinn] of a use function... (GM, Section 12, p. 55)

By contrast, Nietzsche wants to demonstrate that examining the history of punishment genealogically we come to the realization that the procedures of punishment antedate the meanings attributed to them (GM II 3). Put differently, the task of genealogy is to show that, although procedures of punishment remain relatively unchanged through time, the purposes to which these procedures are put are different.

This leads us to another aspect of Nietzsche's genealogy which has been misread by Foucault. This relates to the issue of perspectivism and its significance for a "genealogy of morals". Nietzsche's genealogy sets out to demonstrate that 'meanings' (whether these be ideas or morals) are always dynamic creations and not static givens (GM Preface 6). It is always the case that a certain social group defines a specific set of values, which are valid until another group re-evaluates these same values. Arguably, Nietzsche himself engages in such a re-evaluation of values when he undertakes his genealogical enquiries. The insight of Nietzschean genealogy is that all legal institutions, social customs and moral concepts have evolved and are the products of a specific form of will to power. Nietzsche's notion "will to power" (Wille zur Macht) does have the appearance of an ontological claim (see e.g. BGE 36). Whatever the status of this claim, however, its significance lies in its implications; that is to say, Nietzsche employs the notion "will to power" as an analytical principle upon which his genealogy is based. What this principle is meant to show is that "There are no moral phenomena at all, only a moral interpretation of phenomena…" (BGE 108). In other words, the meaning of moral values is dependent upon a given configuration of power relationships. This does not imply that all moral values are senseless; it means that their 'sense' is derived from relations of power. This is where Foucault got it wrong, for he says:

> […] interpretation is the violent or surreptitious appropriation of a system of rules, which in itself has no essential meaning, in order to impose a direction, to bend it to a new will, to force its participation in a different game, and to subject it to secondary rules. (Foucault 1984a, p. 86 – my italics for emphasis)

But, although it is true that, for Nietzsche, no meaning is possible without interpretation and that rules "can be bent to any purpose" (Foucault 1984a, p. 86) – hence the importance of the relevant passage in section 12 of the second essay of *On the Genealogy of Morals*, where the crucial distinction between "Ursprung" and "Zweck" is made – , it is quite wrong to attribute to Nietzsche the view that all interpretation is senseless. Thus, I submit, Foucault failed to appreciate the importance of "meaning" and "interpretation" in Nietzsche's genealogy. At any rate, it is different to believe, as Nietzsche does, that "the whole, long, hard-to-decipher hieroglyphic script of man's moral past" (GM Preface, Section 8, p. 9), "while distinct from any particular interpretation, itself remains nothing other than interpretation" (Schrift 1987, p. 105) and to maintain, as Foucault does, that all interpretations are arbitrary, imposed – as it were – on a set of rules which "are empty in themselves, violent and unfinalized; they are impersonal and can be bent to any purpose" (Foucault 1984a, pp. 85f.). Therefore, whereas Nietzsche maintains that "will to power" is responsible for the definition of any meaning – meaning nonetheless –, Foucault interprets Nietzsche as saying that "will to power" is all there is and that "will to power" operates for its own sake:[11] "humanity…thus proceeds from domination to domination" (Foucault 1984a, p. 85). In this way, Foucault misunderstands the role of power in Nietzsche's genealogy.

So far as the notion of "power" is concerned, there is another significant difference between the Nietzschean and Foucauldian conceptions. Whereas Nietzsche views morality and social-cum-political institutions as the product of the "will to power" of individuals or groups of actors, Foucault considers social and political practices to be the result of strategies without strategists

---

[11] All the same, in a passage noted above Nietzsche does seem to be saying that "will to power" is all there is: "The world seen from within, the world described and defined according to its 'intelligible character' – it would be 'will to power' and nothing else.-" (BGE 36).

(Foucault 1984a, p. 85). In addition, in a number of articles and interviews Foucault emphasizes that the originality of his conception of "power" lies in his understanding of power in terms of "relations of power" (Foucault 1980c, p. 114 and Foucault 1982, pp. 208–226). This conception of "power" implies "freedom", for "slavery is not a power relationship when man is in chains" (Foucault 1982, p. 221). Here "freedom" is conceived in terms of the possibility of resistance. As Foucault says:

> [...] at the heart of power relations and as a permanent condition of their existence there is an insubordination and a certain essential obstinacy on the part of the principles of freedom... (Foucault 1982, p. 225)

According to Foucault's "analytics"[12] of power (in the sense of power relations), there is a constant tension between "relations of power" and "strategies of resistance", this tension being specific to particular circumstances:

> And, in order to understand what power relations are about, perhaps we should investigate the forms of resistance and attempts made to dissociate these relations. (Foucault 1982, p. 211 – my italics)

Importantly, resistance can only be 'local', that is, confined to a particular set of power relations. For example,

> [...] opposition to the power of men over women, of parents over children, of psychiatry over the mentally ill, of medicine over the population, of administration over the ways people live. (Foucault 1982, p. 211)

However, Keith Ansell-Pearson has a point when he says that "Foucault's reading of the role of will to power in the project of genealogy is much too anarchic for Nietzsche's taste" (Ansell-Pearson 1991, p. 121).

Now, in examining how Foucault interprets Nietzsche's notion of the body, we arrive at the conclusion that here, too, Foucault misconstrues the significance assigned to it by Nietzsche. In *Discipline and Punish*, which is Foucault's genealogical work mostly influenced by Nietzsche's *On the Genealogy of Morals*, Foucault follows Nietzsche by employing the concept of "memory". According to Nietzsche, "memory" is responsible for "breed[ing] an animal which is able to make promises" (GM II 1). As he goes on to say:

---

[12] Foucault insisted that he did not put forward a "theory" but an "analytics" of power (see Foucault 1998, p. 82). For a view that Foucault's analyses of power constitute a "theory", albeit in a qualified sense, see Lynch 2011, pp. 14ff.

> That particular task... includes... as precondition and preparation, the more immediate task of first making man to a certain degree undeviating [notwendig], uniform, a peer amongst peers, orderly and consequently predictable. (GM II 2)

This is done by way of a "technique of mnemonics" which holds that "'A thing must be burnt in so that it stays in the memory: only something which continues to hurt stays in the memory'" (GM II 3).

In Foucault's aforesaid genealogical work punishment and discipline create a "memory" both for recent offenders and for all prospective ones. In the seventeenth and eighteenth centuries, Foucault says, this "memory" was engraved directly on bodies through the cruelest rituals of torture:

> A body effaced, reduced to dust and thrown to the winds, a body destroyed piece by piece by the infinite power of the sovereign constituted not only the ideal, but the real limit of punishment. (Foucault 1991, p. 50)

The above quotation refers to Classical punishment. By contrast, says Foucault, in Modern punishment "memories" are inscribed indirectly on bodies by way of the discourse of the social sciences whose task is to discipline bodies. These discourses aim to produce "subjects" with the capacity to make certain choices (rather than others), to initiate certain actions and to resist certain sorts of regulations. Similarly, with regard to sexuality, Foucault has argued that "There was a steady proliferation of discourses concerned with sex...a discursive ferment that gathered momentum from the eighteenth century onward" (Foucault 1998, p. 18). What is specifically interesting is "the multiplication of discourses concerning sex in the field of exercise of power itself" (Foucault 1998, p. 18). Put simply, power produces sexuality or – better – a knowledge of sexuality (*scientia sexualis*) (Foucault 1998, pp. 51–73).

So where did Foucault go wrong? How did he divert from Nietzsche's view of the body? Commenting on Nietzsche's genealogy, Foucault says:

> [...] descent attaches itself to the body. It inscribes itself in the nervous system, in temperament, in the digestive apparatus; it appears in faulty respiration, in improper diets, in the debilitated and prostrate bodies of those whose ancestors committed errors. (Foucault 1984a, p. 82)

As I understand the above quotation, Foucault is actually saying that a genealogical enquiry (whose task is "descent") is concerned with bodies, more specifically with "[...] the metamorphosis of punitive methods on the basis of a political technology of the body in which might be read a common history of power relations and object relations" (Foucault 1991, p. 24 – my italics). But this suggests a genealogy of bodies, whereas Nietzsche practised a genealogy of morals.¹³ Whereas, for Foucault, the body is a passive force, a recipient – as it were – of power (in the form of both discipline and punishment) which moulds it and makes it docile, Nietzsche saw the body as an active force. In other words, Nietzsche saw the body in organic or physiological terms, while Foucault's conception is a very 'thin' one, since he viewed the body as nothing else but a mere substratum on which power operated. In fact, for Nietzsche, it is bodies or organisms which are driven by an instinctual "will to power" (BGE, 13, p. 44); power is not imposed on them. Moreover, in Nietzsche's view, knowledge does not produce the body; rather, it is the body which produces knowledge and moral beliefs. Consider, for example, the following:

> With complete calm we will let physiology and the ontogeny of organisms and concepts determine how our image of the world can be so very different from the disclosed essence of the world. (BGE, 10, p. 18)

In addition, concerning Nietzsche's perspectivism, difference in perspectives is due to physiological and instinctual causes, while a God's eye view is impossible. In a famous passage of On the Genealogy of Morals Nietzsche opposed his perspectivism to modern epistemology as follows:

> From now on, my philosophical colleagues, let us be wary of the dangerous old conceptual fairy-tale which has set up a 'pure, will-less, painless, timeless, subject of knowledge', let us be wary of the tentacles of such contradictory concepts as 'pure reason', 'absolute spirituality', 'knowledge as such': — here we are asked to think an eye which cannot be thought at all, an eye turned in no direction at all, an eye where the active and interpretative powers are suppressed, absent, but through which seeing still becomes a seeing-something, so it is an absurdity and non-concept of eye that is demanded. There is <u>only</u> a perspective seeing, <u>only</u> a perspective 'knowing'; the <u>more</u> affects we allow to speak about a thing, the <u>more</u> eyes, various eyes we are able to use for the same thing, the more complete will be our 'concept' of the thing, our 'objectivity'. But to eliminate the will completely and turn off all the emotions without exception, assuming we could: well? Would that not mean to <u>castrate</u> the intellect? ... (GM III 12)

Therefore, Foucault inverted Nietzsche's conception of the relationship between body and knowledge, shifting the emphasis from a genealogy of 'morals' to a genealogy of 'bodies'.

According to a commentator,

> ... one could characterise Foucault as, on the one hand, attempting to undermine historical sociology with the aid of Nietzschean concepts of the body and power while, on the

---

13 For a similar argument see Lash 1984, pp. 1–17. Lash sees a Deleuzean influence in Foucault's conception of the body.

other, attempting to repair the archaisms of Nietzsche by reference to modern social thought. (Minson 1985, p. 78)

Consequently, whereas Nietzsche's genealogy resembles an historical philology, Foucault has made use of the resources of French linguists (mostly of the structuralist school)[14] and modern sociology. There is a sense in which Foucault is more relevant to the contemporary world, especially to the human and social sciences, for "the Judaeo-Christian components of the modern soul are played down in favour of the transforming impact of the human sciences and social administration on the subjective domain – and on the Christian techniques which may have been formative in that domain" (Minson 1985, p. 80). In short, the importance of Foucault's genealogical works lies elsewhere than that of Nietzsche's.

It is interesting that, whereas Nietzsche believed that the problem of modernity was the collapse of cultural values (nihilism),[15] Foucault's diagnosis of the modern condition showed that what was actually problematical was the hegemony of humanist discourse and the values that emerge therefrom (biopolitics). Epistemologically, Nietzsche was concerned with combating the established philosophies of his day,[16] whereas Foucault focused on the application of philosophical categories. With reference to the social sciences, the aim of Foucault's genealogies was to question such sociological *aeternae veritates* as 'society' and 'individual' by emphasizing their historical development. More importantly, Foucault wishes to show that the formation of 'individuals' has been contemporaneous with the formation of 'society', thereby challenging the assumption of the discipline of sociology that 'society' is a relatively modern phenomenon.

I wish to make one final point. Nietzsche's genealogical analyses marked a break with the philosophical tradition of the Enlightenment in general and Kant's project in particular.[17] For Nietzsche, the irony of Kant's critical philoso-

---

14 Although Foucault never accepted he was a structuralist, the book mostly associated with structuralism is M. Foucault's *The Order of Things: An Archaeology of the Human Sciences* (London and New York: Routledge, 2002) [Original: M. Foucault, *Les Mots et les Choses* (Paris: Éditions Gallimard, 1966)].
15 Nietzsche's theme of the 'death of God' is well-known. See the scene of the madman in GS 125. Cf. Z Prologue 2.
16 Therein consisted his philosophizing with a hammer. See EH, Twilight of the Idols: "How to Philosophize with a Hammer".
17 A scholar who sees Nietzsche's work as a rupture with Kant is Gilles Deleuze (see Deleuze 1986, pp. 89–94). By contrast, David Owen sees Nietzsche's genealogy as a transformation of Kant's critical project (see Owen 1994, pp. 17–32).

phy lies in the fact that 'critique' took the form of 'legislation' (viz. the "categorical imperative"). Kant's critique confined itself to delimiting the laws governing knowledge and the claims to morality, but, in so doing, failed to challenge the value of knowledge and moral ideals per se. So, according to Nietzsche, Kant's thought was an instance of the Enlightenment appearance/reality and subject/object distinctions (GM, I 16, pp. 23–24), which are challenged by means of a genealogical enquiry in the first and second essays of *On the Genealogy of Morals* respectively. These distinctions are facilitated by the 'mythology' which is concealed in language and grammar. Specifically, the modern belief in the separation of the 'subject' (or 'transcendental ego') from 'being' is made possible by the distinction between "doer" and "deed" that the structure of language imposes on us in the form of the subject-predicate dimension. As with the passage of time human beings forgot that it was they who had created linguistic symbols, they came to regard concepts as if they were "aeternae veritates" (GM, I 11, p. 50). In consequence, "[...] the most diverse philosophers unfailingly fill out again and again a certain basic scheme of possible philosophies" (BGE, 20, p. 50). According to Nietzsche, Kant's critical philosophy turned out to be uncritical, because Kant took "grammatical functions" for granted. Therefore, Kant was one of those philosophers whose:

> [...] thinking is in fact not so much a discovering as a recognizing, a remembering, a return and home-coming to a far-off, primordial total household of the soul out of which those concepts once emerged – philosophizing is to that extent a species of atavism of the first rank. (BGE 20)

In directing his genealogy against the Enlightenment (and thereby Modernity), Nietzsche was the first postmodern thinker.[18]

By contrast, I wish to argue, Foucault was part of the modern tradition. As is evident from his essay on Kant "What Is Enlightenment?" (Foucault 1984b, pp. 32–50), Foucault drew on this aspect of Kant's philosophy which concerns itself with how we have become what we are and which examines both the limitations of what we are and the possibilities of our being otherwise. Although he rejected Kant's "analytics of truth", Foucault related himself to – what he considered to be – Kant's "ontology of ourselves". Therefore,

> [...] criticism is no longer going to be practiced in the search for formal structures with universal value, but rather as a historical investigation into the events that have led us

---

[18] I have made this argument in Sembou 2011b. I have drawn on this paper in writing this section. Thinkers like Lyotard, Foucault and Derrida are usually associated with post-modernism, where post-modernism means the rejection of the project of modernity.

to constitute ourselves and to recognize ourselves as subjects of what we are doing, thinking, saying. (Foucault 1984b, pp. 45f.; see also Hutchings 1996, pp.122ff.)

Bibliography

Ansell-Pearson, Keith (1991): *Nietzsche Contra Rousseau: A Study of Nietzsche's Moral and Political Thought*. Cambridge: Cambridge University Press.
Clausewitz, Carl von (1982): *On War*. A. Rapoport (ed.). Harmondsworth: Penguin.
Conway, Daniel (2008): *Nietzsche's "Genealogy of Morals": A Reader's Guide*. London: Continuum.
Deleuze, Giles (1986): *Nietzsche and Philosophy*. London: The Athlone Press.
Dreyfus, Hubert L./Rabinow, Paul (1982): *Michel Foucault: Beyond Structuralism and Hermeneutics*. Brighton, Sussex: The Harvester Press.
Foucault, Michel (1966): *Les Mots et les Choses*. Paris: Éditions Gallimard.
Foucault, Michel (1975): *Surveiller et Punir: Naissance de la Prison*. Paris: Gallimard.
Foucault, Michel (1976): *Histoire de la Sexualité, Vol. 1: La Volonté de Savoir*. Paris: Gallimard.
Foucault, Michel (1980a): "Prison Talk". In: Michel Foucault: *Power/Knowledge: Selected Interviews and Other Writings 1972–1977*. C. Gordon (ed.), C. Gordon et al. (trans.). Hemel Hempstead: Harvester Wheatsheaf, pp. 37–54.
Foucault, Michel (1980b): "Two Lectures". In: Michel Foucault: *Power/Knowledge: Selected Interviews and Other Writings 1972–1977*. C. Gordon (ed.), C. Gordon et al. (trans.). Hemel Hempstead: Harvester Wheatsheaf, pp. 78–108.
Foucault, Michel (1980c): "Truth and Power". In: Michel Foucault: *Power/Knowledge: Selected Interviews and Other Writings 1972–1977*. C. Gordon (ed.), C. Gordon et al. (trans.). Hemel Hempstead: Harvester Wheatsheaf, pp. 109–133.
Foucault, Michel (1980d): "Power and Strategies". In: Michel Foucault: *Power/Knowledge: Selected Interviews and Other Writings 1972–1977*. C. Gordon (ed.), C. Gordon et al. (trans.). Hemel Hempstead: Harvester Wheatsheaf, pp. 134–145.
Foucault, Michel (1980e): "The Eye of Power". In: Michel Foucault: *Power/Knowledge: Selected Interviews and Other Writings 1972–1977*. C. Gordon (ed.), C. Gordon et al. (trans.). Hemel Hempstead: Harvester Wheatsheaf, pp. 146–165.
Foucault, Michel (1980f): *Power/Knowledge: Selected Interviews and Other Writings 1972–1977*. C. Gordon (ed.), C. Gordon et al. (trans.). Hemel Hempstead: Harvester Wheatsheaf.
Foucault, Michel (1981): "The Order of Discourse". In: R. Young. (ed.): *Untying the Text: A Post-Structuralist Reader*. Boston, London, Henley: Routledge & Kegan Paul, pp. 48–78.
Foucault, Michel (1982), "The Subject and Power". In: Hubert R. Dreyfus/Paul Rabinow: *Michel Foucault: Beyond Structuralism and Hermeneutics*. Brighton, Sussex: The Harvester Press, pp. 208–226.
Foucault, Michel (1984a): "Nietzsche, Genealogy, History". In: P. Rabinow (ed.): *The Foucault Reader*. Harmondsworth: Penguin, pp. 76–100.
Foucault, Michel (1984b): "What Is Enlightenment?". In: P. Rabinow (ed.): *The Foucault Reader*. Harmondsworth: Penguin, pp. 32–50.

Foucault, Michel (1990a): "The Return of Morality". In: Michel Foucault: *Politics, Philosophy, Culture: Interviews and Other Writings 1977–1984*. L. D. Kritzman (ed.), A. Sheridan et al. (trans.). New York and London: Routledge, pp. 242–254.

Foucault, Michel (1990b): "Sexual Choice, Sexual Act: Foucault and Homosexuality". In: Michel Foucault: *Politics, Philosophy, Culture: Interviews and Other Writings 1977–1984*. L. D. Kritzman (ed.), A. Sheridan et al. (trans.). New York and London: Routledge, pp. 286–303.

Foucault, Michel (1990c): "Practicing Criticism". In: Michel Foucault: *Politics, Philosophy, Culture: Interviews and Other Writings 1977–1984*. L. D. Kritzman (ed.), A. Sheridan et al. (trans.). New York and London: Routledge, pp. 152–156.

Foucault, Michel (1990d): "The Concern for Truth". In: Michel Foucault: *Politics, Philosophy, Culture: Interviews and Other Writings 1977–1984*. L. D. Kritzman (ed.), A. Sheridan et al. (trans.). New York and London: Routledge, pp. 255–267.

Foucault, Michel (1991): *Discipline and Punish: The Birth of the Prison*. A. Sheridan (trans.). Harmondsworth: Penguin.

Foucault, Michel (1998): *The History of Sexuality, Vol. 1: The Will to Knowledge*. R. Hurley (trans.). London: Penguin.

Foucault, Michel (2000): "Structuralism and Post-structuralism". In: James D. Faubion (ed.): *Essential Works of Foucault 1954–1984. Vol. 2: Aesthetics, Method, and Epistemology*. R. Hurley et al. (trans.). London: Penguin, pp. 433–458.

Foucault, Michel (2002a): "Questions of Method". In: James D. Faubion (ed.): *Essential Works of Foucault 1954–1984. Vol. 2: Aesthetics, Method, and Epistemology*. R. Hurley et al. (trans.). London: Penguin, pp. 223–238.

Foucault, Michel (2002b): "So Is It Important to Think?". In: James D. Faubion (ed.): *Essential Works of Foucault 1954–1984. Vol. 2: Aesthetics, Method, and Epistemology*. R. Hurley et al. (trans.). London: Penguin, pp. 454–458.

Foucault, Michel (2002c): *The Order of Things: An Archaeology of the Human Sciences*. London and New York: Routledge.

Foucault, Michel (2004): *Society Must Be Defended: Lectures at the Collège de France, 1975–76*. M. Bertani and A. Fontana (ed), D. Macey (trans.). London: Penguin.

Hatab, Lawrence J. (2008): *Nietzsche's "On the Genealogy of Morality": An Introduction*. Cambridge: Cambridge University Press.

Hutchings, Kimberly (1996): *Kant, Critique and Politics*. London, New York: Routledge.

Janaway, Christopher (2007): *Beyond Selflessness: Reading Nietzsche's "Genealogy"*. Oxford: Oxford University Press.

Messinger, H./Türck, G./ Willman, H. (eds.) (1993): Langenscheidt Standard German Dictionary. Berlin, Munich: Langenscheidt.

Lash, Scott (1984): "Genealogy and the Body: Foucault/Deleuze/Nietzsche". In: *Theory, Culture and Society: Explorations in Critical Social Science* 2(2), pp. 1–17.

Lynch, Richard A. (2011): "Foucault's Theory of Power". In: D. Taylor (ed.): *Michel Foucault: Key Concepts*. Durham: Acumen, pp. 13–26.

Minson, Jeffrey (1985): *Genealogies of Morals: Nietzsche, Foucault, Donzelot and the Eccentricity of Ethics*. Basingstoke: Macmillan.

Nietzsche, Friedrich (1969): *Thus Spoke Zarathustra: A Book for Everyone and No One*. R. J. Hollingdale (trans.). Harmondsworth: Penguin.

Nietzsche, Friedrich (1974): *The Gay Science*. W. Kaufmann (trans.). New York: Random House.

Nietzsche, Friedrich (1990): *Beyond Good and Evil: Prelude to a Philosophy of the Future*. R. J. Hollingdale (trans). Harmondsworth: Penguin.

Nietzsche, Friedrich (1992): *Ecce Homo: How One Becomes What One Is*. R. J. Hollingdale (trans.). Harmondsworth: Penguin.

Nietzsche, Friedrich (1994*)*: *Human, All Too Human*. M. Faber and S. Lehmann (trans.). Harmondsworth: Penguin.

Nietzsche, Friedrich (1994): *On the Genealogy of Morality*. K. Ansell-Pearson (ed.). C. Diethe (trans.). Cambridge: Cambridge University Press.

Owen, David (1994): *Maturity and Modernity: Nietzsche, Weber, Foucault and the Ambivalence of Reason*. London, New York: Routledge.

Owen, David (2007): *Nietzsche's "Genealogy of Morality"*. Stockesfield, UK: Acumen.

Owen, David (2008): "Nietzsche's Genealogy Revisited". In: *Journal of Nietzsche Studies* 35/36, pp. 141–154.

Pizer, John David (1990): "The Use and Abuse of 'Ursprung': On Foucault's Reading of Nietzsche". In: *Nietzsche-Studien* 19, pp. 462–478.

Schrift, Alan D. (1987): "Between Perspectivism and Philology: Genealogy as Hermeneutic". In: *Nietzsche-Studien* 16, pp. 91–111.

Sembou, Evangelia (2011a): "Foucault's Genealogy", 10th Annual Meeting of the International Social Theory Consortium, University College Cork, Ireland on 16–17 June.

Sembou, Evangelia (2011b): "Nietzsche's Critique of the Enlightenment: Nietzsche's Genealogy of Morals", 18th International Conference of the Friedrich Nietzsche Society, Queen Mary, University of London, 9–11 September.

White, Richard (1988): "The Return of the Master: An Interpretation of Nietzsche's 'Genealogy of Morals'". In: *Philosophy and Phenomenological Research* 48(4).

Notes on Contributors

Tom Angier is a Lecturer in Philosophy at the University of Cape Town. His main research interests are in Ethical and Political Theory, and he has historical interests focused on the Nineteenth Century and the Ancient Period. His first monograph is entitled *Either Kierkegaard / Or Nietzsche: Moral Philosophy in a New Key* (2006), and his second *Technē in Aristotle's Ethics: Crafting the Moral Life* (2010). He has written on Alasdair MacIntyre's analysis of tradition, and is preparing a volume on the history of evil in the ancient period. Email: tom.angier@uct.ac.za

Keith Ansell-Pearson is a Professor of Philosophy at the University of Warwick and is currently a Visiting Senior Research Fellow in the Humanities at Rice University. His research interests centre on two main areas of philosophical inquiry: the philosophies of life and nature and philosophy as a way of life. He has authored and edited books on Nietzsche, Bergson, and Deleuze. His book *Heroic-Idyllic: Nietzsche's Search for Philosophy* is forthcoming with Bloomsbury Press in 2015. With colleagues in Melbourne he has been awarded a "Discovery Project" grant for a three year project on the re-invention of philosophy as a way of life. Email: K.J.Ansell-Pearson@warwick.ac.uk

Rebecca Bamford is an Assistant Professor of Philosophy in the Department of Philosophy and Political Science at Quinnipiac University. Her main research interests lie in nineteenth century philosophy, ethics, social and political philosophy, and the history and philosophy of science and mind. She is the author of articles on ethics, on Nietzsche's political philosophy, and on problems in contemporary bioethics. Her work in progress includes books on Nietzsche's *Dawn*, and on Nietzsche's relevance to contemporary Philosophy of Science and Mind. Email: rebecca.bamford@quinnipac.edu

Nandita Biswas Mellamphy is an Associate Professor in the Department of Political Science at Western, specializing in critical and radical political theory and the history of political thought from antiquity to post-modernity. She is also an affiliate member of the Department of Women's Studies and Feminist Research and has served as Associate Director of the Centre for the Study of Theory and Criticism (Western). Her research interests are situated at the intersection of political theory, cultural theory, and continental philosophy. Her topics of study include post-humanism, technopolitics and digital media culture. She is author of *The Three Stigmata of Friedrich Nietzsche: Political Physiology in the Age of Nihilism* (2011), and has written several articles on Nietzsche's political thought. She is currently working on a book on tracing humanist, trans-humanist and post-humanist currents in Nietzsche's political philosophy. Email: mathesis.universalis@gmail.com

Daniel Conway is a Professor of Philosophy and Humanities at Texas A&M University. He has lectured and published widely on topics pertaining to nineteenth century philosophy, social and political philosophy, environmental philosophy, philosophy and literature, and philosophy of religion. He is the author of *Nietzsche's Dangerous Game* (1997), *Nietzsche and the Political* (1997), and *Reader's Guide to Nietzsche's* On the Genealogy of Morals (2008). He is the editor of the four-volume series *Nietzsche: Critical Assessments of Leading Philosophers* (1998), the four-volume series *Søren Kierkegaard: Critical Assessments of Leading Philosophers* (1992), and *Kierkegaard's* Fear and Trembling: *A Critical Guide* (2014). He is the co-editor of *The Politics of Irony: Essays in Self-Betrayal* (1992, with J. Seery), *Nietzsche und die antike Philosophie* (1992, with R. Rehn), *Nietzsche, Philosophy, and the Arts* (with S. Kemal and I. Gaskell, 1998), and *The History of Continental Philosophy*, Volume II (with A.D. Schrift, 2010). Email: conway@philosophy.tamu.edu. Website: http://philosophy.tamu.edu/html/bio-Conway.html

Renato Cristi is Professor of Philosophy at Wilfrid Laurier University, Waterloo, Ontario, Canada. His research interests are social and political philosophy, legal philosophy, metaphysics and the history of philosophy. He is the author of *Le libéralisme conservateur: Trois essais sur Hegel, Hayek et Schmitt* (1993), *Carl Schmitt and Authoritarian Liberalism* (1998), *Hegel on Freedom and Authority* (2005) and *El Pensamiento Político de Jaime Guzmán* (2011). Work in progress includes a book on Nietzsche's aristocratism and Theognis. Email: rcristi@wlu.ca. Website: http://web.wlu.ca/philosophy/index.php?staff=rcristi&page=home

Don Dombowsky is an Assistant Professor in the departments of politics and international studies and philosophy at Bishop's University. He is the author of *Nietzsche's Machiavellian Politics* (2004) and co-editor of *Political Writings of Friedrich Nietzsche: An Edited Anthology* (2008). He has also published articles in the *Journal of Nietzsche Studies* and *Nietzsche Studien: Internationales Jahrbuch für die Nietzsche-Forschung* as well as in other Canadian and European journals. His *Nietzsche and Napoleon: The Dionysian Conspiracy* will be published by the University of Wales Press in 2014. Email: ddombows@ubishops.ca.

Christian J. Emden is Professor of German Intellectual History and Political Thought at Rice University. Emden is on the editorial boards of *Modern Intellectual History* and *Zeitschrift für Kulturphilosophie*. His current research is concerned with political realism and the modern state from Kant to Max Weber, Carl Schmitt, and Hannah Arendt and with the demands of political citizenship in a postnational world. He is the author of *Nietzsche's Naturalism: Philosophy and the Life Sciences in the Nineteenth Century* (forthcoming 2014), *Friedrich Nietzsche and the Politics of History* (2008), *Walter Benjamins Archäologie der Moderne: Kulturwissenschaft um 1930* (2006), and *Nietzsche on Language, Consciousness, and the Body* (2005). Together with David Midgley he edited *Changing Perceptions of the Public Sphere* (2012) and *Beyond Habermas: Democracy, Knowledge, and the Public Sphere* (2012). Email: emden@rice.edu. Website: german.rice.edu

Lawrence J. Hatab is Louis I. Jaffe Professor of Philosophy and Eminent Scholar at Old Dominion University. His research interests include Nietzsche, Heidegger, and ancient philosophy. He is the author of *Nietzsche's "On the Genealogy of Morality": An Introduction* (2008), *Nietzsche's Life Sentence: Coming to Terms with Eternal Recurrence* (2005), *Ethics and Finitude: Heideggerian Contributions to Moral Philosophy* (2000), *A Nietzschean Defense of Democracy: An Experiment in Postmodern Politics* (1995), and *Myth and Philosophy: A Contest of Truths* (1990). He is currently writing a book on language. Email: lhatab@odu.edu

Razvan Ioan is a PhD student at the University of Leiden in the Netherlands. He is completing his thesis on the *Turn to the Body in Modern Philosophy: Spinoza, Schopenhauer and Nietzsche*. His current research interests include critiques of metaphysics, epistemology, modern and early modern philosophy of science and political philosophy. Email: r.ioan@umail.leiduniv.nl

Manuel Knoll is a Professor of Philosophy at Boğaziçi University, Istanbul, Instructor (Lehrbeauftrager) in political theory at the Munich School for Political Science, Member of the Instituto "Lucio Anneo Séneca" of Universidad Carlos III de Madrid, Privatdozent for Political Theory and Philosophy at Munich University (LMU) and co-publisher of *Widerspruch. Münchner Zeitschrift für Philosophie*. He has lectured and published widely on topics pertaining to ancient, modern and contemporary political philosophy and ethics, in particular ancient and contemporary theories of justice, Plato, Aristotle, Machiavelli, Nietzsche, Rawls and Walzer, social philosophy and critical theory. He is author of *Aristokratische oder demokratische Gerechtigkeit? Die politische Philosophie des Aristoteles und Martha Nussbaums egalitaristische Rezeption* (2009), *Theodor W. Adorno. Ethik als erste Philosophie* (2002). He is the co-editor of *Niccolò Machiavelli – Die Geburt des Staates* (2010), and *Das Staatsdenken der Renaissance – Vom gedachten zum erlebten Staat* (2013). Email: Manuel.Knoll@lrz.uni-muenchen.de. Website: www.manuelknoll.eu

Donovan Miyasaki is an Associate Professor of Philosophy at Wright State University in Dayton, Ohio. His current research focuses on the political implications of Nietzsche's critiques of free will, agency, and the morality of improvement (*Besserungs-Moral*). His recent publications include "The Equivocal Use of Power in Nietzsche's Failed Anti-Egalitarianism," forthcoming in *Journal of Moral Philosophy*, "Nietzsche's Will to Power as Naturalist Critical Ontology," *History of Philosophy Quarterly* (2013), "Breeding as Natural Morality: A Critique of Eugenics as Taming," forthcoming in *Nietzsche and the Becoming of Life*, (ed. V. Lemm, 2014), and "Nietzsche contra Freud on Bad Conscience" in *Nietzsche-Studien* (2010). Email: d.miyasaki@wright.edu. Website: http://wright.academia.edu/DonovanMiyasaki

Paul Patton is Scientia Professor of Philosophy at The University of New South Wales, Sydney, Australia. His current research deals with the relationship between normative and historical questions in French poststructuralist political philosophy (Deleuze, Derrida, Foucault) and in left-liberal analytic political philosophy, especially Rawls. He is the author of *Deleuze and the Political* (2000) and *Deleuzian Concepts: Philosophy, Colonization, Politics* (2010). He is editor of *Nietzsche, Feminism and Political Theory* (1993) and *Deleuze: A Critical Reader* (1996). He is co-editor of *Political Theory and the Rights of Indigenous Peoples* (2000), *Between Deleuze and Derrida*, (2003) and *Deleuze and the Postcolonial* (2010). Email: prp@unsw.edu.au. Website: https://hal.arts.unsw.edu.au/about-us/people/paul-patton

Phillip H. Roth is a PhD candidate at the Hochschule für Politik München – Bavarian School of Public Policy and is a Research Associate in the political theory department there. His dissertation focuses on the concept of legislation in Nietzsche's philosophy. Research interests include: ancient and modern moral and political philosophy (especially Plato, Spinoza, Kant, Nietzsche, Derrida), philosophy of law, aesthetics and Jewish studies. Work in progress includes a volume on modern and contemporary theories of power in the social sciences (ed. with U. Weiß). Email: roth@hfpm.de. Website: http://hfpm.academia.edu/PRoth

Evangelia Sembou holds a B.A. from Queen Mary, University of London, a M.Sc. from The University of Edinburgh and a D.Phil. from the University of Oxford. She wrote her doctoral thesis on G. W. F. Hegel's *Phenomenology of Spirit*. She has taught political theory and philosophy at the University of Oxford, and philosophy in the faculty of Continuing Education at Birkbeck, University of London. Her research interests include Hegel, history of political philosophy, continental political philosophy and social theory. She has published articles on Hegel in *History of Political Thought*, the *Jahrbuch für Hegelforschung* and the *Bulletin of the Hegel Society of Great Britain* as well as an article on Hegel and Foucault in an edited collection of conference proceedings. Her books include *'Midwifery' and Criticism in G. W. F. Hegel's "Phenomenology of Spirit"* (2012), *Plato's Political Philosophy* (2012), *Modern Theories of Politics* (2013) and an edited collection, *Political Theory: The State of the Discipline* (2013). She is now writing a contracted book, *Hegel's Phenomenology and Foucault's Genealogy*. Email: evangelia.sembou@hotmail.com

Tamsin Shaw is an Associate Professor of European and Mediterranean Studies and Philosophy at New York University. She received both her B.A. and Ph.D. from Cambridge University. She was formerly an Assistant Professor of political theory in the politics department at Princeton University, where she held the Lawrence S. Rockefeller University Preceptorship. She has also previously been a Junior Research Fellow at King's College, Cambridge, and a member of the School of Social Science at the Institute for Advanced Study, Princeton. She is the author of *Nietzsche's Political Skepticism* (2007) and has also published articles on Nietzsche and Max Weber. She is currently working on debates about the impact of secularization on European culture. Email: tamsin.shaw@nyu.edu. Website: tamsinshaw.com

Barry Stocker is an Assistant Professor in the philosophy stream of the Department of Humanities and Social Science at Istanbul Technical University, and is a Senior Honorary Research Associate in the Department of Philosophy at University College London. His research interests are in history of philosophy particularly continental European philosophy since Kant, ethics, political theory, aesthetics, and philosophy and literature. He is the author of *Derrida and Deconstruction* (2006), *Kierkegaard on Politics* (2014), and is co-author of *Rousseau on Language: Two Perspectives* (2014). He is the editor of *Post-Analytic Tractatus* (2004) and *Derrida: Basic Writings* (2007). Work in progress includes a book on Foucault and liberty. Email: Barry.Stocker@itu.edu.tr. Websites: http://stockerb.wordpress.com. http://istanbultek.academia.edu/BarryStocker

Rolf Zimmermann is a former professor of philosophy at the University of Konstanz, Germany. His research interests include ethics, political philosophy, history of moralities, Nietzsche and politics. He is the author of *Philosophie nach Auschwitz. Eine Neubestimmung von Moral in Politik und Gesellschaft* (2005); *Moral als Macht. Eine Philosophie der historischen Erfahrung* (2008). His book chapter "National Socialism – Bolshevism – Universalism. Moral Transformations in History as a Problem in Ethics" in *Nazi Ideology and Ethics* (eds. W. Bialas/L.Fritze, 2014) is complementary to his contribution in this volume. Email: pohl-zimmermann@t-online.de. Website: www.prof-rolf-zimmernann.de

Name Index

Abel, Günter 10, 34, 227–228, 237–238
Abbey, Ruth 189, 192, 277–278, 285, 418, 428
Acampora, Christa Davis 117, 132, 170, 290, 304, 309, 428, 430
Acemoglu, Daron 136
Adkins, Arthur W. H. 416, 428
Aeschylus 356, 422
Alcibiades 201, 278
Alcoff, Linda Martín 60, 62–63, 74, 75, 76
Alexander, Jeffrey 348, 379
Anaximander 115
Andresen, Joshua 225, 237
Anderson, Elizabeth S. 166, 169
Angelescu McVey, Laura 169
Angier, Tom 32, 405–430, 449
Ansell-Pearson, Keith 1–2, 30, 33, 56, 69, 75–76, 89, 132, 234, 237, 242, 258, 264, 269–286, 309, 310, 316, 340, 342, 279, 384, 403–404, 415, 428–430, 438–439, 441, 446, 448–449
Apollo 81, 86, 175, 180–181, 183, 438
Appel, Fredrick 4, 5, 33, 118, 126–127, 132, 174, 184, 192, 215, 217, 237, 316, 340, 418, 428
Arendt, Hannah 36, 44–45, 53, 56, 61, 205, 207, 450
Arangio-Ruiz, Vincentius 340
Arneson, Richard J. 159, 169
Arnheim, M. T. W. 175, 178, 192
Aristotle 22–24, 35, 129, 188, 226, 238, 244, 246, 254, 264, 385, 449, 451
Arnold, Matthew 140, 151–152, 342
Aschheim, Steven E. 48, 56
Ashworth, Philip A. 208
Assoun, Paul-Laurent 399, 403
Augustus, Emperor 13
Austin, John 148

Baberowski, Jörg 53, 56
Bach, Johann Sebastien 422
Baehr, Peter 209
Baeumler, Adolf 17
Baier, Annette C. 326–327, 340
Bamford, Rebecca 25, 26, 59–76, 449

Bataille, Georges 77, 206, 207
Bauch, Bruno 173, 192
Baviera, Johannes 340
Beethoven, Ludwig van 417, 422, 424
Benson, Bruce 288, 309
Bentham, Jeremy 148, 434
Benz, Ernst 239, 264
Bergeron, Louis 204, 207
Bergk, Theodor 177
Bergmann, Peter 315, 340
Berkowitz, Peter 177, 192, 288, 309
Berlin, Isaiah 142, 152
Berry, Jessica 212, 224, 228, 238
Bertani, Mauro 34, 152, 447
Bertram, Ernst 173, 198–200, 208
Bianquis, Geneviève 208
Bishop, Paul 75, 343
Bismarck, Otto von 12, 16, 46, 175, 185, 200–202, 320
Blanchot, Maurice 23
Blondel, Eric 387, 404
Bluche, Frédéric 195, 208
Boghossian, Paul 378
Bonaparte, Louis-Napoleon (Napoleon III, Emperor of the French) 2
Bonaparte, Napoleon (Napoleon I, Emperor of the French) 29, 195, 198, 204, 333
Borgia, Cesare 198, 201–202, 263, 333
Brandes, Georg 3, 28, 173, 202, 207–208, 259, 264
Brassier, Ray 87–88
Breazeale, Daniel 89
Bridgham, Fred 57
Brobjer, Thomas H. 2, 33–34, 93–97, 111, 242–243, 260, 264, 316, 340, 384–386, 404, 410, 413, 428–429
Brose, Karl 262, 264
Brusotti, Marco 1, 34, 238
Buffiere, Félix 180, 192
Burckhardt, Jacob 4, 25, 33–34, 139, 152, 173–174, 179, 193
Burchell, Graham 34, 111, 152, 286
Burke, Edmund 16, 173
Butler, Judith 81, 88–89

Caesar, Gaius Julius 13, 47, 149, 193, 198–202, 206–208
Caliban 74
Cameron, Frank 186, 192
Camiller, Patrick 35
Campbell, Timothy 285
Cancik, Hubert 176, 192
Capuzzi, Frank 310
Card, Claudia 323, 340
Carlyle, Thomas 239
Carnot, Lazare 16, 149
Caro, Adrian Del 67–68, 73, 75, 430
Carr, Edward Hallett 313, 340
Carrière, Jean 194
Caspari, M. O. B. 152
Castoriadis, Cornelius 117, 132
Catiline (Lucius Sergius Catalina) 199
Cavell, Stanley 16, 33
Cervantes, Miguel de 15
Charles the Bold, Duke of Burgundy 13
Chase, Michael 286
Churchill, Winston 56
Cicero, Marcus Tullius 22, 24
Clark, Maudmarie 42, 56, 101, 111, 153, 156, 169–170, 224–225, 227, 230, 238, 256, 263–264, 288, 310, 337, 340, 342
Clausewitz, Carl von 435, 446
Cohen, Joshua 378
Cohen, Mark 89
Cohn, Paul V. 57
Cole, Philip 323, 340
Collins, George 34
Conant, James 16, 33, 191, 193
Condren, Conan 325, 340
Connolly, William E. 4–5, 25, 33, 95, 111, 135, 152
Conway, Daniel 2, 30, 34, 48, 156, 169, 211, 221, 233, 238, 241–242, 264, 287–311, 429–430, 432, 446, 450
Constant, Benjamin 12, 23, 33, 141–142, 152, 195, 203, 208
Cox, Christoph 83, 89
Craig, Edward 410, 412, 428
Craiutu, Aurelian 209
Crick, Bernard 153, 342
Cristi, Renato 25, 28, 135–137, 152, 173–194, 450
Curley, Edwin 341

Dahl, Robert 191
Dannhauser, Werner J. 220, 238
Danto, Arthur Coleman 1, 34
Darwin, Charles 87, 139, 244, 265, 307, 395
David, Paul A. 169
Deaton, Angus 162, 169
Del Caro, Adrian 67–68, 73, 75, 132, 342, 379, 430
Deleuze, Gilles 18–19, 21–22, 25–26, 34, 77, 80–82, 87, 89, 95, 111, 444, 446–447, 449, 452
Derrida, Jacques 18–19, 22–23, 25, 34–35, 433, 435
Descartes, René 265, 276
Detwiler, Bruce 3–4, 34, 145, 152, 174, 193, 259, 264, 288, 310, 315, 328, 340
Dickey, Laurence 341
Dienstag, Joshua Foa 350, 379
Diethe, Carol 132, 342, 379, 384, 404, 430, 448
Dingel, Molly J. 66, 76
Doering-Manteuffel, Anselm 53, 56
Dombowsky, Don 2, 4–5, 12, 25, 29, 33–34, 47, 62, 76, 97, 135, 152, 173, 174, 185, 186, 192, 193, 195–208, 215, 230, 234–235, 238, 242, 260, 264, 315, 340, 450
Dostoevsky, Fyodor 198
Dreyfus, Hubert 432, 436, 446
Dudrick, David 42, 56, 337, 340
Dufraisse, Roger 203–204, 208
Duncker, Max 57, 176, 193, 343
Dworkin, Richard 159, 169

Easterlin, Richard 162, 169
Eden, Robert 19, 34, 345, 379
Eliade, Mircea 18
Elias, Norbert 32, 406, 423, 424–426, 428
Ellis, Geoffrey 203–204, 208
Eliot, George (Mary Ann Evans) 411
Emden, Christian J. vi, 31, 207–208, 313–344, 424, 425, 428, 450
Emerson, Ralph Waldo 16–17, 36, 239
Engels, Friedrich 137
Englund, Steven 200, 208
Epictetus 30, 275, 277, 279, 281–282, 284, 286
Epicurus 274, 277, 279, 280–281
Esposito, Roberto 285

Etter, Annemarie 260
Euripides 3
Eze, Emmanuel Chukwudi 127

Faber, Marion 448
Faubion, James D. 447
Ferguson, Adam 145, 147, 150, 152
Ferrini, Contardo 340
Ferry, Luc 418, 428
Fisher, Herbert Albert Laurens 195, 204, 208
Fitzpatrick, Sheila 56
Fleischmann, Eugene 345, 379
Fontana, Alessandro 152, 447
Fontana, Biancamaria 33, 34, 152, 208
Foot, Philippa 288, 310
Förster, Bernhard 52
Förster-Nietzsche, Elisabeth 1
Fossen, Thomas 399, 404
Foucault, Michel 18–20, 22, 25, 27, 30, 32–35, 77, 81, 88, 107, 111, 136–137, 145, 152, 208, 269, 274–278, 283–286, 405, 428, 431–448, 451–452
Frei, Christoph 330, 341
Frenzel, Ivo 14, 34
Freud, Sigmund 21, 452
Friedländer, Saul 52, 56
Friedrich II of Hohenstaufen, Holy Roman Emperor 201–202
Friedrich III, German Kaiser 16
Friedrichsmeyer, Sara 76
Fritzsche, Peter 56
Fukuyama, Francis 347–348, 379
Furlani, Guiseppe 340

Gall, Lothar 318, 341
Gaskell, Ivan 429–430, 450
Gast, Peter, *see* also Heinrich Köselitz 279
Gaugroker, Stephen 340
Gemes, Ken 343, 405, 408, 409, 428
Gerhardt, Volker 40, 56, 265
Gerner, Andrea 19, 34
Gersdorff, Carl von 176
Geuss, Raymond 314, 341, 379, 405, 408–9, 415, 429
Geyer, Manfred 56
Gilman, Sandor 206, 208
Gladstone, William Ewart 142
Gobineau, Arthur de 402

Goethe, Johann Wolfgang von 12–13, 15, 149, 174, 198, 202, 239, 263, 402, 417
Golffing, Francis 89
Golomb, Jacob 17, 34, 48, 56, 76
Goltz, Colmar 195, 208
Gordon, Colin 446
Gray, John 35, 153
Gregor, Mary J. 153, 341
Gregorovius, Ferdinand 196, 208
Grote, George 141, 152, 153, 175–176, 193
Grotius, Hugo 148, 152
Guay, Robert 409, 429
Guizot, François 141–142
Gundolf, Friedrich 197, 208
Guttari, Félix 21, 34, 95, 111
Gutting, Gary 286
Guzzoni, Alfredo 264

Haase, Marie-Luise 89, 240, 246, 258, 264
Hadot, Pierre 279–280, 286
Haeckel, Ernst 11
Halliwell, Stephen 214, 219, 238
Hamlet 351
Hand, Sean 404
Handwerk, Gary 286
Hardin, Russell 326, 341
Hardy, Thomas 14–15, 36
Harris, Jose 344
Hart, H. L. A. 230–231, 238
Hartmann, Jacob Wittmer 217
Hartung, Gerald 345, 379
Hatab, Lawrence J. 10, 19, 25, 27, 29, 34, 45, 56, 61–62, 76, 113–123, 156, 169, 175, 177, 184, 190–193, 288, 294–295, 310, 316, 341, 405, 409, 418, 429, 432, 447, 551
Hawthorne, Nathaniel 16
Haydn, Joseph 422
Hayek, Friedrich 109, 136, 137, 152, 450
Hazareesingh, Sudhir 201, 208
Hedrick, Charles 193
Hegel, Georg Wilhelm Friedrich 4, 239, 318, 320, 332, 341, 343–344, 450, 452–453
Hegemann, Werner 203, 208
Heidegger, Martin 89, 263–264, 288, 310, 451
Heine, Heinrich 7, 202, 208, 389

Heit, Helmut 1, 34
Hellbeck, Jochen 55–56
Hennis, Wilhelm 19, 34, 345, 348, 379
Heraclitus 115
Herder, Johann Gottfried von 239
Herold, J. Christopher 195, 201, 208
Hesiod 115, 178
Higgins, Kathleen M. 429, 430
Hitler, Adolf 54–55
Hobbes, Thomas 118, 142, 148, 330, 341, 343, 385
Hofmann, Etienne 152
Hofmannstahl, Hugo von 173
Hollingdale, Reginald J. 57, 76, 89, 132, 153, 170, 208, 242, 264, 310, 342, 429, 447–448
Hollis, Margaret 344
Holtman, Robert B. 204, 208
Holub, Robert C. 59, 62–63, 67–68, 73, 76
Holzer, Angela 189–190, 193
Homer 115, 174, 180
Horstmann, Rolf-Peter 342, 379
Humboldt, Wilhelm von 23, 27–28, 135–153
Hume, David 126, 136, 145, 148, 150
Hunt, Lester H. 25, 34, 105, 111, 136–137, 152, 288–289, 295, 310, 316, 325, 340–341
Hunter, Ian 197, 340–341
Hurley, Robert 34, 285, 447
Hussain, Nadeem J. Z. 334, 338, 341
Husserl, Edmund 276
Hutchings, Kimberly 431, 446–447
Hutter, Horst 279, 286

Ingram, David 269, 286
Ioan, Razvan 31, 383–404, 451
Ivison, Duncan 74, 76
Izzard, Eddie 129

Janz, Curt Paul 176, 184, 193
Jaeger, Werner 179, 193
Janaway, Christopher 219, 238, 290–293, 304, 306, 310, 334, 341, 343, 407–408, 410, 414–415, 429, 432, 447
Jaspers, Karl 288, 310
Jean-Paul (Johann Paul Friedrich Richter) 239

Jensen, Anthony K. 174, 178–179, 184, 192–193, 211
John, King of England 25

Kahan, Alan S. 25, 34
Kahneman, Daniel 162, 169
Kail, Peter J. E. 405, 408–410, 412, 429
Kant, Immanuel 49, 84, 107, 127, 136, 141–142, 153, 249, 273–274, 313, 317, 321–322, 324, 330, 338, 341, 424, 426, 444–445, 447, 450, 452–453
Katsafanas, Paul 114, 132
Kaufmann, Walter 29, 34, 41, 56, 70, 76, 89, 132, 153, 170, 174, 185, 193, 208, 242, 264, 286, 288, 310, 311, 414, 419, 429, 447
Kaulbach, Friedrich 251, 264
Kekes, John 323, 341
Kelly, Donald R. 204, 208
Kemal, Salim 421, 423, 429–430, 450
Kennan, George F. 49
Kerr, Robert 173
Khlafa, Jean 34
Kittsteiner, Heinz D. 327, 342
Klement, Kevin C. 407, 429
Klossowski, Pierre 77, 199, 208, 211, 238
Knobe, Joshua 162, 170, 413, 429
Knoll, Manuel 1–36, 173, 186, 193, 211, 215, 217, 226, 236, 238, 239–266, 309, 378, 451
Koenig, Barbara A 66, 76
Kohn, Hans 209
Korsgaard, Christine M. 329, 342
Köselitz, Heinrich, see also Peter Gast 173, 195
Koskenniemi, Martti 330, 342
Krell, David Farrell 310
Kritzman, Lawrence D. 447
Krochmalnik, Daniel 48, 57
Krug, Gustav 176
Krulic, Brigitte 316, 342
Kwinter, Stanford 89
Kyrnos 173, 185, 187, 190

Lampert, Laurence 241, 243, 246, 256, 265, 295, 310
Lane, Helen R. 34
Langbein, John H. 132

Large, Duncan 57, 76, 311
Lange, F. A. 221
Langewiesche, Dieter 318, 342
Lapoujade, David 89
Laruelle, François 26, 77–89
Lash, Scott 443, 447
Lassmann, Peter 344
Laun, H. van 286
Lawrence, George 36, 153
Le Bon, Gustave 204–205
Lee, Sandra Soo Jin 76
Lehmann, Stephan 448
Lehrer, Ronald 76
Leiter, Brian 2, 35, 57, 101, 105, 111, 153, 162, 170, 289–290, 293–295, 310, 316, 323, 331, 335, 338–342, 378, 405, 408–410, 412–415, 429–430
Lemm, Vanessa 135, 153, 169–170, 173, 186, 193, 212, 225, 227–229, 236, 238, 316, 342, 452
Lenin, Vladimir Ilyich (V. I. Ulyanov) 52
Lennox, James 76
Lennox, Sara 138, 153
Leslie, Donald M. 207
Locke, John 25, 27–28, 128, 132, 136, 141, 155
Loeb, Paul S. 290–291, 304, 309–310, 406, 411, 415, 429
Long, A. A. 282, 286
Louis XI, King of France 13
Lovitt, Carl R. 207
Luban, David 124, 132
Lucretius (Titus Lucretius Carus) 262
Lukács, György 408, 429, 430
Luther, Martin 207
Lynch, Richard A. 441, 447
Lyotard, Jean-François 445

Macey, David 34, 152, 447
Machiavelli, Niccolò 4, 24, 35, 148, 153, 313–314, 328–330, 337, 342, 451
MacIntyre, Alasdair 239, 265, 449
Macpherson, C. B. 132
Madison, James 126
Magnus, Bernd 429–430
Maistre, Joseph de 16
Malthus, Thomas 395
Mandel, Siegfried 208

Mandelbaum, Maurice 407
Mann, Thomas 18, 49, 173
Mannheim, Karl 406
Mariátegui, José Carlos 60
Markham, Felix 204, 208
Marquis of Posa 179
Martí, José 74
Marti, Urs 316, 342
Martin, Alfred von 173–174
Martin, Luther H. 286
Martin, Nicolas 49, 57
Marx, Karl 4, 21, 80, 137–138, 304, 317
May, Simon 288, 293, 295, 310, 341–342, 429
McCloskey, Deirdre N. 136, 153
McCormick, John 380
McMurrin, S. M. 170
Mayer, J. P. 36, 153
Meinecke, Friedrich 261, 265
Mellamphy, Dan 81, 88–89
Mellamphy, Nandita Biswas 19, 26, 77–89, 135, 153, 449
Mellamphy, Ninian 89
Melville, Herman 16–17
Meneander 13
Menoeceus 274
Menger, Carl 137
Messinger, Heinz 438, 447
Metternich, Klemens von 16
Metzler, J. B. 192, 342
Middlemore, Samuel George Chetwynd 33, 152
Middleton, Christopher 3, 35, 259, 265
Mill, John Stuart 24–25, 28, 35, 44, 136–139, 141, 153
Minson, Jeffrey 444, 447
Mirabeau (the Younger), Honoré Gabriel Riqueti, Comte de 149, 320
Mises, Ludwig von 12–13, 35, 137
Mitchell, J. M. 152
Mitzman, Arthur 345, 379
Miyasaki, Donovan 25, 28, 155–170, 211, 451
Molinari, Gustave de 136
Mommsen, Theodor 149
Mommsen, Wolfgang J. 317, 342
Montaigne, Michel de 22–23, 339
Montesquieu, Charles-Louis de Secondat, Baron de la Brède et de 136, 146, 272

Moore, Gregory 395, 402, 404, 413, 429
Morgenthau, Hans J. 313, 330, 341–344, 347–389
Morris, Edward Joy 208
Morris, Ian 175, 177, 185, 193
Morton, Adam 323, 342
Mouffe, Chantal 321, 342
Mullarkey, John 87, 89
Müller, Karl-Otfried 193
Müller-Lauter, Wolfgang 43, 57, 262–263, 265, 392, 404
Murphy, Jonathan 34
Murray, Oswyn 33, 152
Mushacke, Hermann 177

Nauckhoff, Josefine 342, 430
Negri, Antimo 176, 193
Nehamas, Alexander 214, 238, 242, 265, 288, 310, 410, 429
Neocleous, Mark 272–273, 286
Nipperdey, Thomas 318, 343
Nisbet, H. B. 341
Norman, Judith 328, 342, 379, 384, 404, 430
Norton, Robert E. 208
Nussbaum, Martha 35, 159, 160–161, 166, 170, 264, 315–316, 343, 384, 404, 451

Ober, Josiah 193
Ockham, William of 236
Odysseus 332
Oedipus 332, 356
Oehler, Max 192–193
Oehler, Richard 173
Ogden, C. K. 344
O'Keeffe, Dennis 152
Oksala, Johanna 283–284, 286
Ottmann, Henning 2, 35, 175, 190, 193, 215, 217–218, 238–239, 253, 263, 265, 316, 343
Otto, Walter 181, 193
Owen, David 5, 35, 156, 170, 258, 265, 290–291, 294–295, 307, 311, 316, 343, 350, 370, 372, 379, 432, 444, 448
Oz-Salzberger, Fania 152

Pâdurean, Vasile 184
Palmer, R. R. 207

Palmowski, Jan 318, 343
Pangle, Thomas 380
Parkes, Graham 343, 400, 404
Parsifal 263
Pascal, Blaise 282
Patton, Paul 19, 25, 27, 74, 76, 93–111, 242, 452
Paul, Saint (Saul of Tarsus) 307
Payne, Eric F. J. 179
Pearson, Joseph 34
Pericles 23, 149
Petersen, Ulrik Enemark 330, 343
Peukert, Detlev 19, 35
Pinder, Wilhelm 176
Pippin, Robert B. 311, 316, 331, 343, 428, 430
Pius VII, Pope 196, 203
Pizer, John David 438–439, 448
Plaß, Hermann Gottlob 176, 194
Plato 6–9, 23–24, 29–30, 211, 213–220, 222–224, 226, 233, 237–238, 244, 246, 251–254, 258, 260, 262–265, 278, 332, 433, 451–453
Pliny (the Younger, Gaius Plinius Caecillius Secundus) 277
Poellner, Peter 331, 343
Polybius 24
Porter, James I. 176, 194
Promotheus 356, 422
Prospero 74
Pufendorf, Samuel 330, 343
Pugliese, Joseph 60, 76

Quine, Williard Van Orman 331, 343

Rabinow, Paul 286, 432, 436, 446
Radkau, Joachim 19, 35
Raico, Ralph 35
Railton, Peter 331, 343
Rand, Ayn 137
Rapoport, Anatol 446
Raskolnikov 198
Rasmussen, Dennis C. 272, 286
Rawls, John 28, 109, 111, 141, 155, 159–160, 170, 451–452
Ray, Winifred 208
Reckermann, Alfons 1, 35, 242, 265
Reder, Melvin W. 169

Rée, Paul 76, 307, 407, 411
Reginster, Bernard 41, 57, 331, 334, 338, 343, 420–422, 430
Reis, Hans 341
Rémusat, Mme de (Claire Elisabeth Jeanne Granvier de Vergennes de) 207
Renaut, Alain 418, 428
Riccobono, Salvator 340
Richards, Grant 208
Richardson, Brian 99, 153, 342
Richardson, John 159, 170, 335, 338, 343, 429–430
Richardson, Sarah S. 76
Richter, Melvin 209
Ridley, Aaron 290, 292, 294, 304, 306–307, 311, 342, 379, 399, 404
Riehl, Aloys 173, 194
Robertson, Simon 343
Robinson, James 136
Rochette, Désiré-Raoul 176, 194
Rolph, William 389, 395–396, 404
Roodt, Vasti 3, 33–36, 57, 111, 193, 264–265, 316, 344, 404
Rosen, Michael 378
Rosen, Stanley 215, 238
Rosenkranz, Karl 318, 343
Rosenthal, Bernice G. 48, 57
Roth, Guenther 153, 278, 344, 378
Roth, Phillip H. 25, 29, 211–238, 452
Rouse, Joseph 314, 331, 336, 343
Rousseau, Jean-Jacques 16, 33, 60, 148, 365, 385
Roux, Wilhelm 492–498, 403–404
Ruehl, Martin A. 315, 343
Runciman, David 327, 343

Salaquarda, Jörg 89
Salomé, Lou 197, 208
Sanders, Will 74, 76
Santaniello, Weaver 76
Sappho 177
Sawangfa, Onnicha 169
Scaff, Lawrence 346, 379
Schaberg, William H. 68, 76
Schacht, Richard 33, 193, 238, 266, 304, 310–311, 337, 342–343, 408, 430
Schank, Gerd 404
Scheuermann, William E. 313, 343

Schirnhofer, Resa von 206
Schoeman, Marinus 70, 72, 76
Schopenhauer, Arthur 7, 12, 40, 43, 49, 60, 213, 215, 221, 227, 233, 238, 246, 248, 252, 262, 273, 350–351, 359, 379, 426, 451
Schiller, Friedrich 12–13, 179, 242
Schirnhofer, Resa von 206
Schlegel, Friedrich 191
Schmidt, Jochen 252, 265
Schmitt, Carl 54, 57, 318–319, 343, 347–348, 379
Schmitz, Frederick J. 310
Schönherr-Mann, Martin 35, 193
Schrift, Alan D. 62, 76, 440, 448
Schuett, Robert 330, 344
Schulte, Michael 344
Schumann, Robert 422
Schumpeter, Joseph 137, 191
Schuringa, Christoph 409, 428
Schutte, Ofelia 60–64, 68–69, 73–76, 328, 344
Schwab, George 343, 379
Schwaabe, Christian 19, 35
Schweitzer, Frank 178
Sembou, Evangelia 20, 32, 431–448, 452
Sen, Amartya 159, 170
Seneca (the Younger), Lucius Annaeus 274–275, 277
Senellart, Michel 34, 152
Seung, T. K. 198, 209
Shafir, Gerson 348, 354, 380
Shapiro, Gary 300, 311
Shaw, Tamsin 2–3, 19, 31, 35, 316, 338, 344, 345–380, 462
Sheehan, James J. 318, 344
Sheridan, Alan 34, 208, 286, 447
Siemens, Herman W. 2–3, 33–36, 47, 57, 93–94, 105, 111, 117, 133, 156, 170, 193, 242, 264–265, 316, 344, 386, 404
Silverthorne, Michael 341, 343
Simondon, Gilbert 82–83, 89
Sinhababu, Neil 57, 170, 316, 340–342, 429–430
Skinner, Quentin 342
Smith, Adam 136–137, 142, 145, 148, 150, 286
Smith, Anthony-Paul 87, 89

Smith, Brittain 71, 75–76, 286
Smith, Daniel W. 208, 238
Smith, Douglas 57
Smith Zweig, Jacqueline 169
Socrates 7, 29, 175, 182–183, 214–216, 219, 220, 252, 274, 277–278, 307
Soll, Ivan 213, 222–223, 238
Solomon, Robert C. 288, 294, 311, 405, 409–410, 428, 430
Sombart, Werner 49, 57
Sommer, Andreas Urs 239, 244, 252, 260, 265
Sophocles 222
Spencer, Herbert 11, 137–139, 183
Speirs, Ronald 344, 379, 429
Spinoza, Baruch 142, 330, 385, 451–452
Sprung, Mervyn 70
Staël, Germaine de 196, 209
Staten, Henry 304, 306, 311, 417, 419, 421–423, 430
Stalin, Joseph (Iosif Vissarionovich Dzhugashvili) 52
Steen, Mark 34
Stegmaier, Werner 48, 57, 211, 223, 238–239, 241, 244, 246, 265
Stendhal (Henri Beyle) 196, 202
Stern, Sheila 33, 152
Stern, Tom 200, 209
Stocker, Barry 1–36, 44, 135–153, 173, 211, 239, 309, 378
Stoekl, Allan 207
Strauss, David 307
Strauss, Leo 18, 24, 199, 209, 347–348, 380
Strawson, Peter Frederick 51, 57
Strong, Tracy B. 1, 3, 35
Suits, Barnard 163–164, 170
Swanson, A. J. 17
Switek, Malgorzata 169

Tacitus, Publius Cornelius 145
Taine, Hyppolite A. 4, 11, 139, 271, 286
Taormina, Mike 89
Taylor, Charles 191, 194
Taylor, Dianna 447
Taylor, Quentin P. 137, 153
Temkin, Larry 158, 170
Tenbruck, Friedrich 348, 353, 359, 380

Theognis 28, 173–194, 450
Thiele, Leslie Paul 258, 266, 315, 344
Thomas, Alan 418, 430
Thucydides 23, 329, 337
Titunik, Regina 348, 380
Tocqueville, Alexis de 4, 13–15, 24–25, 34, 36, 136, 138, 141, 151, 153, 272
Toews, John Edward 318, 344
Tomlin, Humphrey 208
Tomlinson, Hugh 34, 89
Tongeren, Paul J. M. van 117, 133, 226–227, 229, 231, 238, 288, 311, 404
Tönnies, Ferdinand 324, 344
Treitschke, Heinrich von 203, 209
Tribe, Keith 379
Trotsky, Leon (Lev D. Bronstein) 52–53, 57
Tsouna, Voula 280, 286
Tuck, Richard 152, 341
Tucker, Benjamin 136
Tully, James 343
Tugendhat, Ernst 51, 57, 238
Türck, Gisela 438, 447
Turner, Bryan 362

Ure, Michael 59–61, 76, 286

Vacano, Diego A. von 213–214, 238
Vaihinger, Hans 338, 344
Vernant, Jean-Pierrre 117, 133
Vico, Giambattista 145
Villa, Dana 24–25, 36, 136, 153
Viroli, Maurizio 329, 344
Vogt, Ernst 179, 194
Voltaire (François-Marie Arouet) 16, 149, 272

Wagner, Cosima 6, 244
Wagner, Richard 12, 180, 213, 291, 198, 307, 417, 422, 426
Walker, Leslie J. 143, 342
Walker, Sandra 39
Wallraff, Charles F. 310
Warren, James 286
Warren, Mark 4–5, 36, 131, 133, 155–156, 170, 316, 326, 344, 428
Weber, Max 19, 24, 26, 31, 36, 45, 50, 53, 57, 136, 153, 313–314, 319–324, 329, 344, 345–380, 450, 453
Welcker, Friedrich Gottlieb 177, 194

White, Alan 256, 266
White, Richard J. 306, 311, 436, 448
Wilcox, John T. 333, 344
Williams, Bernard 2–3, 36, 316, 342, 344, 356, 379–380, 405, 428, 430
Williamson, Eugene 15, 36
Williamson, George S. 315, 344
Willmann, Helmut 438, 447
Wistrich, Robert S. 17, 34, 48, 56
Wittich, Claus 153, 344, 378
Wolin, Richard 328, 344
Wolin, Sheldon 141, 153
Woloch, Isser 195–196, 209

Wood, Allen W. 341
Würzbach, Friedrich 173

Yeats, W. B. 18
Young, Julian 179, 194, 280, 286
Young, Robert 446

Zachriat, Wolf Gorch 253, 266
Zantop, Susanne 76
Zavatta, Benedetta 36
Zimmerman, Rolf 25–26, 39–57, 453
Zimmern, Helen 57
Zittel, Claus 243, 266

Subject Index

ability 109, 159, 162, 163, 164, 165–166, 168–169, 189, 195, 200, 213, 216, 236, 329, 392–393
absolutist 12
activity 82, 87, 114, 117–118, 122, 163, 179, 184, 198, 202, 220, 255, 276–277, 280, 288, 299–301, 331, 364, 385, 389, 390, 393–396, 390–400, 417, 421
action, actions 21, 41, 44, 54, 61, 63–64, 72, 98–102, 117, 121, 143, 143–144, 151, 157, 159, 163–164, 166, 175, 184–185, 188, 221, 231, 235, 273, 279, 314, 323, 326–327, 329–333, 336, 351–354, 356, 359–361, 364–366, 374–375, 397, 400, 410, 432, 442
aesthetics, aesthetic 12, 29, 32, 98, 117–118, 211–215, 218, 220–224, 228, 231–232, 236, 239, 245, 277, 283–284, 288, 315, 317, 319, 331, 351, 357, 365, 375–376, 385, 416–417, 421, 423–424, 426, 452–453
agency 98–99, 146, 190, 273, 335, 371, 452
ἀγαθῶν, *see* good
agôn, *see* agon
agon 127, 167, 178–179
  agones 125
  agonistai 125
  agôn 3, 420, 423
agonism 184
agonistic, agonistics 5, 27, 45, 113, 115–119, 121–127, 129–131, 164, 418
agreement (communal) 101–102, 123, 225–226, 228, 230, 232–233, 235, 367
Alexandrian 182
America, American 5, 13, 16, 22, 126, 128, 141–142, 363, 366, 370
  Americas 136
  American Indians 128
  Latin America 60
  Native American 66
  North America 27, 97
amoral, *see* moral
amor fati 198, 257–258, 308
anarchic 181, 141
anarchism 366

anarchist 136
anarchistic 27
anarchy 105, 195
ancestry 8, 15, 413, *see also* descent, *Entstehung*, genealogy, *Herkunft*
ancients 23, 142–143, 145, 148, 275, 284–285
Anglo-American, Anglophone, Anglo-Saxon 1, 3, 5, 77, 124, 185, 242, 316
animal, animals 39, 42, 83, 85, 99–100, 116, 205, 212, 214, 220, 222, 226–227, 244–250, 290, 295, 336, 350, 352, 396–397, 403, 441
animalistic 226, 347
animality 212, 224–232, 365
anthropocentric 79, 225
anthropological 4, 216, 241, 246–253, 255, 260, 262, 314, 330
anthropology 128, 240, 244
anthropomorphisms 228
anti-authoritarian, *see* authoritarian
anti-biological, *see* biological
Antichrist 298
anti-Christian, *see* Christian
antidemocratic, *see* democratic
anti-egalitarian, *see* egalitarian
anti-egalitarianism, *see* egalitarian
anti-eudaimonism, *see* eudomomism
anti-hedonistic, *see* hedonistic
anti-heroic, *see* heroic
anti-moral, *see* moral
anti-parliamentary, *see* parliament
anti-pluralistic, *see* pluralistic
antique 139, 141–142, 144–145, 148–151
antiquity 151, 176, 198, 201, 246, 276, 283, 449
anti-political, anti-politicality 2–3, 27, 94, 105–106, 113, 131, 174, 179, 185, 192, 242, 317, 425
anti-realism, *see* realism
anti-Semitism 11, 52
Apollinian, Apolline, Apollonian 7, 26, 79, 182, 221–222, 355–356, 419
archaic 12, 221, 289

Subject Index

aristocracy 8, 13–15, 18, 24–25, 28, 135, 138, 142, 174–179, 181, 184–190, 203, 206, 218, 253, 258–260, 368–369, 385–386, 397, 417
aristocratism 173–174, 180, 189, 191–192, 450
aristocrat, aristocrats 14, 23–24, 174–175, 177–178, 180–181, 183, 185–189, 250
aristocratic 3–4, 8–25, 18–19, 25, 28–29, 46, 117, 122, 126, 129–130, 135, 141, 150, 157, 171, 214, 227, 243, 258, 260, 295–296, 368–373, 390, 414–416, 423–424, 428
aristocratic radicalism 3, 10, 28–29, 173–209, 259
Aristotelian 151
art 178, 181, 173, 211, 214–215, 219–223, 228, 235, 245, 248, 251–252, 274, 276, 280, 283–284, 295, 315, 339, 351, 376, 391, 399, 402, 416–420, 422–423, 426–427
art-forms 356
artist, artists 7, 29, 188, 200, 205–206, 211, 213, 215–216, 218–219, 220, 223, 228, 247–248, 255, 261, 263, 279, 283, 417, 419–420, 422
artistic, artistically 214, 220–222, 227–228, 236, 249, 371, 419–424, 426
arts 115, 214, 219, 279, 283, 422, 424–425
artwork 222
ascetic 116, 173, 245, 273, 290, 295, 297, 305–306, 308, 334, 338–339, 352, 357–358, 360–361, 365, 371, 397, 402
asceticism 276, 361
assembly, assemblies 12, 125, 204
Asia 128, 136
Asian 67, 70
assimilation 158, 160–161, 167, 169, 206, 275, 395
Athenian 23, 141, 172–173
Athenians 23, 182
Athens 13, 23, 33, 141, 147, 191
Attic 181
atomism 82, 221
authoritarian 17, 26, 39, 45, 47, 50, 56, 136, 186, 190, 203, 206, 315, 317, 319, 322, 324, 326, 328, 362
    anti-authoritarian 21

authoritarianism 19, 87
authoritative 292–293, 351, 356–357, 359, 361
authoritatively 183
authority 3, 21, 47, 54–55, 87, 105, 110, 118, 121, 130–131, 135–136, 147, 177, 182, 186–188, 191, 202–204, 230, 249, 258, 263, 288, 291, 294–295, 297, 299–300, 302–304, 306, 308–309, 319, 324, 345, 348, 357, 371, 406
    authorities 49, 107, 120, 339, 348
autonomous 86, 108, 122, 151, 156, 249–250, 256, 328, 336, 409, 427
autonomy 82, 128, 249–250, 329, 332, 336, 437

Bacchic, *see* Dionysian
bad (as moral concept) 22, 63, 70, 120, 142, 173, 177, 182, 231, 248–250, 263, 276, 278, 282, 290, 323, 337, 389–390, 402, 407
barbarian 146
barbarians 104, 145, 157
barbaric 127, 145–146
barbarism 188
beast 245, 371
    blonde beast 371
    beastly 296
    beasts 6, 157, 245, 295, 397, 407
    blonde beasts 6
beast of prey, beasts of prey 6, 245, 295–296, 407
Bildung 186–187, 418
Bildungsbürgertum 340
bioethics 66, 449
biological 52, 71–72, 79, 179–180, 244, 255, 336, 396–418
biologism 62
biologist 395
biology 376, 389, 391, 403, 413, 415–416
biopolitics 30
bios 284
bio-political 30, 60, 269–286
bio-politics 434
blond beast, *see* beast
body 32, 71, 89, 234, 254, 256, 275, 278, 339, 360, 383, 392–394, 397–398, 426, 441–443

Subject Index — 467

bodies 20, 83–84, 102–103, 240, 270, 435, 442–443
Bolshevism 39, 48, 50–56
Bolshevik 52–54
Bolsheviki 55
Bolsheviks 53
Bolshevist 55
Bonapartism 12, 18, 29, 47, 62, 195–209
Bonapartist 29, 135, 199, 202–206
Bonapartists 12

Caesarism 18, 21, 199, 203, 207
Caesarist 21, 39, 135, 195
Caesaristic 199
Calvinism 361, 362, 373
Calvinist 361
capability 131, 159
    capabilities 155–156, 159, 166
capacities 72, 99, 92, 145, 300
care of self, care of the self 30, 59, 269–286, see also self-care
    epimeleisthai 277
caste, castes 139, 166, 181, 252, 259, 260, 361, see also rule of Manu
categorical imperative 249, 324
Catholic, Catholicism, Catholics 319–320, 361
Catholic Church 96, 196, 319
charisma 319, 353, 355, 371–372
charismatic 31, 50, 186, 203, 349, 353, 359, 371–373
chiasmic 87
chiasmus 78, 84–86, 88
Chinese 26, 67, 69–70, 285
Christian 9–10, 14, 30, 43, 46, 48, 122, 174–175, 196–197, 202, 240, 245–246, 248, 250, 255, 261–263, 275, 278, 281–282, 287–290, 292, 297–298, 303–304, 306, 308, 313, 324, 329, 332, 334, 339, 345, 352, 357, 372, 405, 407, 411–412, 416–417, 427, 444
    anti-Christian 196, 202, 206
    post-Christian 278
Christians 61, 241
Christianity 44, 46, 52, 68, 70, 117, 190, 245–246, 249, 251, 262, 275, 277, 282–283, 308, 387

church, churches 15, 30, 56, 96, 135, 196, 202, 261, 319, 322, 333
citizen, citizens, citizenry 27, 97, 102–103, 107–111, 118, 124–125, 130–131, 140, 143–144, 187, 203–204, 216, 237, 253, 261, 277, 320–321, 329, 450
citizenship 24–25, 96, 109, 123, 129
Civil Code 12, 29, 203
civil compact 143
civil law 12, 147–148, 434
civil life 54
civil rights 142
civil self 151
civil peace 104, 317, 321
civil rights 10
civil society 102, 136–137, 145, 148, 150, 225, 320
civil state 226
civil war 52
civility 188, 272
civilization 14, 49, 146, 188, 197, 227, 261
civilized 106, 146, 245, 423
clan 106
class, classes (economic or social) 11, 13–15, 24–28, 32, 44, 53, 55, 64, 71–73, 88, 108, 142–143, 149, 151, 174, 177–179, 189, 203–204, 206, 216–218, 234, 273, 281, 303, 354, 364–365, 401, 406, 414–416, 421, 423–427, 433
classical liberalism, see liberalism
cognitive 85, 138, 141
cognition 79
colonial 26, 59–76, 151
    postcolonial 74
colonialism 26, 59–60, 62–63, 67–68, 73, 128
colonialist 62, 67–68, 73, 128
colonization 26, 59, 68, 73–75
colonize 75
colonized 26, 60, 70, 73
colonizer, colonizers 60, 74–75
colonizing 65–67, 73, 75
command 128, 181, 184, 217, 249, 334, 366
commanded 147, 271
commander, commanders 185–187, 211, 251
commanding 180, 183, 259, 335, 399
commandments 200

commands 47, 81, 157, 165, 182, 305, 373, 419
commercial 13, 23, 28, 100, 135–136, 145, 148, 150–152, 174, 269–272, 416
commercial society 100, 135–136, 145, 148, 150–152, 269–272
commonwealth 8, 226, 260
communal 226, 229
communitarian 272
communitarian tyranny, see tyranny of the majority
communitarianism 23
community 51–55, 101, 103, 119, 146, 166, 187, 216, 225–227, 229–232, 234, 237, 279, 322–324, 326, 368
   moral community 31, 314, 315–322, 323–324, 326
   political community 9, 25, 94, 254, 260
competition 167–168, 174, 178, 396, 402, 423, 433
conflict, conflicts 19, 45–47, 54–55, 64, 101, 113, 116, 121–122, 124, 126, 138, 160, 178, 181, 200, 229, 318, 332, 365, 392, 398, 426–427, 434, 439
conformism 234, 269
conformity 28, 140, 144, 152, 236
conqueror, conquerors 6, 102, 325, 371
conquest, conquests 6, 14, 156, 167, 168, 420
conscience 22, 42, 100, 104, 120, 197, 214, 245, 255, 271–273, 276, 278, 290, 323, 334, 368, 421, 432
consciousness 85, 115, 146, 224–225, 227, 245, 318, 326, 332, 350
conservative, conservatives 3, 16–18, 29, 136, 139, 142, 173–174, 204, 259, 315, 325, 340
   ultraconservative 24
constitution (political) 24, 46, 50, 195, 199, 203, 204, 252
constitutional (political) 39, 45–46, 50, 54, 56, 102–104, 110, 122, 144, 148, 253, 318, 320
constitutional law, see law
contempt 116, 173, 189, 207, 234, 271, 278, 287, 296, 372, 424
contemptible 255, 346, 368–369
contract 113, 118, 128–129, 145, 367

contractarian, contractarians 6, 128
contractualist, contractualists 6
cooperate 143
cooperation 101, 143–144, 151, 313, 395
cooperative 151
cosmological 99, 257
cosmopolitan 313
cosmopolitanism 282
courage 8, 140, 258, 369
courageous 263
criminal, criminals 65, 110, 198–199, 272
criminal law, see law
critical history, see history
critique 5, 10, 11, 19, 20, 39–40, 43–46, 48–49, 55–56, 64, 117, 123, 126, 136, 158, 191, 198, 206–207, 214, 217, 223, 225, 239, 255, 261, 270, 272–273, 278, 287, 294, 298, 309, 319, 322, 335, 347, 349, 383, 393, 396, 399, 401, 405, 407–409, 411–412, 415–416, 418–419, 436–437, 445
cultivate, cultivated, cultivating 41, 115, 128, 146, 150, 185–186, 196, 269, 271, 277, 279–281, 285, 299–300, 301
cultivation 15, 165, 178, 270, 276, 334
   self-cultivation 59, 70, 72–73, 274
culture, cultures 2–3, 6–7, 9, 11, 15, 24, 32, 49, 63, 71, 74, 84, 94–95, 98, 101, 103–106, 115–117, 121, 123, 128, 136–140, 145, 149–153, 156, 174–175, 179–184, 186–189, 192, 197–198, 206, 216, 220–221, 233–235, 245, 247–249, 251–252, 272, 278–279, 292, 329, 347–348, 350, 355, 357, 360, 383–384, 402, 418–419, 424–426, 428, 453
custom, customs 13–14, 23, 62, 96, 107, 140, 146–148, 157, 197, 234, 236–237, 323–324, 328, 336, 390–393, 395, 398, 400, 403, 411, 439
   Sitte 156, 188, 236
customary 145–148, 156
Cynics 274

Darwinian, Darwinians 11, 138, 396
Darwinism 11, 138, 239, 244, 246–247
   Neo-Darwinism 138
Darwinist 241, 244
death of God, see God

Subject Index — 469

decadence 65, 118, 191, 195, 302, 383–384, 395, 404
  Entartung 384
decadent, decadents 69, 174, 187, 191, 301, 401–402
decay 9–10, 31, 46, 105, 246, 298, 303, 319, 366
deconstruction 433
deconstructive 432
degenerate, degenerates 65, 247, 293, 302–303, 396, 398, 401–403
degenerated 365, 367
deification 180
deity 180–181, 360
Deleuzean 443
Delphic 274, 276
democracy 3–5, 9–10, 12–16, 22–25, 27–28, 39, 45–46, 50, 56, 62, 93–111, 117, 122–127, 129–132, 138, 140–142, 144–147, 151, 173–175, 179, 186–187, 190–195, 203, 205–207, 316–321, 326, 328, 371, 385–386, 403, 418, 424
democratic 3–5, 9–10, 12–17, 19, 22, 25–27, 29, 44–47, 49, 51–52, 77, 93–94, 97–98, 102–105, 107–110, 113, 117–118, 122–124, 126–127, 129–132, 136, 146, 149, 152, 156, 173–175, 179, 184, 186, 191–192, 195–196, 201, 203, 234–235, 246, 315, 317, 320, 347, 383, 389–391, 394, 396, 399
  antidemocratic 5, 62, 203
democrats 175, 179, 180, 186
descent 8, 241, 244, 389, 414, 389, 414, 433, 438, 442, *see also* ancestry, *Entstehung*, genealogy, *Herkunft*
desert 160–161, 166
despot 80, 328
despotism 10, 19, 203
devaluation 227, 263
devalue, devalued, devalues, devaluing 8, 145, 245, 250, 278, 415
dialectical 55, 78, 86–87, 182–183
dictatorial 45, 50
dictatorship 13, 195, 203
difference, differences 8, 19, 21, 27, 85, 87, 110, 113, 115, 123, 129, 146, 158–161, 168, 217, 222, 244, 246, 253, 259, 275, 332, 380, 391, 393

difference principle 159–160
dignity 97, 160, 177, 184, 246, 252, 282, 347, 363, 370–371, 377–378
Dionysiac, Dionysian 7, 26–27, 79, 83, 84, 86, 175, 181–182, 196, 198, 201, 205, 221, 351, 356, 358–359, 419–420
  Bacchic 181
discipline 143, 183, 186–187, 190, 202, 273, 285, 291, 332, 369, 442–443
displeasure, *see* pleasure
distribution, distributions 95, 130, 160–161, 164–166, 243, 313, 321, 360–362, 364
distributive justice, *see* justice
doctrine, doctrines 9, 54, 99, 115, 195, 214, 222–223, 228, 241, 243–244, 255, 258, 354, 360, 363, 365, 367, 394, 395–396, 409–413.
doctrinal 78
dominate, dominated, dominating, domination 25, 42–43, 45, 49, 54, 68, 73, 79, 81, 83–84, 86–87, 105, 114, 116, 123, 131, 141, 150, 166, 168–169, 190, 225, 245, 295, 301, 322, 334, 389, 391, 393–395, 397–399, 403, 416, 417–418, 421, 425, 433, 438, 440
Dorian, Doric 174–175, 177, 181, 189
drives 114–115, 117, 122, 181, 183, 200–201, 221, 226, 245, 270, 330, 336, 399–400, 411, 420
duty, duties 102, 142, 156, 165, 228, 230, 246, 254, 273, 275, 326, 371
dynastic 196, 203, 321
dynasty, dynasties 8, 144, 402

earth, earthly 6, 30, 42, 48, 96, 120, 128, 188, 205, 233, 240, 248–249, 263, 280–281, 294, 325, 346, 350, 352, 358, 364, 366, 368, 370, 410, 417
economic 24, 28, 88, 108, 135, 137, 141, 148, 150–151, 156, 159, 161, 166, 169, 191, 199, 206, 269, 314, 318, 322, 361, 364, 366, 423, 435
economics 97, 137
economists 366
economy 123, 137, 269, 287, 302, 304–305, 333
  homo economicus 145
  political economy 23, 142, 143–144, 352

education, educational 8, 16, 105, 109, 137, 140, 144, 187, 189, 200, 245–246, 251, 253, 299, 321–322
egalitarian, egalitarianism 3, 5, 10–13, 15, 19, 23, 25, 27–28, 39, 43, 46, 50–51, 55, 107–109, 126–127, 129–130, 135, 148, 151–152, 155–170, 181, 205, 254, 259, 418, 424
    anti-egalitarian, anti-egalitarianism 26, 28, 46, 50, 127, 141, 169, 203, 206, 234, 338, 415
    non-egalitarian 18, 236
ego 60, 282, 445
    egoism 91, 275, 375
    non-egoism 276
    unegoism 407
    egoistic 98, 243, 289, 375
    unegoistic 91
    egoistical 201
    unegoistical 282
egotism 150
election, elections 96, 110, 123–124, 371
electoral 105, 142
elite, elites 8–9, 11, 18, 25–26, 29, 44, 118, 129, 141, 148, 156–158, 190, 260
elitism 17–19, 21, 49, 126, 129–130, 141, 191
elitist 17–18, 24, 26, 44, 50, 122, 141, 149, 156, 186, 283, 316, 328
emancipated 198
emancipation 53, 127–129, 186, 273, 320
empire, imperial 195, 186, 195, 201, 204, 206
    German colonial 58
    Holy Roman Empire of the German Nation 12, 202
    Kaiserreich 46, 49, 425
    Napoleonic 195–196, 201, 203–204
    Roman Empire, Imperial Rome, *imperium Romanum* 199, 206
    Second (German Hohenzollern) Empire, Imperial Germany 62, 308, 317–320
    empire of law, *see* law
Enlightenment 13–14, 20, 27, 32, 96, 104, 106–107, 127–128, 137, 145, 148, 150, 206, 248, 327, 444–445
enslavement 6, 65, 104, 325
Entstehung, 433–434, 436, 438–439, *see also* ancestry, descent, genealogy, *Herkunft*

Entartung, see decadence
Epicurean, Epicureans 277, 279–281, 337
epics 222
epimeleisthai, see care of the self
epistemic, epistemically 31, 161, 292, 339
epistemology, epistemological, epistemologically 63, 175, 191, 224–227, 331–332, 337, 443–444, 451
equality 14–16, 24, 28, 39, 43–47, 52, 54, 56, 84, 86, 103, 117, 126–131, 141, 147, 155–162, 165–168, 173, 184, 195, 203–207, 245–246, 253–254, 260, 325, 330, 354, 364, 424–425
estate, estates 7, 206, 252–253, 259–260
eternal recurrence, eternal return 8, 21, 77, 83, 239, 257–258
ethic 203, 271, 278, 324, 329, 372–373
ethicist, ethicists 269, 273
ethical, ethically 30, 60–61, 63–64, 70–75, 94, 125, 142, 150–151, 175–176, 270, 276–277, 282–283, 323–324, 326, 328, 332, 243–244, 356, 359–361, 364–366, 371–372, 449
    metaethical 314, 337–340, 347
    pseudo-ethical 364
    supra-ethical 328
ethics 52, 59, 70, 72, 150, 174, 184, 269–271, 274, 276–277, 283–284, 313, 324, 329, 361–362, 383, 437, 449
    metaethics 337–339
ethos 97, 157, 175, 184, 203, 283, 322
eudaimonic 31
eudaimonism 348, 368
    anti-eudaimonism eudaimonistic 348, 361, 366
eugenic 138, 190
Europe 8–9, 11–12, 22, 26, 44, 64–65, 67–75, 103, 109, 148–149, 196–197, 199, 202, 246, 251, 278, 281, 328, 363, 374, 425
European, Europeans 8, 16, 26, 65–69, 72, 75, 93, 97, 103, 128, 141–142, 174, 185, 199, 205–206, 245–246, 250–251, 279, 319–320, 326, 340, 345, 423
    non-European 128
evaluate, evaluates, evaluated 42, 48, 162, 250–251, 300, 406, 413
    re-evaluates 439

evaluation, evaluations, evaluating 72, 101, 156–157, 161, 203, 250–251, 305, 347, 409, 411–412
  reevaluating, re-evaluation, revaluation 148, 197, 199, 202, 250–251, 370, 408–409
  evaluative 158, 405, 408–409, 412, 414–416, 426
  evaluator 42
evil 42, 56, 61, 72, 116, 140, 157, 184, 236, 250, 274, 285, 290, 292, 299–300, 323–324, 333, 337, 356, 370, 378, 397, 449
evolution, evolutionary, evolutionistic 60, 95–96, 106–108, 125, 136, 138, 142, 148, 244, 247, 321, 325, 333, 367–368, 391–392, 394–395
excellence 13, 115, 129–130, 190, 192, 198, 308, 419
exceptional 28, 69, 121, 186, 199, 220, 227, 229, 247, 260, 263
experiment, experimental, experiments 110, 147, 205, 228, 249, 257, 271, 285, 335
extra-moral 231–232, 289, 308

factory 7, 65, 69, 72, 252
fallacy 406–407, 436
  genetic fallacy 32, 405, 407–408, 412, 416, 423, 426
family 14–15, 52, 106, 146, 204, 301, 307, 415, 423–424
Fascism 17–18, 79, 86
Fascist, Fascistic, Fascists 1, 17–18, 27, 48–49, 78–80, 85–88
feudal 14–15, 149, 176, 189
feudalism 15, 189, 203
flourish, flourishes 242, 253, 334
flourishing, flourished 4, 24, 64, 110, 151, 157–158, 162–163, 178, 226, 278, 280, 294, 298, 300–301, 330, 334
forces 20–21, 23, 80–84, 86, 88, 115–118, 120–122, 131, 135, 189, 196, 221, 279, 289, 305, 354, 366, 375, 395, 423, 434, 438–439
Foucauldian 285, 440
Franco-Prussian War 12, 424, 426
free spirit, *see* spirit

freedom 12, 23, 60, 62, 65, 75, 102, 104, 116, 118–119, 131–132, 138, 166, 169, 181, 187, 189, 198, 203, 229, 255, 273, 275, 278, 280, 283–284, 335–336, 417, 441
  positive freedom 164
French Revolution 2, 13, 16, 46, 49, 52, 107, 141, 149, 195, 197, 205–206, 410
friend, friends 22, 187, 279–280
friendship 202
future 8, 26–27, 47–48, 63–64, 71, 94–95, 103–104, 106, 110, 118, 149, 174–175, 187–188, 205, 233–234, 242, 248–249, 251, 254, 259, 263, 271, 279, 282, 289–290, 303, 308, 317, 325–327, 336, 348, 352, 354, 364, 369–370, 401, 436

genealogist, genealogists 4, 294, 408, 411, 432–436
genealogy, genealogical 20, 31–32, 42, 81, 120, 126–127, 177, 181, 289, 290, 322, 327, 335, 388–399, 405–430, 431–445
  see also ancestry, descent, *Herkunft*
genetic 21, 138, 294, 405–406, 408, 411, 413, 426
genetic fallacy, *see* fallacy
Germany 2, 12, 49, 52, 62, 67–68, 96, 124, 145, 317–320, 326, 342, 406, 425
Goethean 201
genius, geniuses 6–8, 29, 41, 44, 69, 183–184, 186–187, 195–197, 199, 202, 212, 215–216, 218, 221, 224, 227, 233–234, 239, 241, 243, 248–249, 252–255, 262, 317, 406, 423
goal, goals 4, 7, 9, 42–43, 48, 65, 72, 96, 99, 107, 114, 140, 144, 155–156, 161, 165, 201, 212, 223, 234, 236, 241, 243, 247–50, 252–253, 259–261, 279–280, 291–292, 320, 347, 358, 363, 366, 368–370, 373, 391, 396–397, 436
god 10, 31, 44, 46, 85, 126, 147, 180, 200, 240, 244–245, 249–250, 258, 261–262, 276–277, 281–283, 308–309, 321, 351, 354, 358, 360–361, 366, 372–373, 375, 411, 443
  death of God 10, 30, 46–47, 240, 249, 261, 263, 444

gods 177–178, 181, 222, 237, 240, 262, 277, 280, 356–357, 375, 417
good, goodness, goods 4–6, 8–9, 23, 27–28, 31, 42, 46, 56, 61–63, 68, 70, 100, 107, 109–111, 116, 135, 142–143, 156–158, 160, 162–167, 177–178, 182, 184, 188, 190, 216, 218, 224, 226, 231–234, 236, 241, 243, 248–253, 256, 258–260, 270–274, 277–278, 281–282, 285, 292, 299, 306–307, 322–330, 332–333, 337, 351, 364, 368, 373, 389–390, 407, 417–419, 421, 423–424, 427–428
  ἀγαθων 175
Greece 115, 141–142, 180, 186–187, 220–221
Greek, Greekness 3, 6, 28, 41, 45, 59, 106, 115–117, 121, 123, 125, 127, 146, 178–179, 181, 184, 186–187, 189, 211, 213, 220–221, 239, 246, 252, 276–278, 283, 331, 356–357, 420, 422–423, 427, 433
guilt, guilty 124–126, 157, 245, 271–273, 290, 234, 356, 405
government, governments, governmental 9, 12, 21, 23–24, 56, 97, 102–110, 113, 118, 123, 125–126, 130, 137, 142–143, 145, 147, 179, 186, 195, 202, 205, 316–317, 321, 386, 423
grammar 85, 445
Great Politics, *see* politics

happiness 56, 70, 114–115, 162–168, 222, 227, 233–234, 253, 256, 270, 274, 346, 349, 352, 354, 357, 363, 366, 417
health, healthy 8, 59, 61, 64–73, 75, 116, 118, 127, 157, 183, 202, 245, 254, 256, 258–259, 271, 290, 293–296, 298–299, 302, 304, 309, 331, 334, 346, 368, 384, 298, 401–403, 421
  unhealthy 54, 60, 62, 66, 240, 293–294
hedonism, hedonistic 31, 99, 339, 347–348, 350, 354, 363, 365–366, 368–370, 376–377
  anti-hedonism, anti-hedonistic 347–348, 369, 373
  non-hedonistic 349–351, 354, 360–363, 366–367, 369–370, 373–375, 377–378
Hegelian 318
hegemony 173–175, 181, 184–185, 385, 444

herd 3, 42, 70, 157, 183, 189, 200, 205, 216–218, 234, 295, 333–334, 338, 346, 363, 417
  herd morality 234
Herkunft 190, 389–390, 414, 416, 433, 438, *see also* ancestry, descent, genealogy
homo plebeius, see plebeian
heroic 13, 22–23, 28, 70, 149–152, 175, 185, 241, 283, 417, 422
  anti-heroic 28
  non-heroic 31
hierarchy, hierarchies, hierarchical, hierarchically 8, 19, 21, 27, 29, 32, 43, 61, 63, 69, 104, 127, 158, 190, 204–206, 216, 218, 253, 259–260, 276, 323, 383, 390–391, 393–394, 397–399, 402–403, 438
higher 4, 8, 9–10, 18, 29–30, 43–45, 58, 52, 54–55, 60, 72, 95, 104, 108, 117, 146, 157, 164, 183, 186, 188, 191, 205, 212, 217–218, 223, 226, 240–243, 245–249, 251, 254–256, 258–263, 270, 285, 288, 292, 332, 335, 365, 368–370, 372, 388, 397, 399 401, 415, 417
history, critical 63
history, monumental 63, 75
Hobbesian 328
Homeric 145, 180–181, 183–184, 222, 416
homo economicus, see economy
human rights, *see* rights
humane, humaneness 221, 272, 249, 373, 377
humanity 20, 30, 52, 66, 71, 94–96, 105–106, 108, 157, 160–161, 171, 212, 216, 222, 231–233, 235, 241, 244–247, 250, 260, 271, 279–281, 326, 330–333, 335, 347, 368–369, 372, 401, 424, 440
humankind 19, 94–95, 106, 108, 241–242, 246–249, 262, 290, 292, 298, 303, 308

ideal type, ideal types 39, 45–47, 50, 53–54
ideology, ideologies, ideological, ideologically 3, 11, 39, 53, 61, 72–74, 87, 195, 199, 225, 329
immoralism, immoralist, immoralistic, immoralists 15, 30, 196, 272, 276, 287–311
immorality 196, 202, 275

imperial, *see* empire
Imperialism, imperialistic 202, 206, 326
impotence 99, 101, 163, 167, 169, *see also* powerlessness
indigenous 66, 73–76, 147
individualism, individualist, individualistic 15–16, 23, 29, 39, 44, 56, 135, 137, 149, 152, 160, 173–175, 185, 203, 242, 249, 261, 331, 365
individuality 15, 42, 131, 138, 180, 185
inequality 8–9, 54, 156–157, 159, 162, 165–168, 246, 253, 260, 354, 364, 424
inferior 61, 120, 129–130, 166, 183–184, 189, 250, 253, 323, 438
injustice, *see* justice
instinct, instincts, instinctual 48, 84, 96, 100, 118, 157, 162, 182–183, 186, 200, 226, 245, 290, 293, 296–297, 302, 305, 333–334, 340, 366, 399–403, 417, 432, 443
institution, institutions, institutional, institutionalized 10, 13–15, 20, 23–25, 46–47, 54–55, 69, 75, 95–97, 103–109, 113, 116–118, 131, 135–136, 139, 142–143, 148, 151, 159, 162, 175, 185, 187, 192, 199, 201–203, 205–206, 232, 234, 278, 314, 316, 319, 321, 324, 332, 335, 362, 365, 367, 386, 390–391, 398, 400, 403, 419, 434–437, 439–440
intoxication 66, 106, 175, 181–182, 358, 417, 419, 422

Jewish 46, 48, 51–52, 54, 185, 206, 250–251, 405–407, 410, 452
Judaea 46
Judaism 51
Judeo-Christian 175, 313, 323–324, 332, 334, 339
jurisdiction 272
jurisprudence 123, 148
just war, *see* war
justice 93, 96–97, 101, 109–111, 117, 119–122, 129, 137, 157, 159, 165, 253–255, 313, 315–316, 325, 332, 334, 360, 367, 417, 451
 injustice, injustices 9, 95, 120–121, 125, 144, 353–354, 432
 distributive justice 4, 253–255

justification, justifications 2, 8, 31, 51, 63, 73, 102, 109, 118, 125, 149, 192, 223, 232–233, 242, 260, 308, 318, 320, 325, 345, 349–350, 352–357, 359–364, 366, 368–369, 373, 374–377, 424

Kaiserreich, see Empire
Kantian 32, 43, 55, 313, 324, 326–327, 330, 332
 Neo-Kantian 173
knowledge, knowledgeable 7, 14, 69, 78–79, 83–86, 88, 98, 114, 135, 182–183, 188, 211, 216, 221, 223, 228, 235, 248, 252, 273–274, 276, 278, 284–285, 321, 350–351, 388, 402, 405–406, 427, 432, 436–438, 442–443, 445
Kultur, see culture

last man 31, 246, 345–380
Latin America, *see* America
law 8, 12, 24, 30, 54–55, 82, 87, 97, 102, 104, 110, 118–121, 135–136, 139–141, 146–150, 171, 199–200, 204, 211–212, 220, 226–227, 229–232, 236, 249–250, 260, 271, 274, 276, 287, 302, 313, 324, 330, 338, 366–367, 370, 434
 common law 124
 constitutional law 46, 54
 empire of law 171
 Manu, law of 8–9, 147, 149, 260, 293
 natural law 8, 121, 330, 367
 Roman law 12, 323
 law-giver, law-giving 43, 47, 69, 215, 218, 223, 226, 233, 236–237, 251, 263, 274, 303
laws 13, 29, 64, 75, 85, 102, 110, 116, 120, 151, 162, 204, 221, 226, 229–232, 272, 274, 278, 297, 316, 331, 436, 445, 452
leader, leaders 17, 19, 23, 31, 54, 61, 130, 175, 186–187, 364, 371–373, 377
leadership 16, 23, 50, 54, 186–187, 203, 349, 371–373
Legal Positivism 148, 231–232, 367
legislation 29, 123, 142, 181, 211–238, 445, 452
 self-legislation 188
legislator, legislators 181, 200, 205, 212, 215–216, 230, 235, 279

liberal, liberalism 4–5, 9, 10–13, 15–20, 23, 25–28, 39, 44–45, 47, 50, 55–56, 74–75, 93–95, 104, 107–109, 113, 131, 135–142, 149–152, 156, 160, 169, 191, 201, 254, 262, 318, 322, 324–326, 347, 363, 377, 452
   classical liberalism, classical liberals 12, 27, 135–153, 155
liberation 9, 59, 60–62, 65, 73, 105, 129, 188, 283, 291
   self-liberation 70
libertarian, libertarianism 22, 136–137
liberty 14, 22–25, 30, 140–143, 145–146, 160, 181, 315, 437, 453
   negative 142
   positive 142
   of the ancients 23, 142, 145
   of the moderns 23, 142, 151
libidinal 86–87
linguistic, linguistically 77, 85, 225–226, 377, 445
Lutheran 14, 424

Machtstaat 366
majority 9, 24, 44, 97, 138, 144–145, 169, 185, 217, 255, 289, 323, 418
mankind 19, 45, 51–53, 100, 217, 232–233, 251, 254, 263, 352, 368, 396, 417
Marxism 23, 43, 77
Marxist, Marxists 20, 22, 87, 205
masses 6, 8, 17, 61, 97, 118, 178, 183, 186–187, 217, 230, 245, 247, 247, 250–252, 259–260, 320–321, 362
master, masters 6, 11, 31–32, 45, 65–66, 68, 73–74, 78–79, 82, 84–87, 102, 104, 188, 197–198, 201, 217, 229, 233, 235, 360, 371–372, 375, 389–392, 394–395, 410, 415, 436, 439
   master morality 45, 233, 235, 410, 439
   morality of masters 31
mastering 83–86, 391–393
mastery 65–66, 73–79, 82, 85–88, 115, 119–120, 198, 276, 439
   self-mastery 15, 201, 258, 273–274
materialist, materialism 18, 26, 31, 77–89, 137–138, 224, 413
maximin 159
mechanics 78, 81, 83–84

mechanical 71, 143, 182, 375
medical 387, 423
medicine 59, 64, 441
mediocre 9, 22, 43, 183, 245–246, 260
mediocrity 43–45, 138, 173, 250, 325
metaethical, *see* ethical
metaethics, *see* ethics
metaphor, metaphors, metaphorical, metaphorically 32, 96, 195, 150, 228–231, 236, 238, 299, 371, 387, 420
metaphysical 18, 21, 29, 40, 114, 120, 129, 181, 216, 248, 273, 275, 281, 322, 328, 332, 338, 340, 353–354, 360, 410, 433, 434
metaphysics 7, 18, 20, 211, 215, 235–236, 248, 273, 288, 336, 433, 435, 438, 450–451
militarism 14, 17, 49, 195, 202, 207, 426
militarization 29
military 6–7, 18, 23, 54, 105, 140, 145, 195–196, 203–204, 206, 252, 277, 320, 371, 423
Mitleid, *see* sympathy
monarchical 11, 16, 173
monarchist 144
monarch, monarchy 12, 14, 24, 145, 147, 196, 205
monumental history, *see* history
moral psychology 155–156, 162, 315–316, 427

Napoleonic 196, 200–206, 317–318
narrative, narratives 128, 239, 241, 318, 351, 354, 356, 359, 363, 374, 408, 415, 426
National Socialism 48, 50–51
nationalism 11, 15, 49–50, 139, 324, 325–326
nationalist, nationalists 16, 49, 326
Native American, *see* America
naturalism 13, 42, 84, 128, 148, 161, 293, 314, 329–338, 414
Nazi, Nazis 17, 50, 52, 54–55, 384
Nazism, 26, 39, 50–55, *see also* National Socialism
negative liberty, *see* liberty
Neo-Darwinism, *see* Darwinism
Neo-Kantian, *see* Kantian
Neo-Stoic, *see* Stoic
newspapers 151

nihilism 8, 251, 279, 338, 444
nihilists 241
noble, nobles 9, 14, 46, 155–158, 160–162, 165–169, 176, 182–187, 189–190, 197, 200, 214–215, 217, 229, 235, 237, 245, 250–251, 260, 280, 292, 295–296, 300, 323, 356, 376, 390, 397, 414–417, 419, 421
nobility 8, 15, 29, 53, 174, 176, 190, 204, 206, 251, 323, 370, 414, 424
noblesse 200
non-egalitarian, *see* egalitarian
non-egoism, *see* egoism
non-European, *see* European
non-hedonistic, *see* hedonistic
non-heroic, *see* heroic
normative, normatively 2–3, 28, 41–45, 54–55, 137, 155, 157, 159, 161, 243, 313–314, 316, 320, 322, 326–327, 329–339, 345, 349, 355, 357–359, 409, 411–412, 452
norms 46, 51, 54–55, 117, 192, 287, 322, 324, 326–327, 330–331, 339, 350–351, 359, 414, 419, 437
North America, *see* America

obedience 26, 148, 181, 183–187, 230–231, 283, 324, 348
obedient 273
obey, obeys 81, 200, 217, 230, 259, 334, 346, 348, 397
obligation, obligations 53, 61, 144, 157, 160–161, 275–276, 282, 326, 348, 361, 366, 370
oligarchs 24, 188
oligarchy 29
Olympian 7, 16, 180–181, 183, 241, 243, 252, 262
ontology 83, 214–215, 218, 224, 234, 445
ontological 61, 224, 411, 439
organic 42, 82, 85, 99, 143, 334–338, 390, 394, 398, 443
organism, organisms 32, 84, 87, 391–396, 398, 402–403, 443
original position 159
Overman, over-man 8, 10, 21, 25, 239, 240–243, 255, 258, 261–263, 368
superhuman 185

Superman, super-man 198, 239, 246, 368
trans-humanist 450
Übermensch 29–30, 45, 202, 206, 239–266, 368–369, 436

pain 144, 256–257, 347, 350–351, 368
parliament, parliamentary 19, 124, 174, 205, 320
anti-parliamentarianism 195, 206
pathos of distance 131, 168, 178, 259, 372
peace 70, 101, 104, 118, 120, 123, 196, 225, 281, 292, 303, 317, 321, 352, 417
peaceful 50, 101, 123, 181, 271
perfectionism 16, 95, 156, 242
perfectionist 94, 242, 258
perception 84–85, 104, 212–214, 220, 223–224, 234, 301, 317, 322, 325, 362
perspectivism 123, 175, 214, 222, 439, 443
perspectivist 191
pessimism 256, 368
pessimistic 75, 330, 345, 350, 356
Physiocrats 148
physiological 32, 69, 85, 88, 301, 305, 383–388, 390–391, 399, 401–402, 410, 413, 443
physiology 31–32, 64, 153, 383–404, 413, 443
Platonic 13, 17, 19, 23–24, 30, 214–219, 222–224, 233, 237
Platonically 187
Platonism 18, 215, 218, 222–223, 233
Platonist 18, 21, 29, 214, 217
pleasure, pleasures 30, 65, 98, 100, 114–115, 149–150, 271, 275–276, 280, 284, 334, 346–347, 349, 352, 368, 374
displeasure 274
plebeian 14, 24, 175, 182–183, 188, 217, 414
homo plebeius 177–178
plebeians 28, 178
plebs 175–178, 184
plebiscite, plebiscites 195, 203–204
plebiscitary 29, 50, 196, 204–205
pluralism 5, 13, 19, 21, 161, 168–169, 316
pluralist 3, 135
pluralistic 169
anti-pluralistic 160
polis 106, 173, 216, 219, 226, 237

political community, see community
political economy, see economy
political technology 273, 442
political theology, see theology
politician 50, 142, 329, 371
politics, grand 8, 100, 108, 251
politics, great 47–48, 205, 389, 402–403
polity 29, 145, 151, 317, 326, 330
positive liberty, see liberty
post-Christian, see Christian
postcolonial, see colonial
postmodern 4–5, 129, 135, 191, 445
postmodernism 445
postmodernist 32
poststructuralist 80, 442
priest, priests 11, 136, 149, 240, 245, 250, 287, 295–297, 301–303, 305–306, 308, 397, 410
Priester 45
priestly 245, 296–297, 303, 305–306, 415
principium individuationis 180–181
private 9, 10, 97, 101, 105, 144, 199, 317, 321, 365
proletarian 55
property 95, 97, 100, 102, 104, 109, 127, 128, 135–136, 141–142, 147, 164, 182, 206, 399
Protestant, Protestantism 14, 318, 362
Prussia, Prussian 12, 15, 96, 139–140, 144, 318, 425
pseudo-ethical, see ethical
psychological 29, 60–61, 64, 66, 74–75, 99, 101, 123, 159, 162, 164, 169, 198, 211–228, 290, 331, 334, 349–350, 352, 354–356, 358–359, 405, 408, 410, 412–413, 415–416
psychologically 231, 349–350, 353, 374
psychologism 406
psychologist 298, 409
English psychologists 407, 411
psychologizing 330
psychology 59, 61, 155–156, 161–162, 164–165, 201, 213, 215, 315–316, 330–331, 334, 339, 352, 354, 376, 408, 414–415, 419, 427
public 45, 54, 95, 98, 102–103, 110, 117–118, 136–137, 140, 185, 196, 204–205, 211, 317–320, 322, 334, 339, 365, 367, 423
punishment, punishments 16, 20, 110, 119, 147, 356, 377, 390, 398, 408, 411–412, 417, 439, 442–443
punitive 104, 442

race, races 6, 51–52, 54, 75, 95, 127, 142, 188, 278, 333, 346, 371, 401, 433
racial, racially 11, 17, 54–55, 66, 67, 106, 128, 138, 326, 333
rank, ranks 7, 8–9, 32, 42–44, 158, 179, 205, 217–219, 223, 243, 250, 252–256, 258–260, 263, 390–391, 414–415, 425
rebellion 46, 78–79, 86–87, 123, 135, 410
redemption 7, 52, 70, 96, 213, 248, 282, 290, 373
redistribution 95–96, 165, 364
reevaluating, re-evaluation, revaluation, see evaluation
religion 2, 9, 18, 48, 96–97, 104–105, 143, 196, 205, 221, 245, 248, 275, 277, 280, 317, 320–321, 333, 347, 349, 354–355, 358–359, 361, 364–365, 371, 384, 386, 409, 424, 450
Renaissance 68, 70, 185, 191, 196–197, 201–202, 263, 315
republican 13, 16, 22–24, 50, 191, 203
republicanism 12, 22–24, 26, 142, 148, 151
resistance, resistances 20, 30, 61–62, 67–70, 74–75, 79–80, 82, 86, 88, 113–116, 119, 122, 159, 161–169, 262, 269–286, 289, 291, 335, 420, 422, 437, 441
ressentiment 16, 157, 235, 323, 360, 364, 407, 410, 412, 415
revenge 46–48, 60, 98, 100, 119–121, 157, 163, 263, 296, 364, 402
revolutionary 16, 22, 52–53, 55, 78–80, 86, 95–96, 174–175, 318, 365, 425, 432
rhetoric, rhetorical 61, 127–129, 131, 149, 152, 212, 225, 228, 239, 304, 347, 399, 412, 414, 419
rights 9, 11, 15, 19, 25, 45, 47, 51, 54–55, 69, 73–74, 93, 101, 103, 126–128, 135–136, 140–142, 147–148, 156, 159–160, 203–204, 212, 226, 233, 235, 246, 254, 256, 260, 303, 316, 325, 351, 363, 367, 385, 438

Roman law, see law
Rousseauian 197
ruled 200, 216, 217, 276, 372, 410
ruler, rulers 18, 24, 29, 109, 188, 197, 216–217, 313, 315, 328–329, 348, 372
rules 55, 117, 124–125, 164, 183, 186, 188, 190, 229, 275, 283, 419, 434–435, 440

Saint-Simonists 326
sameness 130–131, 160
secularism 105, 345, 347, 349, 363, 377
secularized 175, 317–319, 321, 373
secularization 3, 105, 345–347, 362, 374, 376, 453
secularizes 321
sciences 10, 20, 64, 244, 279, 376, 385–389, 391, 413, 436, 442, 444, 452
scientific 40, 115, 176, 228, 244, 298, 341, 354, 394–395, 400, 413–414, 433
Schopenhauerean 351, 359, 374–375
self-actualization 41–42
self-care 274, 276, see also care of self
self-creation 118, 127, 129, 131
self-cultivation, see cultivation
self-interpretation 43, 46–48
self-legislation, see legislation
self-liberation, see liberation
self-mastery, see mastery
self-overcoming 259, 274, 288, 291–292, 296, 299, 368
Simondonian 86
Sitte, see customs
slave, slaves, 7, 11, 21, 31–32, 45–46, 65, 78, 102, 119, 122, 127, 141, 156–157, 178, 181, 183–184, 188, 212, 216–217, 229, 233–234, 250, 252, 259, 281, 289, 300, 323, 360, 368–369, 397, 410, 415–416
   slave morality 45–46, 119, 122, 156–157, 212, 233–234, 289, 360, 397, 410, 415–416, 439
   morality of slaves 178, 250
   slave revolt 36, 300, 323, 410
slavery 7–8, 24, 65, 71, 118, 206, 216, 234–235, 252, 259, 325, 397, 419, 441
slavish, slavishly 155–158, 234, 414, 418, 427, 439
socialism 10–11, 48, 50–51, 71, 73, 97, 136–137, 141, 171, 318, 324–325, 364

socialist 9, 53, 69, 71, 95, 108–109, 347, 363–364, 367, 371
Socratic 29, 182, 220, 274
solitude 64, 216, 275
sovereign 12, 121, 148, 188, 222, 226, 228, 244, 313, 336, 442
   sovereign individual 325–329, 336, 436
sovereignty 12, 19–21, 144–145, 182, 196, 203, 205–206, 212, 321
species 2, 51–52, 83–86, 94, 108–109, 138, 180, 183, 241–242, 244, 246–248, 285, 287, 295, 302, 333, 388, 391, 396–397, 399–400, 402, 413
Spinozist 198
Stalinism 53, 55
Stalinist 52–53
Stoic, Stoicism 201, 270, 274, 281–284
   neo-Stoic 60, 150
stratification 129–130
suffering 15, 21, 31, 46, 98, 149–150, 222, 240, 248, 257, 263, 271, 295, 334, 345–380, 411, 417, 420
suffrage 44, 46, 97, 127, 141–142, 195, 203–204, 206
superman, see overman
supra-ethical, see ethical
sympathetic 120, 270–271, 274, 288
sympathy 70, 98, 125, 141, 150, 271, 363, 378, 411, 414
   Mitleid 150, 270, 396, 407

tekhne 277
theodicy, theodicies 31, 345, 347–349, 352–363, 365, 367, 369, 373–377
theology 183, 318, 384
   political theology 175, 180
therapeutic 26, 59–60, 63–64, 66–68, 70, 72–73, 75, 280–281, 402
therapeutics 279–280
therapy 59–61, 64, 68, 71–72, 74, 269, 285
totalitarianism 17, 26
Traditionalism 17–18
tragedy 13, 20, 115, 181–182, 211, 235, 331–332, 356, 438
tragic 20, 175, 221–222, 235, 331, 366, 421–423
transcendental 84, 86, 327, 329, 360, 445
Transcendentalism 17

Transcendentalist 16
tyranny 122, 126, 164, 271, 326
tyranny of the majority 24, 44, 138
    communitarian tyranny 272
    tyrant, tyrants 23, 188, 203, 328–329,
Übermensch, *see* overman

universalist, universalism 16, 43, 49, 51–56, 128, 313, 333, 425
universality 128, 169, 232, 303
unhealthy, *see* healthy
ultraconservative, *see* conservative
utilitarian, utilitarians 21, 31, 43, 44, 183, 348, 367, 439
utilitarianism 43, 152, 346, 366, 368
unegoism, *see* egoism
unegoistic, *see* egoistic
unegoistical, *see* egoistical

virtue 16, 70–71, 99, 101, 149, 150, 183, 196, 198, 206, 255–256, 273, 327, 339, 356, 422
    virtù 70, 195–196, 337
    virtue ethics 150, 313, 329
    virtue ethicist 269
virtues 13, 28, 49, 64–65, 70, 101, 119, 140–141, 144, 151–152, 158, 183, 188–189, 196, 216–217, 274, 290, 299–300

warrior, warriors 9, 53, 157, 250, 260, 416
Whig 25, 173
wickedness 23, 98, 256
will to power 8, 10, 40–57, 77, 82, 87, 95, 113–133, 164, 334, 395, 397, 400, 417, 420–421, 423, 434, 439–440, 443
workers 26, 64–67, 69–75, 183, 190, 204, 354

yes-saying 235, 306

www.ingramcontent.com/pod-product-compliance
Lightning Source LLC
Chambersburg PA
CBHW062005180426
43198CB00037B/2388